The Medieval Theologians

The Medieval Theologians

Edited by

G. R. Evans
University of Cambridge

BLACKWELL
Publishers

Copyright © Blackwell Publishers Ltd 2001
Editorial matter and arrangement copyright © G. R. Evans 2001

First published 2001

2 4 6 8 10 9 7 5 3 1

Blackwell Publishers Ltd
108 Cowley Road
Oxford OX4 1JF
UK

Blackwell Publishers Inc.
350 Main Street
Malden, Massachusetts 02148
USA

British Library Cataloguing in Publication Data

A CIP catalogue record for this book is available from the British Library.

Library of Congress Cataloging-in-Publication Data

The medieval theologians / edited by G. R. Evans.
    p. cm.
    Includes bibliographical references and index.
    ISBN 0–631–21202–7 (alk. paper) — ISBN 0–631–21203–5 (pbk. : alk. paper)
    1. Theology—History—Middle Ages, 600–1500. 2. Theologians. I. Evans, G. R.
(Gillian Rosemary)

    BR253 .M38 2001
    230′.09′02—dc21   00–060793

Typeset in 10 on 12.5 pt Galliard
by Graphicraft Limited, Hong Kong
Printed in Great Britain by MPG Books Ltd, Bodmin, Cornwall

This book is printed on acid-free paper.

Contents

Preface   vii
List of Contributors   ix
Introduction   xiii

PART I   THE END OF THE ANCIENT WORLD

1   Augustine of Hippo   *John Rist*   3
2   Boethius, Cassiodorus, Gregory the Great   *Charles Kannengiesser*   24
3   Postpatristic Byzantine Theologians   *Andrew Louth*   37

PART II   THE CAROLINGIANS

4   Bede the Theologian   *Benedicta Ward*   57
5   Carolingian Theology   *Willemien Otten*   65

PART III   A MEDIEVAL "RENAISSANCE"?

6   Berengar, Roscelin, and Peter Damian   *G. R. Evans*   85
7   Anselm of Canterbury   *G. R. Evans*   94
8   Peter Abelard and Gilbert of Poitiers   *Lauge O. Nielsen*   102
9   Bernard of Clairvaux, William of St. Thierry, the Victorines
      Emero Stiegman   129
10   The *Glossa Ordinaria*   *Jenny Swanson*   156
11   Peter Lombard   *Marcia L. Colish*   168

PART IV   THE HIGH MEDIEVAL DEBATE

12   Saint Bonaventure   *Michael Robson*   187
13   Thomas Aquinas   *Fergus Kerr*   201
14   Later Medieval Mystics   *Oliver Davies*   221
15   Academic Controversies   *Takashi Shogimen*   233
16   Duns Scotus and William Ockham   *Alexander Broadie*   250

PART V DISSENT

17	The Waldenses *Euan Cameron*	269
18	Dualism *Gerhard Rottenwöhrer*	287
19	Ecclesiology and Politics *Matthew S. Kempshall*	303
20	Wyclif and Lollardy *Stephen Lahey*	334

CONCLUSION

21	Robert Kilwardby, Gabriel Biel, and Luther's Saving Faith *G. R. Evans*	357
22	Augustine, the Medieval Theologians, and the Reformation *Paul Rorem*	365
	Index	373

Preface

This is a companion volume to *The Modern Theologians*, edited by David Ford, first published in 1989, which entered a much-revised second edition in 1997. Yet in a sense it cannot be a companion, for its subject-matter makes its premises radically different. David Ford can write of "the global scope of Christian theology, its diversity amounting often to fragmentation."[1] He can write of "theologies." The authors discussed in this volume would not have understood what he meant. They would have recoiled from the very idea of "diversity"; it was difficult enough for them to come to terms with the idea that some matters might be "indifferent," *adiaphora*. They would not have approved of fragmentation at all, because it would have betokened schism and the loss of the one faith. Paradoxically, although it was as true for the Middle Ages as for the period since the nineteenth century, that Christian theology has engaged "immense intellectual energy," the thrust of the labor has changed. The authors in this volume wanted to protect, to preserve, to clarify, certainly, but not to change the heritage handed on to them. Their efforts are directed at *holding off* challenge; if they are seen to *make* it, that is largely by accident, and the dissident is frequently to be heard protesting that he said, or intended to say, nothing new, nothing different, that he has been misunderstood.

It is a pity that the "missing volume" or volumes, on Reformation and post-Reformation theologians, are not yet to hand. An immense gulf of expectation and assumption separates the end of the Middle Ages from the nineteenth century and it would be impossible to attempt to bridge it here, except to point to the accompanying shift in the intellectual aspirations and social patterns. A writer cannot but be of his time, especially when the times require him to be up to date and saying something new if he is to be taken seriously. Perhaps the single most important alteration which took place from the nineteenth century was the move from disapproving of innovation to valuing originality.

Unity and continuity are of the essence of the faith and no greater strain has been put upon the survival of Christianity than that which has been created by the modern expectation that a leading thinker will be saying something new.

That has led to extreme positions, to separatist claims, to challenges to the very persistence of God as he has always been understood to be ("process theology"), which in the centuries with which this volume are concerned would have got a theologian branded a heretic. The running concern of medieval authors about the relationship of Christian learning to the secular, scientific, or philosophical, was to avoid contamination. The modern theologian may embrace the challenge enthusiastically and try to establish a new relationship in which Christianity moves within the scientific or philosophical parameters of secular scholarship. Such inculturation took place of course from the earliest Christian period. The difference lies in the recognition that it is doing so and the willingness that it should.

It is important here not to lose sight of the immense stretch of time the volume covers. More than a thousand years is a great many generations. And while many of the nineteenth- and twentieth-century theologians were able to correspond with one another and read one another and engage in contemporaneous argument, driving change and experimentation forward, our theologians could do that only on a limited scale. They were working conceptually in something theologically much closer to the Augustinian "City of God." Their fellow theologians might be *antiqui* as easily as *moderni*, and accessible to them only patchily in extracts from their writings or by reputation.

The flavor, then, is different. And so to some degree is the prose of the authors of the chapters in this "second" volume. They have been trying to find not a new way of putting something but a way of explaining clearly how things looked to an author writing (usually) in Latin in an age which was in many respects another world.

In one respect the two volumes have identical purposes. An introduction to a theologian or a group of theologians is of use to readers coming new to his work only if it helps them to think in a way appropriate to the thinkers in question. To understand what preoccupied the medieval theologians is the first step to reading them on their own terms and entering into their concerns. The authors of the chapters in this volume have tried to bring to the surface not only the themes which were topical or fashionable when an author was writing, but also the way he approached his task and the stimuli or challenges he faced.

Note

1 *The Modern Theologians*, ed. David Ford (Blackwell, 1997), p. ix.

Contributors

Alexander Broadie is Professor of Logic and Rhetoric in the Philosophy Department, University of Glasgow. His publications include *Notion and Object: Aspects of Late-Medieval Epistemology* (1989), Robert Kilwardby OP, *On Time and Imagination* (ed. and trans., 1993), *Introduction to Medieval Logic* (2nd edn., 1993), *The Shadow of Scotus: Philosophy and Faith in Pre-Reformation Scotland* (1995).

Euan Cameron is Professor of Early Modern History, University of Newcastle upon Tyne. His recent books include *The European Reformation* (1991, with subsequent reprints) and *Waldenses: Rejections of Holy Church in Medieval Europe* (2000).

Marcia L. Colish is the Frederick B. Artz Professor History at Oberlin College, Ohio. Her recent publications include *Medieval Foundations of the Western Intellectual Tradition, 400–1400* (1997), *Peter Lombard* (2 vols., 1994; winner of the Haskins Medal, Medieval Academy of America), and *Remapping Scholasticism* (2000).

Oliver Davies is Reader in Systematic Theology at the University of Wales, Lampeter. His recent publications include *Meister Eckhart: Mystical Theologian* (1991) and *Meister Eckhart: Selected Writings* (1994).

G. R. Evans lectures in History and Theology in Cambridge. She was British Academy Research Reader in Theology 1986–8. Her publications include *Philosophy and Theology in the Middle Ages* (1993), *Getting It Wrong: The Mediaeval Epistemology of Error* (1998), and *Bernard of Clairvaux* (2000).

Charles Kannengiesser is C. E. Huisking Professor Emeritus of Theology, University of Notre Dame, Indiana. He currently lectures in Canada and Australia. An expert in patristics, he has published widely on Athanasius and the Alexandrian tradition. His recent publications include *Arius and Athanasius* (1991) and *The Bible in Early Christianity: A Handbook of Patristic Exegesis* (forthcoming).

Matthew Kempshall is Lecturer in Medieval History at Lincoln College, Oxford. His recent publications include *The Common Good in Late Medieval Political Thought* (1999) and a contribution to *Translations of Medieval Philosophical Texts: Ethics and Political Philosophy* (2000).

Fergus Kerr is Regent, Blackfriars Hall, Oxford, and Honorary Senior Lecturer in the Faculty of Divinity, University of Edinburgh. His recent books include *Theology After Wittgenstein* (2nd edn. 1997) and *Immortal Longings: Versions of Transcending Humanity* (1997).

Stephen E. Lahey is Assistant Professor of Philosophy, Le Moyne College, Syracuse NY. His recent publications include *Metaphysics and Politics in the Thought of John Wyclif* (forthcoming), entries on medieval logic in the *Cambridge Dictionary of Philosophy* (1999), and articles on Wyclif, Ockham, and Maimonides in *Journal of the History of Ideas*, *Franciscan Studies*, and *American Catholic Philosophical Quarterly*, respectively.

Andrew Louth is Professor of Patristic and Byzantine Studies in the University of Durham. His recent publications include *Denys the Areopagite* (1989) and *Maximus the Confessor* (1996).

John M. Rist is Professor Emeritus of Classics and Philosophy, University of Toronto, and currently Visiting Professor at the Institutum Patristicum Augustinianum, Rome. His recent books include *Augustine: Ancient Thought Baptized* and *Ancient Thought from Plato to Dionysius*.

Lauge O. Nielsen is a Senior Lecturer at the Institute for Church History and Vice-Dean of the Faculty of Theology, University of Copenhagen. He is the author of *Theology and Philosophy in the Twelfth Century* (1982), as well as writing on theology and natural science in the late medieval and early modern period. For the last few years he has worked on the early fourteenth-century Franciscan, Peter Auriol.

Willemien Otten is Professor of the History of Christianity in the Department of Theology at Utrecht University. Her recent publications include *Eriugena East and West* (ed. with B. McGinn, 1994) and numerous articles in books and journals, including *Harvard Theological Review*, *Vigiliae Christianae*, *Theological Studies*, and *Dutch Review of Church History*.

Michael Robson, OFMConv., is Dean and a Fellow of St. Edmund's College, Cambridge, and the College's Director of Studies in the Faculty of Divinity. He is a Fellow of the Royal Historical Society. His recent publications include *Saint Francis of Assisi: The Legend and the Life* (1997), *The Franciscans in the Medieval Custody of York* (1997), and contributions to five other volumes on the history of religious life and schools as well as articles in a range of Franciscan journals.

Paul Rorem is Benjamin B. Warfield Professor of Ecclesiastical History at the Princeton Theological Seminary. He is the editor of *Lutheran Quarterly* and co-author of *John of Scythopolis and the Dionysian Corpus* (Oxford Early Christian Studies, 1998).

Gerhard Rottenwöhrer is an Extraordinary Professor in Munich. His recent publications include *Unde malum?: Herkunft und Gestalt des Bösen nach heterodoxer Lehre von Markion bis zu den Katharern* (1986) and *Zeichen der Satansherrschaft: Die Katharer zu Verfolgung, Mord- und Strafgewalt* (1996).

Takashi Shogimen is a former Research Fellow, Clare Hall, Cambridge. Recent publications include "William of Ockham and Guido Terreni" in *History of Political Thought* (1998) and "The Relationship between Theology and Canon Law" in *Journal of the History of Ideas* (1999).

Emero Stiegman is Professor Emeritus of Religious Studies at Saint Mary's University, Halifax, Nova Scotia. His recent books include *On Loving God by Bernard of Clairvaux, with an Analytical Commentary* (1995).

Jenny Swanson is author of *John of Wales* (1989).

Benedicta Ward is a sister of the Community of the Sisters of the Love of God. She is Reader in the History of Christian Spirituality in the University of Oxford and a Fellow of Harris Manchester College, Oxford. Her most recent books are *The Venerable Bede* (1990) and *High King of Heaven: Aspects of Early English Spirituality* (1999).

Introduction

G. R. Evans

What unites the "medieval theologians" is in part an artificial division of time, which has traditionally separated them from the "Fathers" and the "Reformation authors" at either end. These dividing lines will not bear the strain of much scrutiny. Augustine and Gregory the Great had a sense of living in a time of change, but they certainly did not see themselves as moving from a "patristic" to a "medieval" world. And while Luther was undermining old certainties he looked back to Gabriel Biel not forward to a "modern world." But that thousand years, a longer period than the "modern" period since the sixteenth century, and full of change in theological priorities, has a certain unity nonetheless. Taken as a whole, it can be seen to have dealt with big issues, moved things onward.

"Faith in" the crucified and risen Jesus of Nazareth had to take a definitive shape in the first generations after his death. It was, perhaps, enough for the salvation of the individual to "believe in him," that is, to trust in a person. But this faith had to be communicated; the believer had to be able to explain to others what he believed, or there would be no new Christians. When St. Paul urged Christians to be ready to give reasons for the faith that was in them, he was setting in train a process of immense length and complexity. A map had to be made of what that faith consisted in, its intellectual as well as its affective content.

During the first Christian centuries this "faith" faced a series of challenges. "Statements of faith" had to be made by a Church simultaneously wrestling with the question of its very identity and the related question of its authority to make such statements. The Nicene Creed of 325 is one of the most significant for succeeding generations, and every clause reflects the heat of battle, in which the position stated was established. One of the themes of this book is the continuation of such debates and the raising of new challenges.

In the fifth and sixth century the Roman Empire collapsed and the Greek-speaking East and the Latin-speaking West increasingly went their own ways. In the East, the early ecumenical Councils were regarded as definitive. The Orthodox view that nothing should be added after this period largely placed a stay upon enlargement of the theological remit in the Greek East. Effort there went principally into the development of a mystical neoplatonism, and a powerful if not always intellectually rigorous spirituality. In the West, the early explorations of disputed questions left unfinished business. The task that remained (as the West saw it) was partly to expand the scope of the study of theology and partly to improve the exactness with which theological ideas could be discussed.

For Boethius in the sixth century, *theologia* was strictly confined to topics which were also, in a sense, philosophical. They included the being and nature of God and his attributes; the way in which he is able to be both "three" and "one"; and the creation of the world. Ancient philosophers had discussed those topics, too; they were not in themselves exclusively Christian issues, although Christian thinkers put upon them an interpretation which made them distinctively Christian. The patristic period had discussed the Incarnation exhaustively, but mainly from the point of view of the question whether God could truly have become man without demeaning his divinity. The medieval interest in that dilemma remained, but the focus shifted to enquiries into why it had been *necessary* for him to do so, and what had been *achieved*.

A number of questions remained, and in a sense followed on, taking the debate into the realm of ecclesiology. If Christ restored mankind by his death and resurrection, why is there still work to do? Why is there still sin in the world? What is the role of the Church and the sacraments? What will be the end of all things? Hugh of St. Victor in the twelfth century described as the *opus restaurationis*, the work of restoration and all that follows from it, in terms of a theology of the Church and sacraments. The medieval millennium was the principal period of the full development of the theology of the Church and of the sacraments, and it prompted an unprecedented sophistication of debate about the *polity* of the Church and its relation to the State.

The Framework of Study

The Middle Ages, stretching for our purposes from the fifth century to the sixteenth, was also the period when theology took shape as a subject of increasingly formal academic study. At the beginning of our period theology was done mainly in two contexts. It was part of the teaching office of the Church. There, it took the form of catechetics and preaching. In the early Church, the homily was characteristically a "Bible study," although it could be extremely wide-ranging in the topics which presented themselves on a reading of the texts. Augustine and Gregory the Great were always conscious that the bishop had a special responsibility for maintaining and spreading and defending the faith. Both were lengthy and frequent exegetical preachers.

The second context was apologetic, meeting the questions people raised about the faith. Some of these were novel; some already had a long history and can still be found in one form or another age after age. They became a problem only when those who took a view at odds with orthodoxy persisted in it when they were told it was not sound. For then that opinion became a heresy. A good deal of the theological unraveling and development of the patristic and medieval periods consists of this type of argument against determined opposition.

After the end of the ancient world, the pattern of scholarship changed. Because of the collapse of the educational infrastructure the necessity (which Cassiodorus and Boethius had already recognized), was to preserve and hand on a tradition of intellectual life which was no longer being naturally sustained by a society increasingly under pressure from the barbarian invasions. Once Benedict had provided the necessary Rule, and monastic life began to develop, learning tended to enter the cloister. Bede, in his monastery in the north of England in the seventh century, lived on the other side of a divide. He was trying to recapture what had now been lost. In this he was assisted by the travelings of Benedict Biscop, who brought him copies of books held in the library of Monte Cassino. This mother-house of the Benedictine Order thus made available resources which the energetic Bede was able to use in his scriptural commentaries and in his writings on the natural world. Somewhat different in cast were the cathedral schools of the Carolingian period. These existed to train the clergy attached to cathedrals. The Emperor Charlemagne was particularly anxious to ensure that cathedral canons reached an acceptable educational standard and lived according to rule, so that the cathedrals were well served.

The medieval period saw the rise of the universities. They grew out of a time of enlargement and experimentation. Individual masters of note, especially from the end of the eleventh century, began to attract students in some numbers as they traveled and taught in northern France. At first the focus was the leading individual, the notable or charismatic teacher. The cathedral schools provided some geographical stability in this period of change. Monastic schools with their relatively static populations were less well placed to assist. Towards the end of the twelfth and the beginning of the thirteenth centuries the new schools gradually took on an institutional framework and began to reward their students with degrees (*gradus*), partly to meet a need for a clerical "civil service," with professional masters to teach future generations.

Our "medieval theologians," then, worked in a succession of different types of environment for learning. One of the most obvious changes was the shift from a situation in which the ordinary citizen of standing was an educated man, to a world in which the educated man was the exception and normally a monk or cleric. It was not until the end of our period that the secular citizen was commonly to be literate again, and able to become an intellectual leader.

Most of the authors in this book have it in common that they thought and wrote in Latin when they did theology. Latin was not a language well-designed for the purpose. It is not as natural a philosophical vehicle as Greek and there had been a problem about devising a vocabulary in which to do Christian theology at all. Cicero and Boethius had made significant contributions there, but the continuing life of the Latin language, its stretching to fit new needs, continued Christian century by Christian century.

Where the best minds of the day are professional Christian theologians of one sort or another, the climate of scholarship encourages the setting of what might otherwise be other concerns within the framework of Christian theology. For example, Robert Grosseteste and Henry of Langenstein alike used the discussion of the creation story in Genesis as a peg upon which to "hang" discussion of the whole span of natural science. Optics, for example, comes in appropriately at the point in Genesis where light is divided from darkness.

Similarly, debates arising in other subject areas meet their most powerful challenges when a point of faith appears to be set at risk. It was this abrasion, this rubbing up of one study against another, which perhaps did more than anything else to drive Christian learning onward from the cloisters to the universities. A common scholarly language geared to doing theology was likewise a unifying force and the vehicle of a search for exactitude.

The Theological Parameters

From the time of the forming of the canon, the main Christian study was the Bible. There was always a sense that it was a text with an authority like that of no other. But beside it traveled a body of Christian and secular literature which also carried "authority." Selected authors slowly came to be regarded as Fathers, first Augustine, Jerome, Ambrose, Gregory the Great (by Bede), then Bede himself, in the eyes of those who came after him. This process seems to have come to a natural end early in the twelfth century. A few figures, Anselm, Bernard of Clairvaux, Hugh of St. Victor, found their way for a time into collections of extracts or *florilegia*. But they never became established as "Fathers" in their own right and in effect the list was "closed" with Bede.

Bede's careful assembly of existing opinions of earlier Christian authors known to him – Augustine, Gregory, Boethius – formed the basis of future Scriptural commentary. That was itself to be worked over by future generations engaged on much the same task, but with an increasing number of "authorities" to take into account. A text was "an authority" whose weight depended on the author's standing as Christian or secular. It was a continuing challenge to determine what could be "used" of Cicero and of other classical *auctores*. It was also a challenge to decide where to place reliance among the views of Christian authors. That became a far more pressing and nearly disastrous challenge when the remainder of Aristotle reached the Latin West in the twelfth and thirteenth centuries.

The text of the Bible in Jerome's Latin Vulgate version was taken to be the inspired Word of God, dictated by the Holy Spirit. Jerome had insisted that he did not regard his translation as itself inspired, but the methods of textual analysis used by medieval scholars depended heavily upon the assumption that the words could be examined as minutely as though they had been placed directly on the page, in the Latin, by God himself. This stood at the pinnacle of a hierarchy. This reliance upon the sacred page encouraged a corresponding though lesser respect for the written "authority" of the great Christian authors, Augustine, Gregory the Great, Jerome himself, and in due course Bede; and, on another (subsidiary) level, for the classical authorities who, although they had not been Christians, were yet ancient and respected. It fostered an idea of *auctoritas* which was formative for Christian theology.

A line gradually came to be drawn between the high authority of the early Christian 'Fathers" and the more modest authority ascribed to more recent writers. In the twelfth century it was still possible to include in collections of extracts portions of more recent writers such as Anselm of Canterbury, Hugh of St. Victor, Bernard of Clairvaux. Authors still alive carried less weight than those who had died. The division between *antiqui* and *moderni* then became a subject of debate.

Much of medieval textual criticism is devoted to the resolution of apparent contradictions in the text of Scripture, and there, it was essential to ensure that everything was "saved," nothing merely rejected; but even where the disagreement was between mere "human authors" some device for settling it had to be arrived at. Where respected opinions conflicted, an attempt had to be made to reconcile them. It was not until very late in the Middle Ages that it became possible to dismiss an opinion as merely human and possibly wrong.

The arrival in the eleventh century of a strong new interest in dialectic was important here. On the one hand, it prompted a debate about the respective roles of reasoning and this reliance upon "authority" in determining theological questions. On the other, it generated new theological questions, as we see in the disputes created by the teachings of Berengar and Roscelin. Access to more of Aristotle's logical works in the twelfth and thirteenth centuries heightened the power of these questions to disturb. For example, questions about the soul began to fly about, as well as opinions on other matters which the authorities made various abortive attempts to suppress in a series of condemnations during the thirteenth century.

Dealing with Awkward Questions: Heretics and Dissidents

For Christian theology continued to be formed in the medieval as in the patristic period by the asking of awkward and persistent questions. It was still the case that heresies were defined as such not when a question potentially challenging orthodoxy was posed, but when it was sustained by a determined and often charismatic figure.

In Augustine's day issues were raised in turn by the Donatist schism (with its implications for the doctrine of the Church and of ministry); the dualist heresy of the Manicheans (which threw into question the omnipotence of God); and the Pelagian heresy (which presented a difficulty about the necessity of the death of Christ, as well as undermining the doctrine of the sacraments). In each case, not all the implications of these ideas were clear at the outset and it was only as Augustine and others grappled with them that their drawbacks for orthodoxy became clear. In these pages other heresies of the patristic period hover in the background, and sometimes in the foreground of the work of our theologians. We meet the Arians, Eutyches and Nestorius, the Monophysites and the Monothelites, still shaping debate.

In the Carolingian period the most notable challenge was once more to the theology of the sacraments, in the debate over the nature of the Eucharistic change. In the eleventh century that issue became topical again, when Berengar forced the clarification which led to the formulation of the doctrine of transubstantiation.

In 1054 the Eastern and Western Churches divided in a schism which has still not been mended. In the twelfth century there was a revival of a latter-day "Manicheism" in the dualist Albigensian heresy. There was an anti-establishment movement which challenged the authority of the Church and the very necessity of the sacraments, led by Waldes, whose followers became known as the Poor Men of Lyons or the Waldenses. This last type of challenge became increasingly important in the later Middle Ages, evolving into the Lollard movement, which shared similar preoccupations with the imbalance of power in the Church.

Ecclesiology and Theology

Further ecclesiological issues were raised with great force in the West when the balance of power between Church and State shifted and a strong doctrine of papal plenitude of power began to emerge within the Church itself, partly as a result of the Investiture Contest leading up to the Council of Worms in 1122. Matters essentially of discipline – simony and clerical celibacy – became contentious, because they involved property. Within the Church there was a running battle between papal monarchy and episcopal collegiality during the later medieval centuries.

In a sense these were all matters of governance, of the structural elements of ecclesiology. But there was a deeper theological challenge, in the return to the ancient dilemma about the balance between charism and order. In the early Church there had been two threads of development, that led by the Spirit moving in individuals and that which placed the emphasis on the safety of a steady orderliness in the Church.

The Philosophical Parameters

In the academic arena there was challenge, too. It is surprising how much popular interest there appears to have been in the squabbles of scholars; at least, it was certainly feared that such disagreements could put stumbling-blocks in the way of the ordinary faithful. That presumes that members of that community would be able to get a sense of the issues. That in its turn would require us to ask how. St. Bernard spoke of that danger a good deal when he was confronting Peter Abelard. One clue to the way in which it might be possible for the uneducated who did not speak Latin, and did not read at all, to understand the thrust of the often abstruse disagreements of scholars, is the high interest these disputes appear to have commanded as theater. In the early sixteenth century crowds would gather to watch theologians throw accusations at one another.

In Boethius's day philosophy and theology (identified together as *theologia*) covered much the same ground. Both dealt with the existence and nature of God, unity and trinity and creation. They shared a preoccupation with the difficulty of accepting that the supreme being could have any close encounter with his creatures and that he could have humbled himself to become man. The remainder of the later theological "syllabus" was in play too of course. But it was not until the twelfth century that Hugh of St. Victor put in a nutshell the contrast between the *opus creationis* and the *opus restaurationis*. He pointed out that the existence and nature of God, the Trinity and the creation, were all matters which could be discussed by the use of reason alone if necessary. Discussion of the incarnation and the restoration of mankind and the role of the Church require a knowledge of revealed historical events, that is, of the text of Scripture and the application of reasoning to that text.

This duality of "reason" and "authority" was much in the minds of authors of the high Middle Ages. It made for an increasingly systematic and purposeful treatment of issues. Epistemological concerns were never far from the minds of late medieval scholars; technical vocabulary was increasingly refined; there was a new detail, density, and complexity in the treatment of familiar topics. Twelfth-century authors can be read "direct." For the thirteenth century the modern reader needs a crib, and Aquinas himself was conscious that he was living in an age when the proliferation of questions made it hard to see which was wood and which was tree. Beyond that stage the increasing technical refinement began to become counterproductive to the point where a Peter Ramus in the sixteenth century cried out for radical simplification.

Scholasticism, Humanism, and Renaissance

There has long hung about the study of medieval thought a group of terms which we must touch on for the sake of clarity. The terms "schoolmen" and "scholastic" have tended to be used of the writers and writings of the later Middle Ages, from the period when the universities came into being. They are probably best avoided now; they have been debased into a vocabulary with con-notations of obscurantism, and of preoccupation with minute division of topics into problems which could be addressed with remorseless methological rigor but limited inventiveness. That does not do justice to the scope the system gave for the best minds of the day to explore and even to play with ideas.

There remains some value in the contrasting of a "scholastic" with a "mon-astic" mode of doing theology. From about the late twelfth century (with excep-tions such as Bonaventure) theologians tended to embrace one road or the other, writing works of spirituality or works of philosopical theology but seldom both. The contrast is sharp in the ways in which the interpretation of Scripture was handled. But even here it does not pay to seek to make the divisions too tidy. The Franciscan and Dominican scholars who were the leaders of the day in homiletic were also among the most rigorous and talented of the "scholastics."

When we turn to ideas of humanism and renaissance we come to an unavoidable limitation of this volume. It concentrates on the work of individuals and chiefly upon those who now appear first and foremost "theologians." But throughout our period theology was not only the leading study, commanding the respect and effort of the brightest of each generation; it also affected, indeed permeated, most other studies. So if we want to understand whether there was such a thing as medieval "humanism" we must not only look at the evidence of revival of a love of the writings of the secular classical authors, but also examine the development of the doctrine of man at the hands of the theologians. Similarly, if we seek in the twelfth century and beyond the marks of a "renaissance" breadth of interest in skills and topics revived and rediscovered, we have to consider mathematical and scientific endeavors (and much else) in their contemporary theological framework. The treatment of the six days of creation by Robert Grosseteste and later by Henry of Langenstein becomes a *tour de force* of stitching into the fabric a huge range of scientific subjects.

It cannot all be done in one book. The critic will notice omissions from the list of authors treated here and of topics of importance too. We have set out principally to provide an accessible introductory volume for the reader relatively new to this scene and to provide a picture of the ways in which this thousand years of endeavor fits together.

The question with which this story must leave us is whether the medieval theologians simply went too far down a road which was a high road until the thirteenth century but in the end petered out as a mere track. Or did the sixteenth-century changes destroy a mature study as it reached its full fruition?

The End of the Ancient World

1   Augustine of Hippo
    John Rist

2   Boethius, Cassiodorus, Gregory the Great
    Charles Kannengiesser

3   Postpatristic Byzantine Theologians
    Andrew Louth

Augustine of Hippo

John Rist

Introduction

The writings of Bishop Augustine, a man predestinate, as his first biographer put it, and the most influential Christian theologian after St. Paul, mark the transition from the ancient world to the Latin Middle Ages, and set the Western theological tone for more than a thousand years.[1] Those writings form no fully tidied theological system, for as Augustine tells us himself, his thought developed. But Augustine wants to emphasize some parts of that development more than others, and in any case his own warnings on the matter were normally overlooked by his medieval successors. Hence the medieval Augustine is by no means the real Augustine, but a more homogenized figure, and insofar as we moderns give an account of a developing Augustine, we are distorting the figure known in the Middle Ages. Insofar as we see Augustine as a system-builder, however, we also indicate the origins of much later controversy, for on a number of important issues both sides of the argument could find something in their favor somewhere in Augustine – and if not, like Eriugena, they might try to circumvent him. Already by the time of Anselm, Augustine's account of love and the will had been significantly misconstrued, and few were aware of the nature of the problems underlying his accounts of God's omnipotence or the efficacy of Baptism, or of the tension between his reading of St. John on God's love and of St. Paul on predestination. No account of the effects and influence of Augustine can ignore the challenge of the relationship between the genuine and the supposed beliefs of the bishop of Hippo. At the beginning of the third millennium we are in a better position to face that challenge than were the medievals.

Formative Stages

Born in 354 in Tagaste (now Souk Ahras in Algeria) to the as yet unadventurously Christian Monnica and to Patricius – a local notable and still a pagan – Augustine was educated at nearby Madaura, former home of the racy and Platonizing novelist Apuleius, then at the African metropolis of Carthage. Here he eventually became a professor of rhetoric, first met philosophy through reading Cicero's *Hortensius*, which he said later filled his soul, for a while, with an "incredible burning desire" for God and Wisdom (rather than for a political career), and after a brief period of sexual turbulence settled down with a lower-class woman who bore him a son they named Adeodatus.

He also became a Manichean, and though only an "auditor," not a strict devotee, maintained a connection for ten years with this semi-Christian group which owed allegiance, in a manner which varied somewhat from place to place, to the third-century Mesopotamian prophet Mani. Manicheanism attracted him for its apparent rationalism, its insistence that nothing should be taken on faith, that the Christian scriptures had been corrupted by Jewish interpolations, and most enduringly by its claim to dissolve the problem of the origin of evil, especially moral evil. When we sin, they told him, it is not really we who sin – for we are a particle of pure light encased in a body – but another substance which sins within us. We ourselves, and the cosmos as a whole, are a battleground for the endlessly indecisive battle between the spirits of Good and Evil.

Like many another careerist from the provinces – and spurred by the idleness of his students who evaded paying their fees – Augustine moved to Italy in 383, first to Rome, where perhaps aided by his Manichean connections he made a number of influential contacts among the Senatorial and often determinedly pagan aristocracy, and then next year to Milan, center of the western Empire, where he was called to the Chair of Rhetoric – which he later dubbed the Chair of Lying.

The move proved unexpectedly decisive, for in the Christian oratory of Bishop Ambrose, himself a careerist turned powerful prelate, he met not only a new and fascinating literary form, but a new reading of Christianity. Most unusually as yet in the theologically largely backward West, Ambrose read and was influenced by Greek theology in the tradition of Origen, the learned third-century master of Alexandria. From this tradition he acquired and conveyed to Augustine the practice of reading the Old Testament allegorically – which helped resolve Manichean doubts about its worthiness – and the notion that God must be recognized as immaterial Spirit. In common with most others in the West, Augustine had been brought up to think of God as a vast and all-pervasive material substance.

In Milan too, though not directly through Ambrose, Augustine met platonism at first hand, or rather the neoplatonism of another third-century Alexandrian, Plotinus. His guide was a certain priest, Simplicianus, "spiritual father" of Ambrose himself and to become his successor as bishop. Augustine tells us that in the first instance it was through a man "swollen with monstrous vanity" – and probably a pagan – that he began to read a smallish number of "Platonic books," and that through Simplicianus he realized that in these books "God and his Word," though not the Incarnation, are implied (*Confessions* 7.9.14). Put otherwise he came to believe that neoplatonism provides the necessary immaterial principles to expound a coherent and worthy theism but that it could not motivate its adherents to live aright. It offered a metaphysics but no theology of historical time; it lacked the realization that Christ is the only Way from this world to the Heavenly City, even though the Platonists might descry that City from afar.

With his doubts about the Bible – even its non-Ciceronian style – assuaged through Ambrose, about the nature of God by platonist immaterialism, and about the necessary disregard for social success by Victorinus (the Roman rhetorician of an earlier generation who had translated Plotinus into the Latin which Augustine had read and who had received the unexpected answer "Yes, in a way" to the famous question, "Do walls then make a Christian?"), Augustine followed Victorinus in seeking baptism. After losing confidence in the supposed rationalism of the Manicheans – in particular he had come to recognize the force of his friends' mockery of Manichean astrology – he had temporarily fallen back on the Skepticism of Cicero, some of which would be influential on the development of his theory of belief, but which in general he soon found good Platonic reasons to defuse.

Joining Augustine in baptism were his son Adeodatus and his close friend Alypius (later also to be a bishop in Africa). His concubine had been sent back home, where she may have become a nun, but this had occurred rather earlier, with the enthusiastic support of Monnica, who had followed her successful son from Tagaste and was still urging him to a socially useful marriage: a necessary step for his future career in public life. Marriage with the mother of his child was not only politically inconvenient but legally impossible.

Augustine was convinced of Christianity well before he was prepared to accept baptism: in his way, he thought, were his engrained habits of sexual excess and his inability to lead a proper married life, and it took the example of others who had radically abandoned the world to push him, via strange stories of desert Fathers and a rather Plotinian mystical experience in Milan, to the point of conversion. But this conversion was to be uncompromising: he would afford no further indulgence to his sexual weaknesses, but establish a lay monastic community with his friends, who too were to tame their worldly appetites – in the case of Alypius not least for the brutalities of the gladiatorial shows. After a preliminary retreat in Cassiciacum, where he began to write Christian philosophy, he returned to Africa via Ostia, where before her death he shared with Monnica a second mystical experience in which Plotinian motifs remained but the backdrop was the Communion of the Saints. Once arrived home, he established his lay community where he could enjoy the "leisure in which to divinize oneself" (*deificari in otio*; *Letter* 10.2): an attitude which he later found distasteful.

Philosophy and the Bible

Before long Augustine was constrained to the priesthood as the intended successor of Valerius, the Greek-speaking bishop of Hippo Regius whose diocese had become a stronghold of the schismatic "party of Donatus," with which Augustine was to become locked in the first of those ecclesiastical battles which determined both his personal career and the nature of much of his writing. For though he was a prolific author, the great bulk of Augustine's output, with the exception of the *Confessions*, the *Literal Commentary on Genesis, The Trinity*, and the *City of God*, was in response to present and immediate demands, from a circle which began with his personal friends and widened to Africa as a whole, then spread throughout Latin-speaking Christianity and even, eventually, began to reach the Greek East. Of this massive collection – Augustine's only non-Christian book, in his Manichean days, had been *On the Fine and the Fitting* – a very large section has survived: treatises, hundreds of letters and more than 500 sermons. Only the latter genre is ill-represented: Augustine seems to have preached and published over 8,000.

Augustine's thought is unsystematic, and as he well knew, it developed over time. At the philosophical and theological level that development may be seen roughly as a steady modification of the metaphysics of Plotinus when it appeared in irreconcilable conflict with the Bible and the Catholic tradition insofar as Augustine knew it. But his knowledge of philosophy and theology, certainly when compared with his prominent Greek contemporaries, was limited – which gave his original talent more unfettered opportunities. Near the end of his life he composed a work called *Reconsiderations*, in which he offered further justification, and to some degree correction, of most of his treatises; he was particularly concerned to show that his work could offer no comfort to the followers of Pelagius, to whose refutation he had devoted much time and energy over the last twenty years of his life, and whose view that we are given, in baptism, sufficient grace to live the good life, without further and continuing divine assistance, he considered a star example of human pride: that pride taking the form of supreme confidence in the moral efficacy of one's own strict ascetic practice. For after the Fall, Augustine had come to believe in 396, in the course of thinking through enquiries of his old mentor Simplicianus about the exegesis of Romans 9, we are free only to sin. We are the spiritually lame who can walk only with God's assistance.

At his conversion Augustine had only a quite limited knowledge of the Bible. Ambrose had suggested he study Isaiah, and he had found it too difficult (*Confessions* 9.5.13). But shortly after being ordained priest in Hippo, he asked his bishop for time to study the Scriptures, which he needed above all in his role of preacher, not least against the Manicheans and the Donatists, and with that further modification of platonism began. He had always known that the platonists – ignorant of the Word made flesh – could only talk, not live, the good life, and that at best they catered for only a limited few. But he had accepted from them that happiness, understood as human flourishing and being perfect in the image and likeness of God – by which he soon understood the whole Trinity – was possible in our earthly life. That optimism was soon to fade; even the saints, he came to believe, were shown by Scripture to be liable to sinful thoughts and potentially damaging fears throughout their lives. Under platonic influence too he had confounded the world of intelligible Forms with the Christian heaven. Above all he had ignored, with the neoplatonists, the importance of history, because the neoplatonists knew nothing of the Incarnation and the Resurrection of the body, nor of the workings of God's will through the Old Testament.

On such issues, Augustine soon become convinced, the Platonists must yield to the manifest teachings and authority of Christ, and Augustine, who from the beginning professed himself only interested in "God and the soul" (e.g. *Soliloquies* 1.2.7), found that our bodily history and destiny meant that the Platonic concern with the soul – rather than with that inexplicable but unique and indeed "miraculous" (*City of God* 22.24) body–soul "mixture" which after 411 he identified as a *persona* – also needed modification: once he could say simply that we are "a rational soul using a mortal body" (*The Life-Style of the Catholic Church* 1.27.52), that at the Resurrection there will be no flesh (*Faith and the Creed* 10.24), and in his earliest commentary on Genesis that Adam and Eve were not intended to procreate physically. All such ideas were to yield to Augustine's deepening attention and comprehension of Scripture. "What I want is for it to be healed as a whole, for I am one whole. I do not want my flesh to be removed from me for ever, as if it were something alien to me, but that it be healed, a whole with me" (*Sermon* 30.4).

Yet Augustine's reading of Scripture was never strait jacketed into a system: his emphases vary, sometimes in ways which defy total assimilation, depending on which Scriptural text is uppermost in his mind or the subject of his commentary. After 400 in particular his emphasis on God as Love in commenting on John's Gospel and Epistle defies complete harmonization with his emphasis on God's justice, mercy, and predestination in his comments on Romans. And Augustine's widening and deepening knowledge of Scripture never erased his particular predilection for special texts: Genesis, the Psalms, the Pauline Epistles, and at times St. John.

Faith and Reason

The twelfth-century distinction between philosophy and theology is not only non-Augustinian; it is more generally nonpatristic. There is a sense in which Augustine could think of Plato and Plotinus as both philosophers and theologians: a Christian "theologian," most commonly at that time, is a type of metaphysician, except that through God's Revelation in Scripture and in the tradition of the Church he has more data. The origin of evil cannot be fully comprehended without knowledge of the fall of the angels, though its causes – pride, envy, and self-will – have been partly understood by the pagan philosophers. "Theology" and "philosophy" are concerned with the same enterprise: to understand the nature of God, the nature of the world and man's place in that world. The Christian notion that man is made in the image and likeness of God is the answer to a variety of "philosophical" as well as "religious" or "theological" questions.

But Augustine's claim to be a Christian philosopher, that is, both a Christian and a philosopher, would not have gone uncontested. Opponents of Christianity, as to some extent of Judaism, had long argued that Christians relied not on demonstration but on faith. Two centuries before Augustine, Galen had remarked, "had I been a follower of Moses or of Christ I would not have offered you a demonstration, I would have said 'Just believe.'" So at the very least Augustine was called on to offer a convincing explanation of the relation of reason and faith, for although he thought that unbelieving philosophers – especially platonists – can learn much by intelligent practice of their trade, it is not enough for happiness and salvation.

To resolve the problem of reason and authority, Augustine both restated the relationship between faith (or belief) and reason – in a manner which called in question the traditional Platonic contrast between knowledge and belief – and also offered a reasoned account of the nature of proper authority: the motto of the whole enterprise was "Unless you believe, you will not understand" – from the Latin Septuagint version of Isaiah 7:9[2] – for while faith seeks, understanding finds (*The Trinity* 15.2.2). In theology, at least, faith in this life is the necessary prerequisite to understanding; in the next life it will be superseded by it. For now, however, while "on the way," we live in hope.

Augustine had conceded to the Skeptics that in our present mode of existence the possibility of strict knowledge is limited: to such areas as logic, mathematics, certain forms of direct perception, and most importantly to awareness of our own existence as thinking if fallible beings ("I am mistaken, therefore I am"). Normally we live by belief alone, not only in religion, but in our entire daily lives. It is by belief in the authority of Cicero himself that we know that he executed a number of the Catilinarian conspirators in 63 BC. It is by belief in our mother that we know who is our father and we believe on the authority of midwives and others who is our mother. So since we must live, for the most part, not by knowledge but by justified belief, it is entirely reasonable to follow those with the relevantly legitimate authority. In the case of religion it is the Scriptures, and for their authority it is the Church: Augustine tells us that he would not have believed the Gospels were it not for the authority of the Catholic Church (*Against the Epistle of the Foundation* 5.6).

Augustine defines belief as "thinking with assent" (*Predestination of the Saints* 2.5), and by assent he means something like what the Stoics, whom he knew chiefly through Cicero and Varro, had meant when they spoke of assent to a proposition. But Augustine is very conscious that we do not merely assent to what is rational; we often decline to do so because we do not want to. So that to understand belief, and the legitimate authority to which we can rationally give credence, we not only need to understand the propositional content of our proposed theological beliefs, but to want to hold them. In other words – and here we find ourselves face to face with Augustine's account of the devastating effects of the Fall of Adam – our beliefs are affected not only by our present *ignorance*, and by our fallen and vicious habitual desires, but more fundamentally by our inherited weakness (*infirmitas*) under temptation. For such *concupiscentia* is the condition of our fallen "will";[3] if we were holy our *concupiscentia* would be our *caritas*, our love of God and neighbor.

Love, Grace, and Knowledge

Human nature, and above all human love, which should be directed to God, is corrupted in Adam, and being weakened, falls prey to the accumulated weight of evil – to what Augustine calls "carnal" habits. Such habits are also disorderly, and Augustine calls on God to prioritize his loves: *ordinate in me caritatem* (Song of Songs 2:4). Instead of being "slaves of God," we are liable, without God's help, to be slaves of the Devil: citizens not of the City of God – with a love of what is unchanging, eternal, and the free property of all as God's gift – but of the secular city, where perverse self-love, and its corresponding greed, is directed towards the temporal and changing, to our own will rather than to the will (and with it the perfect nature) of God the Trinity.

But what is Adam to us? We, believes Augustine, are somehow one in Adam, just as the redeemed will be one in Christ. As his life progressed, Augustine came to hold that each of us is a combination of two natures, one communal, or in Adam, and by adoption potentially in Christ, and one our own personal life. From Adam, or as member of a fallen race, we have inherited our weakness of intellect – we see through a glass darkly – and our wandering perversity of love. Once Augustine seems to have been closer to the "Pelagian" position that we are able at least to seek God's help in our now deformed condition. After his attempts in 396 to answer Simplicianus' questions on Paul's Epistle to the Romans, he became convinced that the Scriptures themselves bear out a different and darker reading – despite his attempts to save his earlier account of "free will" – that for us to act rightly, not to be weighed down by our perverse loves and carnal habits, our "wills" – that is our basic set of loves and hates – must be "prepared by God." The specific Latin (*voluntas praeparatur a Deo*, from Proverbs 8:35) may not appear before about 412; the idea itself is much earlier. Grace, Augustine had told Simplicianus (1.2.13), is the "achiever of a good will."

Yet for all the inadequacy Augustine identifies in our capacity to will the right, and to love the right, it is in this area of human motivation – as in his view that Platonic Forms are thoughts (not concepts) in God's mind – that his deeply Platonic construction of Christian metaphysics is to be seen most clearly. Augustine was always certain as a Christian that the core of any philosophically adequate justification of Christianity must be Platonic (plus a modicum of Stoicism, strained through neoplatonism to remove the vitalism and pantheism). For platonism alone talked both of an immaterial world and of man's love for the Good; if Plato and Plotinus had overestimated the power of that unaided love to "persevere to the end," their insight that man has the capacity to be inspired by the love of an immaterial God, and that such inspiration alone is adequate to bring us progress – at least before the Fall – in the spiritual life is fundamentally correct. The point is so important that Augustine should speak for himself. From many examples, the following, from different stages of his career, faithfully represent his thinking:

Men cry out that they are blessed when they embrace with great yearning the beautiful and longed-for bodies of their wives, or even of prostitutes, and shall we doubt that we are blessed in the arms of truth. (*On Free Will* 2.13.35)[4]

Too late have I loved you, beauty so old and so new. (*Confessions* 10.27.38)

Give me a man in love: he understands what I mean. Give me a man who yearns: give me a man who is hungry: give me a man travelling in the desert, who is thirsty and sighing for the spring of the eternal country. Give me that sort of man; he knows what I mean. But if I talk to a cold man, he does not know what I am talking about. (*On John's Gospel* 26.4)

But this transformed theory of platonic *Eros*, in heterosexual language, in which Love is eventually, as in *The Trinity* (15.20.38), identified as the Holy Spirit, is never detached from its realistically Christian context. We do not live, as Adam lived, in a world transparent to and for the love of God, but in what in the *City of God* is dubbed "this darkness of social life" (19.6). And in that darkness, where Christ and his Cross – the latter grows on Augustine's consciousness as he develops – are the only Way and baptism is the gateway to Eternal Life, God's help is constantly required; our love is too weak on its own, and indeed, as Augustine had also pointed out to Simplicianus, we cannot determine the circumstances in which we shall fall in love. Hence our final text on love must be that from the *Confessions* which drew down the condemnation of Pelagius: "Love, who are always ablaze . . . enkindle me. Give what you command and command what you will." The *Confessions*, composed shortly after the theological analysis of Augustine's replies to Simplicianus, presents the personal working out, in Augustine's own calling by God, of the theology of grace first developed in those replies.

If our wills and our loves require God's support, the same is true of our fallen intellect. Augustine's account of human learning is platonic, in the by now authorized version of Plotinus. He seems to have toyed with the pre-existence of the soul – required by Plato himself for epistemological reasons among others – but he certainly soon abandoned that unChristian possibility in favor of a rather Plotinian view that we are aware in our ongoing "memory" of "impressed notions." How many such notions exist is not entirely clear, but Augustine speaks at different times of ideas of eternal law, of numbers, of wisdom, of a just law impressed on the human heart and of the good itself. Such impressed ideas are rules by reference to which we can both form concepts and make judgments, moral and nonmoral.

In the platonic manner, Augustine holds that for knowledge first-hand experience is essential: that is why we can only have beliefs about historical events in the past. That is why we need such immediate access to the impressed ideas, but though we all have such ideas, we are not always able to make use of them: for that we require illumination from the Teacher, that is, from Christ. The effect of such illumination is that our internal awareness is awoken by the light of God. The Good, that is, enables us to see what is in fact in front of our eyes (whether physical or mental). Augustine observes that we do not understand words if we do not know that to which they refer (this is a major topic of *The Master*), and that we do not understand texts unless we can read them in the right light. Otherwise we should understand the Scriptures merely by reading them through. Often divine illumination takes the form of our being induced to comprehend what we previously did not want to know.

So the illumination of the mind is not merely the light shining on impressed ideas, but the presenting of such ideas in a way that is compelling to the thinker. Such a theory, of course, is "platonic," and in no way to be compounded, in its originally Augustinian form, with any kind of exposition of Aristotle's "active intellect." Indeed Augustine, like most of the Fathers, had only a limited knowledge of Aristotle. He tells us that he had read the *Categories* without a master, but he was perhaps too easily persuaded by Plotinus that Aristotle's hylemorphic theory of soul and body as form and matter does insufficient justice to the required account of the soul.

Thus far we have seen Augustine reconciling skepticism about knowledge with a platonic theory of impressed ideas, itself grounded on the claim that by introspection we reach the ground of our being. But at every turn we are confronted with his insistence that in our pride and self-love, and in the *concupiscentia* and *ignorantia* that are the results of the Fall, even in the baptized, we are unable to secure happiness in this life and can only hope for salvation if God's assistance is available.

Augustine himself, as we have seen, always claimed only to be interested in "God and the soul." But here is a problem. Augustine believes that we are created, as Genesis had it, in the image and likeness of God, and by that he understood, though not immediately, that we are the image of the whole Trinity. Clearly an image and likeness is only intelligible if we have an idea of the original, but for us, as Paul had it, the possibility of knowledge of God is only through a glass darkly. So how are we to proceed? In his later life Augustine became convinced that we must perforce begin to think about the Trinity through ourselves as an image: we must attempt to understand God through the "memory," intelligence, and will or love that we ourselves exhibit – though there is certainly no formal theory of the analogy of being in Augustine or in any other patristic writer. Such is the project of *The Trinity*, a work on which Augustine toiled for many years (404 to after 420), continually being held up, to the irritation of some of his friends, by what he considered the more pressing problems of his pastoral office.

God's Nature

But why should we believe in a God at all, especially in view of the problem of evil which had so concerned Augustine in his Manichean days that he had then found himself forced to agree that God must not be omnipotent, must be what he would later call "cruelly weak" (*Unfinished Work* 1.120)? Yet Augustine says in the *Confessions* (e.g. 6.5.7) that he never doubted God's existence; the problem was always with his nature and our sources of knowledge of that nature. He even suggests – in a world in which there were few atheists in the modern sense (that is, individuals who deny God's existence) rather than in the ancient sense (in which both Aristotle and Epicurus were deemed atheists in that they deny the existence of God's providence, of his care or love for mankind) – that the most plausible explanation for any denial of God's existence is that some people are so morally corrupt that they need to convince themselves of atheism.

Yet there are arguments for God's existence in Augustine, most particularly that from *On Free Will* (Book 2) which is the precursor of Anselm's ontological argument – if indeed that really is an argument for God's existence rather than for his necessary characteristics if he exists. In *On Free Will* Augustine argues from the existence of our minds to the existence of God as an immaterial substance. Roughly the argument is that although our minds are the highest thing in us, yet they are capable of identifying what is higher than themselves, above all Truth: higher because eternal and unchanging. That might seem to lead to a static, even impersonal God like the platonic Form of Goodness, but Augustine now avails himself of the neoplatonic claim that if such a Truth exists, it must exist in a mind, and that mind cannot be human, because it could not then be eternal and unchanging. Such a mind must indeed be that than which nothing greater can be conceived.[5]

Such an argument, built on the basic certainty of my own existence as a thinking being – Augustine, as we have seen, believes he can dispose of skeptical claims that we do not know our own existence as beings of this sort – will give us a neoplatonic God, though Augustine does not use the typical Plotinian language so to describe him. Augustine's God is not identified as "beyond Being," but as "being itself" (e.g. *Expositions on Psalms* 135 (134)): the terms are closer to the formulation of Porphyry than to that of Plotinus, though mediated to Augustine through Victorinus (*Against Arius* 4.19). Though Augustine never accuses Plotinus of the crude fallacy of proposing in the phrase "beyond Being" a God who does not exist, he seems to have been nervous of such language and to prefer the less spectacular "highest being" (*City of God* 12.2; cf. *Sermon* 117.5 for *summus deus*) or "true being." But above all, of course, immaterial Being.

But such talk and such neoplatonizing arguments about God's existence get nowhere near the Christian divinity, the Trinity in Unity. We have already seen how Augustine was aware from his Milanese days that the neoplatonists knew nothing of the God of history, the God of the particularism of the Old Testament, the God of the Incarnation and Resurrection. But there are other features of the Christian God which seem to have caused him even more trouble in his attempts to amalgamate Christianity with neoplatonic metaphysics. Classical philosophy – though Augustine was hardly aware of it – had no developed concept of omnipotence, yet omnipotence in some acceptation is an essential attribute of the God of both the Old Testament and the New. Certainly the neoplatonists thought that somehow the world is entirely dependent metaphysically on the One, the first principle; without the One nothing could exist. But in contrast to the Christians they could not envisage the possibility of God without a world. They could no more imagine a creation *ex nihilo* than could the pantheist Stoics; that possibility had in effect been ruled out since the time of Parmenides. But although Christians too, when philosophizing in the Greek tradition, had much difficulty in coming to terms with the idea of omnipotence (to which they alluded daily in their prayers), by Augustine's time, and in Augustine himself, they are clear that it is indeed a divine attribute.

Despite creation *ex nihilo* (the only plausible Christian substitute, now long rejected, was creation *de deo*, that is, from God's own substance[6]), the specifics of Augustine's doctrine of omnipotence are far from transparent; hence a source of much confusion for his later readers, particularly if they are inclined to believe in his near theological completeness. What seems clear to Augustine is that God's omnipotence must indicate not merely that he had made heaven and earth – early accounts of omnipotence stress physical power – but also entail that his will cannot be thwarted: which leaves the problem of how his "will" is to be understood. The apparent starkness of Augustine's emphasis on the will, however, is somewhat diminished by his recognition of the distinction between what God directly causes and what he merely allows. And what he allows must be governed by the laws of logic (for God himself is Truth). Thus the existence of angels, and of human freewill (which itself depends on man's being a genuine image of God, at least in Adam, and to a degree even in our fallen race), is incompatible with the necessary moral goodness of the whole creation.

The Fall also introduces problems of the relationship between God's justice and God's mercy. How could God wish everyone to be saved, if some are not? And how can it not be the case that some (indeed many) are damned, if God is to be just? Indeed how are some to be *saved* if God is just, for all deserve punishment? If some are saved, why are all not saved? Certainly God is omnipotent, but in what does his omnipotence consist? Augustine, largely unaware, as we have seen, of the philosophical roots of his own problems about omnipotence, and that he is treading almost untrodden philosophical territory, unknowingly compounds those problems by the nature of many of his literary projects: different emphases relevant to the problem of predestination can be discerned in comments on different Scriptural texts – on John or Paul, for example – and Augustine's reputation has suffered in various ways by the popularity of his short *Encheiridion*, a work not among his very latest, but easy of access and a source for overheated and careless phrases not to be found elsewhere.[7]

Problems with omnipotence arise not only because of different emphases in interpreting different parts of Scripture; they are also called out by the very notion of assimilating the Bible and Catholic tradition and practice on the one hand to the traditions of the philosophers on the other. Augustine talked about foreknowledge and determinism – a legacy from the debates of the Stoics and Skeptics – long before he became conscious of the specifically Christian, though obviously related problems of predestination,[8] and it is by no means clear that his account of God's foreknowledge (or more strictly, since God as immaterial is beyond time, of God's knowledge) can be squared with his Scripturally based accounts of predestination: accounts, that is, not merely of what God knows but of what God does. For the core of much of his argument against philosophical determinism, for example in *On Free Will*, is that knowledge of future contingents does not entail the determination of those future contingents. But the doctrine of predestination precisely does involve this, as Augustine himself says when he defines predestination as "God's foreknowledge *and preparation* of those acts of kindness by which those who are saved are saved" (*On the Gift of Perseverance* 14.35).

Baptism and the Church

It is clear to Augustine that only a remnant of our fallen race (the *massa damnationis*) is saved – though illustrating our ignorance of God's ways he told Simplicianus that if he were to guess who were saved, God would laugh him to scorn (1.2.22). But if some are saved – and of that Augustine is secure, even if his account of the atonement is relatively undeveloped, combining something of Ambrosiaster's ransom theory (especially in his earlier writings) with intimations of the "satisfaction" theory of Anselm – how can he be so sure that all are not? Doubtless the reasons are in part historical; Christians in times of persecution had been far from normally inclined to suppose that their persecutors would repent and seek baptism, the gateway to eternal life. But this empirical claim is closely tied to doctrines about baptism itself, in Augustine as well as in many of his predecessors. For above all in north Africa baptism was considered essential for salvation, and although Augustine occasionally suggests (as in *On Baptism* 4.22.29) not only that exception is to be made for martyrdom, but that "conversion of the heart" may suffice, he is more normally inclined to wonder whether even the penitent thief had not in fact been baptized.

Old Testament worthies apart, membership of the Catholic Church is normally a prerequisite for salvation. Even baptism in and of itself is not enough, else the schismatic Donatists of north Africa could be secure. Augustine knows, and rigorously interprets, the famous text of Cyprian (*Letter* 73.21) that outside the Church there is no salvation. Yet although normally baptism and Church membership are required for salvation, they are not of course sufficient; we have already seen how Augustine does not know God's will in the matter, and could not divine it. What he does know, of course, without knowing its limitations, is his theology of the necessity of baptism; hence another problem he bequeathed to the Middle Ages, that of the fate of unbaptized infants, subject, as he tells Jerome (*Letter* 166.4.10), to a very light penalty: such that it is certainly better for them to have been born than not.

As for the Church and its actual membership, Augustine adopted a thesis of the unorthodox Donatist Tyconius, whose scriptural exegesis he greatly admired: that as Tyconius has it in his first "Rule" (on "The Lord and his Body") – rejecting the sectarian notion current among the Donatists themselves that the visible Church is the Church of the pure – the visible Church is a mixed body, partly the body of the Lord, partly the body of Satan. Those baptized are on the right route, but many are called and few are chosen, and Church members, like the traveler from Jerusalem to Jericho, may be mugged *en route* (*Sermon* 131.6).

One of the side-effects of Augustine's mature thinking along these lines was its implication for the work and responsibilities of a bishop: his role is to get people into the Churches, to preach to them and minister the Sacraments. It is not his business to be too scrupulous about the depth and sincerity of the belief of his flock – though, in enabling God's grace to work on those he wills, he will certainly castigate outrageous sins and sinners, and he will be held to account if he does not.

It is clear that for Augustine, however undeveloped his theory of the Atonement, Christ is not merely an *exemplum*. Were he merely that, Augustine would on his own account be a Pelagian. Man always needs God's help, as we have seen, and membership in the Church is his normal means of providing it. In a late work (*On Correction and Grace* 11), Augustine fleshes out the theology of how this help is bestowed. Adam before the fall was always capable of doing good; he had the capacity not to sin (*posse non peccare*), and that capacity was the result of a condition established by God (who thus offered an *adiutorium sine quo non*). But now after the Fall, the *felix culpa*, we are of course much worse off than Adam – needing further divine assistance, the *adiutorium quo* – but paradoxically that further assistance will bring us to a better state than Adam could have attained: a state in which we cannot sin (*non posse peccare*); a quasi-divine condition which we reach by a kind of divinization. Here Augustine makes use of an idea widely developed in the Greek Fathers since Origen and Athanasius: our adoption by God as Paul had described it. It is sometimes said – perhaps largely for reasons of denominational polemic – that there is no significant theory of divinization in Augustine; that notion is false.[9] Echoes of Irenaeus and Athanasius are obvious in such comments as "He who is God was made man – who was about to make gods of those who were men" (*Sermon* 192.1.1).

To work for his mediocre flock, to be the means by which God's grace can take hold of those he wishes, is the "burden" of the bishop. For bishops are an external sign of the invisible Church, and they are linked, in Augustine's view, in an Apostolic succession. As to how they function as a group, his views are somewhat fluid. The Donatist "bishops" are certainly outside the true Church because they are a parochial African splinter-group, out of communion with Rome, the see which possesses the bodies of Peter and Paul. But Augustine's views of the precise nature of the supreme authority of the Roman see are unclear. With the African bishops as a whole he was delighted to secure the support of Rome against the Pelagians, but such support, though viewed as final (*causa finita*), was sought as a backup to decisions already reached by the African bishops themselves in local councils. For though Augustine was a universalist, he was not a centralist. He had little time for appeals by African clergy to Rome against decisions of their own bishops; indeed the African bishops in general determined to forbid such appeals.

Sin and Virtue

What kind of good life should the clergy encourage in their flocks? The antisectarian direction of Augustine's later teaching might lead us to suppose that though he himself lived a monastic life, and hoped that his clergy would be monks, his demands would not be too severe. Yet we must distinguish between the ideal and the expectation. Augustine's demands were high, even to the point – detested in late Roman society – of expecting masters not to have sex with their slave-girls; to which he admitted that the most likely reply would be "Can I not do what I like in my own house?" (*Sermon* 224.3.3).

As the number of his sermons indicates, Augustine was nothing if not a preacher. Even before becoming a bishop, he had been asked, contrary to local practice, to preach to the evidently ill-informed African episcopate on the Creed. His sermons, though hugely popular, were imbued both with an explicit moral message, and with the clear outlines of the basic theology behind that message. As we should expect, that theology is above all of our need for God's grace if we are to be freed from our present "carnal habits," and to be endowed with *caritas* rather than subjected to various forms of the *concupiscentia* which has become our second nature. Augustine devotes much time to explaining the psychological condition we are now in: our divided selves being the victims both of the sin of Adam – the guilt but not the subsequent weakness of which is removed by baptism – and of the personal sins to which that weakness invariably exposes us.

In his earlier days as a preacher and controversialist Augustine pointed frequently to what St. John calls the "triple concupiscence" (1 John 2:16). Specific references to such concupiscence fade away after about 400, though the themes survive in other phrases, and may be treated as typical. The triple concupiscence may be identified roughly as (a) the lust for power (*libido dominandi*) – naturally the mark of fallen public, but not exclusively public life – (b) the lust for bodies and in general the desire to "enjoy" oneself physically and idolatrously, that is, without reference to the superior claims and implications of the love of God – and (c) the abuse of the intellect summed up by the traditional term *curiositas*: a desire to know what it is not proper to know. The core of the triple concupiscence is pride, or apostasy from God. Its antidote is Christian humility, which must be linked with the recognition of our dependence on God and our love for him as our creator and redeemer. For Augustine, who had always been deeply concerned with the problem of the origin of moral evil, the root of that problem is not that we are material but that we are created. But we do not want to accept our creation; we want – this is both an inevitable risk of our creation from nothing and the ultimate source of our evil acts – to be creators of ourselves. Only by adoption as sons of God can we be logically and theologically freed from such risks. Then we shall no longer wish to impose sins on our bodies or to use our bodies sinfully.

In identifying pride as the source of sin, Augustine is able to carry through another part of his "project" for the assimilation of traditionally platonic ideas into a Christian framework. For alongside such Scriptural texts as "The beginning of all sin is pride" (e.g. *On Genesis against the Manichaeans* 2.5.6 from Ecclesiasticus (10:9–15)), we may set a passage from Plotinus' *Ennead* 5.1.1, where the soul's evil and pride (*tolma*) is the wish to rule itself and belong to itself: the wish to rejoice in its own power. Such power, Augustine tells us in *On Free Will* (3.25.76), the soul enjoys as if she were a god. But for Augustine only the true God should be "enjoyed."

Rejoicing in one's own power in despite of God will reveal itself, in many texts and not least in *On Free Will*, in a failure to recognize that goods are to be shared, not simply appropriated. Pride, Augustine tells us in the *Literal Commentary on Genesis* (11.15.19–20), rejoices in private goods; it is a perverse self-love (Augustine can distinguish this from a respect for the self which derives from our common creation in God's image) to identify what is common with the private: private and hence a source not of unity for mankind but of division.

The second aspect of the triple concupiscence has contributed much to Augustine's ill-repute in more contemporary quarters. As we have seen, his views on the relation, within the human person, between the soul and the body developed over time, but he was always concerned with the attitude of the soul to the body's needs and desires, not least its sexual desires. When we consider Augustine's attitude to the institutions of social life, we shall look at the effects of this on his view of marriage, but we should notice here that he never underestimates the importance and ambiguity of sexuality.

On strictly platonic principles, love and sexuality being features of our most basic nature as given by God, their misuse is liable to be particularly revealing in its personal and social consequences – though not necessarily among the more sinful of human errors. Sexual sins are not, in Augustine's view, caused by the body struggling against the soul; they are caused by the perverse attitudes of the soul itself, which thus imposes them on the body. Notoriously, he thinks that the phenomenon of unwanted erections and impotence is part of the penal condition we are in: we are not even able to control our own bodies, so weak has the soul become. Our unwanted sexual disarray is a striking symbol of the disharmony of our soul–body relationship as a whole. It is thus hardly surprising that Augustine is well aware of problems of sexual exploitation: another form of the arrogant misuse of others.

The third aspect of the triple *concupiscentia* is *curiositas*, a traditional vice among the pagans as well as the Christians, typically associated, for example, with the desire to discover, by magic or astrology, what we should not know. Augustine's attitude to *curiositas* may seem to suggest an unjustifiable curb on man's legitimate desire to know and understand the world in which he lives, but we have only to allow that there are certain things which we ought not to know, such as, for example, how a baby would react to various forms of torture, to realize that Augustine is raising a serious question. The moral issue is not whether *curiositas*, in some form, is a vice, but what are the specific limits of *curiositas*: what is it right for us to know and not to know? It was to remain highly contentious what Augustine thought proper subjects of Christian study – such study being primarily governed by what it could contribute to an understanding of the Scriptures – and where the edge of some form of *curiositas* had been reached. Discussion of such matters in *On Christian Teaching* had a decisive impact on debates about a Christian scholarly curriculum for centuries.

It would be seriously misleading if, in approaching morality through the "triple concupiscence," we gave the impression that Augustine's is primarily an ethics of prohibition; rather it is an ethics of the inspiration of the Good, though an ethics in which fear is the beginning, but not of course the end, of wisdom. Augustine claims to know of few if any instances where fear has played no part in a man's conversion to Christianity (*On Catechizing the Simple* 4.7–9), but that fear is intended to give way to love of God, and hence through God to love of neighbor – the value of the "neighbor" depending on his nature as the image of God and the product of God's will.

In his treatment of love as the basis of the virtues, Augustine transcends not only traditional Stoic rationalism, but in the strictness and uncompromising nature of his position, platonism as well. From almost the beginning of his Christian career, in what is in other respects too an advance warning of the future direction of his thought, he already claimed in *On the Life-Style of the Catholic Church* (1.15.25) that all the virtues are modes of love – not as the Stoics had argued, modes of right reason, though Augustine would be the last to hold them to be contrary to reason. Hence the notorious slogan, perhaps misused even by Augustine himself in dealing with ecclesiastical opponents, "Love and do what you wish." To attain the standards of that "love," however, would be to achieve a human perfection possible only in another life. "Love and do what you wish," far from being a license for situation ethics, is nothing less than a call to mankind to want to want what God wishes, loves, and commands, and to conform our actual wishes and practices to those second-order wants. Nor does it prevent Augustine from holding to certain moral absolutes: such as the strict prohibition on lying, even in a good cause.

Public and Social Life

Turning from private morals to public life and to political and social institutions, we see how Augustine's identification of pride (compounded in the Devil by envy of mankind) as the root of all evils, takes the form less of greed and more prominently of the *libido dominandi*, the lust for power, the desire, as Augustine was inclined to put it (*On Music* 6.13.41), to have someone's soul (not merely his body) under one's control. As with any political thinker, Augustine's utterances on public life must in the first place be set against his contemporary society, and the late Roman Empire bore little resemblance to the *poleis* of classical Greece where political science and philosophy began. Yet for all that, and while Augustine sums up his age and "the darkness of social life" in which we normally live by commenting that the typical power of one man over another is that of a master over a slave, it is remarkable how in many ways the Platonism of Augustine's metaphysics has its fiercer analogue not only in his ethics but even in his political thought: not least in his account of the degraded features of much of public life. Like Plato in the *Republic* (which he had only seen in translation), Augustine took the view – reinforced by influences not only fron Stoicism but from apocalyptic Christianity itself – that we are all at least *en route* to being either slaves of the good and of God or of evil and the Devil; that there is no third City; that a guide to the true nature of society can be found in looking at the opposite ends of the apparent political spectrum: the City of God, of which according to the Psalmist glorious things are spoken (Ps. 86:3), and the prime example of the secular City which – to the presumed horror of not a few of Augustine's contemporaries – was the City of Rome and the Roman Imperial system: even, at least potentially for most of Augustine's career, the *Christian* version of that system. Caesaropapism of the variety espoused in his praise of the Emperor Constantine by the historian Eusebius and many who came after him soon seemed shallow to Augustine.

From the very first pages of the *City of God*, Augustine contrasts the cult of power, the religion of the secular city demonstrated paradigmatically by Rome itself, with the worship of the Christian God. The Letter of James (4:6) tells us that God resists the proud and gives grace to the humble; the poet Virgil, speaking for Rome herself, emphasizes that her mission is to spare the conquered and beat down the proud. But the sense of "proud" is now quite different: the proud, for Augustine, are those who defy the true God and substitute their violent and salacious idols; for Virgil they are those who oppose Rome's rise to domination. Beneath the gloss of heroic poetry and debased panegyric Augustine discerns a more sinister story.

Echoing not the poets but Rome's own secular historians, in particular Sallust, Augustine explains how Rome's rise to domination must be understood in terms of the inherently vicious character of fallen man himself. It was Sallust who had popularized the phrase "lust for power" in historical writing, and Augustine follows him in explaining how that lust enabled the Romans to discipline other, but lesser, vices – until supreme power had been attained. And within the drive for power of the Roman community as a whole, at first hidden but then surfacing in a struggle to the death among the leading men, is the search for individual glory and honor, but a search which resolves itself into the pursuit of a personal despotism.

Indeed that hidden goal had long since revealed itself in the brutality and arrogance which had disfigured Roman history even in its early and more "heroic" period: the whole is marked by rape, by the reduction of the poor to slavery, by endless executions and floggings, and a ceaseless desire for war and further conquest. The pretext and "goal" is a kind of peace; the reality is the death of countless thousands of people. The Emperor Nero marks the culminating point – or nadir – of the entire process: even glory is now despised, while greed for domination is all that remains (*City of God* 5.19). Such success, Augustine concludes platonically and in the words of Cicero, merely affords the tyrant the miserable opportunity to sin the more gravely because now unpunished. Here we reach the tyrannical man of Plato's *Republic*, and certainly Augustine emphasizes how he is torn apart by his insatiable but conflicting cravings. But he adds something specifically Christian to the earlier picture: the tyrant, seeking to be divine, as to a degree are all sinners including Augustine himself (*Confessions* 2.1.1), puts on a diabolical unity: a blasphemous image of the unity of God.

The Roman Empire is the most recent, and the most successful, of secular societies. In its Christian guise it at least suppresses vice and allows Christianity to be preached, but there is no reason to think that in "Christian times" evil-living will cease or even that persecution is at an end – and the fall of the Empire would merely mean that some new form of godless structure would take its place.

But while the Christian Empire lasts, what should be its attitude to non-Christians? Augustine's views vary: he had no misgivings about the suppression of pagan practice, though it appears that he had no interest in compelling conversion. Nor does he suggest that direct attempts be made to pressure Jews; they will be converted at the end of time. In the case of heretics and schismatics, however, his attitudes grew more severe, colored by his long struggle with Donatism, and by his increasing satisfaction that Donatist terrorism – directed both against Catholics and against fellow Donatists who might wish to convert – could be forcibly suppressed by the Imperial power. Eventually he concluded that the Donatists should be "compelled to come in," since in religion as elsewhere evil habits can only be broken by a *disciplina* which encourages the heretic to "recognize the truth which he had overlooked." But though the Church must persecute the schismatic "brother" (*Letter* 173.10), Augustine (who normally also disliked the practice of torture) remained opposed to his execution – which would needlessly deprive him of the chance of repentance.

Augustine is pessimistic about the prospects of the secular city: its institutions, which include judicial torture and slavery, are bitter, and the good man is constantly longing to flee to the monastery – of which in defiance of his own theories about the ubiquitous repetitiousness of human sin, Augustine is at times too sanguine. But such flight, he insists, is often to be rejected: soldiers and administrators are advised to stay at their posts. The agonizing decisions, the ambiguous occasions where one has to choose where no choice can give much immediate satisfaction or comfort, are part of our present penal condition. If current forms of slavery were abolished, Augustine would doubtless maintain, other versions of domination would replace them. The solution lies not in institutional reform but with the human heart: an unfortunate disjunction which tended to perpetuate systemic injustice or "structures of sin" – and not untypical of ancient thought as a whole.

The Christian society in which we must live while on the road (*in via*) to our eternal destiny will have its monks and nuns, but the vast mass of its population will be married laity. Yet marriage itself, a divine institution ordained by God for the perpetuation of the human race, lies also between the two worlds: between the City of God and the secular city. Its purpose even before the fall (Augustine eventually determined) was the procreation of legitimate children, and associated with this are two other goods, the loyalty of the spouses to one another, and the *sacramentum*, that symbol of unity in a fallen world which indicates the unequal partnership between Christ and his Church (Eph. 5:23).

Yet the essence of marriage is the friendship of the spouses, the *maritalis affectio* – which is why it is the consent of the parties and not consummation which makes the marriage: a friendship to be developed in a particular circumstance. Yet in a fallen world even friendship is a mixed blessing: Adam himself sinned "so as not to be severed from his only companion" (*Literal Commentary on Genesis* 11.42.59; *City of God* 14.11). Friends, as we would put it, can easily become cronies.

Augustine has a high view of marriage, and demands fidelity equally of both partners, but though he is prepared to say (*The Good of Marriage* 3.3) that "there is a certain dignity in our fervent pleasures when a man and a woman come together realizing that they are parents," he has failed to find a clear theory of the goodness of sexuality apart from its obvious necessity for conception. Some at least of his difficulties are caused by a more general problem: the belief, common to most ancient thinkers, that pleasure should exclusively be enjoyed as the indirect effect of an activity rather than as in part at least constitutive of an end in itself.

Combine the lack of any claim that within the context of an appropriate lifestyle pleasure can be a necessary good for those who experience it with Augustine's belief that somehow original sin is transmited from one generation to another and that sexual behavior, like all human activities, is liable to take the form of one party exploiting the other, and a darker side of the institution of marriage will develop. At times it may appear more like one of God's ways of bringing good out of evil – though that, of course, is not Augustine's considered view. On the other hand Augustine avoids the modern "heresy" of uniquely separating at least some forms of sexual activity from the effects of original sin.

Looking to the Future

There is no place in our limited survey to pursue such ambiguities further, but the mere mention of them highlights the basic problem in reading and comprehending Augustine as a whole – and helps us to understand both why his legacy is so important and why it is so controversial. Augustine grew up in a largely pagan culture – which gave way as he lived to what was to be the Christian Middle Ages. In his education he was soaked in Latin (but not Greek) classical literature – Virgil, Terence, Cicero – and in the Greek philosophers, above all the neoplatonists. On top of this was grafted his growing Christianity, so that he emerged bestriding the Latin West almost as a summation of the past. Already in his lifetime he came close to being an oracle, and he himself, recognizing such a destiny, did his best in writing his *Reconsiderations* to present an exaggerated uniformity in his views. But there is a difference between the mature Augustine and the growing Augustine, and even the mature Augustine was still in course of growth.

Augustine read Virgil and Plotinus, Cicero and Tyconius; his successors largely read Augustine, and assumed that they could take over his thought without going through the stages that had made it what it was. And in adopting that attitude, in assuming that Augustine had largely replaced his own past, they were inclined to think that too many loose ends had been tidied up. But the real Augustine had not entirely reconciled God's justice with his mercy, let alone St. Paul with St. John; he had not decided the best account of the origin of the soul; he had wavered on the role of pagan writings in Christian culture; he had left unfinished business on the details of sexual morality and hence on marriage, as well as on the wider relationship between soul and body. And the list is still incomplete: Augustine had left no finished account of man's metaphysical as distinct from his moral identity – or lack of it; he had left unfinished his account of the nature of divine illumination and of the relationship between our love and our overall "mindset"; he had not reconciled foreknowledge, freewill (however understood), and predestination. On many of these themes he had made great advances while remaining aware of much further work to do. As he says of his extraordinarily influential discussion of the Trinity and of its analogues in human psychology, he wanted people both to think carefully about what he had said and to correct his errors in a way appropriate to a Christian.

The Augustine we have displayed was not always the Augustine seen by his successors. I have argued elsewhere that Augustine would have had little difficulty in updating his work to meet much, though not all, recent criticism. Later Augustinians might find their difficulties greater.[10] The medieval Augustine was not always the most philosophically or theologically powerful Augustine, and in some matters he became a "false friend" or even an opponent of the real Augustine. But to say as much is only to say that Augustine's legacy is both what he did, said, and intended, and what he was assumed to have meant. To deny either the one or the other Augustine is to impoverish the history of theology.

Notes

1 In the present limited chapter it is possible only to scratch the surface. Thus important topics will be treated inadequately or even omitted altogether. I have attempted a limited rectification of this in the suggestions for further reading.

2 The earliest reference is *The Master* 11.37.

3 *Concupiscentia* has several senses in Augustine. Early on it normally means lust; later it often denotes that weakness of will which is a consequence of the fall.

4 I have retained this traditional but misleading translation for the Latin *De Libero Arbitrio Voluntatis* simply because it *is*

traditional. A more accurate rendering would be *On Human Responsibility*.

5 The origin of the argument, as pointed out by du Roy (1966: 245 n. 5), seems to be a passage of Cicero (*Tusc. Disp.*, 1.26.65).

6 For rejection of such ideas in Augustine see *On Free Will* 1.2.5, *Soliloquies* 1.1.2, etc.

7 Cf. Rist (1994: 272 n. 43). At a similar date (ca. 421) can be found in *Against Julian* 2.8.23 the sole instance in Augustine of the phrase *servo arbitrio*.

8 The two are still apart in *City of God*, Book 5.

9 See especially Capánaga (1954: 745–54); Bonner (1987: 206).

10 Rist (1994: ch. 8).

Some Further Reading

(Including works mentioned in an abbreviated form in the notes. In some important areas of Augustine's thought, for example on the Trinity, there is no up-to-date synoptic work.)

Bochet, I., *Saint Augustin et le désir de Dieu* (Paris, 1982).

Bonner, G., "Augustine's Doctrine of Man: Image of God and Sinner," *Augustinianum* 24 (1984): 495–514.

Bonner, G., "The Desire for God and the Need for Grace in Augustine's Theology," in *Congresso Internazionale su S. Agostino* 1 (Rome, 1987): 203–15.

Brown, P. R. L., *Augustine of Hippo: A Biography* (London, 1967).

Burnaby, J., *Amor Dei: A Study of the Religion of St. Augustine* (London, 1938).

Capánaga, V., "La deificación en la soteriologia agustiniana," *Augustinus Magister* II (Paris, 1954–5): 745–54.

Drobner, H. R., *Person-Exegese und Christologie bei Augustinus* (Leiden, 1986).

Du Roy, O., *L'intelligence de la foi en la Trinité selon saint Augustin* (Paris, 1966).

Fredriksen, P., "Beyond the Body/Soul Dichotomy: Augustine on Paul against the Manichees and the Pelagians," *Recherches Augustiniennes* 23 (1988): 87–114.

Hölscher, L., *The Reality of the Mind: Augustine's Philosophical Arguments for the Human Soul as a Spiritual Substance* (London/New York, 1986).

Huftier, M. "Libre arbitre, liberté et péché chez s. Augustin," *Recherches de théologie ancienne et médiévale* 23 (1966): 187–281.

Kirwan, C., *Augustine* (London, 1989).

Lawless, G. and Dorans, R. (eds), *Augustine and his Critics* (London, 1999).

Markus, R. (ed.), *Augustine* (Modern Studies in Philosophy, New York, 1972).

Matthews, G. B. (ed.), *The Augustinian Tradition* (Berkeley, 1999).

O'Connell, R., *The Origin of the Soul in St. Augustine's Later Works* (New York, 1987).

O'Daly, G. P., *Augustine's Philosophy of Mind* (London, 1987).

O'Donovan, O., *The Problem of Self-Love in Saint Augustine* (New Haven and London, 1980).

Rist, J. M., *Augustine: Ancient Thought Baptized* (Cambridge, 1994).

Schmitt, E., *Le mariage chrétien dans l'oeuvre de saint Augustin. Une théologie baptismale de la vie conjugale* (Paris, 1983).

Solignac, A., "La condition de l'homme pécheur d'après saint Augustin," *Nouvelle Revue Théologique* 78 (1956): 359–87.

Te Selle, E., *Augustine the Theologian* (London, 1970).

Van der Meer, P., *Augustine the Bishop* (English trans., London/New York, 1961).

Boethius, Cassiodorus, Gregory the Great

Charles Kannengiesser

Three emblematic figures – Boethius (d. 524), Cassiodorus (d. ca. 580), and Gregory I (d. 604) – pronounce the farewell to antiquity experienced in Italy by Roman society during the sixth and seventh centuries. All three were as much rooted in the postclassical culture of the Empire as they were, along their respective family traditions, infused by Christian values and ideals. From the vantage point of a high-level education they succeeded in retrieving significant values of a long-forgotten past for contemporary generations in danger of being engulfed in the turmoil of barbaric invasions. Their fundamental achievement was not only to convey those values through an epochal change, but to reformulate them in an original way, marked by their consistent awareness of themselves and of their inherited identity. As a clear-minded rhetor, Boethius exercised his logical strength in a rigorous control over Aristotelian and other philosophical sources. As a versatile commentator on biblical books, on political events and juridical institutions of his time, Cassiodorus summarized much of the traditional Roman wisdom, challenged by breakups of history. As a born leader, Gregory developed a visionary capacity of opening the future beyond the boundaries of his own civilized world, when the very foundations of it seemed fatally shaken.

These three figures tower over their generations. The first dug deeply into the past to reach the most elementary components of coherent thought in the classical mode, grammatical items as well as mental categories, able to structure the minds of people uprooted from their imperial inheritance. In old age the second effected astonishing shifts in his public appearance from the political to the religious sphere, by which he prepared and announced the medieval power of the church in the West. The third, on the threshold of a new century, inaugurated the public discourse of Christian leadership which would prevail during the millennium of the Middle Ages. To compare them with each other would be idle and superficial, but to focus on their genuine creativity may highlight the capacity of individuals at all times to put their mark on changing times.

Boethius (ca. 480 to 524/6)

Symmachus, an offspring of the *gens Anicia* (not to be confounded with his ancestor of the same name, who defended a dying paganism in Milan when the intransigent Ambrose governed the local community of Nicene Christians), was Prefect of Ravenna, patrician and head of the senate under Theoderic, and he was the sponsor of most of Boethius's education. Soon the gifted pupil married his daughter. As an orator, Boethius excelled in philosophical debate and more generally as an exponent of the liberal arts. His teaching of the Latin and Greek classics, or his special interest in mathematics and astronomy, displayed all the gifts of a superlative thinker constantly positioned at the critical edge of an inquisitive mind. He represents a sort of anticipated Leonardo da Vinci figure, at least in his technical inventiveness, but lacking the impulses of a Renaissance in his day. With Symmachus he took sides in supporting the Ostrogothic regime and gaining the senatorial party for that attempted *realpolitik*. His two sons were raised to the consulship by Theoderic, the "King of the Ostrogoths," who was at once "Patrician of the Romans" and "Governor of Italy."

Theoderic ruled Italy for three decades. Ennodius paid tribute to him for having reconciled Italy with its tormented past. At Theoderic's court in Ravenna all major functions were discharged by Romans. He ruled the two nations of the Goths and the Italians with Roman authority, whereas the Senate continued primarily to serve the old aristocracy of the country. As a son of a senatorial family, Boethius would never have entered into a fatal confrontation with Theoderic's administration, had political intrigue and confessional intolerance not poisoned their relationship. In a period of clashes between Catholic orthodoxy and heterodoxy, the Arian Theoderic had always expressed deep respect for Nicene church leaders. His rare intrusions into internal Church affairs, mainly due to the polemics occasioned by episcopal elections, showed a constant political wisdom. In many of his letters he expresses a sincere deference to ecclesiastical dignitaries. When visiting Rome in the year 500, he was enthusiastically received by the Pope, the Senate, and the whole population.

Only in the later years of his reign did Theoderic change for the worse. Catholic extremists inflicted persecution on Arian groups all over Italy. Exasperated by the political agitation which was degenerating into religious warfare, the Barbarian ruler displayed despotic characteristics. When Emperor Justin prescribed Arianism throughout the Empire in the year 523, Theoderic felt the measure as a direct menace to the Goths, the more as the Roman Senate supported Byzantine rule. A climate of suspicion developed in Ravenna, in which it became easy to convince the King that a plot was organized against him by some senatorial factions. It was in that troubled environment that Boethius, one of the chief officers of the crown, decided to write in defense of Senator Albinus, the suspected instigator of the alleged plot. In a like act of protest, if not of sheer provocation, he also published an anti-Arian tractate *On the Trinity*. It was enough to get him thrown into prison, and during his year-long captivity he composed a lengthy essay, the *Consolation*, in the form of a conversation with a personified Philosophy. After a summary trial, he was executed in 524, his father-in-law Symmachus meeting the same fate. Two years later, Theoderic himself succumbed to an attack of dysentery on the very day, the seventh of the kalends of September, on which he had decreed that all Catholics were to be ejected from their churches.

Boethius's *Consolation of Philosophy* is a book about the purpose of life. It is written in a pattern of alternating prose and verse which proved attractive to medieval listeners and encouraged some imitations of the genre, such as Jean Gerson's *Consolation of Theology*. Boethius asks whether a providence is in charge of the universe, and if so whether it is benevolent and powerful and can bring things to a good outcome. He also looks at the evidence that things might be at the disposal of mere Fortune, whose fickleness places human beings always at risk of an abrupt reversal of their fortunes. These are spheres where philosophy is also theology, at least in the sense of the term familiar in the ancient world. Boethius begins from a Stoic viewpoint, seeing the universe as proceeding inexorably from cause to effect, with no scope for more than an illusion of human freedom. He moves, with Philosophy's help, to a position in tune with a Christian platonism in which he owes much to Proclus. The soul is to seek its Creator, the One who is above all change, and who has nothing to do with evil. All goods are one and the pursuit of happiness is the pursuit of unity with the One who is the Good. Eternity he sees as the complete, simultaneous, and perfect possession of endless life (*interminabilis vitae tota simul et perfecta possessio*, Cons. V.6). Boethius owes a substantial debt here to the first part of Plato's *Timaeus* (all that was then accessible in the West). Providence now begins to look different, a force which permits things we do not perceive as good at the time, but which prove to be right for us. Boethius thus comes to a different kind of acceptance from the Stoic, and to hope. Philosophy reminds Boethius that it is unwise to trust the notoriously unreliable Fortune. Boethius thus creates a systematic account of human destiny which leaves out the Christian elements of sin and its remission, redemption, and eternal life. He thought with Plato that the soul exists before the conception of the individual as a human body. But he does not hold a full-blooded doctrine of the transmigration of souls, and in fact there is nothing in his platonism which is ultimately incompatible with Christian faith.

He also took a grand overview of what he saw happening about him in his own day. The mastery of Greek which had enabled previous geneations to read the Greek philosophers for themselves was growing much less common among the educated. So he conceived the plan of translating the whole of Aristotle and Plato into Latin. That was cut short by his execution, and the fact that he had got as far only as the first elements of Aristotle's logic and had not rendered any of the platonic dialogues was greatly to affect the culture of the Western world until the remainder of Aristotle was turned into Latin in the twelfth and thirteenth centuries. Plato's arrival in the West was even later, and for more than a millennium scholars depended largely upon the mediated Plato of Augustine and others. With these translations belong the *De Arithmetica* and *De Musica*, both heavily dependent upon Greek sources, and especially upon the *Arithmetic* of Nicomachus of Gerasa, of importance for the medieval study of the *quadrivium,* or four mathematical arts (as Boethius himself labeled them).

Although it was to philosophy he seems to have turned in the condemned cell, five theological essays survive which show Boethius to have been Christian. Some of them had periods of importance in medieval theology. He wrote *On the Trinity,* a work which medieval readers would naturally compare with Augustine's book of the same title. Indeed, he drew attention to Augustine as a source in the Prologue. But his approach was different. He was more of a self-conscious logician and he tried to approach the mystery with the aid of reason and with a fresh vocabulary. He was the first to attempt a comprehensive treatment in Latin. In *On the Trinity,* on "Whether Father, Son and Holy Spirit are substantially predicated of the Trinity," Boethius explores concepts of form, unity and plurality, identity and difference. He makes the point that the Aristotelian "categories" apply differently to God. In the Godhead all accidents are substantive. (God is not "good," but "goodness.") Only relation exists absolutely between the Persons of the Trinity. Like Augustine, Boethius stresses that the persons of the Trinity are equal, but he takes further the question of how equals can differ, for Father, Son, and Holy Spirit are not identical. The two "trinitarian treatises" were probably written close together. The *De Trinitate* is much the more developed.

In the *De Hebdomadibus* he explored a version of the demonstrative method, providing a list of "self-evident" truths or truths derived from such *communis animi conceptiones* to be applied, by those wise enough to comprehend them, to the solving of a problem: "How substances are good in virtue of their existence without being substantial goods." The topic is the implication of Plato's belief that the good transcends being, so that everything which exists derives from the good. Boethius asks whether good things are good in the same way as the highest Good, or whether their goodness is merely an attribute.

His book against Eutyches and Nestorius deals with two principal Christological heresies. *Against Eutyches and Nestorius* was prompted when about 513 a Greek bishop wrote to Pope Symmachus to encourage the adoption of points in addition to the Chalcedonian formula. Boethius was there in person during the resulting debate. He learned of the "Nestorian" view that Christ is both of and in two natures and the Monophysite view ("Eutychian") that Christ is of two natures, but not in two natures. He addressed himself to the underlying questions about "nature," and "person" and their relationship. He defines "person" as "the individual substance of a rational nature" (*naturae rationabilis individua substantia,* C. *Eut.* 3) and argues, in accordance with the views of Maxentius, that Christ is indeed also one person of two natures; that there is one nature of the Incarnate Word; and that the incarnate Lord is "one of the Trinity." He believed that this can be said without implying that God can suffer or that there is plurality in the divine being. Here he had an eye to the Christological controversy which had been going on in the Eastern half of Christendom, and in Greek, and which was creating fresh controversy when its conclusions had to be put into Latin.

The brief *On the Catholic Faith* deals with the themes of the creed.

Cassiodorus (ca. 485 to 580)

Born into the senatorial aristocracy, Flavius Magnus Aurelius Cassiodorus Senator personified until his death the fully assumed *romanitas*. His family owned much land in Calabria, with ancestral ties to Syria. "His grandfather had been the friend of Aetius and notary to Valentinian III, his father filled high office under Odovacar and Theoderic, governed Sicily as *consularis*, administred his native provinces of Lucania and Bruttii as *corrector*, and from 503 to 507 held the splendid office of *praetorian prefect*" (Deanesly, 1956: 33). As a civil servant of the highest rank, his unshakable determination was to secure in Italy a future for the good of society and public order through an alliance with the Ostrogoths. The members of Roman nobility never found in him an ally in their obstructive maneuvers against the Ostrogothic administration. As a lay Catholic he considered the church as a first-rate warrant of sociocultural values amidst the disruption and misfortunes caused by invading Barbarians.

At the age of 15, at the court of Theoderic in Ravenna, he was one of his father's *consiliarii* and, a few years later, *quaestor sacri palatii* (507–11) in charge of the stylistic correction of Theoderic's edicts, then *consul ordinarius* (514). Not yet in his forties he replaced Boethius in the office of *magister officiorum* (523). In that capacity he "headed the administration. He controlled the minor court officials, the soldiers of the royal household, the reception of foreign embassies and the conduct of foreign affairs, the *cursus publicus* and the buying of food supply. Under him worked the counts (*comiticaci*), the old *agentes in rebus* under a newer name: they supervised provincial officials and various government departments" (Deanesly, 1956: 38). After Theoderic's death, he became praetorian prefect (533–7), his career culminating in the title of Patrician. He assisted Amalasuntha, the mother of Theoderic's young son, Athalaric, in a regency which was to last for several years. A political option of such magnitude itself illustrates the properly Cassiodorian farewell to antiquity, namely as a realistic choice made by a man of far-reaching strategies. However, it is in his literary initiatives and in the spiritual domain of his Christian commitment that paradoxically this man of action produced his most significant legacy. Indeed his written work testifies to his future-oriented mindset. In an imposing collection of documents, the *Variae*, he intended to secure for future generations an archival documentation of history in the making as he experienced it. In order to preserve his political option from misunderstandings in his lifetime and after his death, he composed the *Chronica*, a chronicle of Roman history. Unfortunately lost, except for a few poor extracts, is his *History of Goths* in 12 volumes, which was supposed to consolidate the historical foundation of Gothic ruling in his day. In the same line of political apologetics, he engaged in a critical self-identification by commenting on his family tree, the *Ordo generis Cassiodorum*.

On a more theoretical level, having retired from public life in 540 when Belisarius occupied Ravenna, Cassiodorus composed a treatise *On the Soul*. It marked at once a personal conversion to spirituality and an original stance in a broadly debated issue of his time.

Approximately at the same time he decided to give himself a systematic education in biblical matters by studying, paraphrasing, and rewriting Augustine's commentary on the Psalms. To that *Expositio Psalmorum* he dedicated his leisurely hours during eight years, from 540–8.

After a studious residency in Byzantium (ca. 540–54) he created the "Vivarium" on his own Calabrian property, a center for higher learning of his own conception (a projected institute of theology in Rome never materialized because of Gothic warfare). His pupils and co-workers were monks. Their practical exercises concentrated in a *scriptorium*. For less educated recruits he conceived a handbook, from 551 to 562, the *Institutiones divinarum et saecularium litterarum*, in two volumes. Around 90 years of age, he also composed for them and for a broader readership *Complexiones in Epistulas et Acta apostolorum et Apocalypsin*, adding to it a carefully expurgated edition of Pelagius's *Commentary on Romans*. At last, circa 580, his concern for a spotless transmission of ancient manuscripts by the copyists of the Vivarium urged him to publish a guideline *De orthographia*. He died among his monks aged 95.

Some fragments of *Discourses* by Cassiodorus are also preserved, such as his *Panegyricus* for Eutharic and Theoderic, of 519; and his speech for the wedding of Witigis and Matasuntha in 536.

As a giant on the cultural scene of the vanishing Roman Empire in the Latin world Cassiodorus represented a creative force for centuries to come, because he joined his admiration for ancient Rome with an equal fascination for the epochal changes underway during his lifetime. In his writings as in his public office he pursued his objectives with a sense for the paradigmatic challenges implied in them. He was not a man of unfinished business. In 538 his friends suggested to him to produce a set of official documents illustrating (and justifying) his political action in the *Variae*: he collected 468 search archives, mainly letters, in 12 volumes, which he enriched with political and philosophical comments, a work proper to serve as model for top-level bureaucracies during the whole medieval period.

At an earlier time, in 519, his *Chronica* reached the same status of a paradigmatic precedent for late medieval historians, such as that of Hermann von Reichenau. Stretching from Adam to the very year of its composition, the overview of world history exploited classical sources like Livy and Aufidius Bassus, older chronicles and contemporary testimonies. The author's synthesis was again characterized by the extreme extension of the topics covered and by its focus on a future-oriented strategy, namely to reconcile Goths and Byzance.

A similar mediation between past and future operates at the core of Cassiodorus's spiritual work. In *De anima*, initially composed as the thirteenth book of *Variae* between 538 and 540, the author primarily relies on Augustine, not without calling on more recent authorities like Claudianus Mamertus, which made the work an attractive resource for later scholars such as Hincmar of Reims. The *Expositio psalmorum*, Cassiodorus's major achievement in biblical exegesis, not only presents a luminous retrospective of patristic interpretations around the central *Enarrationes* of Augustine, but again it testifies how Psalms could be explained in the spirit and the Latin diction of the sixth century. By his way of discussing traditional issues about the Psalter, the author eloquently demonstrated that, beyond the decay of classical culture in his day, there was a valuable source of human and Christian self-understanding to be preserved for future generations. Bede and many other interpreters absorbed the lesson long before the *Expositio* was printed for the first time in 1491. As a farewell to Antiquity the work could not have been more clearly focused on the learned allegorism of the patristic period, nor could it more obviously invite a critical repraisal of that ancient hermeneutics. It still does today.

Cassiodorus became the arch-educator of the Middle Ages through his methodological introduction of the *Institutiones divinarum et saecularium litterarum*, the "Study of Divine and Secular Literature" consisting for him not only in a consistent appropriation of Holy Scripture, but in the practice of the liberal arts as well, down to the managing of gardens and of medical care. The author's matter-of-fact attitude inspired recipes for practical action which had an immediate appeal long after his death, and his scholarly pedagogy would attract the attention of distinguished teachers like Alcuin and Raban Maurus. The same could be observed in *De orthographia*, in which the precepts of ancient latin grammarians are discreetly repeated with a precise awareness of the technical difficulties encountered by latter-day copyists. Alcuin learned the practical lesson. The theological veteran of the Vivarium, having humbled himself to the most elementary level of scholarly work, became seminal for the unthinkable millennium before him.

Gregory I (ca. 540 to 604)

By birth a Roman, in a time of calamity, when the "end of the world" – a traditional and local world – daily seemed at hand, Gregory stands out in the judgment of history as the ultimate representative of ancient Rome. His individual embodiment of the spirit which for centuries had secured the prestige of the main capital city in postclassical antiquity opened for Rome the unthinkable possibility of a new universal leadership beyond its own collapse. If in Gregory's purposeful contribution to that unpredictable future there was any articulate farewell to antiquity, it can only be translated in the terms of his immediate action. Contrary to Boethius and Cassiodorus, whose teaching may have comforted him in his own public dedication, he never became an unwilling spectator of a political drama beyond his control. He remained center-stage on a scene of worldwide relationships for all his 14 years in the papal office. His supreme power in that position was unquestionable, though even today an enigma remains. Gregory made history, but it is not always clear how much he loved the power he exercised. He seems to have identified with his office in such an unselfish way that his spiritual message kept its pristine vigor throughout his most compromising political engagments. Rarely, if ever, was Christian mysticism so intensely involved in wordly affairs without losing its genuine inspiration. Gregory's writings offer some clues for interpreting him and his actions, but in their own way they participate in the mystery of his spiritual creativity. In regard to ancient Christianity, through his fervently catholic parents, he was bound to a traditional worldview, largely expressed in his pastoral and exegetical thought; however, he remained polarized by the "End," as he called the unknown future, not in the desperate fanaticism of cult members, but with the inspiring imagination of a leader fully responsible in his immediate decisions. In short, the uniqueness of Gregory's historic achievement – and thereby of his farewell to antiquity – resides in his integral and unified synthesis of ancient Roman virtues and medieval newness.

Born circa 530, of wealthy parents belonging to senatorial nobility, he counted Pope Felix III among his ancestors, possibly also Pope Agapet I. His father, Gordianus, served as administrator of one of the seven Roman *regiones*. His mother, Silvia, was so devout as to be later (with two sisters-in-law) proclaimed a saint by popular consent. Young Gregory absorbed what was left of classical education in the turmoil of the day. Benefiting from his father's position, he learned more in law and government than in classical humanities; however, he missed an initiation into the Greek language. Soon after 570, probably in 573, after he had reached the required age, he was nominated *praefectus*, which means chief civil official, of the city of Rome. His father having passed away and his mother having entered a convent, he found himself to be the richest bachelor as well as the highest official in town. Following the example of Ambrose in fourth-century Milan and of some other prestigious figures, he turned a radical conversion into a religious lifestyle. His father's property was invested in the founding of six monasteries in Sicily and in alimonies for the Roman poor, the bulk of the local population. He transformed his parents' estate in the very city of Rome, on Monte Celio, into another monastery, into which he entered himself and became a humble monk for several years. One can only speculate about the personal benefit of that voluntary seclusion, the precise community ruling in the place, one guesses, being of a Benedictine type. One possible assumption would be that Gregory occupied his mind as a self-appointed ascetic by reading sacred Scripture. A comprehensive reading of the Bible, with an uncommon capacity to memorize it, was to infuse all his later writings. Strikingly enough, a tradition based on popular witnessing (as encapsulated in the story-telling of Bede) ignored all of Gregory's monastic education; but it described him strolling one day on the forum and noticing some prisoners from Anglia exposed for sale, a premonitory encounter linking Gregory's first steps in asceticism with one of his final, most spectacular, initiatives as a church leader.

In 579, Pope Pelagius II ordained Gregory as a deacon, nominated him as his secretary (*apocrisiarius*), and sent him to Constantinople, where Tiberius II was emperor and Eutychius patriarch. Rome was in utter distress, plagued by flood and epidemics, and permanently on the verge of being attacked by the Lombards. Gregory's mission was without result. First, Tiberius II, then his successor Emperor Maurice, were not prepared to rescue the old capital in the West, despite Gregory's insistent requests. During six years, the latter immersed himself in the big city life on the Bosphorus, living in a community of Latin monks, talking with heretics, multiplying contacts with high-level officials, a close friend of Theoctista, the new emperor's sister. He also met foreign visitors, such as Bishop Leander of Seville, who would remain his ally in the future, but who, on the spot, induced him to write down the homilies, the *Moralia*, which he used to deliver for his host community. Another visitor, Anastasius, the former patriarch of Antioch, transmitted to him first-hand information about the latest theological storm which had made him flee from Syria. That Gregory learned some Greek during his stay in the East is highly probable, but he never gives evidence of it. He returned to Rome with empty hands, though in his head was an invaluable knowledge of Byzantine administration and of the whole fabric of imperial constitution in his day. From 590 to 595, he buried himself again in the monastery of St. Andrew on Monte Celio, serving as the head of the community and focusing with his monks on biblical studies. He wrote several commentaries, in particular the *Moralia in Job*, a classic for all medieval generations. His expertise on the Greek church allowed him to put an end to a controversy among the bishops of Istria, while the natural qualities of his highly responsible and clear-minded eloquence would have multiplied for him opportunities to intervene in difficult circumstances, had his life not changed forever in 590, when public acclaim called on him as the replacement of the deceased Pelagius. After six months came the approval of the Byzantine emperor. A reluctant deacon Gregory was consecrated Pope in St. Peter on September 3.

As a sort of programmatic statement, the new pope dedicated to his "brother and fellow-bishop" John of Ravenna *Regulae Pastoralis Liber*, which in itself would suffice to demonstrate the author's inner synthesis of ancestral *romanitas* and post-imperial *christianitas*. Indeed there was engraved in each line Gregory's farewell to the type of antique church behind him with its redundant discourse and its institutional illusions.

The Prologue starts with a well-composed statement, by which the reader should feel securely conducted from step to step. Each section opens with an introductory consideration, its outline clearly formulated. The whole exposition addresses first of all bishops, and it intends to improve their awareness of the duties and challenges of their office. The author speaks to them directly out of his personal experience. He shows a remarkable gift for psychological analysis in exhorting them to improve their moral values. He speaks in tones of a leader whose authority in the matter is unquestionable, as he projects into his writing the whole idealistic dedication of his monastic self. He recollects his past, expresses his fears and hopes, and positions himself in a programmatic way for the papal ministry, the highest office in their familiar world.

Actually, the whole essay was conceived as a practical commentary on biblical references relative to pastoral care. Scripture, when not expressly quoted, impregnates Gregory's personal statements, thereby legitimizing his own prescriptions. A symbolic interpretation of biblical images is constantly at work. In line with an exegetical tradition which had started with Philo and Origen of Alexandria, the parts of the priestly vesture become symbols of spiritual behavior in II.1–3; also the bricks of Ezekiel 4:1–3 symbolize the teaching of the faithful. The reading of Scripture appears to be the sole resource for preachers, as Gregory insists in III.

Interestingly enough, part IV, also on preaching, is entirely written from the viewpoint of the congregation, not of the preacher himself, as in Augustine's *De doctrina christiana*. Indeed the different categories of faithful require appropriate forms of pastoral care. From chapter to chapter, Gregory punctuates his advice with biblical quotations. His own thinking on the concrete experience of pastoral care is shown as deriving from Scripture.

In Gregory's vision, the pastoral role shared leadership with the powerful in a quintessentially spiritual dedication, now "as by God's will all high authority in this world is inclined to reverence toward religion," *quia auctore Dei ad religionis reverentiam omne iam praesentis saeculi culmen inclinatur* (I.1). In that "world," "church" was in the process of integrating the sacred *and* the secular order of reality. The late sixth-century pontiff was already conceiving his public discourse in something approaching a medieval atmosphere, in which the inner structure of the church no longer needed a proper apologetic description, nor needed to be defended against a hostile "world." Gregory was exercising authority on a top level of responsibility and with such an insight for the needs of his subordinates and such an intimate determination to side with them that he would always introduce himself as the lowest servant of those for whom he stood in office, *servus servorum*. A careful reading of the *Regula Pastoralis* is essential for catching the soul and spirit of Gregory's pontificate.

The complete history of Gregory's pontifical tenure need not be narrated, but there is no doubt that in all his initiatives the new pontiff secured a new future for the Roman church. Being the first monk in the papal office, he pushed to the extreme the implanting of Benedictine monasteries in the territories under his ruling and, whenever it was possible, he found it convenient to impose celibacy on catholic clergy. He actively supported the elimination of dissident groups, such as the remainder of Donatists in Africa, or the Arians among the Lombards. He urged the conversion of Jews, though he defended their civil liberties. His missionary activity concentrated on the suppression of paganism in Sicily and Corsica. It crossed the Channel in 595, when Gregory sent the prior of his former community on Monte Celio, the future Augustine of Canterbury, to Britain for the conversion of the English. Inside the hierarchical constitution of the Church, his juridical skills worked marvels, as can best be seen in reading his letters, more than 800 of them, carefully edited soon after his death. Gregory was a manager of ecclesiastical goods and interests with an extraordinarily realistic lucidity in practical matters. He was an expert in human psychology, able to address distant, even totally unknown correspondents with a direct and convincing touch. His crystal-clear unselfishness in the administration of papal patrimony equalled his watchful awareness in political matters. His meeting with the Lombard King Agilulf on the steps of St. Peter's was a victory emanating from his innermost moral strength, but more outstanding than any other quality of this resourceful leader was Gregory's effective generosity in social matters. From the first day of his conversion to asceticism until he died, his religiously motivated "option for the poor" was more than a pious slogan; it was a burning issue at the top of his daily agenda. Employing for charity the common procedures of economic life in his time, he ordered and carefully organized distributions of basic provisions on a large scale. For securing immediate relief to a broad spectrum of local society he called on ancient principles of patronage when offering food and assistance to the most helpless victims of the ongoing epochal changes in contemporary Rome. His sanitary measures for fighting plagues, as well as his multiple interventions for ransoming Roman citizens held prisoner by Barbarian warlords, testify to his ability to face the worst scenarios with prompt effectiveness.

Gregory's literary legacy was to become a primordial resource for spiritual enlightenment during the medieval age. What Shakespeare means for English language up to the present day, Gregory represents for the Christian discourse of the Middle Ages and beyond. For he "surfed" from one linguistic register to another in his playful oratory, alternating and contrasting them with the same dexterity, and many phrases of his invention entered the popular psyche, being used as catch-phrases and references by many authors throughout the centuries. In his relentless dictation of letters and homilies, he accumulated his own *ktema eis aei,* his "achievement forever," which, more than Thucydides' historic analyses, would carry ethical values of antiquity over into the Barbaric kingdoms of nascent Europe.

His most extensive and most popular writing was the collection of 35 *libri morales,* or *Moralia sive expositio in Job,* presenting in written form the sermons delivered to latin monks in Constantinople during 595. Medieval authors used to quote them as *Magna moralia.* Benedictine scribes copied them in all their monastic settlements equipped with a proper *scriptorium.* Today they are available in major collections of primary texts, such as the *Corpus Christianorum, Series Latina* (no. 143, ed. M. Adriaen); or *Sources Chrétiennes* (nos. 32, 212, 221, ed. A. Bocognano). A dedicatory letter, with some autobiographical remarks explaining the origin and the genre of the work, is joined to a "Preface," which shows how the author's thought remained rooted in an understanding of the biblical books fixed long before him. It seems obvious that Gregory intended to explore the meaning of Job for his contemporaries in strict conformity with patristic hermeneutics, whereas his intensely personalized commitments of the day impose on him themes and overtones never heard before. In a narrative and sometimes prolix exposition, this commentator would address several generations of readers with a familiar, already medieval voice. "We should first reach out to the roots of history, so that we may afterwards satiate our mind with the fruit of allegories" (I.x.21, *debemus prius historiae radicem figere, ut valeamus mentem postmodum de allegoriarum fructu satiare*). From Book III until the end, the spiritual significance centered on ethical values, what Gregory calls the Book of *allegoriae,* of Job is emphasized with all the procedures learned from the Fathers. Gregory addresses the human tragedy of his day, a show of senseless violence, of countless innocent deaths, of inhuman brutality, but also the vices which go with it, betrayals, greed, pride, and so forth, all leading to social injustice and abuse of power.

Never does the commentary result in a scholarly explanation, nor does it contain any traces of an abstract system of theology. It offers a substantial, very coherent presentation of Christian spirituality, entirely empirical in its inspiration, based on the author's own experience. With an acute sense of human psychology, Gregory describes the common experience of potential readers like an eye-witness of what they had to go through, calling on them with an attractive eloquence.

The doctrine of the *Morals on the Book of Job* is based on a mystic notion of Godhead: given the poor state of the human mind since the Fall of Adam and Eve, we forever face the Unknown. Only negative assertions are thinkable in proper theology. Augustine had already been of that same opinion. Contemplation of divine realities is given by divine grace. Its beneficiaries are called to a state of reception – a challenge enough by itself – more than proceeding to a deliberate intellection. They may reach a blurred and uncertain vision, a "nocturnal" apprehension of the supernatural. They remain people of desire, not of possession, even at the extreme limit of their inner journey, when their soul finds itself *reverberata*, at once blinded and repelled by divine bliss (*Mor.* 5.58; 16.38, 24.11–12, etc.; *In Ez.* 2.2.12 . . .). In fact, Satan would always try to oppose spiritual progress, at least in the limits tolerated by God. Finally, what happens depends on our free determination. Temptations must be overcome, which occasions a greater purification, a deeper humility, a more personal conversion. *Compunctio* means regret for any past failure, but also tears of joy *in jubilo* for the divine grace received (Job 33:26; cf. *Mor.* 24.10). Ultimately, love alone gives us the right understanding, *per amorem agnoscimus* (*Mor.* 10.13), a love which Gregory would expressly celebrate in his *Homilies on the Gospels* and in the *Commentary on Ezekiel*.

The 22 *Homilies on Ezekiel* (CCSL no. 142, ed. M. Adriaen) were delivered in the basilica of the Lateran during 593 and published eight years later. Again they are filled with vivid echoings from ongoing warfare, with the horror and distress of impending disasters; but, more than the *Morals*, they vibrate with an Augustinian sense of the inner life. Gregory rests on the African bishop's basic notions leading the human soul towards divine transcendency, not without giving them a new relevance, galvanized as he was by his own desire of the Beyond and his vision of the End. The 40 *Homilies on the Gospels* (Migne, *Patrologia Latina*, 76, 1075–1312), each of them for a different gospel passage, date from around Easter 591. In a colloquial style, again close to the popular simplicity in many of Augustine's sermons, the Pope speaks the language of the humblest among his flock. With the exception of the more dogmatic Homily 17, delivered for a small group of bishops in the baptisterium of the Lateran, Gregory preached all these *Homilies on the Gospels* on Sundays and feastdays in the different station-churches of Rome. Due to various circumstances or to the chosen text to be commented, he spoke from seven minutes to a full hour. Having written his text in advance, but weakened by sickness, he could not himself deliver the first 20 popular sermons, but he presided over their public reading by a *notarius*. Intentionally composed as models for fellow-preachers, the gospel homilies of Gregory became indeed a paradigm for medieval preaching. Of Gregory's comments on the Old Testament, in addition to his books on Job and Ezekiel, only the homilies on Canticle 1.1–8 and 1 Kings (CCSL no. 144, ed. P. Verbraken) survive. Four books of *Dialogues*, at least inspired by Gregory (F. Clark, *The Pseudo-Gregorian Dialogues*, 2 vols, 1987) and enormously influential during the Middle Ages, offer in Book II an extensive biography of Benedict of Nursia and a summary of Gregory's eschatology in Book VI. With the latter contribution, the imaginary projection of the biblical universe, bound to a notion of universal salvation, reached a level of narrative intensity never to be surpassed for over a millennium, until Western Enlightenment challenged the foundations and processes of such mythical thinking.

Bibliography

S. J. B. Barnish, "The Work of Cassiodorus after his Conversion," *Latomus*, 48 (1989): 157–87.

S. J. B. Barnish, trans., Cassiodorus, *Variae* (one-fourth) (Liverpool, 1992).

J. C. Cavadini, ed., *Gregory the Great: A Symposium*, Notre Dame Studies in Theology, 2 (Notre Dame, 1995).

H. Chadwick, "The Authenticity of Boethius's Fourth Tractate, *De fide catholica*," *JTS*, n.s. 31 (1980): 551–6.

W. V. Cooper, trans., Boethius, *The Consolation of Philosophy* (New York, 1943). See also translations by R. Green, 1962, 1976; V. E. Watts, 1969; S. J. Tester 1973; J. Watson, 1984.

M. Deanesly, *A History of Early Medieval Europe* (London and New York, 1956).

F. H. Dudden, *Gregory the Great: His Place in History and Thought* (London, 1905; New York, 1967).

G. R. Evans, *The Thought of Gregory the Great* (Cambridge, 1986).

L. W. Jones, trans., *An Introduction to Divine and Human Readings by Cassiodorus* (New York, 1946).

L. W. Jones, "The Influence of Cassiodorus on Medieval Culture," *Speculum*, 20 (1945): 433–42; see also *Speculum*, 22 (1947): 254–6.

M. L. W. Laistner, "The Value and Influence of Cassiodorus' Ecclesiastical History," *Harvard Theological Review*, 41 (1948): 51–67.

R. Macpherson, *Rome in Involution: Cassiodorus' Variae in the Literary and Historical Setting* (Poznan, 1989).

R. A. Markus, *Gregory the Great and His World* (Cambridge, 1997).

H. F. Steward, E. K. Rand, and S. J. Tester, trans., *Boethius, The Theological Tractates: The Consolation of Philosophy* (Loeb, 1918).

P. G. Walsh, trans., Cassiodorus, *Explanation of the Psalms*, Ancient Christian Writers, vols. 51–3 (1990–1).

Postpatristic Byzantine Theologians

Andrew Louth

Post-Chalcedonian Christology

To speak of "postpatristic Byzantine theology" is to accept an understanding of the Fathers which is at odds with that of Eastern Orthodox theology, for which the "Fathers" are those who have received the Gospel from the Apostles and passed it down to later generations: it is, therefore, a category constantly renewed, stretching from the apostolic period to the present day.[1] If, however, one is concerned to mark off Byzantine theology from contemporary developments in the West, the term "postpatristic" is useful.

At the Synod of Chalcedon (451), the bishops prefaced their definition of faith with the words "following the holy fathers." Its immediate connotation was probably the fathers of the three Ecumenical Synods, the decisions of which had just been rehearsed, as well as Cyril of Alexandria, whose synodical letters had been endorsed, and Leo of Rome, whose famous tome to Flavian of Constantinople had also been accepted; it does, however, set down a rule for the conduct of theological reflection that was to be determinative for the future. One effect of the emergence of the notion of patristic authority was the compilation of *florilegia*, collections of extracts from the Fathers on topics of current interest, which become increasingly important for the formulation and presentation of theological doctrine. Examination of these *florilegia* (vastly facilitated by Alois Grillmeier's authoritative survey of this genre of theological literature in volume 2, part 1, of his monumental *Christ in Christian Tradition*)[2] reveals two things: first, not surprisingly, that the bulk of these *florilegia* are concerned with Christology, which was to dominate theological reflection from the fifth to the seventh centuries (to the ninth, if one accepts the judgment of the protagonists themselves, that the iconoclast theology was ultimately a matter of Christology); but secondly, that most of these *florilegia* are in Greek, the Latin contribution being relatively minor. These facts are significant, for the Synod of Chalcedon meant different things to East and to West. If accepted at all (and many in the East never accepted it), it was accepted in the East as a synod that had endorsed the teaching of Cyril; in the West, however, it was accepted as the Synod that had endorsed the teaching of Leo, and, as such, accepted much more wholeheartedly. In the East, Chalcedon opened up a period of Christological debate; in the West, in contrast, it more or less closed a chapter of Christological controversy. But for both East and West, Chalcedon inaugurated (or at least set its seal on) an era of theology that looked to the Fathers for guidance.

This very fact causes the path of theology to divide between the Latin path of the West and the Greek path of the East (though the latter path itself almost immediately divides, and mingles with other linguistically determined paths, those of the new Christian vernaculars of the East: Syriac, Coptic, Georgian, Armenian, and so forth), for the Fathers the Greeks looked to were those who wrote in Greek, whereas the Fathers the Latins looked to were those who wrote in Latin – supplemented by translations, mainly from the late fourth and early fifth centuries (Jerome, Rufinus, Julian of Eclanum), only fitfully added to later on (notably in the ninth century by Eriugena).

The Fathers of the "Golden Era" (roughly, up to the Synod of Chalcedon) had looked directly to the Scriptures for their authority, so that, though one can distinguish different exegetical traditions (which do not, however, correspond at all exactly to the already existing linguistic divide), it is still the same mountain range, as it were, to which the Fathers, in this narrow sense, look back. Their followers, for whom the ultimate authority of the Scriptures was mediated by the interpretation of the Fathers, looked back across different mountain ranges – that of the Greeks and that of the Latins – so that a much greater divergence imposes itself. The Greek patristic mountain range has many more peaks than the Latin – Irenaeus, Origen, Athanasius, the Cappadocian Fathers, Cyril – whereas the Latin range is dominated by awesome peak represented by Augustine. It is not surprising that one of the early Latin *florilegia* is of extracts from Augustine compiled by Vincent of Lérins; though Cyril looms large in the Christological *florilegia* in the East, he does not dominate in the way Augustine tended to. The ways of Latin and Greek theology are beginning to diverge, though it will be long before this divergence is thought to amount to opposition.

This divergence between East and West is aggravated by the much greater theological activity in the East from the sixth century onwards, which can be explained, in part, by the continuance in the East, in however battered a form, of the public structures of the Roman Empire, including the educational system (the initial collapse of which Patriarch Nikephoros dated to the early eighth century).[3] The two topics that dominated theological debate in the sixth century – Origenism and Christology – aroused little interest in the West, save for the alarm caused by the apparent abandonment of Leo's Synod (of Chalcedon) by the condemnation of the Three Chapters and the decrees of the Fifth Ecumenical Synod (Constantinople II, 553).

Christological developments were dominated by the desire of the Emperor to heal the schism between Christians in the East caused by the Synod of Chalcedon.[4] The main plank of this policy was the theological position, generally known as "Neo-Chalcedonianism" (though better: Cyrilline Chalcedonianism), that sought to interpret the definition of Chalcedon in the light of Cyril's theology. Notable representatives include John of Caesarea ("the Grammarian"), who engaged in controversy with Severus of Antioch, the greatest theologian of his age and determined opponent of Chalcedon, and Leontios of Jerusalem; it became imperial policy under the Emperor Justinian. This theological position rested on three points: first, the clarification that the hypostasis of the Incarnate Christ is the Son of God, the Second Person of the Trinity; secondly, agreement that Cyril's favourite formula for Christ, μία φύσις τοῦ Θεοῦ Λόγου σεσαρκωμένη ("one incarnate nature of God the Word"), is capable of an acceptable interpretation; thirdly, acceptance of the theopaschite formula, "one of the Trinity suffered in the flesh." This position is more than a theological compromise: it had profound implications for both Christian devotion and theological reflection. Devotionally, it focuses on God's embracing of suffering for our salvation: as the hymn *Only-Begotten Son* (sung since the ninth century at every celebration of the eucharistic liturgy in the Byzantine rite, attributed to Justinian, but perhaps by Severus) puts it, "you were crucified, Christ God, by death trampling on death, being one of the Holy Trinity, glorified with the Father and the Holy Spirit, save us!"

Theologically, it led to continued reflection on the nature of the person, or *hypostasis*. Throughout the century, there were repeated attempts to define more closely what is meant by person, in distinction from nature. The distinction between οὐσία and ὑπόστασις, first made by Basil the Great in the fourth century in the context of Trinitarian theology, was developed by sixth-century theologians: οὐσία was identified with φύσις, and their meaning elucidated by drawing on classical and late antique logic (not least current developments among the logicians of sixth-century Alexandria); ὑπόστασις, however, having no currency in classical logic, needed separate attention, which concentrated on the explanation of *hypostasis* as "mode of existence" (τρόπος ὑπάρξεως), suggested (though not followed up) by the Cappadocian Fathers. This development will reach its apogee in the seventh century, in the thought of St. Maximos the Confessor, who uses the distinction to solve the problems posed by the monenergists and monothelites, and further develops this notion of the personal, hitherto discussed solely in relation to Trinitarian theology and Christology, in the context of anthropology.

Origenism

The other topic of theological reflection in the sixth century was Origenism.[5] Aspects of Origen's own thought had been condemned even during his lifetime, but the late fourth century saw much interest in his speculations, in the Alexandrian Didymos the Blind, and among the Cappadocian Fathers, but especially in the pupil of the Cappadocians, the monk Evagrios. Evagrios' development of Origen's ideas quickly led to his condemnation within a few years of his death in 399, but the way Evagrios used Origen's ideas (not least his metaphysical ideas) to provide a theoretical context for his understanding of the ascetic struggle of the monk and his attaining of the goal of contemplation and deification was to prove enduringly popular in monastic circles. Evagrios, along with Origen and Didymos, were anathematized at the Fifth Ecumenical Synod of 553, and a series of "Origenist" propositions condemned.[6] The Origenist position condemned envisaged a primal state in which all rational beings were united with one another and God as a "henad"; through a failure of contemplation these rational beings fell, became souls and were embodied in the cosmos, where they were, through asectic struggle, to seek to regain their former state. One of the souls remained in unbroken contemplation of God, and this soul, eternally united to the Word through such contemplation, descended to unite itself with a human body in the Virgin's womb, to assist souls in their restoration to their primal state, to which state all rational beings will eventually return, even the demons (ἀποκατάστασις παντῶν), and in which state they will become equal to Christ (ἰσοχρίστοι). Such ideas were still popular in the seventh century, when they received patient and sympathetic refutation by St. Maximos the Confessor.

Liturgical Theology: Dionysios and Romanos

But apart from theological controversy, the sixth century saw two figures of great importance for the development of Byzantine theology. One of these was the (probably) Syrian monk who wrote under the name of St. Paul's Athenian convert, Dionysios the Areopagite, the other, perhaps the greatest poet of the Byzantine period, Romanos the Melodist. Romanos' importance lies in his expressing in popular and memorable form the drama and doctrine of Christian salvation.[7] This he did through the poetic genre of the *kontakion*, a kind of verse sermon of which, if he did not create it, he was the greatest exponent. In these long, dramatic poems, that were chanted as sermons during the "sung service", the vigil that formed part of the "Cathedral Office" on Great Festivals and some Sundays, Romanos drew on the rich typology provided by the Old Testament to express the wonder and meaning of the Incarnation, the Paschal mystery, other mysteries of Christ's life, and examples of his teaching, as well as the glory of the saints, and to mark other events, earthquakes and the rebuilding of Hagia Sophia, when the people of Constantinople needed to turn to God in supplication or praise. In his kontakion for Christmas (by legend, his first, revealed miraculously), he depicts the reception of the magi thus:

> "Therefore now receive, holy Lady – receive those who have received me,
> for I am in them as I am in your arms;
> I did not leave you and yet I came with them."
> She opens the door and receives the company of the magi.
> She opens the door – she, the unopened
> gate through which Christ alone has passed.
> She opens the door – she who was opened
> and yet in no way robbed of the treasure of her purity.
> She opened the door, she from whom was born the door,
> > a little Child, God before the ages.[8]

It is difficult to underestimate the influence of Ps.-Dionysios the Areopagite in Byzantine theology: his world vision focused on the liturgy, many of his theological and philosophical notions, and not least his arcane ontological language were eagerly embraced in the East.[9] He first emerges in 532, quoted (or misquoted) in support of those who continued to reject Chalcedon (the so-called monophysites) at a meeting, called by Justinian to explore the possibilities of union between Orthodox and monophysite. After some initial hesitation, he found ready acceptance among the Orthodox, too; a process greatly assisted by publication of an edition of the works of the Areopagite by the learned bishop of Scythopolis, John: an edition with prologue and annotations, making plain (among other matters) Dionysios' impeccable Chalcedonian credentials.[10] The works of the Areopagite are presented as having survived from a much larger corpus, the titles of which are referred to in the works that are extant.

These extant works are an account of the workings of the divine economy through angelic agency in the *Celestial Hierarchy*, an account of the principal liturgical rites – Baptism, Eucharist, and the consecration of Chrism, Ordination (episcopal, priestly, and diaconal), Monastic consecration, and the Funeral service – in the *Ecclesiastical Hierarchy*, an examination of the names by which we praise God in the *Divine Names*, what seems to be an epitome of all this (in terms still disputed), in which the way of denial of attributes to God (apophatic theology) is emphasized, in the *Mystical Theology*, and ten letters.[11] The language and concepts are drenched in late Athenian neoplatonism of the kind associated with the fifth-century *diadochos* of the Platonic Academy, Proklos, and the last *diadochos*, Damaskios. Dionysios was to prove the channel through which many late neoplatonic ideas and much terminology entered the Byzantine tradition, not least the distinction between apophatic and kataphatic theology (theology of denial and affirmation), which provided a vocabulary for a distinction that had long been established in Greek theology (for instance in the Cappadocian Fathers and St. John Chrysostom).

He introduced into Greek the word "hierarchy" (which he seems to have invented), meaning, however, not so much graded subordination, but, as he says, "a sacred order and knowledge and activity, being assimilated to God as much as possible" (*Celestial Hierarchy*, 3.1): his vision is of the created order as a theophany, radiating the glory of God and drawing everything into union with him by its beauty manifest in ordered hierarchy. The earthly liturgy, reflecting the angelic liturgy, celebrates the outreach of God's love in creation and redemption, and in responding to that love, humankind, indeed the cosmos itself, is drawn into union with God who is beyond being, a union that is transforming and leads to deification.

In this whole process of being drawn back to God, Dionysios detects a fundamental rhythm of purification, illumination, and union. Dionysios' influence was felt in three areas. First, his philosophical language gave Byzantine theologians a language in which to express their understanding of the transcendence of God, the ordered structure of the cosmos, the nature of prayer and providence, and also, of particular importance, the way in which beings are maintained in existence by participation in God's outflowing activity, which prepares the way for the distinction between God's unknowable essence and his activities (or energies) through which God is known by, and communicates Himself to, creatures. Secondly, Dionysios' threefold rhythm of purification, illumination, and union, by which creatures are drawn into union with God, was quickly adopted by the tradition of Byzantine ascetic theology, which was itself of largely Evagrian inspiration. Thirdly, Dionysios' understanding of the liturgy as reflecting the angelic liturgy (an already traditional theme) and playing out, through symbols both visual and expressed in movement, the movement of God's love towards us, our loving response which finds its goal in rest in God, a movement that reflects both the movement of the cosmos as well as the reconstitution of human inwardness through loving response to God's love: all this profoundly influenced the Byzantine understanding and experience of the liturgy, especially the Eucharistic liturgy.

Maximos the Confessor

The seventh century was a watershed for Byzantine theology. Politically, the Byzantine Empire nearly foundered in face of the loss of its Eastern provinces to the Persian Empire in the early decades of the century (from which near disaster it recovered, owing to Herakleios' generalship), and then its final loss of those provinces to emergent Islam in the second quarter of the century and the constant pressure from the troops and the fleet of the Umayyad caliph during the first 50 years or so of the Umayyad dynasty (founded in 661). The response to this disaster in the capital city of Constantinople was to plunge into heresy: first the Christological heresies of monenergism and monothelitism, and then the heresy (regarded as Christological by both sides) of iconoclasm. But the seventh century also saw one of the high points of Byzantine theology, in the achievement of St. Maximos the Confessor, and the consolidation of his vision among the monks of Palestine, a process that culminated in the many-faceted work of St. John Damascene, in the first half of the eighth century.

St. Maximos was born in 580, probably in Constantinople, and after a sound education and a brief period as head of the Imperial Chancery in the early years of Herakleios' reign, he became a monk, which he remained for the rest of his life.[12] In 626, when the Persian army occupied the Asian coast of the Sea of Marmara, where Maximos' monastery was situated, he, with many others, fled. He spent the next period of his life in North Africa, close to Carthage. In the mid-640s he made his way to Rome, where he was the inspiration behind Pope Martin's calling of the Lateran Synod of 649, which condemned the heresies of monenergism and monothelitism. For this defiance of the imperial will, both Martin and Maximos were arrested and taken to Constantinople, where first Martin and then Maximos were condemned and sent into exile, where they died (Martin in 655 in the Crimea, Maximos in 662 in Lazica, in present-day Georgia), confessors to Orthodoxy. From 640 onwards, Maximos' works were concerned with defining and defending the true doctrine of Christ, against the heresies of monenergism and monothelitism. For him, both were heretical, because both diminished the human nature the Word of God had assumed for human salvation. Drawing on the reflections of the sixth-century theologians, Maximos worked out the implications of what has been called his "Chalcedonian logic," with its distinction between *hypostasis* and *physis*. Whereas nature was determined by the definition (or meaning) of being (λόγος τῆς οὐσίας), person or *hypostasis* was manifest in its "mode of existence" (τρόπος τῆς ὑπάρξεως). Following Aristotle, Maximos related activity to nature, ἐνέργεια to φύσις, so that as Christ had two natures, he must also be conceded two ἐνεργείαι. These activities were united in the person of Christ, but they were united without confusion. Similarly with will: this also belonged to nature, and so there were two wills in Christ. But he made a distinction between natural will, and our actual experience of willing, which in a fallen world involves deliberation, as we make up our mind between conflicting purposes – this Maximos called θέλημα γνωμικόν ("gnomic" will) – and this "gnomic" will is not found in Christ, who knows no moral hesitation. At the root of this lies Maximos' understanding of nature as created by God and therefore something that cannot be opposed to God, something that God need never overrule: this profound grasp of the integrity of created nature is something that underlies his metaphysics and ascetical theology, too.

It is worth pausing for a moment to reflect on the literary genres used by Maximos to expound his theology outside the polemics of the Christological controversy. Maximos was a simple monk; there is no evidence that he ever became abbot or even a priest, though he was clearly revered for his learning, and his wisdom as a spiritual father. Consequently, there are no homilies: still, in the seventh century, one of the commonest genres of theological writing.[13] In fact, all Maximos' writings seem to be occasional: responses to requests from others. Sometimes this is directly so, in the form of a letter, or of a series of responses to a set of questions ("Questions and Answers": *Erotapokriseis*): into this category fall his most demanding works, the *Questions to Thalassios*, and his famous *Ambigua* (*Aporiai* or "Difficulties"). His two brief commentaries – on Psalm 59 and on the *Paternoster* – were probably occasional works also (the commentary on the *Paternoster* explicitly so), as too were his two sets of centuries – the four *Centuries on Love* and the two *Centuries on Theology and the Incarnate Dispensation* (again explicitly so in the case of the *Centuries on Love*, the response to a request from a certain Elpidios, to whom also his *Logos asketikos* was addressed).

In Maximos' writings we are confronted with occasional theology, theological reflection in response to others' questions, the continuation of a conversation, or of monastic catechesis. Of these works, three of them take the form of response to questions about difficulties – the early so-called *Quaestiones et Dubia* (properly: *Erotapokriseis*), the *Quaestiones ad Thalassium*, and the two sets of *Ambigua* (the *Ambigua ad Ioannem* (*Amb.* 6–71) and the little later *Ambigua ad Thomam* (*Amb.* 1–5)): difficulties in passages of Scripture or in the Fathers, especially in the writings of St. Gregory the Theologian (Nazianzen) (all but one of the *Ambigua* are concerned with passages from Gregory). This genre – the "difficulty," dealing with problems in Scripture and, especially, the Fathers – was to become the staple of Byzantine theology: we shall encounter it later in Photios' *Amphilochia* and Psellos' works on Christian theology. Though this genre might look something like the modern scholarly article (or better: note and query), in its origins in Maximos it seems to be primarily monastic: all Maximos' interlocutors are monks, and the bearing of the issues discussed on the pursuit of the Christian (monastic) life is never lost from view.[14] This monastic context is even clearer in the following centuries, for this is a favorite genre of Byzantine monasticism, introduced by Evagrios, that presented food for meditation in a series (or set of series) of 100 (generally brief) chapters.[15] Maximos' two sets of centuries seem each to be an engagement with the legacy of distinguished predecessors: the *Centuries on Love* engaging with Evagrios, and the *Centuries on Theology* with Origen.[16]

Maximos' theology is, then, in presentation and reality mostly a meditative, monastic theology. Despite its occasional character, there lies behind Maximos' theology a profound vision that draws on, and interweaves, the several traditions of Eastern Christian theological reflection to which Maximos claims to be heir. The whole of later Byzantine theology can be seen to be governed by the theological vision of this monk and confessor. In his theological vision, Maximos draws together the ascetic, the theological, and the cosmic dimensions of earlier Greek theology. He is indebted to the ascetic theology of Byzantine monasticism, especially in its Evagrian form, though he is also influenced by the rather different, more affective, tradition of the Makarian Homilies, and shows direct knowledge of the fifth-century Diadochos of Photike, in whom one also finds an attempt to bring the two traditions, the Evagrian and the Makarian, into mutual illumination. To this ascetic tradition, Maximos joins the theological tradition of Athanasius and Cyril, of the Cappadocian Fathers, Basil the Great, Gregory the Theologian, and Gregory of Nyssa: their Trinitarian theology and their Christology, as well as their understanding of the cosmos, and the human person as image of God and bond of the cosmos. This cosmic dimension of Greek theology is deepened by the Dionysian heritage which Maximos embraces enthusiastically.[17] The interweaving of these three traditions is manifest in all Maximos' works, but nowhere more strikingly than in his *Mystagogia*, his commentary on the Eucharistic liturgy. This work, presented as a supplement to Dionysios' *Ecclesiastical Hierarchy*, consisting of what Maximos learned from his *geron* or spiritual father, and reluctantly put in the form of a treatise at the urgent request of one of his friends, sees the whole liturgy framed by the symbolism of the church building within which the liturgy takes place. The church itself, with its division into nave and sanctuary, has multiple symbolic reference: to the cosmos, consisting of heaven and earth, to the human person consisting of body and soul, to the human soul itself, consisting of a contemplative and active part. As Maximos draws out the meaning of the liturgy, it is made apparent that the work of reconciliation, celebrated and effected in the liturgy, resonates both throughout the whole cosmos, as well as in the depths of the human soul. This understanding of the liturgy affected the way in which church buildings were constructed throughout Byzantium, ensuring that the cosmic dimension of the liturgy and the Christian faith became a reality to even the simplest Byzantine Christian.

Maximos' vision had, to begin with, little impact in the capital of the Byzantine world. It was the theology of the capital that he had attacked in his lifetime, and the continuance there of the sway of heresy in the eighth and early ninth centuries, this time iconoclasm, probably meant that Maximos had few readers in the capital during those years. Even in the middle of the ninth century, after the Triumph of Orthodoxy, Maximos' works were only imperfectly known in Constantinople, as is evident from Photios' *Myriobiblion* (or *Bibliotheca*). It was in fact among those staunch defenders of Chalcedonian Orthodoxy (and therefore of the vindication of Maximos' theology at the Sixth Ecumenical Synod of 681), the monks of Palestine, that Maximos' theology was first received and assimilated (as is evident from the fact that to their Christian opponents, the monophysites and the monothelites, they were known as "Maximianists").

In the century following the Islamic conquest of the Middle East and the establishment of the Umayyad Empire with its capital in Damascus in 661, the Orthodox Christians (that is, the supporters of Chalcedonian Orthodoxy) found themselves in a new situation. Hitherto, they had been favored subjects of the Byzantine Empire (indeed, heretics had no civil rights at all): Orthodoxy was imperial policy, and could be (and was) supported by persecution of those who dissented. The Arab conquest changed all that, and Orthodox Christians in the Middle East found themselves just one religious group among many, needing to defend themselves against other Christian groups – monophysites and monothelites, as well as the Nestorians, now part of the same Empire with the fall to the Arabs of Persia – and also other religious groups, such as Jews, Samaritans, Manichees, and eventually Muslims. This forced Orthodox Christians in the Middle East to define and defend the Christian tradition as they had received it. Against other Christians, they had to define and defend their understanding of the nature of the Incarnation; against Jews, they had to defend their understanding of God as Trinity, and their veneration of the True Cross and of the saints, their icons and their relics, all regarded by the Jews as idolatry;[18] against Manichees, they had to defend the doctrine of creation and providence. In all this the monks of Palestine, the most articulate defenders of Chalcedonian Orthodoxy, played a leading role. In order to argue convincingly, they had to know the definition of terms (not least the complex terminology needed in Christology, with its language of person and nature, will and energy) and the principles of logical argument: to meet this need Christian textbooks of logic were produced.[19] This process of defense was also a process of definition. Hitherto, Orthodoxy had been the beliefs and practices of the Orthodox Christian community, defined, where necessary, by Ecumenical Synods; now the whole gamut of Christian belief and practice came under scrutiny, and in defending their beliefs, Christians were also defining them. A good example of this is the defense in the seventh century, long before the outbreak of iconoclasm in the Byzantine Empire, of the veneration of icons against Jewish objections of idolatry. The practice of icon veneration had grown, and come to assume a major role in Christian devotion, both private and public, by the beginning of the seventh century (in 626, for instance, the defense of Constantinople against the Avar-Persian siege focused on the icon of the Mother of God as defender of the city: the kontakion (Τῇ ὑπερμάχῳ Στρατηγῷ) that prefaces the Akathist hymn probably dates from this time). Against Jewish accusations of idolatry, Orthodox Christians had to defend themselves, and pointed out that in the Old Testament veneration of holy men and items used in temple worship was not thought to be contrary to the second commandment, as well as developing the distinction between veneration expressing honor (τιμή), which can be shown to creatures, and veneration expressing worship (λατρεία), which is due only to God.[20]

St. John Damascene

The apogee of this defense and definition of Orthodoxy by the monks of Palestine is to be found in the works of St. John Damascene.[21] His threefold work, the *Fount of Knowledge*, is an epitome of the aspects of this process: the *Dialectica* being the last of the Christian textbooks of logic, and the *De Haeresibus* and *De Orthodoxa Fide*, marking out the true faith and distinguishing it from the many-headed (in fact, hundred-headed) Hydra of heresy. The most popular form of this work – both in John's lifetime and later – seems to have been a collection of 150 chapters, consisting of the early form of the *Dialectica* in 50 chapters, and the 100 chapters of *De Orthodoxa Fide*. But in either form, what is striking is the way in which John presents his work in the monastic form of the century. This clue, often neglected, suggests that we should treat this work as a resource for deepening an understanding of the Christian life, rather than some kind of proto-scholastic venture. Hardly any of the chapters of the *Fount of Knowledge* is original, in the sense of having John as its author: most of the *Dialectica* is drawn from already existing epitomes of classical logic, dependent on the work of the fifth- and sixth-century Alexandrian commentators on Aristotle; the first 80 chapters of *De Haeresibus* is lifted directly from the fifth-century summary of Epiphanios' *Panarion*; and the chapters of *De Orthodoxa Fide* are culled from a wide range of patristic sources. *De Orthodoxa Fide*, especially, is a *florilegium*, without acknowledgment of its sources. But rather than decrying John's lack of originality as an *author*, it is perhaps more to the point to see these works as setting out a pattern of *reading*: selecting from the wealth of the patristic tradition those authors most valued for the various aspects of Christian doctrine. John's labors as scriptural exegete fall into the same category: the commentary on the epistles of Paul is derivative, excerpted from the homilies of St. John Chrysostom's, and the still unedited commentary on the great prophet Elijah is probably similarly derivative (the authenticity of both these works is not beyond question). The same is true of the *Hiera*, or *Sacra Parallela*, a work of massive erudition, gathering together passages from Scripture and the Fathers to illustrate a whole range of theological and ethical concepts (though much work remains to be done on the textual tradition of this work).

The contrast between John's exegetical labors and those of his exact contemporary, the Venerable Bede, is instructive: though Bede, like John, draws heavily on the labors of his predecessors, Bede sought to complete the Latin tradition of commentary by writing commentaries on works, such as Acts and the Apocalypse, not yet commented on by any Latin Father; for John the tradition of commentary is complete, all that remains to do is reap its wisdom.

Monastic Learning and the Liturgy

It was not simply in the realm of the intellectual definition and defense of Orthodox theology that the monks of Palestine played a decisive role in the first century after the Arab conquest of the Middle East. In that same period, the monastic office developed dramatically, and liturgical poetry found its place in the worship of the monks not least in the canon, a series of verses or troparia, fitted into the singing of the nine biblical canticles that constituted the main part of the dawn office (called *orthros*, or matins). Liturgical poetry had already, in the *kontakia* of Romanos and others, become a vehicle for theology in the cathedral office of city churches such as Hagia Sophia in Constantinople. Now liturgical poetry was to find a place in the monastic office, which eventually, after the fall of Constantinople in 1204, supplanted the *kontakion* and the cathedral office altogether (the opening verse, the koukoulion, of the *kontakion* was incorporated in the canon, and came to be known as the "*kontakion*"). The canon originated in Palestine at the beginning of the eighth century, and all the early composers of canons, Andrew of Crete, Cosmas of Maiouma, and John of Damascus himself, had links with Jerusalem and the monasteries of the Palestinian desert. In contrast with the *kontakion*, the canon was less a verse sermon than a verse meditation, in this reflecting its monastic roots.

The work of the monks of Palestine in defining, defending, and celebrating the Orthodox faith seems to have taken some time to be made known in Constantinople. John was known in the capital within years of his death for his opposition to the imperial policy of iconoclasm: at the iconoclast synod of Hiereia in 754, he was condemned along with Germanos, the patriarch deposed by Leo III, and George of Cyprus. But his writings were unknown to Photios, who makes no mention of him in his *Myriobiblion*. His *De Orthodoxa Fide* was, however, translated into Slavonic in the tenth century, so it must have been known in Constantinople by the end of the ninth century. The reception of the theological and liturgical achievement of the monks of Palestine in Constantinople probably took place in the later half of the ninth century, after the overthrow of iconoclasm and the "Triumph of Orthodoxy" in 843. The link may have been the Palestinian monks, Michael the Synkellos and the branded brothers, Theophanes and Theodore, who found themselves in Constantinople during the second period of iconoclasm (815–43) and made common cause with the iconodules, led by the abbot of the Stoudios, St. Theodore. It certainly seems to have been in Studite circles that the new Palestinian monastic office found acceptance in Constantinople, where the canon was developed by Joseph the Hymnographer.

The Impact of Iconoclasm

Iconoclasm itself had an impact on the development of Byzantine theology, though we know virtually nothing about the iconoclast theologians of the capital themselves (we know more about the iconoclast ideas of the second iconoclast emperor, Constantine V, from the fragments of his *Inquiries* preserved in Nikephoros' refutation of them). The second stage of iconoclasm saw a defense of veneration of icons that used Christological language to express the notion that what is depicted, and venerated, in the icon is the *hypostasis* or person (*prosopon*, which also means "face"), not the nature. The iconoclast claim that the only true image of Christ was the eucharist led to clarification on the part of the Orthodox as to the nature of the eucharistic presence: it was real, not symbolic.

But the wider contribution of iconoclasm to the development of Byzantine theology is to be found in the political and economic recovery that began to take place under the eighth-century iconoclast emperors: this ushered in the prosperity of the ninth century which made possible the revival of learning that Lemerle called *le premier humanisme byzantin.*[22]

Photios

So far as theology is concerned, the most important figure of this revival of learning, in which the reestablishment of the monastery of the Stoudios under St. Theodore in the first decade of the century played an important role, was Photios, head of the Imperial Chancery before being appointed patriarch in 858.[23] Photios' contribution to theology has been little studied, save for his accusation against the West of heresy for adding the term *filioque* to the creed, thereby declaring the double procession of the Holy Spirit from both Father and Son. In opposition to this Photios developed the doctrine that the Holy Spirit proceeds from the Father alone. In his letters and "Amphilochia" (i.e., Questions to Amphilochios, metropolitan of Kyzikos), Photios brings his enormous learning to bear on a series of biblical and patristic problems, rather in the manner of Maximos (whose earlier *Ambigua* were addressed to John, like Photios' Amphilochios, bishop of Kyzikos).

Symeon the New Theologian

From the ninth century onwards, Constantinople became a center for theological learning in the Byzantine Empire. It was not, however, only at the university of the Magnaura that such theological study took place. The monasteries themselves, experiencing a revival in the wake of the reestablishment of the Stoudios under St. Theodore, also became centers of theological activity. Much of this activity followed the pattern of John Damascene in reaping the rich harvest of earlier ages. This is true, for instance, of the so-called *Synagoge* or *Evergetinos*, compiled in the eleventh century, under the direction of Paul, the founder of the monastery of the Theotokos Evergetis in Constantinople.[24]

Of far greater influence was a Constantinopolitan monk, a generation earlier than Paul Evergetinos, whose life and writings caused great controversy, such that he was expelled from Constantinople, and spent the last years of his life on the Asian bank of the Bosphoros. This was Symeon the New Theologian (the "New" was probably originally a mark of disfavor, but it was adopted by his disciples as ranking him with the two other "theologians," John the Evangelist and Gregory Nazianzen).[25] His voluminous writings strike a new note of vigor and enthusiasm, and make claims to an authority that cut across the established traditions. In form his writings belong to the the traditional genre of Byzantine monasticism: homilies or catecheses and discourses composed of these, centuries, hymns. He reaffirmed the authority of lived experience, and even called in question traditional hierarchical authority not based on such experience. He emphasized the importance of confession to and guidance by a spiritual father. He recalls his hearers to the living reality of the Gospel, and rails against those who think that the world of the New Testament, with its immediate experience of God's word and the evidence of miracle, has passed. Symeon brought into Byzantium, and into monasticism, the living authority of actual spiritual experience: he also spoke about his experiences, and claimed for himself the authority they conferred. The influence of Symeon is at times somewhat surprising: the patriarch Michael Keroularios, excommunicated by Cardinal Humbert in 1054 in the name of the (deceased) Pope Leo IX, admired Symeon, and took his teaching as supporting his claim to spiritual authority over against the temporal authority of the Byzantine Emperor.

Michael Psellos

The eleventh century saw the Byzantine Empire heading inexorably for disaster. However, far from discouraging theological activity, such unsettled times, as seems rather the rule in Byzantium, witnessed a growing engagement with theological issues. Partly this was a result of the increasing need felt by the Byzantine Empire for Western support, which brought to a head the growing differences between the two parts of Christendom. A concern for such theological issues can be found in writers at the turn of the eleventh century, such as Theophylact, Archbishop of Ohrid,[26] and the Cypriote recluse, St. Neophytos,[27] both of whom also were concerned with scriptural exegesis, and the latter of whom certainly believed that finding the voice of the Fathers was more than a matter of compilation.

Earlier in the eleventh century Michael Psellos, the "consul of the philsophers," held sway in Constantinople as a teacher of renown, and a master of much learning that seemed to have been lost to the Byzantine world, especially the works of the last pagan philosophers of late antiquity such as Proklos, as well as being an adviser in the court of the Emperor himself.[28] Greek Christians had long made a distinction between the Outer and the Inner Learning, the former being the teaching of the classical philosophers and their followers, the latter the mysteries of the Christian Gospel. Psellos seems to have been one of the first to renew acquaintance with the Outer Learning. Despite this, he also had a genuine interest in the Inner Learning, and he managed to avoid being condemned. Not so his disciple, John Italos, who had succeeded Psellos as "consul of the philosophers." Under Emperor Alexios, who began the restoration of the Empire after the disasters of 1071 (the year of the defeat of the imperial forces to the Turks at Manzikert and the loss of Bari to the Normans), John was condemned in 1082 for his attachment to the Outer Learning, and the anathemas against him became part of the *Synodikon of Orthodoxy*, the proclamation of Orthodox doctrine that, since the Triumph of Orthodoxy in 843, had been part of the Church's liturgy for the first Sunday of Lent. In reality, the division between the Outer and the Inner Learning did not separate one kind of Byzantine learning from another: it represented an ambivalence at the very core of the Byzantine mind, for the Inner Learning itself drew heavily on Platonic philosophy for its conceptual vocabulary.

Athos and the Spiritual Theology of Inwardness

Both the split between Outer and Inner Learning, however, and a growing awareness of intellectual developments in the West characterize the intellectual climate of the last century of Byzantium. In a period that saw civil war in Byzantium and the inexorable loss of Byzantine territory to the Ottoman Turks, ending with the loss of the Queen City in 1453, intellectual and theological activity grew apace. Apart from further attempts to secure theological agreement between East and West on issues that now included purgatory, as well as the *filioque* and the authority of the papacy, the principal theological controversy of the fourteenth century was hesychasm, in which the split between Outer and Inner Learning and the divide between East and West were concentrated. From the twelfth century onwards, there had developed in the monasteries of the Holy Mountain of Athos a movement usually called "hesychasm." The word derives from the Greek ἡσυχία, quietness or stillness, and so could characterize any contemplative form of monasticism. In the narrower sense of the fourteenth-century controversy, it refers to a style of monastic life that lays stress on inward prayer or prayer of the heart, and especially the use of the "Jesus prayer" (the standard form being: "Lord Jesus Christ, Son of God, have mercy on me, a sinner"), to achieve such a state of prayer. Once, as a result of long ascetic struggle, a monk has achieved this state of prayer, he knows a state of union with God, in which God is manifest as the uncreated light, as Jesus appeared to his disciples on the Mount of the Transfiguration. The growth of hesychasm, in this sense, owes something to the influence of Symeon the New Theologian, though Symeon himself seems to have known nothing of the Jesus prayer. Claims to such experience were ridiculed by Barlaam, a Greek monk from Calabria, who arrived in Constantinople in 1330, where he became abbot of one of the monasteries, and was involved in negotiations about union between Byzantium and Rome.

Gregory Palamas

The hesychast monks were defended by St. Gregory Palamas, a monk of Mount Athos, who became Archbishop of Thessaloniki in 1347.[29] There are several strands to Palamas' defense of hesychasm. Central is the distinction he makes, drawing on earlier Greek patristic tradition, between the uncreated essence and uncreated energies of God: God in his essence is unknowable, but he makes himself known through his energies, which are not the created effects of God's power, but God himself. It is God's energy, as uncreated light, that the disciples beheld on Mount Tabor, and that the hesychast monks themselves experience. But there are further strands to Gregory's defense. For Gregory, union with God in prayer involves the union of the human person, so that the physical senses share with the intellect in its engagement with God. Barlaam's dismissal of the hesychasts' claim to see the uncreated light of the Godhead as hallucinations ignores this. A further aspect of Gregory's position concerns the nature of God himself. In opposition to Western scholastic ideas where God's essence and existence are identified (so that what God is is identical with that He is), the distinction between the uncreated essence and the energies of God prevents the elision of any distinction between God's energies or attributes, entailed by the Western understanding of God's unity.

It has recently become popular (as a result of Meyendorff's study of Palamas) to say that the controversy between Gregory and Barlaam was simply a dispute within Byzantine theology, a dispute between a reading of Dionysios the Areopagite in terms of the Outer Learning, and a reading in terms of the Inner Learning. It seems likely, however, that the reception of Western ideas in Byzantium was also involved, though it is probable that this process was more complex than it has often been portrayed.

The recent publication in a scholarly edition of Manuel Planoudis' Greek translation of Augustine's *De Trinitate*, made at the end of the thirteenth century,[30] has made it clear that Gregory himself had read and appreciated Augustine, as well as Barlaam, though in ways that are at first sight surprising (e.g., he found in Augustine support for arguments *against* the *filioque*).[31] This process of opening the Latin theological world to the Byzantines continued in the fourteenth century, with a Greek translation of Aquinas's *Summa contra Gentes* being published in 1354, but by then it was probably too late for Byzantine theologians to appreciate Latin theology, which more and more appeared in the role of aggressor in the negotiations for union that the increasingly desperate Byzantine Emperors sought to promote. The last century of Byzantium also saw growing interest in the Outer Learning of the kind for which Psellos had come under suspicion and John Italos condemned, some of which was to blossom in the Italian Renaissance.[32] But with the fall of Constantinople in 1453 all these blooms perished. Greek theology under the Ottomans became defensive, and succumbed to Western categories to an extent far in excess of anything the Byzantines had known. Whatever survived from Byzantium survived in the monasteries, so that the place of the Inner Learning perhaps looms larger in the eyes of posterity than it did to the Byzantines themselves.

Notes

1 See Georges Florovsky, "St. Gregory Palamas and the Tradition of the Fathers," reprinted in his *Bible, Church, Tradition: An Eastern Orthodox View*, vol. 1 of the Collected Works of George Florovsky (Belmont, Mass.: Nordland Publishing Co., 1972), pp. 105–20.

2 Alois Grillmeier, *Christ in Christian Tradition*, II/1 (London: Mowbray, 1987), pp. 51–78.

3 Nikephoros of Constantinople, *Breviarium* 52, ed. C. Mango (Dumbarton Oaks Texts, 10; Washington DC, 1990), p. 121.

4 Best guide: Alois Grillmeier, *Christ in Christian Tradition*, vol. 2, parts 1, 3, 4. London: Mowbray, 1987–96. See also John Meyendorff, *Imperial Unity and Christian Divisions: The Church 450–680 AD* (Crestwood, NY: St. Vladimir's Seminary Press, 1989) (much better than his earlier *Le Christ dans le théologie byzantine*, Paris: Le Cerf, 1969).

5 For sixth-century Origenism, see Antoine Guillaumont, *Les "Kephalaia Gnostica" d'Évagre le Pontique et l'histoire de l'origénisme chez les grecs et chez les syriens*, Patristica Sorbonensia 5 (Paris: Seuil, 1962). Guillaumont's identification of the Origenism condemned in 542 and 553 with the authentic teaching of Evagrius has not gone unchallenged: see Gabriel Bunge, "Hénade ou Monade? Au sujet de deux notions centrales de la terminologie évagrienne," *Le Muséon* 102 (1989): 69–91.

6 Two sets of Origenist propositions were condemned at Justinian's instigation, the first in an edict of 542, addressed to Patriarch Menas and others, the second at the Fifth Ecumenical Synod in 553. The condemned propositions are rather different: those of 542 are primarily concerned with Origenist eschatology, those of 553 with Origenist protology.

7 For Romanos' kontakia, see *Sancti Romani Melodi Cantica Genuina*, eds. P. Maas and C. A. Trypanis (Oxford: Clarendon Press, 1963). For a selection, in English translation with notes and introduction, see St. Romanos, *On the Life of Christ: Kontakia*, trans. Archimandrite Ephrem Lash, Sacred Literature Trust (London: HarperCollins, 1995).

8 Romanos, *On the Life of Christ*, p. 6.

9 For a brief introduction to the Areopagite, see Andrew Louth, *Denys the Areopagite* (London: Chapman, 1989). For more detail, see Paul Rorem, *Pseudo-Dionysius: A Commentary on the Texts and an Introduction to Their Influence* (New York: Oxford University Press, 1993).

10 See Paul Rorem and John C. Lamoreaux, *John of Scythopolis and the Dionysian Corpus: Annotating the Areopagite* (Oxford: Clarendon Press, 1998).

11 Critical edition by B. Suchla, G. Heil, and A. M. Ritter, *Corpus Dionysiacum*, 2 vols., Patristische Texte und Studien 33, 36 (Berlin, New York: W. de Gruyter, 1990–1). (Unreliable) English translation by Colm Luibheid, with notes by Paul Rorem, Pseudo-Dionysius, *The Complete Works*, Classics of Western Spirituality (Mahwah, NY: Paulist Press, 1987).

12 For an introduction to Maximos' life and thought, see Andrew Louth, *Maximus the Confessor* (London: Routledge, 1996). The literature on Maximus is considerable: important works include H. U. von Balthasar, *Kosmische Liturgie: Das Weltbild Maximus' des Bekenners*, 2nd, completely revised, edn. (Einsiedeln: Johannes-Verlag, 1961) (1st edn.: 1941); Polycarp Sherwood OSB, *The Earlier Ambigua of St. Maximus the Confessor and his Refutation of Origenism*, Studia Anselmiana 36 (Rome: Orbis Catholicus, Herder, 1955); Lars Thunberg, *Microcosm and Mediator: The Theological Anthropology of Maximus the Confessor*, Acta Seminarii Neotestamentici Upsaliensis 25, C. W. K. Gleerup–Ejnar Munksgaard: Lund, 1965 (2nd edn. with some revisions: Chicago and La Salle, Ill.: 1995); Walther Völker, *Maximus Confessor als Meister des Geistlichen*

Lebens (Wiesbaden: FranzSteiner Verlag, 1965); and now, Jean-Claude Larchet, *La Divinisation de l'homme selon saint Maxime le Confesseur* (Paris: Le Cerf, 1996). Maximos' works can be found in Patrologia Graeca (ed. J. P. Migne; hereafter "PG"), 90–1; a critical edition of his works is being produced, under the direction of Carl Laga and Carlos Steel, in Corpus Christianorum Series Graeca (Turnhout, 1977–).

13 For the Byzantine homily, see *Preacher and Audience: Studies in Early Christian and Byzantine Homiletics*, eds. Mary B. Cunningham and Pauline Allen (Leiden, Boston, Cologne: Brill, 1998).

14 On the monastic context of *aporiai* and *erotapokriseis*, see Paul M. Blowers, *Exegesis and Spiritual Pedagogy in Maximus the Confessor: An Investigation of the Quaestiones ad Thalassium, Christianity and Judaism in Antiquity* 7 (Notre Dame: University of Notre Dame Press, 1991), pp. 28–94.

15 On the genre of the century, see Balthasar, *Kosmische Liturgie*, pp. 482–4.

16 The other centuries that appear in Migne (PG 90.1177ff.) are mostly a later compilation, mainly drawn from Maximos' *Quaestiones ad Thalassium*.

17 Many twentieth-century theologians, following Fr. John Meyendorff, have attempted to put a distance between Maximos and Dionysios and spoken of Maximos' "Christological correction" of Dionysios. This seems to me overstated: Dionysios needs no "Christological correction," and neither Maximos nor Gregory Palamas provides any.

18 For Christian anti-Jewish literature of the seventh century, see the survey by Averil Cameron, "Byzantines and Jews: Some Recent Work on Early Byzantium," *Byzantine and Modern Greek Studies* 20 (1996): 249–74.

19 On this topic, see Mossman Rouché, "Byzantine Philosophical Texts of the Seventh Century," *Jahrbuch der Österreichischen Byzantinistik*, 23 (1974): 61–76, and other articles by the same author.

20 See the fragments from the works of Leontios of Neapolis, Simon of Bostra, and Jerome of Jerusalem, preserved in the anti-iconoclast *florilegia* of John Damascene and the Seventh Ecumenical Synod. Best modern edition in Hans Georg Thümmel, *Die Frühgeschichte der ostkirchlichen Bilderlehre*, Text und Untersuchungen 139 (Berlin: Akademie Verlag, 1992).

21 Works in PG 94–6. Critical edition by Bonifatius Kotter OSB: *Die Schriften des hl. Johannes von Damaskos*, 5 vols., Patristische Texte und Studien 7, 12, 17, 22, 29 (Berlin: W. de Gruyter, 1969–88).

22 Paul Lemerle, *Le premier humanisme byzantin* (Paris: Presses Universitaires de France, 1971).

23 Works in PG 101–4. Critical edition of homilies by B. Laourdas, Thessaloniki, 1959; of letters and *Amphilochia* by *idem* and L. G. Westerink, 6 vols. in 7 (Leipzig: Teubner, 1983–8); of the *Myriobiblion* (*Bibliotheca*) by R. Henry, 8 vols. (Paris: Les Belles Lettres, 1959–77) (plus index vol. 9, ed. J. Schamp, 1991).

24 Εὐεργετινὸς ἤτοι Συναγωγὴ τῶν θεοφθόγγων ῥημάτων καὶ διδασκαλίων τῶν θεοφόρων καὶ ἁγίων πατέρων, ed. Makarios of Corinth and Nikodemos Hagiorites, Venice, 1783; 7th edn. in 4 vols., Athens, 1983. On the Evergetinos and the monastery, see the volumes edited by Margaret Mullett and Anthony Kirby, *The Theotokos Evergetis and Eleventh-century Monasticism*, and *Work and Worship at the Theotokos Evergetis*, Belfast Byzantine Texts and Translations, 6.1 and 2, 1994–7.

25 Critical edition by J. Darrouzès AA, Basile Krivochéine, et al., Sources Chrétiennes 51, 96, 104, 113, 122, 129, 156, 174, 196 (Paris: Le Cerf, 1957–73).

26 Works: PG 123–6. Critical edition of selected works by P. Gautier, 2 vols., Thessaloniki, 1980–6.

27 See the critical edition of his works, produced by his monastery: Ἁγίου Νεοφύτου τοῦ Ἐγκλείστου, Συγγράμματα, 2 vols. so far, Πάφος: Ἔκδοση Ἱερᾶς Βασιλικῆς καὶ Σταυροπηγιακῆς Μονῆς Ἁγίου Νεοφύτου, 1996–8.

28 Psellos' works still await critical editions. A critical edition is being published in the Teubner library, in which the first volume of Psellos' theological works has been edited by the late P. Gautier (Leipzig: Teubner, 1989).

29 For a modern edition of Gregory Palamas' works (not properly critical), see P. Christou, ed., Γρηγορίου τοῦ Παλαμᾶ, Συγγράμματα,

5 vols so far, Thessaloniki, 1962–92. There is a critical edition of *150 Chapters*, by Robert E. Sinkewicz CSB, Studies and Texts 83 (Toronto: Pontifical Institute of Mediaeval Studies, 1988). For Palamas and the hesychast controversy, see Jean Meyendorff, *Introduction à l'étude de Grégoire Palamas*, Patristica Sorbonensia 3 (Paris: Seuil, 1959); but see also the criticisms of John Romanides, "Notes on the Palamite Controversy and Related Topics," I and II, *Greek Orthodox Theological Review* 6 (1960–1): 186–205; 9 (1963–4): 225–70.

30 Eds. Manuel Papathomopoulos, Isabella Tsavari, and Gianpaolo Rigotte, Ακαδημία Αθηνῶν Βιβλιοθήκη Α. Μανούση 3 (Athens: Κεντρὸν 'Εκδόσεως 'Εργῶν 'Ελλήνων Συγγράφεων, 1995).

31 See R. Flogaus, "Der heimliche Blick nach Westen: Zur Rezeption von Augustins *De trinitate* durch Gregorios Palamas," *Jahrbuch der Österreichischen Byzantinistik* 46 (1996): 275–97; *idem*, *Theosis bei Palamas und Luther*, Forschungen zur systematischen und ökumenischen Theologie 78, Göttingen, 1997; *idem*, "Palamas and Barlaam Revisited: A Reassessment of East and West in the Hesychast Controversy of 14th-century Byzantium," *St. Vladimir's Theological Quarterly* 42 (1998): 1–32; J. Lison, "L'Esprit comme amour selon Grégoire Palamas; une influence augustienne," *Studia Patristica* 32 (1997): 325–32; Josef Lössl, "Augustine's *On the Trinity* in Gregory Palamas's *One Hundred and Fifty Chapters*," *Augustinian Studies* 30 (1999): 61–82.

32 See Steven Runciman, *The Last Byzantine Renaissance* (Cambridge: Cambridge University Press, 1970), and Donald M. Nicol, *Church and Society in the Last Centuries of Byzantium* (Cambridge: Cambridge University Press, 1979).

The Carolingians

4   Bede the Theologian
        Benedicta Ward

5   Carolingian Theology
        Willemien Otten

Bede the Theologian

Benedicta Ward

The Venerable Bede is usually considered today first of all as the father of English history, but in his own times his reputation was primarily as an exegete and theologian. After recent editions and translations of many of his commentaries on the Bible, he is now seen in a clearer perspective as the greatest scholar of his age and the finest theologian between the early Church and the Carolingian age. He was an exact contemporary of John of Damascus: "Bede has illumined the West, Damascene the East with his wisdom," was the comparison made by Cardinal Bellarmine and quoted by Leo XIII in the bull of canonization of Bede in 1899.[1] Connected there with a contemporary Greek theologian, Bede was often shown in frescoes and illuminations surrounded by both Greek and Latin theologians, especially by the four Latin Fathers of the church whom Bede himself had identified as Augustine, Jerome, Gregory, and Ambrose. He was formally acknowledged to have a place among them when he was canonized and given the title "*Doctor Anglorum*."

Bede was not, however, a great systematic theologian but a supreme communicator. He saw himself as "following in the footsteps of the Fathers," by reading their works and absorbing their orthodoxy of doctrine. For Bede, a "Father" was not only one who received truth clearly and steadily but one who transmitted it to others with equal care and grace. Like the Greek and Latin fathers, he knew the scriptures and drew all his theology from them; he read all he could of the expositions of doctrine by his predecessors and absorbed it with remarkable clarity, and he gave his whole life to passing this on to others, as he said, "it was always my delight to learn or to teach or to write".[2]

Bede was no Augustine, Anselm, Aquinas; he made no new contribution to doctrinal definitions of the central tenets of the Christian faith, but the theologian has many tasks, not just the single one of refining doctrine. Bede understood that his task was to receive, verify, and transmit, and in doing so he ensured that the Christianity of the Anglo-Saxons was a continuation of the teaching of his predecessors. There is a double sense in which Bede gave a patristic theological perspective to the Church in Britain: he received the full tradition of the teaching of the Fathers and made it flower in his own life; and he also passed on this tradition to others. He did the second of these in three ways: first, by his work on the Scriptures themselves: secondly by his transmission of the patristic tradition of commentary to the monks, the clergy, and the laity; and thirdly by the way in which he looked at and recorded the early history of the English people. It seems appropriate therefore to consider Bede as a theologian in these three ways in turn; and because the Fathers of the Church are known through their writings, books will be used as pivots to the theme.

First of all, what did Bede do for the central text, the Scriptures? He laid down the true foundations for the study of the sacred page when from childhood he set himself to learn languages in order to read the text of the Scriptures, beginning with Latin, learned from Ceolfrid and Trumbert. He learned Greek later and then made corrections to his early commentaries, notably his commentary on Acts.[3] He tried his best with Hebrew by using the *Commentary on Hebrew Names* of Jerome.[4] Then he read the Scriptures with detailed and continuous care, in the course of the Offices of his community but also by private study, rejoicing especially over the arrival in his monastery of the text of Jerome's vulgate, reflecting the *hebraica veritas*.[5] The book which most of all is connected with Bede's care for the text of the Bible is the *Codex Amiatinus*, now in the Laurentian Library in Florence. It is one of the great books of the world and its appearance shows the care with which it was made: it has 1,030 folios (2,060 pages) of calf skin, each made from one calf, measuring 27.5 by 20.5 inches. It is 10 inches thick and weighs 75.5 pounds, with wrappings about 90 pounds. It is written in double columns in a lovely clear uncial, with a full-page illumination of Ezra the Scribe and also one of Christ in Majesty. It also contains concordance tables, a detailed diagram of the temple in Jerusalem, and three diagrams to explain three ways of arranging the biblical books according to Jerome, Hilary, and Augustine. This magnificant book was, moreover, only one of three, all produced in the scriptorium at Jarrow under Ceolfrid and in Bede's lifetime, as the unique survivor in his age-group in the monastery after the plague.[6]

Why does this great book matter? Because the text is the oldest surviving text of Jerome's Latin translation *iuxta hebraica*, and therefore one of the key biblical texts still for the study of the Bible. It seems likely that behind this project there lies the copy of the Bible called the *codex grandior* made by Cassiodorus at Vivarium in Calabria in the fourth century and which may have been brought to Jarrow by Ceolfrid and is now lost. Bede mentioned it in his treatise *On the Temple*:

> But these are the porches which the senator Cassiodorus, in the picture of the Temple, put in the pandect . . . these distinctions which I have found in Cassiodorus' picture I have taken care to note briefly, reckoning that he learnt them from the Jews of old and that such a learned man had no intention of proposing as a model for our reading what he himself had not first found to be true.[7]

This book gave the idea of a codex, of one huge volume containing all the Scriptures, and possibly also decided its form. But the text was the new text of

Jerome, more recently still brought to Jarrow by Bede's abbot and received by him with enthusiasm:

> He [Ceolfrid] added three new copies of the new translation of the Bible to the one copy of the old translation which he had brought back from Rome.[8]

Of these "three copies," Ceolfrid arranged that two should be for the use of the brothers in his monasteries:

> He [Ceolfrid] caused three Pandects to be transcribed, two of which he placed in his two monasteries in their churches in order that all who wished to read any chapter of either Testament might readily find what they desired.[9]

The third of these books he took with him, intending it as a present for the Pope, when he set out for Rome in his old age. This third copy is now known as the *Codex Amiatinus*:

> when Ceolfrith was about to make his departure for Rome he decided to present it as a gift to St. Peter, the prince of the Apostles.[10]

It proved, however, not to be a direct gift. Ceolfrid died at the monastery of Langes, and his book was taken to Rome; later it was acquired by the monastery of Monte Amiato and the dedication changed. Though it was known as a major manuscript of the Bible, it was not identified as coming from Jarrow until 1890. The inscription had been altered to read:

Cenobium ad eximii merito
Venerabile salvatoris
Quem caput ecclesiae
Dedicat alta fides
Petrus Langobardorum
Extrimis de finibus abbas
Devoti affectus
Pignora mitto mei
Meque meosque optans
Tanti inter gaudia patris
In ceolis memorem
Semper habere locum

"Cenobium ... Salvatoris" had been written over an erasure which now is seen to read "Corpus ... Petri," and "Petrus Langobardorum" was written over an erasure which reads "Ceolfridus Britonum." The true reading identified the book with Bede's Jarrow, reading:

> Abbot Ceolfrid, from Britain, the furthest limits, send my heart-felt offering to the place where rests the body of Peter, whose profound faith made him head of

the Church, hoping that for me and mine there may be a place forever among the joys of our heavenly homeland.[11]

It is impossible not to see Bede's hand in the establishment of the text of this codex. Its history shows even more of the place of Bede and his monastery in the life of the whole Church. First, the materials involved indicate a very rich monastery with skilled scribes. Secondly, it was a monastery with immense care for the Scriptures, with men willing to give time and labor to produce their best texts in three plain books, for scholarly use, in church.[12] Thirdly, such an enterprise needed the time and attention of a great scholar, entirely on top of his material; one such mastermind was Ceolfrid, but it seems very probable that another was Bede. Truth, the grammatical truth of the words, mattered to its makers, and its beautiful execution was a labor of prayer. Bede mentioned the books in his *History of the Abbots*, and there is another account of its history in *The Life of St. Ceolfrid*. Bede mentions the departure of Ceolfrid when he left for Rome with the book also in his commentary *On Samuel*.[13] The greatest work of Jarrow in the days of Bede and a book of importance to the whole church still, should be counted as one aspect of Bede's theological interests.

Secondly, what did Bede do about transmitting the commentaries on the Bible of the Fathers of the Church? He received many such books through Benedict Biscop and Ceolfrid, who collected them in Gaul and Rome, but he not only had books, he followed the advice of Augustine of Hippo[14] and read them. He had access at Wearmouth and Jarrow to over a hundred authors, including Basil (*On the Hexameon*, trans by Eustathios), Cassian, Cassiodorus, Chrysostom, Cyprian, Eusebius, Gregory Nazienzen, Hilary, Isaidore, Origen (*On Genesis*), Prudentius, Rufinus, Sedulius, and especially Augustine, Jerome, Gregory, and Ambrose. Bede absorbed them and used them to give others who did not have access to the texts a way of understanding the Scriptures according to the Fathers, with his own comments and explanations where necessary. Some of the commentaries were his own, where he did not have a patristic text, for example, on Samuel, on parts of Kings, on Habaccuck. Many of these were included in the eleventh-century *Glossa Ordinaria* and remained the standard biblical commentaries for the Middle Ages. Bede wrote with due care for sound theology, pointing out heresies, explaining what they were and why they were wrong. He concentrated, like his predecessors, on the exact grammatical meaning of the text, then on the doctrinal meaning of the passage about Christ, and then gave the moral, interior spiritual meaning of it for the hearer or reader.[15]

The commentaries were sent to friends such as Bishop Acca, or correspondents in both monasteries and convents, for the use of those concerned with understanding and with teaching the word of God in a relatively newly Christian country. But there are also examples of Bede's own application of the patristic tradition in his homilies which commented on the Gospels used in the liturgy. Some of them, such as his homily on the anniversary of the death of Benedict Biscop and his two homilies for the anniversary of the dedication of the church at Jarrow, have interest as relating to local events, but even in these the main part is careful patristic-style commentary on the text of the Gospel used at the liturgy, to bring out the doctrinal meaning and apply it to the hearers. A large group of homilies relate to Lent and Easter, another to Advent and Christmas, presenting the central Christian mysteries of Incarnation and Redemption in accessible and deeply spiritual theology. Later, they were collected by Paul the Deacon[16] into a book of homilies for use in the monastic Office and have therefore constantly been used. In them, Bede himself is looking towards Christ as the Fathers did, and helping others to do the same. Copies of Bede's commentaries and homilies circulated and were copied and read throughout Europe, and eventually in the tenth century in England. They were among the texts requested by Boniface for use in his mission.[17]

Thirdly, Bede wrote theological history in his accounts of saints such as Cuthbert, and preeminently in his last book the *Ecclesiastical History of the English Nation*. In it he placed the lens of the Gospel over the events of the conversion of the English a century earlier, and on every page there is no mere collection of facts but a sustained interpretation of them. As he said in his preface, he wrote "in accordance with the principles of true history,"[18] collecting with infinite care all that could be known from the sources available to him, but placing it within the structure of redemption, "for the instruction of posterity".[19]

Bede is a supreme story-teller. The characters of Augustine of Canterbury, Aidan, Hilda, Oswald, Chad, and many more shine from his page, but always within the light of the Gospel, showing the turning of the *gens anglorum* from paganism into the new life of the redeemed. Bede's *History*, as much as his commentaries, is about "the light that lighteth every man who cometh into the world," and his efforts were directed to see that darkness should not overcome it, now and in England.

All his life Bede continued with this double task of recording the coming of the Good News to the English and assisting in its spread. It was therefore fitting that on his deathbed he still worked within that framework of helping the new nation to become a part of the Kingdom, and it is significant that he was translating the gospel of John into English. The true theological education of the English was a hard and unremitting task, for Bede was above all a "true theologian," and his interest was in the presence of Christ in the continuing Church, in the hearts of each one. He knew the importance of ensuring that conversion was inner as well as outer. It was the realization of the ultimate end of salvation through the theology of faith that Bede wanted to transmit to the Anglo-Saxons, not just theological information about it. He was concerned that every English Christian should know by heart at least the basis of prayer and of belief, in the Lord's Prayer and the Creed:

> it is most certain that all those who have learned to read Latin will know these [Creed and Lord's Prayer] well, but the unlearned, that is to say those who only know their own language, must learn to say them in their own tongue and to chant them carefully. This ought to be done not only by the laity, that is to say those living the ordinary life of the populace, but also by the clergy and the monks, who are experts in Latin. For thus the whole community of the believers

may learn of what their faith consists, and how they ought in the strength of that belief to arm and defend themselves against the assaults of evil spirits. Thus they will learn, as a united chorus of supplicants to God, what above all they should seek from the divine clemency. Because of this I have frequently offered an English translation of the Creed and the Lord's Prayer.[20]

Latin learning, which Bede himself loved and valued so deeply, was something a Christian must assimilate with all his powers in order to use his mind for the glory of God. But Bede was well aware that such learning could become idolatry and a cause of conceit. Beyond the words and the doctrines, however grasped, there was a whole new way of approaching reality that needed to be received and applied. It is this expanding of the mind by discipline in order to know what matters, that lies behind Bede's view of Christian theological education. In the constant effort of the converters of the Anglo-Saxons to tranform and transfigure their polished, sophisticated pagan society into a Christian *koinonia*, this exchange had to take place. This was true, for example, not only of kings and nobles, but also among the nuns and monks of the royal abbeys of England. Great ladies might become abbesses in their own estates and households and continue their great position almost unchanged at the center of things; retired soldiers might enjoy a quiet monastic retreat to their abbey on their estates, but their attention to the brightness, glory, nobility, and generosity that showed their own position, needed realigning in the new way of the cross. In order to enable such people to understand the central matter of the gospel, Bede turned to translation from Latin into their own language. In a letter to Huaetberht, abbot of Jarrow after Coelfrid, when sending him his commentary on the Book of Revelation, Bede wrote:

I think that the indolence of our nation, I mean the English, ought to be taken into account which not long since, that is in the time of Pope Gregory, received the seeds of faith and has cultivated the same remissly enough so far as reading is concerned. I have arranged my plan so as not only to elucidate the sense but also to compress the sentances inasmuch as brevity if it is clear is wont to be fixed in the memory more than prolix discussion.[21]

Bede was no sentimentalist about Christian education and theology. Doctrine mattered and it had to be thoroughly examined at all levels, always, by those capable of it. But Bede was well aware that there were other ways of knowing God as well as the exercise of the intellect. He recorded a long account of a vision of heaven and hell, by an unlearned layman, Drythelm, a married man in Northumbria.[22] He also included in his *History* the story of Caedmon, the first Anglo-Saxon poet, a cowherd who at first could not read, write, or sing.[23] There was also Owine, an East Anglian thane of Queen Etheldreda who, when he went to join the monastery of Chad at Lastingham, carried with him an axe and an adze to show that he wanted no part in the discipline of book-learning; yet it was he who saw and heard the angels who came to take the soul of Chad into heaven, not the more bookish brothers.[24] Learning for Bede must always be concerned with vigorous life in Christ if it was not to fall into the perils of pride. In his commentary on Proverbs, Bede made this point:

> Better is a stupid and simple brother who, working the good things he knows, merits life in heaven, than one who being distinguished for his learning in the scriptures lacks the bread of love.[25]

It was the increase of the love which is Christ that was for Bede the aim of Christian theology, and in his account of the life of the hermit-bishop Cuthbert, Bede adds a revealing comment to the story of Cuthbert and his dying master Boisil:

> "And what, I ask you, is it best for me to read which I can yet finish in seven days?" He [Boisil] replied, "The evangelist John. I have a book consisting of seven gatherings of which we can get through one every day with the Lord's help, reading it and discussing it between ourselves as far as is necessary."

Bede added: "they were able to finish the reading so quickly because they dealt only with the simple things of 'faith that works by love.'"[26]

Learning and passing on knowledge in theology as elsewhere is surely never a matter of accumulating information which will give the person possessing it more status. The word "education" itself is, after all, derived from *educare*, "to draw out," that is, to enable the full potential of a person to be activated and realized. In the Crewian oration in 1993, Seamus Heaney referred to the understanding Robert Frost had of education as not being about getting to a higher class by achieving another level of knowledge, but about allowing perspectives to be so realigned that it becomes possible to establish a critical angle on whatever determines ideas of high and low in the first place. It was this expanding of the mind by discipline in order to know what mattered and to be absorbed by it that lay behind Bede's view of theology. His own final prayer at the end of the *Ecclesiastical History* underlines his application of this:

> and I pray you, merciful Jesus, as you have graciously granted me sweet draughts of the Word which tells of You, so of your goodness, grant that I may come at length to You, the fount of all wisdom, and stand before Your face forever.[27]

Notes

1 Bull of Leo XIII, Urbe et Orbi: *Acta Sanctae Sedis in compendium opportune redacta et illustrata*, ed. V. Piazzesi, XXXII (Rome, 1900), pp. 338–9.

2 Bede, *Ecclesiastical History of the English People*, eds. R. A. B. Mynors and B. Colgrave (Oxford, 1969) (hereafter EHEP), Bk. V, ch. 24, p. 567.

3 Cf. *Expositio Actuum Apostolorum et Retractio*, ed. M. L. W. Laistner, Medieval Academy of America Publication no. 35 (Cambridge, Mass., 1939).

4 Jerome, *De Nominibus Hebraicis*, ed. P. de Lagarde, *Corpus Christianorum Series Latina*, 72 (Turnhout, 1959).

5 Bede, "Lives of the Abbots of Wearmouth

and Jarrow," in *The Age of Bede*, ed. D. H. Farmer (Harmondsworth, 1965), ch. 15, p. 201 (hereafter LA).

6 *Codex Amiatinus*, MS, Biblioteca Medicea-Laurenziana, Florence. Cf. E. A. Lowe, *Codices Latini Antiquiores*, 111, p. 299. Also R. L. S. Bruce-Mitford, *The Art of the Codex Amiatinus*, Jarrow Lecture, 1967.

7 Bede, *On the Temple*, trans. Sean Connolly (Liverpool, 1995), ch. 17, 2, p. 68.

8 LA, ch. 15, p. 201.

9 *Life of Ceolfrid, Abbot of Wearmouth and Jarrow*, trans. D. S. Boutflower (London, 1912), ch. 20, p. 69.

10 Ibid.

11 Bruce-Mitford, *The Art of the Codex Amiatinus*, pp. 5–6.

12 The other two pandects have almost entirely disappeared: "A leaf of one of the other two pandects was discovered by Canon Greenwell, of Durham, in a Newcastle bookshop in 1909; and this with two or three similar leaves, known as the Middleton leaves, are in the British Museum," ibid., p. 1.

13 Bede, *In Primam Partem Samuhelis Libri III*, ed. D. Hurst, *CCSL* 119 (Turnhout, 1969), p. 212.

14 Augustine, *de Doctrina Christiana*, II, viii.

15 For Bede and the rules of Tyconius cf. Bede, *On Revelation, Patrologia Latina*, 93, col. 131.

16 Cf. Cyril L. Smetana, "Paul the Deacon's Patristic Anthology" in *The Old English Homily and its Patristic Background*, eds. Paul E. Szarmach and Bernard F. Huppe (Albany, 1978).

17 *The Letters of St. Boniface*, trans. Emerton (Princeton, 1940), Letter LXXV (91), p. 168.

18 EHEP, Preface, p. 7.

19 Bede, "Letter to Egbert," in *The Ecclesiatical History of the English People*, trans. J. McClure and R. Collins (Oxford, 1994), p. 346.

20 Ibid., p. 347.

21 Bede, *On Revelation*.

22 EHEP Bk. V, ch. xii, pp. 489–99.

23 Ibid. Bk. IV, ch. xxiv, pp. 415–21.

24 Ibid. Bk. IV, ch. iii, pp. 339–41.

25 Bede, *On Proverbs*, in *Proverbia Salomonis*, ed. D. Hurst, *Corpus Christianorum Series Latina*, 119B, xxii, 9.

26 Bede, "Life of St. Cuthbert," in *Two Lives of St. Cuthbert*, ed. B. Colgrave (Cambridge, 1940), p. 183. The codex mentioned here was once thought to be the Stoneyhurst Gospel of John, now in the British Museum, but this is unlikely since it has eleven not seven gatherings.

27 EHEP, Bk. V, ch. 24, p. 571.

Carolingian Theology

Willemien Otten

Introduction

In his well-known collection of essays on history and tradition published in 1993, Eric Hobsbawm introduced a new historiographical concept which he called *the invention of tradition*.[1] His claim was that, when social and cultural movements trace back their roots to ancient tradition, they need not always be taken at their word. For what they call tradition may in fact be a product of recent invention. Hobsbawm's interest seems to have been captured by the fact that movements such as nineteenth-century nationalism gained much faster acceptance when claiming to be in continuity with a distinguished past. Thus his book highlights the important role of tradition precisely as a way to influence the present.

To go from nineteenth-century Europe back to the eighth and ninth centuries is quite a historical leap. More than a leap into a distant past, however, it is a leap into an era in which there was a different conception of the past and of history altogether. As a crucial era in the history of Western Christianity the Carolingian period may well have distinguished itself by first conceptualizing this need to depend on a past. When Alcuin fought the adoptionist Christology of eighth-century Spain, he did so with the full confidence that he represented traditional orthodoxy over ancient heresy. It is tempting to apply Hobsbawm's phrase here and speak about the invention of tradition. Yet whereas this label aptly describes various nineteenth-century developments, it does not cover adequately what happened in the Carolingian age. When Hobsbawm's nineteenth-century nationalists construed the idealized past to which they wanted to return, they had enough historical awareness to do so, including an adequate sense of distance. For they knew that this ideal past had never existed. When the Carolingians looked back, however, they were confronted with an enormous void. This was the dramatic result of the collapse of the Roman Empire in the fifth and sixth centuries CE, which separated them forever from the glory of ancient Rome and the distinguished age of the Fathers.

Yet being the natural educators they were, Carolingian theologians seemed unwilling to stare into this void, as this would lead them on an Orphic quest that was doomed to fail. Instead they projected their vision on the future, a future which would make them share retroactively in the glorious past that was never theirs. Karl Morrison has called this the strategy of *mimesis*.[2] He explained how the Middle Ages generally resisted innovation, unless it could be presented as a reform, i.e., a repeating or following (*mimesis*) of traditional Christian principles and values. This is exactly what most Carolingian theologians did. Ancient tradition became in their hands a useful tool with which to craft a future.

Employing this dual strategy of invented tradition alongside mimetic reform, the Carolingians built a cultural home for themselves which would subsequently be considered Europe's shared Christian heritage. What makes their theological achievement so difficult to assess, however, is that they removed the traces of their own interference so scrupulously that twelfth-century authors could lean on this tradition as if it had always been there. Thus their contribution has long remained unnoticed. The very fact that the Carolingians remained virtually invisible throughout such a crucial process of cultural transmission may well be the greatest testimony to their achievement.

But it is also the reason that they did not always receive appropriate credit. When not played down altogether, Carolingian theology is often seen as a theology marked, if not marred, by controversy. In the following we shall follow the Carolingian controversies more or less in chronological order. We shall begin with the adoptionist controversy. Next we shall deal with the iconoclasm controversy, after which we continue with the eucharistic controversy. We end with the predestination controversy. It is important not to narrow the importance of Carolingian theology to the sum of its controversies. The emergence of different, even divergent, opinions marking the theological landscape can itself be seen as a clear sign of the Carolingians' growing self-awareness. This self-awareness was at the basis of a kind of intellectual confidence by which they were able not just to defend their own positions as in conformity with the Fathers but, on a deeper level, to harmonize the Fathers' different voices in such a way as to create a coherent sense of tradition.

Alcuin (730–804) and the Adoptionist Controversy: The Meaning of Divine Sonship

Of all the Carolingian controversies, the one on adoptionism is probably the most misunderstood. This is a direct result of Alcuin's formidable success in labeling the adoptionist position a heresy. He did so, moreover, in the stigmatizing vocabulary derived from the early Christological debates. Since the weight of the patristic tradition as codified by the Carolingians has only increased since the days of Alcuin, his judgment became progressively harder to resist. Thus his views proved instrumental in confirming and spreading the orthodoxy of Chalcedonian Christology. But was Alcuin right in condemning adoptionism?

Impressed by the original insights of the adoptionists, John Cavadini has recently rehabilitated this Spanish Christology, calling it "the last Christology of the

West."[3] Apparently in Spain an (under)current of western Christological ideas existed which was not influenced by the orthodox position until it became confronted by Alcuin. Cavadini saw this current as a legitimate offshoot of the North African theological tradition, which included Augustine. Why then did it lead to controversy?

The adoptionist controversy started when Elipandus, archbishop of Toledo since 754 CE and Primate of all Spain, spread the view that Jesus was the "adoptive" Son of God. Elipandus' first adoptionist statements seem to have been brought on by a trinitarian dispute with a certain Migetius in the 780s which involved Migetius' view of a relation between the divine *personae* in the Trinity and the historical persons David, Jesus, and Paul. According to Elipandus Migetius held that the corporeal persons David, Jesus, and Paul existed in the Trinity (*tres personas corporeas in divinitate*). This would seem to indicate that all persons of the Trinity had become assumed there through an extension of the Christological paradigm. Following Augustine, Elipandus responded that the second person of the Trinity was not the "person assumed from the virgin" in Jesus, but the one "born from the Father without beginning." Remaining loyal to a one-person Christology, he also avoided the pitfall of Nestorianism, by which Christ was seen as only a human being and thus there would have to be two persons in Christ, one by nature and one by adoption.

When Elipandus was criticized by Beatus of Liebana, the abbot of an Asturian monastery under Moorish control, he began to formulate his adoptionist position in clearer terms. The central difficulty with it lies in the understanding of the term *adoptivus*. For Elipandus, Christ's "adoptive" Sonship meant neither that he had been adopted by God the Father, which would amount to Arianism, nor that he had adopted a human body, as a stronger variant of Christ's assuming flesh. What Elipandus had wanted to say was that, by assuming flesh or body, the Word or Son of God became the first-born in adoption and grace. His reference to adoption functioned as a kind of exegetical elaboration of the self-emptying of Christ in Philippians 2:7, according to which the Son of God took the form of a slave and was made in the likeness of men.

In its Spanish version, then, the debate centered on Christ's human being who was assumed, specifically on the question whether or not he was *adoptivus*. Although Beatus opposed Elipandus, it seems the Christological position of these two Spanish thinkers was part of an integral Western theological development. Its origin may well be the *homo assumptus* Christology found in Augustine's *Encheiridion*, where he uses Philippians 2 to describe the Incarnation in paradoxical terms.

By the late eighth century, however, the debate moved to Urgel in the non-Muslim north, as Elipandus sought help from its bishop Felix to suppress the heresy of Beatus. Felix may have been interested in this Toledan Christology as a way to resist Carolingian control of the Spanish March and maintain at least some ecclesiastical independence. But he soon fell victim to the fierce anti-adoptionist campaign orchestrated by Rome and the Carolingians. While Pope Hadrian I was the first to equate Felix's teaching with Nestorianism, his major charge against

Elipandus' adoptionism was that it alienated the Son from the Father. By stressing the self-emptying of the Word, as Elipandus did, this alienating effect was only increased. When Alcuin became involved, he followed directly in Hadrian's footsteps, as they both judged Elipandus and Felix from an Eastern Christological perspective. Alcuin went even further than Hadrian by suggesting that, as a human being, Christ was a servant who was adopted into Sonship. It thus appears as if the conflict between Hadrian and Alcuin on the one hand and Elipandus and Felix on the other was a conflict between two different theological settings: the paradoxical Christology of the God-Man in the West and the (theo)logical analyses of Christ's two natures in the Eastern Christological debates between Cyrillus and Nestorius. When attacking Felix, Alcuin contented himself with faulting him for his inconsistency, in the same way as Nestorius had once been attacked.

After a first condemnation at the council of Regensburg in 792, Felix and Elipandus were condemned at the synod of Frankfurt in 794. Felix, who was merely guilty by association, was not even deposed until 799, when he took up adoptionism again. Summoned to Aix, he held a lengthy dispute with Alcuin, after which both kept rethinking their views. In accordance with what would soon be standard Carolingian method, Alcuin collected a dossier of patristic references in order to persuade Felix to give up adoptionism. He extensively used a Latin version of the *Acta* of the council of Ephesus (431) for this, which he had found in his home library of St. Martin's monastery in Tours.

For purposes of this chapter it is especially interesting to see how this controversy was both shaped by and shaped Alcuin's own theological views. Born around 730 in England, Alcuin had been persuaded by Charlemagne at a meeting in Padua in 781 to join his court circle of scholars in Aix. He quickly became one of the court's leading figures. His strength was the teaching of the liberal arts, which he saw as foundational for any sound teaching of the orthodox faith. When first faced with adoptionism at the council of Frankfurt in 794, Alcuin simply accepted Hadrian's rejection of it. Even when analyzing the flaws in Elipandus' position at a later time, he still seemed to be fighting Hadrian's view of Elipandus rather than Elipandus himself. For Alcuin the adoptionists considered Christ a man, yet one who was elevated into adoption or grace; hence the charge of Nestorianism. It is only after the face-to-face debate with Felix in Aix in 799 that he elaborated his position by writing seven books against his opponent. His arguments throughout unfold as a simple case of logic, as for him Felix's teaching can only lead to the logical disjunction that Christ's one person is both God and not God at the same time.

For one reading Alcuin from the perspective of the Spanish, his views amount to a simple misreading, as he neglected Felix's interpretation of Philippians 2:6–11. Alcuin could not see Christ as assuming the *forma servi*. While the Spanish focus had been on the unique continuity of substance between the *forma Dei* and the *forma servi*, Alcuin interpreted Christ's self-emptying as a kind of elevation of a man into sonship. Regarding the nature of the union of Christ's two natures as ultimately mysterious, he stressed that it should be recognized to be ineffable.

For one interested in the perspective of the Carolingians, Alcuin's misreading serves as a first example of the creative ways in which Carolingian theologians were to develop their own positions. While Alcuin's objections to adoptionism come out poorly in his books against Felix, they are much clearer in his three books *On the Faith in the Holy and Undivided Trinity*, his final dogmatic work written for Charlemagne in 802. Methodologically this work consists in unacknowledged citations from the Church Fathers, to a degree far exceeding modern plagiarism. Yet at the same time, it lays down a constructive theology of the Trinity, in which the Incarnation holds a central place. Although Alcuin uses Augustine's *On the Trinity*, his focus is not on its famous psychological analogies. Rather than being speculative, this work is meant to instruct teachers and preachers on how to expound orthodox faith. To facilitate their teaching, Alcuin expounds trinitarian doctrine largely in the form of a commentary on the Creed. In this way the doctrine of the Incarnation becomes embedded in the whole of the Catholic faith, of which it is the centerpiece. When expounded correctly, the orthodox faith will bring about a reign of Catholic peace across the Empire, remedying heresy by simply preventing it. Alcuin's view of the Incarnation is that it is a *mirabilis coniunctio* of two natures. While the logic of Christ who became man remains ineffable, its continuous effect is the working of miracles in the world. In Christ God's grace is given out to man so that man, through this same grace, will be forgiven his sins. This conviction lies at the heart of Alcuin's Catholic faith and from it the moral and practical reforms of the Carolingian church seem to follow only naturally.

For the Spanish, the teaching of adoptionism had much to do with proclaiming a continuity of substance between Christ the Son of God and Jesus the Man, its Christology representing a line of development that was Western rather than Chalcedonian. In contrast, Alcuin's theological interest in this matter was not speculative. Accepting Pope Hadrian's criticism of adoptionism, he endorsed this papal view with his own arguments, most of which he borrowed from the Fathers or the *Acta* of the council of Ephesus. Looking to his major work on the Trinity at the end of his life, we find that it looks like a tapestry of patristic citations. Yet its narrative pattern gives us a deeper insight into Alcuin's own Christology. While firmly anchored in Chalcedonian faith, it amounts to a fresh rephrasing of it in a new and more accessible theological language. The result is an exposition of doctrine which runs parallel to the structure of the Creed, as the devotional/theological and the moral/pastoral blend into one. At the heart of Alcuin's faith is the Incarnation as a mystery to be worshiped, reflecting the gift of God's grace to the world.

Thus Alcuin's position gives us a first indication of what Carolingian theology looks like: based on patristic authority, even if at times far-fetched, its doctrinal expositions aim at the sound teaching of the faith. The truth of this faith was reinforced by the Carolingians' claim that only a universal Church could guarantee the *pax catholica*. The tendency to see theological analysis as closely related to the exposition of the faith, a faith which was expressed in the correct worship of the Church, means that the Carolingian discussions were ultimately more about truth as a value by which to live than a proposition to which to assent.

Theodulf (750/60–821) and the Iconoclast Controversy: From Divine Son to Human Saints

Of all the Carolingian controversies, the one on images is the most convoluted. This goes back in part to the complex composition history of the *Opus Caroli* (formerly called the *Libri Carolini*) as the document which came to contain the official Carolingian viewpoint on images. Traditionally attributed to Alcuin, this work has been written instead by Theodulf. Born around 750/60, Theodulf had left Spain to join the Carolingian court, where he quickly became one of Charlemagne's favorite advisers. He became abbot of Fleury and bishop of Orléans in 798.

While the controversy can be simply stated – whether or not to worship images – it appears the theological issues that were at stake involved much more than images alone. Concerning the right interpretation of the Fathers, for example, Theodulf seemed to aim at emancipation not just from the Greeks, but also from the Pope. To avoid controversy with the Roman curia, however, he had to exercise extreme care in presenting his position as flowing naturally from the tradition.

The motive behind the Carolingian focus on the tradition was that Charlemagne's iconoclast position differed from both the Byzantine East and the Pope and that only when presented as "traditional" could there have been any hope for its broad acceptance. As the *Opus Caroli* state clearly in IV 28, this synod (Nicaea II) should have called itself universal only "if it had lacked newness of words and had contented itself with the doctrines of the ancient Fathers." From this implicit accusation, it can be deduced that Theodulf himself claimed to do just that.

The controversy itself unfolded as follows. At the second Nicene Council in 787 the Byzantine East had adopted an iconophile position after having been iconoclast before. The Nicene Council was presided over by Empress Irene on behalf of her young son Constantine VI. Although Pope Hadrian I himself was not present, he had sent a letter to the council and was represented by two legates. After the council, the proceedings reached the court of Charlemagne in a poor Latin translation. Outraged at what they read, the king and his court theologians drew up a quick reply against the Greeks, the so-called *Capitulare adversus synodum*, which was brought to Rome in 792 CE. Meanwhile Theodulf had set out to expand on the *Capitulare*, in an endeavor to bolster the Carolingian position with further evidence from the Church Fathers. Being associated with the Council, however, the Pope was unwilling to condemn its outcome. When he informed the Carolingians, Theodulf carefully re-edited the expanded document, removing references to Hadrian's letter to Nicaea. As they could not present the *Opus Caroli* to the Pope, the Carolingians stored the manuscript in the royal archives.

Leaving the political and cultural ramifications of this controversy aside, it is especially impressive to see how Theodulf succeeded in proving the intellectual validity of the Carolingian position, since he had to use all his (philo)logical skills to counter the Byzantine arguments. We have seen how Alcuin drew on the Latin

Acta of the council of Ephesus to attack Felix. A similar pattern is found in the *Opus Caroli*, whereby it should be noted that Theodulf's own position was even more interwoven with the Fathers than Alcuin's. As his Byzantine opponents had used extensive patristic arguments to defend their iconophile position, Theodulf was not free to select his own sources in defense of his view. He also used the Fathers, many of whom had also been drawn on by the Eastern party, as he contested the Greek interpretation. Only in this oblique way could he put forth the "right," that is, Carolingian view. Thus this controversy was ultimately about much more than images. It was ultimately about the authoritative view of the Fathers, as the Carolingians strove to replace the Byzantine church as the natural heirs of the orthodox faith.

Underneath this confident use of the tradition for purposes of validation, the *Opus Caroli* points to the Franks' remarkable ecclesiological self-awareness and sensitivity, which was based on a set of strong biblical and Christological convictions. Their main objection to the Greek position was that it turned believers away from the Trinitarian God, as the only object worthy of adoration. Moreover, the Greeks wished to substitute lifeless material icons for the saints' real powers. For Theodulf, images were much less worthy than relics, inasmuch as the latter at least were tied to the saints' real bodies. Hence, the adoration of images would lead people into superstition rather than true worship. To underscore this, Theodulf argued that this had always been the position of the universal Church. As it has a living faith, it can resort to the active memory of a living tradition. For Theodulf it was so true that the Church alone can mediate between humanity and God that his ecclesiology borders on the mystical, as he portrayed the Church not just as body of Christ, but as his Bride.

Yet this mystical vision of the Church was not devoid of political motives. If the Church is truly the Bride of Christ, there can be no formal boundaries to her sense of duty. While Theodulf proclaimed the unity of the Western Church as symbolized in the papal see, it is significant that the pope with whom he felt most affinity was not Hadrian, but a past pope of impeccable standing, Gregory I. It is almost as if Theodulf launched on the reputation of Gregory to bypass the authority of Hadrian. While Gregory had tolerated the presence of images in the Church, he had not allowed for their worship, which made his position relatively close to Theodulf's own. Quoting from Gregory's letter, therefore, helped him to neutralize Hadrian's position.

Since a crucial part of the iconoclast controversy concerned the use of the Fathers, it is important to realize that Theodulf became a recognized expert in this strategy. From a letter written by Charlemagne in 798, it appears the king also approached him for patristic evidence in the adoptionist controversy. One of the ways in which Theodulf got the Fathers on his side was by making a careful distinction between the so-called *res Christianorum*, by which he indicated the correct Carolingian middle position on images, with the *ordo testimoniorum*, i.e., a correct line-up of authorities. It remains unclear which came first for Theodulf: the Carolingian position on images or the view that the different Fathers should form one authoritative chain. Deftly molding his evidence, Theodulf was able to craft a case from the Bible and the Fathers in such a way that their combined authority underscored the position of the Carolingians themselves.

Theodulf frequently claimed support from the entire universal tradition of the Church, even though the evidence of Scripture for this erudite biblical scholar still outweighed the patristic tradition. At the same time, the patristic tradition hardly represented a single viewpoint. To use his sources responsibly, Theodulf employed a multilayered strategy. He sometimes called on the entire tradition of the Fathers as a well-rounded whole, preceded by Scripture and continued by the various councils, whereas at other times he contested the authenticity of certain patristic writings used by the Greeks. For this he called again on the authority of a past pope, in this case Gelasius, the presumed author of a list of authorized patristic writings, the so-called *De libris recipiendis et non recipiendis.* When necessary, Theodulf dispensed with the *ordo testimoniorum* altogether. When the Pope faulted Charlemagne for his failure to adhere to chronological order, as he had claimed that the entire apostolic tradition supported Gregory's testimony, the *Opus Caroli* simply left out all patristic support. After all, the *res Christianorum* was also embodied in the Carolingian church who, in her capacity as Bride, was headed not by any reigning pope but by Christ himself.

The point of convergence for the different strands of the iconoclast controversy, such as the notion of the tradition as a preconceived whole, or a universal Carolingian Church seen as the Bride of Christ, is again Christology. The question on images broadens ultimately into one about the power of representation. Whereas the Greeks saw no harm in the presence of icons in the church, as a way for the saint to communicate his power to all those present, Theodulf found this unacceptable. While the first of his objections may well seem the most mundane, it went right to the Christological heart of the controversy. In Theodulf's view, if one failed to make a difference between image and original, i.e., a true saint and his icon, churches would engage in material competition. Would one not try make the images as costly as possible so as to increase the salvific power of the saint in question? Yet his gravest concern was not the costliness, but the morally disruptive and divisive effect of this competition on the unity of the church.

Theodulf claimed that only humanity was created in the image of God, and that further representations were unnecessary. Since humanity's role as "live" representation of the divine was compromised through Adam's Fall, it had to be renewed through the Incarnation of the Word. In Jesus Christ, the Son of God restored humanity's role of *imago Dei.* Since in Christ God had bridged the gap between himself and humanity through love, it is through Christ that God should be worshiped. Material symbols, then, ought not to mislead us through their false semblance, as they detract from Christ's role. This explains the significance of the Cross for the Carolingians, as it represents Christ's power without compromising the inimitable efficacy of his death and resurrection (cf. II.28).

Theodulf rejected the equation of icons with the body and blood of Christ at the Eucharist. Both Christ's body and his blood received in the sacrament, and the believers' faith and confession in the heart, are more true than icons, because they are filled with the truth of Christ himself. Just as the event of the Incarnation collapsed the Old into the New Testament, so it also united the historical tradition of the Fathers with the present situation of the Carolingian Church, who is Christ's Bride. As for this tradition, to underscore its venerability and reliability alike, it had been stored in books and not in images. Just as Moses wrote down the law and did not paint it, so Jesus wrote rather than drew with his finger in the sand.

Theodulf's Christology naturally implied a view of the Trinity as well. In Book III.3 en III.8 as in his *On the Procession of the Spirit* Theodulf advocated the so-called *filioque*, which the Greeks considered a nontraditional Western innovation to the Creed. While Greek authors like Basil of Ancyra and Constantine of Cyprus were able to integrate their adoration of the Trinity with their adoration of images, Theodulf argued that in doing so they overstepped the boundaries separating creatures from their creator. Christ alone is able to bridge this gap, which is symbolized in the *Opus Caroli*'s joint embrace of the *Filioque* and the cross. Recognizing how acceptance of these two is crucial for the unity of a true and universal Church, Theodulf seems to have written his *Opus Caroli* in fact as a long methodological preamble to a Carolingian ecclesiology which has its basis in a reconstructed anthropology. For him, sound faith does not just restore humans to their original role as image of God, but it unites them through Christ in the universal Church. Elevated through grace, this Church which is constituted of sinful humans can yet mystically serve as Bride of Christ.

The Eucharistic Controversy: Radbertus and Ratramnus on the Meaning of Sacrament

It is again the interrelation between Christology and ecclesiology which constitutes the general framework of the debate on the eucharist. Within this framework the different interpretations of Radbertus and Ratramnus each have their rightful place. We shall start again with a short historical survey.

Paschasius Radbertus, who was head of the monastic school at Corbie, was asked by his student Warin, abbot of Corbie's daughter monastery of Corvey in Saxony, to send instructions for his monks on the eucharist. He composed his book *On the Lord's Body and Blood* in 831–3. In early 843, King Charles the Bald came to Corbie for prayer and found himself impressed by the monk Ratramnus. As Radbertus had not supported Charles for the throne, he may have avoided his company. Charles asked Ratramnus a specific question, namely "whether the body and blood of Christ, which the faithful at church receive in their mouth, are present there in mystery or in truth." Ratramnus answered by writing his own *De corpore et sanguine Domini*.

Shortly after Radbertus became abbot of Corbie, he decided to send a revised copy of his book to Charles in an effort to placate him. Meanwhile, Ratramnus had succeeded him as head of the monastic school. As suggested by Ratramnus' modern biographer Jean-Paul Bouhot, the eucharistic "controversy" may well have its roots in the succession of these masters, as their students started comparing teaching styles.

Yet a real controversy never erupted. Although it can be deduced from later correspondence between Radbertus and his former pupil Fredugard that the master had a rather flexible way of arranging his patristic sources, his orthodoxy was never questioned. Only in the tenth century did Heriger of Lobbes observe a discrepancy between their positions which he connected with their following of different authorities. Hence Radbertus came to be seen as Ambrosian and Ratramnus as Augustinian. But it was not until the Reformation, when protestants opposed the Roman Catholic dogma of transubstantiation, that Ratramnus' position was taken up as representing the true Augustinian, i.e., "spiritual" position on the eucharist. Naturally they rejected Radbertus' position. Only during the Reformation, then, did this early medieval debate become a real controversy. But by then religious debate had become interchangable with confessional polemics.

When we return to the Carolingian context, however, all we know is that these two monks had different ways of interpreting the Eucharist. In addition to stressing the importance of this sacrament, the divergence of their positions typically reflects the outburst of creative study in the so-called Carolingian renaissance. Of course, ecclesiastical conflicts did arise under Charles the Bald as well, as is clear from the predestination controversy, but that was not quite the case here.

While the different ways in which Radbertus and Ratramnus used the Fathers may reflect the standard method of Carolingian controversy, it points to a deeper difference in theological hermeneutics as well. We shall use their different approaches to the tradition as a way to assess the deeper Christological and ecclesiological aspects of their sacramental views.

It appears the celebration of the Mass became ever more central to the theology of the early Middle Ages, which itself was typically developed in monastic circles. Rather than separating Christians from the outside world, as baptism did, the Eucharist aimed at centering the Christian community. Even though monks initially were lay persons, due to the various Carolingian reforms the monasteries had rapidly gained prestige as the Christian communities *par excellence*. Hence it may not have been surprising that Ratramnus was asked by the king for advice on such an important matter as the Eucharist.

When we compare the methods of these two theologians, Radbertus' way of integrating patristic arguments into his work represents an older and less scholarly way of monastic reflection, which was both more meditative and more spontaneous. Underlying and preceding their methodological difference, however, was a very different view of the Eucharistic sacrament as *mysterium*. For Radbertus, its most important aspect was the creation of new life, as it inaugurates a kind of incarnation for the church. Through the losing of his own life, Christ gave birth to the church. By reenacting this, the priestly actions at the altar signify a mystery of such profundity that this sacrament encompasses truth and figure at the same time. The density of images and ideas that became jumbled together in Radbertus' "centering" interpretation of the Eucharist had a parallel in the impressionistic way in which he used the Fathers. He felt free to arrange them poetically, as if to match the tide of his reasoning. Rejecting any particular hierarchy, he seemed oblivious to the accusation that his sources might not be authentic and hence, his use of them inaccurate. Could he not always find another source?

Of his predominantly Latin sources, Ambrose had pride of place. Radbertus clearly felt comfortable with Ambrose's imagery, which was incarnational and eschatological alike. From Ambrose's *De mysteriis* he derived the notion of the Eucharist as a miracle defying the order of nature. Yet where Ambrose saw the Eucharist as a follow-up to baptism, Radbertus saw the host as a *viaticum* for him and his monks, a divinely made provision for their lifelong pilgrimage. As the connection with baptism faded into the background, the monks' life-journey came to foreshadow the impending passage from this life to the next, a *transitus* which would bring salvation not just to monks but to all believers.

In contrast, Ratramnus had a much crisper method in wishing to separate out his biblical and patristic evidence from his own interpretation. He thereby showed himself to be dependent on his sources as well, basing his own position explicitly on evidence culled from both. His specific aim was to trace the so-called *vestigia sanctorum patrum*. Through the words of the Fathers he could ultimately trace the source of their inspiration back to the Bible, especially the gospel. When Ratramnus settled on Augustine's *On Christian Doctrine* III.16.55 as his central authority in chapter 33, he appears to have done so mainly because Augustine had based his interpretation on a quotation from Christ in John 6:53. Augustine saw Christ's commanding words about the eating of the flesh and the drinking of the blood as *figurata locutio*, so as to avoid the charge of Capharnaism for partakers of the sacrament. When Ratramnus adopted Augustine's position, how-ever, the effect was that he underscored the difference between the *verba Christi* on the one hand, to which one might add the Fathers, and the *veritas rei* on the other, i.e., Christ's sacrifice itself.

Being much less invested in the Eucharist as a living sacrament, Ratramnus wanted to validate the sacrament through the correct use of patristic and biblical authority. He differed from his predecessor not so much on the centrality of the sacrament as on the need to articulate its meaning based on a linear arrangement of the Fathers' written testimony. In consequence, his way of teaching was much more formal and scripted. More than the spiritual nature of Augustine's interpreta-tion (*figurata locutio*), it was Augustine's choice to prioritize Christ's *words* in the gospel in articulating the meaning of his sacrifice that appealed to Ratramnus. Only in this way could the difference between the sacrament as *figura* and the *veritas rei* of the sacrament be properly maintained.

Although Radbertus considered the sacrament a mystery because it encom-passed both figure and truth, he ultimately came to see it as a miracle uniting both. In his revised treatise he added numerous miracles from the *Vitae Patrum*, as they underscored the efficacious power of the sacrament. If the words of institution as well as the priestly actions at the altar were done according to Church rite, the believer consumed alongside the host also its healing power. Word, deed, and effect cannot be separated in what thus constitutes a mystery of a deeply performative quality. For Radbertus, the new life given by the sacrament adds to the quality of the Church as the body of Christ, as the believers literally become *concorporated* with Christ. Remarkably enough, however, in chapter 4 he also seems to point ahead to the later *extra-Calvinisticum*, by which Christ is physically present in heaven while spiritually present at the altar. Apparently, Radbertus regarded the power of the Eucharist as so all-pervasive that even after Christ had ascended to open the gates of heaven, he could still be present at the altar. Just as truth and figure contract to the mystery of the Eucharist, so Christology and ecclesiology contract to the symbolic but powerful community of the monks, the *locus* of holiness in the Carolingian world.

In the end, two different ecclesiological pictures emerge. For Radbertus the Eucharist was a self-enclosed sacrament, comparable to the closed monastic community in which he lived. While believers would share in its salvific power, for monastic theologians as believers *par excellence* the challenge was to try and "unpack" it, so as to savor all the different shades of meaning it could adopt. This explains the meditative and intimate way in which he used the Fathers. He selected the authors of his choice and cited them in the way he preferred, yet he considered his choices to be neither exhaustive nor exclusive. Given the centripetal effect of the Eucharist as uniting the community, he did not worry about a fracturing of the tradition. Christ himself guaranteed the unity of the Christian community as well as of its tradition, being the pulsating heart of both.

For Ratramnus, an essential difference separated the *veritas rei* of Christ's sacrifice from its reenactment at the altar. As a result the role of faith became increasingly important, as the community should approach the sacrament with due reverence. This sense of revering distance also characterized his use of the Fathers. From permanent peers, they became elevated authorities whose opinions should be carefully weighed and selected. Thus we notice a first crack in the serenity of the monastic sphere. For when monastic meditation becomes misunderstood, there arises the need for a procedure of extrinsic validation whose rules are no longer co-extensive with those regulating monastic life itself. Although it would still be a long time until the Reformation, one begins to see why Ratramnus' approach could gain appeal over time, while Radbertus' devotional approach faded away with the demise of monastic spirituality itself.

Eriugena (810–77) and the Predestination Controversy: The Balance between Grace and Free Will

The final controversy in the context of this chapter is somehow also the most erratic. Among numerous others, it involved two of the most original minds of the entire Carolingian era, namely Gottschalk of Orbais and Johannes Scottus Eriugena. For the latter, however, the controversy in which he became involved was not one which he had sought himself. As we know very little of Eriugena's early life, other than that he was born in Ireland as suggested by his name, and taught at the palace school of Charles the Bald, the importance of this controversy is that it marked his first public appearance. Archbishop Hincmar of Reims had requested that Eriugena be invited to give his opinion on the issue of predestination. As it turned out, it was to be both his first and his last try at theological combat.

This was long after Gottschalk, a monk at Orbais, had not only spread the notion of a so-called double predestination (*gemina praedestinatio*) but, adding insult to injury, had also claimed that this view represented the true Augustinian position. The way in which the controversy was played out between Gottschalk and Eriugena reflects the wider predestination debate only indirectly. In this wider debate one finds all the ingredients of a typical Carolingian controversy, as a substantial theological question became coupled with an argument about the meaning of tradition. The theological question at hand, i.e. predestination, touched again on the nature of the church, yet in this case ecclesiology did not become linked to Christology, but rather to soteriology and anthropology. In the final analysis, this was a debate about the meaning and scope of the divine will; it focused especially on whether God dispenses grace and salvation to all or just a part of humanity.

Instead of following the debate in some detail, as we did before, our focus here is on the interference of Eriugena, as he was no doubt the most brilliant philosophical and theological mind of the Carolingian era. Yet because of the erratic, even artificial nature of the controversy between him and Gottschalk, some historical background is necessary, as they were not the debate's natural opponents. Gottschalk was a monk who had been given to the monastery of Fulda as an oblate. After reaching the age of maturity, he wished to leave the monastery, as he considered monasticism a human institution. Yet Abbot Hrabanus Maurus, who may not have liked to see his astute young pupil leave, tried to dissuade him through unfair means by accusing him of heresy. When the synod of Mainz allowed Gottschalk to leave, he went on to Orbais and Corbie. In 845–6 he could be found at the court of Count Eberhard of Friuli. After returning to the north, his teaching was condemned at the synod of Mainz in 848. Hrabanus, by now archbishop, sent Gottschalk back to Hincmar of Reims with a letter detailing the charge of double predestination, by which it was implied that God had selected not just those he wanted to save, which was the Church's position, but also those he wished to condemn. In the latter case, abstaining from sin and obeying the Church could not alter one's fate. Charles the Bald condemned Gottschalk in 849 at Quierzy and his writings were burnt, while he himself was imprisoned at Hautvillers. Far from being isolated, Gottschalk kept up correspondence and was supported both at Orbais and Corbie.

Although one can see the theological danger implied by Gottschalk's view of a double predestination, his aim was not to undermine the church, but rather to underscore its need for an active missionary policy. This explains Gottschalk's own missionary journeys and his preaching of baptism to peoples at the edge of Carolingian society. At the heart of the ecclesiastical conflict that ensued, therefore, there may well have been a difference between the interest in ecclesiastical power and politics of some, notably Hincmar of Reims and Hrabanus Maurus, and the evangelizing activities of the more outward-looking Gottschalk.

After his initial treatise *Ad reclusos et simplices*, in which he warned against Gottschalk's views, Hincmar of Rheims was to restate his own position on predestination twice. Various other parties became involved as well, among whom were Florus of Lyons and Prudentius of Troyes. Ratramnus of Corbie was asked by Charles the Bald to procure a dossier of patristic references, in which he supported Gottschalk. The debate had gone on for almost a decade until Eriugena published his *On Divine Predestination* in 851. His intervention was rather unusual, as it touched on the actual subject-matter of the debate only obliquely. Eriugena simply used the occasion to kill two birds with one stone: by unfolding his own views, he condemned Gottschalk's position. Although Hincmar and his allies dismissed Eriugena's intervention as inaccurate, one wonders whether it was much different from the way Theodulf had judged the Greeks on the matter of iconoclasm. It may well signal the end of the Carolingian renaissance that this intervention could form a serious threat to Eriugena's career, as in the end his treatise literally pleased nobody. It was only through the protection of Charles the Bald that he could he pursue his teaching and research activities, culminating in his massive dialogue, the *Periphyseon*.

While Gottschalk was truly interested in exploring the issue of double predestination which he considered Augustinian, and Hincmar and his allies were truly interested in proving the adequacy of single predestination, it seemed the agenda of neither party held much attraction for Eriugena. In this sense, the predestination conflict, while comparable to previous ones, is yet more complicated, as for Eriugena the topic provided the occasion rather than the subject of the debate.

Hincmar had asked Eriugena to refute Gottschalk's thesis that God's predestination is double (*gemina est praedestinatio*), namely of the elect to eternal rest and of the reprobate to death. His underlying request to Eriugena was thus to disprove Gottschalk's claim that this was in accordance with Augustine's views. When asked this question before, both Ratramnus of Corbie and Prudentius of Troyes had answered in the affirmative. To them Gottschalk indeed seemed to tread on solid Augustinian ground.

Perhaps for this reason, or maybe simply because he was of a different stature from most of his peers, Eriugena did not proceed in the usual Carolingian way, setting off one quotation or interpretation of Augustine against another. Instead, his approach was to elevate the discussion to a higher theoretical plane. In fact, he raised it to the highest plane of all, i.e., God. According to Eriugena, predestination and prescience did not make a difference, as far as God's nature was concerned. It is from the perspective of God's nature, then, that Eriugena wanted to perceive and analyze all things, as this would give a "substantial" rather than a "relative" view. Seen in this way, predestination could not be double, because God's nature itself is one. In the same way, it is true that the double command for humans to love, which implies love of God as well as love of neighbor, can yet have its root in God's undivided Love.

By elevating the entire discussion on grace and free will to the level of God's nature, Eriugena seemed to endorse the idea of a single predestination. Yet he did so in quite a different way from the way Hincmar might have wished when he first asked him to refute Gottschalk. For Eriugena was to regard predestination not as single, in the sense of "opposed to double," but rather as one and simple, thereby transcending Gottschalk's view of an *opus bipertitum* altogether. While Eriugena recognized a difference within God's predestination, this was not the same as a division. For God chooses actively to give beatitude to some, while he merely permits others to attain damnation on account of their own sinful pride.

More important than the content of Eriugena's refutation of Gottschalk, however, was his method, or rather, the way in which he managed to unite content and method in his treatise. By wishing to transcend any doubleness in God, it seemed Eriugena ultimately desired to unify all methods by which one can try to know God. This explains his famous teaching in chapter 1 that true philosophy is true religion and vice versa. For him, there is no real difference between the divine authority of codified revelation found in the biblical text and/or the Church Fathers, and the reasoning process through which this revelation is scrutinized by the human mind. It should thus not come as a surprise that Eriugena did not distinguish between God's existence, his necessity, his being, and his will, as they are ultimately all the same, namely God. Eriugena vehemently rejected any and all idea of necessity seen as an extrinsic principle by which God could in any way be compelled. For him, God's being simply is (identical with) his will and his necessity.

This principle of a continuous divine identity underlies all Eriugena's thinking about predestination. In this way God's prescience could thus seamlessly transmute into his predestination for Eriugena. After all, God's nature is undivided and substantive. When in the Preface to *On Divine Predestination* Eriugena emphasized how the things that are not, cannot be known or foreknown by God, he did so not because he saw God's prescience as somehow deficient, but because he recognized that God is substantive. Since every substance must be in something, it simply cannot be in nothing.

Having considered divine predestination extensively from the perspective of God's one and undivided substance, Eriugena also explored it from the aspect of humanity, as he analyzed human free will. His view of humanity's substance mirrors his view of the divine substance, of which it is after all the image. In humanity, therefore, to will, to be, and to know are also essentially one. Quoting extensively from Augustine's *On Free Will*, Eriugena maintained that humans have a free choice of the will (*liberum arbitrium voluntatis*) even after Adam's sin but that, as is the case with every good thing, they can choose to make bad use of it.

Finally, what was perhaps most novel and important in Eriugena's way of reasoning was his introduction and intensive use of rhetorical strategies. Thus he demonstrated how the terms predestination and prescience could be applied to God only by transference from the level of creation to the level of the creator. This transference may be carried out on the basis of a likeness with God, as when we say that humans are made in the image of God who rules his creation through grace, or by contrariety to God, as when we say that God predestines some to evil. Through *enthymema* this merely indicates how their human wills can do evil. It is the rhetorical strategy of *enthymema* which Eriugena used to great effect in his attempt to counter Gottschalk's interpretations of Augustine. For Eriugena, where Augustine speaks about a negative predestination, Gottschalk simply fails to recognize that Augustine meant this *e contrario*. Thus Gottschalk developed too literal a reading of Augustine which amounts in fact to a misreading. Even when some people seem predestined to evil, Eriugena holds that one can legitimately conclude only that God has foreknown their evils, but not that he has actively predestined them.

Towards the end of his treatise it appears Eriugena foreshadowed Anselm's reasoning in *Why God Became Man* by arguing on the basis of a preconceived order of nature with an inherent law of justice which encompasses both the human and the divine. Inside this order God has put clear boundaries to all creatures, including the malice of the impious which is not allowed to stretch into infinity. In order to teach humanity to abide by those same boundaries but also to curb this malice, God ultimately sent his Son to liberate humanity. It is here in chapter 18 that the issue of Christology comes in for Eriugena.

As we said above, however, Hincmar was not pleased with Eriugena's treatise and neither was anybody else. While this may reflect the more combative atmosphere of ninth-century polemics, of which Gottschalk was an even more serious victim, it also reflects the idiosyncrasy of Eriugena's own unique reasoning talent which transcended the genre of controversy altogether. Although he can be faulted for not giving a fair share to Gottschalk's views, he opened up an entirely new genre of theological reasoning, which through the use of dialectic was to strive for internal coherence more than polemical success. After Eriugena's *Periphyseon*, which remained largely unread during his own lifetime, we will have to wait until Anselm before a similarly independent and self-sufficient brilliance is found. With the writings and reasoning of Eriugena, therefore, the Carolingian era appears to have reached both its climax and its end.

Conclusion: Consensus Through Controversy

At the end of this chapter it is useful, if challenging, to ask what common themes we can find in the various controversies that justify our subsuming them under the heading of "Carolingian theology." While it was not our intention here to unfold what might be called "true Carolingian doctrine," there is enough commonality in the way the various controversies are framed in this period for it to be possible to observe a theological consensus at least on some points.

First of all, what all the participants in the four controversies which we discussed had in common was their *method*. The method they universally adopted was to proceed through citations from the Fathers. They did so often in ways which would have to be judged unacceptable by modern standards, quoting the words from the Fathers as if they were their own. Yet for Carolingian authors, this was a tribute to the Fathers rather than an illegal appropriation of texts that were not theirs. It is precisely because they reasoned from an assumed continuity with the patristic tradition that they were able to proceed in this informal and intimate way. At the same time, we also see the innocent use of the Fathers being questioned and a more formal attribution of sources beginning to replace it, as in the eucharistic controversy between Radbertus and Ratramnus.

In terms of *theological content*, it is rather more difficult to find what the various controversies precisely have in common. One way of putting it is to say that all of them involved the *relation between Christology and ecclesiology*.

The adoptionist controversy was most outspoken on this point, as the problem of divine Sonship defined the debate throughout. For Alcuin, belief in the incarnation as the mysterious connection between human and divine enabled humans to share in Christ's grace, uniting them as sinners in the church that is his body. Alcuin's ecclesiological view was as practical as his Christology was mystical, as it is precisely respect for the incarnation as a mystery that allows for worship.

The nature of this worship is what was at the heart of Theodulf's concerns in his *Opus Caroli*. Worship belongs to God and not to the images of saints. Humans themselves are *imagines dei* and hence worthier than any icons. Whereas through sin this image-character of humanity became polluted, it is cleansed through Christ's sacrifice, as he is the *imago dei* par excellence. Worship should therefore use only the symbol of the cross, to acknowledge the dependence of all Christians on their Savior. The awareness of this dependence leads to an intimacy by which the Church is not just seen as the body of Christ, but as his Bride. Because of its bridal character, in the eyes of the Carolingian research team that worked on the *Opus Caroli* the Western Church was much closer to Christ than the Byzantine East.

Christ's sacrifice was the subject-matter of the eucharistic debate between Radbertus and Ratramnus. The centrality of the sacrament being undisputed, the difference between them was more on the level of ecclesiology than of Christology. The question that arose for them is to what extent one can still recapture this sacrifice and how to assess its ultimate meaning for the church during the interval between Christ's ascension and his eschatological *parousia*. While for Radbertus the salvific effect of Christ's sacrifice, which gave life to the Church once, remains tangible in the mystery on the altar, renewing this life with every breaking of the bread, Ratramnus seemed more hesitant in linking the gospel words about Christ's sacrifice directly to the sacrament. Following Augustine, he favored a figurative interpretation of the sacramental mystery. Thus he allowed the Eucharistic sacrament to protect its life-giving and recreating power.

Finally, the life-giving element of divine grace was at the heart of the conflict on predestination between Gottschalk and Eriugena. Here the connection between Christology and ecclesiology contracts to soteriology, as the central question here dealt with the freedom of the human will. While Gottschalk, who like Ratramnus faithfully but literally followed Augustine, held to a double predestination, i.e., of those who God wanted to give life and of those he condemned to eternal damnation, for Eriugena this was not acceptable. The reason is not that he held to a single predestination, as Hincmar did, but that predestination can only be one and simple, as it coincides with God's being, his knowing, and his willing. While Eriugena did not elaborate on his ecclesiological position, it may be assumed that he accepted the authority of the church. Even so, for him this authority paled before the divine justice with which God saves some, but permits others to squander their birthright of *imago dei*. Just as God, humans are free to choose, even despite sin, and not even God forbids them to forgo their salvation.

Notes

1 See E. Hobsbawm and T. Ranger (eds.), *The Invention of Tradition* (Cambridge: Cambridge University Press, 1993), pp. 1–14 ("Introduction: Inventing Traditions").

2 See K. Morrison, *The Mimetic Tradition of Reform in the West* (Princeton: Princeton University Press, 1983).

Select Bibliography

Angenendt, A., *Das Frühmittelalter: Die abendländische Christenheit von 400 bis 900* (2, durchgesehene Auflage; Stuttgart: Kohlhammer, 1995).

Bouhot, J.-P., *Ratramne de Corbie: Histoire littéraire et controverses doctrinales* (Etudes augustiniennes: Paris, 1976).

Bullough, D. A., "Alcuin and the Kingdom of Heaven: Liturgy, Theology, and the Carolingian Age," in U.-R. Blumenthal (ed.), *Carolingian Essays. Andrew W. Mellon Lectures in Early Christian Studies* (Washington, DC: Catholic University of America Press, 1983), pp. 1–69.

Cavadini, J. C., "The Sources and Theology of Alcuin's *De fide sanctae et individuae trinitatis*," *Traditio* 46 (1991): 123–46.

Cavadini, J. C., *The Last Christology of the West: Adoptionism in Spain and Gaul, 785–820* (Philadelphia: University of Pennsylvania Press, 1993).

Cristiani, M., "La controversia eucaristica nella cultura del secolo IX," *Studi medievali, serie terza*, IX (1968): 167–223.

Cristiani, M., "La notion de loi dans le *De Praedestinatione* de Jean Scot," in R. Roques (ed.), *Jean Scot Erigène et l'histoire de la philosophie*. Papers of the Laon colloquium, July 7–12, 1975 (Paris: CNRS, 1977), pp. 277–88.

Driscoll, M. S., *Alcuin et la pénitence à l'époque carolingienne* (Münster: Aschendorff, 1971).

Freeman, A., "Theodulf of Orleans and the *Libri Carolini*," *Speculum* 32 (1957): 663–705.

Ganz, D., "The Debate on Predestination," in M. Gibson and J. Nelson (eds.), *Charles the Bald: Court and Kingdom: Papers based on a Colloquium held in London in April 1979* (Oxford, 1981), pp. 353–73.

Liebeschutz, H., "Development of Thought in the Carolingian Empire," in A. H. Armstrong (ed.), *The Cambridge History of Later Greek and Early Medieval Philosophy* (Cambridge: Cambridge University Press, 1967), pp. 565–86.

Marenbon, J., "Carolingian Thought," in R. McKitterick (ed.), *Carolingian Culture: Emulation and Innovation* (Cambridge: Cambridge University Press, 1994), pp. 171–92.

Meyer, H. B., SJ, "Alkuin zwischen Antike und Mittelalter: Ein Kapitel frühmittelalterlicher Frömmigkeitsgeschichte," *Zeitschrift für katholische Theologie* 81 (1959): 306–50, 405–54.

Otten, W., "Eriugena's *Periphyseon*: A Carolingian Contribution to the Theological Tradition," in B. McGinn and W. Otten (eds.), *Eriugena: East and West: Papers of the Eighth International Colloquium of the Society for the Promotion of Eriugenian Studies, Chicago and Notre Dame, 18–20 October 1991* (Notre Dame: Notre Dame University Press, 1994), pp. 69–93.

Otten, W., "The Texture of Tradition: The Role of the Church Fathers in Carolingian Theology," in I. Backus (ed.), *The Reception of the Church Fathers in the West: From the Carolingians to the Maurists*, vol. I (Leiden: Brill, 1997), pp. 3–50.

Pelikan, J., *The Christian Tradition: A History of the Development of Doctrine*, vol. 3: *The Growth of Medieval Theology (600–1300)* (Chicago: University of Chicago Press, 1978).

Schrimpf, G., *Das Werk des Johannes Scottus Eriugena im Rahmen des Wissenschaftsverständnisses seiner Zeit: Eine Hinführung zu Periphyseon* (Munster: Aschendorff, 1982).

Sullivan, R. E., *"The Gentle Voice of Teachers": Aspects of Learning in the Carolingian Age* (Columbus: Ohio State University Press, 1995).

A Medieval "Renaissance"?

6   Berengar, Roscelin, and Peter Damian
G. R. Evans

7   Anselm of Canterbury
G. R. Evans

8   Peter Abelard and Gilbert of Poitiers
Lauge O. Nielsen

9   Bernard of Clairvaux, William of St. Thierry,
the Victorines
Emero Stiegman

10   The *Glossa Ordinaria*
Jenny Swanson

11   Peter Lombard
Marcia Colish

Berengar, Roscelin, and Peter Damian

G. R. Evans

The eleventh century saw a revival of interest in the big theological questions of the patristic period, the nature of God, the Trinity, incarnation. A prompter here was undoubtedly the changed quality of the interest of scholars of the day in the study of grammar and logic which was throwing up technically challenging questions. There was also a return to characteristically Carolingian concerns, in the form of discussion of the Church and the sacraments. Here, too, fresh insights were generated by the study of grammar and logic but there were also political pressures. There was contemporary controversy over simony (which was happening because of the wish to buy high office in the Church) and clerical celibacy (the failure of which was leading to pressure to provide for clergy children). This was also the age of a heightening of awareness that the relationship of Church and State was changing. What was known as the "Investiture conflict" reached its height at the turn of the century and in the two decades afterwards. It was brought to crisis point by the practice of kings and emperors seeking to enlarge their role in the appointment of bishops. This was a natural enough temptation, since with a bishopric went lands and influence and the bestowal of a bishopric was a powerful instrument of patronage. But royal persons were not ordained ministers and it was gradually becoming clear that they went beyond their authority in seeking to intrude upon the sacramental aspects of the making of bishops by giving the ring and pastoral staff to the new "shepherd." This lengthy dispute about the line which was to be drawn between the temporal and the spiritual spheres ran on to the Council of Worms of 1122 and beyond, and its resolution prompted a signal development of the theologies of Church and sacrament.

The famous names of the eleventh century in theological debate include Lanfranc and Berengar on the sacramental controversy, Roscelin of Compiégne and Peter Damian on the Trinity. We are in a difficulty about where to "put" Anselm of Canterbury because his writings have an importance beyond their age. Although much of the subject-matter of this chapter was of significance in his work, he must have a chapter to himself.

Berengar of Tours

Berengar came from a family which had a tradition of supplying canons to serve St. Martin's Tours. He set up as a professional teacher and became secretary to the Count of Anjou, enjoying a patronage which gave him a certain position and notability.[1] By 1049 the content of his teaching was attracting worried attention. In a letter to the King of France, Theoduin of Liège expressed anxieties that Berengar was saying that the Eucharist was not the body and blood of Christ, and further that he was questioning the very efficaciousness of the sacraments. Moreover, said Theoduin, he was arguing that the handing over of the episcopal staff did not convey the authority of the office.[2]

Theoduin of Liège wrote against Berengar to Henry I of France, accusing him of introducing ancient heresies into modern times, by saying that "the body of Christ" is not a body so much as a shadow or figure of his body; he and others destroy legitimate marriage, and do their best to overturn the baptism of infants, he continues. He sees it as imperative that they be publicly confuted.[3]

These are the concerns of an "establishment" which fears that an attack is being made upon the authority of the Church. Such talk was to become the connecting thread of a series of schismatic and heretical movements in the twelfth century. The Waldensians, for example, were to be heard along much the same lines. There was certainly justification for the fear that if Berengar, a successful teacher, was indeed giving a lead of this sort, he might win followers and do damage. It is not clear that he was, at least not on all these themes. But Berengar was a good speaker, and persuasive, so that the Bishop of Langres was alarmed at the way in which his ideas were catching on, affording, in his view a public stumbling-block: *haec communis virtus, haec publica fortitudo, commune et publicum malum sit.*[4]

When Berengar wrote in his own defense a little later, he was conscious of the accusation that he had been a stumbling-block to the faithful. What is the difference between a prophet saying something unpopular and a voice which speaks out in that way but is regarded as a heretic?[5] he asks. Berengar insisted that he was speaking as his conscience made him,[6] and in taking that line he was setting out on a road which was ultimately to lead to the debates of the Reformation about the balance between individual conscience and the duty to submit to the teaching of the Church. Hugh of Langres says that Hugh should not presume to think for himself (*singulariter sentire*); he has a duty to concur with Christian and canonical faith.[7] It seemed a sound principle to assert that what is familiar is more probable than what is strange.[8]

It was partly Berengar's fault that controversy swelled. He became involved in arguments with the higher clergy. To Adalman of Liège he wrote indignantly to say that he had been accused of Manicheism and that his view of the body and blood of Christ in the Eucharist did not deserve that accusation.[9] Ascelin, Dean of Chartres, wrote to him about such a dispute.[10] He tried to find himself allies, among them Lanfranc, to whom he wrote a letter seeking to stir him into taking an interest in some points of Eucharistic controversy.[11] His letter became known, and it may even for a time have done Lanfranc's reputation for uprightness and orthodoxy some harm to have been so conspicuously associated with him. In 1050 the two met, at Brionne, but we do not know what Lanfranc was thinking before he wrote his book on the controversy.

In 1059 Berengar was summoned by the Pope to answer for his views at a Council at Rome. At a plenary session of the Council, he was presented with a demand to swear to a confession of faith on the Eucharist devised by Cardinal Humbert. His writings were condemned and burned. That gave the Church authorities a document which they could disseminate in the places where Berengar's ideas had become known, and thus they sought to end discussion and suppress his contentious views.

Berengar was not silenced. He said that he had been *forced* to swear, and argued that an oath taken under duress was not binding. He continued teaching the same ideas in the old way. If anything, he became more polemical. Portions of a treatise of this period survive, and in it he attacks the Pope and Humbert personally.

There was no immediate rejoinder, for there was a new Pope in 1061 and it was Lanfranc not he who took up the debate. Lanfranc wrote his treatise *On the Body and Blood of Christ* in the early 1060s, while he was abbot of St. Stephen's, Caen, and that helped to take the debate onto a new "platform" of respectability.

How did Berengar and his opponents "position" themselves over the Eucharist? Why did the issues strike them in this way? Berengar was aware of the debate of a generation or two earlier, in which the Carolingian scholars Paschasius Radbertus and Johannes Scotus Eriugena had been involved. He mentions their names in a letter to Lanfranc;[12] Paschasius he mentions to Adelman.[13]

It is a characteristic of theological debate that subjects of perennial or repeated controversy may reappear in different guises and with different thrusts age by age without those engaged in the later conversation being conscious of the way the question has changed. A case in point is the use by both sides in the sixteenth-century debate of Augustine's thoughts on faith and works, without either side apparently realizing that the problem he was addressing was rather different from theirs. In the sixteenth century the question was what was pleasing to God and would be rewarded with salvation; in Augustine's day it was whether the catechumen ought to give up his bad habits while he was under instruction, or could wait to begin on good works until after he had been baptized. The concerns of Paschasius Radbertus and his contemporaries had been with the contrast of figure with reality, the image with the literal.

It was known that there had been controversy a few generations earlier about the nature of the "change" which made the bread and wine the body and blood of Christ, when the words of consecration were said, when a priest said Christ's words, "This is my body" (I Corinthians 11:24). Augustine's idea was that a sacrament is a holy sign (*sacrum signum*).[14] That is because it is an outward and visible sign of an inward and spiritual grace. A sign is not itself the thing it signifies. It points to something else.

It was this which the Carolingian controversy had settled upon as a focus of the debate as to where the "reality" then lay. The thing signified, the body and blood of Christ, is in fact the more "real," however powerfully the senses may be disposed to believe the evidence presented to them that they are looking at and tasting bread and wine.

But there was less clarity about the difference it now made in the eleventh century that there was a far more sophisticated understanding of the philosophy of language. Berengar was certainly aware that there was a difference, at least in the standard terms in which others of his generation would put it. He speaks in his letter to Adelmann of the balancing of reasoning and authority.[15]

There was also a new sense of the implications of the rules derived from Aristotle's *Categories*, which recognizes that although, by definition, accidents may alter (for that is the nature of accidents), the substance does not, or else it would have become a different substance.

In the Eucharistic change, when bread and wine "become" the body and blood of Christ, the accidents, the appearance, and smell of the bread and wine remain the same but the substance is believed to be changed, from that of bread and wine to that of the body and blood of Christ. There is *trans-substantio*, to use the twelfth-century terminology.

Like so many in the history of the Church who were eventually categorized as heretics, Berengar began by asking an important question, and continued to ask it in the face of official assertions that he had better stop asking it because he was upsetting the faithful. His opponents and the generation after them traveled a very long way down the road of definition and clarification of what became the doctrine of transubstantion. The formation of, and insistence upon, this doctrine was to have immense consequences for the later Middle Ages.

But not everything Berengar said had to be "opposed." He was at one with Lanfranc in understanding the Eucharist as a mystery, a celebration, a liturgical act. He accepted the definition of a sacrament as a holy or sacred sign (*sacrum signum*). He helped to encourage awareness that although the sacraments are all instruments or vehicles of grace, they are specific and each sacrament makes present the particular reality it signifies.[16] The reason why there was a rash of treatises on the Eucharist in the late eleventh and twelfth centuries was partly that Berengar had made people interested in the subject. The interest of the authors of these treatises ran about in a number of directions, some involving mere curiosity. Scripture says that Christ's risen body is in heaven, but in the consecrated host it is also physically on earth. It is there in its entirety in each host, and yet it may simultaneously be in many such hosts. The totality of the consecrated hosts, taken over time, greatly exceeds in quantity the size of Christ's body. If Christ is "really" in each host, what happens if a mouse eats a fallen crumb? Does grace work to the salvation of the mouse? Treatises were written, for example, by Hugh, Bishop of Langres (*On the Body and Blood of Christ against Berengar*).[17] The fullness of divine power exceeds the grasp of the senses, he points out, and the human senses cannot embrace by their own perceptions that which informs them. He accuses Berengar of crudely saying that there is no change in the bread and wine and that it is merely an intellectual device or construct to deem the bread to be the body of Christ. It is a sign, but a mere sign. In this, "you create a stumbling-block for the whole Church," he accuses.

This was the age in which it became more clearly realized than before that a high doctrine of the sacraments goes with a high doctrine of the Church, that sacramentology and ecclesiology develop together. The link was made highly visible by those who prompted debate by challenging the need for the sacraments and the Church.

Talking to "Unbelievers"

As potent a formative influence in theology as controversy in which heresy comes to be defined (and consequently orthodoxy too), is exchange of opinion with those of other faiths. Peter Damian's *Letters* include a lengthy *epistola* which is a treatise in itself, indeed one of the dialogues with Jews which were to become popular in the next generation. Letter 1 is addressed to Honestus. It purports to be in response to a request from him for material with which he may meet the arguments of the Jews.

There is a strong consciousness in Peter Damian's text of the danger such arguments can present. They can bring down the faith if they are successful. They are stumbling-blocks to the faithful and consequently dangerous to salvation. So rebutting them is important. These are not merely interesting intellectual challenges.

It was a commonplace of such dialogues with "unbelievers" that the author would begin by finding common ground. In the case of "pagans" only reason would do. In conversations of the twelfth century with the Albigensian dualists, only the New Testament would do, for they held that the Old Testament was the work of the "evil" God. For discussions with the Jews, the Old Testament is the common scriptural authority on which the disputants can rely.

Peter Damian was born in 1007 at Ravenna. In his youth, he became a secular master. About 1035 he took the decision to become a monk and entered the monastery of Fonte Avellana. There he became so noteworthy as a teacher that he was moved to Pomposa, where the monks apparently stood in need of a good schoolmaster.[18] He became Cardinal-Bishop of Ostia in 1057. In this movement from one world of teaching to another, and ultimately into high office in the Church, Peter Damian was a man of his time. (Lanfranc and Anselm followed similar progressions.)

Peter Damian became above all a "monastic" scholar, writing on topics of spirituality as well as what was to become "academic" theology. There are letters, sermons, saints' lives, prayers, poems, and treatises, which he sent to his contemporaries.[19] He was also interested in the politically heated issues of the time, the debate on simony and the controversy about clerical celibacy, on both of which he had things to say. On simony, which he characterizes as a dragon "spewing forth its venom," he sees the Archbishop of Ravenna as a dragon-slaying knight of Christ.[20]

In methodology and stance, he tended to the side of the conservatives. In his book on divine power he says that he is angry with contemporary "dialecticians" whose challenges seem to place the Virgin Birth in question. Present in 1059 for Berengar's confession, he "stood for" sacramental realism against Berengar.

The Divine

Peter Damian's *On Divine Omnipotence*, addressed to Desiderius, Abbot of Monte Cassino, is the first book of the Middle Ages on divine power. The question whether God can restore lost virginity was, it seems, a teaser used to entertain students in the schools. Yet it is also a very serious question, indeed it is a problem with many layers, only some of them philosophical, and it is much bigger than it seems. There is an area of potential relevance to the Blessed Virgin Mary, still virgin though pregnant and remaining virgin after giving birth.[21]

On one interpretation, it asks whether God can restore those who are fallen, and so it is soteriological, a question about redemption. On another interpretation, it asks whether God can go against the natural order and therefore it is a question about miracles. On a third view, it is a question about the course of history. Can God, who is eternal, cause things which have happened in time not to have happened? Can God undo the past? That takes the questioner into the realm of divine foreknowledge and predestination. On a fourth interpretation, it is a question about divine sovereignty and it asks whether there is anything an omnipotent God cannot do.

This last aspect was of interest to Anselm of Canterbury, too, in his *Cur Deus Homo*. There he pauses to point out in his preliminary remarks that the interaction of will, power, and necessity will underlie the whole discussion of the treatise. It is perhaps here, above all, that the new expertise in logic might be expected to be brought to bear. But Peter Damian's touch as a logician is light, much as was that of Anselm of Besate. This Anselm played with logical riddles in his *Rhetorimachia* of 1046.[22] His keen enjoyment of sophistry and parody did not prevent him from casting doubt on the freedom of God's acts with all the serious sense of the importance of the question which Peter Damian was asking in his own treatment.

Is there anything an all-powerful God cannot do? He cannot deceive or be deceived. He cannot be unjust. He cannot act unwisely. He cannot die or destroy himself. He cannot act in any way which is contrary to his goodness.[23] Anselm of Canterbury would say that to act in any such way would be for God to act against his own nature, and that would be not a power but an impotence. And there are many things logically impossible which God can do, because they are good and he is both good and all-powerful.

Peter Damian's approach to the dialogue with the Jews is, appropriately, to cite the Old Testament so as to seek to show the Jews that Christians are right in their interpretation. He points out Old Testament evidence for the presence in

Christ of both the weakness of humanity and the power of divinity. "What do you have to say to that, Jew? By what shameless daring can you avoid such obvious, such divine statements?"[24] he challenges. His main topic – for it was the principal point on which Jews and Christians differed – was the question of the incarnation, central to Christianity. But Peter Damian also discusses ceremonies, circumcision, the Sabbath, unclean foods (46ff.).

Jews, like any other reasonable beings, could be argued with not only on the basis of authority but also by reasoning. Peter Damian accordingly gives up a section of his Letter to the arguments from "reason" which can be brought to bear in persuading the Jews of the truth of the Christian view of the faith. Here he concentrates on trying to persuade the Jews that the reason they suffer from persecution is that they were the murderers of Christ; and that they should take that as evidence that they were *at fault* in killing him, for it follows from that that he was indeed the Messiah. But the section of "reasoning" is comparatively brief and Peter Damian deliberately does not attempt anything logically sophisticated. "As I attempted to take into account your lack of training, I did not try to employ the flowers of rhetorical eloquence, nor the sharp arguments of the dialecticians," (74) he says firmly.

Roscelin of Compiègne

Roscelin of Compiègne resembled Berengar in being a controversial figure who made his name by challenging the great and by writing or teaching on subjects so controversial that he appeared to be conjuring with heresies.

The self-appointed opponent of Anselm of Bec and Canterbury, Roscelin of Compiègne also attacked Lanfranc, and later Peter Abelard, with apparently a similar wish to make himself famous by being seen to be engaged in debate with those whose names were already known. Roscelin taught Peter Abelard as a young student.[25] In the case of Anselm, his contention was that Anselm had been teaching that there were three Gods not one. It appears that Anselm had been making the point that when we call a single person "white" and "literate" we do not mean that there are two people, even though "white" and "literate" (*albus, grammaticus*) could, in Latin, be used as nouns as well as what we should now call adjectives (for Roman grammarians regarded both as a single part of speech).

Prompted by rumors already spread by Roscelin, the monk John wrote to Anselm of Canterbury to ask him to clarify exactly what he had been teaching on the Trinity. "What belief do you hold about the three persons of the Godhead, which it would not shame you to write down for the common benefit of Christians?"[26] He describes Roscelin as paraphrasing Anselm in this way: "If the three Persons are only one thing, and not three, like three angels or three souls, so that the divine will and power are altogether one thing, then the Father and the Holy Spirit were incarnate with the Son." Roscelin suggests that Lanfranc is teaching the same thing.

Anselm responded relatively calmly at first. He explains in a letter in reply that what he says is either to be understood with reference to the Persons or with reference to God as one. If Roscelin is speaking of the three Persons then he is speaking "superfluously," since clearly those three are three. If he is saying that there are three substances that is another story, and Anselm promises that he will tell it when he has more leisure.[27] But Anselm became alarmed by Roscelin's continuing criticism and questioning. He wrote to Fulk of Beauvais (letter 136) asking him to defend him against Roscelin at the Council of Reims, and also to defend the good name of Lanfranc.

There are one or two other surviving texts which help to round out our picture of Roscelin and his teaching. A letter from Theobald of Étampes to Roscelin explores various canon law points, and there is a similar letter from Ivo of Chartres.[28]

In 1092 Roscelin was called to defend his teaching on the Trinity at the Council of Soissons. He, like Peter Damian, revived and altered the direction of contemporary exploration of the theology of the Trinity.

Notes

1   Margaret Gibson, *Lanfranc of Bec* (Oxford, 1978), ch. 4, pp. 64–5.
2   Patrologia Latina (ed. J. P. Migne; hereafter "PL"), 146.1439–42, Theoduin of Liége, Letter to Henry I of France.
3   PL 146.1439–42.
4   PL 142.1327.
5   Berengar, *Rescriptum contra Lanfrannum*, ed. R. B. C. Huygens, Corpus Christianorum Continuatio Medievalis Brepols (Turnhout, 1977–), lxxxiv, A, B, pp. 35–6.
6   Berengar, *Rescriptum contra Lanfrannum*, p. 40.
7   PL 142.1333–4.
8   Berengar, *Rescriptum contra Lanfrannum*, p. 41.
9   J. de Montclos, *La controverse eucharistique du xième siècle*, Spicilegium Sacrum Lovaniense 37 (Louvain, 1971).
10 PL 150.67–8.
11 PL 150.63.
12 PL 150.67–8, and 63.
13 Montclos, p. 533.
14 *De civitate dei*, 10.5.
15 Montclos, p. 537.
16 Montclos, pp. 393–4.
17 PL 142.1325–34.
18 I. M. Resnick, *Divine Power and Possibility in St. Peter Damian's De Omnipotentia* (Leiden, 1992).
19 Peter Damian, *Letters*, 3 vols., ed. Owen J. Blum (Washington, DC, 1989, 1990, 1992), vol. 1, letter 12, to a bishop called John.
20 Ibid., letter 3.
21 Resnick, p. 47.
22 Anselm of Besate, *Rhetorimachia*, ed. K. Manitius, MGH Historica 2 (Weimar, 1958), p. 181.
23 Resnick, p. 4.
24 Damian, *Letters*, vol. 1, letter 1 (31).
25 Epistola ad Abaelardum, ed. J. Reiners, *Der Nominalismus in der Frühscholastik* (Münster, 1910) (Beitrage zur Geschichte der Philosophie des Mittelalters, Series Munster (hereafter "BGPMA"), 8, 5). F. Picavet, *Roscelin, philosophe et théologien d'après la légende et d'après l'histoire* (Paris, 1911).
26 Anselm, *Anselmi opera omnia*, 6 vols., ed. F. S. Schmitt (Rome/Edinburgh, 1938–68), letter 128, III.270–1.
27 Ibid., letter 129.
28 Picavet, pp. 115, 117.

Bibliography

Anselm of Besate, *Rhetorimachia*, ed. K. Manitius, MGH Historica 2 (Weimar, 1958), p. 181.

Berengar, *Rescriptum contra Lanfrannum*, ed. R. B. C. Huygens, CCCM, lxxxiv, A, B.

Damian, Peter, *Letters*, ed. Owen J. Blum (Washington, DC, 1989, 1990, 1992), 3 vols.

Gibson, Margaret, *Lanfranc of Bec* (Oxford, 1978), ch. 4, pp. 64–5.

Macdonald, J., *Berengar and the Reform of Sacramental Doctrine* (London, 1930).

Montclos, J. de, *La controverse eucharistique du xième siècle, Spicilegium Sacrum Lovaniense* 37 (Louvain, 1971), pp. 393–4.

Picavet, F., *Roscelin, philosophe et théologien d'après la légende et d'après l'histoire* (Paris, 1911).

Resnick, I. M. *Divine Power and Possibility in St. Peter Damian's De Omnipotentia* (Leiden, 1992).

Roscelin of Compiègne, *Epistola ad Abaelardum*, ed. J. Reiners, *Der Nominalismus in der Frühscholastik* (Münster, 1910) (BGPMA, 8, 5).

Theoduin of Liège, Letter to Henry I of France, PL, 146.1439–42.

Anselm of Canterbury

G. R. Evans

Anselm of Canterbury was a thinker of independent mind, and at the same time careful not to disturb the security of a faith he believed to be a settled thing. The result was the creation of an entirely fresh approach to a number of existing issues.

He was born an Italian, at Aosta, in 1033. His father died when he was a young man, and he set off, as others of his generation were doing, towards the north, in search of what we should now call a higher education. This was a period of "wandering scholars," when those in search of opportunities to study tended to seek out famous teachers rather than going to study at a particular "school." There were as yet no universities. The only established "schools" were those attached to cathedrals. (Charlemagne had insisted that the education of a cathedral's clergy should be of a good standard, and his policy had on the whole been successful.)

There was an exception. At Bec, a new foundation of Benedictine monks, an innovative kind of school had been set up by Lanfranc. The founder of Bec, whose name was Herluin, was not himself a learned man, but Lanfranc, like Anselm, was an educated and able Italian. He had settled, intending to lead a monastic life in the new community with Herluin, and had opened a school to which the sons of the local nobility came flocking. Not all these by any means intended to be monks. That made the school unusual, because it was the consistent pattern of Benedictine monastic life that schooling was provided only for the children given to the monastery by their parents, to equip them for a life of prayer and reading conducted in Latin. There were no "open" monastic schools as a rule.

Bec drew Anselm, after he had been wandering for about three years. He found Lanfranc lecturing on works of classical logic and rhetoric, as well as teaching the study of the Bible. It was already a convention that the grounding in Latin extended not only to "grammar" (learning the language and its structure) but also to logic, the classical art of argument, which had survived into this period chiefly in the works of Boethius and Cicero, since most of Aristotle's logic was not to become available in Latin in the West until the twelfth century, and, to a limited degree, to the study of rhetoric. Here, too, the available classical text-books of the period were limited in number, but Cicero's *On Invention* was used and the anonymous *Rhetorica ad Herennium*, which was then believed to be by Cicero. The interest of the study of rhetoric for Lanfranc seems to have lain in the fact that here, too, was an art of argumentation, although directed at persuasion rather than at proving.

As a pupil, Anselm stood out. He could see for himself that he was his master's intellectual equal and he began to face a problem about the decision where he was to spend the rest of his life. He had come to the view that he wanted to be a monk. If he stayed at Bec there would inevitably be rivalry. The alternative was to go to Cluny, then a fashionable "reformed" monastery, where a great deal of emphasis was placed upon the routine of daily life and little on the things of the mind. That would have meant giving up the world indeed, because it would have cut him off from his growing intellectual interests. He decided in the end to stay at Bec, and in due course Lanfranc left for the monastery at Caen and then to be Archbishop of Canterbury, leaving Anselm in charge of the teaching.

Anselm was his natural successor as schoolmaster, but under him the schoolroom changed. Bec was a successful monastery and it was attracting a good number of new monks. Anselm concentrated on teaching them and he developed in them capacities which made them all appear to the historian Orderic Vitalis like "seeming philosophers".

It was among his monks that, after ten years of study, chiefly in the Bible and the works of Augustine, Anselm wrote his first book, the *Monologion*.[1] He described it as a meditation on the divine being. It was a convention of the ancient and medieval world for an author to pretend that he had written only because others had pressed him to do so, but when Anselm describes how his monks had asked for the book, it is hard not to believe him. His method of teaching them had been to hold a form of debate with them very like the Socratic, though lacking in the Socratic devices of point-scoring and making a fool of one's opponent. The group had reflected purposefully together on the nature of God and these were the results. It is possible to get a sense of the atmosphere of these discussions and the intensity with which the group worked, from a passage in the *Life* of Gundulf, who later became Bishop of Rochester. It is described there how Anselm would sow the seeds of ideas and Gundulf would water them with his tears.

Anselm's method was to invite his monks to begin from what they themselves knew of the good, and to climb upwards in their thought to higher and higher goods until they began to glimpse, not God himself, for he is ultimately beyond human comprehension, but a clearer idea of what he must be like.[2] That led him on to consider other aspects of the divine nature and then to examine the mystery of the Trinity. This principle that God is the best and greatest of all things follows on from the notion adumbrated in the Proslogion that God is that than which nothing "better" can be thought.

Anselm's chief model at this early stage of his authorship remained the works of Augustine, and it is apparent throughout the *Monologion* that Anselm had been borrowing from Augustine's work *On the Trinity*. Augustine took the view – which has come back into fashion in the late twentieth century – that when the Bible says that man is made in the image of God it means that human nature also reflects in some way the Trinitarian character of the Godhead. For example, Augustine thought he saw in the way will, memory, and understanding are all present in a single person, an image of the manner in which God may be three and still one.

This "Augustinianism" was not eradicated when his old master Lanfranc made Anselm stop and think about his methodology. Anselm took up a position which gave him an independence of approach for the rest of his life. When he had finished the *Monologion* he sent a copy to Lanfranc (who was by now Archbishop of Canterbury), to ask him for his comments. There was a long silence and he had to prompt a reply by asking former monks of Bec, who were now at Canterbury in Lanfranc's community there, to press for an answer. Lanfranc took the view that although there was nothing Anselm had said which was out of tune with Augustine's teaching, it was inappropriate for him to be putting so much into his own words. He said that he should be quoting Augustine's authority and keeping close to the text of his source. Anselm clearly came to his own conclusions about this advice, because the *Monologion* was put into circulation, certainly with his direct approval, but without such notes and citations. And thereafter Anselm continued to write his books in his own way.

This was a decision of some importance. This was not an age in which it was acceptable to depart from express authority. A considerable proportion of monographs and, by definition, all commentaries, depended upon earlier texts which were their sources. Anselm was no rebel, but he began to develop a theological method which placed great confidence in quiet reasoning. He was confident that any reasonable person, presented with a clear explanation of the truths of faith, would be able to accept them. It was a view he was to find less easy to sustain as time went on and he gained painful experience of live theological controversy. But certainly at the outset, working among his respectful and enthusiastic monks at Bec, he had no reason to believe that everyone would not welcome a good, clear account with similar enthusiasm.

Indeed, he says as much in his *Proslogion*. That was to be his next book. He came to write it because after he had finished the *Monologion* he was left with a sense of intellectual dissatisfaction. He was conscious that in the *Monologion* he had constructed "a chain of many arguments" and that appeared to him to be untidy.[3] So he began to search for "a single argument" which would prove not only that God exists but all the other things Christians believe about him.

This search proved a distraction. He found that he could not concentrate at prayer and he began to think that the enquiry was a temptation of the Devil. But eventually there was a "eureka" moment and there burst upon him an insight. This was the ontological proof for the existence of God which has the merit of being unique among the arguments that there is a God. Aquinas placed it in a category of its own. It is worthy of remark that Anselm began with that question at all. Anselm was unusual in struggling philosophically with the question whether

God exists. It was not a question which troubled Augustine; and Anselm, too, knew no one (as far as we know) who did not believe in God. These were not centuries of atheism or agnosticism but of an almost universal belief.

The ontological argument (chapters 2–4) runs thus. Anselm points out that everyone – even the Fool of the Psalms (53:1) who thinks there is no God – is able to formulate in his mind the notion of "that than which nothing greater can be thought." But it is also, and equally, possible for everyone to distinguish between the "thought" of such a thing, taken simply to be an idea; and the thought of such a thing as a reality. But for that than which nothing greater can be thought to exist in reality is obviously greater than for it to exist only as an idea. This is the point at which Anselm makes a move in his argument which still divides his critics. He says that it follows that that than which nothing greater can be thought must therefore exist in reality. It is not unimportant here that (although he almost certainly had no direct knowledge of Plato),[4] he was working with an idea of "reality" which was fundamentally platonist. To a platonist the movement from idea to reality takes place at a level where the idea is itself more real than any particular exemplification.

His discovery excited Anselm and he says that he believed it would give others the same joy.[5] So he wrote it into a new book, prefacing it with a devotional chapter which is itself an important clue to the context in which he envisaged that the argument would best be understood. In the remainder of the *Proslogion* he went on to develop the argument to show that all the divine attributes – goodness, mercy, justice – can be arrived at by the same reasoning, and he concludes with a reflection on the nature of heaven, in which he suggests that it must, by definition, involve a continuation of the legitimate joys of earth. Thus, someone who runs fast in this life will still enjoy running fast in the next.[6]

Meanwhile, he was continuing with the steady teaching of his monks. One of the most important of the tasks this included was grounding them in the skills they needed for the study of the Bible. Until Peter Lombard's *Sentences* largely took over from the Bible as the main "textbook" of theological study in the thirteenth century, this was the fundamental task. Anselm's idea was to teach a method, an alertness to questions of language and logic, which would enable the student to understand whatever portion of the text he was reading. This was not at all like the patient progression through the text passage by passage of the traditional commentator, and it made no use at all of extracts from patristic authorities.It was thus a quite different method of exegesis from that which was to evolve in the twelfth century into the *Glossa Ordinaria*.

Anselm applied the skills and ideas he had learned from the study of grammar and logic to resolving vexed questions of signification in the text of Scripture. In this early period of his writing he composed four little treatises in this area, all taking the form of "dialogues" between "Master" and "Pupil."

The first, the *De Grammatico*, stands a little apart because it is solely concerned with a technical question on which the classical textbooks of grammar and logic differ. Anselm's question is whether the word "literate" (*grammaticus*) is a substance or a quality).[7] The others, the books *On Truth, On Freedom of Choice, On the Fall of Satan,* take one or two passages of Scripture and analyze them. In the case of the treatise on the fall of Satan the key passage is John 8:44, which describes Satan as not "standing fast in the truth."

Anselm develops the themes of truth and "rightness" (*rectitudo*) progressively through the three little treatises.[8] The first, *On Truth,* was, he says, prompted by a sense of unfinished business on the part of his pupils. The *discipulus* begins by reminding him that the question "What is truth?" had been left hanging in the *Monologion.*[9] As Anselm explores the notion it becomes clear that his central idea is that truth is a "rightness," so that there can be truth of actions as well as of statements, and a statement is true if it says that what is so is so. In the treatise on freedom of choice the discussion moves on to the right exercise of the will, and it is then but a step to the situation of Satan and his failure to persevere in acting in a way which is in conformity with this understanding of truth.

With the completion of this group of treatises, Anselm's period of quiet happiness as a theologian and philosopher began to come to an end. He found that he had become a controversial figure, as we saw in the section on Roscelin.

Anselm was distressed. He did not want the faithful led astray and naturally no one wants to see himself publicly misrepresented. This episode led to his writing *On the Incarnation of the Word.* It is unlike any of his other books, in that it survives in at least two versions, possibly more. Anselm's habit was not to let his books out of his hands until he had got them right, and he did not share Augustine's taste for *retractationes,* because he had no need to consider them. But here there was a first attempt to explain rationally to Roscelin that he had misunderstood what Anselm had been teaching, and then bewilderment at the discovery that here was someone apparently more interested in the controversy than the truth. For Roscelin went on accusing Anselm of heresy. And in the end Anselm wrote a book not merely on the issue Roscelin had raised, indeed, not primarily about that at all, but on the question how it was possible for the Son to be incarnate if the Father and the Holy Spirit were not also incarnate.

This disturbing period coincided with Anselm's translation from Bec to the Archbishopric of Canterbury, as Lanfranc's successor. He did not want to be Archbishop. He was thrown into a world of politics where he lacked the pragmatism and the necessary skills, as well as any taste for such a life as he now had to lead in confrontation with the king, William Rufus. The king, for his own reasons, wanted Anselm to acknowledge the anti-pope as the true Pope. But Anselm had already given his loyalty to Urban II and he was not prepared to change it. That would, in his eyes, have been a breach of "right order" (*rectus ordo*). The quarrel took him into exile, and led to further disagreements with the next king, during the course of which Anselm had to go into exile again, and came to realize that he had unwittingly allowed William to try to invest him in a manner which was in breach of the principle that the secular authority could play no sacramental part in the making of a bishop.

This was the period of Anselm's mature writing. His erstwhile pupil Gilbert Crispin was now Abbot of Westminster, and it seems possible that during the time when he feared that he might be chosen as Lanfranc's successor, Anselm may have spent some time staying at Westminster with Gilbert, keeping out of sight. Gilbert himself was writing a book in the form of a Disputation between a Jew and a Christian. It was a topical issue; this was a generation in which Jews and Christians were actively engaged in debate and Jews were sometimes converted. The chief difference between them (theologically speaking and from the point of view of an eleventh and twelfth set of priorities), was that the Jews would not accept that Christ was God incarnate. Their monotheism rejected that. It may well be that this stimulated Anselm's own interest in the questions he addressed in the *Cur Deus Homo*, "*Why God Became Man.*" And the theme followed on naturally from the one he had just been exploring in the final version of the *De Incarnatione Verbi.*

The *Cur Deus Homo* was written over an extended period; Anselm was never a rapid writer. He took it with him into exile. He chose the dialogue form once more, but this time the conversation was between himself and Boso, another of the Bec monks, and not between "master" and "pupil." Boso plays the part of the "unbeliever." They begin with a hypothesis. Anselm says that he will set out to show that even if Christ were taken out of the equation altogether it would be necessary to bring him back, so as to give a coherent account of the manner in which the human race was able to be restored to the position and purpose for which God created it. Important here is his continuing assumption that there is a rightness to things, a *rectitudo*, a divine harmony, which is divinely ordained and cannot ultimately be frustrated, for God is omnipotent and he always wills what is right. This gives an emphasis (characteristic of the period but particularly marked in Anselm) to the notion of fittingness (*convenientia; decentia*). "Fittingness" is powerful in his frame of reference. Anselm points out near the beginning of the *Cur Deus Homo* that three things, "will," "power," and "necessity," are closely associated in the solutions he proposes; here too is a familiar theme of his thought brought to maturity.

The argument of the *Cur Deus Homo* begins by asking what problem was created by the fall of Adam and Eve. God could not simply forgive them, Anselm argues, because his own "honor" was diminished by what they had done. (This is an assumption much colored by the fact that Anselm had lived most of his adult life in a feudal world in northern Europe and took this to be a constant, an absolute, rather than a principle applicable only for a brief period of the history of political thought and in a limited geographical area.)

Something therefore had to be done to make things right again, to restore right order (*rectus ordo*). Could God himself have intervened? The objection to that is that he was not the debtor. To pay oneself a debt someone else owes is not to discharge the obligation of the other person. This patterning of "owe" and "ought" is important as an indicator that Anselm was still thinking in his earlier terms of things "having to be as they ought to be" in order for them to be "true."

Could God have used an angel? But the angel would, again, not have been the debtor. Could God have used a human being? There the difficulty was that all human beings, who certainly were debtors, were now tainted with original sin, and were simply not able to do what was required. Logically, the only possibility was for a being who was both God and man to do what was needed, for only he both owed the debt and was able to discharge it. And so we come back to the incarnate Christ, who was indeed the only solution.

Anselm's last years – and the works of his maturity were written when he was in his sixties and seventies – were taken up with two or three main themes. In 1098, while he was in exile at the papal court, seeking the Pope's backing for his stand against the King of England, he was called on by Pope Urban II to frame a rebuttal of the arguments of the Greeks who were attending the Council of Bari. This was an important issue. In 1054 a schism had begun, dividing the Eastern and Western Churches. The division was in reality mainly political, and it turned in some measure upon Greek indignation about the claims of the Bishop of Rome to primacy over the four patriarchs of the East. There were, however, old theological disagreements, and it was these which were the "presenting symptoms" of the division.

The most important of these was the debate about the inclusion of the *filioque* clause in the Creed. This began in the West in the Carolingian period and it made a considerable difference to the "structure" of the Trinity. The original version of the Creed had said that the Holy Spirit proceeded from the Father. The Western version said that he proceeds from the Father and the Son. The Greeks objected to this because it was an addition to the Creed, and in their tradition that would have stood strongly against it even if they had believed that it was theologically correct. But they said forcefully that it was not correct, because, in their view, it pointed to two "origins" or "principles" in the Trinity, Father and Son, and the Father should stand alone in that position. This was a notion heavily dependent on the Pythagorean and neoplatonist influences of the idea that unity is metaphysically better than plurality, which were particularly strong in the theology of the old Eastern half of the Empire, where the direct study of texts in Greek had continued to be relatively easy.

Anselm asked for a few days to prepare his riposte, and we have a version of it in his treatise *On the Procession of the Holy Spirit*, which he completed four years later. He knew nothing of the history of the dispute, either in the eleventh century or earlier. He approached the problem straightforwardly as one of reason. His argument turns on symmetry. Only if the Spirit proceeds from the Father and the Son do we have a situation in which each Person of the Trinity is peculiar to himself and each has an attribute which he shares with the other two. Only the Son has a Father; only the Father has a Son; only the Spirit does not have a Spirit proceeding from himself. But both the Father and the Spirit do not have a Father; both the Spirit and the Son do not have Son; and both the Father and the Son have a Spirit proceeding from themselves.

In these last years of his life Anselm also went back to the subject of free will, linking it now systematically with the "most famous question," as he calls it, of the relationship between human freedom of choice and divine foreknowledge and predestination and the action of grace.

On his deathbed Anselm was still hoping to complete a book on the origin of the soul, for, as he said, if he did not do so, he was not sure than anyone living would be able to.

Anselm's influence in his own time and in the period after his death was perhaps greater, ironically, in the area of his spiritual writings than in that of his speculative theological writings. There are many manuscripts of his devotional works and a vast penumbra of spurious imitative spiritual writings attributed to him with confidence during the Middle Ages. His theological and speculative writing had the disadvantage for the next generation that its close argument made it less easy to use in short extracts or quotations than the writings of others working in more conventional ways. But his achievement there is not readily measured by counting the manuscripts. The work lasted. In time the importance of his ideas became clear; philosophers and theologians have continued to wrestle with his arguments not for their antiquarian interest but for their intrinsic value and importance until the present moment.

Notes

1 *Proslogion*, Prologue, *Anselmi opera omnia*, 6 vols., ed. F. S. Schmitt (Rome/Edinburgh, 1938–68), I, p. 7.
2 *Monologion*, 1, S I, p. 13.
3 *Proemium*, S 1, p. 93.
4 Even of the *Timaeus*, which was in limited circulation within a generation in Calcidius' version.
5 *Proemium*.
6 Chs. 24–6.
7 S 1, p. 145. Aristotle, *Categories*, I; Boethius, *In Cat.*, I, 1, Patrologia Latina, 64.167, *Denominativa vero dicuntur quaecunque ab aliquo solo differentia casu* (that is, both substantive), while the grammarians say one is a substance and the other a quality.
8 S 1, p. 176.
9 *Monologion*, 5, S 1, p. 181.

Bibliography

The Works of the St. Anselm, eds. F. S. Schmitt and R. W. Southern (Rome–Edinburgh, 1938–68), 6 vols.

Memorials of St. Anselm, eds. R. W. Southern and F. S. Schmitt (Oxford, 1969).

The Works of St. Anselm, trans. and ed. Brian Davies and G. R. Evans (Oxford, 1998).

Anselm, Aosta, Bec and Canterbury, eds. David Luscombe and G. R. Evans (Sheffield, 1996).

G. R. Evans, *Anselm and Talking About God* (Oxford, 1978).

G. R. Evans, *Anselm* (Chapman, 1989).

R. W. Southern, *St. Anselm and his Biographer* (Cambridge, 1963).

R. W. Southern, *St. Anselm: A Portrait in a Landscape* (Cambridge, 1997).

Peter Abelard and Gilbert of Poitiers

Lauge O. Nielsen

Numerous teachers of high intellectual standing made the schools of Northern France famous in the first half of the twelfth century, but contemporaries were not slow to recognize the leading roles played by Peter Abelard and Gilbert of Poitiers.[1] When John of Salisbury wanted to prove that indisputable advances in science had been made during his lifetime he focused on the contributions made by the most prominent of his teachers, viz., Abelard, Gilbert, and the logician Adam Parvipontanus.[2] Some believed that as theologians Abelard and Gilbert were two of a kind. This was the view of the most influential ecclesiastic of the time, the Cistercian abbot, Bernard of Clairvaux, who succeeded in getting Abelard convicted of heresy in 1140 and a few years later attempted – but failed – to elicit a papal condemnation of Gilbert.

Writing at about the same time as John of Salisbury, in the 1150s, the German Cistercian Otto of Freising, then Abbot of Morimond, inserted a long digression into his chronicle of the deeds of his nephew, the Emperor Frederick I. In this he gave an account of the careers of Abelard and Gilbert and sketched their thinking. Otto's obvious motive for straying from his main subject was to show that the similarities between the two leading theologians were more apparent than real. According to Otto, the circumstance that Gilbert as well as Abelard had been renowned masters of both logic and theology, and that both had put logical concepts and reasoning to use in their theological works, should not overshadow the much more significant fact that they had been men of very different molds and had entertained widely divergent conceptions in theology. Moreover, Otto did nothing to hide his admiration for Gilbert, whose sole fault, in Otto's eyes, had been his parsimonious and cryptic manner of expression, whereas he thought less highly of Abelard, who was full of himself and eager to amuse the students by his ready wit.[3]

To a modern historian Otto's stance is not without appeal. Dissimilarities between Abelard and Gilbert spring to eye much more readily than similarities. First, their lives and careers ran very different courses. Whereas Abelard's life had all the ingredients of drama, and he experienced great successes as well as terrible defeats, Gilbert's biography is on the surface much less spectacular, and his career could serve as an ideal for the successful twelfth-century theologian. Secondly, the surviving works of the two theologians are markedly different both in contents and in style. Apart from his logical commentaries and glosses Abelard authored mainly treatises in which he argued his own points of view. Gilbert's literary remains, on the other hand, consist of commentaries which do not purport to present the persuasions of the commentator but the views of the author whose works he expounded. Thirdly, Abelard's manner of exposition is much more readily accessible than Gilbert's. This is due not only to their different choices of literary genre, i.e., the independent treatise as opposed to the commentary, but also to their talents as writers. Abelard's style is clear – sometimes deceptively so – and he displays an unusual talent for coining fortunate phrases and for inventing similes of explanatory nature. Gilbert's style, on the other hand, is pedantic and possesses little of the elegance of Abelard's writings; parsimony and precision were his primary concern.

In the following the lives and the literary remains of the two theologians will be outlined. After this, some of the main features in the two theologians' works will be presented. In view of the very different natures of their writings and the complexity of their thought it is not particularly meaningful to simply compare their divergent opinions on various issues of importance in theology; this would inevitably result in a rather shallow picture. Abelard's theology developed over a period of twenty years, and the detailed charting of this development is still outstanding.[4] Nonetheless, Abelard's method in theology and the overriding direction of his thought are clearly visible already in his first work of theology. Accordingly, an attempt will be made to track the main line of argument in this work. The basic principles and overriding motives of Gilbert's thought are voiced only in his commentaries, and here he abstains from presenting a comprehensive account or even a summary of his basic ideas. This means that the reader is required to reconstruct the position from which Gilbert interpreted the authoritative writings he commented on. Evidently, it is not possible to give an exhaustive account of Gilbert's theology in this connection;[5] instead focus will be on selected aspects of Gilbert's theological thought that may serve to illustrate his contribution to theology. Finally, even on such a strictly limited basis it should prove possible to identify some points on which the two theologians were in basic agreement as well as some of the differences that separated them.

Peter Abelard's Biography

More is known about Abelard's life than about perhaps any other scholastic, and this is largely due to his autobiography, the rightly famous and fascinating *Historia Calamitatum*. Since the narrative in this work does not go beyond approximately 1129–31, the last ten years of his life are, as is often the case with medieval intellectuals, shrouded in obscurity, and must be reconstructed on the basis of the few pieces of information that can be gleaned from remarks in his own works or from those of his contemporaries.[6]

Abelard was born around 1079 in Le Pallet[7] in Brittany, and in spite of being the eldest son he chose to pursue the career of a scholar. Among his early teachers the most prominent were the notorious Roscelin, with whom Abelard stayed for a long time in Loches and Tours, and William of Champeaux, who was the leading master in Paris. Wanting to gain a reputation – as well as money – for himself, Abelard set up school from around 1102, and for the next ten years he taught either in Paris or in the vicinity of Paris. Up to this point Abelard lectured on dialectics, which is to say grammar and logic, and he proved his true standing by defeating his former master, William of Champeaux, in a controversy over the nature of universals.[8]

After a more or less voluntary return to his native Brittany Abelard took up the study of theology in 1113, and he became a pupil of Anselm of Laon who was the leading theologian of the time. During his rather short stay in Laon Abelard became positively impatient with Anselm. In order to demonstrate Anselm's lack of intellectual clarity Abelard started to lecture on the prophet Ezekiel and, according to his own testimony, he soon outshone the master of the school. Anselm answered the challenge by simply expelling Abelard from Laon. Consequently, Abelard had to go back to teaching dialectics, and in Paris he landed the prestigious position of master at Notre Dame. From that point Abelard led the life of a respected scholar until around 1117, when the dire consequences of his romantic involvement with Héloïse brought this period in his life to a close.

The highly dramatic and moving tale of the two lovers has been told innumerable times since Abelard's own account,[9] and it was of consequence for the future direction of Abelard's professional career. Having suffered mutilation at the hands of Heloise's enraged uncle, Abelard became a monk and took refuge in the abbey of St. Denis. Here he appears to have returned to the study and teaching of theology, and the literary fruit of his labors was his first written work of theology, the so-called *Theologia "Summi Boni"*. The reception accorded to Abelard's book was anything but favorable. Soon Abelard was accused of heresy by two former students of Anselm of Laon, and he was summoned to a council in Soissons in 1121. Here the papal legate condemned Abelard's book to the flames and sentenced Abelard to perpetual confinement in a monastery other than his own. In spite of the severity of the sentence, the consequences were not altogether unbearable. Soon afterwards Abelard was allowed to settle in a place of his own near Nogent-sur-Seine, and here he built an oratory dedicated to the Trinity.

Quite predictably, Abelard's great fame as a teacher attracted a throng of students to his new and remote abode, and already in 1122 Abelard was teaching again. The first oratory was replaced by a much bigger and more durable building which was consecrated to the Holy Spirit ("The Paraclete"). The following five years Abelard was allowed to pursue his scholarly activities. According to Abelard's less than explicit account, this quiet period was eventually brought to an end by the rising antagonism of some monastic reformers. Facing yet another onslaught,

Abelard took refuge in Brittany, where he became abbot of a remote monastery inhabited by a flock of rough and unruly monks. In spite of great difficulties and even threats to his life Abelard remained in the secluded place for no fewer than six years.

Precisely when Abelard returned to Paris is not clear, but it would seem that by 1133 he had settled there again and that he took up teaching logic as well as theology. We do not know whether Abelard's final period of teaching was without interruption, and whether he taught logic concurrently with theology. At any rate, he had been in Paris for some years when he had to face his final ordeal.

Sometime in the late 1130s the Cistercian William of St. Thierry read two theological treatises that had originated in Abelard's school. One of these works was by the master himself, whereas the other seems to have been an edited report of Abelard's oral teaching. According to William, the two works were very similar in contents, and both reeked of heresy. William immediately drew up a refutation of Abelard's theological aberrations, and in order to put political weight behind his attack he enlisted the assistance of the bishop of Chartres as well as his long-time friend Bernard of Clairvaux. A private meeting with Abelard persuaded Bernard that William had been correct in his assessment of Abelard's theology, and soon Bernard began preaching in public against the Parisian master. Naturally, Abelard was incensed at Bernard's slanderous attacks, and through the Archbishop of Sens he challenged Bernard to a public debate which would settle the matter once and for all. Bernard accepted the challenge with a great deal of apprehension; engaging Abelard, the renowned master of dialectics, in open debate did not appeal to Bernard who had no scholastic training. Finally, it was decided that the matter should be dealt with at the council of Sens in 1140. In order to avoid confronting Abelard in an open discussion Bernard called a private meeting in the evening before the day of the debate, and in this the bishops who attended the council took part. Here Bernard managed to secure the condemnation of what he and William perceived to be Abelard's views. On the following day Abelard was presented with a list of condemned propositions which he was required to either defend or repudiate. This put Abelard in an impossible situation, since he had nothing to gain from either defending propositions that had already been condemned or repudiating what was supposedly his own view. Having been outwitted by Bernard, Abelard chose the only course of action left open to him and appealed to the pope. If Abelard had entertained any hope that his appeal would win him a real opportunity to present his case, disappointment soon set in. While he was still on his way to Rome, his adversaries won the pope's approval of the condemnation, and in letters to Bernard of Clairvaux and the Archbishop of Sens, Pope Innocent II condemned Abelard to perpetual silence while his followers were to be excommunicated.[10]

Having been irrevocably defeated Abelard sought the protection of Peter the Venerable, the powerful Abbot of Cluny, and through his compassion and kindness Abelard's last two years became more tolerable than they might otherwise have been. Abelard died on April 21, 1142.

Abelard's Writings

The main body of Abelard's speculative writings may roughly be divided into two groups.[11] The first consists of his writings on logic, which are closely related to his activities as a teacher of dialectics. Besides early commentaries on the textbooks commonly used in the schools of the time, Abelard composed an original and monumental handbook called the *Dialectica*. Only fragments remain of a second and greatly expanded handbook on logic, which is usually known by the title *Logica*. Though the dating of Abelard's logical writings is by no means uncontroversial there are grounds for claiming that these works were composed before Abelard was censured in Soissons, i.e., before 1121.[12] After this incident Abelard appears to have written sparsely on logical matters; in fact, what has been preserved of Abelard's later logical writings is limited to a few commentaries which seem to stem from his teaching at the Paraclete.[13]

The second main group of Abelard's writings consists of his theological works. After the condemnation of the *Theologia "Summi Boni"* Abelard concentrated on theology, and with some justification it may be said that for next twenty years much of his time was spent on demonstrating the injustice of the condemnation and reclaiming his orthodoxy. Far from giving up the project undertaken in the *Theologia "Summi Boni"* Abelard put immense effort into revising the book. The second version of the controversial work is now known as the *Theologia Christiana* and is a rather unwieldy expansion of the original which dates from approximately the mid-1120s. The third version, the so-called *Theologia "Scholarium,"* was released for general circulation in the latter half of the 1130s, and though it was based on the previous version it was a great improvement over its predecessor in having both a much tighter structure and a wider scope.

Just how much work Abelard put into his *Theologia* emerges from the number of different "redactions" in which the work has been transmitted. The two latter versions, i.e., the *Theologia Christiana* and the *Theologia "Scholarium,"* are attested to in numerous different stages of development, and this indicates that the writing and revising of the *Theologia* was a process that continuously occupied the author for twenty years. Even after the publication of the third version Abelard continued to correct and expand on the work.

Another of Abelard's theological works also relates to his defense of his theological program, and this is the so-called *Sic et Non*. The main body of the work consists of quotations from the Church Fathers which have been arranged in groups that focus on particular points of doctrine. As indicated by its title, the aim of the work is to demonstrate that the evidence of tradition is anything but unanimous inasmuch as conflicting views on even central issues are to be found in the authoritative writings of the Fathers.

The prologue to the *Sic et Non* is Abelard's only "autographic" contribution to the work. Here he shows how the observation of a few rules of interpretation may assist the theologian in avoiding the impasse that would otherwise result from conflicting testimonies of authority.[14] In itself the prologue is an early and very original introduction to hermeneutics. Seen with respect to Abelard's personal development, however, the prologue comes across as Abelard's elaborate proof that the theological method followed in the first version of the *Theologia* is dictated by the tensions inherent in the tradition of the Fathers. Linking the *Sic et Non* to Abelard's first condemnation is also supported by its time of composition; the first version dates from the time immediately after the condemnation in Soissons, whereas Abelard prepared the second and final version concurrently with the composition of the *Theologia Christiana*.

During Abelard's last sojourn in Paris he wrote a commentary on Paul's epistle to the Romans and various works such as the unfinished dialogues between a philosopher, a Jew, and a Christian on the good life.[15] Just before the Council of Sens, Abelard composed an innovative treatise on sin and penance as well as vice and virtue, and this he entitled *Scito teipsum*. Unfortunately only the first book and the very beginning of the second book have been preserved, and there is room for speculation that it might belong to Abelard's unfinished works. The salient point of the work is to advocate the view that moral judgment rests not on external deeds but on the intentions of the doer. Nevertheless Abelard stressed that a moral code based on intentions is of limited use in the courts of law, and conceded that the judicial system is inextricably tied to external deeds and evidence. Abelard also realized that morals have nothing to do with eternal salvation, which rests squarely on God's predestination.[16]

After the second condemnation Abelard wrote several smaller pieces of an apologetic nature and he also went back to revising the *Theologia "Scholarium."*

The *Theologia "Summi Boni"*

Though Abelard's *Theologia "Summi Boni"* treats of one of the traditional subjects of Christian theology, the author's approach is far from traditional. In order to appreciate the novelty and significance of the work it is absolutely essential to keep in mind the basic question which Abelard wished to answer.

At the very outset of the work Abelard notes that Christ, the Wisdom of God Incarnate, described God or the single divine substance by giving him the three names of "Father," "Son," and "Holy Spirit." To Abelard it is clear that these names denote God's power, wisdom, and goodness. Abelard justifies linking the personal names to precisely these divine attributes by observing that God is the supreme and perfect good, and that supreme perfection is based on the coming together of these three attributes; power without wisdom would be wanton, just as the combination of power and wisdom without goodness would imply harmful and destructive egotism.[17] The primary task facing Abelard is to identify the reasons why precisely the personal names of "Father," "Son," and "Holy Spirit" were given to the one God who is powerful, wise, and good.

Outlining the basic presuppositions of his subsequent discussion, Abelard observes that the personal names should not be taken at face value inasmuch as none of these names is said of God in the same way as it is of created beings. As

Abelard explains – and later elaborates on – in talking of God we cannot but use names that were originally given to creatures for the sole reason that we have no language proper to the divine. Furthermore, given the uniqueness of the divine being, this transfer of names from the sphere of creatures to God greatly affects the signification of the terms, and, as Abelard points out, without paying close attention to these shifts in meaning the theologian is bound to go astray (1.1–5).[18]

It should be clear that Abelard's manner of addressing the theological questions of the divine Trinity in the *Theologia "Summi Boni"* strongly reflects his background in dialectics. To him, the basic task is one of linguistic analysis, viz., to locate the ultimate reasons for applying the names of "Father," "Son," and "Holy Spirit" to the divine being and, consequently, to discover the true meaning of these terms when said of God. The primary problem for Abelard is not what kind of entity a divine person is, or why God's absolutely unitary nature allows of the characteristics of the three persons. Though, in the course of his argument, Abelard deals with several aspects of the Trinity in terms of ontology, he consistently endeavors to maintain his linguistic approach.

Abelard's treatment of the question posed is not without ambiguity, but in the main it proceeds by three steps. The first consists in charting the testimony of authoritative tradition. In so doing Abelard adopted a much more comprehensive view of tradition than the one generally accepted by his contemporaries, and the main reason for this is that his ultimate answer relies on what he found in the writings of the ancient philosophers. Secondly, he confronts several arguments that some dialecticians of his time had raised against the divine Trinity. Entering into this debate in the *Theologia "Summi Boni"* was required for two reasons. Obviously, it gave Abelard an opportunity to distance himself from the doctrinal aberrations of members of his own profession which might reflect badly on his own work.[19] Equally, he used this discussion to clarify the fundamental terms involved in the Trinitarian question. The third step in Abelard's treatment consists in delineating the true meaning of the Son's generation from the Father and the procession of the Holy Spirit from both Father and Son. At this final stage Abelard is in a position to answer the main question of why God is named "Father," "Son," and "Holy Spirit."

The testimony of tradition

Assessing the testimony of tradition, Abelard observes that the Trinity is attested to by two channels: the prophets of Israel and the philosophers of antiquity. Going over the pertinent passages in the Old Testament Abelard makes a point of linking the naming of the second person in the Trinity as "God's Word" (*verbum Dei*) to the testimony of Moses and refers to Augustine for its proper interpretation. Since God does not utter sounds, "God's Word" should not be taken in the literal sense, but as figurative speech, and Abelard finds that it is synonymous with the name "God's Wisdom" (*sapientia Dei*) (1.14–16 and 1.25–9).

After his rather cursory treatment of the Old Testament testimony, Abelard turns to the ancient philosophers. That the philosophers perceived the triune nature of God was, according to Abelard, due to their superior reason, which is a gift of God. That some of the philosophers were heathens and of low moral standing does not impair the veracity of their perception – just as Solomon's fall from true religion did not take away his wisdom. Nevertheless, as Abelard is careful to point out, in general the philosophers were men of the highest moral standing (1.30ff.).

With respect to recognizing the Trinity Abelard accords a place of prominence to Plato, who perceived the Trinity more clearly than any other philosopher. Plato not only described the second person in the Trinity as the mind or the Son of God, but in the *Timaeus* he also intimated the nature of the Son's generation and identified the Holy Spirit. However, Plato's description of the Holy Spirit is, as Abelard notes, in need of interpretation. Plato talked of a soul of the world (*anima mundi*), but, according to Abelard, this characterization makes no sense, since the world as a whole cannot possess a single soul. For this reason Plato's description should not be taken at face value; it must be regarded as figurative speech. Relying heavily on Macrobius and Augustine, Abelard concludes that Plato's "world soul" is a veiled reference to the third person in the Trinity. As Abelard emphasizes, there was nothing improper about Plato's using figurative speech, and his metaphor was well chosen. By this name Plato indicated that the Holy Spirit is the benevolent organizer of the created universe and the bringer of every good in much the same way as the animal soul is the vitalizing principle of animated beings (1.36–46).

The logical aspects of the trinity

As an introduction to his refutation of contemporary dialecticians Abelard delivers a long praise of the science of dialectics: in itself dialectics is of incomparable value, and this is not in the least diminished by its being misused by ignorant and ill-willed practitioners. Abelard recognizes that he must meet his adversaries on their own ground and rely on arguments which rest only on human reason, since this is the only sort of argument which they accept. In elaborating such a rational defense of Christian faith, the theologian should not, according to Abelard, aspire to reach truth itself. Since God as the ultimate truth is not directly known, the theologian must be content with advancing something that has a semblance of truth and appears convincing. Accordingly, for Abelard, rational theology cannot and should not be conceived of as a substitute for revealed theology; it is rather an exposition and defense of what is implied by revelation, and as such it does great service to the spreading of true religion (2.26–7).

Outlining the basic terms of the debate on the Trinity, Abelard observes that the ternary of persons should under no circumstance be construed as compromising the absolute unity of the divine being. Since the divine substance is absolutely simple, the three persons cannot be seen as parts of a whole. Equally, the simplicity of the divine substance prohibits viewing the three persons as formal principles that inform divine being as a substrate. Finally, God is not subject to accidental determinations, and for this reason the divine persons cannot be regarded as accidental or mutable forms in which divine nature participates. In other words, the divine substance or essence is, according to Abelard, absolutely simple, singular, and individual, and this prohibits viewing the relationship between divine nature and divine persons in accordance with any mode of composition that is known from created beings (2.33–4).

On the other hand, Abelard explains, simply identifying the three divine persons with the divine essence will not do either. Each of the persons has its own proper characteristic, and the common feature of these personal "properties"[20] is that they are relative: the Father is not from anybody else and begets a Son; the Son is from the Father and is born; the Holy Spirit proceeds from both Father and Son (2.30 and 2.41–2).

Uniting absolute unity and personal trinity is not without its problems, and this is borne out by the objections of the dialecticians. To Abelard it is evident, however, that the fundamental flaw of these objections is that they assume that it is possible to talk of the divine in much the same way as of created beings. But, according to Abelard, this is not true at all. Given that divine nature is unique and not immediately perceived, it is necessary to talk of the divine in a circumspect manner, and this was recognized by the ancient philosophers who stressed that divine nature possesses its own manner of speech (*modus loquendi*) (2.64–5). Exemplifying the difference between ordinary speech and statements about God, Abelard focuses on the term "substance" (*substantia*) which, when said of created beings, designates that the object subsists by itself and is subject to accidental determinations. When said of God, on the other hand, the very same term retains only the first meaning inasmuch as God is his own being and is not subject to changeable properties (2.34 and 2.66). An even more telling example Abelard finds in the fact that it is possible to predicate something of God by means of a verb. By its very nature a verb designates time, but time does not at all apply to the divine being, who is eternal and immutable. Consequently, verbs simply loose this aspect of their signification when used of God (2.70).

In pointing out this fundamental lack of congruence between human speech and divine nature, Abelard has no intention of denying that it is possible or legitimate to talk of God in human language. Rather Abelard's point is that when talking of God, it is imperative to keep in mind that terms have been transferred from the realm of creatures to that of the uncreated, and that this transfer should observe certain principles. One of these principles is that there must be some commonness or similarity between the signification of the word in its primary use, i.e., when said of creatures, and its semantic import when said of the divine (2.71–2 and 2.77–8). An obvious example of this is Abelard's charting of the meaning of "substance." Secondly, it is possible to talk of God by means of similes, which is to say in figurative terms. Of this Abelard provides a few examples when dealing with the generation of the Son, but probably the most telling is his interpretation of Plato's world soul. In both cases it is, according to Abelard, imperative to pay attention not only to the similarity that is indicated by the terms used, but also to the dissimilarity which is necessarily implied by any word or statement said of God. Accordingly, to Abelard, all talk of God is by nature ambiguous and requires careful linguistic interpretation.

Observing these guidelines for theological explanation, Abelard proceeds to explain why the dialecticians' objections to the divine Trinity are fallacious.[21] In so doing Abelard exerts all his dialectical skills, and in particular he focuses on the different ways in which one may distinguish between what is the same and what is different. The immediate reason for this – highly abstract – investigation is that his opponents seem to share the conviction that the three persons cannot be mutually different if they are the same substance, or, conversely, that they cannot be the same substance if they are truly different persons. In order to refute this line of argument, Abelard strives to find a sense in which it is reasonable to claim that something which is fundamentally the same may also be different from itself. At the end of his rather long inquiry, Abelard comes up with one way of distinguishing between "the same" and "the different" which appears to fit the Trinity.

In all Abelard distinguishes between six different ways in which something may be said to be the same. Of immediate importance is the sense in which something is the same with regard to definition. In this connection "definition" should not be interpreted in the strict sense, i.e., as definition by proximate genus and difference, but as synonymous with "adequate description." Explaining this, Abelard adduces that "body" and "corporeal substance" are the same with regard to definition, inasmuch as the two expressions are semantically equivalent and provoke the same understanding in the mind of the hearer. On the other hand, "colored substance" is no adequate description of "body" since color does not form part of the semantical "contents" of "body," even though – in the external world – every body is colored. Accordingly, what is the same by definition is also the same numerically and essentially, inasmuch as the same object is adequately described by both terms or expressions (2.84–5).

Parallel to this, Abelard charts the different ways in which something is said to be different. Again the main weight of the investigation is on what is different with regard to definition. Exemplifying this kind of difference Abelard focuses on the terms "man" and "animal." Though both terms can be used as names of any particular human being and enter into the complete definition of man, viz., "man is a rational animal," it is not the case that they are the same with respect to definition. The word "animal" is obviously said of many living beings that are irrational and not humans. On the other hand, terms that are different by definition do not require that the particular object of which they are said, should be different either numerically or essentially (2.96–7). In other words, that a substance such as Socrates is rightly called both "man" and "animal" does not imply that he is different from himself either numerically or substantially.

Rebutting the dialecticians' objections, Abelard employs this distinction of definition or – as Abelard also calls it – of "property" in order to provide an insight into the relationship between nature and persons in God. Whereas the divine nature is a simple essence and as such an absolute unity, there is diversity in God solely insofar as the persons differ with respect to their quasi-properties. According to Abelard, there can, however, be no conflict between, on the one hand, divine nature and, on the other, divine persons since unity in nature is an identity in substance, while trinity in persons is a ternary of properties. In other words, in agreement with what has been shown to be true of things – or rather words – that differ with respect to definition or property, the divine persons cannot compromise the unity of divine nature or substance. Moreover, as true numbering is linked to substance, Abelard believes there to be no doubt that the unity of the divine nature is real or substantial, while the trinity of persons is in a certain sense accidental. For this reason it is not warranted to conclude that there are three beings (*tria*) because there are three persons (*tres*) (3.4–3.5).[22]

Against the dialecticians Abelard demonstrates that they completely fail to grasp the subtle difference between the substantial and the personal in talk of God. According to Abelard, nobody should deny that the Father is almighty and that the Son is almighty, but this does not entail that the Father is the Son. The reason for this is, as Abelard points out, that the context is not taken into account. In the premises, the predicate term "almighty" refers to the unitary essence, whereas the terms in the conclusion point to the personal characteristics (3.38–9).[23]

The naming of the divine persons

In the third part of the *Theologia "Summi Boni"*[24] Abelard is finally in a position to answer his initial question of why God is designated by the names "Father," "Son," and "Holy Spirit." Concentrating first on the Son's generation, Abelard notes that the Son of God is born from the Father as wisdom proceeds from power. In and of itself power is not wisdom but, conversely, wisdom is a certain kind of power, i.e., the power to discern. In other words, there would not be wisdom unless there was power, but the converse does not hold good (3.56). This relationship does not imply that one element precedes the other or that they are of unequal standing, merely that they are different by way of definition. Elucidating what this implies for the understanding of the Son's generation, Abelard explains that a simile to this relationship is to be found in a waxen seal where there is a difference of property or definition between the wax itself and the image that is impressed on the wax, whereas the unity of the object is unimpaired.[25] Abelard finds another parallel in the way in which a species, e.g., man, is said to be born from a genus, e.g., animal, and this he elaborates on by combining the testimonies of Boethius and Mercurius Trismegistus, who had been one of the key witnesses to the pagans' perception of the Trinity (3.52–3). Moreover, Abelard also claims the authority of Christ. Describing himself, Christ had said that he was the Son of God, which is the ancient philosophers' description, whereas he never used the title "the Word of God," which is the prophets' term for the second person in the Trinity. This is no coincidence according to Abelard. By adopting the philosophers' term Christ showed that the philosophers had intimated the Son's generation much more clearly than the prophets, who had spoken in coarse terms so as to accommodate their unlearned audience (3.66–7).

Elaborating on his understanding of the Son's generation, Abelard proceeds to expound several of the traditional Trinitarian formulas. In all instances he strives to show that the distinction of definition is a golden key to unlocking seemingly offensive traditional formulas, and that their true meaning is uncovered through linguistic analysis (3.60ff.).

Dealing with the procession of the Holy Spirit from the Father and the Son, Abelard explains that God's goodness springs from his love (*caritas*), and that this love has two aspects. Firstly, one may view God's love as simply the love which resides in God, i.e., His affection (*affectus*). Secondly, God's love may be considered insofar as it brings about good effects (*effectus*). According to Abelard, the two are closely related inasmuch as God's affection is the cause of God's turning to creation with gracious gifts. Abelard finds that what is implied by saying that the Holy Spirit proceeds from Father and Son is precisely this relationship between God and creation which is founded in divine goodness. If creation were only based on divine power there would be no loving providence or care. However, since divine power is moderated by divine wisdom, God encompasses his creation with love and providential care, and for this reason it is no coincidence that creation is associated with the Holy Spirit in particular (3.88–9).

Abelard was fully aware that his interpretation is not without its problems. Clearly, linking the procession of the Holy Spirit to creation seems to confound what is eternal, i.e., the divine Trinity, and what is temporal, i.e., creation. In order to resolve this apparent confusion Abelard resumes his discussion of Plato's world soul. One of the more serious difficulties with identifying the Holy Spirit and the Platonic world soul is that the latter is claimed to have been brought forth in time, and this would imply that, in Plato's view, the divine Trinity is temporal. But Abelard does not agree with this interpretation. In his view Plato used the word "soul" (*anima*) and not "spirit" (*spiritus*) – even though God is spirit – for the sole reason that he wanted to focus on God's beneficial effects in creation and to stress that God takes care of His creation in much the same way as man's soul cares for his body. A similarly limited view of the Holy Spirit is, as Abelard notes, found in the writings of somebody as highly respected as Augustine. That God's love or His affection is primarily something eternal and arises from the interaction between power and wisdom is simply something that Plato took for granted in the *Timaeus* (3.94ff.).

At this point[26] Abelard is at long last in a position to answer the main question of why God is rightly designated by the three names of "Father," "Son," and "Holy Spirit." Since these terms designate God's power, wisdom, and goodness they might seem superfluous or even misleading. But, as Abelard stresses, this is not the case at all. Whereas "power," "wisdom," and "goodness" are absolute terms, the personal names are relative terms. Accordingly, what these terms indicate is that God's power is related to and is accompanied by His wisdom (3.86), and that God's wisdom relates to His power in such a way as to give rise to love and, as its effect, to impart goodness to creation (3.91). Consequently, the three personal names of "Father," "Son," and "Holy Spirit" teach man something of the utmost importance about God and induce man to turn to God in gratitude.[27]

Assessment of Abelard's exposition

Abelard's *Theologia "Summi Boni"* reads like a single continuous argument even though it is true that the author digresses and repeats himself on more than one occasion. On the surface its goal is a fairly modest one, viz., to investigate the meaning of God's personal names. However, seen against the background of Abelard's conception of man's cognition of God and the nature of theology, the task Abelard sets himself in the *Theologia "Summi Boni"* takes on importance. Human language reflects created reality and is badly suited to talk about God; for this reason, an indispensable part of theology consists in unravelling the import of statements about God, and this can be accomplished solely by way of linguistic analysis. In short, Abelard's *Theologia "Summi Boni"* is intended as a model of genuine theology that is not limited to merely repeating the formulas of tradition but attempts to elicit their true meaning and thus to make the faithful understand what they believe.

In spite of Abelard's efforts to bolster his interpretation by persuasive argument, his efforts were – as already mentioned – not appreciated, and in the understanding of Otto of Freising the Council of Soissons had convicted Abelard of Sabellianism inasmuch as he had "attenuated" the divine persons.[28] Though it makes little sense to reduce the *Theologia "Summi Boni"* – or Abelard's theology as a whole – to a simple list of more or less orthodox opinions, it cannot be denied that some passages in Abelard's exposition make his adversaries' reaction at least understandable.[29] On the other hand, it is equally certain that most of his contemporaries were simply incapable of grasping Abelard's sophisticated line of reasoning, and that the central message of his work was best understood by his students.

Gilbert of Poitiers' Biography

Not much is known of Gilbert's early life. He was born around 1085 in Poitiers, where he received his elementary education. Subsequently, he completed his training in the seven liberal arts under the famous masters Bernard and Thierry of Chartres, after which he arrived in Laon to study theology under Anselm. We do not know precisely when Gilbert was in Laon, but it is not unlikely that he met Abelard. Apparently, Gilbert left Laon before Anselm's death in 1117 and returned to Poitiers where he became a canon in the beautiful Romanesque cathedral. Gilbert was not content to stay in Poitiers and obtained a position in Chartres around 1124. At some point Gilbert became chancellor in Chartres, and he filled this position as late as 1137. Shortly afterwards Gilbert moved to Paris where he taught dialectics and theology in the cathedral school. He remained in Paris until his appointment to the bishopric of Poitiers in 1142. There is no evidence that Gilbert continued teaching after becoming bishop, and it seems that Gilbert's time as bishop was taken up with reclaiming the rights and privileges of a hitherto neglected see.

In 1146 two of Gilbert's archdeacons accused him of entertaining heretical views on the divine Trinity. In order to further their cause they sought an audience with Eugenius III, but the pope postponed dealing with the matter until the following year. Subsequently they enlisted the assistance of Bernard of Clairvaux, and the first formal hearing took place in Paris in 1147. Here Bernard acted on behalf of the accusers while Gilbert emphatically denied having propagated unorthodox views. Since Gilbert's writings were not available, the pope decided to postpone the matter for another year. Gilbert's case was resumed in the early spring of 1148 in a consistory which was held after the close of the council in Reims. On this occasion Gilbert faced a formidable opposition; besides Bernard of Clairvaux, who acted as official accuser, the opposition counted several of the most important French theologians and ecclesiastics, such as Sugear of St. Denis, Robert of Melun, and Peter Lombard. Nonetheless, Gilbert's prospects were not totally ominous. The *curia* had scant sympathy with Bernard and wished to curb his influence, and Gilbert's case was a golden opportunity for defying Bernard.

On the first two days of the process Gilbert debated with Bernard and managed not only to display his own learning but also to embarrass his adversary. While Bernard relied on thin collections of short excerpts from the writings of the Church Fathers – so-called *florilegia* – Gilbert demonstrated his intimate and extensive knowledge of the entire works of the Fathers. After the debate on the second day the papal counsellors decided that they had heard enough and that their judgment would be forthcoming. To Bernard this development was anything but promising, and falling back on the strategy that had made him victorious in the Abelard case he convened a meeting of his supporters in the evening. Here Bernard drew up a confession of faith which was endorsed by the participants and later conveyed to the pope with the express clause that the confession was nonnegotiable. As the *curia* got wind of Bernard's move they were deeply angered by Bernard's attempt to preempt their decision, and protesting to the pope they claimed that Bernard was preparing a schism in case Gilbert was acquitted. Facing this serious charge, Bernard was forced to retreat, and he assured the pope that the confession of faith was intended solely as a clarification of the issues that had been debated. Being under pressure from two sides[30] Eugenius was forced to arrive at a decision both parties could accept. Accordingly, he endorsed Bernard's confession of faith and charged Gilbert with bringing his works on Boethius' theological treatises into agreement with Bernard's confession.

After this Gilbert returned to his see, and he died in Poitiers on September 4, 1154.

Gilbert's Writings

No more than three works can be ascribed to Gilbert with certainty, and they are all commentaries.[31] In his youth Gilbert composed a commentary on the Psalms which he supposedly asked Anselm of Laon to correct. Dating from Gilbert's years as a master there is a commentary on the Pauline letters as well as a commentary on Boethius' theological treatises. Of these works the two biblical commentaries are still available only in medieval manuscripts.[32] However, this should not be taken to imply they were without influence; they were extensively used by Peter Lombard in his biblical commentaries and were generally known in the Middle Ages as "the medium-sized commentaries" (*media glossatura*).

Gilbert's commentaries are all cast in the same literary mold. The defining characteristic of the type of commentary cultivated by Gilbert is that the authoritative text commented on is woven into the text of the commentary. The advantage of this compositional style is that the original text and the commentary form a single continuous text which is easy to read. In addition, this type of commentary gave the author full liberty to expand his exposition of any particular passage without regard for the physical space that would be available on the page. In this respect the *lectio continua* commentary marked a great advance over the so-called marginal commentary that had been current in the school of Laon; here the commentary is placed as explanatory notes in the margins while the text commented on occupies the center of the page. On the other hand, composing commentaries in which the original text and the commentary form an integral whole, required a substantial effort of the author who had to take every word of the original into account and make transitions as imperceptible as possible. In order to avoid confusing the reader as to whether he was reading the words of the original author or the commentator, the authoritative text was often either underlined or otherwise emphasized in the medieval manuscripts.

Gilbert's Theology

In his commentary on Boethius' treatise *De Trinitate* Gilbert confronts some (*aliqui*) who claim that the divine essence consists of three parts, and who assign omnipotence to the Father, wisdom to the Son, and goodness to the Holy Spirit. In Gilbert's view, this opinion rests squarely on a rule that is proper to natural science but does not obtain in theology. Of created objects it is true to say that a difference in properties is due to a difference in formal principles; for example, one and the same person is colored because of his corporeality and is clever because of his rationality. However, this rule does not apply to the divine inasmuch as it is a fundamental rule in theology that the divine essence is absolutely simple and without parts (61,1ff. and 169,64ff.).[33]

That Gilbert's criticism is directed at Abelard and his school is hardly a matter for speculation, just as it is clear that Gilbert had read Abelard with great attention and realized that his position was significantly different from that of Sabellius. In Gilbert's view, Abelard's interpretation of the Trinity makes little sense unless some sort of distinction is assumed to exist between divine omnipotence, wisdom, and goodness. To Gilbert, however, this is a straightforward mistake, albeit an understandable one. What Abelard failed to realize is that what is universally true in the world of created being does not automatically hold true when talk is of God. Like natural philosophy, which deals with created objects, theology is an autonomous science that has its own rules, and one should avoid transferring rules from one science to another without proper justification.

Gilbert's rejection of Abelard's view of the Trinity is indicative of some of the principles that govern his own theological thought. First, in Gilbert there is a conscious effort to discover the proper natures of the single sciences and to investigate their mutual relationships. Secondly, Gilbert is as convinced as Abelard that careful linguistic interpretation of theological statements is required in order to avoid falling into heresy or sheer nonsense. Thirdly, in theology it is, according Gilbert's perception, imperative to recognize that Christian faith does not conform to the modes of thought which are natural to man, and that theological explanation is of necessity partial and should not aspire to exhaust its subject matter.

The science and language of theology

Commenting on Boethius' division and description of the sciences, Gilbert accepts that theology derives some of its defining characteristics from its object. Thus theology is said to be without motion and matter because the divine essence is devoid of matter and not subject to change. On the other hand, Gilbert takes exception to Boethius' claim that theology should be called "intellectual" because of the way in which the object of theology is perceived. Gilbert agrees that theology has a proper mode of cognition but this is not adequately described by this term since, according to Gilbert, intellectual cognition is properly a perception of created objects and their formal constituents (85,97ff.). In his commentary on Boethius, Gilbert does not elaborate on his understanding of the nature of theological cognition, but in his commentary on the *Corpus Paulinum* he deals extensively with this topic.

To Gilbert theological cognition cannot be separated from faith, and it derives many of its defining characteristics from the association with faith. Christian faith does not fall within the precinct of man's natural abilities but is a divine gift which is directly bestowed by God and is due solely to God's liberality. Some of the faithful hold their religious persuasion without grasping the realities that underlie the confession of faith, and these believers Gilbert terms the small ones (*parvuli*). To others God bestows not only faith but also a perception of the grounds of faith, and believers of this higher order Gilbert calls the spiritual ones (*spirituales*). The sole cause of the spirituals' superior cognition is that they are illuminated by God, and in Gilbert's understanding this illumination that is associated with faith is not primarily affective but very much rational. Firstly, it is man's rational faculty or the intellect that is enlightened by God, and, secondly, it is illumination that enables the spiritual believers to rationally expound and defend the mysteries of faith. Accordingly, what divine illumination brings about in spiritual believers is nothing but theological cognition or the science of theology, and this science or perception may be called "intellectual" for the obvious reason that it is the intellect which is illuminated by God.[34]

Just like the other sciences, theology is, as Gilbert underlines, governed by rules. Some of these rules are proper in the sense that they are valid only in theology, whereas other rules are common to theology and some other speculative science. With Gilbert the distinction between proper and common rules is a general characteristic of sciences and, consequently, of theology. An example of a rule that is proper to theology Gilbert finds in the principle that the three divine persons who are mutually diverse, are one and the same essence; this could never obtain in the created world where every single person has a separate essence. On the other hand, the nature of rules that are common to or shared by several sciences, is not without ambiguity in Gilbert. Obviously, axioms of logic are common insofar as they are of universal validity. But other rules are said to be common in the sense that they originally belong to one science, and subsequently they are transferred to and put to use in another science. In order for such a rule to have validity in the latter science, it is, as Gilbert stresses, required that there is some agreement between the objects of the two sciences, and that the rule is adapted to the objects of the posterior science (115,1ff.).

The importance of distinguishing between what is proper and what is common is also at the forefront in Gilbert's deliberations on the nature of theological language. Gilbert is in complete agreement with Abelard that it is impossible to construct a language that is particular to theology, and, consequently, the perceptions of theology must be phrased in ordinary human language. According to Gilbert, however, the basic structure of man's language reflects the ontological conditions of creatures. When talking of created objects an ordinary predicative statement such as "Socrates is white" reflects Socrates' ontological constitution. In this particular case the subject term, which is a proper noun, has been given to Socrates on the basis of his total and individual form, whereas the predicate term indicates one of Socrates' formal principles, i.e., the form of whiteness which causes Socrates to be white.[35] In Gilbert's – and, of course, Boethius' – terminology the ontological distinction between the thing that is, and the formal principles by which the object is what it is, is voiced in the distinction between *id quod est* and *id quo est*. Every created thing is, in Gilbert's view, composite in the sense that the object is determined by its inherent formal principles which endow their subject with being something. Some of these forms are substantial in the sense that they cause a thing to come into being, while others are accidental in the sense that they endow their subject with properties that may change without affecting the continued existence of the object. It is this basic ontological composition between *id quod* and *id quo* in the sphere of created reality that is reflected by simple predicative statements and discloses the composite nature of human language.

Obviously, the close interrelationship between human language and the ontological constitution of created objects is of paramount importance when talk is of God. God is absolutely simple, and this means that in the divine there is no plurality of formal principles, and, consequently, there is no distinction between *id quod* and *id quo*. This entails that the very simplicity and singularity of divine nature is at odds with the structure of human language. But talk of God is possible only in human language. For this reason it is, as Gilbert underlines, imperative that the theologian is continually aware of this incongruity and strives to spell out the true or deeper meaning of statements about God.[36]

Even though numerous names are used to describe God, this should not be taken to imply that God's being or essence is divided into parts. When God is said to be "powerful," "wise," or "good," it is absolutely necessary to explicate that the several names point to one and the same divine being. The reason for using several names for God is, according to Gilbert, to teach man something about God by describing the divine being under different aspects which are known from creation. In other words, the plurality of divine names serves primarily a pedagogic aim and is justified for the sole reason that God as the highest good encompasses all perfections that are present in creation. Examples of another sort of divine name are "omniscient" and "ubiquitous," which designate not only divine being but also something that is external to the divine essence. They indicate the way in which God relates to creation and should not be assumed to designate divine being in itself, since the solitary divine being is eternally immutable and does not acquire new properties with the advent of creation (169,82ff.).

Gilbert also recognizes the need to talk of God by means of figurative speech or similes. What is characteristic of Gilbert's treatment of such deliberately "improper" speech is that he takes great care in explaining the theoretical foundation of similes. To Gilbert it is fully possible to ascribe to God characteristics that belong primarily to creatures. In such cases one should keep in mind, though, that by predicating such an attribute of God, no adequate description of God is obtained. The true import of such an attribution is that God as the cause of creation possesses in an eminent manner what is present in creation as his effect.

To Gilbert, however, similes in the precise sense of the term are much more interesting than the straightforward transfer of names from creation to creator. The point of similes is, according to Gilbert, to illustrate some state of affairs in the divine by means of a relationship that is found in creation. Similes of this more complicated kind involve four terms and two relationships. A highly telling example of this Gilbert finds in Paul's letter to the Hebrews (1:3) where Paul describes Christ as the brightness (*splendor*) of God's glory (*gloriae*) and the express image (*figura*) of divine reality (*substantiae*). Since brightness and image in the created world are not directly comparable to Christ or the second divine person, Gilbert is persuaded that a highly sophisticated line of thought is intimated by these names. What the simile is intended to convey is that as brightness relates to the source of light so the Son of God relates to the Father. In other words, Paul compares a relationship in the world of creatures to the relationship between Father and Son in the divine. Comparisons of such relationships are well-known to Gilbert from Boethius who termed this type of mathematical relationship "*proportionalitas.*" The point of the simile is obviously to highlight the fact that the Son comes from the Father, and that they are coeternal, in the same way as brightness is a concomitant of light, and as light is never without brightness. On the other hand, it is, according to Gilbert, just as important to keep in mind that similes are never perfectly adequate, and that they always contain an element of dissimilarity. In Paul's example, according to Gilbert's interpretation, brightness is not as lucid as the source of light, which means that this particular simile fails to bring out the consubstantiality of Father and Son. Accordingly, this aspect of the divine relationship should be illustrated by means of other similes. For this purpose Gilbert adduces that a human offspring and its ancestor are equal with respect to being man, i.e., they are consubstantial, and that this agrees with the relationship between God the Father and God the Son. However, in this simile the points of dissimilarity are that a human father and his son are not coeval, and that they are numerically different with respect to substantial being, i.e., they are two human beings, while Father and Son in God are both eternal and numerically one God. Accordingly, though similes may illustrate some aspects of the divine they are of necessity also incongruous to the divine, and for this reason, Gilbert argues, several similes are required in order to depict the complex and yet simple nature of divine nature, and, like statements about God, similes are always in need of careful interpretation.[37]

Gilbert's interpretation of the Trinity

With Gilbert the unity and absolute simplicity of the divine essence is a given, and for this reason expounding the divine Trinity becomes a matter of attempting to show how there may be a ternary of mutually different persons in a single and noncomposite being.

The pivotal point of Gilbert's deliberations on the nature of the divine persons is the conviction that the word "person" retains a major part of its signification when applied to the divine persons. In the world of creatures, according to Gilbert, the word "person" designates an object that has proper being in the sense that it cannot be composed with anything else, i.e., enter into composition with something else and become part of a more comprehensive totality. This is true of the object itself as well as of its ontological principles, which is to say its inherent forms that endow the object with being and make the thing into what it is. That an object is a person and has this special kind of singularity is, as Gilbert explains, revealed by the so-called externally affixed accidents. Accidents of this kind do not endow the object with being in the proper sense of the word, i.e., they are not inherent formal principles, but are the circumstances in which the object is situated. Exemplifying this, one may say that Socrates' being a father or his living in a particular house in Athens are external in comparison to Socrates' ontological constitution, inasmuch as they do not make Socrates into an object of a particular kind; they merely describe Socrates' position in the world. Nonetheless, these external accidents are indicative of Socrates' being a person inasmuch as they demonstrate that Socrates is unique in the sense that no other object is situated in precisely the same circumstances as Socrates or relate to other things in the world in the very same way. For this reason it is true to say of created persons that they are persons because of their inherent being that is singular and individual or incommunicable. However, the particular status of persons is demonstrated by the way in which they relate to other objects in the universe, and these relationships Gilbert classifies as externally affixed accidents for the sole reason that they do not endow the person with being or being something.[38]

It is obvious to Gilbert that the word "person" is primarily given to created persons, and that its significance is somewhat modified by its transfer to the realm of the divine. The fact that the divine persons are one and the same essence or being clearly violates the stipulation that persons are supposed to be separate beings and possess their proper and incommunicable formal principles. In contrast, the divine persons are different insofar as they relate to each other; the Father relates to the Son by way of generation (*generatio*), the Son relates to the Father by being born (*nativitas*), and the Holy Spirit relates to Father and Son by being their mutual bond (*connexio*). These relationships clearly belong to what, in the world of creatures, is classified as externally affixed accidents. In the divine, however, these relationships are, as Gilbert points out, not only indicative of the difference existing between persons but they are also the causes of this difference (148,67ff.). With regard to the definition or significance of the word "person" this means that there is only partial agreement between what "person" signifies in the created sphere, and what it implies in the divine. The source of the mutual difference of the divine persons is not their being but their divergent and externally affixed characteristics which not only demonstrate but also cause the mutual difference between the divine persons.

Since the personal relationships in the divine fulfill this double purpose, it is, according to Gilbert, legitimate to view them as personal properties, and thus one may consider them as principles that together with the divine essence or being constitute the single divine persons (156,45ff.).[39] In talking of the divine relationships as of personal properties or characteristics one should keep in mind, though, that they are not parts of the divine essence or in any other way formal components that enter into composition with the divine nature.

Gilbert's classification of the personal relationships in the divine as externally affixed might lead one to suspect that he would agree with Abelard that the ternary of persons is in some way accidental in comparison to the real or substantial unity of the divine essence. But this is not the case. To Gilbert it is a matter of the utmost importance to stress that each of the personal properties in the divine are accompanied by true unity, and that the Trinity of persons is no less "real" than the unity of the divine essence. For this reason Gilbert rejects Abelard's distinction between "*tria*" and "*tres*" and claims that the personal properties as well as the divine persons are numerically "three" in the masculine (*tres*) as well as in the neuter (*tria*) (176,28ff. and 178,83ff.). In the same vein Gilbert maintains that the word "person" is not a relative term when said of a divine person. This is due to the fact that the personal properties cause the divine persons to be what they are, and this is reflected in the substantial or *per se* manner in which "*persona*" is predicated of the three persons (152,23ff.).

By insisting on both the true numerical unity of the divine and the equally real numerical ternary of persons, Gilbert obviously gives up reaching a final answer to the question of how God is both one and three. His interpretation of the personal relationships in the divine is also far from providing a solution to the problem of how the absolute simplicity and singularity of divine nature can be reconciled with a true ternary of divine persons. This might be seen as a sign of failure on Gilbert's part, but this is not how Gilbert saw things. To him it is absolutely evident that the divine Trinity is a mystery and remains so in this life (148,77ff.). Theological exposition or the intellectual perception of faith does not in any way dissolve the mystery because intellectual cognition of things divine is strictly partial, as Gilbert underlines. On the other hand, this does not imply that the efforts of the theologian are in vain. To Gilbert the point of theology is to delineate the mystery in rational terms and thus to elucidate the mystery as far as possible. This requires an extensive training on the part of the theologian in the sciences, and one of the main tasks of the theologian consists in making clear the true meaning of statements about God and determining the appropriateness of similes. On this basis, Gilbert stresses, it is possible to refute heretics and assist the small ones in acquiring some understanding of the grounds of faith.[40]

Abelard's and Gilbert's Contributions to Theology

It should be clear that Abelard and Gilbert shared several convictions of principal importance in theology. They both agreed that the primary object of theology, namely divine nature, is incommensurable with the structure of human language, and that theological perception can be expressed only in terms of human language. Equally, to both this entails that linguistic and logical analysis are indipensable tools in theological work. Accordingly, it was as theologians that Gilbert and Abelard insisted on the necessity that theologians master grammatical and semantical analysis as well as logic. Likewise, both of them made a point of stressing that the authoritative writings of tradition should be read with a keen eye to the context, just as they demonstrated the importance of identifying and properly expounding figurative speech in Scripture as well as in the writings of the Church Fathers.

In spite of their agreement on these points of principle, it cannot be denied that Abelard and Gilbert differed significantly in the way they put them to use. One highly revealing example of this is their very divergent ways of elucidating the word "person" as applied to the divine. In explaining this, Abelard built on his protracted investigation into the different meanings of the terms "same" and "different," just as he attached major importance to his grammatical simile. To Gilbert semantical analysis was no less important than to Abelard. Nonetheless, Gilbert's analysis is markedly different insofar as, ultimately, it was founded on a perception of the ontological criteria that justify ascribing this term to objects in the created world as well as in the divine.

This difference between the two theologians was of consequence for their different explanations of why it is legitimate to talk of personal properties in God. Both recognized that there are no personal properties in God if the term is taken to designate inherent forms. Equally, they agreed that the personal properties are derived from the relationships existing between the three persons, and that ascribing personal properties to the divine persons is only warranted insofar as they are understood as reflections of the personal relations. However, Abelard's analysis of what "person" signifies in the divine does not assist him significantly in explaining why it is warranted to talk of personal properties in God; in fact, it is difficult to avoid the impression that he accepted this usage solely on the basis of tradition. Gilbert, on the other hand, was able to provide a fuller explanation since his analysis had furnished him with the distinction between inherent and circumstantial or externally affixed accidents, and ascribing personal properties to the divine persons became less problematic insofar as it could be justified on the basis of the way in which externally affixed accidents relate to the divine persons.[41]

Partial agreement between Abelard and Gilbert is also apparent in their views of the nature of theology. They agreed that God's unique being far surpasses the capacity of man, and that man's perception of the divine is strictly limited in this life. Equally, they shared the conviction that the purpose of theology is to explicate what is believed. To both, this exposition and elucidation is rational in the sense that it brings at least some understanding of the contents of confession.

Nonetheless, Abelard and Gilbert differ significantly in their perceptions of the sources of theological cognition. To Abelard revelation is not limited to Scripture and ecclesiastical tradition but includes the legacy of the respectable philosophers of antiquity. In some respects, Abelard found, the thinkers of antiquity surpassed the prophets of Israel, and an example of this is their description of the relationship between Father and Son in God. This does not imply that the philosophers, in Abelard's view, had a higher standing than the prophets, but merely that God also used the philosophers as channels of revelation by granting them superior intellectual capacity.

To Gilbert theological cognition is intimately linked to faith and is a direct gift of God in the same way as faith. This means that Gilbert viewed theology as a part of the order of salvation as well as a necessary element in the life of the church, and in this respect – as in most others – he closely followed his intellectual mentor, Augustine. To Gilbert, however, this fundamental view of theological cognition as a special gift of grace did not imply that theology is in any way less rational or intellectually demanding than the other sciences. In fact, to Gilbert the rationality of theology is such that in very important respects theology has to correct the perceptions of other sciences, which is to say the perceptions of philosophy or natural man.[42] As regards the testimony of the philosophers of Antiquity, Gilbert was convinced that as heathens they had nothing substantial to contribute in matters divine.

Another and much more elusive difference between Abelard and Gilbert can be discerned in their treatments of the divine Trinity. Gilbert's manner of dealing with this issue reveals that his primary objective was to rationally identify the core of the mystery. This is to say that Gilbert's efforts were primarily directed at finding a way to talk of the Trinity which would exclude linguistic ambiguities and superficial difficulties of logic. By establishing the basic terms and the fundamental rules, Gilbert did not think that he had solved the mystery of the Trinity. He was convinced, however, that he had identified and delimited the persisting core of the mystery.

Abelard's treatment of the divine Trinity is, in principle, not very much different from Gilbert's. Abelard did not pretend to solve the problem of how three persons are one in nature, or how one nature agrees with a ternary of persons. On more than one occasion he expressly granted that these questions must of necessity remain without final answers in this life.[43] What Abelard did claim was that he had provided preliminary answers to these questions, and, in general, he maintained that the theologian's task is to find answers that are as close to the truth and as convincing as possible. For this reason the similes he invented in the *Theologia "Summi Boni"* and later elaborated on were intended to assist believers in approaching the truth; and this is true even of Abelard's highly abstract similes that were drawn from the sciences of grammar and logic.[44]

Putting this rather subtle difference between Abelard and Gilbert into rather crude – and easily misunderstood – terms, one may say that Abelard's treatment of the Trinity is "positive" in the sense that it is directed towards finding as much of an answer as is possible in this world. Gilbert's treatment, on the other hand, is less positive or optimistic insofar as his main concern was to outline the very core of the Trinitarian mystery.

In their own time, Abelard and Gilbert suffered the misfortune of being misunderstood by most of their intellectual peers. To Abelard the consequences of this were much more severe than to Gilbert. Nevertheless, both theologians also enjoyed the very good fortune of having bright pupils who understood the main lesson of their masters, that is, that theology should aspire to clarity of thought as well as expression. Through these pupils Peter Abelard and Gilbert of Poitiers gave a new and enduring direction to theology as it was cultivated in the medieval schools.

Notes

I wish to thank Dr. Russell L. Friedman, University of Copenhagen, for his valuable comments on this chapter.

1 Here the common modern spellings of the names of the two theologians will be used. However, the historically correct forms seem to be "Petrus Abaelardus" and "Gilbertus Porreta"; see Mews (1988) and Pelster (1944–9).

2 See John of Salisbury (1929), p. 119, where John underlines that only fools will reject something true simply because it was advanced by a modern author such as Abelard, Gilbert, or Adam.

3 See Otto of Freising (1974), pp. 224–6.

4 Abelard's *Theologia* occupied him for the last twenty years of his life. Though much of the groundwork has been laid by Mews (1985a), (1987a), and (1987b), a detailed interpretation of the intellectual development reflected in the various "redactions" of Abelard's *Theologia* has not been undertaken yet.

Obviously, this is not the place to try to fill this gap, and it must be granted that a presentation of Abelard's theology based only on the first version of the work cannot do full justice to his thought.

5 A fuller account of Gilbert's theology and philosophy as well as the methodological problems posed by Gilbert's writings is to be found in the first part of Nielsen (1982).

6 An accurate summary of Abelard's biography as well as the ambiguities of Abelard's autobiographical account is supplied by Marenbon (1997). Major biographies have been written by Grane (1970) and Clanchy (1997).

7 His later epithet "*Palatinus*" was derived from his place of birth.

8 For this debate on universals, see, e.g., Marenbon (1997), pp. 174ff., and de Libera (1996), pp. 148ff.

9 It was Abelard's autobiography which prompted the subsequent exchange of letters between Heloise and Abelard. The correspondence is easily accessible in Abelard (1974).

10 The pope's precipitate decision of the appeal case was not too surprising inasmuch as Bernard had been instrumental in bringing about the recognition of Innocent as pope in the 1130s and was the pope's confidant.

11 For a survey of Abelard's literary legacy, see Mews (1995). Abelard authored not only didactic works but also hymns and a monastic rule for Heloise and her nuns.

12 For the disagreements among modern historians on the dating of Abelard's logical writings, see Luscombe (1988) and Marenbon (1997).

13 There are indications that Abelard composed a work on grammar in the same period, but so far not even fragments of this work have come to light; cf. the discussion in Marenbon (1997), pp. 50ff.

14 The majority of these rules appear already in the *Theologia "Summi Boni."*

15 These works, just as the various reports of Abelard's oral teaching, would clearly have to be considered in order to present a more comprehensive account of Abelard's theology; in this connection consideration of space prevents a closer examination.

16 The *Scito teipsum* is rich in original ideas and observations but its main line of argument is not always clear; cf. however Marenbon (1997).

17 Abelard considers the divine Trinity as something naturally known to man, but his reasoning on the mutual implications of power, wisdom, and goodness amounts to a semi-proof of the triune nature of God, and, in this respect, he may be said to have "anticipated" Richard of St. Victor's proof based on the nature of love.

18 References to the *Theologia "Summi Boni"* are enclosed in parentheses and have the form "1.9," which refers to section 9 in book 1.

19 Abelard's former and long-time teacher, Roscelin, had propounded a view of the Trinity according to which the divine persons were three separate beings whose unity consists in having one will. This view seems to have been inspired by Roscelin's nominalistic viewpoints in logic. It was strongly opposed by leading theologians such as Anselm of Canterbury, and Roscelin was convicted of heresy in Soissons in 1092. To Abelard, whose association with Roscelin was public knowledge, it was evidently a matter of importance to distance himself from Roscelin's theological ideas, and he apparently attacked Roscelin quite openly even before the publication of the *Theologia "Summi Boni."* Roscelin became aware of his former student's attack and replied in a very ill-spirited letter to Abelard.

20 Abelard is very careful to underline that, in talking of personal properties in God, the theologian does not attribute any kind of forms to God or the divine persons, and that it is much less misleading to talk of what is proper to the divine persons (2.104–5).

21 Abelard's refutation of the dialecticians' objections is particularly revealing of the close interrelationship between logical analysis and theological reflection in his thought.

22 With Abelard it appears to be axiomatic that the neuter indicates the substantial aspect, while the masculine and the feminine imply the personal. This distinction was widely employed in later discussions of the hypostatic union; cf. Nielsen (1999).

23 Abelard often stressed the importance of taking the context into account, since this is the only way to ascertain what the terms denote or stand for. This contextual approach is also found with Gilbert and later it was greatly refined; see Rosier (1994).

24 The division into books in the *Theologia "Summi Boni"* is slightly off as compared to the development of Abelard's argument, and this is due to the fact that Abelard chose to let his responses to the adversaries' arguments be the framework for his exposition.

25 In later versions of the work Abelard elaborated on this simile; see Bonanni (1996).

26 In actual fact, Abelard presents his general conclusion already in the conclusion to his investigation into the nature of the Son's generation. Thus he establishes first the relative nature of "Father" and "Son," and only

after this is the relative nature of "Holy Spirit" or "*donum*" established.

27 Abelard openly admits that one of the more obvious difficulties with his exposition is that linking the personal names to the attributes of power, wisdom, and goodness would seem to pave the way for claiming that there are more than three persons in God. Why shouldn't God's attributes of justice and ubiquity be regarded as divine persons? Abelard answers by pointing out that the number of divine persons is established by revelation, and that God's motive for revealing the Trinity was to describe divine goodness and to incite gratitude in man and to further religious worship. In order to accomplish this God did not need to introduce more than three persons since this number is sufficient for indicating the supreme good and for enabling man to understand the nature of divine persons without falling victim to misconceptions (2.114–16).

The same line of thought is at the bottom of Abelard's famous grammatical simile. According to this the ternary of persons may be likened to the fact that one and the same person may be viewed as both the speaker, the one spoken to, and that of which others talk. This simile, Abelard thought, is particularly apposite inasmuch as it prevents the misconception that God is more than three persons (2.108–9).

28 Otto of Freising (1974), p. 226. Gilbert's criticism of Abelard's Trinitarian doctrine seems to point in the opposite direction, i.e., towards tritheism, but it is not clear which version of the *Theologia* Gilbert had read; see below, section 6. Judging from Abelard's – admittedly biased – account in the *Historia Calamitatum* the proceedings at the council were utterly confused and gave Abelard no opportunity to present his case.

29 An example of this is Abelard's brief description of the Incarnation. Thus Abelard maintains that the statement that God's wisdom became incarnate is equivalent to saying that God became incarnate in order to teach man by the spoken word as well as by his bodily example (3.45).

30 Obviously, the importance of the close personal relations between Eugenius and Bernard should not be overlooked in connection with Gilbert's trial.

31 For a fuller list of works that have been or might be ascribed to Gilbert see Nielsen (1982), pp. 42ff. To these should be added the *sententiae* which were published by Häring (1978–9).

32 One of the great challenges in editing Gilbert's biblical commentaries is the fact that the author quotes extensively from the writings of the Church Fathers, and that innumerable brief quotations are implicit and have been fitted seamlessly into the text.

33 References to Gilbert's commentaries on Boethius are enclosed in parentheses and have the form "61,1," which refers to page 61, line 1 in Häring's edition.

34 See Nielsen (1982), pp. 115ff. Gilbert does not spell out whether illumination brings about new knowledge in the sense of directly imparting new knowledge or in the sense of enabling the illuminated intellect to discern the reasons for belief. In this respect Gilbert is no less clear than many other thinkers who belong to the Augustinian tradition.

35 Gilbert's analysis is somewhat more complicated, but this is not of immediate importance in this connection; cf. Nielsen (1982), pp. 47ff.; de Rijk (1987) and (1988–9) as well as Knuuttila (1987) and (1993), pp. 75ff.

36 See Nielsen (1982), pp. 158ff.

37 See van Elswijk (1966), p. 266 n. 1, or Nielsen (1982), p. 135 n. 77, for the pertinent text from Gilbert's commentary on Paul.

38 For this, see Nielsen (1982), pp. 58ff.

39 To Gilbert, this shift from relationship to personal property is facilitated by the fact that, with Gilbert, the science of "mathematics" classifies externally affixed accidents in the same manner as inherent formal principles; cf. Nielsen (1982), pp. 92ff.

40 Gilbert's notorious and – even in his own work – "paradoxical" distinction between "*Deus*" and "*divinitas*" strongly indicates the ultimate insufficiency of theological explanation. For a discussion of this distinction, see Nielsen (1982), pp. 158ff.

41 This difference between Abelard's and Gilbert's theological conceptions is certainly also due to their divergent positions in dialectics: Abelard had ties to the school of the so-called "*vocales*," whereas Gilbert belonged to the moderate realists; see Iwakuma (1992).

42 To Gilbert it is perfectly clear that theology is of the greatest importance for a true understanding of created nature, and that theology modifies many of the natural perceptions of man; for this, see Nielsen (1982), pp. 136ff.

43 In the 1130s Walter of Mortagne took exception to the provocative claim made by some of Abelard's students that their master had rationally explained the divine Trinity. Abelard hastened to ascertain that his *Theo-logia* did not lend support to this mistaken impression; see Mews (1987b), p. 217, and cf. Mews (1985a), pp. 146ff.

44 From Abelard's treatment of the Trinity it appears that, in his view, divine attributes such as power, wisdom, and goodness are much more readily understood than the divine persons and their relationships. Without this presupposition it would be nearly impossible to understand Abelard's argument in the *Theologia "Summi Boni."*

Bibliography

Abelard, Peter (1950), *Historia Calamitatum*, ed. J. T. Muckle. Medieval Studies, 12, pp. 162–213.

Abelard, Peter (1969a), *Opera Theologica*, vol. 2, ed. E. M. Buytaert. Corpus Christianorum, Continuatio Mediaevalis, vol. 12. Turnhout.

Abelard, Peter (1969b), "Theologia Christiana," in Abelard (1969a), pp. 69–372.

Abelard, Peter (1970), *Dialogus inter Philoso-phum, Iudaeum et Christianum*, ed. R. Thomas. Stuttgart.

Abelard, Peter (1971), "Scito teipsum," in Luscombe (1971).

Abelard, Peter (1974), *The Letters of Abelard and Heloise*, trans. B. Radice. Harmondsworth.

Abelard, Peter (1976–7), *Sic et Non*, eds. B. Boyer and R. McKeon. Chicago/London.

Abelard, Peter (1987a), *Opera Theologica*, vol. 3, eds. E. M. Buytaert and C. J. Mews. Corpus Christianorum, Continuatio Mediaevalis, vol. 13. Turnhout.

Abelard, Peter (1987b), "Theologia 'Summi Boni,'" in Abelard (1987a), pp. 83–201.

Abelard, Peter (1987c), "Theologia 'Scholarium,'" in Abelard (1987a), pp. 309–549.

Bonanni, S. P. (1996), "Parlare della trinità. Lettura della 'Theologia Scholarium' di Abelardo." *Analecta Gregoriana*, vol. 268. Rome.

Clanchy, M. T. (1997), *Abelard: A Medieval Life*. Oxford.

de Libera, A. (1996), *La querelle des universaux: De Platon à la fin du Moyen Age*. Paris.

de Rijk, L. M. (1987), "Gilbert de Poitiers: ses vues sémantiques et métaphysiques," in Jolivet and de Libera (1987).

de Rijk, L. M. (1988–9), "Semantics and Metaphysics in Gilbert of Poitiers: A Chapter in Twelfth-Century Platonism." *Vivarium*, vol. 26, pp. 73–112, and vol. 27, pp. 1–35.

Dronke, P. (ed.) (1988), *A History of Twelfth-Century Western Philosophy*. Cambridge.

Ebbesen, S. and R. L. Friedman (eds.) (1999), *Medieval Analyses in Language and Cognition*. The Royal Danish Academy of Sciences and Letters, "Historisk-filosofiske Meddelelser," vol. 77. Copenhagen.

Gilbert of Poitiers (1966), *The Commentaries on Boethius by Gilbert of Poitiers*, ed. N. M. Häring. *Studies and Texts*, vol. 13. Toronto.

Grane, L. (1970), *Peter Abelard: Philosophy and Christianity in the Middle Ages*. London.

Häring, N. M. (1978–9), "Die 'Sententiae Magistri Gisleberti Pictavensis Episcopi.'" *Archives d'histoire doctrinale et littéraire du moyen age*, tom. 45, pp. 83–180, and tom. 46, pp. 45–105.

Iwakuma, Y. (1992), "'Vocales,' or Early Nominalists." *Traditio*, 47, pp. 37–111.

John of Salisbury (1929), *Metalogicon*, ed. C. C. I. Webb. Oxford.

Jolivet, J. (1969), "Arts du langage et théologie chez Abélard." *Études de philosophie médiévale*, tom. 57. Paris.

Jolivet, J. and A. de Libera (eds.) (1987), "Gilbert de Poitiers et ses contemporains. Aux origines de la 'Logica Modernorum.'" *History of Logic*, 5. Naples.

Jolivet, J. (1997), *La théologie d'Abélard*. Initiations au Moyen Age. Paris.

Knuuttila, S. (1987), "Possibility and Necessity in Gilbert of Poitiers," in Jolivet and de Libera (1987), pp. 199–218.

Knuuttila, S. (1993), *Modalities in Medieval Philosophy*. London.

Luscombe, D. (1971), *Peter Abelard's "Ethics."* Oxford.

Luscombe, D. (1988), "Peter Abelard," in Dronke (1988), pp. 279–307.

Marenbon, John (1997), *The Philosophy of Peter Abelard*. Cambridge.

Mews, C. J. (1985a), "Peter Abelard's (Theologia Christiana) and (Theologia 'Scholarium') Re-examined." *Recherches de Théologie ancienne et médiévale*, tom. 52, Louvain, pp. 109–58.

Mews, C. J. (1985b), "On the Dating of the Works of Peter Abelard." *Archives d'histoire doctrinale et littéraire du Moyen Age*, tom. 52, pp. 73–134.

Mews, C. J. (1987a), "Petri Abaelardi Theologia 'Summi Boni'. Introduction," in Abelard (1987a), pp. 15–81.

Mews, C. J. (1987b), "Petri Abaelardi Theologia 'Scholarium'. Introduction," in Abelard (1987a), pp. 203–308.

Mews, C. J. (1988), "In Search of a Name and Its Significance," *Traditio*, vol. 44, pp. 171–200.

Mews, C. J. (1995), *Peter Abelard*. Authors of the Middle Ages, II, 5 – Historical and Religious Writers of the Latin West. Aldershot.

Nielsen, L. O. (1982), *Theology and Philosophy in the Twelfth Century*. Acta theologica Danica, 15. Leiden.

Nielsen, L. O. (1999), "Logic and the Hypostatic Union: Two Late Twelfth-Century Responses to the Papal Condemnation of 1177," in Ebbesen and Friedman (1999), pp. 251–79.

Otto of Freising (1974), *Gesta Frederici seu rectius Cronica*, ed. F.-J. Schmale. Ausgewählte Quellen zur deutschen Geschichte des Mittelalters, Bd. 17. Darmstadt.

Pelster, F. (1944–9), "Gilbert de la Porrée, Gilbertus Porretanus oder Gilbert Porreta?" *Scholastik*, Bd. 19–24, pp. 401–3.

Rosier, Irene (1994), *La parole comme acte: Sur la grammaire et la sémantique au XIIIe siècle*. Paris.

van Elswijk, H. C. (1966), *Gilbert Porreta: Sa vie, son oeuvre, sa pensée*. Spicilegium Sacrum Lovaniense, tom. 33. Louvain.

Bernard of Clairvaux, William of St. Thierry, the Victorines

chapter 9

Emero Stiegman

Running parallel to Anselm of Canterbury's innovative drive, as continued by Abelard's generation of "schoolmen," was a great movement of theological summation and renewal centering on monastic life. The new "scholastic" system in formation would become so normative in succeeding centuries as to replace the monastic style, rendering it opaque, virtually deprived of the title *theology*. One of the successes of twentieth-century scholarship has been the recovery, identification, and reevaluation of this "monastic theology."

From the initial triumph of monasticism in the fourth century, through its flowering in the twelfth, it was inevitable that theology should become monastic. Other than bishops, the virtuosi of religious reflection were monks, functioning in an elite environment – addressing monks, offering a biblical interpretation of the experience of monks. These writers assumed their community to be the Church. In the twelfth century, roughly calculated as from 1075 to 1200, the tradition achieved an impressive maturity.[1] The roll of honor is long, including authors from among the traditional Benedictines (e.g., Rupert of Deutz, Peter the Venerable, Peter of Celle, Arnald of Bonneval). But, among both monks and the quasi-monastic canons regular, it was the powerful movement of reform that channeled the energy of religious thought. Outstanding were the Cistercians and the Victorine canons. Here, we will focus on the Cistercians Bernard of Clairvaux and William of St. Thierry and on the regular canons Hugh and Richard of St. Victor. To view their work merely as preparation for a subsequent movement – i.e., as "early scholastic" – would be to misread it.

Monastic theology can be differentiated from that of the schoolmen in its source, its objective, and its method – though it is easy to exaggerate the differences of these two modes of religious thought and, perhaps unwisely, to disengage them.

The supreme source for both was the Bible – for the monks, as that which was devoutly sung in the *opus Dei*; for the "schoolmen," as required proof-texts in their argumentation. The monasteries were well stocked also with patristic manuscripts in which a theology could be found that had flowed into the Middle

Ages.[2] The monks trusted it more simply than the "schoolmen." In later generations, particularly among the sixteenth-century reformers, a decayed scholastic
theology would be criticized for lacking contact with the patristic heritage.[3] Out
of esteem for St. Bernard's theological approach, some Renaissance humanists
would dub the abbot "Last of the Fathers."[4]

The objective of monastic reflection upon Bible texts was contemplative prayer
(*contemplatio*). For the *magistri* of the schools, different pastoral concerns and
the need for precise doctrine led, instead, from *lectio* to *disputatio*. The quest for
order was pervasive. Monastic writers plotted the lines of an *ordinatio caritatis*
(cf. Song 2:4), the ordering of all reality to the love that originates in God and
must return to God.[5] To the early scholastics, the more urgent problem of order
was dialectics, the rules of discursive reasoning.

The two styles differed also in method. While the schoolmen struggled to
understand the data of faith through a more extensive application of dialectic –
standing, as it were, on the traditional *credo ut intelligam* (I belive so that I may
understand) – monastic theologians showed greater confidence in the more concrete and synthesizing appeal to experience: *credo ut experiar* (I believe that I may
experience). Though they argued for the revelatory function of love, in which
alone God was "known," they did not denigrate the role of reason. This difference in method made for contrasts in the use of language. The monk's purpose
could be achieved only in the full linguistic range of poetic prose, the manner of
language of the Bible itself. The schoolmen, instead, believed that precise doctrinal definition was possible only in the abstract vocabulary of analysis. Their
efforts, through several generations, would produce – for better and for worse –
the technical vocabulary of scholasticism.

In the twelfth century, the two ways of doing theology thrived side by side,
though at the beginning the entry of early scholasticism had met with some
hostility. Its use of dialectic had not always been free of what Landgraf called
frenzied indiscrimination.[6] Jean Leclercq finds in monastic authors such as John
of Fécamp, Peter Damian, and Lanfranc "a certain fear" of dialectics as applied to
sacred texts.[7] Resistance to a growing trend toward speculation may explain why
even St. Anselm, powerfully innovative in his effort to introduce an increased but
balanced application of dialectic to the quest for religious knowledge, is poorly
represented in many monastic libraries of the period.[8]

The writings of twelfth-century monastic theology lie on the earlier side of a
significant cultural divide, the replacement of earlier platonizing modes of thought
by later scholastic adaptations of the writings of Aristotle. Only a philosophical
naiveté would pronounce the older literature less valuable on that account.

Bernard of Clairvaux

No medieval theologian offered a clearer vision of the operations of grace *within*
and *through* human nature itself than St. Bernard. The theological anthropology
supporting his doctrine was common to the monastic tradition, but nowhere did

its power to illuminate emerge so strongly as through the psychological astute-ness and linguistic mastery of the Abbot of Clairvaux.

Bernard is the "cloistered" monk who traversed Europe resolving a papal schism, who upbraided pope and emperor, dislodged archbishops from their sees, pur-sued heretics, and preached the Second Crusade, all the while writing prolifically and leading the broadest reform in monastic history. He is the aggressive polemi-cist who exhibits the energy of his era and suffers its myopia as his readers today suffer the limitations of vision of their own age. To read him as theologian, one does well to turn away from the highly-colored surface of twelfth-century con-frontations – acknowledging its potential for distraction – and to seek out, in-stead, the contemplative who escorted Dante to the throne of the Trinity. The two personae are sometimes difficult to reconcile. In the man of action, we find contradictions;[9] in the theologian (when he is given a hearing), consistency, depth, and heuristic strength.

Bernard (b. 1090) sprang from the lower nobility of Burgundy. At the age of 22, he interrupted a literary education to join the "new monastery" at Cîteaux, entering with the thirty companions he had gathered. Abbot Stephen Harding sent this young man of legendary magnetism, only two years later, to found the monastery of Clairvaux. The Cistercian reform became the great cause in Bernard's life. Much of his intervening in ecclesiastical politics would be in the interest of his own foundations, even (it seems) when this objective was unacknowledged;[10] and the largest part of his literary output would take the form of sermons to his monks.

The eight large volumes of Bernard's works include the series of 86 *Sermons on the Song of Songs*, recognized as the masterpiece of the genre, *Sermons on Differ-ent Topics*, *Sermons on the Liturgical Year*; tracts such as *The Steps of Humility and Pride*, *Apologia to William of St. Thierry*, *On Precept and Dispensation*, *On Loving God*, *On Grace and Free Choice*; and 547 letters, which the author col-lected and reedited before his death in 1153.[11] In a generation of ambitious Latinists, Bernard was a stylist without superior.

Observing his manner, as he assumes the role of watchdog of orthodoxy against Abelard and Gilbert of Poitiers, one would hardly suspect that he is himself a theologian whose originality and intellectual daring sometimes surpass theirs. He was drawn into these and other controversies, sometimes inadvisedly, through the insistence of alarmed friends, who saw him as heir to the doctrinal authority that passed from Anselm of Canterbury to the School of Laon and its masters, Anselm of Laon and William of Champeaux.[12]

Bernard's opposition to the *magistri* of the cathedral schools was highly quali-fied. His own theological education, derived in large measure from reading the Fathers, was strengthened through close contact with former schoolmen like William of Champeaux and his great friend William of St. Thierry. He promoted the careers of scholars like Peter Lombard, Robert of Poule, and John of Salis-bury; and, among those seeking his theological counsel was Hugh of St. Victor.[13] One of his interventions demonstrates his concern about exactness in doctrine and his feeling of responsibility as a theologian: he wrote an unsolicited letter to the canons of Lyons opposing, in fine dialectical form, their doctrine of the Immaculate Conception of Mary.[14] When circumstances required, Bernard's argumentation moved with a brisk logic; his distinctions were sharp, his definitions precise. Drawing overly simple contrasts between monastic and scholastic theology can obscure such facts.

The image of Bernard as a reactionary obscurantist in his confrontation with Abelard and Gilbert is, one may suspect, a partisan construct; something of it may be history's revenge for the undeserved image of his opponents that he himself projected, in the acrimonious style that was Christendom's traditional dialogue with "heretics": they were rationalists devoid of faith.[15] Disposing of both notions is, for our present purposes, more urgent than reviewing the two trials for a judgment; because, whereas nothing of what distinguishes St. Bernard the theologian occurs in its finest form in these trials, misconceptions about a great religious thinker have persisted.

Bernard's deepest concerns will be discovered, not in assessing his role as *defensor fidei* against his adversaries, but in seeking in their doctrine what disturbed him as a contemplative monk.[16] For instance, if we hold a matter of faith as the best available hypothesis, an opinion – an *aestimatio* (or *existimatio*, as Abelard said) – then reason becomes the final arbiter, and the monk's mystical ascent loses its grounding.[17] A similar dynamic is present in the rejection of Abelard's view of the reason for the Incarnation.[18]

Abelard was condemned at the Council of Sens (1140). Eight years later, at the Council of Reims, the conflict with Gilbert of Poitiers was resolved, this time with less deference to Bernard from the pope and the bishops.[19] Later, in sermons 80–2 on the Song of Songs, as the abbot reminisced on the debate, Gilbert's preoccupation with the linguistic problem of predication (the question of universals) was dismissed in the face of perceived threats to the metaphysical soundness of doctrines such as God's simplicity[20] and the soul's affinity to God (*naturarum tanta cognatio*)[21] – postulates in Bernard's contemplative system.[22] We must look for the root and trunk of the abbot's theology, then, not in his well chronicled public disputes, but in writings where he controls the agenda.

Christology

At the heart of Bernard's thought is Christology. The emphasis this author places on the humanity of Christ reflects the monastic tradition of *lectio divina*, a private meditative reading of Scripture which draws a reader imaginatively into the event; it is a new emphasis in theological literature.[23] He believed that the reason for the Incarnation included God's wish to be known by us. He writes,

> I think this is the principal reason why the invisible God willed to be seen in the flesh and to converse with humans as a human. He wanted to recapture the affections of carnal beings who were unable to live in any other way, by first drawing them to the salutary love of his own humanity, and then gradually to raise them to a spiritual love.[24]

Bernard's treatment of "the carnal love of Christ" sets him apart. Working in the tradition of Origen's commentary on the Song of Songs, he nevertheless overrules the rejection he finds there (and in Gregory of Nyssa) of the flesh (*caro*).[25] In the flesh we are bonded to Christ. The Word became flesh and dwelt among us to show God's lovableness, to attract our human love. The flesh, then, may be other than that *caro* which resists *spiritus* (Rom. 8:1). "That carnal love which eliminates the carnal life is good."[26] Bernardine expressions of this love can be strikingly lyrical: "I recognize you, Lord Jesus, so beautifully formed [*formosus*] in my very form!"[27] Martin Luther exclaimed (1537) that there was "no friendlier word on earth" than Bernard's phrase naming Christ "bone of my bone and flesh of my flesh" (Gen. 2:23).[28]

God's lovableness is ever before us in the *memoria Christi*, in which the mysteries of Christ's life – commemorated in Bernard's sermons of the liturgical year – and the hope of his promises are revisited. This vivifying memory is the work of the Holy Spirit.[29]

Anthropomorphic language about God, when referred to the Incarnation, is the literal truth: in Christ, God has human feelings, hands, feet, and lips. In the Sermons on the Song of Songs, the Christ who is spouse of the Church makes it possible to speak in quite physical ways of the eternal Word as bridegroom of the soul.

St. Bernard is the principal literary source of that tender devotion to the humanity of Christ found in Western piety, from the Nativity crèche of Francis of Assisi to the oratorios of J. S. Bach. The frequent denaturing of this piety into devotionalism represents a failure to follow our devout theologian as he advances from the *memoria Christi* to the invisible ever-present resurrected Lord. In Bernard's pedagogy of the Incarnation, Christ incites a carnal love only as the gracious starting point of an ascent:

> Afterwards he showed them a higher degree of love when he said, "It is the Spirit who gives life, the flesh profits nothing" [John 6:64]. I think Paul had reached this level when he said: "Even if we once knew Christ in the body, we know him thus no longer" [2 Cor. 5:16]. Perhaps this was also true of the Prophet who said: "A Spirit before our face is Christ the Lord" [Lam. 4:20]. When he adds: "Under his shadow we will live among the heathen," he seems to me to speak on behalf of the beginners, in order that they may at least rest in the shade since they know they are not strong enough to bear the heat of the sun. They may be nourished by the sweetness of his humanity since they are not yet able to perceive the things which are of the Spirit of God [1 Cor. 2:14]. The shade of Christ, I suggest, is his flesh which overshadowed Mary and tempered for her the bright splendor of the Spirit [Luke 1:35].[30]

The carnal love of Christ is to become rational and then move on to a spiritual love.[31] Bernard makes his point succinctly speaking of Mary Magdalene at the Easter tomb. " 'Do not touch me, for I have not yet ascended to my Father [John 20:17].' As if to say he could be touched by her, and wished to be, only after his ascension."[32] The mystery of Christ's life most celebrated in the abbot's preaching was the Ascension.[33] Beyond piety, what is set forth is a doctrine on the soteriological role of the human Christ and of the relation of Jesus to the eternal Word.

The question of Christ's relation to those human beings who do not know him is taken up with surprising clarity in the tract *On Loving God*. The advance to perfect love of God is traced here in the human person as such, in *homo* or *consors naturae* (Dil. 23), in one gifted with reason (Dil. 4). All people can respond to the loving God redemptively at work within them. Those who do not know Christ, the *infideles,* may have faith nevertheless, even while not enjoying awareness of the direct way to God, which is Christ.[34]

Ecclesiology

Bernard's ecclesiology is of a piece with his mystical doctrine.[35] His concentration upon the Word and the soul as bridegroom and bride of the Song of Songs is justified, he insists, only in so far as the individual soul is a member of the Church, the true bride of Christ (Eph. 5:32).[36] This vision of oneness among the members he continually links to the doctrine of Christ's Mystical Body, rejoicing over the unity of the Church on earth and in heaven.[37] The ecclesial sense is strong, shown both in contemplative sermons and in *Five Books on Consideration,* where Bernard counsels his former pupil, Pope Eugenius III, to resist the aggrandizement of an imperial papacy and claim only what is "of apostolic right."[38] Prelates are to exhibit the motherly virtues of Jesus;[39] and heretics are to be persuaded, not persecuted or put to flight.[40]

But for all his engagement in the institution, Bernard held, as Congar has said, a very monastic idea of the Church.[41] The Church was preexistent among the angels.[42] Humans are called to fill their fallen ranks, joining "the Church of the perfect."[43] What John saw (Rev. 21:2–3) coming down from heaven, the new Jerusalem, adorned as a bride for her husband, was the Church.[44] It exists now in exile on the earth, which is "the land of unlikeness."[45]

A traditional patristic view holding members of the Church to be of three orders (*ordines*) had devolved into the concept of three grades of perfection (*gradus*), in which the lowest belonged to the laity. In applying essential Christian categories to the monastery – especially in referring the ecclesial imagery of the Song of Songs to monks – Bernard joined this trend.[46] He shared his era's unexamined notion of the place of the laity.

The sacraments of the Church occupy little space in the saint's writings. But when in about 1125 Hugh of St. Victor wrote to him, submitting three questions on Baptism, Bernard responded with a compact tract (letter 77), uncharacteristically academic, in the manner of the schoolmen.[47] In Hugh's treatment of Baptism in his *De Sacramentis,* we find not only many of Bernard's ideas but some of his precise language.

The abbot speaks of the Eucharist rarely and with little of his characteristic affectivity.[48] He must content himself, he laments, with the "husk of the sacrament" instead of the kernel of the Word.[49] For, "what does eating his flesh and drinking his blood mean other than being mindful of (*communicare*) his passion and imitating the life (*conversationem*) he led in the flesh?"[50] Faith in what was later to be labeled the real presence was never in question.[51] But the abbot of Clairvaux would allow no one to lose sight of the Church itself, the bride of Christ and one body with him, as the great Sacrament, with discrete specifications of its essence in the liturgical sacraments. Posterity has argued over his idea of causality in the sacraments but has paid scant attention to his emphasis upon their communicative sign-value.[52]

Anthropology

The exhortation to listen and to reflect is constant in Bernard the contemplative. His theological anthropology has an existential starting-point in self-knowledge, where we discover the majesty of what we are in creation and the misery of our sinfulness. The tension between the two becomes an incitement to return to the Creator's plan and become, gradually, what we *are*. In its abiding con-sciousness of the human reality as God's image, as therefore called in its very nature from the moment of creation to respond to an ineffable love, Bernard's concept of the human being is markedly optimistic. His only concern is that the self in relation to God will fail to discern the source of its beauty: "There are two facts you must know: first, what you are; second, that you are not that by your own power."[53] Failure here will produce a false self, one "twisted" to forming *propria*, things we see as our own (*ad propriam retorquere*); we become divided and lose our *selves*."[54] The tension disappears when, in the perfect love of God, there is no longer any "gnawing concern over what is ours" (*nulla mordente cura de proprio*).[55]

Bernard's confident view of human nature – his faith that the resources sup-plied by a loving God pour into us (from God's freedom and not from our merit) with the predictability of the processes of plant growth – is expressed in the optimistic imagery of the early twelfth century, when natural growth was the dominant metaphor.[56] He finds the "root" of fraternal charity (Luke 10:27) in a certain primordial reciprocal attraction among humans: it "takes on, as if from the moisture of the soil, the force of vegetation, through which, as grace breathes down from above, it bears the fruit of a caring concern [*pietatis*]."[57]

The imagery of flower and fruit are used even to gloss Paul's statement, "All that does not proceed from faith is sin" (Rom. 14:23): "Hence there is no fruit without flower or good work without faith" – a way of saying that the flowering of our nature is the work of redemptive grace.[58] To map the process of growth in divine love – the action of God within the soul – he studies the experience of humans as such rather than of Christians. His models in the tract *On Loving God* (*De diligendo Deo*) are the *infideles*, and in them he traces the "natural" move-ment of the soul from self-love to the perfect love of God.[59]

When Bernard speaks of nature, the role of divine grace is never in doubt. The *affectio naturalis*, evolving as love grows but never eliminated, is an eros planted in the soul; it can be satisfied only in God.[60] *Agape* (1 John 4:8) exercises its agency through this eros.

> I said above that God is the reason [*causa*] for loving God. That is right, for he is the efficient and final cause of our love. He offers the opportunity, creates the affection, and consummates the desire. He makes himself, or rather he is made [cf. John 1:14], lovable; . . . His love prepares and rewards ours. [61]

To be distinguished from redemptive grace (*gratia salvans*), then, is the grace received in creation itself (*gratia creans*), the divine love that constitutes us what we are, images of God. By nature we love, but only by grace (*gratia salvans*) do we love the good.[62] Sin has weakened us but not changed what we are. For strength(*virtus*) we need an added grace: "Grace sets in order what creation has given, so that virtues (*virtutes*) are nothing else than ordered affections."[63]

Bernard reflects, not upon the hypothetical possibility of God's declining to elevate humanity by withholding grace, but upon the actuality of God's presence in grace to the human person. A "merely human" level of humanity, then, has never existed.[64] A century later, the scholastics would postulate the abstraction "nature" in order to form a metaphysical theory of the "supernatural," clarifying God's absolute freedom and the unexacted quality of grace.[65] Bernard uses a different language,[66] one that can be seen to avoid the danger of an extrinsicist view of divine–human relations present in the later theoretical effort.[67]

Not drawn to metaphysical systematization, the author, nevertheless, had a view of body–soul unity that was a rough functional equivalent of theories that Aquinas would develop.[68] The body was so essential to human integrity, he opined, that the soul could not love God totally until reunited with the body in the General Resurrection.[69] One of his most used scriptural tags was, "The corruptible body weighs down the soul" (Wis. 9:15); but he adds, "because of love, not heaviness"[70] – i.e., not through its materiality but through the involvement of a sinful will. The immortality by which we are a likeness of God is compromised, he laments, in the death of the body.[71]

Yet there are ambiguities. The body's closeness to the things of earth, in the transitoriness common to material things, places us in the danger of forgetting our true home. Eve, tempted by the sensible fruit (*pulchrum . . . delectabile . . . suave*), lost her heavenly orientation.[72] The soul must avoid "attachment to earthly things, all of which return to the earth."[73] Bernard could see no intrinsic worth in the fleeting things of the temporal order.[74]

A further problem posed by the body was its sexuality. No fault attached to the use of sex in marriage (*propriam amplecti coniugem*), Bernard says.[75] But many other expressions seem to contradict this. He did not see how the *amplexus maritales* could stand together with *sanctitas*.[76] In *libido* there is sin; therefore, he said, Mary was not conceived immaculate.[77] He condemned the irrationality of coitus (*ille intemperans ardor in coitu*) and spoke of unclean seed (*de immundo conceptum semine*).[78] At several points in interpreting the Song of Songs (his *canticum spirituale*), he dismissed the idea that its imagery involved sexual feeling, "something corporeal."[79] With this, he perpetuated a difficulty in perceiving, specifically in the spousal intimacy of sex, a supernal sign value in marriage.[80]

Bernard observes, bemused, that we live under "an agreeable constraint" (*favorabilis vis*) and bear the yoke of voluntary servitude.[81] This contradiction he explains by appeal to the classic anthropology that distinguishes between our being *images* of God and our having a *likeness* to God (Gen. 1:26). The tension between the two gives a characteristic dynamism to early Cistercian thought on the human condition.[82]

The abbot offers a systematic exposition of the theme in *On Grace and Free Choice* (*De gratia et libero arbitrio*), a work that becomes part of the theological tradition.[83] He demonstrates originality with respect to his predecessors, Augustine and Anselm of Canterbury, particularly in his triple distinction of the states of liberty:[84] The divine image in the soul is found in *liberum arbitrium*, our freedom from necessity, our self-determined assent on the basis of rational judgment; our likeness to God, lost in sin, consists of two elements – freedom from sin (*liberum consilium*) and freedom from misery (*liberum complacitum*) – a freedom that fixes the will in the good and eliminates all disturbance.[85] The Grace of Christ restores *liberum consilium*, our ability to avoid sin, but the full *liberum complacitum* is reserved for heaven, with brief foretastes in this life.

Later, in his *Sermons on the Song of songs* (SC 80–3), Bernard deliberately rearranges the schema, setting a more obvious Pauline pattern (Rom. 3:2; Col. 1:15; Gal. 4:22, 31; etc.), while maintaining the same dynamic.[86] Christ is the image of God; but, because we are made *in* this image, we are capable of participating in the truth, wisdom, and justice of the Word. We have something of the dignity (*magnitudo*) and uprightness (*rectitudo*) of the Word, but in sin we lose this uprightness.[87] On the other hand, our likeness to the Word – i.e., simplicity, immortality, and freedom – is clouded but not lost.[88] Our freedom is caged by sin, and our immortality – through the death of the body and the changefulness of the will – is compromised.

Again one encounters this writer's awe before the mystery of human grandeur, though a brief sketch cannot convey the careful metaphysical argumentation he assembles. If he failed in his anthropology to transcend the monastic charism, he also supplied deep insights into the truth that the dynamism of grace is present in our very nature as created.

Epistemology

In Bernard's epistemology, the Augustinian concept of free choice (*liberum arbitrium*), with its integration of reasoning and freedom, is central.[89] The author strongly defends reason. The will, he writes, is a "rational movement"; and though reason, its mate, is "in some sense its follower," the will is "never moved without reason"; moreover, "there can be no wisdom in a creature except through reason."[90] Not infrequently the strong philosophical undercurrent of his writing rises to the surface.[91] His two concerns respecting reason are that its limits may be ignored – he inveighs against "the scrutinizer of majesty" (Prov. 25:27) – and that it may be isolated from a more comprehensive wisdom.

Both worries are addressed in his teaching that only in love is there a true knowledge of God. He quotes Gregory the Great's maxim, "Love itself is a knowing [*notitia*]."[92] He tells aspiring contemplatives, "He is present to God who loves God, insofar as he loves."[93] Or, "Charity is your vision."[94] Bernard's affectivity must not be allowed to mask his orientation to vision, or knowledge.[95]

In the epistemology of the abbot of Clairvaux, faith is an invitation to inquire, not the frustration of our urge to know. "Faith is a kind of voluntary, yet certain, foretaste [*prelibatio*] of the not yet apparent truth."[96] The object of Christian faith and the guarantor of its certitude is the divine Word as substantial Truth (John 17:17). The author concludes that, in the synesthesia of the spiritual senses, to hear the word (Rom. 10:17) is to see.[97] "Even to believe is to have seen."[98]

The directionality implicit in "foretaste" receives much attention. Faith is dynamic, linked to desire; it is the seed of experience. "What they [beginners] do not experience, let them believe, so that one day, by virtue of their faith, they may reap the harvest of experience."[99] But first, faith must beget desire, for "understanding is the fruit of faith; perfect love, of desire."[100] The *intellectus fidei* cannot rest in theology. Faith calls all to move toward fuller religious experience.[101]

For Bernard, this is not so much exhortation as doctrine, valid for all believers; but the assertion is offered in the language of images. "We who walk by faith (2 Cor. 5–7) live in the shadow of Christ."[102] "The shadow of faith that tempers the light to the weakened eye is good."[103] The rhetoric strives to communicate "an integral knowing,"[104] a "tasting of the good."[105] This disciplined theology of the imagination (as Leclercq calls it), demanding all the resources of poetry, is oriented to experience.[106] The abbot continually asks his readers to match what he writes to what they have gone through: "If you turn your attention to your own experience, . . ."[107] Or, "About this, let your experience teach you."[108]

In the abbot's writings, religious experience – a large and balanced concept – is an epistemological principle, one that seems to have lain fallow through vast stretches of the subsequent history of theology. While distinguishable from reason and faith, experience subsumes and reconciles the two. Reason, even when guided by faith, needs a broader knowing. Faith needs to grow toward a more direct knowing. In experience, both are completed. Experience, on the other hand, needs both reason and faith as reality checks.[109]

Bernard calls the Song of Songs, which he reflects upon as a comtemplative discourse (*theoricus sermo*), "the book of experience."[110] The tradition had spoken of two books in which God made himself known to us, the book of creation and the book of Scripture.[111] Bernard's declaration that experience is a third revelatory book is a significant doctrine.[112] It is the preeminent distinguishing mark of his thought.

By religious experience Bernard means knowledge of divine things through direct contact. About contemplative themes, he says, "They regard divine things and, except to those who experience them (*expertis*), they remain altogether unknown."[113] Contact is through the spiritual senses, which (in keeping with the tradition from Origen) means "by affection, not the hand; by desire, not the eye;

by faith, not the senses."[114] The experiential knowledge in which souls know God is *sapientia*, "wisdom by which they taste what they apprehend through the intellect."[115]

This experience involves all faculties. To receive the kiss of the Bridegroom, then, one prepares "her reason for the gift of insight, her will for that of wisdom."[116] "Its reality lies in the affections [*affectibus*]; it is attained, not by reason, but by a con-forming [*conformitate*]" – i.e., by taking on the form of the Word.[117] In the Song, we read of "a harmony not of voices but of wills."[118]

Not only the content of religious experience is incommunicable, but experience as such. Joy over the approach of the Word is "a song that only the singer can hear."[119] We read words from the bride of the Song; yet, "We do not understand what she is saying, because we do not feel what she feels."[120] Regarding imperfect souls: "Since they experience [*sapiunt*] less, they understand less."[121]

The indispensable noetic value of religious experience is not limited to contemplation. We note that, in his tract on Baptism, Bernard was able to postulate a saving faith offered to non-Christians who were just, by assuming that their experience was open to God.[122]

Bernard is one of the major mystics of the West. Here we have described his thought according to theological themes, even though admirers in his day saw these components in a different perspective. When the Cistercian Geoffrey of Auxerre spoke of him as "that great theologian" (*magnus ille theologus*), it was with specific reference to the abbot's masterpiece of contemplation, the *Sermons on the Song of Songs*.[123] We have, therefore, at every turn associated these theological elements with the abbot's quest of contemplative prayer.

Within the writings of St. Bernard, largely in homiletic form, lies an original, comprehensive, and cohesive "theology of experience." This author represents what may be the fullest Western realization of "the anthropological turn," the conviction that the mystery of the human person is correlated to the mystery of God.[124] The abbot's insights into the meaning of the data of faith left to later generations the task of valid extrapolation to life outside the monastery – "the problem of principle in the relation between the world and the kingdom."[125] But, even here, the stand Bernard took on the book of experience pointed to a solution and opened the way to development.

Expression of the Cistercian spirit did not stop with the abbot of Clairvaux but extended to several writers of theological significance. Aelred of Rievaulx (ca. 1110–67), the "Bernard of the North," produced the preeminent transposition of pagan concepts of friendship into Christian categories. Guerric of Igny (1080–1157), in 54 liturgical sermons, expounded a rich Pauline spirit-Christology (1 Cor. 15:45). Isaac of Stella (ca. 1100 to ca. 1175), of English origin like Aelred, and like Guerric a former schoolman, incorporated into his contemplative anthropology insights on the body from the school of Chartres. He advanced early Cistercian reflection on the Mystical Body and added to the tradition of the white monks a strain of Dionysian apophatic mysticism.[126] No one, however, was as close to the mind of Bernard as his friend William of St. Thierry.

William of St. Thierry

In the twelfth century, the profoundest theology of the Trinity, the most systematically developed anthropology of Image and Likeness, and the furthest probe into the relationship between love and knowledge belong to the Cistercian William of St. Thierry.

Born in Liège (ca. 1080), William attended one of the cathedral schools, probably that of Reims. Like many schoolmen of the generation, he experienced a "conversion" from academic theology and entered the Benedictines at St. Nicasius of Reims, eventually becoming abbot of St. Thierry (ca. 1120). He had met St. Bernard, perhaps as early as 1118, and spent a long convalescence with the young abbot in day-long conversations when the two were in the infirmary of Clairvaux.[127] Over Bernard's long resistance, he left his abbacy in 1135 and joined the new Cistercian monastery of Signy. The close enduring friendship of these two kindred spirits creates for posterity a difficulty in discerning, on many issues, the personal source of doctrines they hold in common. Several of William's writings were attributed to Bernard; only in the twentieth century has scholarship discovered the individuality and the stature of the abbot of St. Thierry.

William's first works were *The Nature and Dignity of Love*[128] and *On Contemplating God*.[129] He contributed to the Eucharistic debates of the day with his tract *On the Sacrament of the Altar*.[130] At Signy (ca. 1137–9) he wrote the *Exposition on the Song of Songs*,[131] perhaps his finest achievement, offering his understanding of union in the Holy Spirit. Also from these years is *The Nature of the Body and the Soul*,[132] where we learn that the human body is the image of the universe as the soul is the image of God. The *Exposition on the Epistle to the Romans*[133] remains close to Augustine and Origen and contains the germ of the mystical doctrine flourishing in many other works, such as the *Meditations*.[134] He discusses faith, the vision *per speculum in aenigmate* (in 1 Cor. 13:12), in his *Mirror of Faith*[135] – faith leading to mystical contact (*credo ut experiar*) – and in the *Enigma of Faith*[136] – reason's exploration of faith (*credo ut intelligam*).[137] In his last years he wrote the *Golden Epistle*[138] to the Carthusians (*Epistola ad fratres de Monte-Dei*), his best-known work, treasured as a summary of medieval mystical teaching. A manual of excerpts from Augustine (the *Sententiae*) has been lost; but two other of his *florilegia*, drawn up at Bernard's request, one from St. Ambrose,[139] the other from St. Gregory the Great,[140] survive.

With the sophistication of his theological schooling, William gently repairs imprecisions in the treatment of the Eucharist by a fellow monk, Rupert of Deutz. But, to counter the influence of Abelard, he incites the bishops and his friend Bernard to full attack.[141] For the work of a bold speculative theologian, William's vigorous expressions of diffidence in unaided reason are notable, reminding one of his conversion from the schools.[142]

We can distinguish three key ideas in his theology, though we cannot separate them: (1) *imago* and *similitudo*, (2) *imago trinitatis*, and (3) *amor* and *intellectus*.

First, he brings the classic anthropology of Image and Likeness, as he receives it through Augustine and the Western Fathers, to unparalleled doctrinal articulation.[143] With sin, the image of God in which we are created (Gen. 1:26) is damaged and our likeness to God lost. The image of God in us is our original participation in the divine nature, bestowed by *gratia creans* (the concept we have met in Bernard).[144] "This," writes William, "is the condition of the good mind, still sterile of those fruits of understanding [*intelligentiae*] and wisdom which it awaits from illuminating grace."[145] This second grace makes clear, by its name, the contemplative orientation of William's thought.

Humans, made *ad imaginem Dei*, find their model in Christ, who is the very Image of God. But, what characterizes our author's anthropology is his shift of focus from *Deus* to *Trinitas*. He writes:

> The holy soul is reformed to the image of the Trinity, the image of the one who created her, even in the way of his beatitude. For the illuminated and attracted will (that is, intellect and love and the disposition toward enjoyment) is in some way, with respect to experience [*affectionum*], three persons, even as is said and believed about the Trinity in God.[146]

A platonizing view of the soul, not unique to him, gave William two important postulates: first, that there is a higher and lower level of soul (his *anima* and *animus*), and second that knowledge and affectivity are complementary. "It is clear," he writes, "that there are three conditions of those who pray, or three kinds of prayer – animal, rational, and spiritual [cf. 1 Thess. 5:23; 1 Cor. 2:14]."[147] The third, however, is "no longer called likeness but unity of spirit."[148] These levels require a progressive conformity of the will to God's will; but, in the complementarity of the cognitive and affective, our transformation is tied to a vision of God: "We will be like him because we will see him as he is" (1 John 3:2).

On earth we must move toward a *similitudo Dei* that will be complete only in heaven. There, "where, even as in the Father and the Son, seeing is the unity itself, so also between God and humans will the seeing be our likeness." He explains further: "The Holy Spirit, the unity of the Father and the Son, is also the love between God and the human being, and their likeness."[149]

This bold tenet, that the love of humans for God *is* the Holy Spirit, distinguishes William's trinitarian theology. As the persons of the Trinity are subsistent relations and the Holy Spirit is the union of Father and Son, so our own union with the Trinity – when this is consummated as a *cognitio amoris* (that knowledge which is love) – is the Holy Spirit, the reciprocal knowledge of Father and Son.[150] For William, the Holy Spirit is the very community of the Trinity, a relation that is communicated to us in an *unitas spiritus* (1 Cor. 6:17). He holds, in effect, that our ascent to God is *per Filium, in Spiritu, ad Trinitatem*.[151] As Augustine's trinitarian mysticism centers on Christ, William's centers on the Holy Spirit.[152] We read: "The love of God, or the love that is God, the Holy spirit, infusing itself into a human's love and spirit, draws him to itself (*afficit eum sibi*); God, then, loves himself in the human being and makes him his spirit and love, one with himself."[153]

This divinization is qualified: even in our total acceptance of the Spirit's unifying action, we are limited by our capacity to receive. The unity by nature in the Trinity becomes our unity with it by grace.[154] Then, what we receive is "a certain likeness [*effigies*] of his knowledge" – still a knowledge by participation.[155]

The knowledge William speaks of is our love for God – the kiss, the embrace, the union, our *similitudo*, which (he insists) *is* the Holy Spirit. He sees the same mutuality in our love and knowledge of God as he finds in the persons of the Trinity. Writing of the Spirit as the unity of Father and Son, he prays, "The author and ordainer of the unity by which we are one in ourselves as well as in you is the same Holy Spirit."[156] The key here is William's understanding of the intersubjective character of the trinitarian *unitas spiritus*. This relation to God he generally calls our *intellectus amoris*; it receives classic formulation in his maxim, "Love itself is our knowledge" (*Amor ipse intellectus est*).[157]

This Johannine insight (1 John 4:7) became the principle according to which William regulated his approach to God, one in which love was the soul's sensor. It underlay a sometimes excessive uneasiness in the face of his generation's growing fascination with dialectics. Yet it did not retard the intellectual pace of his own work.

Déchanet may be right in explaining the strange slightness of William's reputation: for centuries, his innovative ideas were deliberately "protected" by incorporation into, or association with, the *oeuvre* of his friend St. Bernard, where they received a broad contextual reading.[158] To the enrichment of theology, these ideas, which have their own clarity and force, have begun to emerge.

Hugh of St. Victor

Like the Cistercians, the canons regular of the abbey of St. Victor were intent on religious renewal. Their founder, William of Champeaux (d. 1121), was in the direct intellectual line of Anselm of Canterbury and his disciple at Bec, Anselm of Laon. William retired from the school of Paris to dedicate himself to a canonical life emphasizing poverty and contemplative prayer. Soon educational needs in the quickening urban environment turned the new abbey into the epicenter of a restless early scholasticism.

Hugh of St. Victor, the most renowned in a long list of Victorine masters, is the era's outstanding example of the attempt to render theology scientific while maintaining its monastic character. He may have been born in Saxony, sometime after 1090. Very prolific in many academic genres, he began writing after 1120; he died in 1141. No recital of this encyclopedist's doctrines can match in importance his methodological contributions. Working from the standpoint that God is manifest in all his works – a vision fostered by the mystical insights of Dionysius the Pseudo-Areopagite, though largely Augustinized – Hugh concluded that the entire range of human learning should be viewed as preparation for theology.[159] In his *Didascalicon*, he organized all knowledge (his *philosophia*) in that perspective.[160] In writing the first of the medieval *summae* (summaries of doctrine), *The*

Mysteries of the Christian Faith, he again stood upon a seminal organizing principle, distinguishing the content of biblical revelation according to God's founding work (*opus conditionis*) and restoring work (*opus restaurationis*).[161] By enlarging for theology the humanistic base already latent in monasticism, and by augmenting the function of sanely applied dialectics, Hugh's writings contributed in a unique way to keeping Victorine theological reflection within the lines of Catholic orthodoxy and, thereby, to ensuring the general acceptance of what developed into the scholastic method.

Among the generation's many schemes for classifying sciences, Hugh's *Didascalicon* stands out as the most original since Aristotle.[162] He makes no advances in the disciplines tabulated but draws them together in a symbolic inclusiveness. Bernard of Clairvaux, from his cloister, aware of the danger of *curiositas*, committed his monks exclusively to the most direct way to God.[163] Hugh, addressing theologians of a new society, exhorted them to "learn everything."[164] The universe itself was a book written by the finger of God (*scriptus digito Dei*).[165] All secular learning was to be enlisted in the cause of a correct reading of the Bible, the starting-point of theology; and theology was to be directed to a *sapientia* which contemplated "the only primordial reason for things."[166] Truth is found in all disciplines, but theology is "the perfection of truth."[167]

Books 4, 5, and 6 of the *Didascalicon* treat of the interpretation of Scripture. We are to understand the biblical text as history, allegory, or tropology, "as reason requires" (*prout ratio postulat*).[168] One who finds allegorical or mystical meanings (*mysticam intelligentiam et allegoriarum profunditatem*) when none are implied is as blameworthy as one who ignores them when they are there.[169] The edifice of meaning rests on the double foundation of history – a foundation in the earth – and allegory, which forms the lower part of the rising structure.[170]

First, for theological as well as linguistic reasons, the historical, or literal, meaning supports all others.[171] Hugh's attention to the literal meaning, evinced in the help he sought from Jewish scholars, marked a significant moment in medieval exegesis.[172] Virtually no one since Jerome had shown a similar preoccupation. Hugh's Victorine disciple Andrew (d. 1175) would carry the project forward.

In moving on to allegory, the second foundation of meaning, Hugh speaks of the "many mysteries" of the faith revealed in the *sacra pagina* of the Bible. These become his subject in the doctrinal summa "The Mysteries of the Christian Faith." Here he links the mystic deeds done (*facta mystica*), or allegory proper, with the mystic deeds to be done (*facienda mystica*), or the moral meanings of tropology. Upon such a foundation rests the divine reality God wishes to reveal, an ultimate meaning towards which the other meanings tend. Only in the attaining of this reality is the work of restoration, the subject of all the Bible, finally complete.[173]

Historians have paid less attention to this mystical dimension of Hugh's theology than to those elements of his thought that are of significance for early scholasticism. Folded into our author's understanding of tropology was *contemplatio*.[174] The three treatises on Noah's Ark, written between 1125 and 1130, are the clearest "exhibits" of Hugh the contemplative.[175] Here again, the importance of the work lies more in its symbolic inclusiveness – its distinctive ordering of monastic contemplation to the new theological model of scholasticism – than in the author's analysis of mystical consciousness.[176]

Hugh's interest in Noah's Ark sprang from his conviction that an adequate literal reading of a Bible text, one that informed us of what had happened in history, was necessary for reaching spiritual meanings. He provides a drawing of the ark (based on Gen. 6), now lost but described in his text.[177] The conception is of a multivalent symbol of the earth, of salvation history, and of our present sharing, through contemplation, of eternal life in the risen Christ. It is a mandala of mystic consciousness.[178]

Hugh, the great teacher, excelled in a medium beloved of the Dionysian strain in his era – i.e., the use of symbols, which he defined as "the assembling, or interconnecting, of visible forms [*coaptatio visibilium formarum*] in order to exhibit something invisible."[179] The symbol could effectively suggest what reason groped for.

An important postulate, also shared throughout the twelfth century, lay behind his architectonic distinction between God's founding work and his restoring work. Our redemption in Christ, including the ascetical process of striving to accept it, was a "restoration" (*opus restaurationis*) in the sense that it returned us to the original state of creation, before sin; here, reaching out to God in contemplation was (even as to Bernard and William of St. Thierry) "natural."

Among other eminent Victorines some, like Walter (ca. 1180) and Absolon (d. 1203), reacted in a strongly negative way to the new theology; others, like Andrew, Achard (d. 1160), Richard (d. 1173), and Godfrey (d. after 1194), followed the constructive direction established by Hugh. None matched the master in his integration of mystical ascent and reliable doctrine as these grew out of a careful literal reading of the Bible.

Richard of St. Victor

The most outstanding of Hugh's disciples was a mystical theologian who, in important areas, surpassed his master. Richard of St. Victor (d. 1173) was a Scot about whose life we know little. Though he left no doctrinal *summa*, his treatise on the Trinity is a major development of insights from Augustine and Dionysius. With Hugh's scholastic sense of order, Richard assembled and further elaborated the monastic mystical tradition into a highly articulated system. His profound treatment of contemplation, the most complete of the century, is a landmark in the growth of Western mysticism.[180]

Richard's numerous works cover many themes. In all, however, it is impossible to disengage personal contemplative elements (his main thrust) from doctrinal ones. He was less preoccupied than Hugh with the literal meaning of the text; yet, he served the Victorine project of biblical education with many scriptural commentaries and a huge encyclopedic reference called *The Book of Selections*.[181] His two most influential mystical tracts were *The Twelve Patriarchs*[182] and *The*

Mystical Ark,[183] generally referred to as *Benjamin minor* and *Benjamin major* respectively. Another such treatise, *The Four Degrees of Violent Charity*,[184] uncovers the experiential foundation of his richly speculative *De Trinitate*.[185] What God reveals in the dynamic of human love is perceived as a privileged analog of the Trinity. The surest access, then, to the theology of this early-scholastic *magister* is through the monastic contemplation of the Victorine canon.

The anthropological basis of Richard's contemplative work was the "image-and-likeness" thought common in monasticism. But our author joins to this the Boethian epistemology (Hugh had used it) which divides what may be known into *naturalia, intelligibilia,* and *intellectibilia* (*quod . . . in propria semper divinitate consistens*).[186] The last of these three categories allows him to speak of things that are of God alone. Onto this grid he fits the classical monastic ascetical and mystical concerns – e.g., a stress on self-knowledge. In the author's various configurations of the soul's ascent, there is an inner consistency and as strong an integration of ascetical and contemplative elements as may be found in the literature.

The Twelve Patriarchs is a manual teaching the means to spiritual growth. Seven necessary virtues are exemplified in the patriarchs born to Jacob's wives Leah and Rachel, with omission of the four born of their maids (Gen. 29–49). The soul must finally come to know Benjamin, contemplation; but first, it must undergo a gradual preparation for communion with the beautiful Rachel, wisdom.

For a fuller unfolding of theory, one turns to Richard's contemplative master-piece, *The Mystical Ark.* "Contemplation," we read, "is the free penetration of a mind, suspended in awe, into the manifestations of wisdom."[187] Therefore, contemplation is a knowledge continuum that moves from the *sensibilia* known in imagination, to the *intelligibilia* known by reason, to the ineffable *intellectibilia* apprehended only by the higher understanding.[188] Each of these ways of knowing operates in two registers, one remaining within its own power, the other by addition of an attraction to the power above it.

Working from his central image, the Ark of the Covenant (Exod. 25:18–22 and Isa. 6), Richard envisions the two six-winged Seraphim hovering above the ark as figures of six types of contemplation. They are the contemplation (1) of *sensibilia* through the imagination, and (2) of the ideas of these visible things in the imagination but also "according to reason," the higher power; the contemplation (3) of qualities in invisible things (*intellibilia*) by reason, and (4) of spirits by reason "but not according to reason"; finally, contemplation, by the higher *intelligentia*, (5) of God – *supra sed non praeter rationem* – and (6) of the Trinity, which is *praeter rationem*.[189]

Though Richard gives a Christological interpretation of the Ark elsewhere, here in *The Mystical Ark*, to the surprise of commentators, he makes no explicit mention of Christ.[190]

In the last book of the tract – a discussion of the relation of grace and human effort, observed in three ways of experiencing contemplation – the author moves from his focus on the intellectual dimension of contemplative progress to the love which enlightens. Here, in the *excessus mentis*, "when the mind is in total forget-fullness of itself [*mens . . . penitus obliviscitur*]," contemplation is pure joy.[191]

The phenomenon of human loving is that effulgence of the divine in creation where Richard sees God as triune. The *De Trinitate*, his major doctrinal treatise, is eminently mystical. More than the work of predecessors from whom he borrowed (Augustine, Ps.-Dionysius, Gregory the Great, and Anselm), his is a theology of interpersonal relations.[192] The Dionysian postulate *bonum est diffusivum sui* begins a reasoning process: among the attributes of God, whose existence is proven early in the treatise, is goodness as *summum bonum*.[193] Such goodness must go out to another (*in alterum tendat*) and be returned; therefore, it is charity.[194] In the personal God, who *is* all that God possesses, this charity must be personal. From human love, in whose fullness we experience goodness, happiness, and glory, we conclude to a plurality of Persons in God.

Lest it be thought that the reciprocal character of God's love is satisfied in his love of creatures, Richard invokes the concept *caritas ordinata*: the highest charity cannot be addressed to a limited being and lack a divine consort.[195] The argument from goodness is repeated for happiness and for glory. That the divine Persons are three derives from the idea that, in the perfection of charity, the adequate beloved is *condilectus*, one willing to share the love received: *oportet ut pari voto condilectum requirat*.[196]

What is remarkable in this trinitarian theology is the dialectical connection between its psychological insights and the rational strength of its doctrine. Richard's capacity for observing the dynamics of human love is increased by the trinitarian faith that resonates in the effort. In varying degrees, that quality characterizes all the writings of the Victorine mystic. He is a finer theologian for being an insightful psychologist.

Even so rapid a survey of the great Cistercians and Victorines should suggest that, in the surge of twelfth-century renewal and reform, the thinkers who stood at the boundary of two theological eras embodied the maturation of a millennium's reflection. Its unresolved tensions would be addressed in the name of a growing laity and a diversifying society. Perhaps something of monastic theology, in the existential immediacy of its grounding in experience, could not be accommodated in the rising "scientific" theology. Nevertheless, its buried treasure would remain as a resource for theologians yet to come.

Notes

The following abbreviations for Bernard's works are used in the notes: Csi. (*De consideratione libri V*); Dil. (*Liber de diligendo Deo*); Div. (*Sermones de diversis*); Ep. (*Epistolae*); Gra. (*Liber de gratia et de libero arbitrio*); MalV (*Vita s. Malachiae*); OS (*Sermo in festivitate omnium sanctorum*); Pre. (*Liber de praecepto et dispensatione*); Quad. (*Sermo in quadragesima*); QH (*Sermo super psalmum "Qui habitat"*); SC (*Sermones super Cantica Canticorum*); Sent. (*Sententiae*).

1 Jean Leclercq, "The Renewal of Theology," in Robert L. Benson and Giles Constable, eds., *Renaissance and Renewal in the Twelfth Century* (Cambridge, Mass.: Harvard University Press, 1982), 68–87. Leclercq's periodization extends to 1174 (pp. 69–70).

2 Jean Leclercq, "Médiévisme et unionisme," *Irénikon* (1946), 6–23.

3 See e.g. Steven Ozment, "Humanism, Scholasticism, and the Intellectual Origin of the Reformation," *Continuity and Discontinuity in Church History: Essays Presented to George Hunston Williams* (Leiden: Brill, 1979), 133–49.

4 Oliver Rousseau, "S. Bernard, le dernier des Pères," *Saint Bernard théologien: analecti sacri ordinis cisterciensis*, 9 (Rome, 1953), 300–308.

5 Bernard McGinn, *The Presence of God: A History of Western Christian Mysticism* (New York: Crossroad, 1991–), vol. 2: *The Growth of Mysticism*, (1994), pp. 149–57, on the *ordinatio caritatis*. This multivolume work will be cited by volume and page only.

6 Artur Michael Landgraf, "Der hl. Bernhard in seinem Verhältnis zur Theologie des 12. Jahrhunderts," in J. Lortz, ed., *Bernhard von Clairvaux, Münch und Mystiker: Internationaler Bernhardkongress, Mainz 1953* (Viesbaden, 1955), pp. 44–62.

7 Jean Leclercq, "S. Bernard et la théologie monastique du XIIe siécle," *Saint Bernard théologien*, 7–23, at 8–9.

8 H. Weisweiler, *Das Schriftum der Schule Anselms von Laon und Wilhelms von Champeaux in deutschen Bibliotheken* (Münster, 1936), pp. 244–7.

9 Jean Leclercq, *A Second Look at Bernard of Clairvaux*, trans. Marie-Bernard Saïd, CS 105 (Kalamazoo, Mich.: Cistercian Publications, 1990), p. 45.

10 For Cistercian intervention in the episcopal succession at York, for example, when Bernard vilified and displaced the incumbent, St. William of York, see David Knowles, "The Case of St. William of York," *The Historian and Character* (Cambridge: Cambridge University Press, 1963), pp. 76–98; Jean Leclercq, *A Second Look at Bernard of Clairvaux*, pp. 38–40.

11 The critical edition is *Sancti Bernardi Opera*, ed. Jean Leclercq et al. (Rome: Editiones Cistercienses, 1955–77), here referred to parenthetically (volume: page, line) after the standard abbreviations of his works (by numbered paragraphs). Translations, when taken from the Cistercian Fathers series, are acknowledged as CF, with volume number. Similarly, the Cistercian Studies series appears as CS.

12 Jean Châtillon, "L'influence de S. Bernard sur la pensée scholastique au XIIe siècle," *S. Bernard théologien*, 268–88, at 275.

13 G. R. Evans, *The Mind of St. Bernard of Clairvaux* (Oxford: Clarendon Press, 1983), pp. 138–47, lists the many petitioners and their questions.

14 Ep. 174 (7:388–94). Châtillon, "L'influence," pp. 276–7. See Bruno Scott James, trans., *The Letters of St. Bernard of Clairvaux* (London: Burns Oats, 1953), pp. 289–93. For numbering in James, see pp. 523ff.

15 See Bernard's Ep. 190 to Innocent II (8:17–40), preceded by a shorter letter to the Innocent, Ep. 189 (8:12–16).

16 N.-M. Häring, "Saint Bernard and the Litterati of His Day," *Cîteaux: Commentarii Cistercienses*, 25 (1974), 199–222, at 216–18. Evans, *The Mind of Saint Bernard*, pp. 147–73, reviews the dispute with Abelard as it occurs in the primary sources. Edward Little, "Bernard and Abelard at the Council of Sens, 1140," *Bernard of Clairvaux: Studies Presented to Dom Jean Leclercq* (Washington, DC: Cistercian Publications, 1973), 55–71, offers recent views which demythologize the confrontation.

17 Abel. 9 (8:25, 15–24).

18 Evans, *The Mind of St. Bernard*, pp. 154–6, finds duplication of some of the imagery in Anselm's *Cur Deus homo?* in Bernard's letter to Innocent II, Ep. 190.25 (8:38, 11–12). Cf. *Anselmi Opera*, II.51.20–1.

19 See N.-H. Häring, "The Case of Gilbert de la Porrée, Bishop of Poitiers (1142–1154)," *Mediaeval Studies*, 13 (1951), 1–40, at 12–13. Geoffrey of Auxerre, in *Vita Bernardi* 3, 12–14 (PL 185, 310–11), gives a Cistercian account of both struggles, against Abelard and against Gilbert. (The abbreviation "PL" will hereafter be used for the series "Patrologia Latina.")

20 SC 80.6 (2:281, 12–13): "Divinitate," inquiunt, "Deus est; sed divinitas non est Deus." [etc.]

21 SC 80.2 (2:277, 22–3).

22 See N.-H. Häring, "The Case of Gilbert de la Porrée," pp. 12–13.

23 Ewart Cousins, "The Humanity and the Passion of Christ," in Jill Raitt, ed., in collaboration with Bernard McGinn and John

Meyendorff, *Christian Spirituality: High Middle Ages and Reformation* (New York: Crossroad, 1987), 375–91, at 376–7. Cousins offers earlier examples from Peter Damian, John of Fécamp, and especially Anselm of Canterbury.

24 SC 20.6 (1:118, 21–6; CF 4:152): Hanc ego arbitror praecipuum invisibili Deo fuisse causam, quod voluit in carne videri et cum hominibus homo conversari, ut carnalium videlicet, qui nisi carnaliter amare non poterant, cunctas primo ad suae carnis salutarem amorem affectiones retraheret, atque ita gradatim ad amorem perduceret spiritualem.

25 McGinn, 2:174.

26 SC 20.9 (1:120, 22–3): Bonus tamen amor iste carnalis, per quem vita carnalis excluditur, contemnitur et vincitur mundus.

27 SC 25.9 (2:168, 22): Quam formosum et in mea forma te agnosco, Domine Jesu!

28 See SC 2.6 (1:12, 1–2) [Puto enim spernere me iam non poterit os de ossibus meis, et caro de carne mea], alluded to by Franz Posset, "Divus Bernhardus: Saint Bernard as Spiritual and Theological Mentor of the Reformer Martin Luther," in John R. Sommerfeldt, ed., *Bernardus Magister: Papers Presented at the Nonacentenary Celebration of the Birth of Saint Bernard*, CS 135 (Kalamazoo: Cistercian Publications and *Cîteaux, Commentarii Cistercienses*, 1992), 515–30, at 530. The author cites WA 45:304, 1–3 (stenogram), lines 9–14 (print).

29 Dil. 13 (3:130, 10–12).

30 SC 20.7 (1:119, 4–14; CF 4, 152–3): Monstrabat autem postea eis altiorem amoris gradum, cum diceret: Spiritus est qui vivificat, caro non prodest quidquam. Puto huc ascenderat iam qui dicebat: Etsi cognovimus Christum secundum carnem, sed nunc iam non novimus. Fortassis et Propheta nihilominus in hoc ipso stabat, cum diceret: Spiritus ante faciem nostram Christus Dominus. Nam quod subiungit: Sub umbra eius vivemus inter gentes, mihi videtur ex persona incipientium addidisse, ut quiescant saltem in umbra, qui solis ferre ardorem minus validos se sentiunt, et carnis dulcedine nutriantur, dum necdum valent ea percipere quae sunt Spiritus Dei. Umbram siquidem Christi, carnem reor esse ipsius, de qua obumbratum est et Mariae,

ut eius obiectu fervor splendorque Spiritus illi temperaretur.

31 SC 20.9 (1:120, 22–4).

32 SC 28.9 (1:198, 11–13): Noli me tangere: nondum enim ascendi ad Patrem meum. Quasi vero cum iam ascenderit, tunc tangi ab ea velit aut possit. For a fully explicit exposition of the idea, see SC 75.6–9 (1:250–2).

33 Jean Leclercq, "Le mystère de l'Ascension dans les sermons de saint Bernard," *Collectanea Ordinis Cisterciensium Reformatorum*, 15 (1953), 81–8.

34 Bernard writes of "the ones who take a salutary short-cut . . . choosing the shortened and shortening Word," Dil. 21 [CF 13B, p. 23]. Qui salubri compendio cauti sunt . . . verbum abbreviatum et abbrevians eligentes" (3:136, 26–7). See Emero Stiegman, "An Analytical Commentary," in *On Loving God by Bernard of Clairvaux*, CF 13B (Kalamazoo, Mich.: Cistercian Publications, 1995), 43–219, at 54–7.

35 Yves Congar, "L'écclésiologie de S. Bernard," *Saint Bernard théologien*, 136–90.

36 SC 12.11 (1:67, 22–5); SC 68.1 (2:196, 21–2).

37 The communion of saints is a motif heard throughout Bernard's work; see especially OS 5.6 and 11 (5:365 and 369–70).

38 Csi 2.10 (3:418, 1–2): Esto, ut alia quaecumque ratione haec tibi vindices, sed non apostolico iure. Jaroslav Pelikan, *The Growth of Medieval Theology (600–1300)* (Chicago: University of Chicago Press, 1978), pp. 300–1, summarizes Bernard's position.

39 SC 23.2 (1:139–40); 41.6 (2:32); Sept. 1.2 (4:346). See Caroline Walker Bynum, *Jesus as Mother: Studies in the Spirituality of the High Middle Ages* (Berkeley: University of California Press, 1982), ch. 4.

40 SC 64.8 (2:170, 11–15).

41 Yves Congar, "L'écclésiologie de S. Bernard," *Saint Bernard théologien*, 136–90, at 179.

42 SC 27.6 (1:186, 2–8). See Helmut Riedlinger, *Die Makellosigkeit der Kirche in den lateinischen Hohenliedkommentaren des Mittelalters. Beiträge zur Geschichte der Philosophie und Theologie des Mittelalters* [BGPTMA] 38, 3 (Münster, i.W., 1958). The author, listing parallel passages of Bernard's SC and Origen's commentary,

pp. 156–7, finds the model in Origen. For the role of the angels, which Congar ("L'écclésiologie de S. Bernard," p. 151) sees as determinative of Bernard's ecclesiology, see also SC 7.4–5; 19, *passim*; 31.5; 41.3–4; 52.6; 62.1; 68.4; 76.7; 77.3–4; 78.1–2.

43 SC 14.5 (1:78, 26–7): Ecclesia ergo recumbit intus, sed Ecclesia interim perfectorum. Spes tamen est et nobis. The "congregation of the just," at SC 68.3 (2:198, 16). But, in SC 38.5 (2:17, 16–17), only in heaven will the Church be immaculate.

44 SC 27.6 (1:185, 25 to 186, 2).

45 The Church tries "to maintain its likeness [to God] in the land of unlikeness": *in regione dissimilitudinis retinere similitudinem*. SC 27.6 (1:185, 22–3).

46 Henry deLubac, *Éxégèse médiévale: Les quatre sens de l'écriture*, 2 parts in 4 vols. (Paris, 1959–64), II, 576–8. The author traces the theme from Origen, through Augustine, to Gregory the Great and the middle ages.

47 Ludwig Ott, *Untersuchungen zur theologischen Briefliteratur der Frühscholastik unter besonderer Berücksichtigung des Viktorinerkreises*. BGPTMA 34 (Münster: Aschendorff, 1937). Bernard's response is studied at pp. 495–548. Hugh Feiss, OSB, "Bernardus Scholasticus: The Correspondence of Bernard of Clairvaux and Hugh of Saint Victor on Baptism," *Bernardus Magister*, 349–78, at 359. The author translates letter 77 (7:184–200).

48 René-Jean Hesbert, "Saint Bernard et L'Eucharistie," *Mélanges Saint Bernard* (Dijon, 1953), 156–76, at 160, 167.

49 SC 33.3 (1:235, 11–13): Me oportet interim quodam sacramenti cortice esse contentum, carnis furfure, litterae palea, velamine fidei.

50 QH 3.3 (4:394, 21–3): Quid autem est manducare eius carnem et bibere sanguinem, nisi communicare passionibus eius, et eam conversationem imitari, quam gessit in carne?

51 See MalV 57 (3:360, 10–12): Bernard says, admiringly, that Malachi faced down one who presumed to say that in the Eucharist there was only the sacrament and not the substance of the sacrament (*rem*

sacramenti) . . . not the actuality of the body (*non corporis veritatem*). In QH 3.3 (4:394, 21–395, 2) he says it is the body of Christ that we receive (*dominicum corpus accipimus*).

52 William Courtenay, "Sacrament, Symbol, and Causality in Bernard of Clairvaux," *Bernard of Clairvaux*, 111–22, reviews later discussions on Bernard's notion of sacramental causality.

53 Dil. 4 [CF 13B] (3:122, 8): Utrumque ergo scias necesse est, et quid sis, et quod a teipso non sis.

54 Dil. 6 (3:124, 7–10): Impossibile est . . . ad Dei convertere voluntatem, et non magis ad propriam retorquere eaque sibi tamquam proprie retinere. And, loss of self: Ubi se dedit, me mihi reddidit. Dil. 15 (3:132, 10–11); or, regarding spousal union: . . . nil proprium, nil a se divisum habentibus. SC 7.2 (1:31, 25).

55 Dil. 32 (3:146, 24–5).

56 Regarding the era, see Gerhart B. Ladner, "Terms and Ideas of Renewal," *Renaissance and Renewal*, 1–33, at 13. M.-D. Chenu, *Nature, Man, and Society in the Twelfth Century* (Chicago: University of Chicago Press, 1968), pp. 18–24.

57 SC 44.4 (2:46, 24–9): Annon hinc denique amor proximi radicem trahit, de quo in lege mandatur: Diliges proximum tuum sicut teimpsum? Ex intimis sane humanis affectibus primordia ducit sui ortus fraterna dilectio, et de insita homini ad seipsum naturali quadam dulcedine, tamquam de humore terreno, sumit procul dubio vegetationem et vim, per quam, spirante quidem gratia desuper, fructus parturit pietatis.

58 SC 51.2 (2:84, 26–85, 1): Itaque nec sine flore fructus, nec sine fide opus bonum. In the Augustinian tradition, Bernard can shift perspectives on concupiscence, from its bondage in sin, as here, to its character as a drive that grace may put in order, as in most of *On Loving God*. See my discussion in "An Analytical Commentary," pp. 146–50.

59 Stiegman, "Analytical Commentary," pp. 51–9, on Bernard's equating the *infideles* to human nature.

60 See Bernard McGinn, "God as Eros: Metaphysical Foundations of Christian Mysticism," in Bradley Nassif, ed., *New Perspectives on Historical Theology: Essays in*

Memory of John Meyendorff (Grand Rapids, Mich.: Eerdmans, 1955), 189–209. Origen is the source of this transcendent view of eros (pp. 194–7).

61 Dil. 22 (3:137, 17–21): Dixi supra: causa diligendi Deum, Deus est. Verum dixi, nam et efficiens, et finalis. Ipse dat occasionem, ipse creat affectionem, desiderium ipse consummat. Ipse fecit, vel potius factus est, ut amaretur; . . . Eius amor nostrum et praeparat, et remunerat.

62 Gra. 16 (3:178, 2–6): Porro ipsum ut esset, creans gratia fecit; ut proficiat, salvans gratia facit; ut deficiat, ipsum se deicit. Itaque liberum arbitrium nos facit volentes, gratia benevolos. Bernard McGinn, "Introduction" [to Gra.] in *The Works of Bernard of Clairvaux, Volume Seven: Treatises III, On Grace and Free Choice* and *In Praise of the New Knighthood* (Kalamazoo, Mich.: Cistercian Publications, 1977), 3–50, at 25 n. 71. The author believes the Augustinian *creans–salvans* distinction was made popular by Bernard.

63 Gra. 17 (3:178, 9–11): Simplices namque affectiones insunt naturaliter nobis, tamquam ex nobis, additamenta ex gratia. Nec aliud profecto est, nisi quod gratia ordinat, quas donavit creatio, ut nil aliud sint virtutes nisi ordinatae affectiones.

64 Anders Nygren, *Agape and Eros*, trans. Philip S. Wetson (Philadelphia: 1953), p. 650, criticized Bernard's view of love as "far too human." M. C. D'Arcy, *The Mind and the Heart of Love: Lion and Unicorn. A Study in Eros and Agape* (New York, 1947; 1956), p. 245, responds that where agape eliminates eros, "there is no man left."

65 Bernard Stoeckle, *Gratia supponit naturam: Geschichte und Analyse eines theologischen Axioms* (Rome: Orbis Catholicus, Herder, 1962). At pp. 91–8, the author discovers a precursor of the idea in Maximus the Confessor (580–662).

66 A. Van den Bosch, "Présupposés à la christologie Bernardine," *Cîteaux in de Nederlanden*, 9 (1958), 5–17, at 5.

67 Gregory Baum, *Man Becoming: God in Secular Experience* (New York: Herder and Herder, 1970), pp. 1–36, credits twentieth-century Catholicism's progressive escape from "extricism" to the philosopher

Maurice Blondel's seminal work *L'action* (1893); meanwhile, Chrysologue Mahamé, "Les auteurs spirituels dans l'élaboration de la philosophie blondelienne (1883–1893)," *Recherches de science religieuse*, 56, 2 (1968), 231–4, demonstrates St. Bernard's direct influence in the philosopher's text.

68 Pierre Rousselot, *Pour l'histoire du problème de l'amour au moyen âge: Beiträge zur Geschicte de Philosophie des Mittelalters, Texte und Untersuchungen* 4/6 (Münster i/ Westfalen, 1908), p. 53 n. 1. The author expresses surprise at coming to this conclusion.

69 Dil. 31–3 (3:145–7).

70 SC 81.7 (2:288, 10): Corpus quod corrumpitur aggravat animam, sed amore, non mole.

71 SC 82.3 (2:294, 7–8): Etsi non privatur vita, vitae tamen beneficium suo corpori iam non sufficit vindicare.

72 SC 82.4 (2:294–5).

73 SC 82.3 (2:11–12): appetentia terrenorum – quae quidem omnia ad interitum sunt. Also, Csi 5.26 (3:489, 12–14), where Bernard sees "the soul depart from itself into the transient beauty of this world."

74 M.-D. Chenu, *L'évangile dans le temps* (Paris, 1964), p. 448.

75 Pre. 15.42 (3:282, 25–7).

76 Ep. 174.7 (7:391, 19).

77 Ibid., 21–3.

78 SC 82.5 (2:296, 7) and HM5 2 (5:69, 6–7).

79 SC 31.6 (2:223, 1–9): Vide autem tu, ne quid nos . . . corporeum seu imaginarium sentire existimes. See also SC 40.1 (2:24, 12–17); SC 46.1 (1:56, 9–19); SC 53.3 (2:97, 27–8), where we read: Verum non decet istiusmodi corporeas phantasias imaginari, praesertim tractantes hoc Canticum spirituale.

80 E. Ann Matter, *The Voice of My Beloved: The Song of Songs in Western Medieval Christianity* (Philadelphi: University of Pennsylvania Press, 1990), pp. 31–4.

81 SC 81.7 [CF 40] (2:288, 16–17): Est enim necessitas haec quodammodo voluntaria. Est favorabilis vis quaedam.

82 Maur Standaert, "La doctrine de l'image chez saint Bernard," *Ephemerides Theologiae Lovanienses*, 23 (1947), 70–129, esp. 118–21.

83 McGinn, "Introduction" to *On Grace and Free Choice*, pp. 39–45. The treatise is esteemed by Peter Lombard, Thomas Aquinas, and Bonaventure.

84 Ibid., pp. 40–1. Broadly speaking, Bernard reaffirms the Augustinian tradition.

85 Gra. 3.6–5.15 (3:170–7).

86 Michael Casey, *Athirst for God: Spiritual Desire in Bernard of Clairvaux's Sermons on the Song of Songs*, CS 77 (Kalamazoo, Mich.: Cistercian Publications, 1988). At pp. 160–70, Casey demonstrates the mystical direction of SC 80–3 – a highly plausible reason for Bernard's change of scheme.

87 SC 80.2–3 and 4–5 (2:277–9 and 279–81).

88 SC 81.2–5 (2:284–7) and 82.2–6 (2:292–6).

89 McGinn, "Introduction" to *On Grace and Free Choice*, p. 8, notes the evolution of this category: not until Aquinas is *liberum arbitrium* replaced by *voluntas*.

90 Gra. 3 (3:168, 1–9): Porro voluntas est motus rationalis, et sensui praesidens, et appetitui. Habet sane, quocumque se volverit, rationem semper comitem et quodammodo pedissequam: non quod semper ex ratione, sed quod numquam absque ratione moveatur . . . Neque enim prudentia seu sapientia inesse creaturae potest, vel in malo, nisi utique per rationem.

91 In "Analytical Commentary," pp. 51–9, I illustrate this.

92 Div. 29.1 (6/1:210, 11) and Sent. 3.127 (6/2:249, 20). In Gregory, *Hom. in Ev.* 27.4 (PL 76:1207A). See Robert Javelet, "Intelligence et amour chez les auteurs spirituels du XIIe siècle," *Revue d'ascétique et de mystique*, 37 (1961), 273–90, 429–50.

93 Pre. 20.60 (3:293, 4): Prasens igitur Deo est qui Deum amat, in quantum amat.

94 SC 82.8 (2:297, 21): Caritas illa visio.

95 See M.-P. Delfgaauw, "La lumière de la charité chez saint Bernard," *Collectanea Ordinis Cisterciensium Reformatorum*, 18 (1956), 46–67, 306–20.

96 Csi. 5, 3.6 (3:471, 7–8): Fides est voluntaria quaedam et certa prelibatio necdum propalatae veritatis.

97 SC 28.7 (1:197, 4–6); and SC 59.9 (2:140, 16–17): Etsi fides ex auditu, sed ex visu confirmatio est. The idea is developed in John Sommerfeldt, "Bernard of Clairvaux on the Truth Accessible through Faith," in E. Rozanne Elder, ed., *The Joy of Learning and the Love of God: Studies in Honor of Jean Leclercq*, CS 160 (Kalamazoo, Mich.: Cistercian Publications, 1995), 239–51, esp. at pp. 241–6.

98 SC 70.2 (2:208, 28–9): Et credidisse enim, vidisse est.

99 SC 84.7 (2:306, 24–6): Credant quod non experiuntur, ut fructum quandoque experientiae fidei merito consequantur.

100 Ep. 18 (7:67, 24): Intellectus igitur est fructus fidei, perfecta caritas desiderii.

101 See SC 62.6 (2:159, 3–21); SC 83.1 and 2 (2:298–9).

102 SC 31.10 (1:225, 25): Vivimus proinde in umbra Christi qui per fidem ambulamus.

103 SC 31.9 (1:225, 12): Et bona fidei umbra, quae lucem temperat oculo caliganti. See E. Stiegman, "The Light Imagery of Saint Bernard's Spirituality and Its Evidence in Cistercian Architecture," in *The Joy of Learning*, 327–88, for the doctrine underlying Bernard's imagery of shadow and light (pp. 334–62).

104 SC 8.5 (1:39, 3–4): Si enim integre cognovissent, . . .

105 SC 85.8 (2:312, 23–4): . . . si quis sapientiam saporem boni diffiniat.

106 "The Renewal of Theology," p. 85. Jean Leclercq, *Recueil d'études sur S. Bernard et ses écrits*, 3 vols. (Rome: Edizioni di storia e letteratura, 1962–9), 3:213–66. The author studies the aesthetics of Bernard's biblical language.

107 SC 1.9 (2:6, 22): Ceterum vos, si vestram experientiam advertatis, . . .

108 Csi. 5.11, 24 (3:486, 18): Doceat te de hoc experimentum tuum.

109 On experience as stabilized by the norms of faith, see SC 28.89 (1:197–8); Quad. 5.5 (4:374, 20–1).

110 SC 1.3 (1:4, 9): . . . acceditur ad hunc sacrum theoricumque sermonem. SC 3.1 (1:14, 7): Hodie legimus in libro experientiae. Jean Leclercq, "Aspects spirituels de la symbolique du livre au XIIe siècle," in *L'homme devant Dieu: Mélanges offerts au Père Henri DeLubac*, 3 vols. (Paris: Aubier, 1962), 2:63–72, studies Bernard's use of *liber experientiae*.

111 DeLubac, *Exégèse médiévale*, 1: 121–5.

112 McGinn, 2:185 and 186, calls this "significant innovation" a "real contribution." This concept of experience was latent already in Origen, as shown by Marguerite Harl, "Le langage de l'éxperience religieuse chez les pères grecs," *Rivista di storia e letteratura religiosa*, 15 (1977), 5–34, at 26.

113 SC 41.3 (2:30, 15): Divina sunt et nisi expertis prorsus incognita sunt.

114 SC 28.9 (1:198, 13–14): Et utique poterit [tangere], sed affectu, non manu; voto, non oculo; fide, non sensibus. For Origen, see McGinn, 1:121–4, 239–40.

115 SC 9.3 (1:44, 3–5): [spiritus] sapientiae qua gustent quod intellectu apprehenderint.

116 SC 8.6 (1:39, 29–40, 1; CF 4): . . . paret e regione duo labia sua quae sponsa est, intelligentiae rationem, sapientiae voluntatem.

117 SC 67.8 (2:193, 29–194, 1): Res in affectibus, nec ratione ad eam pertingitur, sed conformitate. For the joining of the affective and the voluntary in *affectus* (or *affectio*), see my "Analytical Commentary," pp. 93–5.

118 SC 1.11 (1:8, 1): voluntatum, non vocum consonantia.

119 SC 1.11 (1:8, 2–3): Sola quae cantat audit.

120 SC 67.3 (2:189, 28–9): Nescimus quid loquitur, quia non sentimus quod sentit.

121 SC 19.7 (1:112, 10–11): Sed enim adolescentulae, quoniam minus sapiunt, minus et capiunt. For a variant, SC 22.2 (1:130, 7–8).

122 Hugh Feiss, *"Bernardus Scholasticus,"* pp. 353–4, presents Bernard's position in Ep. 77 to Hugh of St. Victor.

123 Leclercq, "S. Bernard et la théologie monastique," p. 16 n. 1.

124 The expression is from Bernard McGinn, "The Human Person as Image of God: II. Western Christianity," in Bernard McGinn and John Meyendorff, eds., *Christian Spirituality: Origins to the Twelfth Century* (New York: Crossroad, 1986), 312–20, at 328.

125 Yves Congar, *Lay People in the Church: A Study for a Theology of Laity*, trans. Donald Attwater (Westminster, Md.: Newman Press, 1965), p. 86.

126 McGinn, 2:284–96; also, Bernard McGinn, "Introduction" in *Three Treatises on Man:* *A Cistercian Anthropology* (Kalamazoo, Mich.: Cistercian Publications, 1977), pp. 1–100; Bernard McGinn, *The Golden Chain: A Study in the Theological Anthropology of Isaac of Stella* (Washington, DC: Cistercian Publications, 1972).

127 William records the episode in his *Vita Bernardi*, 12.59 (PL 185:225–66, at 259BC).

128 De natura et dignitate amoris, PL 184, 379–407.

129 De contemplando Deo, PL 184, 365–80; edition by Jacques Hourlier in *Sources chrétiennes* [SCh] 61. I cite critical editions of William by page and line number.

130 De sacramento altaris, PL 180, 341–66.

131 Expositio altera super Canticum Canticorum [Cant.], PL 180, 473–546; edition by J.-M. Déchanet in SCh 82. William is the probable author also of the *Brevis commentatio in priora duo capita Cantici Canticorum*, PL 184, 407–35.

132 De natura corporis et animae [Nat. corp.], PL 180, 695–726.

133 Expositio in Epistolam Pauli ad Romanos, PL 180, 547–694.

134 Meditativae orationes [Med.], PL 180, 205–48.

135 Speculum fidei [Spec.], PL 180, 365–98; edition by J.-M. Déchanet in SCh 301.

136 Aenigma fidei [Aenig.], PL 180, 397–440; preferred edition by M.-M. Davy, *Guillaume de Saint-Thierry: Deux traités sur la foi: Le miroir de la foi, L'enigme de la foi* (Paris: Vrin, 1959).

137 McGinn, 2:228.

138 Epistola ad fratres de Monte-Dei [Ep. Frat.], PL 184, 307–54; edition by J.-M. Déchanet in SCh 301.

139 Commentarius in Cantica Canticorum e scriptis S. Ambrosii collectus, PL 15, 1849–98.

140 Excerpta ex libris S. Gregorii Papae super Cantica Canticorum, PL 180, 441–74.

141 William's personal response was his *Disputatio adversus Petrum Abaelardum*, PL 180, 259–82.

142 Jean Châtillon, "William of Saint Thierry, Monasticism and the Schools: Rupert of Deutz, Abelard, and William of Conches," in *William, Abbot of St. Thierry: A Colloquium at the Abbey of St. Thierry*, trans.

Jerry Carfantan (Kalamazoo, Mich.: Cistercian Publications, 1987), 153–80 at 171–2.

143 David N. Bell, *The Image and Likeness: The Augustinian Spirituality of William of St. Thierry* (Kalamazoo, Mich.: Cistercian Publications, 1984), pp. 17–18, regarding excessive claims of Eastern influence.

144 Bell, pp. 89, 96–8.

145 Cant. 174; SCh 82:356: Ipse est bonae mentis status ex gratia creante, sterilis adhuc ad intelligentiae et sapientiae fructibus: quos expectat ex gratia illuminante.

146 Med. 12.14; PL 180, 246D: Reformatur enim anima sancta ad imaginem Trinitatis, ad imaginem eius qui creavit eam, etiam ipso modo beatitudinis suae. Nam illuminata voluntas et affecta, id est intellectus et amor, et fruendi habitus, sicut de Trinitate Deo dicitur et creditur, Quodammodo tres sunt affectionum personae.

147 Cant. 13; SCh 223:84–5: Tres ergo status esse orantium, vel orationum, manifestum est: animalem, rationalem, spiritualem.

148 Ep. Frat. 262; SCh 223:352–3: . . . ut non jam similitudo, sed unitas spiritus nominetur.

149 Aenig. 6 (Davy edn., 96): Ubi etiam sicut in Patre et in Filio, que visio, ipsa unitas est; sic in Deo et homine, que visio, ipsa et similitudo futura est. Spiritus sanctus unitas Patris et Filii, ipse etiam caritas est similitudo Dei et hominis.

150 See e.g. Spec. 106; SCh 301:176.1–2: Ea vero cognitio quae mutua est Patris et Filii, ipsa est unitas amborum, qui est Spiritus sanctus.

151 McGinn, 2:269.

152 Bell, p. 253.

153 Ep. Frat. 170; SCh 223:278: . . . et amans semetipsum de homine Deus, unum secum efficit et spiritum ejus et amorem ejus. Note also Ep. Frat. 266 (SCh 82:354): . . . hoc idem homini, suo modo fit ad Deum, quod consubstantiali unitate, Filio est ad Patrem, vel Patri Filium.

154 Nat. corp.; PL 180, 722D.

155 Bell, p. 228, cites Cant.; PL 180, 479B.

156 Med. 6.7; PL 180:224AB: Unitatis vero, qua in nobis vel in te unum sumus, auctor et ordinator est idem Spiritus sanctus.

157 Ep. Frat.; PL 184:336A (SCh 173). Also, Cant.; PL 180:499C (SCh 76). Odo Brooke, *Studies in Monastic Theology*

(Kalamazoo, Mich.: Cistercian Publications, 1980), pp. 27–30.

158 Jean-Marie Déchanet, "A Comment," in *William of St. Thierry: A Colloquium*, 254–7.

159 Hugh wrote *In Hierarchiam celestem commentaria* [In Hier.], PL 175, studying the Dionysian work.

160 G. R. Evans, *Old Arts and New Theology: The Beginnings of Theology as an Academic Discipline* (Oxford: Clarendon Press, 1980), studies also similar, if less comprehensive, twelfth-century efforts – e.g., in diagrams on pp. 15–16. On the *Didascalicon* [Did.], see the edition of Henry Buttimer, *Hugonis de Sancto Victore. Didascalicon: De Studio Legendi* (Washington, DC: Catholic University Press, 1939), cited as Buttimer.

161 *De Sacramentis* [De Sac.], PL 176:173A–618B.

162 McGinn, 2:370.

163 See e.g. Hum. 28 (3:38, 2–29); Dil. (3:136, 24–7).

164 Did. 6.3 (Buttimer, 115:19–20): Omnia disce, videbis postea nihil esse superfluum.

165 *De tribus diebus* 3 (PL 176, 814B).

166 Did. 1.4 (Buttimer, 11:14–20): Diximus philosophiam esse amorem et studium sapientiae . . . quae sola rerum primaeva ratio est.

167 In Hier., Prol. (PL 175, 928A): Hic autem summa philosophiae est, et veritatis perfectio.

168 Did. 5.2 (Buttimer, 96:18).

169 *In Salomonis Ecclesiasten*, Praef. (PL 175, 115A).

170 Did. 6.4 (Buttimer, 118:18–26).

171 Grover Zinn, "*Historia fundamentum est*: The Role of History in the Contemplative Life According to Hugh of St. Victor," in George H. Shriver, ed., *Contemporary Reflections on the Medieval Christian Tradition: Essays in Honor of Ray C. Petry* (Durham, NC: Duke University Press, 1974), 135–58.

172 Beryl Smalley, *The Study of the Bible in the Middle Ages*, 2nd edn. (Notre Dame: University of Notre Dame Press, 1964), pp. 83–105. Cf. de Lubac, *Exégèse médiévale*, seconde partie 1, chs. 4 and 5.

173 De Sac. 1, Prol., 6 (PL 176, 185CD): Super haec ante omnia divinum illud est ad quod ducit divina Sriptura sive in allegoria,

sive in tropologia, . . . in quibus constat cognitio veritatis et amor virtutis: et haec est vera reparatio hominis.

174 Did. 5.9 (Buttimer, 109:23–5).

175 (1) *De arca Noe morali*, (2) *De arca Noe mystica*, and (3) *De vanitate mundi* (PL 176, 617–740).

176 McGinn, 2:383.

177 De arca mor. 1.2 and 3 (PL 176, 622B–26B, 629D); De arca myst. 1, 9, and 15 (PL 176, 681A–84A, 696C–97B, 702AC).

178 Grover Zinn, "Madala Symbolism and Use in the Mysticism of Hugh of St. Victor," *History of Religions*, 12 (1973), 317–41, e.g. at 322–3.

179 In Hier. 3 (PL 175, 960D).

180 McGinn, 2:405.

181 Edition by Jean Châtillon, *Richard de Saint-Victor: Liber exceptionum. Texte critique avec introduction, notes et tables* (Paris: Vrin, 1958). See also PL 196.

182 *De praeparatione animi ad contemplationem: Liber dictus Benjamin minor* (PL 196, 1–64). McGinn, 2:593 n. 188, notes that in some manuscripts the work is named, more correctly, *Liber de duodecim patriarchis*.

183 *De gratia contemplationis . . . hactenus dictum Benjamin major (De arca mystica)* [Benj. maj.], (PL 196, 63–202).

184 Edition of G. Dumeige, *Ives: Épitre à Severin sur la charité. Richard de Saint-Victor. Les quatres dégrés de la violente charité.*

185 *De Trinitate: Texte critique avec introduction, notes et tables*, ed. Jean Ribaillier (Paris: Vrin, 1958) [De Trin.]. Also, PL 196.

186 Boethius, *In Isagogen Porphyrii Commenta 1.3* (ed. Brandt in *Corpus Scriptorum Ecclesiasticorum Latinorum*, 48:8–9).

187 Benj. maj. 1.4 (PL 196, 67D): Contemplatio est libera mentis perspicacia in sapientiae spectacula cum admiratione suspensa.

188 For imagination and reason, see Ben. maj. 1.3–4 (PL 196, 66C–68C).

189 Book 1 of Ben. maj. In books 2, 3, and 4, these six types of contemplation are studied.

190 McGinn, 2:410–11. Note, however, that Richard's intellectual model, Dionysius (see McGinn, 1:162), often speculated in seeming independence of biblical texts.

191 Ben. maj. 5.5 (Pl 196, 174BC).

192 Ewart Cousins, "A Theology of Interpersonal Relations," *Thought* 45 (1970), 56–82.

193 De Trin. 2.16–19 (Ribailler, 123–6).

194 De Trin. 3.2 (Ribailler, 136.9–10): Oportet itaque ut amor in alterum tendat, ut caritas esse queat.

195 Ibid. (Ribailler, 137.29–30): Oportuit divinam aliquam personam persone condigne, et eo ipse divine, consortio non carere.

196 De Trin. 3.11 (Ribailler, 147.39): Summe ergo dilectorum summeque diligendorum uterque oportet ut pari voto condilectum requirat, pari concordia pro voto possideat.

Bibliography

Bell, David. *The Image and Likeness: The Augustinian Spirituality of William of St. Thierry*. CS 78. Kalamazoo, Mich.: Cistercian Publications, 1984.

Van den Bosch, A. "Présupposés à la christologie Bernardine." *Cîteaux in de Nederlanden*, 9 (1958), 5–17.

Brooke, Odo. *Studies in Monastic Theology*. Kalamazoo, Mich.: Cistercian Publications, 1980.

Casey, Michael. *Athirst for God: Spiritual Desire in Bernard of Clairvaux's Sermons on the Song of Songs*. CS 77. Kalamazoo, Mich.: Cistercian Publications, 1988.

Châtillon, Jean. *Richard de Saint-Victor: Liber exceptionum. Texte critique avec introduction, notes et tables*. Paris: Vrin, 1958.

Déchanet, J.-M. *William of St. Thierry. The Man and his Work*, trans. R. Strachan. Spencer: Cistercian Publications, 1972.

Delfgaauw, M.-P. "La lumière de la charité chez saint Bernard." *Collectanea Ordinis Cisterciensium Reformatorum*, 18 (1956), 46–67, 306–20.

Evans, G. R. *Old Arts and New Theology: The Beginings of Theology as an Academic Discipline*. Oxford: Clarendon Press, 1980.

Evans, G. R. *The Mind of St. Bernard of Clairvaux*. Oxford: Clarendon Press, 1983.

Javelet, Robert. "Intelligence et amour chez les auteurs spirituels du XIIe siècle." *Revue d'ascétique et de mystique*, 37 (1961), 273–90, 429–50.

Leclercq, Jean. "S. Bernard et la théologie monastique du XIIe siècle." *Saint Bernard théologien. Analecta Sacri Ordinis Cistercienses* 9. Rome (1953): 7–23.

Leclercq, Jean. "The Renewal of Theology." In *Renaissance and Renewal in the Twelfth Century*, eds. Robert L Benson and Giles Constable with Carol D. Lanham. Cambridge, Mass.: Harvard University, 1982.

Leclercq, Jean. *A Second Look at Bernard of Clairvaux*, trans. Marie-Bernard Saïd. CS 105. Kalamazoo, Mich.: Cistercian Publications, 1990.

McGinn, Bernard. "Introduction." *On Grace and Free Choice by Bernard of Clairvaux*, trans. Daniel O'Donovan. Kalamazoo, Mich.: Cistercian Publications, 1988.

McGinn, Bernard. *The Presence of God: A History of Western Christian Mysticism*. Vol. 2: *The Growth of Mysticism*. New York: Crossroad, 1994.

Sommerfeldt, John R., ed. *Bernardus Magister: Papers Presented at the Nonacentenary Celebration of the Birth of Saint Bernard*, CS 135. Kalamazoo, Mich.: Cistercian Publications and *Cîteaux, Commentarii Cistercienses*, 1992.

Stiegman, Emero. "An Analytical Commentary." *On Loving God by Bernard of Clairvaux*. CF 13B. Kalamazoo, Mich.: Cistercian Publications, 1995.

Zinn, Grover. "Mandala Symbolism and Use in the Mysticism of Hugh of St. Victor." *History of Religions*, 12 (1973), 317–41.

The *Glossa Ordinaria*

Jenny Swanson

The *Glossa Ordinaria* was an apparatus of annotations to the Latin Bible, which became standardized towards the middle of the twelfth century and remained standard until the eighteenth century. It was printed frequently between the fifteenth and eighteenth centuries, usually with the *Postillae* of Nicholas of Lyre and the *Additiones* of Paul of Burgos. These printed editions were very substantial, filling six folio volumes.

The term *glossa* is an ancient one, which dates back to the time of the Greek grammarians. These scholars, commenting on Greek texts, used *glossa* to mean both a word which required particular explanation, and also the explanation itself. This second meaning is the one which was carried forward into the Middle Ages, and indeed into modern times. It is important, nowadays, to distinguish between firstly a gloss (*glossa*) or individual comment, secondly the Gloss or *Glossa*, meaning the ever-growing body of comment which became attached to the Bible from patristic times, and thirdly the *Glossa Ordinaria*, that particular sequence of explanatory material which became standard apparatus to the Bible in the mid-twelfth century. The term *Glossa Ordinaria* is in fact a modern one: twelfth- and thirteenth-century scholars simply used the term *Glosa*.

From the time of the earliest Christian writers, the term *glossa* or gloss has been used to mean an explanation of something in the Bible. Beyond that, however, the word *glossa* has meant quite different things at different points in Christian intellectual development. To early Christian writers, a gloss meant simply an explanation of some tricky or unclear word in the text of the Bible. The explanation might be needed because the word was foreign to the reader, was no longer part of everyday speech, was a technical term unfamiliar to the current audience, or was used in an unfamiliar way. Whatever the reason, these early glosses normally comprised only one word each – almost more a translation than an explanation – and could be fitted easily between the lines of the text, or in the margin opposite the relevant line.

Over time, many individual scholars added glosses of their own, and the numbers grew until the *glossa* could no longer be comfortably fitted into and around the text. Eventually they were gathered in separate books: Bible-orientated combinations of dictionary and encyclopedia, which could be used alongside a Bible. Initially they appeared in the same order in which they had once appeared in the text, so that the reader could – if he wished – work through the two texts steadily from front to back. This method of textual organization particularly suited readers who were studying a specific biblical book or section in its entirety, or who were reading the Bible for their own information or for personal devotion.

Later, as abilities to redesign the structure of books became more developed, the separated sets of glosses were rearranged and became available alphabetically. This format, more closely akin to a modern dictionary or encyclopedia, was particularly suitable for scholars who wished to examine the ways in which a particular word might be used in the Bible, to check on a word without remembering its exact reference, or to compare the ways in which a word was interpreted in different places in the text. It was a format more useful for purely scholastic purposes: for those wishing to make an intellectual point in a sermon or a lecture, in an argument or in a biblical commentary of their own. The two styles of separate gloss, independent of the Bible text, each had their own advantages for different types of user. They also shared the advantage that they were not so unwieldy for the reader to manage.

However, both separate versions of the Gloss had the disadvantage that the reader did not know for sure which words of the biblical text had entries in the Gloss, and which did not, without going through a tedious process of constant cross-checking between volumes.

This, then, was the dilemma faced by twelfth-century scholars. A Gloss separated from the biblical text itself might be less unwieldy than one large, all-embracing volume, and availability in different formats might allow users to select that most appropriate to their purposes, but in reality a Gloss without the corresponding biblical text was useless, like footnotes without the main page of a modern text. The Bible and the *Glossa* belonged so closely together that their separation was unnatural. A further complication was provided by the greatly increasing size of the Gloss, particularly for certain books, when compared to the size of the original biblical text. At first the *glossa* were simply concrete definitions of the difficult words in the text. As not all were difficult, the *Glossa* was naturally much smaller than the Bible. This began to change when the original meaning of the *glossa* was expanded, before the ninth century, to include any historical, geographical, or biographical facts which might help the user to understand the text. At this period, the encyclopedic format was becoming popular in other fields. It was inevitable that collection and organization of facts connected to the Bible should take place, and the size of the *Glossa* expanded dramatically.

The *glossa* later came to include expository or explanatory sentences, until by the twelfth century the term *Glossa* came to mean a complete running commentary on some part of the Bible. An apparatus on this scale was not really suited to the independent, alphabetized format which was to develop in other fields of learning. Yet it was so unwieldy that, if it were possible to squeeze it in around the text of the Bible itself, that text became effectively unreadable. Copying was also a difficulty, as it was all too easy for a scribe to confuse the text and the notes, and unwittingly to include, in the text, sections of the notes which should not be there. The possibility and risk of such textual corruption became a real concern as the Middle Ages developed: eventually a papal decree (of 1588, by Sixtus V) declared that copies of the Vulgate should no longer include marginal notes, as they were too confusing to readers.

There was only one sensible solution to these multiplying difficulties with the Bible and its associated and expanding glosses: reorganization. By the middle of the eleventh century the necessary tools existed. Now that it is possible to trace an outline history of the developing *Glossa*, it can be seen that this is indeed a history of developing organization. Each new tool made available to scholars – improved textual layout, improved systematization and organization of material, improved techniques of comparison and analysis – was quickly applied to the developing Gloss on the Bible, the heart of Christian thought and scholarship. In the twelfth century, these improvements and refinements gave scholars the *Glossa Ordinaria*.

For many years it was believed that this text was the work of the late Carolingian scholar Walafrid Strabo (d. 849), which had come into common use through the schools of the twelfth century. That this could not be so was demonstrated by a number of papers written before the Second World War, and was clarified by Beryl Smalley in *The Study of the Bible in the Middle Ages* (1940). Yet the myth was repeated in many books and encyclopedias of the later twentieth century, and even posted on the Internet in the 1990s. Therefore it seems worthwhile to summarize the evidence here.

Before 1900, there was relatively little study of medieval biblical commentaries, and many of the conclusions formed by nineteenth-century scholars, and often repeated subsequently, were simply based upon inadequate evidence. The tradition of Walafrid Strabo's authorship of the *Glossa Ordinaria* is a good example of this. Some commentaries by Strabo (on the Psalms and Canonical Epistles) survive, as do certain glosses (on some of the prophets) which appear to come from his circle, even if they are not by Strabo himself. Berger, writing in 1893, detected a similarity between these and early portions of the *Glossa* on certain biblical books, and concluded that the nucleus of the *Glossa*, on those books at least, derived from Strabo, even if he could not be credited with having written the whole thing. However De Blic showed, in the late 1940s, that the similarity came about because both Strabo and the authors of the early Gloss had drawn from the same group of patristic authorities: beyond that, the two had made quite different selections of extracts and handled them quite differently. So there were in fact two independent minds or groups of minds at work in the commentaries on those particular books.

The Gloss on the Pentateuch required separate examination. Several eleventh- and twelfth-century writers – for example Manegold of Lautenbach – quoted "Strabus" on Genesis and Exodus, and some parts of the Gloss on these books were attributed to him both in manuscripts and in printed editions. The tradition of Strabo's partial authorship was therefore an old one, which could have come about in one of two ways. Firstly, Strabo might have produced the Gloss on the Pentateuch, combining patristic extracts with his own original contributions and signing the latter himself. Secondly the Gloss might be the work of a later scholar or group of scholars, who used a commentary by Strabo among many other sources. De Blic demonstrated the truth of the second option. Strabo did produce commentaries on the Pentateuch, explaining in his own preface that his aim was to abridge the much longer works of his master Rabanus Maurus. So by his own admission he aimed to summarize established work rather than to produce new work of his own. The glosses attributed to "Strabus" in the Gloss were shown by De Blic to be extracts from his derivative commentaries. Apart from these few dozen short quotations on Genesis, Exodus, and the Pentateuch, the glossators chose not to include any of Strabo's work, preferring to use a variety of quite different sources. In fact Walafrid Strabo was well known to medieval scholars as an abbreviator of Rabanus Maurus, rather than anything else. They were prepared to copy and to quote Strabo's work, but in at least six surviving manuscripts, ranging in date from the ninth century to the twelfth, this was explained as being due to lack of access to the original works of Rabanus, which were considered to be of much higher quality.

Some scholars have suggested that, even if Strabo had nothing to do with writing the *Glossa Ordinaria*, he might have deserved credit for the layout. However, all the genuine works ascribed to Strabo are written out continuously, and bear no resemblance to the distinctive layout of the *Glossa Ordinaria*, which does not appear until much later. So Strabo, like many other scholars of his day, was merely an unwitting contributor to the *Glossa Ordinaria*. He wrote commentaries which were primarily summaries of his own master's works, and a number of short extracts from these were included in the developing *Glossa* by scholars of a later generation. By no stretch of the imagination can he be credited with the authorship of even the Carolingian *Glossa*, let alone the *Glossa Ordinaria*.

Yet in some ways the roots of the *Glossa Ordinaria* do lie in the late Carolingian period. The purpose of the *Glossa Ordinaria*, as it developed in the eleventh and twelfth centuries, was not to be innovative. It did not represent the cutting edge of contemporary theology, but rather came into existence to organize and make available the body of established work which had built up over almost a thousand years. It was intended as a study aid for beginners in theology; students just embarking upon the study of the Bible. It was not until the twelfth century that it became common for students to go on to higher studies in the Bible, in law or in medicine. In all these fields, the standard work of reference became a text and commentary laid out as an integrated, glossed page.

Margaret Gibson ("Carolingian Glossed Psalters") has clearly shown that the ancestor and forerunner of these standard texts, where layout and structural organization are concerned, was the luxury Glossed psalter of the Carolingian period. Around two dozen of these survive, although some are mere fragments. In their day they were technically innovative. Unlike a "school text," where notes were interlinear and could be altered or expanded by the owner at some later date, the annotations to these Glossed psalters were clearly and elegantly written, and in a different script from the main body of the text. The pages were carefully ruled to allow for the marginal gloss, which was ruled and written at half spacing compared to the text. These developments made the core text easier to read, and kept the annotations next to the relevant sections of the text, but discouraged expansion and development. Such volumes did not encourage readers to add their own thought or to contribute new information. They were designed for a reader in a passive mode of study and were of little use to the relatively few theological scholars of the ninth and tenth centuries. But they were well suited to the Carolingian noblemen who commissioned such volumes, and proved equally appropriate to those embarking on the study of theology in the twelfth century universities.

The establishment of theology courses as a standard in the universities was an important factor in the development of the *Glossa Ordinaria*, which was itself an important study aid if such courses were to succeed. The schools of the late eleventh century supplied the teachers of these courses – one-time pupils themselves, now risen to scholastic eminence. They also supplied the scholars who developed what was to become the *Glossa Ordinaria*. To produce a useful commentary upon the whole Bible was an extensive and intricate task. Some biblical books had had one or more commentaries attached to them well before the Carolingian period. Books such as the Psalms and the Pauline Epistles had been the subject of many commentaries, and were a popular subject for early twelfth-century masters seeking to establish themselves. For such books, a process of selection and combination was required from the twelfth-century glossators. Other books had been less popular with scholars, and had little or no commentary attached. These needed the traditional body of glosses expanded, or completely new bodies of comment written. Throughout these two very different processes, the goal was that of balance – of creating an integrated and authoritative apparatus to the whole of the Vulgate.

In order to do this meaningfully, it was first necessary for twelfth-century scholars to establish the correct text of the Vulgate. Efforts in this direction led to new understanding of the problems of textual criticism, and Christian scholars once again began to consult with their Jewish counterparts on the text of the Hebrew originals. This was to become an important feature of developing twelfth-century exegesis.

In parallel with this process of textual correction, there was a vast process of selection, organization, and extension of the glosses from previous centuries. It was too large a task for any one scholar or any single team: a number of twelfth-century scholars undertook different portions of the task. It has been possible to discover the names of many of these twelfth-century contributors, who represent the apex of nearly a thousand years of biblical scholarship, and also the names of many of their predecessors, from whose combined work they selected and developed material.

The textual layout and structures which were used to create the *Glossa Ordinaria* were already in existence in the Carolingian period. So were many of the comments and explanations which were eventually incorporated into the *Glossa*

Ordinaria, although the two elements did not come together for several hundred years. Although the *Glossa Ordinaria* can not be attributed to Walafrid Strabo himself, many of the roots of the work do extend back to his period.

Carolingian scholars such as Alcuin, Claudius of Turin, Rabanus Maurus and his pupil Walafrid Strabo, had labored to produce commentaries on various books of the Bible. These commentaries mostly comprised connected sequences of quotations from surviving patristic works, rather than original exposition. There were some attempts to mark the sources of individual sections, but often this was not even attempted, and any names of sources were easily lost in copying. The work of this group was important because they did succeed in producing some kind of commentary for almost all the books of the Bible. In doing so, they discovered a number of inconsistencies in the patristic tradition.

More original ninth-century scholars, such as Paschasius Radbertus and John the Scot, Haimo and his pupil Heiric of Auxerre, and Remigius of Auxerre, followed these up and went on to compare and criticize different commentaries, and thus to renew the tradition of scholarly comment as opposed to mere quotation of past opinion. This development, fueled by the scholarship of the Carolingian period, stalled with the death of Remigius in ca. 908. It was to be well over a hundred years before any other important biblical commentary was produced. The contents of the *Glossa* also stalled and largely stagnated, until revived by the development of the cathedral schools in the eleventh century. It was this development which led to the need and desire for an up-to-date *Glossa*, and created the personnel able to fulfill this need.

Fulbert of Chartres (d. 1028), the leading teacher of the early eleventh century, seems to have done much to refuel the development of the *Glossa*. He was skilled in exposition, and his pupil Berengar of Tours (ca. 999 to 1088) produced a set of glosses on the Pauline Epistles, which survive in fragments. Berengar's friend and colleague, Drogo of Paris, is probably the author of another set of glosses on the Pauline Epistles, written at a similar period and using a similar method. These two sets of glosses were collected with many others on the same book, all patristic or anonymous except for a third set which can be identified as the work of Lanfranc of Bec, once a pupil of Berengar's. In this set, Lanfranc used very similar methods to Berengar, and to Drogo of Paris.

St. Bruno of Chartreux, who taught at Rheims before he withdrew from the world in 1086, seems also to have had an important influence; he commented on both the Psalter and the Pauline Epistles, and the Gloss on the Psalter by Gilbertus Universalis is only one of the works which we know depended directly on Bruno's Gloss.

Manegold of Lautenbach, for many years a teacher at Paris, also produced commentary on the Psalter and Pauline Epistles, although only a fragment of the latter survives. It is difficult to assess his contribution to the Gloss, as so much of his work is now missing. However, elements of his work were borrowed by Anselm of Laon, one of the great figures of early twelfth-century intellectual life. Beryl Smalley believed that this borrowing indicated a master–pupil relationship between Manegold and Anselm.

Anselm of Laon (d. 1117) and his brother Ralph (d. 1134) were conducting a flourishing school by about 1100. They had great influence upon other theologians of their day, and also played a very important part in the next stage of the development of the *Glossa*. Anselm himself began the enormous task of attempting a Gloss upon the whole Bible: he was a masterly teamworker, and received much help from other members of his school. He died before his task was completed, but it is clear that he had, and was known to have, the whole task in mind. Peter the Chanter, writing fifty years after Anselm's death, still regretted that he had died before he had fulfilled his aim. Anselm's contribution was important in two ways; firstly through the Gloss he produced with the help of his associates, and secondly because he seems to have established the idea that there should, and could, be a complete, contemporary gloss upon the Bible.

It has been possible to trace three further early twelfth-century scholars who made significant contributions to the development of the Gloss. Lambert of Utrecht, who taught between ca. 1080 and ca. 1120, produced a commentary on St. Paul which was rich in historical *exempla*, and circulated with some of Anselm's works in the later twelfth century, as part of a popular compilation by Robert of Bridlington.

In Paris, Peter Lombard and Anselm's pupil Gilbert of Poitiers continued to work on the Scriptures in the manner developed by Anselm and his school. Smalley states that they represent the transition between the period of scattered cathedral schools, and the centralization of studies in the University of Paris. Until this point, most scholars who contributed to the developing biblical Gloss concentrated on one of two aspects: either they focused on producing study aids through different or better compilation of past work, or they produced independent exegesis. The key development of the late eleventh/early twelfth century was that both elements now proceeded simultaneously. In the Carolingian period it had been necessary for a generation of scholars to concentrate on compilation, before a second generation could become sufficiently knowledgeable and confident to begin to compare, contrast, comment, and eventually be led on to independent exegesis. At the turn of the twelfth century, the intellectual environment was very different. Scholars and schools were more numerous, and education and learning were available outside the particular atmosphere of the monastic schools. The number of available texts was increasing, and new methods of thought and of analysis promoted a more critical and disciplined approach to the body of surviving work.

This is the period when a *Glossa Ordinaria* became necessary. It was necessary as a core textbook for use in theology courses in the developing universities. It was necessary as an established point from which the more original scholars could depart: a baseline from which they could make their theoretical journeys, and which would help them give directions to their intellectual followers. Roman Law and canon law also had a need for such a *Glossa Ordinaria* during the twelfth century, and both these subjects also produced one. The development of these documents was intensively studied and well understood by the middle of the twentieth century, when the process of development of the biblical equivalent was still relatively unclear. Because the development of the glossed core texts for these fields began relatively late, and took place relatively quickly in a university atmosphere, different glosses and elements within them were much more clearly attributed, and the attributions were better preserved. Tracing of their development and authorship was a much more straightforward task, and understanding of which scholars had made which contributions, and when, could be obtained relatively easily.

The situation was quite different for the biblical *Glossa Ordinaria*. Its vast bulk, and the fact that its roots extended back through almost a thousand years of scholarship, meant that the authorship of many individual portions of the Gloss had been long lost by the twelfth century. Even once it had been established that the development of the *Glossa Ordinaria* was a multistage process, rather than the work of Walafrid Strabo alone, there was the challenge of discovering how many stages of development there were, and what they involved. Then there was the issue of the scholars who had contributed to the process: we know that there were very many, but not exactly how many. We know the names of some, but not necessarily what each one did. Many others remain unknown.

Throughout the twentieth century, a few modern scholars have worked to unravel the pattern, the process, the nature and scale of the contributions produced by individual medieval scholars. Now, at the beginning of the twenty-first century, the outline becomes clear. As has already been seen in this chapter, glosses or explanatory notes to the Vulgate were well established even in the Roman period. Separate commentaries on individual portions of the Vulgate were also produced by many patristic scholars. Works written in an encyclopedic format became increasingly popular after the time of Isidore of Seville (560–636). This style influenced the scholars of the Carolingian Renaissance, who contributed to the development of the biblical *Glossa* in two main waves which spread over a full century. The first wave were primarily compilers who delighted in rediscovering and gathering together a bulky collection of mainly patristic material, some of which would have been lost to us without their intervention. Through their collecting and compiling, they discovered some parts of the Bible which had received much commentary, often contradictory, and other parts which had been largely ignored. The second wave were able to capitalize upon the works of their predecessors, both by tackling critically the contradictions already exposed, and by producing original commentary on sections of the Bible which had hitherto had relatively little discussion.

The death of Remigius of Auxerre (ca. 908) marked the beginning of a period with few developments in biblical commentary and thus few opportunities for development of, or improvements to, the *Glossa*. This situation altered with the establishment of the cathedral schools in the eleventh century, which brought changes in every element of western European scholarship. New learning and new techniques of scholarship led to an explosion of biblical commentary, and eventually to establishment of standard university courses on theology, which naturally took the Bible as their core and central textbook. The students on these courses could not plunge, untrained and undirected, into the steadily swelling sea of available biblical commentary: they needed a reliable apparatus which would combine the best of contemporary scholarship with the best from the accumulated body of the previous thousand years. This they got in the form of the *Glossa Ordinaria*. That this met its intended purpose is indicated by its success and by the fact that it did become established, being often reproduced and often used.

The "final production" of the *Glossa Ordinaria*, as opposed to the frequently changing Gloss of previous centuries, was very much a twelfth-century event. It would have made little sense outside this context. Like the developments of the Carolingian period, it was a two-generation task, although unlike that earlier flood of expansion and organization, the two generations did not have differing agenda. The second generation of Carolingian scholars had relied on the first to produce their raw material, in the form of extensive compilation. The scholars of the eleventh century already had the Carolingian apparatus of compilation and criticism to hand, together with their new tools of grammar and dialectic. They were therefore well-equipped to continue the process on several fronts at once: making further selection of good contemporary comment, pruning out the less relevant and more repetitive of the older material, and creating new glosses to fill the gaps which they perceived.

The central figure in the process was Anselm of Laon, who was once believed (by Migne among others) to have written the interlinear glosses in the *Glossa Ordinaria* while Strabo had produced the marginal glosses. Although this legend may reflect the historical reality of a ninth/twelfth-century blend in the *Glossa Ordinaria*, and a largely dual-stage process of development after the patristic period, it is as implausible as the myth of Walafrid Strabo as single author. Smalley carefully showed that this attempt at separation into two discrete sets of glosses – the marginal and the interlinear – was imaginary. No manuscript has ever been found which contained one but not the other, so they had no separate existence. The claim that the marginal glosses were a separate and more extensive set which explained whole passages, while the interlinear glosses were explanations of single words in the text, is also demonstrably false. Smalley confirms that the biblical Gloss is divided in exactly the same way as that on the *Corpus Iuris*: on a practical basis, with shorter glosses put between the lines and longer ones on the margins, because they fitted better onto the page when organized in this way. No clear differentiation can be made on the basis of nature, content, or date, but only upon the length of individual glosses. They are certainly all integral parts of the same whole.

What was the nature of Anselm of Laon's true involvement? He was a critical figure in the process of creating the *Glossa Ordinaria*. Peter the Chanter commented upon his unfinished plan to gloss the whole Bible, although he died before completing it. We know from other sources that Anselm was definitely responsible for the sections of the *Glossa Ordinaria* which covered St. Paul and the Psalter, and probably responsible for the section on the Fourth Gospel. His circle also made major contributions: his brother Ralph of Laon compiled the Gloss on St. Matthew, and his pupil Gilbert the Universal produced the Gloss on the Pentateuch and the Greater Prophets and Lamentations, before becoming Bishop of London in 1128.

The author of the Gloss on the Lesser Prophets is not yet firmly identified. Robert of Bridlington, writing in the 1150s, attributed it to Gilbert the Universal. Another twelfth-century author believed it was written by Ralph of Laon. Even twelfth-century scholars who were confident that the *Glossa Ordinaria* was intimately connected with the intellectual circle of Anselm of Laon, were not always agreed on which member of the group had been responsible for which particular book.

The Gloss on the Apocalypse has been connected with Gilbert de la Porrée, and the Gloss on Acts with a "Master Alberic" who may be Master Alberic of Reims, a pupil of Anselm and possibly a friend of Gilbert the Universal. Many of the biblical books have no twelfth century name associated with their Gloss, and it is not enough to assume that the known contributors, such as Anselm and Ralph, produced the apparatus to other books without receiving the credit. Although they may have done so, as yet there is not enough evidence to make an informed judgment. In some cases, it seems clear that they definitely did not produce the Gloss to particular books. Peter Comestor stated that neither Ralph nor Anselm of Laon glossed the Gospel of St. Mark.

The Gloss produced by Anselm and his assistants was not the only attempt at a contemporary twelfth-century gloss. Although there is evidence that their version was being copied in Paris before 1137, it had not yet won the status of a standard text. It was quoted as "Anselm" or "the glosses of Gilbert the Universal," or even without attribution. There are surviving examples (e.g. MS Grenoble 32) of Glosses set out in just the same way, with marginal and interlinear annotation, but with quite different material. So until the 1140s at least, Anselm's *Glossa* was just one apparatus among several which aimed to fill the same need. The need seems to have been clearly perceived.

The responsibility, or credit, for establishing Anselm's *Glossa* as the standard seems to belong to Gilbert of Poitiers and Peter Lombard, both famous Parisian scholars of the mid-twelfth century. Both built upon this *Glossa* in their own works. Gilbert of Poitiers expanded the patristic glosses from Anselm's Gloss on St. Peter and the Psalter. His popular expansion came to be known as the *Media Glosatura*. Peter Lombard also expanded the Gloss on these two biblical books while carefully following Anselm's text as his nucleus. His work, the *Maior* or *Magna Glosatura*, was written between 1135–6 and 1142–3, and seems to have displaced all the other glosses for these books, becoming the main schools text. This brought Anselm's version of the *Glossa* to increased prominence. Gilbert de la Porrée and Peter Lombard seem to have used Anselm's *Glossa* in their oral teaching, thus introducing it to a whole generation of Parisian scholars. Lombard's *Sentences* finished 1152 and at once a standard textbook for the teaching of doctrine, used not only his own *Magna Glosatura*, but also Anselm's *Glossa*. This gave greatly increased authority to the apparatus of Anselm and his collaborators, and ensured that *de facto* it became the *Glossa Ordinaria* of future decades and centuries.

A generation of Parisian scholars became familiar with Anselm's *Glossa* through lectures, references in popular and dynamic new textbooks by eminent teachers of the day, and the increasingly available numbers of copies of the *Glossa* itself. Naturally they wished to emulate the work of men like Peter Lombard, and produce glosses upon what had indeed become the *Glossa Ordinaria*. Smalley tells us that the earliest known example of a gloss upon the *Glossa Ordinaria* is a series of lectures on the Gospels, given by Peter Comestor at some time before his appointment as Chancellor in 1168.

Already, by this date, a glossed Bible had come normally to have one particular set of prefaces and glosses – the *Glossa Ordinaria*, which contemporary scholars simply called *Glosa*. Other versions might be referred to as *"vetus glosa,"* an older version. Small details of the *Glossa Ordinaria* varied from copy to copy, but no major additions or changes were made. Printed editions, when they appeared, remained virtually unaltered. The *Glossa Ordinaria* spread from Paris through Latin Christendom.

The question of the sources of the *Glossa Ordinaria* is a thorny one, and with good reason. Each book had a separate developmental history: not only were there different "final authors," but in each case the author, whose name we may or may not now know, was drawing on a separate body of traditional material and sources. The glossators had to select heavily from the body of existing apparatus, in addition to introducing comments of their own. They left no methodology: it is hard for a modern scholar to establish the bases upon which they made their selection, or even to be sure how many previous compilations were available to help with the task for any given Bible book.

The Gloss on St. Paul was based on an earlier compilation, as it has many glosses in common with the Lanfranc–Berengar–Drogo collection mentioned earlier in this chapter. Smalley suggested that the Gloss on the Pentateuch might be connected to much earlier collections which combined Isidore, Rabanus, and Walafrid Strabo. The Gloss on the Gospels has been shown to contain traces of some eighth-century glosses. Generally the glossators seem to have worked from earlier collections, rather than from the original patristic sources. It is unclear whether this was a matter of convenience or necessity. Convenience was probably a consideration, but the glossators may also have felt a conscious preference for the distilled essence of earlier generations of thought. They did not want to produce a completely new and original *Glossa*, but rather to draw upon and summarize the combined tradition of material already available. The *Glossa Ordinaria* was intended simultaneously as an explanatory apparatus and as a history of a thousand years of previous apparatus. The glossators made a point of quoting a wide range of authors dating from the third to the early twelfth centuries, from the Latin Fathers to Lanfranc and Berengar.

Smalley very properly said that we cannot really discuss the value of these extracts as they appear in the *Glossa Ordinaria*, because the needs and purposes of the glossators are too remote from our judgment. But we can deduce something of how their value was perceived in their own day, and that perceived value was immense. The *Glossa Ordinaria* was developed primarily as an essential summary-apparatus to the Bible. This it successfully became, being an essential textbook which scholars of many future generations could, and would, use as the foundation of, and departing point for, their own developing ideas and interpretations. The *Glossa Ordinaria* was not without its critics, naturally. Despite its great popularity, it had limitations which contemporary scholars were quick to recognize. Petrus Manducator felt that the gloss was often either too brief or too long-winded. Robert of Melun felt that abbreviation of individual glosses had rendered their sense confusing or misleading. Later twelfth-century scholars generally saw it for exactly what it was – an intermediate textbook. In an ideal world the student, having used the *Glossa Ordinaria*, would then follow up the originals of the individual glosses within the package, in order to obtain fuller knowledge of them. The most committed of scholars, Stephen Langton among them, can be shown to have done this. Many others would never reach this stage, but could still learn an enormous amount through the medium of the *Glossa Ordinaria*. In summary, it was an enormous success, fulfilling exactly the need at which it had been aimed. It was the foundation of many twelfth- and thirteenth-century lecture courses, was still being referred to in sermons of the seventeenth century, and was owned and used by John Donne, who made many allusions to it in his *Divine Poems*.

References

G. R. Evans, *The Language and Logic of the Bible: The Earlier Middle Ages* (Cambridge: Cambridge University Press, 1984).

Margaret Gibson, "Carolingian Glossed Psalters," in *The Early Medieval Bible*, ed. R. Gameson (Cambridge: Cambridge University Press, 1994), 78–100.

M. T. Gibson, "The Twelfth Century Glossed Bible," *Papers Presented to the Tenth International Conference on Patristic Studies Held in Oxford in 1987*, ed. E. A. Livingstone, *Studia Patristica* XIX–XXIII (Leuven, 1989), 232–44.

Beryl Smalley, "Some Gospel Commentaries of the Early Twelfth Century," *Recherches de théologie ancienne et médiévale*, 45 (1978), 153ff.

Beryl Smalley, *The Study of the Bible in the Middle Ages*, 3rd edn. (Oxford: Oxford University Press, 1984).

ch**a**
pter
11

Peter Lombard

Marcia L. Colish

Born ca. 1095/1100 in the Novara region, Peter Lombard entered the historical record in the early 1130s when Bernard of Clairvaux met him in Italy and urged him to study theology in France. Peter did so, first at Rheims and, then in 1136, at Paris. Probably an extern student of Hugh of St. Victor, he was in any case thoroughly versed in Victorine theology and in the teachings of other recent and current schools and masters. Peter began his own teaching career in ca. 1142. He became a canon of Notre Dame by 1145, subdeacon in 1148, deacon after 1150, and archdeacon by 1156. He taught until 1159, when he became bishop of Paris, dying in that office July 21/22, 1161.

The Lombard was both a biblical exegete and a systematic theologian. His surviving exegetical works are commentaries on the Psalms (before 1138) and on the Pauline Epistles, or *Collectanea* (1139–41, with a second redaction 1155–8). Not extant but attested indirectly are commentaries on most of the other biblical books. Exegetical material, derived especially from the *Collectanea*, plays a prominent role in Peter's systematic theology, the *Four Books of Sentences* (two redactions, final edition 1155–7), where he assigns it to the appropriate subject-matter headings, and is also found in his 30 known sermons.

As an exegete, Peter did more than any other twelfth-century theologian to develop a scholastic, as distinct from a monastic, approach to Scripture. He agrees that the Psalms should be read morally, Christologically, and ecclesiologically. But his Psalms commentary has far wider aims. Peter treats the Book of Psalms as a composite text containing Psalms of different types, whose connection with other Psalms in the same subcategory needs to be flagged. He provides an *accessus* to each Psalm and to the Book of Psalms as a whole. He notes, and tries to resolve, textual discrepancies arising from the transmission of the Psalms through regional Psalters that sometimes predate and differ from the Vulgate. He sees a need to weigh conflicting authoritative readings. Sometimes he finds them reconcilable. When such is not the case, he analyzes the authorities and offers principled reasons for preferring one to another. Rather than glossing the Psalms to incite devotion, he extracts doctrine from them, mainly ethical and sacramental.

In some cases he retains the solutions arrived at in the *Sentences*; in other cases he substitutes revised positions in his later work.

These traits also mark the *Collectanea*. But in glossing Paul Peter goes much farther. He views the apostle not only as a rich source of authoritative doctrine on many topics but also as the first working Christian theologian. As such, his teaching is subject to the same kind of historical and logical evaluation as scholastic exegesis applies to postbiblical authorities. Peter reads Paul literally, the sole exception being the apostle's identification of Antichrist with Nero in II Thessalonians. Rejecting this interpretation, Peter substitutes his own moral and allegorical understanding of Antichrist. Other areas in which he thinks Paul's authority should be relativized or rejected in the light of the transitory or circumstantial situation in which he preached are the subjection of women, the preference for celibacy over marriage, and permitting disparity of cult in marriage.

Peter's *Collectanea* reflects quite thoroughly the interplay between his exegesis and systematic theology. The second redaction of the *Collectanea* contains revisions informed by the teachings of John Damascene, whom Peter was the first Latin theologian to use in 1154 after his translation from Greek; he draws on this authority even more extensively in the *Sentences*, especially in Trinitarian theology and Christology. Apart from the carryover of subject matter, the *Collectanea* witnesses the further development of Peter's methodology for critiquing authorities that reappears to such influential effect in the *Sentences*.

The Lombard first framed his pedagogical program using the *Collectanea* as his teaching text but soon replaced it with the *Sentences*. Even more than his exegesis, this was the work giving Peter enduring stature as a theological authority for the next four centuries. As a textbook the *Sentences* takes the form of a sentence collection, assembling authorities and arguments to buttress each point covered. This genre of theological literature, invented in the first half of the twelfth century, was in wide use in Peter's day. Masters experimented with it in the effort to devise a systematic curriculum suited to the training of professional theologians. In their sentence collections they presented the material they thought their students needed to know, organizing it so as to display the interconnections among Christian doctrines and their relative importance. In adducing authorities they used to support the positions they defended, and in criticizing authorities supporting positions they opposed, masters articulated their own views while teaching students to think theologically, and critically, about the legacy of the Christian tradition, also demonstrating how insights from other disciplines could contribute to the theologian's work.

One reason for the Lombard's long shelf-life is that, among recent and current scholastics using that genre, his sentence collection was the most comprehensive, balanced, and coherent of those available. In addition to logical and theological clarity and a comparative absence of redundancy, Peter provides organizing themes orchestrated throughout the *Sentences* that link its parts. In his preface, he takes an Augustinian idea, the distinction between signs and things, use and enjoyment, and gives it a new assignment. Where Augustine draws this distinction to guide budding exegetes in applying the liberal arts to interpreting Scripture, Peter extends sign theory to sacramental signs as well as to the verbal signs in the biblical text. For him, Scripture, sacraments, created goods, and the discipline of theology itself are to be used, not enjoyed as ends in themselves; their goal is the enjoyment of God and the eternal communion of the blessed with Him in heaven.

Moving to the actual schema of the *Sentences*, Peter devotes the first of his four books to the deity. He includes proofs of God's existence, expressing thereby his conviction that natural reason can yield valid theological knowledge. The Lombard launches his doctrine of God with the distinction between nature and person in the Trinity, a topic requiring, for him, refinements in the use of theological language. He ends Book 1 with the attributes possessed by the deity as such and those he manifests in his relations with created beings. This sets the stage for Peter's consideration of the creation, angels, human beings, their nature before and after the fall, and the effects and transmission of original sin in Book 2. Peter devotes Book 3 to the redemption. Christ's incarnation and the union of divine and human natures in his person command detailed attention. Here, he applies the terminological specifications he had adopted in discussing nature and person in the Trinity in Book 1. Christ's human nature and moral aptitudes undergird Peter's treatment of the atonement and ethics. The Savior's efficacious and exemplary functions in the Christian life connect Book 3 with the sacraments, the main theme of Book 4. After a clear definition of sacraments in general, Peter treats the rites of the church deemed sacramental in his day, placing his stamp of approval on the septiform principle. Book 4 concludes with last things and the permanent assignment of souls to their posthumous destinations in hell and heaven, purgatory having been considered earlier as a pendant to the sacrament of penance.

If this coverage and organization of his material proved to be influential, so too was Peter's extensive and apposite choice of authorities and the incisive and knowledgeable analysis he applies to them. With respect to contemporaries, he sometimes provides a crisp statement of consensus views, whether they have recently emerged or are of long standing and whether they require defense against heresy or against alternative orthodox positions deemed unpersuasive, irrelevant, or outdated. Peter often finds new ways of conceptualizing questions that other thinkers had raised but failed to resolve. At other times he polemicizes on issues on which no contemporary consensus existed. He sometimes plays a major role in the emergence of a new consensus, or at least articulates the terms in which questions continued to be debated. In addition to making apt use of philosophy and the liberal arts, where he deems them helpful, Peter draws heavily on canon law, especially in his sacramental theology. This, too, gives Lombardian theology a fresh, broad-gauged, and distinctive look.

In summarizing the main outlines of that theology, its most emblematic note is that the branch of Western theology Peter thought needed the most massive overhaul was the doctrine of God. He objects to platonizing theologies of all kinds. He opposes immanentalist and emanationist views of the deity and has no use whatever for negative theology. These concerns reflect his own intellectual proclivities and not merely the desire to refute conclusions of Christians led astray by platonism. Peter is convinced that the theological subject of subjects is the transcendent deity and the unmanifested Trinity; theology is not just about God's manifestation of Himself *ad extra*. In developing this theme in his Trinitarian theology, Peter's task was complicated by the absence in his day of a common and speculatively adequate vocabulary for distinguishing the divine nature from the Trinitarian persons. He dislikes the term "substance" in this context, denoting as it does the Aristotelian understanding of a being that is a composite of matter and form, since it is not apposite to God as a unitary spiritual being. Perforce, he must use "substance" because it is in the creed. But he understands it exclusively as the essence of any being, whatever it happens to be, and applies it only to the divine nature shared equally by the Trinitarian persons. That divine nature he defines as absolute being, being as such. As for the terms apposite to the Trinitarian persons, they must, for Peter, denote exclusively the persons' attributes in relation to each other in the eternal unmanifested Trinity. The only terms meeting this criterion are the traditional ones of unbegotten, begotten, and proceeding. When Trinitarian persons act *ad extra*, Peter emphasizes, it is the Godhead that acts, although its functions may be delegated to this or that person. Since the Godhead is immutable and incommutable, its workings in nature and in humankind are its effects and not participations of the divine being. These activities are not expressions of any inner necessities of the divine nature, but free. And, the divine nature is always greater than any manifestation God may make of it in the creation. God is never exhausted or circumscribed by anything He does *ad extra*. He acts, to be sure, to create, to sustain, to govern, to empower, and to sanctify mankind; but His role as a God of agency in these respects never overrides or subsumes his transcendent reality as a God of essence.

With this doctrine of God in mind, over against purely or primarily economic understandings of the deity, Peter launches into his proofs of God's existence. Prefacing them with the *invisibilia dei* passage from the Epistle to the Romans and starting with data found in the visible world whose causes inductive reason can infer, he also imparts a metaphysical look to this topic. Peter has no doubts about the powers of reason in this connection, or in the applicability of its use by pagan philosophers. He offers four proofs. The first is an *a posteriori* proof from effects to causes and from causes to a first cause, and from design and order in the universe to a first cause that is an intelligent and supreme orderer. The second is an *a posteriori* proof from motion to an immutable ground of being. Here Peter begins to shift from physical to metaphysical analysis. It is not how the deity acts, as a cause, that is the crux of this proof, but his intrinsic nature. The analysis of being offered in the second proof undergirds the third and fourth proofs. In the third proof Peter notes that there are degrees of being and degrees of goodness in the universe. A supreme being is required as the cause of this hierarchy. And, this supreme being cannot be merely the highest term in the hierarchy. It must be a being that transcends the hierarchy. In the fourth proof Peter observes that created beings are composite and changeable. Thus, creatures must have a ground of being that is simple and unchanging. In all, Peter's proofs point to a deity who utterly transcends his creation. While creation is ontologically dependent on him, he is radically independent of it. The priorities and posteriorities in these proofs refer, primarily, to the order of being, not the order of time. There is much grist for the mills of metaphysicians in these proofs, as well as for those of natural theologians.

For Peter, these conclusions are demonstrable by natural reason and they enable theologians to elicit several basic divine attributes; but reason cannot prove that God is three in one. With respect to the Trinity, reason at best can offer analogies, especially the Trinitarian analogies in the human soul. As analogies, they always fall short of what they resemble and they require revelation and faith to be appreciated. Apparent parallels to the doctrine of the Trinity found in pagan philosophers are the shadow, not the reality. In any case, these parallels refer to economic descriptions or similitudes of the Trinitarian persons. The analogies acceptable to Peter, by contrast, speak to the intratrinitarian relations of the Father, Son, and Holy Spirit. And, critical to this analysis is a concept of relation purged of the Aristotelian acceptation of that term as an accident that may, or may not, be predicated of a substance susceptible of modification by accidents. Such an idea is totally inapposite to the deity. Peter replaces it with a grammatical definition of relation, as found in relative nouns like left and right. Such relatives, comprehensible in the light of their correlatives, provide helpful insight into the relations among the Trinitarian persons.

Peter next takes up the divine nature shared by the Trinitarian persons in relation to the created universe, accenting God's ubiquity, the compatibility of God's providence, predestination, and foreknowledge with contingency and free will, and whether God can do other, and better, than he does. With respect to God's ubiquity in the natural order, he is not present in creatures substantially but as their ground of being, enabling them to carry out their natural functions; God's presence in the incarnate Christ is the exception proving the rule. Likewise, in the order of grace, God communicates not himself but a *virtus* or power that leaves intact the creaturely status of the rational beings to whom he grants it; here, the Eucharist is the exception proving the rule. God is less ubiquitous in the charismatic order than in the order of nature since not all people receive his grace and those who do may reject it; those who accept it do not always act with it to the same degree or in the same way. But in neither case is God's ontological grounding of the natural or charismatic order a participation of the divine nature.

Peter treats the issue of providence, foreknowledge, and predestination in relation to free will from a metaphysical perspective, considering how it sheds light on the divine attribute of omniscience. Although we can distinguish the ways He manifests it, God's knowledge is intrinsically total, simple, and eternal. Foreknowledge is God's knowledge of everything that will ever happen, regardless of what causes it. Providence, which Peter calls disposition, is God's governance of the universe, including His foreknowledge of the natural laws He intends to create before He puts them in place. Predestination is the grace of preparation which God grants to the elect, His salvation of them when they cooperate with it, and His knowledge from all eternity of who they will be. Peter acknowledges that predestination is causative and that its decree is unchanging. But divine foreknowledge is not *per se* causative. God does cause some of the things He foreknows. But He also foreknows things that will occur contingently or by the free will of rational creatures. The fact that God creates some beings with the capacity for contingent or voluntary action in no sense limits God's knowledge or His role as a cause, for He freely creates such beings as they are and He knows exhaustively what they will do. The main point Peter makes here is that God's omniscience is not limited or defined by the operations of his creatures as secondary causes.

Peter's argument that God can do other, and better, than He does offers a parallel analysis, referring the issue to God's omnipotence. Similarly, he seeks to show that God's actual arrangements in the temporal world do not exhaust His power, and that in ordaining them, He does so freely. Peter defines God's omnipotence not as God's power to do anything at all but as His power to do whatever He wills. What He does do is just and good. But He is not constrained by His justice and goodness in exercising His power. Further, the choices He actually makes do not limit what He might have done, or what He yet might do. For God, in principle, is always capable of doing more than He actually does do. In elaborating this argument, Peter calls upon the teaching of the twelfth-century nominalists – not to be confused with thinkers denying the extramental referata of universals later in the Middle Ages – on the consignification of nouns in oblique cases and verbs in past and future tenses with nominative nouns and present-tense verbs. This analysis yields the conclusion that what was once possible to God is always possible to Him. In addition to this creative use of contemporary semantic theory, Peter here states a principle animating his doctrine of God more generally, the distinction between God's ordained and absolute power. His most striking articulation of this doctrine is the assertion that, although Christ was born, crucified, and resurrected once for all, God could, if He willed it, replicate those events.

Moving to Peter's account of creation, he is antipathetic to the project, popular with some contemporaries, of considering how or whether the cosmogenetic doctrine of Plato's *Timaeus* squares with the Book of Genesis. His own discussion draws exclusively on the exegetical and patristic traditions. His main contributions in this field are threefold: he finds a cogent way of including angels within a primarily hexaemeral account of creation. He also finds a way of combining the six-day Genesis account with a modified doctrine of creation *simul*. And, he finds a way of presenting creatures in an order reflecting their relative metaphysical status, while retaining the standard biblical model, which does not order creation in this way.

For Peter, God and God alone creates the universe *ex nihilo*. He rejects exemplary causation, however understood, along with preexistent matter, and the assignment of particular cosmogenetic roles to different Trinitarian persons. Since God did not need to create the universe, why did He do so? So that rational creatures may come to a knowledge and love of Him and enjoy eternal felicity, Peter answers. Everything else in the universe was created for its utility to rational beings in achieving that end. Objecting to platonic anthropology, Peter does not devalue the human body. God gave us both bodies and souls so that mankind could serve as a microcosm of creation. Thus, in loving and serving God in body and soul we bring the whole creation back to Him; and it is metaphorically redeemed and glorified in us. This notion lays the foundation for the thoroughly Aristotelian anthropology Peter develops later in the *Sentences*; in both the creation and the redemption of mankind, soul and body are integrally united.

As for the timetable of the creation, Peter holds that angels and primordial matter were created simultaneously and before everything else. Then, the other creatures were produced according to the biblical six-day plan. During the hexaemeron God also created seminal reasons as causes of subsequent developments. The Lombard's account of creation is literal, straightforward, and streamlined, displaying no interest in the scientific anomalies it contains. Here, as in his treatment of cosmogenesis itself, he shows no desire to wear the hat of the natural philosopher.

The question of when the angels were created was debated in Peter's day and not all accepted his solution. But contemporaries largely agreed with his views on the nature and attributes of angels and on why they constituted an important theological topic. That consensus centered on the angels' reason and free will, their use of these faculties in their decision to fall or not to fall, and the felt need to argue that, once confirmed as good or as fallen, their moral states were unchangeable. What Peter adds to this common agenda is an analysis of angelic free will, defined as the capacity to choose good or evil without violence or constraint, that lays the groundwork for his treatment of human free will before and after the fall, the states of the souls of the blessed and damned, and a key feature of his Christology. The good angels remained loyal to God, he argues, because they freely chose to cooperate with divine grace. The fallen angels fell not only because they freely chose disobedience but also because God subtracted or withdrew His grace from them. This absence of grace then became an unalterable condition of the fallen angels, making it impossible for them to repent. The good angels, confirmed in virtue, continue to receive grace and continue to cooperate with it, thus continuing to grow in virtue. In neither case has the angels' free will been abrogated. Rather, it has been intensified; the angels of either sort now experience no conflicting desires. Thus, they will exclusively what they want, without violence or constraint. And thus, they continue to deserve the treatment they receive. With respect to the good angels, another distinction emerges. Their merit, as confirmed, does not change qualitatively. But it continues to improve, quantitatively, as their opportunities for manifesting virtue increase in the course of time. This distinction between quality and quantity resurfaces in Book III in Peter's description of the human Christ as a moral agent whose virtue is always perfect; His life, death, and resurrection do not increase that virtue qualitatively but merely multiply His opportunities for displaying it. And, the permanence of the damned and blessed in their hellish and heavenly states is justified by the view that, continuing to will evil and good exclusively, they continue to merit their fates. Finally, Peter's argument that the good angels continue to grow in virtue points to their constitution as changeable creatures. In this respect, although they are composed of pure spirit, they are distinguishable from God, who is immutable.

Disclaiming that the study of human nature before the fall is a frivolous pursuit, Peter offers a naturalistic, if lean, account of the creation of Adam and Eve and of their physical and spiritual life in Eden. As a pendant to the analysis of free will now applied to the primal parents' fall, Peter adds that their motivations, although equally deliberate and intellectual, differed. Eve consented to the misuse of knowledge; Adam to the misuse of wisdom.

Once fallen, mankind became subject to physical suffering and death, the inability to exercise sexual functions without lust, concupiscence understood as misdirected love more generally, and ignorance. But, for Peter, the most serious consequence of original sin is the depression of the will. While he staunchly asserts that fallen humanity remains free to reject grace and while, reactivating a theme dormant for eight centuries, he avers that conscience, a spark of reason inclining us toward the good, remains present even in the worst of sinners, he holds that our postlapsarian freedom to choose good or evil without violence or constraint has been deactivated. We continue to need grace, both prevenient and cooperating, in order to will the good. But grace is not a substitute for free will. What grace does, in conjunction with free will, is to enable the free will to become a good will. Peter sees free will and grace acting synergistically. Virtue is a good quality of the mind, a disposition inclining us to live rightly. Both grace and free will are needed to activate this disposition. The Lombard analogizes grace to rain, free will to the earth, and virtue as a mental disposition to a seed. The fruit borne by the seed is virtue understood as the good intentions and actions that ornament the soul of the moral agent and that are accounted meritorious in him. There can be no merit without free will. And, when God rewards the meritorious, He rewards not Himself but the virtues that moral agents have made their own ingrained character traits.

That process, however, must be conducted under the conditions of labor applying to postlapsarian mankind, inherited willy-nilly. In considering how original sin, and its consequences, are transmitted from parent to child, Peter stresses that parents are the cause only of the bodies of their offspring. God directly creates each person's soul, a soul good on account of its divine creation. It contains the rational faculties, free will included. How, then, can parents transmit the guilt, the punishment for sin, and the inclination to sin to souls they do not create themselves? Peter answers that parents, perforce, pass on to their children a flesh that has been corrupted by the fall, along the lines of the inheritance of acquired characteristics. This vitiated flesh bears with it the inclination to sin. In due course, it will make the sexuality of their children inoperable without lust. And, thanks to the intimate union between the human body and soul, the vitiated body engendered by the parents will fuse with the innocent God-given soul in the womb and corrupt it as well.

This account, harsh as it seems, at least has the merit of reinforcing the major point Peter makes about human nature. It was as a unit of body and soul that we were created. It was as a unit of body and soul that we fell. It was, also, as a unit of body and soul that we were afflicted with the consequences of original sin. While the fall depresses the will more than any other faculty, it also vitiates the body. At the same time, it is as an integral unit of body and soul that we will be redeemed and glorified. This principle informs God's chosen mode of human redemption in the incarnation of Christ. It also informs God's ordinance for the extension of Christ's saving work in the ethical and sacramental life of the Church.

There are three main topics in the field of Christology on which the Lombard takes a stand. The first is the hypostatic union. There were three orthodox accounts of it taught at the time: the *assumptus homo* theory, the subsistence theory, and the *habitus* theory. Peter acknowledges that all receive support in the Christian tradition. He also finds them all problematic. In explaining why, he applies the lexical clarifications he had developed in treating the doctrine of God. The first theory suggests that there are two persons or three substances in the incarnate Christ; the second suggests that His human nature was divinized in the hypostatic union; the third suggests that His humanity was accidental and partible from His divinity once assumed. Having outlined their perceived deficiencies, Peter declines to choose among them, concluding that the best course of action is to leave the matter open pending further investigation. The most he has to say is that the Word took on a human body and soul not yet in existence and not yet joined to each other before His human nature was united impartibly to His divine nature and person. This union was not accidental and did not alter either His divine or His human nature. He has one person only, a divine one. Peter stresses the full consubstantiality of the human Christ with the rest of humanity. Although, like His mother, He was exempted from original sin, Christ took on mortality, one of its consequences, and the capacity to suffer temptation. At the same time, the Lombard endows the human Christ with a quasi-superhuman psychology, arguing that the human Christ knew, by grace, everything that the Word knows, by nature. In this respect, Christ was not entirely like us in all but sin; the psychology of temptation and virtuous choice were necessarily different in His case than in ours. The same claim also makes it difficult for the Lombard to argue convincingly that the human Christ had the virtues of faith and hope, despite the incomplete knowledge that defines these virtues.

In treating Christ's saving work, Peter reflects a strong tendency, visible in his ethics as well, to accent the internalizing of the Christian message in the lives of believers. Thus, while his theology of the redemption retains an objective dimension in its view of what Christ accomplishes and what redeemed mankind receives, he emphasizes the subjective side of the transaction. Christ's role, in offering His perfect virtue and perfect obedience to God, is not to change God's mind about mankind but to catalyze our own capacity to love, in response to His love for us. The reception of Christ's redemption also mitigates the inclination to sin that remains a consequence of the fall in believers, making less arduous the recuperation of the image of God in the human soul that is the goal of the ethical and sacramental life.

Although the part of his ethical doctrine concerning sin and vice is presented in Book II, while his analysis of virtue is placed in Book III, under the heading of the moral aptitudes of the human Christ, much of what Peter has to say on ethics is consistent, if not totally so. Aside from the lack of symmetry between the human Christ and other human beings just noted, another major point on which Peter gives with one hand and takes with the other is the question of whether natural virtue is possible. On the face of it, most of the evidence suggests a negative answer, since one of the hallmarks of Lombardian ethics is the principle that all meritorious acts require the collaboration of free will and grace. At the same time, another central feature of Peter's ethics is his stress on intentionality as the essence of ethical acts and as the critical determinant of a moral agent's ethical status. While he holds that some acts are intrinsically immoral and that good intentions should ordinarily be expressed in good, and appropriate, actions, he maintains that, present or absent external expression, inner intentionality remains of the essence. It is not temptation, or the contemplation of temptation, but the conscious and voluntary decision to reject or to succumb to it that counts, whether one acts out that decision or not. This view leads Peter to dismiss out of hand the privative theory of evil, replacing it with the theme of our willed fall into the *regio dissimilitudinis*, in which we deliberately obscure God's image in ourselves.

At the same time, intentions cannot be severed from the ends they serve. We cannot serve an objectively good end by wrongdoing. Good deeds require good faith. Leaving aside faith as a theological virtue, which would require consent to specifically Christian teachings, Peter thinks that good faith means the absence of hypocrisy as well as good intentions in a positive sense. He concedes that non-Christians are capable of expressing it, in their own virtues and in their service to their neighbors inspired by natural piety. So, the virtuous pagan rears his head in the *Sentences*, if briefly.

In Christian ethics, his real subject, Peter preserves the distinction between God as transcendent and His effects in creatures in His mission *ad extra*. Neither grace, in general, nor the gifts of the Holy Spirit, in particular, enables Christians to participate in the divine nature. The virtues and merits which that grace and those gifts help us acquire are, and remain, purely human attributes. This is so whether the virtues are cardinal, theological, or gifts of the Spirit. Peter gives an abbreviated account of the first and third types of virtue. A parallel between them is that, in both cases, some virtues or aspects of virtue, needed for this life only, do not endure, while we bring others from the *via* to the *patria*. One of the gifts of the Spirit is knowledge. Peter does not clarify how it is similar to, or different from, knowledge as a product of our natural rational endowment.

Peter is far more interested in the theological virtues, agreeing that faith and hope are ordered to our life *in via* and that charity alone endures. Faith attracts most of his attention, reflecting his felt need to understand faith both as an epistemic state and as a virtue. The first of these issues was debated; Peter adopts the definition of faith as below knowledge and above opinion, adding that it deals only with theological objects of knowledge. On faith as a virtue he states the consensus position, distinguishing faith as intellectual assent to a body of theo-logical propositions held to be true, from faith as assent to what someone says because he is trustworthy, from faith that saves. The latter involves adhesion to God in love and confidence and a faith that works in love. Peter adds that the faith that saves may be proportioned to the intelligence and education of the believer. But it must embrace the propositions of the creed, however imperfectly they are grasped.

Giving a standard definition of charity as love of God for His own sake and love of self and neighbor for God's sake, Peter manifests his taste for hierarchy by positing four grades of charity: incipient, proficient, perfect, and most perfect, the latter describing the saints in heaven. He also hierarchizes the gradation of goods under the heading of charity. We should love God the most, as the supreme good. We should love the souls of rational creatures next, for they have an eternal destiny. We should love the human body next, for it is intimately linked to the soul and it is likewise destined for future glory. Thus, its health and self-preservation are legitimate goods. Finally, we should love the things below us in the creation, insofar as they conduce to the body's well-being. This ladder of love recapitulates, in the return to God, Peter's metaphysical and moral hierarchy of creation. He concludes his discussion of charity with the distribution of practical assistance, recognizing the finitude of means at anyone's disposal. Dissenting from the principle of need as the prime determinant, he substitutes relationship, from parents to other relatives to one's household to neighbors to compatriots, ending with enemies. He includes enemies nor merely to comply with the biblical injunction to love them but also to reinforce the point that, as a theological virtue, charity transcends natural obligations.

Peter's most important contribution to sacramental theology in Book IV is his retention and refinement of Hugh of St. Victor's redefinition of sacraments in general, not just as visible signs of invisible grace but as signs that resemble what they signify and that mediate divine grace, making it effective in the inner lives of recipients. Peter uses this same Victorine definition of sacraments as a rationale for rejecting Hugh's claim that Old Testament rites are truly comparable with salvific Christian sacraments. Sacraments contain and convey grace objectively when administered in the appropriate way, by the appropriate minister, with the appropriate intention. The ability of the recipient to receive and make fruitful use of the grace mediated by sacraments depends, in turn, on the faith and intention he brings to their reception. Lacking the correct faith and intention, he receives the sacramental medium alone, the *sacramentum tantum*, but not its spiritual content, the *res sacramenti*. For Peter, the Christian's journey back from the *regio dissimilitudinis* of sin is concretely moved along, and not just signposted, by the sacraments.

In presenting sacramental theology Peter begins with baptism, confirmation, the Eucharist, penance, and unction, sacraments received by all Christians, followed by holy orders and marriage, sacraments received only by some Christians. In each case, while he discusses the conditions that validate the administration of sacraments, he is concerned primarily with how the sacraments work to heal and sanctify their recipients. He is also interested in removing obstacles to sacramental grace and widening access to these rites. He insists on the repeatability of all but baptism, confirmation, and holy orders and treats the departures from earlier theory and practice that this policy entails as rational, pastoral, and theological desiderata. The individual sacraments he discusses at greatest length are baptism, the Eucharist, penance, holy orders, and marriage. In most cases this emphasis reflects the condition of current debates.

Consistent with his wish to make sacramental grace widely available, Peter admits baptism by desire and by blood as well as by standard administration, and supports the consensus view that, in an emergency, anyone may validly administer baptism so long as he or she intends what the Church intends by the rite. Given his stress on the necessity of correct intentionality for valid reception, he faces a dilemma with infant baptism and judges it an exception to that rule. In infants, baptism is valid on a purely objective basis. Infants receive baptism's ablution of sin and a fund of grace that remains latent in them until they are mature enough to decide whether or not to collaborate with it. While Peter's treatment of baptism indicates his support for the necessity of this sacrament, it is nonetheless in this context that he restates the principle that God always transcends His ordinances for mankind. Although baptism is required for us, in the final analysis, God will save whomever He wills to save, baptized or not.

Eucharistic theology was controversial in Peter's day not only because of the need to defend orthodoxy against heretics who rejected the real presence doctrine or the sacrament altogether but also because orthodox theologians had trouble explaining Eucharistic doctrines on which they agreed. While attending to debates surrounding the administration of the Eucharist, Peter is drawn especially to those reflecting metaphysical or semantic difficulties attached to the belief in the real presence. He addresses two main questions: which body – the resurrected body or His historical body – did Christ give His disciples at the Last Supper, and how can we explain both the change in the bread and wine when they are turned into the body and blood of Christ at the consecration and the elements' retention of the attributes of bread and wine despite that change? On the first topic, he supports the unpopular view that Christ gave His historical body to His disciples. On the second, he insists that the issue be framed in the Aristotelian language of substance and accidents. The change the elements undergo is substantial. The physical attributes of the consecrated elements are accidents. The problem, as Peter notes, is that these accidents no longer have a substance subtending them, serving as a material substratum in which they can inhere. Yet, they subsist, inhering in no substance. Peter is no more successful than anyone else at the time in resolving this anomaly. But he poses it clearly indeed, convinced that it must be explained in Aristotelian terms.

Agreeing that unbelieving recipients receive to their condemnation, jeopardizing their capacity to profit from the Eucharist, Peter at the same time asserts that nothing such recipients do or intend changes the Eucharist's objective content; otherwise, mere mortals would be able to frustrate God's gracious ordinance with respect to the sacrament. For the same reason, the Eucharistic ministry of immoral priests remains valid. Peter disallows only the Eucharistic ministry of heretics, excommunicates, or schismatics. However correctly they may have been ordained, such priests cannot validly administer the sacrament.

The centrality of the recipient, and the role of the sacrament in his inner life, emerge even more forcefully in Peter's treatment of penance. He insists that penance should be available as often as penitents need it. He is a staunch contritionist in the current debate on when, in the three-part sequence of contrition, confession, and satisfaction, the penitent's status is changed in God's eyes. Confession he regards as optional; and, if a penitent cannot find a worthy priest to whom to confess, he may choose a discreet and judicious lay person. This position locates Peter within the orthodox consensus, but near its radical fringe. He is thoroughly mainstream in imposing harsh punishment on priests who violate the confidentiality of confession. Most important, he sees penance as a transaction between the penitent and God. Insofar as there is a necessary minister of penance, it is the penitent's own conscience.

In considering holy orders, Peter rejects the canonists' tendency to treat clerics as functionaries with particular job descriptions, qualifications, and impediments, instead offering a rich theological understanding of ordination as a sacrament. Each of the seven grades of orders signifies, and makes efficacious in the recipient's ministry, the varying modes of service in Christ's own ministry. When this *res sacramenti* is internalized by a properly disposed recipient, it has two effects: it empowers him to perform his pastoral functions *vis-à-vis* his congregants and it grants him the grace enabling him to reify this *imitatio Christi* in his inner life. The ordinand likewise receives the gifts of the Holy Spirit. It is this accent on the inner spiritual meaning of ordination, for the recipient, that distinguishes Peter on holy orders. Uninterested in the jurisdictional relations among prelates or in church–state relations, he does note that there are official functions in the church that convey rank without being grades of holy orders. These include prophecy, poetry, musicianship, and foresight. Individuals exercising these functions may, in some cases, be lay persons; Peter dignifies them for their contributions to the inspiration and edification of the Christian community.

The final sacrament he treats, and at considerable length, is marriage, also perhaps the single most controversial sacrament in his day. There are notable parallels here with his treatment of penance, in that he sees an initial, intentional, and constitutive stage in the sacrament, then followed by physical expression, or not. Thus, in the debate over what makes a marriage valid, sacramental, and indissoluble, Peter supports the present consent of the spouses, not the future consent exchanged at their betrothal or the consummation of the marriage after the fact. Despite the difficulties it may entail, he does not shrink from the logic of his position and admits the validity of clandestine marriage, the parties having no impediments. While his contritionist stance on penance did not, in the event, prevail, Peter's doctrine of marriage formation did help to define an emerging consensus on that subject.

Reasoning that marriage is the vocation to which most Christians are called, Peter removes obstructions to it so far as possible. Generous on the matter of remarriage, both for the widowed and for people whose marriages have been rendered nugatory by the extended absence or presumed death of their spouses or by their spouses' sexual dysfunction, the Lombard is impatient with the discussion of conditions impeding or nullifying marriages. Still, he imposes a lucid order on this subject. He begins by considering conditions impeding consent or leading to defective consent, such as coercion, fraud, and error. He next treats the positive attributes of marriageable persons, insofar as they have not ceded their rights freely or to forces beyond their control. Under the heading of involuntary or congenital impediments he places sexual dysfunction and insanity. All other impediments, such as servile status, vows, disparity of cult, age, cognation, and affinity, he treats as deriving not from the nature of things but from choice, accident, or conventional rules subject to change.

Consistent with both his emphasis on marital intentionality and on the hylomorphic constitution of human nature, Peter sees both the union of minds and hearts and the typical subsequent union of bodies as sacramental, these unions signifying the spiritual and institutional unions of Christ and the Church respectively. This position simultaneously upgrades the spiritual bonding and marital affection of spouses and treats their sexual relations as upright and sinless when ordered to the goods of marriage. But it is here, as well, that the Lombard's theology of marriage proves to be sub-sacramental, in terms of his definition of sacraments in general. For, in his estimation, neither the spiritual nor the physical union of spouses is a means of grace, however much marriage may be a school for virtue. Marriage remains a sign of a sacred thing but it does not effect what it signifies in leading spouses from the *via* to the *patria*.

Peter's treatise on last things outlines the culmination of that journey. His eschatology is noteworthy for his refusal to countenance unanswerable questions or wild-eyed apocalyptic speculation. He therefore omits discussion of Antichrist, although he had developed a cogent interpretation of the topic in his Pauline exegesis, beginning his end-of-time scenario with the general resurrection and the second coming of Christ. With the last judgment and the assignment of souls to heaven and hell, he has two main points to make. There are four types of souls. Saints who have demonstrated their supererogatory merit and sinners who have rejected grace to the end are already judged, and saved and damned respectively. Sinners less comprehensively evil will be judged and condemned; the repentant who died penitent but without having fully expiated their sins, will be judged and saved after a purgatorial interim.

Peter's second point integrates last things into the larger themes informing the *Sentences*. Not only do the damned and saved manifest the city of man and the city of God eternally, they also illustrate the outcome of the doctrine of signs and things, use and enjoyment as applied to the Christian life. Nor does Peter neglect to connect this topic with his overarching doctrine of God. In describing hell and heaven, his central thesis is that God's consignment of souls to these realms is just, in line with the freedom of the will that sinners and saints exercised in this life and continue to exercise in the next. Thus, they continue to merit their punishments or rewards. Like the angels confirmed in the good, the saints experience no obstacles in their willing of the good. Having completed their return from the *regio dissimilitudinis*, they have recovered their true humanity. By the good use of earthly things, they have moved through and beyond signs and *utilia* to the direct knowledge and love of God Himself, whom they can now enjoy forever without mediation. This end-point, for the blessed, still preserves Peter's vivid sense that there are two distinct kinds of beings here who are now joined in loving communion.

Both the strengths of the Lombard's achievement, the questions he deliberately leaves open, the debates he resolves, those he fails to resolve, and the areas in which he does not press the logic of his position to its ultimate conclusion, all provided a wealth of problems and opportunities for later theologians. So did the many *loci* in the *Sentences* that proved hospitable to the new philosophical and scientific materials whose translation from Arabic and Greek lay on the immediate intellectual horizon of Western Christendom. The tradition launched by the Lombard was well served by the fact that his masterwork has a schema and a methodology that could accommodate these new materials and the new debates they engendered, in whatever camp his commentators might plant their standards. First in the cathedral schools of twelfth-century France and then in the theological faculties of universities across Europe, later theologians rapidly made the *Sentences* the basis of their own teaching. From this vantage point, the Lombard's *Sentences* did more than any other text to shape the discipline of medieval scholastic theology.

Bibliography

Primary Sources

Peter Lombard. *Collectanea in omnes d. Pauli apostoli Epistolas,* ed. J. P. Migne. *Patrologia latina cursus completus,* 191–2 (Paris, 1880).
——. *Commentarium in Psalmos Davidicos,* ed. J. P. Migne. *Patrologia latina cursus completus,* 191 (Paris, 1880).
——. *Sententiae in IV libris distinctae,* 2 vols., 3rd rev. edn., ed. Ignatius C. Brady (Grottaferrata, 1971–81).

——. *Sermones* 4, 7–8, 12–13, 21, 23–5, 32, 35–6, 43, 45, 67–8, 72, 80, 99, 111–12, 115, ed. J. P. Migne. *Patrologia latina curses completus,* 171 (Paris, 1893). [misattributed to Hildebert of Lavardin].
Van den Eynde, Damien, ed., "Deux sermons inédits de Pierre Lombard." *Miscellanea Lombardiana* (Novara, 1957), pp. 75–87.

Secondary Sources

Bertola, Ermenegildo. "I commentari paolini di Pietro Lombardo e la loro duplici redazione." *Pier Lombardo,* 3, 2–3 (1959): 75–90.
——. "Il problema delle creature angeliche in Pier Lombardo." *Pier Lombardo,* 1, 2 (1957): 33–54.
——. "Il problema di Dio in Pier Lombardo." *Rivista di filosofia neo-scolastica,* 48 (1956): 135–50.
——. "La dottrina della creazione nel *Libri Sententiarum* di Pier Lombardo." *Pier Lombardo,* 1, 1 (1957): 27–44.

Blomme, Robert. *La doctrine du péché dans les écoles théologiques de la première moitié du XIIe siècle* (Louvain, 1958).
Buytaert, Eligius M. "St. John Damascene, Peter Lombard, and Gerhoh of Reichersberg." *Franciscan Studies,* 10 (1950): 323–43.
Châtillon, Jean. "La Bible dans les écoles du XIIe siècle: "In *Le moyen âge et la Bible,* eds. Pierre Riché and Guy Lobrichon (Paris, 1984), pp. 163–97.
Clerck, D. E. de. "Droits du démon et nécessité de la rédemption: Les écoles d'Abélard et de

Pierre Lombard." *Recherches de théologie ancienne et médiévale*, 14 (1947): 32–64.

Colish, Marcia L. "Gilbert, the Early Porretans, and Peter Lombard: Semantics and Theology." In *Gilbert de Poitiers et ses contemporaines*, eds. Jean Jolivet and Alain de Libera (Naples, 1987), pp. 229–50.

——. *Peter Lombard*, 2 vols. (Leiden, 1994).

——. "Peter Lombard and Abelard: The *Opinio Nominalium* and Divine Transcendence." *Vivarium*, 30 (1992): 139–56.

——. "Peter Lombard as an Exegete of St. Paul." In *Ad litteram: Authoritative Texts and Their Medieval Readers*, eds. Mark D. Jordan and Kent Emery, Jr. (Notre Dame, 1992), pp. 71–92.

——. "*Psalterium Scholasticorum*: Peter Lombard and the Development of Scholastic Psalms Exegesis." *Speculum*, 67 (1992): 531–48.

——. "Systematic Theology and Theological Renewal in the Twelfth Century." *Journal of Medieval and Renaissance Studies*, 18 (1988): 135–56.

Delhaye, Philippe. *Pierre Lombard: Sa vie, ses oeuvres, sa morale* (Montréal, 1961).

Evans, G. R. *Old Arts and New Theology: The Beginnings of Theology as an Academic Discipline* (Oxford, 1980).

Ghellinck, Joseph de. "Le traité de Pierre Lombard sur les sept ordres ecclésiastiques: Ses sources, ses copistes." *Revue d'histoire ecclésiastique*, 10 (1909): 290–302, 720–8; 11 (1910): 29–46.

Gilson, Étienne. "Pierre Lombard et les théologies d'essence." *Revue du moyen âge latin*, 1 (1945): 61–4.

Hamesse, Jacqueline, ed. *Thesaurus Librorum Sententiarum Petri Lombardi*. Series A: Thesaurus Patrorum Latinorum, Corpus Christianorum (Turnhout, 1991).

Häring, Nikolaus M. "The Interaction between Canon Law and Sacramental Theology in the Twelfth Century." In *Proceedings of the Fourth International Congress of Medieval Canon Law*, ed. Stephan Kuttner (Vatican City, 1976), pp. 483–93.

Hödl, Ludwig. "Der Transsubstantiationsbegriff in der scholastischen Theologie des 12. Jahrhunderts." *Recherches de théologie ancienne et médiévale*, 31 (1964): 230–59.

Landgraf, Artur Michael. "Die Stellungsnahme der Frühscholastik zur wissenschftlichen Methode des Petrus Lombardus." *Collectanea Franciscana*, 4 (1934): 513–21.

Lobrichon, Guy. "Une nouveauté: Les gloses de la Bible." In *Le moyen âge et la Bible*, eds. Pierre Riché and Guy Lobrichon (Paris, 1984), pp. 93–114.

Macy, Gary. *The Theologies of the Eucharist in the Early Scholastic Period: A Study of the Salvific Function of the Sacrament according to the Theologians c. 1080–c. 1220* (Oxford, 1984).

Santiago-Otero, Horacio. "Pedro Lombardo: Su tesis acerca del saber de Cristo hombre." *Miscelánea José Zunzunegui (1911–1974)* (Vitoria, 1975), pp. 115–25.

Schmidt, Martin Anton. "Das Sentenzenwerk des Petrus Lombardus und sein Aufstieg zum Muster- und Textbuch der theologischen Ausbildung." In *Handbuch der Dogmen- und Theologiegeschichte* (Göttingen, 1982), 1: 587–615.

Schneider, Johannes. *Die Lehre vom Dreieinigen Gott in der Schule des Petrus Lombardus* (Munich, 1961).

Schupp, Johann. *Die Gnadenlehre des Petrus Lombardus* (Freiburg im Breisgau, 1932).

Zeimentz, Hans. *Ehe nach der Lehre der Frühscholastik: Eine moralgeschichtliche Untersuchung zur Anthropologie und Theologie der Ehe in der Schule Anselms von Laon und Wilhelms von Champeaux, bei Hugo von St. Viktor, Walter von Mortagne und Petrus Lombardus* (Düsseldorf, 1973).

The High Medieval Debate

part 4

12 Saint Bonaventure
    Michael Robson

13 Thomas Aquinas
    Fergus Kerr

14 Later Medieval Mystics
    Oliver Davies

15 Academic Controversies
    Takashi Shogimen

16 Duns Scotus and William Ockham
    Alexander Broadie

Saint Bonaventure

Michael Robson

ch a p ter

12

Bonaventure was born at Bagnoregio, between Viterbo and Orvieto, about 1217. When he was seriously ill as a child, his mother made a vow to Saint Francis of Assisi and he attributed his recovery to the saint,[1] who had interceded for him on other occasions.[2] In addition to his indebtedness, he reflects that the rise of the Friars Minor resembles the growth and development of the Church, which began with simple fishermen and was later enriched with the most illustrious doctors. He believes that the fraternity was established by Jesus Christ and its ranks included scholars, one of whom was Alexander of Hales, a prominent master in the Faculty of Theology at the University of Paris.[3] Bonaventure received his primary education in the friary at Bagnoregio and then proceeded to Paris where he completed his studies in the Faculty of Arts. He was clothed in the habit of the Friars Minor in 1243 and, after studying under Alexander of Hales, Jean de la Rochelle, Eudes Rigaud and William of Melitona, he was appointed as the fifth master of the friars' school in 1252. His 21 years in the University of Paris ended when he was elected as the seventh minister general of the fraternity on February 2, 1257. He led the rapidly expanding fraternity, which he endeavored to keep faithful to the founder's ideals. On May 28, 1273 he was created cardinal bishop of Albano by Gregory X, who consecrated him on November 11 or 12 of that year. At Lyons he was busy with the preparations for the council to be held there in the following summer. He died during the council on July 15, 1274. His writings[4] have interested theologians, philosophers, biblical scholars, devotional writers, and historians of preaching and the Friars Minor.[5] Each of these areas merits fuller attention. This study focuses on the roots of his theology and samples[6] the three main areas of his work. The *Breviloquium*[7] illustrates his articulation of the principal questions of theology. The *De praeparatione ad missam*[8] exemplifies his devotional writings and the friars' role as promoters of euchatistic piety, a sacrament which was at the heart of the liturgical life in friaries. The *Collationes de septem donis Spiritus sancti*[9] express the anxieties felt by many friars about the application of the newly recovered Aristotelian corpus at the University of Paris and the need to maintain due balance between faith and reason.

The Foundations of Theological Study

Medieval theologians worked within an environment suffused by a profound reverence for the Scriptures. The division of the Scriptures into chapters, the proliferation of biblical commentaries, concordances, aids for study, and the quest for the establishment of the authentic manuscript tradition of the sacred text testify to the activities of scriptural scholars. The range and character of the biblical commentaries from the early friars' school have been described by I. Brady and B. Smalley.[10] Scriptural studies laid the foundation for the study of scholastic theology, and from 1243 to 1245 Bonaventure attended cursory lectures on the whole Bible, and between 1247 and 1249 the ordinary lectures, in which the master gave a more profound exegesis of the sacred book. In 1248, still a bachelor, he lectured on *The Gospel of Luke*,[11] which he subsequently revised, and later produced *Commentaries on Ecclesiastes* and the *Gospel of Saint John*. Biblical imagery and quotations pervade his theological writings and many of his treatises open with the words of Scripture, such as the *Breviloquium, Soliloquium, De reductione artium ad theologiam*, and *Itinerarium mentis in Deum*, quoting Ephesians 3:14–19 and James 1:17.

Bonaventure urges the theologian to maintain an appropriate order and to commence with the study of the Scriptures in the letter and the spirit. The Scriptures enjoy a primary authority[12] on account of their divine origin,[13] which is summarized:

> the whole of Scripture is the heart of God, the mouth of God, the tongue of God, the pen of God, *a scroll that had writing on back and front* (cf. Apocalypse 5:1).[14]

Unlike the other sciences, the Scriptures are not handed down by human research, but through divine revelation.[15] A firm faith in the revealed truth is a prerequisite for the theologian; the true faith may never disagree with the Scriptures, which are inspired by the Holy Spirit.[16] In the *liber creaturae*, which was offered to Adam and Eve for their guidance, God communicated efficaciously. When Adam and Eve abandoned their innocence, they lost the power to read this book clearly. Divine providence then saw fit to supply the further testimony of another book, the *liber Scripturae*, which was written in accordance with divine revelation.[17] The Scriptures illuminate the world and possess the power to restore it toward the knowledge, praise, and love of God.[18] They are concerned with the work of redemption[19] and offer a knowledge which moves humanity towards the good and withdraws it from evil.[20] Their central role is manifest in the *Breviloquium*, whose prologue provides a summary of the way in which the Bible is to be used. The hypothesis that this prologue was constructed like a university sermon has been advocated by J. G. Bougerol,[21] whose view gains some credence from part 1, chapter 1, which has the appearance of a beginning rather than a continuation.[22]

After firmly rooting his teaching in the Bible, the theologian is to be guided by the general councils of the Church and the writings of the Fathers; a spirit of harmony pervades these authorities.[23] The writings of these theological luminaries, revered as saints by Bonaventure, help the theologian to understand the Scriptures, whose obscure passages they elucidate.[24] The Eastern Fathers are Dionysius, Gregory Nazianzen, Gregory of Nyssa, John of Damascus, Basil the Great, Athanasius, and John Chrysostom; the Latin Fathers are Hilary, Gregory the Great, Augustine, Ambrose, and Jerome.[25] Just as John of Damascus is hailed as the *doctor Graecus*, Augustine is the *praecipuus doctor Latinus*[26] and the *egregius doctor*.[27] The bishop of Hippo is by far the most influential Father whom Bonaventure treats as an encyclopedic authority,[28] citing him more than 3,050 times and pronouncing his *Confessiones, De Trinitate, De Genesim ad litteram,* and *De civitate Dei* to be the finest expositions on time, matter, forms, the production of things, God, the soul, and the nature of creation.[29]

After the Fathers' writings come the masters' *Summae*, which expound the saints' teaching.[30] More modern theologians, whose writings were already being quoted with authority in the schools of Paris, are cited liberally; the fact that many of these theologians and pastors had a reputation for sanctity of life augmented their authority and influence. Anselm, Richard of Saint Victor, and Bernard of Clairvaux are announced as the medieval successors to Augustine, Gregory the Great, and John of Damascus in theological exposition, preaching, and contemplation, with Hugh of Saint Victor excelling in all three areas.[31] The influence of William, abbot of Saint-Thierry, who subsequently joined the Cistercians, has been examined.[32] Alexander of Hales, who taught Bonaventure between 1243 and 1245, receives special praise and is portrayed as his *pater et magister . . . bonae memoriae*.[33]

While the Scriptures express what is to believed by Christians, the theologian presents the deposit of revelation in intelligible terms,[34] making the transition from the credible to the intelligible.[35] Bonaventure appeals to the authority of Augustine's *De utilitate credendi*:

> what we believe we owe to authority,
> what we understand we owe to reason.[36]

He proposes to show that the science of theology lacks neither true unity nor sound organization:[37] theology is the only perfect wisdom. This is the point at which philosophical knowledge ends, whereas theology goes on to consider the supreme Cause, God, as the remedy of sin, the reward of merit, and the goal of human desires. Bonaventure concludes that all Christians should be aflame with longing to acquire this knowledge.[38]

The Scriptures contain the words of everlasting life and were recorded not only that the human race might believe, but also attain everlasting life. The mendicant theologian is advised to reach out in a spirit of pure faith to God so that he might understand the Scriptures,[39] which should be approached in a spirit of utmost reverence and be accompanied by the cross of Jesus Christ.[40] None but the humble, pure, faithful, and attentive can comprehend the Scriptures and, conversely, vices impede the search for an understanding of the revealed truth; pride[41] and curiosity are singled out for particular attention as obstacles to the work of the theologian.[42] The tradition of the holy man receiving mystical insights is exemplified by St. Francis, who was given theological insights and by affective love entered where theologians with their science stand outside.[43] In keeping with the founder's wishes, Bonaventure regards theological studies as a route to maturity and integrity:

> the purpose of theology is that we become virtuous and attain salvation [*haec doctrina est, ut boni fiamus et salvemur*]. This is accomplished by an inclination of the will rather than naked speculation.[44]

As minister general he continued his predecessors' policy of insisting that friars sent to study and teach theology should be clothed in the appropriate dispositions. The general constitutions laid down the criteria governing the selection of students for Paris: they should be of good reputation, meek, and peaceful among their confrères.[45]

The *Breviloquium*, 1256/7

Beginning with his *Commentary on the Four Books of the Sentences of Master Peter Lombard*, Bonaventure compiled several works of scholastic theology, including his *Quaestiones disputatae de scientia Christi* and *Quaestiones disputatae de mysterio Trinitatis*. Bonaventure explains that the materials on the major questions of theology are so widely scattered in the writings of both the saints and the doctors that it would take students an undue amount of time to read these sources. Moreover, *novi theologi* often dread the Scripture itself, feeling it to be as confusing, disordered, and uncharted as an impenetrable forest.[46] For this reason he yielded to the students' request for guidance and wrote his *Breviloquium*, which explores the theology of the Trinity, the creation, the fall, the Incarnation, grace, the sacraments, and the last judgment. The Incarnation is expounded in the fourth part, underlining the pivotal role played by Jesus Christ who redeems and perfects the created order. Themes from the patristic and medieval world are blended in this mosaic, which includes order[47] and the power of the divine example.[48] Particular attention is paid to the perfection of the divine remedy, the mode of redemption and the theme of *convenientia*.

Bonaventure's *Commentary on the Sentences* discusses the reasons for the Incarnation,[49] a question already addressed in the friars' schools at Oxford under Robert Grosseteste in the early 1230s[50] and Paris under Alexander of Hales and Jean de la Rochelle in the early 1240s,[51] and then developed by a succession of Franciscan masters.[52] Bonaventure's terminology is precise and he does not confine himself to the view that the Incarnation was solely a response to the Fall. The focus is, instead, placed on the divine benevolence, generosity, and perfection in the work of creation[53] and redemption:

what greater act of benevolence than for the master to redeem the slave *by taking the nature of a slave* [Philippians 2:7]? This is a deed of such unfathomable goodness that no greater proof of mercy, benevolence and friendship can be imagined.[54]

The *Deus-homo* becomes humanity's neighbor, brother, friend, and teacher[55] and gives himself in the passion as the price of redemption, thereby manifesting his charity and benevolence.[56] The perfection of the creation is matched by that of the redeemed order.[57] Adam and Eve were the crowning glory of the created order[58] and this is denoted by the fact that they were fashioned on the sixth day with its connotations of perfection. Similarly, the *Deus-homo* who completes the "world redeemed," came in the sixth and last age[59] and was crucified on the sixth day.[60] The Incarnation demonstrates the closeness of the bond between the Creator and fallen humanity and this is reflected in the lexicon of friendship, which is restored by a most amicable mediator capable of uniting Creator and creature.[61]

The view, articulated by Saint Augustine[62] and others, that the Devil was a key player in the drama of salvation, was buried deep in the medieval consciousness. Saint Anselm's rejection of the theory of the Devil's rights was not immediately accepted in the schools,[63] and vestiges of the old formula appear in Bonaventure's earlier[64] and later writings.[65] In the early Franciscan school the *Cur Deus homo* supplants Augustine's *De Trinitate*,[66] although both Anselm and Augustine are credited with the teaching that it was more congruous for the human race to be redeemed through satisfaction than through any other method.[67] Justice,[68] honor,[69] and satisfaction are complementary themes, three sides of a triangle, which express the ordered way in which God deals with humanity in search of redemption,[70] and this takes a particular form:

> as the restoring principle [God] created humanity in an orderly fashion, so must he restore him in an orderly manner. He must repair humanity in a way which safeguards freedom of the will, the honour of God and the order of the universe.[71]

Through pride and disobedience Adam and Eve denied honor to God[72] in a manner where they were bound.[73] The order of divine justice, wisdom, power, and honor show the appropriateness of the restoration of the human race through satisfaction.[74] The divine honor is restored by satisfaction, whose definition is derived from the *Cur Deus homo*. If sin were forgiven without satisfaction, it would remain without any compensation for the honor taken away from God;[75] the divine honor calls for deeds of satisfaction and punishment to atone for sin.[76] The credentials of the agent of restoration are reviewed and it is concluded that:

> God alone could make satisfaction for the whole human race and humanity alone was bound on account of its sin. Therefore it was most appropriate that humanity should be restored by the God-man, born of Adam's stock.[77]

The *Deus-homo* paid back the obedience which he had not stolen and offered a supremely pleasing sacrifice[78] and, ascending to the Father and repairing the fall of the angels, he increased the Father's honor.[79]

Themes of appropriateness or fittingness play a central part in the formulation of the theology of Bonaventure. Any hint that the redemption had to take place in a particular manner is carefully avoided and instead the emphasis is placed upon the theme of *convenientia*,[80] favored by Augustine and those who shaped the Christology and soteriology of the Franciscan schools at both Paris[81] and Oxford.[82] Bonaventure emphasizes the congruity of redemption achieved through the Passion,[83] and holds that no other way was so fitting, so adapted alike to the Redeemer, redeemed, and the nature of salvation. Fallen humanity could not have recovered its excellence, its friendship with God, and purity of soul except through the divine mediator. The human race came into being through the Uncreated Word and sinned by failing to heed the Inspired Word. Accordingly, it rose from sin through the Incarnate Word.[84] The most congruous means of restoration are applied by God, and the Incarnation is presented in terms of a reversal of the process of the Fall.[85] Because the human race had fallen through the suggestion of the Devil and the consent of a deceived woman, it was appropriate that the process of healing involved a good angel promoting the good and a virgin believing and consenting. The medicine corresponds to the disease, the restoration to the fall, and the remedy to the injury. A quotation from Gregory the Great, that contraries are cured by contraries, is frequently invoked.[86] Adam and Eve had sinned through aspiring to be as wise as God, desiring to enjoy the fruit of the forbidden tree. To heal fallen humanity by a fitting remedy the *Deus-homo* wished to be humiliated and to suffer on a tree.[87]

De praeparatione ad missam, ca. 1260

Saint Francis revived the spirit of the Gospel on his journeys throughout Italy, and his powerful gestures and persuasive words brought the teaching of Jesus Christ to life. As a member of a fraternity, whose impact was reinvigorating the Church throughout Christendom, Bonaventure's writings were intended to foster a personal response, drawing the readers into scenes from the Gospel and persuading them to identify themselves with Jesus's friends.[88] In his first few years as minister general he produced a series of devotional texts, including the *De perfectione vitae ad sorores, Itinerarium mentis in Deum, Lignum vitae, De triplici via, Soliloquium,* and *De regimine animae*. These treatises gave him an opportunity to dwell on the crib, the Cross, and the Eucharist, which had been central to the life of Saint Francis and, like Saints Anselm and Bernard, he worked within the tradition of an affective piety. The prologue to the *Itinerarium mentis in Deum* underlines the different dispositions required by those who read his devotional works:

> the reader . . . should not believe that reading is sufficient without unction, speculation without devotion, investigation without wonder, observation without rejoicing,

work without piety, knowledge without love, understanding without humility, endeavour without divine grace.[89]

Nonetheless, the way in which particular themes appear in both devotional and scholastic treatises is exemplified by the restoration of the divine honor, which is applied primarily to the passion and death of the *Deus-homo*. This is also featured in the examination of the fruits of the Eucharist,[90] which are the preservation of devotion to God, love for neighbor, and inner contentment.[91] These themes form the basis of the *De praeparatione ad missam*, which helps priests to reflect upon the sacred office entrusted to them and to assist them in the devout and fruitful celebration of the Eucharist.

The first chapter opens with a reference to the Pauline injunction to approach the sacrament with an appropriate recollection (1 Cor. 11:28). The first of the four preparatory steps requires the celebrant to consider the strength of his faith. The doctrine of transubstantiation, which had been declared an element of the Church's teaching in the first canon of the Fourth Lateran Council, is set forth. The bread and wine, teeming with symbolism, signify the unity which is effected by the sacrament. The centrality of the Eucharist is underlined:

> take away this sacrament from the Church, and what will be left in the world apart from error and infidelity . . . The Christian people will be scattered . . . But, through this sacrament, the Church endures, faith is strengthened, Christianity and the worship of God flourish.[92]

In the second section the celebrant is urged to examine his intentions and dispositions lest his celebration be vitiated by sin. He is persuaded to confront his weaknesses and is enjoined to ensure that he had not lapsed into grave sin or had the intention of sinning since his last confession. Those who receive the Eucharist with such flawed dispositions jeopardize their hopes of eternal salvation and are compared with Judas, the perennial symbol of ingratitude and treachery. The number of priests who persist in the celebration of the Eucharist, despite their defects, is bewailed. In contrast, Saint Francis's emphasis upon due respect for everything pertaining to the Eucharist finds a home in Bonaventure's exhortation that altar vessels and linen should be clean and dignified, mirroring an inner purity on the part of the celebrant.[93] In the third section the celebrant is instructed to assess the love and fervor with which he approaches the altar, lest he approach unworthily (1 Cor. 11:29–30). Reflecting St. Francis's own advice, Bonaventure maintains that venial sins are a potential obstacle to the communion between Creator and creature and he recommends that all lukewarmness, disorderliness, and carelessness be banished. The celebrant is left in no doubt that his sacred office should be exercised for the benefit of the Church in thanksgiving for the blessings bestowed by God. A prominent place is assigned to the protracted meditation on the Passion,[94] which is expanded in several treatises, such as chapter 6 of the *De perfectione vitae ad sorores*. While the Eucharist is a sacramental celebration of the sacrifice offered on the Cross of Calvary, Bonaventure underlines the fact that Jesus Christ suffered only once and that his death was sufficient for all sins, which lay in the past and the future; the Body of Jesus Christ is mystically offered to the Father daily as an antidote to sin. So close is the connection between the sacrifice of the Cross and that of the altar that everything in the Mass represents the passion.[95]

The fourth section prompts the celebrant to review his motivation, scrutinizing his love, desire, disposition, and the necessary intention. The defective dispositions of priests are deplored; too many of them approach holy orders for unworthy reasons, such as the pursuit of financial gain, the satisfaction of ambition, and the accumulation of riches. Instead, the mendicant friar, vowed to a life of poverty, challenges the celebrant to make God the goal of his wishes and desires, as his tonsure indicates.[96] The celebrant should endeavor to ensure that his sacramental celebration becomes a paradigm for his whole life:

> through your participation in the sacred liturgy the name of God should be sanctified in you, so that by your holiness of life the worship and honour of God may increase on earth.[97]

The second chapter deals with the last preparatory acts, the first of which is a confession of sins, expressing the link between the two sacraments articulated in canon 21 of the Fourth Lateran Council and the 1260 general constitutions of the Friars Minor;[98] the two sacraments are also treated in successive chapters of the *Breviloquium*.[99] A thorough and candid confession is strongly recommended and the practice of a vague and general confession, in which sins are camouflaged, is castigated. The son of a physician, Bonaventure employs medical imagery for sin and its sacramental remedy, exhorting the celebrant to open his wounds to his spiritual doctor for sacramental healing.[100] After the recitation of the penance assigned by his confessor, the celebrant should devoutly read Psalms 83, 84, 85, 115, and 129 with their own versicles and prayers. As he proceeds to the altar he is advised to associate himself with Jesus Christ going to his cross. Recollection is required for the prayers and the celebrant should be clothed in the right intentions, with the desire to give due thanks and reverence to the Creator. A profound sense of humility and compassion for the death of Jesus Christ are identified as appropriate dispositions.[101]

Collationes de septem donis Spiritus sancti, 1268

Some of Bonaventure's writings are polemical and address questions which were being debated in the schools. Scruples about the observance of the Rule of the Friars Minor and the rationale for the mendicant lifestyle shape the *Epistola de tribus quaestionibus ad magistrum innominatum* and *Quaestiones disputatae de perfectione evangelica* in the middle of the 1250s. The mendicant controversy at the University of Paris stimulated the *Apologia pauperum*, where he expounded the friars' ideal against the attacks of Gérard d'Abbeville. Bonaventure was commissioned to compose the *Legenda maior Sancti Francisci Assisiensis*, which was intended to serve as the authoritative interpretation of the founder's life. The study of philosophy in friars' schools was vigorously defended by both Jean de la Rochelle,[102] the second master at Paris, and Bonaventure.[103] In the hierarchy of authorities, it occupies the fourth place, that is, after the Scriptures, the Fathers, and the theologians.[104] That balance, however, was seen to be disturbed on occasion. Although Aristotle is declared to be the most excellent of the philosophers,[105] some of his ideas, such as the eternity of the world, had been pronounced incompatible with Catholic teaching in the 1250s.[106] The growing influence of the newly recovered Aristotelian corpus in the Faculty of Arts and the excessive claims advanced by the radical Aristotelians and Averroists in the 1260s caused further concern. Bonaventure, who combated any suggestion that philosophy was self-sufficient, responded to this new danger in his *Collationes de praeceptis decem*, delivered between March 6 and April 17, 1267, and in his *Collationes de septem donis Spiritus sancti*, preached between February 25 and April 9, 1268.

Grace, the fear of God, piety, knowledge, fortitude, counsel, intellect, and wisdom are explored in the *Collationes de septem donis Spiritus sancti*. In the eighth *collatio* the proper exercise of the intellect is treated, and only in the later stages does Bonaventure raise three philosophical errors, two of which had already been pinpointed in the *Collationes de praeceptis decem*.[107] These excesses are deemed heretical and opposed to the *causa essendi*, the *ratio intelligendi*, and the *ordo vivendi*. The first error is to posit the eternity of the world, which undermines divine dominion. It presupposes a circle of movement and time and is refuted by the evidence of the Scriptures (Gen. 1:1). The treatment of this error concludes with an appeal to 2 Maccabees 7:28.[108] Earlier Bonaventure had protested that this error perverted the whole of the Scriptures and denied the Incarnation, providing one of his rare autobiographical references:

> as a student in the Faculty of Arts I learned that Aristotle taught that the world was eternal; when I heard the reasons and arguments [advanced in favor of this view] my heart began to consider how this could be.[109]

The second error consists of a fatal necessity, which issues in determinism. Rooted in a movement of the stars, it maintains that those born under a particular constellation will necessarily become thieves, wicked or good. This is at variance with the doctrine of free will, merit, and reward and entails the belief that God is the origin of all evil.[110] The third error concerns the unity of the human intellect and this is regarded as the worst, which also embraces the two earlier beliefs because it denies the root of distinction and individuation.[111] Among the implications of this claim are the denial of the truth of faith, the salvation of souls, and the observance of the commandments. It declares that the worst person is saved and the best damned.[112]

Bonaventure's intervention in this debate has been deemed instrumental in the censures imposed more than two years later, on December 18, 1270, by Étienne Tempier, Bishop of Paris, upon certain rationalistic propositions.[113] Despite this episcopal judgment, the attack was renewed with greater vigor in the *Collationes in Hexaemeron*, which contains a more sustained criticism of an undue reliance upon philosophy. In the early *collationes* there is a further concentration upon these errors. Scriptural texts from Genesis are cited to disprove the theory of the eternity of the world, which was attributed to Aristotle by the Greek Fathers and all the Arabic commentators. Bonaventure adds that nowhere does Aristotle argue that the world had a principle or a beginning, and he even criticized Plato's views on creation. This error begat the teaching concerning a single intellect, which is also attributed to Aristotle by his commentator. Because Aristotle had been such an excellent guide on certain questions, some could not believe that he could be erroneous on this question.[114]

Bonaventure's response to these excesses and heresy was to exhort the theologian to pass beyond philosophical knowledge and to seek the attainment of wisdom through the development of God's gifts. For example, the last of the *Collationes de septem donis Spiritus sancti* is devoted to the gift of wisdom, which is incompatible with the forces inimical to the Gospel. The theologian, spurning vain wisdom, is instructed to pursue true wisdom. The crucifixion stands as a rebuke to the wisdom of this world and reveals the divine wisdom. The *Deus-homo* rose and ascended in order to school humanity in true wisdom and to establish it in the hearts of women and men.[115] The argument of the Devil is contrasted with that of Jesus Christ; the former is destructive and the latter is constructive and leads to redemption.[116] The vices which mar the pursuit of truth and wisdom are identified in the first of the *Collationes in Hexaemeron*; carnality, cupidity, malice, and cruelty are ranged against the divine law. The prevalence of presumption and curiosity are at the root of the problems besetting the Faculties of Arts and Theology and herald a return to Egypt, the biblical symbol of captivity. The errors circulating in the schools and their remedy are presented:

> theologians have attacked the life of Christ as related to morals, and the teachers in the Faculty of Arts have assaulted the doctrine of Christ by their false statements. A beginning should be made from the centre, that is, from Christ. For He Himself is the mediator . . . , holding the central place in everything. Hence it it necessary to start from Him if someone wants to reach Christian wisdom . . .[117]

In Him are hidden all the treasures of wisdom and knowledge and He is the central point of understanding. This center produces knowledge and serves as a tree of life, the symbol of redemption. This emphasis on the centrality of the *Deus-homo* is presented as the antidote to the philosophical errors circulating in the schools.[118] Bonaventure concludes that the human thirst for knowledge must be subordinated to the search for wisdom and holiness.[119]

Conclusion

Bonaventure's funeral in the church of the Cordeliers at Lyons was attended by the pope, the cardinals, and bishops.[120] He was canonized by Sixtus IV on April

14, 1482 and declared a doctor of the Church by Sixtus V on March 14, 1588. He defended the friars' need to study theology and philosophy in preparation for their ministry of preaching and laid down principles to guide their studies. His attitude towards Aristotle, saluted as the *princeps et dux* of the *peripatetici*,[121] has exercised the minds of several historians of medieval philosophy, including Étienne Gilson and Fernand Van Steenberghen. Mendicant themes emerge in his writings, such as the poverty experienced by the *Deus-homo*, who invites Christians to a life of voluntary poverty.[122] Bonaventure's writings were quoted by subsequent masters in the Franciscan schools at Paris and Oxford, such as Walter of Bruges, John Pecham, William de la Mare, Matthew of Acquasparta, Roger Marston, William of Ware, Gonsalvus Hispanus, and Richard of Middleton. He addressed the questions of the contingency of the Incarnation[123] and the Conception of Saint Mary in an independent manner,[124] which helped to create a climate in the Franciscan school for John Duns Scotus's fuller exposition of these questions.[125] Bonaventure was regarded as one of the major theologians in the thirteenth century, and treatises like the *Itinerarium mentis in Deum, De triplici via*, and *De reductione artium ad theologiam* have long been recognized as classics. Despite the rise of a circle of friars who promoted the writings of Scotus, Bonaventure's enduring popularity is reflected in one of the most important Franciscan libraries in the Middle Ages and in the testimony of William Woodford. When an inventory of the library of the Sacro Convento, Assisi, was compiled in 1381, it contained numerous manuscripts of the major writings of Bonaventure, including spurious treatises.[126] Fifteen years later Woodford's *Defensorium* lists the masters of the Franciscan school and reports that Bonaventure wrote the *Apologia pauperum, super Sententias egregie et alia multa fecit*.[127] By the end of the fifteenth century Bonaventure's writings started to appear among the early incunabula, and between 1588 and 1596 a first edition of his *opera omnia* in seven volumes was printed at Rome by command of Sixtus V.

Notes

I am indebted to Professor J. A. Watt, Revd. Dr. B. Chaberski, OFMConv., and Fr. Alban McCoy, OFMConv., who have kindly read earlier drafts of this study and made valuable comments.

1 Bonaventure, "Legenda minor S. Francisci," c. 7, no. 8, in *Legendae S. Francisci Assisiensis saeculis XIII et XIV conscriptae* (Analecta Franciscana, 10), Quaracchi, Florence, 1926–41, pp. 653–78, 678.

2 "Legenda maior S. Francisci," prol., no. 3, in ibid., pp. 555–652, 558.

3 *Idem*, "Epistola de tribus quaestionibus ad magistrum innominatum," nos. 14, 18, ed. F. M. Delorme, "Textes franciscains," in *Archivo italiano per la storia della pietà*, 1 (1951), pp. 179–218, 216, 217–18.

4 *Doctoris Seraphici S. Bonaventurae opera omnia ed. studio et cura PP. Collegii a* S. *Bonaventura ad plurimos codices mss.emendata, anecdotis aucta, prolegomenis scholiis notisque illustrata*, 10 vols., Quaracchi, Florence, 1882–1902. Cf. J. G. Bougerol, ed., *Sancti Bonaventurae Sermones Dominicales* (Bibliotheca Franciscana Scholastica Medii Aevi, 27), Grottaferrata, Rome, 1977.

5 Cf. Z. Hayes, "Bonaventure: Mystery of the Triune God," in *The History of Franciscan Theology*, ed. K. B. Osborne, New York, 1994, pp. 39–125; M. Haren, *Medieval Thought: The Western Intellectual Tradition from Antiquity to the 13th*

Century (New Studies in Medieval History), London, 1985, pp. 161–71; B. Smalley, *The Gospels in the Schools c.1100–c.1280*, London, 1985, pp. 118–240; D. Monti, trans., *Works of Saint Bonaventure, V: Writings Concerning the Franciscan Order*, New York, 1994.

6 Three of Bonaventure's writings have been selected for brief comment. His other treatises are generally mentioned only in the briefest terms because such a project precludes a fuller exposition.

7 "Breviloquium," in *S. Bonaventurae opera omnia*, V, pp. 199–291.

8 "De praeparatione ad missam," in *S. Bonaventurae opera omnia*, VIII, pp. 99–106.

9 "Collationes de septem donis Spiritus sancti," in *S. Bonaventurae opera omnia*, V, pp. 455–503.

10 I. Brady, "Sacred Scripture in the Early Franciscan School," in *La sacra scrittura e i francescani* (Pontificium Athenaeum Antonianum), Rome, 1973, pp. 65–82; Smalley, "The Gospels in the Paris Schools in the Late 12th and Early 13th Centuries," in *Franciscan Studies*, 39 and 40 (1979 and 1980), pp. 230–54, 298–369.

11 Salimbene de Adam, *Cronica*, ed. G. Scalia (Scrittori d'Italia, 232–3), Bari, 1966, p. 435.

12 "Collationes in Hexaemeron," 19, nos. 6, 7, 15, in *S. Bonaventurae opera omnia*, V, pp. 421, 422.

13 *Breviloquium*, prol., no. 2, p. 201.

14 *Collationes in Hexaemeron*, 12, no. 17, p. 387.

15 *Breviloquium*, prol., 5, no. 3, p. 207.

16 Ibid., p. 5, c. 7, no. 5, pp. 260–1.

17 "Quaestiones disputatae de mysterio Trinitatis," q. 1, a. 2, conc., in *S. Bonaventurae opera omnia*, V, pp. 54–5.

18 *Collationes in Hexaemeron*, 13, no. 12, pp. 389–90.

19 "Itinerarium mentis in Deum," c. 4, no. 5, in *S. Bonaventurae opera omnia*, V, p. 307.

20 *Breviloquium*, prol., 1, no. 2, p. 203.

21 Bougerol, *Saint Bonaventure: Breviloquium, prologue*, texte latin de Quaracchi et traduction française (Bibliothèque bonaventurienne, Introduction Générale), Paris, 1967, p. 67.

22 *Breviloquium*, p. 1, c. 1, no. 2, p. 210.

23 *Collationes in Hexaemeron*, 9, nos. 21–2, p. 375.

24 Ibid., 19, nos. 10, 15, pp. 421–2.

25 Ibid., 9, no. 22, p. 375.

26 "III Sententarium," d. 3, p. 2, a. 2, q. 1, conc., in *S. Bonaventurae opera omnia*, III, p. 86.

27 *Breviloquium*, p. 7, c. 2, n. 4, p. 282.

28 Bougerol, *Introduction a l'étude de S. Bonaventure* (Bibliothèque de Théologie, Série 1, Théologie Dogmatique 2), Paris, 1961, pp. 68–72.

29 *Epistola de tribus quaestionibus ad magistrum innominatum*, no. 16, p. 217.

30 *Collationes in Hexaemeron*, 19, nos. 6, 15, pp. 421–2.

31 "De reductione artium ad theologiam," no. 5, in *S. Bonaventurae opera omnia*, V, p. 321.

32 Bougerol, "Saint Bonaventure et Guillaume de Saint-Thierry," in *Antonianum*, 46 (1971), pp. 298–321.

33 "II Sententiarum," Praelocutio, in *S. Bonaventurae opera omnia*, II, p. 2.

34 "I Sententiarum," proemium q. 2, conc. ad ob. 4, in *S. Bonaventurae opera omnia*, I, p. 11.

35 *Breviloquium*, p. 1, c. 1, no. 4, p. 210.

36 "Christus unus omnium magister," no. 2, in *S. Bonaventurae opera omnia*, V, p. 568.

37 *Breviloquium*, prol., 6, no. 6, p. 207.

38 Ibid., p. 1, c. 1, no. 3, p. 210.

39 Ibid., prol., nos. 1, 4, pp. 201–2.

40 *Collationes in Hexaemeron*, 13, no. 5, p. 388.

41 *Breviloquium*, prol., 4, no. 3, p. 206.

42 *Christus unus omnium magister*, no. 22, p. 573.

43 *Legenda maior S. Francisci*, c. 11, no. 1, pp. 605–6.

44 *Breviloquium*, prol., 5, no. 2, p. 206.

45 M. Bihl, "Statuta generalia Ordinis edita in Capitulis generalibus celebratis Narbonae an. 1260, Assisii an. 1279 atque Parisiis an. 1292. (Editio critica et synoptica)," c. 6, nos. 14–15, in *Archivum Franciscanum Historicum*, 34 (1941), pp. 13–94, 284–358, 72.

46 *Breviloquium*, prol., 6, nos. 4, 5, p. 208.

47 Ibid., p. 4, c. 9, no. 2, p. 249.

48 Ibid., p. 4, c. 1, no. 3; c. 4, c. 9, no. 2, pp. 241, 250.

49 *III Sententiarum*, d. 1, a. 2, q. 2, pp. 21–8.

50 Robert Grosseteste, *De cessatione legalium*, eds. R. C. Dales and E. B. King (Auctores Britannici medii aevi, 7), 1986, pp. 119–33.

51 Alexander of Hales, *Summa Theologica*, IV, lib. 3, Quaracchi, Florence, 1948, q. 2, no. 23, pp. 41–2.

52 Cf. J. M. Bissen, "De motivo incarnationis Disquisitio historico-dogmatico," in *Antonianum*, 7 (1932), pp. 314–36.

53 *Breviloquium*, p. 2, c. 10, no. 5, p. 228.

54 Ibid., p. 4, c. 1, no. 2, p. 241.

55 *Itinerarium mentis in Deum*, c. 4, no. 5; c. 5, no. 2, pp. 307, 308.

56 *Sancti Bonaventurae Sermones Dominicales*, no. 13, pp. 264–5.

57 *Breviloquium*, p. 4, c. 10, nos. 2–3, p. 251.

58 Ibid., p. 2, c. 2, no. 4, p. 220.

59 Ibid., p. 4, c. 4, no. 4, pp. 244–5.

60 *Collationes in Hexaemeron*, 15, no. 17, p. 400.

61 *Breviloquium*, p. 4, c. 1, no. 4, pp. 241–2.

62 Augustine, "De Trinitate", 13, cc. 12–14, nos. 16–18, in *Corpus Christianorum, Series Latina* 50A, ed. W. J. Mountain, Turnhout, 1968, pp. 402–7.

63 R. W. Southern, *Saint Anselm and his Biographer*, Cambridge, 1963, pp. 93–7.

64 *III Sententiarum*, d. 19, a. 1, q. 3, conc., p. 406.

65 *Collationes in Hexaemeron*, 1, no. 30, p. 334.

66 Cf. M. Robson, "The Impact of the *Cur Deus homo* on the early Franciscan School," in *Anselm: Aosta, Bec and Canterbury: Papers in Commemoration of the Nine-Hundredth Anniversary of Anselm's Enthronement as Archbishop, 25 September 1993*, eds. D. E. Luscombe and G. R. Evans, Sheffield, 1996, pp. 334–47.

67 *III Sententiarum*, d. 20, a. 1, q. 2, conc., p. 420.

68 *Breviloquium*, p. 2, c. 7, nos. 1, 4; p. 3, c. 4, nos. 1–5, pp. 224, 225, 233–4.

69 Southern, p. 89, remarks that Anselm was outstanding among theologians for the emphasis he laid on the honor of God.

70 *Breviloquium*, p. 7, c. 3, no. 3, p. 283.

71 Ibid., p. 4, c. 9, no. 2, p. 249.

72 "*Collationes de septem donis Spiritus sancti*," 6, no. 17, p. 486.

73 *Breviloquium*, p. 4, c. 9, no. 3, p. 250.

74 *III Sententiarum*, d. 20, a. 1, q. 2, p. 419.

75 Ibid., d. 20, a. 1, q. 2, no. 4, p. 420.

76 *Breviloquium*, p. 7, c. 3, no. 3, p. 283.

77 Ibid., p. 4, c. 1, no. 4, pp. 241–2.

78 Ibid., p. 4, c. 9, nos. 2–4, pp. 249–50.

79 "Lignum vitae," no. 37, in *S. Bonaventurae opera omnia*, VIII, p. 82.

80 Cf. Hayes, "The Meaning of *Convenientia* in the Metaphysics of St. Bonaventure," in *Franciscan Studies*, 34 (1974), pp. 74–100.

81 Alexander of Hales, q. 2, nos. 10–23, pp. 25–42, where a series of questions *de convenientia incarnationis* is examined.

82 S. Wenzel, "Robert Grosseteste's Treatise on Confession, 'Deus est,'" in *Franciscan Studies*, 30 (1970), pp. 218–93, 244.

83 *III Sententiarum*, d. 20, a. 1, qq. 1–6, pp. 416–32.

84 *Breviloquium*, p. 4, c. 1, nos. 1–4, pp. 241–2.

85 E. Cousins, "The Coincidence of Opposites in the Christology of St. Bonaventure," in *Franciscan Studies*, 28 (1968), pp. 27–45.

86 *Breviloquium*, p. 4, c. 3, nos. 3, 4, p. 243.

87 Ibid., p. 4, c. 9, no. 4, p. 250.

88 *Lignum vitae*, no. 8, pp. 72–3, where the readers are urged to accompany the Holy Family into their Egyptian exile in spirit and to shed tears at the image of the mother and her frail young and beautiful child.

89 *Itinerarium mentis in Deum*, prol., no. 4, p. 296.

90 *Breviloquium*, p. 7, c. 3, nos. 3–5; p. 6, c. 9, nos. 6–7, pp. 283–4, 275.

91 Ibid., p. 6, c. 9, nos. 2–3, 6, pp. 274, 275.

92 De praeparatione ad missam, c. 1, nos. 1–4, pp. 99–100.

93 Ibid., c. 1, nos. 5–7, pp. 100–1.

94 *Legenda maior S. Francisci*, c. 4, no. 3, p. 572, where Bonaventure reports that at first the friars did not have breviaries. Then the cross served as their book, which they examined by day and night. The cross quickly became a central element of the friars' iconography, as the lower church of San Francesco, Assisi, demonstrates.

95 *De praeparatione ad missam*, c. 1, nos. 8–13, pp. 101–4.

96 *Breviloquium*, p. 6, c. 12, no. 3, p. 278.

97 *De praeparatione ad missam*, c. 1, nos. 14–19, pp. 104–5.

98 "Statuta generalia Ordinis edita in Capitulis generalibus celebràtis Narbonae an. 1260, Assisii an. 1279 atque Parisiis an. 1292," c. 4, no. 23, pp. 58–9.

99 *Breviloquium*, p. 6, cc. 9 and 10, pp. 273–6.

100 Ibid., p. 6, c. 1, nos. 1–6, pp. 265–6.

101 *De praeparatione ad missam*, c. 2, nos. 1–5, pp. 105–6.

102 Baldwin ab Amsterdam, "Tres sermones inediti Joannis de Rupella in honorem S. Antonii Patavini," in *Collectanea Franciscana*, 28 (1958), pp. 33–58, 50–1.

103 *Epistola de tribus quaestionibus ad magistrum innominatum*, nos. 15–16, p. 217.

104 *Collationes in Hexaemeron*, 19, nos. 6–10, pp. 421–2.

105 *II Sententiarum*, d. 1, p. 1, a. 1, q. 2, conc., p. 22.

106 *Breviloquium*, p. 2, c. 1, no. 2, p. 219. Cf. B. M. Bonansea, "The Question of an Eternal World in the Teaching of St. Bonaventure," in *Franciscan Studies*, 34 (1974), pp. 7–33.

107 *Collationes de decem praeceptis*, 2, no. 25, p. 514.

108 *Collationes de septem donis Spiritus sancti*, 8, nos. 16–17, pp. 497–8.

109 *Collationes de decem praeceptis*, 2, no. 28, p. 515.

110 *Collationes de septem donis Spiritus sancti*, 8, nos. 16, 18, pp. 497–8.

111 Ibid., 8, nos. 16, 19–20, pp. 497–8.

112 *Collationes de decem praeceptis*, 2, no. 25, p. 514.

113 Haren, p. 161. Brady, "Background to the Condemnation of 1270: Master William of Baglione, O.F.M.," in *Franciscan Studies*, 30 (1970), pp. 5–48.

114 *Collationes in Hexaemeron*, 6, nos. 4–5, p. 361. Cf. Bougerol, "Aristotle et saint Bonaventure," in *Études Franciscaines*, 21 (supplément annuel) (1971), pp. 7–17, and "Dossier pour l'étude des rapports entre saint Bonaventure et Aristotle," in *Archives d'histoire doctrinale et littéraire du moyen âge*, 31 (1974), pp. 135–222.

115 *Collationes de septem donis Spiritus sancti*, 9, nos. 1–4, pp. 499–500.

116 *Collationes in Hexaemeron*, 1, nos. 26–7, pp. 333–4.

117 Ibid., 1, nos. 6–11, pp. 330–1.

118 Ibid., 1, nos. 15–17, 24, pp. 332–3.

119 Ibid., 19, nos. 3–4, p. 420.

120 *Chronica XXIV Generalium Ordinis Minorum* (1209–1374) (Analecta Franciscana, 3), Quaracchi, Florence, 1897, p. 356.

121 *II Sententiarum*, d. 1, p. 1, a. 1, q. 1, conc., p. 17.

122 "Commentarius in evangelium S. Lucae," c. 2, no. 15, in *S. Bonaventurae opera omnia*, VII, pp. 47–8.

123 *III Sententiarum*, d. 1, a. 2, q. 2, pp. 21–8.

124 Ibid., d. 3, p. 1, a. 1, q. 1, pp. 61–4.

125 A. B. Wolter, "John Duns Scotus on the Primacy and Personality of Christ," in *Franciscan Christology* (Franciscan Institute Publication, Franciscan Sources, 1), ed. D. McElrath, 1980, pp. 139–82; and *John Duns Scotus: Four Questions on Mary*, Santa Barbara, 1988.

126 C. Cenci, *Bibliotheca Manuscripta ad Sacrum Conventum Assisiensem*, II, Assisi, 1981, pp. 781–2.

127 E. Doyle, "A Bibliographical List by William Woodford, O.F.M.," in *Franciscan Studies*, 35 (1975), pp. 93–106, 96, 100.

Thomas Aquinas

Fergus Kerr

I

Thomas Aquinas, born in 1224/6 at Roccasecca, the family castle (now ruined) midway between Rome and Naples, in what was then the county of Aquino, in the Kingdom of the Two Sicilies, died on March 7, 1274 at the Cistercian abbey of Fossanova (now a national monument, occupied by Conventual Franciscans), no great distance away. Though most often associated with the great university of Paris, Thomas never lost touch with his roots in the Kingdom of Naples; his subsequent work shows how much he was indebted to his background and upbringing. His mother Theodora came of an aristocratic Neapolitan family. His father Landulph, one of Frederick II's barons, belonged to a minor branch of the Aquino family. There were at least nine children of the marriage, four boys and five girls. Aimo, the eldest son, took part in an expedition sent to the Holy Land by Frederick II, was taken prisoner, and eventually ransomed by Pope Gregory IX in 1233, remaining loyal to the papacy for the rest of his life. Rinaldo, the second son, at first on Frederick II's side, deserted him when he was deposed by Pope Innocent IV in 1245, and was tortured to death on the emperor's orders. Marotta, the eldest sister, became a nun; three of the others married and remained close to Thomas for the rest of his life. From the outset, then, Thomas was familiar with the stress on a family caught up in the conflict of allegiance between the papacy and Frederick II.

In 1231 Thomas was sent to school at the nearby Benedictine abbey of Monte Cassino, as an oblate and at first with his own nurse. His mother tongue was presumably a Neapolitan dialect. For the next seven or eight years, he was trained in Latin liturgical and biblical-patristic culture. Famously, the child often used to ask his teachers, "What is God?" In March 1239, however, hostilities between emperor and pope intensified, leading to Frederick II's being excommunicated; his troops occupied the monastery, most of the monks were expelled, and Thomas was sent home. Yet these years, at an impressionable age, initiated Thomas into centuries of tradition, even if Monte Cassino was not enjoying its most intellectually flourishing period at the time. Very different as his own theology would be, as he practiced the newer methods of the schools (biblical commentary and disputed questions), Thomas was brought up in the monastic tradition of *lectio divina*, as his later writings often reveal.

From autumn 1239 until spring 1244, at another impressionable age, Thomas was a student at the university of Naples, the first university founded independently of the Church (in 1224) as part of Frederick's campaign to outmaneuver the influence of the Pope. Presumably following the usual course in the seven liberal arts, Thomas studied under a certain Master Martin, otherwise unknown, who taught grammar and logic, and under Master Peter of Ireland, known to have a particular interest in Aristotle's works. Naples, at the time, was an outpost of the culture that flourished at Frederick's court in Palermo, where translations from Arabic and Greek were provoking a remarkable renaissance of intellectual life (Frederick himself spoke Arabic fluently).

Remaining close to his family for the rest of his life, even to the extent of once finding them financial assistance, Thomas had firsthand knowledge of the civil and political turbulence of the times. Formed in his early years in traditional monastic study of Scripture, as well as the writings of Augustine and Gregory, by the time he was twenty he had also been exposed to a culture in which Catholic theology was being opened up to the pagan world of Aristotle communicated through Muslim scholarship. Never giving up his interest in patristic theology, he also belonged to an intellectual milieu in which Jewish and Islamic learning was as admired as Christian thought.

In 1242/3, no doubt attracted by their ideal of a contemplative way of life that issues in preaching and teaching, Thomas sought to join the Dominicans. As he would write, much later, citing Gregory as his authority, "it is better to give the results of one's contemplation to others than simply to practise contemplation on one's own" (*Summa Theologiae* II-II, 188, 6). Founded by St. Dominic (ca. 1172–1221), and granted papal approval in 1216, the Order of Preachers had been present in Naples for some years. Being clothed in the Dominican habit in Naples, Thomas remained for the rest of his life a friar of the Roman province of the Order. It is not known where he passed the year of noviciate required by the constitutions of the Order, or indeed whether he even did so, since at the time the Order's practice was often to profess entrants *usque ad mortem* with little probation. Thomas, anyway, was soon sent to Paris, where he must have completed his study of the liberal arts, and attended lectures at least by his older confrere Albert the Great, since his transcription of the course survives.

The next and final major influence on Thomas's intellectual formation were his years of study under Albert. In June 1248 the Order decided to found a *studium generale* in Cologne, an international college for Dominican friars and others who might attend their courses. Albert the Great (d. 1280, over 80 years old), who had been teaching in Paris since 1240, was sent back to Germany to take charge of the new venture. Thomas was sent with him; they probably arrived in time to witness the laying of the foundation stone of Cologne cathedral. In Cologne, he seems to have worked as assistant to Albert, continuing to transcribe his course on Ps.-Dionysius's *Divine Names* and also his exposition of Aristotle's *Nicomachean Ethics*. He may have started teaching: his commentaries on Isaiah, Jeremiah, and Lamentations, his first theological works, seem to date from this period. As *cursor biblicus* his function would have been to "run through" the text with the students; no doubt he attended lectures on Scripture by Albert, in which doctrinal questions raised by the text would have been considered in depth. These years of apprenticeship in Cologne were the final stage in Thomas's formation as a theologian. He must have been ordained priest during this period (1250/1 if canon law was observed), though no record of this survives.

In September 1252 Thomas returned to Paris to lecture on Scripture and then on Peter Lombard's *Sentences*. He immediately found himself at the center of a storm of controversy. The theology faculty was riven with strife as a result of the resentment against the friars, on the part of the secular masters, the diocesan clergy who hitherto occupied the principal chairs. The often extremely acrimonious antimendicant feeling in the faculty would dog the whole of Thomas's career in Paris. The friars were regarded as instruments of centralizing papal policy; though the university was of course a pontifical institution, and drew students and professors from far afield, they were not welcome. In 1253 the secular masters twice suspended classes, partly in the hope of blackmailing the mendicants, who however refused to stop teaching. It did not help that, in 1254, the Franciscan Gerard de Borgo San Donnino published a book proclaiming that the third age of the world had begun around 1200, implying that the friars were the prophets of this "new age." The work was examined and declared heretical, all copies to be publicly burnt. Hostility to the friars reached such a fury that in 1256 the Dominican priory had to be guarded night and day by royal troops.

The *Sentences* (definitively published 1155/8) gather into a single volume the views (*sententiae*) of the Fathers of the Church on the main topics in Christian doctrine. This had been the standard textbook for theological instruction since 1223/7 (and would remain so into the sixteenth century, until supplanted by Thomas's own *Summa Theologiae*). Thus, in 1253–6, Thomas expounded the main themes in Christian doctrine, arranged in the light of the creeds but very much in terms of the patristic inheritance, itself of course the product of meditative reading of Scripture. Lecturers, however, raised questions and interwove considerations well beyond Lombard's text. The text of the commentary which Thomas composed at this time, the *Scriptum super libros Sententiarum*, cites Aristotle over 2000 times (nearly half from the *Ethics*), which suggests how much he sought to rethink theology in the light of the new philosophical ideas.

The study of Aristotle was repeatedly forbidden, though little heed seems to have been paid to successive interdictions; in 1252/5, at all events, the arts faculty in Paris finally received authorization to teach all of Aristotle's work. For the rest of Thomas's life there would be hostility between the arts faculty and the theology faculty in Paris over how to deal with the new ideas. At some point, probably in this period, he decided to integrate the writings of Aristotle with Christian doctrine – as if he felt called to ensure that Islam should not win by philosophy the hegemony it failed to win by military force. His first venture, the short treatise *De ente et essentia,* extant in more than 179 manuscripts, is heavily indebted to Avicenna, Ibn Sina (990–1037), the Muslim thinker whose work he had no doubt met at university in Naples. It expounds the metaphysical doctrines held in common by Christians, Jews, and Arabs at the time, and already displays all the fundamental ideas in philosophy which Thomas would subsequently explore and exploit. Most notably, while Albert seems to have been fascinated more by *what* things are and how they reveal God's hand, Thomas is more interested in the fact *that* things are at all; already, as throughout the rest of his work, he sees the very existence and activity of things as the best evidence of the existence and activity of God in them. Far from having to defend the freedom of creatures against God, or vice versa, as so many theologians find it necessary to do, Thomas saw no need to put the two in competition: as he would say much later, consistently with his view all along, he was puzzled by theologians who "seem to draw a distinction between what springs from grace and what from freewill, as if the same effect could not come from each" (*Summa Theologiae* I, 23, 5).

In September 1256 Thomas was appointed to one of the principal divinity chairs in Paris. His inaugural lecture ("Rigans montes") speaks of the theologian's – relatively minor and yet honorable – place in the communication of divine wisdom; it shows signs of his indebtedness to the neoplatonic Christianity mediated by the writings of Dionysius the Areopagite, perhaps testimony to the influence on him of Albert. A second lecture ("Hic est liber mandatorum Dei"), probably delivered next day, is in praise of Holy Scripture. As he came into his maturity as a teacher, it is as if he wanted to signal his debt and voice his gratitude to the traditional biblical-patristic culture which he inherited. Further, more personal exploration of theological method is to be found in his incomplete commentaries on Boethius's *De Trinitate* and *De Hebdomadibus.* As Thomas reads him, Boethius is taking divine revelation for granted and testing how far philosophical reasoning can bring the believer to deeper understanding of the Christian faith. It is as if the young professor was verifying the legitimacy of using reason to display the coherence of revelation – indeed, at the point where Boethius applies his method to the study of the doctrine of the Trinity, Thomas abandons his exposition, as if he now felt free to go his own way.

During these years (1256–9), we have the greater part of the disputed questions *De Veritate* in a version dictated by Thomas himself; apart from truth itself this collection of 29 disputations deals with divine knowledge, divine ideas, the Word, providence, predestination, the Book of Life, angelic knowledge, the human mind as locus of the image of the Trinity, teaching and learning, prophecy, ecstasy, faith, inferior and superior reason, synderesis, conscience, Adam's knowledge of God before the fall, the soul's knowledge after death, Christ's knowledge, as well as the good, the will, free will, our sensual nature, the emotions, grace, the justification of the unrighteous, and the grace of Christ. No doubt much tidied up, this mass of writing is a record of disputations that actually took place on various occasions in the schools and thus gives us a glimpse of the pedagogy of the time; but much of the material surely reveals the interests that preoccupied Thomas as he developed his own distinctive theological positions.

At the same time, he also started to write the exposition of "the truth of the Catholic faith" (the proper title) that would be known as the *Summa contra Gentiles*. A study house had been established in Barcelona to train Dominican friars as missionaries to work among Muslims and Jews. According to tradition, the *Contra Gentiles* was composed as a handbook of Christian apologetics for missionaries in Muslim Spain and North Africa. Much of it survives in his own handwriting; we can see how much he revised it, and he obviously was free to take his time over it. The first three of the four books investigate how far the truths of the Christian faith can be expounded on the basis of principles available to nonbelievers; only in the fourth do the arguments depend on specifically Christian revelation. In effect, the purpose seems to be to show how Christian doctrine harmonizes with and indeed satisfies the intellectual longings to know the truth that Thomas found exemplified in the philosophical tradition now opened up more richly than ever by the discovery of the ancient Greek texts. "Although the truth of the Christian faith . . . surpasses the capacity of the reason, nevertheless that truth that the human reason is naturally endowed to know cannot be opposed to the truth of the Christian faith," Thomas contends; the implication of which is that for us "to be able to see something of the loftiest realities, however thin and weak the sight may be, is a cause of the greatest joy" (Book I chs. 7 and 8).

Returning to his own province in summer 1259 Thomas remained in Naples, Orvieto, and Rome until 1268, completing the *Contra Gentiles*, writing a commentary on Job, creating the liturgy for the Feast of Corpus Christi, composing his own commentary on Dionysius' *Divine Names*, and starting the *Summa Theologiae*, his most celebrated work. He started to write a second commentary on Lombard's *Sentences*, of which part survives, but soon decided to design an entirely new work, to introduce beginners to Christian doctrine, setting it out in an orderly way, considering how "newcomers to this teaching are greatly hindered by various writings on the subject, partly because of the swarm of pointless questions, articles, and arguments, partly because essential information is given according to the requirements of textual commentary or the occasions of academic debate, partly because repetitiousness has bred boredom and muddle in their thinking" (*Summa Theologiae* I, Foreword). While at Viterbo he lived in the same priory as William of Moerbeke, the translator (from Greek) of so many of the texts which excited Thomas. Among much else, he wrote a commentary on Aristotle's *De Anima*, in conjunction evidently with his exposition in the *Summa* of the human soul as locus of the image of God. During this period he was able to use various monastic libraries, no doubt including Monte Cassino, to compile the *Catena aurea*, a commentary on the gospels put together from patristic sources, Greek as well as Latin. In these years too he produced the ten discussions assembled as *Quaestiones disputatae de potentia*: perhaps his deepest and most elaborate reflection on the doctrine of creation (the first six) and the doctrine of the Trinity (the remaining four).

From September 1268 until April 1272 Thomas lectured again in Paris, producing a stream of commentaries on Aristotle culminating with the *Ethics* and

Metaphysics, as well as producing his commentary on the *Liber de causis*, his lectures on the Fourth Gospel, the *Quaestiones disputatae de Virtutibus*, most of which may easily be related to the *secunda pars* of the *Summa Theologiae*, which many regard as his finest achievement of all.

Thomas still had to defend the right of the friars to teach; but the controversies now came more from the greatly expanded arts faculty, where Siger of Brabant was chief exponent of what would be labeled "Latin Averroism." The theories of Averroes, Ibn Rushd (1126–98), the Muslim philosopher known simply as "the Commentator," had reached Paris about 1230: acknowledged as a fine exponent of Aristotle, his ideas went into the amalgam represented by Siger and others, with philosophical implications that were incompatible with Christian doctrine. Aquinas wrote his *De unitate intellectus, contra Averroistas Parisienses* in 1270, refuting Siger's interpretation according to which Aristotle denied the existence of a mind in each human being. By this time, however, many of his colleagues in the theology faculty had grave doubts about the wisdom of Aquinas's attempts to integrate Aristotle's philosophy into Christian theology.

In June 1272 – the university was on strike – Thomas returned to Naples, to set up a *studium generale*; he completed further commentaries on Aristotle, wrote up his lectures on the Epistles of St. Paul, and got some way into the *tertia pars* of the *Summa* before having a mystical experience on December 6, 1273, after which he ceased to do theology: "I cannot do any more. Everything I have written seems to me as straw in comparison with what I have seen." He was considered well enough to set out in February 1274 to attend the Council of Lyons, diverted to his niece's house *en route*, where he fell seriously ill, had himself transported to Fossanova, where he died within about a month.

II

Preeminently the greatest theologian in Paris in the thirteenth century, Thomas actually spent less than 15 years there, in three bursts, as novice and student 1245–8, and in two stints as teacher, 1252–9 and 1268–72. He spent far more of his life between Naples and Rome, presumably preaching in the vernacular over a wide area, being designated a preacher general in his province in 1260, teaching young friars who were not destined to go to any of the great international universities, and twice being called upon to establish study houses (at Santa Sabina, Rome, in 1265 and in Naples in 1272), with responsibility for organizing courses, etc.

Thomas was never an aloof academic. For one thing, as noted already, academic life in Paris was extremely turbulent during each of his sojourns and he was involved in the controversies; but evidently he was also trusted as an administrator by the friars who knew him best. He was also frequently consulted by more than one pope. While some of the treasured anecdotes make him out to be absent-minded (not noticing what food was being placed before him or that his plate had been taken away, suddenly breaking his silence by thumping on the table when dining with the King of France, exultant that he had thought of how to refute the Manichees, etc.), his unworldliness should not be exaggerated: the Buddha-like serenity attributed to him in much of the iconography is belied by the furious display of intellectual energy and passion in the surviving manuscripts in his own handwriting.

From his student days in Naples until his last year of teaching in Naples Thomas was obviously engaged in reading and interpreting Aristotle. In the last five years of his life he was so preoccupied with expounding Aristotle that it is astonishing to recall that he found time and energy also to produce his commentaries on St. John's Gospel and St. Paul's Epistles as well as the commentary on the *De Causis* and of course the *Summa Theologiae* itself. Even materially, as the chronology suggests, the more deeply he focused on his most innovative and personal theological work (the *Summa Theologiae*), the more frenziedly (almost) he struggled with Aristotle's pagan philosophy while juggling all the time the two great New Testament theologians, John and Paul, and maintaining his interest, through the *De Causis*, in the neoplatonic patristic tradition in which all Catholic theology was rooted.

It is misleading to regard him as a Christian Aristotelian, if that is to ignore his permanent indebtedness to the Fathers, and in particular to Augustine and Gregory, and also to whatever he could learn about Greek patristic sources, and thus his indebtedness to Scripture as read in that tradition and in the liturgy.

On the other hand, by the time that he was developing his own distinctive theology, in his second spell as professor in Paris (1268–72), Thomas was undoubtedly suspected by colleagues of conceding too much, in his endeavor to deal with Aristotle's philosophy by integrating it into Christian theology. In December 1270 the Bishop of Paris, Stephen Tempier, issued a clear condemnation of radical Aristotelianism. In 1272 the arts faculty (not the theology faculty!) petitioned the Dominicans not to remove Thomas from Paris. (They also sent a letter after his death in 1274 asking for copies of various works that he had promised for their library; indeed they even asked for his body to be sent back to Paris – they were far more favorable to Thomas's work than most of the theology faculty!)

In 1277 the new Pope John XXI, Peter of Spain, a prolific writer on philosophical and scientific subjects including commentaries on Aristotle and Dionysius, ordered an inquiry, but Tempier had already set up his own commission of 16 theologians to examine "errors" current in the arts faculty and to consider the doctrines of Giles of Rome (an Augustinian Hermit, taught by Thomas) and Thomas himself. The commission worked suspiciously fast: on March 7, 1277 a list of 219 theories allegedly taught in the Arts faculty was condemned by the bishop; then 51 theories taught in the theology faculty and especially by Giles of Rome were drawn up – many of them clearly Thomas's; Giles was asked to recant but defended them instead, and consequently was refused his license to teach. One of the theses was that of unicity of form, plainly the one that concerned the bishop most. All the available theologians seem to have been brought together then to discuss a number of theses maintained by Thomas, in particular that same thesis. All but two condemned it – the two Dominican theologians, presumably standing out in favor of their distinguished colleague. All was set for a condemnation of Thomas's ideas. It is not clear why it did not happen. John of Vercelli, Master of the Order, happened to be in Paris at the time; he probably intervened to insist that the case should be referred to Rome. It seems likely too that Albert the Great lent his authority to defend Thomas. What we do know is that, when John XXI died in May 1277 (the ceiling of his study collapsed on his head), the seven cardinals gathered to elect a successor (it took them six months) ordered Tempier to proceed no further.

Late in 1279, the Franciscan William de la Mare excerpted and criticized 117 propositions from the writings of Thomas, in a document known as the *Correctorium,* which was officially adopted by the general chapter of the Franciscans in 1282, stating that copies of the *Summa* were not to be provided "except for reasonably intelligent lectors." In Oxford the Dominican archbishop of Canterbury Robert Kilwardby issued his own list on March 18, 1277, unambiguously affecting Thomas, condemning the unicity of form thesis outright. The Dominicans acted quickly against their confrère – in 1278 he was translated as a cardinal to the see of Porto in Italy where he died a year later. That put a stop to the Dominican condemnation of Thomas but Kilwardby was succeeded at Canterbury by the Franciscan John Pecham, a zealous reforming bishop but another longstanding inveterate critic. In 1284 he called the Oxford divinity faculty together and had them formally confirm Kilwardby's condemnation of 1277, including in particular the "unicity of form" thesis. In 1286 Pecham had that thesis declared heretical – and in the same year the Dominicans at their general chapter declared that, while not every Dominican need necessarily agree with every position taken by Thomas, nevertheless everyone should defend his theology as a legitimate theological option.

The subsequent history of the impact of Thomas's theology does not concern us here: the commentators in the sixteenth century (Cajetan, John of St. Thomas, Suarez), the revival in the late nineteenth century at the behest of Pope Leo XIII, the diverse and even incommensurable interpretations currently available. It remains that, however celebrated his reputation as the "Angelic Doctor," as *doctor communis,* particularly since the revival of Thomism in the late nineteenth century, Thomas's theology has always been in contention; all his life he was involved in controversy.

III

There is much more to Thomas than his interest in Aristotle. But since, in his own day as well as in late nineteenth/early twentieth century Thomism, his attempt to integrate Aristotelian themes was so contentious, something more needs to be said.

Consider, in particular, the theory of the unicity of substantial form. The question at first seems harmless enough. Most generally, are the preceding forms annihilated by the arrival of the intellectual soul? In other words, if we may think of ourselves as capable of nourishing ourselves and of reproduction, as plants are, and also of sensation and other activities as animals are, what happens when we recall that we are also rational? On Aristotle's view, espoused by Aquinas, these constitute a hierarchy of vital activities in such a way that human beings, in virtue of their rationality, can exercise also the vital activities of an animal. Human beings, so to speak, are rational all the way down. Certain inconveniences in this hylomorphism may suggest themselves to the modern mind; for his contemporaries, however, the troubling question was about the status of the dead Christ's body in the tomb. According to the hylomorphic conception of body/soul unity that he took from Aristotle, Thomas held that the intellectual soul is the only substantial form of the human being. His adversaries appealed to a plurality of forms and posited, in addition to the rational soul, a *forma corporeitatis*, a corporeal form, that remained the same, inhering in the body both before and after death. In this way they could ensure the continuity between the two states of Christ's body – abandoned, they feared, in Thomas's hylomorphic theory. He, of course, never doubted the identity of Christ's body before and after death; but he appealed to the doctrine of hypostatic union. Christ's body, living or dead, had no hypostasis other than that of the Word; the hypostatic union of the person of the Word with his soul and body did not cease at Jesus's death. There was no need to appeal to a mysterious "corporeal form" when we have it as a defined doctrine of the Church that the hypostatic union remains beyond death (cf. *ST* III, 50, 5). For Thomas, Aristotle's radically antidualistic conception of body/soul unity at the metaphysical level, far from leaving him with something other than Christ's dead body in the tomb, only brought out further implications of the doctrine of hypostatic union. The theologians who suspected him of heresy were the ones who needed the superfluous philosophical notion of a hypothetical *forma corporeitatis*; Aristotle's much simpler philosophical anthropology cleared the way for much more direct reliance on Christian dogma.

There are many other ways in which ideas from Aristotle clarified points of Christian doctrine for Aquinas, For example: he believed at an early stage that one of the implications of the doctrine of hypostatic union was that the knowledge that Christ enjoyed in his human nature was intuitive – that he did not need to work through to the truth by inference from the better to the less well known. The better he understood Aristotle, however, the more clearly Aquinas came to see that, if the man Jesus did not work things out *componendo et dividendo*, in effect by putting two and two together, he must after all have been something other than truly human (cf. III, 9, 4).

Again, late in his career, when he considered the nature of charity, he brought the Fourth Gospel – "I call you friends" – into relationship with the account of true friendship in the *Nicomachean Ethics* which allowed him to find a sense for the divine gift of the virtue of charity which was more than mere doing good and yet not necessarily best represented on the model of mystical marriage (cf. II-II, 23, 1).

Most notable of all, however, is the way in which Aristotle's *Ethics* enabled Aquinas to supplement, or replace, traditional accounts of the spiritual and moral life in terms of keeping or breaking the Commandments, with his lengthy and detailed theological ethics of the development of character. The most original part of the *Summa Theologiae*, perhaps even the point of writing it, is the deeply Aristotelian account in the *secunda pars*, of the moral agent's growth in virtue towards the beatitude which alone assuages our desire for happiness.

IV

Clearly, work on the unfinished *Summa Theologiae* was only a small part of the enormous amount of writing that Thomas did. Mostly, his writing derives from lecture courses on Scripture and from analysis of and commentary on philosophical texts. The *Summa* did not have much influence in his own day: indeed it is arguable how much of an impact it has ever had. Since it is his latest work, it seems right to devote attention to it and highlight features that may be said to represent what is most characteristic of Thomas's thought and of most continuing interest.

The *Summa* is intended to "hand on what relates to the Christian religion in a way that is appropriate to educating beginners" (prologue). Thomas wants to "pursue what relates to *sacra doctrina* as briefly and lucidly as the matter permits." It is far from clear who these "beginners" are. It is often assumed that they must be the young friars whom Thomas was certainly called to instruct when he was Regent-master at Rome in 1265–8, when he started to compose the *Summa*. These would have been run-of-the-mill students who were being trained to preach in the vicinity of the priories in which they had joined the Order; most Dominicans at the time did not proceed to the great international universities but spent their lives preaching and ministering in the neighborhood. Given, on the other hand, that they would certainly not have had copies of the book, or access even to a master copy, it seems plausible to suggest that the *Summa Theologiae* was designed in the first place for those who were to instruct them. Thomas seems to take it for granted that those for whom he was writing already had been taken through the Scriptures in class and had considerable experience of taking part in disputations. The *Summa* reads more like the second-level reflective course which might follow years of studying the biblical and patristic texts, and of hearing doctrinal issues disputed in the schools.

However that may be, the first question deals with the nature and extent of "sacred doctrine." It might be thought, after all, Thomas objects to the thesis which he is to defend, that the *philosophicae disciplinae* which human reason investigates yield enough knowledge of God to make any other teaching superfluous (q. 1). Human beings ought not hubristically to seek to transcend reason (objection 1); as Aristotle says, all beings, including God, are already treated in philosophy (objection 2). These are not factitious objections: in a medieval world pervaded by the Christian religion, with nature as a book revealing the divine presence as much as Scripture itself, it was perfectly reasonable, at the beginning of a reflective appropriation of Christian doctrine, to consider whether it was necessary at all – or at least to say why it was so. It was necessary for our salvation, Thomas contends, that there should be "a certain teaching in the light of divine revelation, besides the philosophical disciplines that are investigated by human reason." First, human beings are directed towards God, an end or destiny that exceeds the comprehension of reason, and since we need to know the end to be able to direct our purposes and actions towards it, certain realities had to be divinely revealed to us that we could not have worked out by reason. Secondly, even the truth about God investigated by reason has come to few, after a long time, and mixed with many errors; yet on knowledge of this truth there depends our entire salvation which is in God – thus even what is knowable about God by reason, in principle, needed to be divinely revealed. There is nothing to stop things treated in the philosophical disciplines in the light of natural reason also being treated by another science in the light of divine revelation – though the theology that relates to sacred teaching differs categorically from the theology which is included in philosophy. Indeed, sacred doctrine is a science that proceeds from principles known in the light of a higher science – which is the science enjoyed by God and the blessed (art. 2). Sacred doctrine or Scripture is founded on divine revelation (ad 2) – *principia revelata a Deo* – so if we are to say, as many do, that Thomas is a foundationalist in theology it has to be said that he founds his theology not on anything natural or philosophical or in any way nontheological but rather on something eschatological – God's self-knowledge as enjoyed by the blessed in heaven, now communicated by divine revelation.

Thomas has a three-part structure in mind: first we shall treat God (*prima pars*); then the movement of the rational creature towards God (*secunda pars*); thirdly Christ who as man is the way for us to be drawn into God (*tertia pars*, cf. q. 2 prologue). God is to be considered not only in himself but also as beginning and end of things, and especially of the rational creature: while Thomas never collapses God and the world into one another he equally never holds them so far apart that he could deal with either independently of the other. After considering God and what proceeds from God according to his will, then, he proceeds next to consider human beings as imaging God in the sense of being agents in achieving the divine beatitude which is their destiny (I-II, prologue): Thomas's theology is entirely dominated by the promise of human participation in God's own blessedness. Thirdly, after considering the virtues and vices, the moral life, by which human beings attain their ultimate destiny, Thomas turns to the "consummation of the entire theological enterprise" – "our saviour the Lord Jesus Christ who has demonstrated in himself the way of truth by which we can reach the beatitude of immortal life by resurrection" (III, prologue).

The third part is, as we noted, unfinished; yet the plan is clear – to treat the moral life as the journey to beatitude (*secunda pars*) in the middle of the treatment of God as beginning and end of all things (*prima pars*) and the treatment of the God-man Christ as the beginning of the new creation (*tertia pars*). The exposition of sacred doctrine, then, has the narrative structure of a journey from God as creator to God as beatifying in raising the dead – from creation to beatitude.

It has been suggested that the overall plan of the *Summa* derives, deliberately or not, from a neoplatonic *exitus/reditus* scheme, in which everything is pictured as coming forth from the origin to which as goal everything returns. It seems more likely, however, that Thomas, consciously or otherwise, had the biblical pattern of creation/resurrection in mind. He explicitly rejected other theological schemes, choosing to expound sacred doctrine *sub ratione Dei*: as being either about God or about what is related to God as beginning and end, *principium et finis* (q. 1, art. 7).

The first part of the *Summa* is itself a three-part consideration of God: what relates to the divine essence or nature (qq. 2 to 26); what relates to the distinction of Persons (qq. 27 to 43); and what relates to the coming forth of creatures from God (qq. 44 to 119). The second part deals with God as the objective reality in which alone beatitude consists (I-II, qq. 1 to 5) and then expounds the moral psychology (qq. 6 to 89), divine law and the dispensation of grace (qq. 90 to 114), and the virtues and vices that constitute the moral and spiritual life that leads to beatitude (II-II). Finally, the third part deals with God incarnate as the way by which everlasting happiness is gained: first the mysteries of the Incarnation, Passion, and Resurrection of Christ (qq. 1 to 59); then the sacraments of Christ by which we achieve salvation (qq. 60 breaking off at q. 90, having discussed baptism, eucharist, and penance); then the destined immortal life to which we come through Christ by rising.

Much attention has been given to I, treating it as natural theology, as an attempt by Thomas to secure the proposition that "there is a God" before embarking on the whole project of expounding Christian doctrine. Given that q. 1 is the prologue to the *Summa*, and that it has already established that "the theology which is part of philosophy" is generically different from "the theology which relates to sacred doctrine" (cf. art. 1, ad 2), and that it is the latter with which the *Summa* is concerned (in contrast perhaps with the *Contra Gentiles*), it is unlikely that Thomas regarded the famous "Five Ways" as an exercise in philosophy. His concern seems rather to steer a way between those who believe that the presence of God is overwhelmingly obvious, naturally self-evident, requiring no further discussion or argument (art. 1), and those who contend that no argument is available or necessary on the grounds that it is solely and purely an article of faith that God exists (art. 2). There is no sign that Thomas was trying to prove the truth of the proposition that God exists to skeptics and atheists, and to do so by appealing to rigorous arguments which might convince them. He is, after all, expounding Christian doctrine in a way that is appropriate to beginners (prologue). Continuing the theme that divine revelation might seem altogether unnecessary on the grounds that so much is already known about God in the philosophical disciplines, Thomas first casts doubt on the arguments invoked by those who find themselves at home in a world that reveals the divine presence at every turn: we have a natural awareness of God as source of our beatitude; anyone who understands what the word "God" means knows that God exists; given that there is such a thing as truth we need no proof that there must be ultimate truth, which can only be God. On the other hand, Thomas is unwilling to concede that nothing in this world could yield any evidence of God's existence: it is simply a matter of faith; as John Damascene says, we have no knowledge of what God is, we can thus have no way of developing an argument; or even if we started from things in the world, since they are finite, they could never sustain an argument in favor of the existence of their having an infinite cause such as God must be. Thomas steers between what were clearly then (as they still are today) extremely tempting views: a naturalistic theism which finds rational argument for God's existence redundant, and an apophatic fideism which regards such argument as impossible. Over against both positions, Thomas airs the possibility that there is no God (art. 3): the existence of evil in the world seems incompatible with there being an infinitely good God; everything in the world makes sense without our supposing that God exists. Thomas picks the two most difficult objections to theism. He then appeals to Scripture: God revealed himself to Moses (Exodus 3:14); and goes on to sketch "five ways" by which God's existence "can be tested" (*probari*): phenomena in the world such as change, causality, contingency, degrees of perfection, and design, show the existence of some prime mover itself moved by none, some first efficient cause, something intrinsically necessary, something which causes being, goodness, and any and every perfection in everything, and something with a mind by which everything is directed to its end – and such items we call "God." It cannot be said that the treatment of the difficulties about the existence of evil and the redundancy of theistic explanation is satisfactory; indeed the whole question is so perfunctorily handled that it is hard to believe that Thomas attached great significance to it. It seems more likely that he was concerned only to challenge the assumption that theistic belief was either so natural that philosophical argument was unnecessary or so much a matter of revelation that it was impossible. In article 3, while invoking the traditional patristic belief that God's existence was a matter of God's self-revelation, Thomas identifies features of the world, quite independent of religion and indeed just the sort of thing with which the philosophical disciplines would be concerned, which imply the existence of something that we might call "God." It is as if the rest of the *Summa* will have to persuade the beginners that the existence of evil is not incompatible with the goodness of God, while the exposition of sacred doctrine itself will have to show them something about the world beyond what the philosophical disciplines explore and explain.

That little enough has been shown in q. 2 seems clear when at q. 3 Thomas immediately asks whether God could be something physical (art. 1). He now embarks on lengthy discussion of how God is *not* – first, then, arguing that there is no difference between form and matter in God, nor between God and his nature or essence, nor between God's being and nature; God is not classifiable (not even in the category of substance); God is "altogether simple," *omnino simplex,* and can in no way enter into composition with anything in the world as if to become part of it. From then on Thomas goes through the traditional divine attributes: perfection, goodness, infinity, transcendence and immanence, immutability, eternity, and unity (qq. 4 to 11).

After this account of how God is in himself, Thomas considers how God is in our experience (*in cognitione nostra*) – how God is known by creatures (q. 12, prologue). In a long discussion, perhaps the most important so far in the *Summa*, Thomas argues against the thesis that no created being could ever see God in his essence – defending himself by citing 1 John 3:2. Given all that has been said about God's absolute simpleness, indeed, it becomes difficult to understand how human beings could ever see Him as He is. Thomas here engages in what had been a very lively debate for decades. He argues that God is certainly seen by the blessed in heaven (art. 1), and not mediatedly but by His own light (art. 2); by grace not by any powers natural to us (art. 4); by our becoming "deiform" (arts. 5 and 6); never comprehending God (art. 7) nor seeing everything in God (art. 8); and all this applying only to the blessed in heaven – nobody in the world could see the divine essence (art. 11); true, we can have a certain natural knowledge of God in this life (art. 12), effectively what we have achieved in qq. 2 to 11; and in the economy of grace a fuller knowledge of God is accessible – "faith is a sort of knowledge" – yet even by the relation of grace we do not have knowledge of God as He is in this life but are joined to Him as to One Unknown (art. 13).

If we have that much knowledge of God in this life, by reason and by the dispensation of grace, we are able to say something about God – which leads to q. 13 and something less than the traditional *de nominibus Dei* and more a methodological defense – steering between the view that we say things of God and creatures neither univocally nor equivocally but analogically (art. 5). The name which is most appropriate to God, it turns out, is "He Who is" – citing the revelation to Moses again (art. 11) – unless it is the Tetragrammaton (ad 1).

Next Thomas turns to what God does in Himself – God's being is his doing, the divine nature is activity: within the divine nature, so to speak, there is knowing (qq. 14 to 18); there is willing (qq. 18 to 25); finally (q. 26) there is beatitude – looking forward to what is to come in the 1a, 2ae – "there is bliss in God *per essentiam* for His being is His doing, in which He enjoys none other than Himself" (I-II, q. 3, art. 2, ad 4).

The topic of God's intrinsic beatitude concludes the discussion of what relates to the unity of the divine essence and opens the way to considering what relates to the trinity of Persons *in divinis* – as if the divine self-enjoyment were the bridge between the consideration of the divine nature and the theology of the divine persons.

Here, instead of starting from the New Testament narrative of the Trinitarian dispensation of salvation, in an historical reconstruction, as modern theologians generally do, Thomas opts for conceptual analysis: first expounding the notion of procession or origination (q. 27), then that of relation (q. 28), preparing the way for that of person (qq. 29 to 43), culminating in q. 43 with a question on the mission of the divine persons: according to what we have seen about the divine presence in everything, we can say that, by knowing and loving, the rational creature by its activity reaches God – thus God is in the creature – but there is a privileged way in which God is said not only to be in the rational creature but even to dwell in him or her as in His temple – so now we are talking about how the rational creature is sanctified – anticipating much that will come much later.

Before we get on to discuss the dispensation of grace and the sanctification of the graced creature we have to consider the coming forth from God of creatures – so from q. 44 to q. 119 we are led through the doctrine of creation: God alone creates (qq. 44 and 45); creation is to do with being radically dependent, not having a beginning; it is the work of God as Trinity (45, 6) and there is a Trinitarian mark on every creature (q. 45, 7). We discuss the angels, qq. 50 to 64; then the seven days of creation, qq. 65 to 74; then the human being, qq. 75 to 102, culminating perhaps in q. 93 with the human being as image of God. There follows a lengthy discussion of how the world is governed, q. 103, with the famous thesis at q. 105, art. 5 (*Deus operatur in omni operante*), introducing Thomas's often repeated insistence that, far from there being any competition between divine freedom and creaturely freedom, our freest acts are precisely the acts in which God's acting is most fully present. Thomas then discusses how creatures work on one another, how angels affect human beings (qq. 106 to 114), how stars and fate affect us (115 and 116) and finally how human beings affect one another – by procreation (118 and 119) – and especially, at some length (q. 117, art. 1), by education.

Whether by nature or under grace, the human creature makes the choices that achieve the blessedness for which he or she is born and which God in Christ has promised and inaugurated in the Holy Spirit. The whole of the second part of the *Summa Theologiae* is, then, an extended account of how as image of God the human being reaches or deviates from that ultimate destiny (prologue to I-II). This ultimate destiny is the divine beatitude which we are empowered to enjoy (qq. 1 to 5); we do so by our choices (6 to 21); integrating and not denying our feelings (22 to 48); developing settled dispositions of character and personality, virtues to be cultivated and vices to be curbed (49 to 89), not forgetting the influence of the Devil (q. 80) and the place of original sin (81 to 89). As rational creatures we live under law (90 to 97), but besides that participation in divine law that we call natural law (94) and the laws that political communities make (95 to 97), there is the Law of Moses (98 to 105) and the New Law of the Gospel (106 to 108), which opens the account of the dispensation of grace (109 to 114). "The most important thing in the Law of the New Testament, indeed that in which its dynamism entirely consists, is the grace of the Holy Spirit given by faith in Christ. Indeed, most radically, the New Law is simply the grace of the Holy Spirit which is given to Christ's faithful" (q. 106, 1). "The very letter of the Gospel would not give life but for the presence within [the believer] of the healing grace of faith" (q. 106, 2). "This grace is communicated to human beings by the Son of God's having become man" (q. 108, 1). "Since grace transcends human nature, it cannot be a substance or substantial form; it is an accidental form of the soul: that which is substantially in God comes to be accidentally in the soul that participates in the divine goodness" (q. 110, 2, ad 2). "God alone makes godlike, by communicating a share in his divine nature by assimilative participation" (q. 112, 1, where Thomas discreetly picks up the Greek patristic theology of grace as "divinization"). "Christ's humanity does not cause grace by its own power but by the power of the conjoined divinity, in virtue of which the actions of Christ's humanity have saving efficacy" (q. 112, 1, ad 1), Thomas immediately contends, citing the doctrine of Christ's humanity as "a kind of instrument of his divinity," which Thomas explicitly takes from the Latin translation of the *Pege Gnoseos* of John of Damascus (675–749), a phrase which recurs more and more, especially in the *tertia pars*.

Having established that the dispensation of grace is "a kind of *habitudo* which is presupposed to the infused virtues, as their origin and root" (q. 110, 3, ad 3), Thomas comes, in the *secunda secundae*, to a detailed account of the virtues and corresponding vices of the moral agent using reason and under grace – starting with the divinely infused or theological virtues, faith, hope, and charity (1 to 46), continuing with the four cardinal virtues classical since Plato: *phronesis* (47 to 56), justice (57 to 122), fortitude (123ff.), and temperance (141ff.). Then, at q. 170, the account concludes of the virtues and vices that concern human beings of whatever condition and status.

Thomas next looks at the ethical considerations in the lifestyle first of those called to be prophets, mystics, charismatics (171 to 178); then what it is like to be called to the active and/or contemplative way of life (179 to 182); to "states" of life (183), the state of perfection, religious life – culminating with a question on being a hermit – a "divine man" (q. 188, art. 8) – or rather with an appendix (q. 189) on the then extremely lively question of who should be allowed to enter religious life. Whether children (189, 5)? Those who are already clerics (art. 7)? Whether one should encourage others to enter religious life (art. 9)? Whether one should enter religious life without consulting many people and without lengthy deliberation (art. 10)? But the allusion to the "divinization" of the human being who has received the gift of the theological virtues faith, hope, and charity, as well as the gifts of the Holy Spirit, and has practiced the cardinal virtues of prudence, justice, fortitude, and temperance, respecting the divine law and delighting in the dispensation of grace – this is surely where the achievement of the unanticipated and unowed grace of blessedness begins in this life – which brings us to the *tertia pars* and the question of the appropriateness of the mystery of God's becoming incarnate.

Citing Ps.-Dionysius (III, q. 1, 1), Thomas maintains that the divine nature is goodness (bounty); whatever is involved in the idea of the good is appropriate to God; what characterizes the idea of the good is that it communicates itself to others – so, as Augustine in the *de Trinitate* confirms, what is most appropriate for the sovereign Good is that it shares itself in a supreme way with the created – "it joins to itself a created nature such that one person comes to be from the trio: Word, body and soul." It was appropriate for God to become incarnate, as John of Damascus says, "so that the goodness, wisdom, justice and power of God should be displayed by the mystery of the Incarnation" (q. 1 *sed contra*). Once again, Thomas draws on Greek patristic sources, bringing them to bear on his conception of the mystery of the incarnate Word as revelation and manifestation of the divine nature.

Only then (q. 1, arts. 2 to 4), does he turn to discuss whether the Incarnation was necessary to redeem sinful humanity. Thomists and Scotists, famously, have disputed about the "motive" (on God's part) of the Incarnation, and usually Thomists cite q. 1, art. 3, where Thomas alludes to Albert the Great and Alexander of Hales who say that even if mankind had not sinned the Son of God would have become incarnate – and on the other side Bonaventure and Odo Rigaldus with whom Thomas aligns himself – Scripture alone lets us know anything about God's will and everywhere in Scripture the Incarnation is related to *sin* – so let us leave it at that: "whatever flows from the will of God beyond all that is due to creatures can become known to us only in Scripture" – which is fine, but given the fact of the Incarnation it is to be seen as a communication befitting and manifesting sheerly divine bounty, so article 1 of q. 3 – it is rather difficult to understand why Thomas comes down so clearly in article 3 – particularly since in article 2 he sketches a variety of considerations regarding the fittingness of the Incarnation.

In qq. 2 to 6 we explore the implications of the hypostatic union; moving in q. 7 to the singular human being Christ and exploring what he must have been like as a moral agent, very much recapping what has been seen previously so that he becomes the paradigm of the story in the *secunda pars*. Appealing to Isaiah 11:2, Thomas recapitulates his account of the moral agent: Christ enjoys habitual grace (art. 1); has the virtues (art. 2); but not faith (art. 3), since he enjoys the *fruitio divina* from his conception; nor hope (art. 4), for the same reason; but the gifts of the Holy Spirit (art. 5), including the gift of fear of the Lord (art. 6); the charisms including prophesy (arts. 7 and 8); indeed the plenitude of grace such that "he is so to speak the universal source in the class of those who have grace" (art. 10). In q. 8, accordingly, Thomas contends, citing Ephesians 1:22, Romans 8:29 and 12:4, etc., that this individual Jesus Christ is also corporate as *caput ecclesiae* – "head of the church." Christ is also head of mankind as a whole (art. 3), citing 1 Timothy 4:10 and 1 John 2:2; including the people of Israel: "the patriarchs, by observing the sacraments of the Law, were carried to Christ by the same faith and love by which we also are brought to him" (ad 3). "Christ alone is the one through whom we have access to the grace in which we stand" (art. 6, ad 3).

Next we consider Christ's knowledge (qq. 9 to 12) and power (q. 13), then the limitations on him, bodily and spiritually (qq. 14 and 15). Thomas continues with the often fairly technical questions much disputed especially at the early councils of the Church, considering the implications of the hypostatic union: in what sense may we say "God is man" and suchlike, very much a conceptual analysis (q. 16); the human nature requiring no human "person" but owing its existence to the divine Person – the *anhypostasis/enhypostasis* of the human nature of Christ (q. 17); monothelitism (q. 18); monoenergism (q. 19).

Next we consider the relationship of Christ to the Father: his being subject to the Father (q. 20); his addressing prayer to the Father (q. 21); his being a priest, as giving holy things to the people and offering their prayers to the Father (q. 22); as the one in whom others are adopted children of God (q. 23); as himself predestined (q. 24). Then we consider Christ's relationship to ourselves: the worship we owe to Christ (q. 25) and Christ as mediator between God and us (q. 26).

If we may recapitulate: in the *prima pars* Thomas considers God's triune being as beginning of all things including the creature made in the divine image; in the *secunda pars* he considers God as the final beatitude which is the end of all things, to be achieved by the human agent by the practice of virtue in the economy of grace; and in the *tertia pars* he considers God as united to humanity in the God-man, planning to continue with what "the Son of God incarnate in a human nature united to himself did and suffered" – foreseeing four sections: his entry into the world (qq. 27ff.); his life in this world (qq. 40ff.); his *exitus* from this world (qq. 46ff.); and his exaltation after this life (qq. 53ff.).

Thus we have questions on the conception, birth, baptism, etc., of Christ, including discussion of the holiness of the Blessed Virgin Mary (qq. 27 to 39): famously, while conceding that the practice in other traditions of celebrating the Conception of the Blessed Virgin liturgically should be tolerated, Thomas did not see the need to hold any doctrine of her "immaculate conception" (cf. q. 27, art. 2).

In qq. 40 to 45 Thomas discusses Christ's life in this world, very much a reading of the Synoptics – his "style" (q. 40); the temptation narrative (q. 41); his preaching (q. 42); his miracles (qq. 43 and 44); and the Transfiguration (q. 45).

The *exitus* from this world (qq. 46 to 52) deals in order with the Passion, death (q. 50) and burial (q. 51), descent into hell (q. 52), and is followed by the *exaltatio Christi* (qq. 53 to 59): resurrection, ascension, being seated at the right hand of the Father and being enthroned as judge.

Thus the *tertia pars* was planned to have three sections: on the Savior himself (qq. 1 to 59); on his sacraments, by which we are saved (qq. 59ff.); and the destiny of immortal life which we reach through him by resurrection (prologue). The first section is divided into the mystery of the Incarnation, exploring the implications of God's becoming man for our salvation (qq. 1 to 26) and, secondly, the things done and suffered by our Savior himself, by God incarnate (qq. 27 to 59). Rephrasing this, the first section deals with the God–man union and its implications (cf. prologue to q. 27); the second with the mysteries of the Word incarnate (cf. prologue to q. 60).

The next stage, then, is to consider "the Church's sacraments as having their efficacy from the World incarnate himself" (prologue to q. 60). Since Thomas abandoned the project, having dealt with baptism (qq. 66 to 71) and confirmation (q. 72 – one question!), the eucharist (qq. 73 to 83), and the sacrament of penance (qq. 84 to 90), we never get to extreme unction, holy order, and matrimony – let alone to the projected final section on the Last Things – though it is all there in the Supplement composed by Thomas's disciples based on his commentary on the *Sentences* from nearly twenty years before.

It may be noted that for Thomas there is no need to introduce a study of the nature of the Church between Christology and the study of the sacraments – for Thomas the *ecclesiae sacramenta* are simply the signs of the grace which effects the believer's sanctification. In q. 60 he places the notion of sacrament very firmly in the category of sign (we should perhaps say: symbol); then as rites of passage in a rudimentary theological anthropology (q. 61); only then insisting that it is by the sacraments of the New Law that we are incorporated into Christ (q. 62) and picking up the early patristic doctrine of sacramental "character," understanding it as "deputing" the individual to take part in the worship of God (q. 63). God alone is the agent of justification which is the inward effect of the sacraments, but there is a subordinate role for the human agent (q. 64). It is appropriate that there should be seven and only seven sacraments, though the eucharist is by far the most important (q. 65).

Baptism is introduced in terms of washing, the symbolism of water, etc. (q. 66); while it pertains most properly to the bishop to baptize, since he is the principal teacher, a lay man and indeed woman and for that matter an unbaptized person may baptize in circumstances of necessity (q. 67); all should be baptized, including infants, but not Jewish children against the will of their parents (q. 68); baptism takes all sin away (q. 69); it is prefigured by circumcision (q. 70) and should be accompanied by teaching (q. 71).

Thomas seems aware of controversy about the origin and necessity of confirmation, though lacks the information which might have enabled him to understand why it drifted apart from baptism; essentially, for him, it marks the passage into young adulthood when the baptized may be expected to stand up for their beliefs in the public arena (q. 72).

The eucharist is introduced in terms of food (q. 73); then as *memoriale Dominicae passionis* (q. 74). Thomas treads carefully through the minefield of theories about the *conversio* of the bread and wine into Christ's body and blood (qq. 75 and 76), contending finally that the accidents of bread and wine remain after the consecration inhering in the accident of quantity (q. 77). Most of the remaining questions deal with issues that are more practical or in the realm of canon law, while the discussion concludes with a skimpy treatment of the eucharistic *rite* – which indicates how differently a modern theologian might approach the whole subject.

One of the main interests in studying a work such as the *Summa Theologiae* is precisely to see how far it differs, in detail and in structure, from approaches more congenial to modern theologians. While it is important to emphasize that it is only one of his many projects, and of course left unfinished, and not at all representative of the commentary and disputation which occupy most of his writing, the *Summa Theologiae* is his last work, in many ways his most original, personal, and mature work, and as a classic of medieval Latin theology always likely to attract new readers.

Bibliography

The best biography now is the introduction by Simon Tugwell to his *Albert and Thomas: Selected Writings*, 1988; the best introduction to evangelical reform, biblical interpretation, teaching methods, etc. remains M. D. Chenu, *Toward Understanding St. Thomas*, 1964; the best account of Aquinas's idea of theology is Per Erik Persson, *Sacra Doctrina* (Swedish 1957, English 1970).

Secondly, we need to see something of what Aquinas does with the God question: Norman Kretzmann, *The Metaphysics of Theism*, 1997; W. J. Hankey, *God in Himself*, 1987; David Burrell, *Knowing the Unknowable God*, 1986; M. J. Dodds, *The Unchanging God of Love: Divine Immutability*, 1986.

Third: perhaps something about the sanctification of the sinner: S. Pfurtner, *Luther and Aquinas*, 1964; above all, Anna Williams, *The Ground of Union*, 1999.

Fourth: "virtue ethics" – for example, Jean Porter, *The Recovery of Virtue*, 1990; Romanus Cessario, *The Godly Image: Christ and Salvation in Catholic Thought from Anselm to Aquinas*, 1990; above all Servais Pinckaers, *Sources of Christian Ethics*, 1995.

General Bibliography

Brian Davies, *The Thought of Thomas Aquinas*, 1992.

Umberto Eco, *The Aesthetics of Thomas Aquinas*, 1986.

John Finnis, *Aquinas*, 1999.

Thomas Gilby, *The Political Thought*, 1958.

D. R. Janz, *Luther on Thomas Aquinas*, 1989.

J. Pieper, *The Silence of St. Thomas*, 1965.

Arvin Vos, *Aquinas, Calvin and Contemporary Protestant Thought*, 1985.

Later Medieval Mystics

Oliver Davies

Amongst all the areas of medieval theology, the mystics hold a special place in the modern world. Relatively few people engage with systematic theologians other than Augustine and Thomas Aquinas, while it is only the specialist who is likely to read the primary texts of canon law or medieval cosmology. Certain of the texts by mystical writers, however, such as the *Revelations* of Julian of Norwich or *The Cloud of Unknowing*, have become spiritual classics, finding a mass market amongst the modern reading public. In the discussion that follows therefore we shall seek to do two things. In the first place we shall offer a survey of medieval mystical thought, pointing to the different schools of spirituality and the diverse contexts in which mystical literature was produced. And secondly, we shall keep an eye on the way in which this literature has been and still is appropriated by the modern mind. In the journey from the author to the reader, every text gathers a history. This is particularly true when the texts concerned are of medieval provenance, and thus belonged originally to a world very different from our own. But most modern readers of these works are likely to be Christians and thus stand within the same hermeneutical community as their original authors and readers. We must recognize therefore that the appropriation of these texts in the modern world generally occurs within a context of ongoing tradition and reflects a greater degree of *engagement* than would normally be the case with most categories of literature. This again constitutes a reason why an account of the ways in which a text is read today can be as important as the recreation of the original environment.

The title of the present chapter well illustrates this point. For most of us, the term "mystic" is likely to suggest a preoccupation with "religious experience," a notion which must further be contrasted with "theology" as the domain of religious belief and thought. An opposition between religious belief or thought and religious experience was, however, fundamentally alien to the medieval world, and thus to the very people who we are here advancing as "mystics."[1] Indeed, it has recently been well argued that an important strain in what we call the medieval mystical tradition is essentially hostile to the concept of religious experience as such, since the knowledge of God is frequently seen in apophatic texts as a knowledge which is precisely other than that knowledge which can be defined as "experience": after all, how can we have "experience" of the one who is not an entity within the world but rather the Creator of it and thus Author of experience itself?[2] The modern category is moreover a seemingly all-embracing one; indeed, we are interested in particular in the diversity and typologies of "religious experience." Those more experiential types of "mysticism" during the Middle Ages are decidedly limited in scope, however; focusing mostly upon visions and auditions which – whether kerygmatic or unitive – are closely bound in with Christian doctrine. The very category of "mysticism," then, is the product of the modern age when experience had begun to emerge as a free-standing concept, and when the religious nature of human kind was seen to involve both elements of experience and elements of belief, though not necessarily in combination.[3] The term "spirituality," even more than "mysticism," belongs to our own day, and frequently has the sense of a set of personal beliefs and values which are in opposition to the outright materialism of our times.[4]

The three types of mystical writing which we discuss below offer a broad chronological survey of the Middle Ages to the extent that monastic literature belongs in the main to the eleventh and twelfth centuries, scholastic writings to the thirteenth and fourteenth centuries, and texts by women to the thirteenth, fourteenth, and fifteenth centuries.[5] Also, each was the product of a particular social environment and was intended for a particular audience. Our first class, the monastic text, grew out of a particular form of consecrated lifestyle, for instance; so that both author and audience shared a spiritual vision and a practical way of life. Inevitably, therefore, a sense of elitism can frequently be discerned in monastic mystical writing, reflecting the extent to which the monk has turned his back on the world and has committed himself to a specialized religious existence.

Monastic literature abounds in hierarchical models of mystical ascent, which map the increasing purification of the soul as it advances towards union with God. Carthusian authors such as Guigo II (d. 1188) and Adam (d. circa 1210), Cistercian writers such as Bernard of Clairvaux (1090–1153) or William of St. Thierry (1075/80–1148) and Augustinian canons such as Hugh of St. Victor (d. 1142) or Richard of St. Victor (d. 1173), are strongly motivated to inspire their monastic audience to ascend to the highest levels of contemplation and love. Also Scripture has a particularly important role in the formation of mystical notions, since *lectio divina* was fundamental to the monk, offering extended periods of reflection on scriptural passages in the light of his own personal commitment to a religious way of life. Monastic spirituality also tended to be suspicious of the more speculative and rationalistic trends which led in the thirteenth century to the establishing of the new universities. Monastic authors certainly did not lack a passionate engagement with Scripture or with questions regarding the nature of the self, but generally preferred a more conservative approach in which the devotional aims of knowledge were more cautiously adhered to.

After the Victorines

The Mystical Ark by Richard of St. Victor (see chapter 9 above) constitutes a kind of "*summa* of contemplation" in its clear articulation of the successive stages of contemplative union with God.[6] It is deeply indebted to the liturgical mysticism of Pseudo-Dionysius, and combines a deeply affective monastic piety with a controlling analysis of the structure of epistemology, as the human mind rises from the knowledge of the material things to immaterial things and finally to truths directly revealed by God. The work of the Victorines, especially Hugh and Richard of St. Victor, anticipated in a number of ways the kind of spirituality which emerged from the new universities which came increasingly to dominate the intellectual landscape of Europe. Powerful social forces of urbanization and the rise of the middle classes, together with the new availability of Greek texts not previously translated or only inadequately so, served to create a sophisticated environment of scholarship and thought which marked a new departure from the monastic schools of the previous century. The universities, and particularly the premier university at Paris, offered a context in which a more rapid exchange of ideas could be embraced and a more open and critical approach be adopted to issues concerned with reason and the nature of the self and the world. Although the relation between the Church and the new learning was not without tension, the newly founded Dominican and Franciscan Orders attempted a *rapprochement* between Christianity and classical philosophy which gave fresh impetus to the Christian mystical tradition.

The strongest expression of this new synthesis of the intellectual and affective cognition of God was the *Journey of the Mind into God* (*Itinerarium mentis in deum*) by Bonaventure (see chapter 12 above). He was born in Italy in 1217 and entered the Franciscan Order in 1243. He studied in Paris under Alexander of Hales, and became a master of theology in 1253 or 1254. In 1257 Bonaventure followed John of Parma as Minister General of the order. His early works were speculative and in the scholastic mold while, from 1257, Bonaventure's works became more spiritual in character. In 1259 he visited Mount La Verna, where Francis had a vision of a six-winged seraph and received the stigmata. There he suddenly understood "that this vision represented our father's rapture in contemplation and the road by which this rapture is reached."[7] Employing the structure of Francis's vision, Bonaventure composed an account of the spiritual life which included diverse elements from previous tradition, resolving them into a new and dynamic christological unity. Rather like Richard of St. Victor's *Mystical Ark*, by which it was undoubtedly influenced, it too constituted a *summa* of the spiritual life.

The *Journey of the Mind into God* begins with a prayer for grace, following the *Mystical Theology* of Pseudo-Dionysius, and sets out the six stages of the journey to God as an ascent through the six powers of the soul: "senses, imagination, reason, understanding, intelligence, and the summit of the mind or spark of conscience."[8] This ascent constitutes also a purification and a reformation of these faculties to their original purity. Broadly, Bonaventure follows the model laid out by Augustine in his *On the Trinity*, whereby the movement towards God begins with our perception of the external world, and then of the mind itself, and finally the restoration of the trinitarian image within us.

For Bonaventure, the "origin, magnitude, multitude, beauty, fullness, activity and order of things" all reveal God to us as the mysterious, trinitarian Creator of the world, so that whoever "is not enlightened by such splendour of created things is blind; whoever is not wakened by such outcries is deaf; whoever does not praise God because of all these effects is dumb."[9] Created things are the "vestiges" of the triune God, and God is revealed both through and in them. But the very process of perceiving objects through the senses, whereby – in medieval tradition – the object is said to reproduce itself in the mind of the observer, itself recalls the eternal generation of the Son within the Trinity.[10] In the same way, the act of judgment, whereby we discern the universal properties of things, is a participation in the unchanging truth of God.

In chapters 3 and 4 Bonaventure turns to the human mind as the place "where the divine image shines forth."[11] The human *mens* (which we translate here as "mind" or sometimes "soul" but which carries the connotations conveyed by modern terms such as "consciousness" and "self") is constituted by three acts or operations, as it wills (or loves), knows (or understands), and remembers itself. These three powers, freed from the perceptions of the external world, show the proximity of the soul to God, since in their operations we see that "memory leads to eternity, the understanding to truth and the power of choice to the highest good."[12] Memory, understanding, and will are also grounded in the Trinity, and so when "the soul considers itself, it rises though itself as through a mirror to behold the blessed Trinity of the Father, the Word and Love: three persons, coeternal, coequal and consubstantial."[13] But frequently the soul is not able to consider itself, since it is dispersed through the senses into the material world.

For Bonaventure, therefore, the theological virtues of faith, hope, and love play a key role in purifying the soul from its compromising attachments to material and external things, and it is the study of Scripture which most furthers the cultivation of these virtues at this stage in the soul's purification and ascent.[14] The further ascent of the soul, which has passed through the vestiges and the image, is "through the light which shines upon our minds."[15] For Bonaventure, an Augustinian, the mind is illumined by divine light and can engage with that light in a sublime act of contemplation. It is now firstly the essential attributes of God which come into view, followed by those proper to the trinitarian Persons. In the former we see God as "primary being, eternal, utterly simple, most actual, and most perfect."[16] This is divine being which is wholly dynamic and wholly self-contained, and by which all particular entities are maintained in existence. Bonaventure argues that this revelation of God's essential attributes as primal being is specific to the Old Testament, where God declared "I am who I am" (Exod. 3:14). In the latter we see God as goodness, which Bonaventure associates with the trinitarian narratives of the New Testament. The Good is self-diffusive, and the highest expression of that principle is the divine generation and self-communication which is revealed to us in the Trinity since in the trinitarian relations "the one diffusing communicates to the other his entire substance and nature."[17]

At this point Bonaventure's thought begins to take on a more distinctly dialectical structure, as he reflects upon the simultaneous identity and distinction which prevails in the Trinity. This trend is heightened as he comes to reflect upon the communication of the trinitarian mystery to us in the person of Christ, in whom "the eternal is joined with temporal man." In him, "the most simple" was united with "the most composite, the most actual with the one who suffered supremely and died, the most perfect and immense with the lowly, the supreme and all-inclusive one with a composite individual distinct from others."[18] And it is upon him that the two cherubs look, who represent the divine Being and Goodness, since Jesus Christ was sent by God and is "eternal life."[19] The final and highest stage of contemplation is reached for Bonaventure when the mind passes beyond even itself. He terms this the *transitus*, or "passing beyond," in which "if it is to be perfect, all intellectual activities must be left behind and the height of our affection must be totally transferred and transformed into God."[20] Here he freely applies the language of crucifixion and resurrection, and affirms that "in this passing over Christ is the way and the door."[21] The object of this contemplation is Christ himself, therefore, "hanging upon the Cross," in whom our cognitive faculties, both intellectual and affective, are totally transformed and are centered upon God.[22]

In many ways Bonaventure's *Journey of the Mind into God* can be seen to reconcile monastic piety, with its characteristic emphases upon embodiment and the will, with the radically intellectualist view of the self which was engendered by the rise of Aristotelianism in the new universities. Indeed, we can read his plea towards the end of the *Itinerarium* that we should 'ask grace not instruction, desire not understanding, the groaning of prayer not diligent reading, the Spouse not the teacher, God not man, darkness not clarity, not light but the fire that totally inflames and caries us into God by ecstatic unctions and burning affections' as signalling the *restoration* of monastic spiritual values within a rationalist environment.[23]

This is much less the case with Meister Eckhart, however, who shared with Bonaventure both the status of a leading scholastic theologian and a commitment to reflection upon the immediacy of God's presence in the world. Eckhart (1260–1327/8) was born in Gotha, near Erfurt, and entered the Dominican Order at 15 years of age.[24] He served as *magister regens* in Paris from 1302–3 and again from 1311–13. The German Dominican school of which he was a leading figure showed the influence in particular of neoplatonist texts, such as the *Book of Causes*, and Avicenna's highly platonizing way of reading Aristotle's *De anima*.[25] One of the chief characteristics of this school was the tendency to combine philosophical and theological positions in a comprehensive understanding of the unity of truth: "all that is true, whether in knowledge, in Scripture or in nature, flows from a single fount, a single root."[26] Although much of Eckhart's work is synthesis, we do not find a restoration of monastic spiritual values in his mystical theology so much as the articulation of a new type of spirituality, predicated upon the assimilation of strongly platonist currents of thought which stressed the primacy of Oneness into a Christian creationist metaphysics.

As we have seen in Bonaventure, the Augustinian understanding of the human mind was one which was open to transcendentalism as the mind engages with its source in the divine light. This Augustinianism is further radicalized in Eckhart, however, who comprehends the relation between creature and Creator in terms of "image" and "word," whereby Eckhart understood a trinitarian dialectic of unity and difference.[27] Thus the human "mind," which is simultaneously our "essence" and our "intellect" (by which again Eckhart means something close to "consciousness"), stands potentially in an immediate relation with God who is himself, for Eckhart, seen as "intellect" or "knowledge." The spirituality of Eckhart, then, is one which focuses upon the capacity of the human mind to realize its potential connaturality with the divine mind by freeing itself from earth-bound images and by entering into its own unified ground, where it already exists in a state of unity with God. Eckhart's spiritual method is also guided by his vocation as a Dominican, which is to evangelize through preaching, and so we find in his work a particular focus upon the sermon as a transformative linguistic performance which guides the congregation to a new understanding of self and world.

It is the philosophical character of Eckhart's mysticism and his engagement with the universal nature of the self which sparked a keen interest in his work in Germany during the nineteenth century, when Idealist philosophers identified in him a kindred spirit. The seeming absence of Christian doctrine in his work when viewed from a particular perspective has also recommended him to those interested in propagating the cause of mysticism without traditional dogmatic belief; and he has seemed to some an ideal interlocutor with some of the speculative systems of the East. But the chief factor that makes this fourteenth-century thinker stand out from his fellow scholastics is not the content of his message but rather the creative skill with which he expresses it. He is one of the first writers of German religious prose, and showed a great ability to present scholastic concepts in vivid and accessible language. This is evident for instance in his use of the metaphor of the "spark in the soul," which represents the human potentiality to know God and which Eckhart conveys with a typical rhetorical élan:

> There is something which is above the created being of the soul and which is untouched by any createdness, by any nothingness. Even the angels do not have this, and even their pure, deep being cannot draw near to it. It is like the divine nature; in itself it is one and has nothing in common with any creature. And it is with regard to this that many teachers go wrong. It is a strange land, a wilderness, being more nameless than with name, more unknown than known.[28]

Eckhart speaks also of "the birth of God in the soul," which represents the transformation of the self through grace, whereby the self is conformed to God's own nature:

> God is present, active and powerful in all things. But only in the soul is he fruitful, for all creatures are only the footprint of God, whereas the soul is by its

nature modelled in God's image. The image must be ennobled and completed by this birth. No creature is responsive to this action of God and to this birth but the soul alone. Truly, whatever perfection enters the soul, whether it be divine, simple light or grace or blessedness, it can only enter the soul through this birth and in no other way.[29]

The "birth" in the soul causes a particular condition of the self which Eckhart refers to as "detachment" or *abegescheidenheit*. This combines both cognitive and ethical aspects, since the "detached" self is freed from the images of material things and is rendered empty of itself and of its own self-centered desires. This unity of the cognitive and the ethical through his understanding of transcendental intellect is deeply characteristic of Eckhart's thinking, and is again something which has recommended him to an age which can be more at ease with the notion of transcendence and the immediacy of God's presence to the self than with the traditional values and expressions of Christian faith.

Despite the strongly philosophical character of his mysticism, which might be thought to have restricted its interest to the universities, Eckhart also preached extensively to congregations of religious women. It is not always clear how much his preaching may have meant to the *mulieres sanctae*, however; and his characteristic stress upon inwardness and intentionality can easily be seen to be a corrective reaction to what may have seemed an excessively external piety of works and performance among the flourishing and vibrant women's communities of the fourteenth-century Rhineland.[30] But the image of the austerely scholastic Eckhart preaching to religious women is a reminder of the extent to which medieval mysticism transgressed boundaries, and how the conceptual structure of the systems which survive in texts today were in close dialogue with the social manifestations of radical religious life which may, for most of us today, be hidden from view.

Medieval women were barred from participating in the universities on account of their gender, but it is appropriate to set the mystical writing of women apart not only from that of the scholastics but also from the writings of monastic men. There are two particular reasons for this. The first is that the medieval women lacked formation in the Latin tradition and therefore tended to write in their native vernacular tongue. This in turn was a recognition of the fact that they were often in closer contact with the vernacular culture of the day than were the men, and we find in a number of women's work important impulses from the world of secular culture. Additionally, women's spiritual writing often shows a greater degree of innovative originality than that of men, who were working more closely within set patterns of thought and expression. Secondly, medieval religious culture was deeply patriarchal to the extent that the assumed human norm was the male. The origins of this trend are complex and lie not only in the influence of a host of scriptural, philosophical, and scientific texts, but also in the structure of society itself, which gave political expression to this ideology. Thus the experience of the medieval woman was that of finding her own self-realization in a world which was structured without her consent, as it were, in which male perceptions of the feminine outweighed women's own self-understanding. Within such an environment it was inevitable that women's mystical writings were closely tied in to bids for the exception of female authority within a male world, most notably the claim to be a recipient of immediate divine communications, as visions or auditions, with a concomitant depreciation (if any were needed) of the individual writer's own intellectual and scholarly powers. Only under such terms was it possible for the female voice to be heard.

Mechthild of Magdeburg was born around the year 1212, and joined a Beguine house in Magdeburg in 1230. After some 40 years in Magdeburg, she moved to the convent at Helfta, which was a leading center of women's piety, where the distinguished Gertrude of Hackeborn was still abbess. Mechthild completed the *Flowing Light of the Godhead* there, and died around 1282.[31] Mechthild first experienced the visions that were to be such an influence upon the first half of her life at the age of 12, and it was her Dominican confessor, Heinrich of Halle, who gave her practical and moral support in the writing of the text that was based upon those visions. This combination of a visionary woman and a learned confessor is in itself characteristic of the collaboration of the sexes during this period, whereby the woman placed herself in the role of a vehicle of divine inspiration, following the model of Deborah or indeed Mary, under the guidance of a male cleric. This relationship was crucial for the protection of a woman, whose visions – as in the case of Mechthild – contained critical observations on the state of the Church.[32] The *Flowing Light of the Godhead* itself is full of images and motifs which distinguish it from the monastic literature with which it might otherwise be thought to have much in common.

As is typically the case with this kind of literature, the boundaries between the visionary and the literary are fluid, not only on account of the spiritualizing of memory, but also because the text itself is seen to be the product of divine inspiration: God declares that his "heart's blood," which shall "flow again" at the end of time, "is written in this book."[33] Indeed, Mechthild's text succeeds in being both literary and mystical at the same time. With great imagination she explores the key motif of "flowing," telling us not only that the book "flowed" from God to herself, but that God's love is an "overflow . . . which never stands still and always flows effortlessly and without ceasing in so sweet a flood so that our small vessel is filled and brims over."[34] The operations of grace and the creation itself are likewise seen in terms of divine "flowing" and "flooding."[35] But this imagery which she uses for the God–world relation is grounded in the dynamic processes that are internal to the Trinity itself. Thus she speaks of the "restless Godhead" of the Father who is an "overflowing spring" and of the Son who is "an ever returning treasure which no one can keep but only the mercy which always has flowed and ever shall flow from God and ever returns in his Son."[36] Her privileging of the language of flowing allows Mechthild to explore and deepen the trinitarian dimension of her spiritual vocation, aligning the created self and uncreated God in a dialectical relation of inflow and outflow.

In addition to this explicitly literary dimension, a further way in which women's writing can be distinguished from that of monastic men is in the personal appropriation of the imagery itself. There is much in Mechthild's *Brautmystik* or "nuptial mysticism" which derives from the Song of Songs, thus recalling the commentaries of Bernard or William of St. Thierry, but the symbolic significance of the imagery is overwhelmed by the existential character of its appropriation. Mechthild enters into an intensely personal encounter with the Bridegroom, who claims her at every level of her being: "O Lord, love me intensely, love me often and long! For the more often you love me, the purer I become. The more intensely you love me, the more beautiful I become. The longer you love me, the holier I become."[37] This new depth of feeling which appears in the writings of thirteenth-century Beguines may well represent the influence upon them of the *Minnesang*, which was the German version of the secular tradition of Courtly Love which popularized a new sensibility of erotic longing. Indeed, we find in Mechthild an echo of the so-called *alba*, detailing the early morning parting of two lovers, and she extensively deploys the imagery of fine dress and dancing.[38] The imagery of embodiment plays throughout her work, and on one occasion she specifically affirms the place of the body against its denigrators, reminding the reader that Christ himself become incarnate.[39] It is in her own flesh too that she feels the sufferings that God brings her, and which she understands to be an inevitable part of the grace she has received in the writing of her book. Suffering for Mechthild, as for many medieval women, is intrinsic to the religious life, and is the primary way in which she knows that she participates supernaturally in the life of Christ.

Julian of Norwich (ca. 1342 to after 1416) also tells us that she has prayed for the physical suffering which marks an understanding of Christ's Passion.[40] And it is the sequence of 15 visions which came to her early in the morning when she lay seriously ill, in May 1373, that are the foundation of her work.[41] This survives in two recensions. The Short Text was probably written soon after the occurrence of the visions and is generally descriptive, while the Long Text was not completed until 1393 at the earliest. In the latter she pursued a thorough and penetrating reflection upon the doctrinal content of the visions, setting out her own mature theological positions. Here too the neoplatonism of the Short Text is replaced with a more incarnational focus upon transformation through the senses. Julian differs from Mechthild to the extent that the unitive character of her visions is worked out not so much at the level of the affections, but rather through understanding, as the anchoress strives to come to terms with questions such as the meaning of the divine love which is shown in the incarnation, and the tension between the universalism implied by God's love for all and the divine judgment given in revelation. The terminology of interpretation ("I conceived," "I understood," "wonder," "marvel," "thus I took it," "I thought," "as to my understanding") sound throughout Julian's text as she strives to penetrate to the true meaning of her visions.

Julian's concerns come together in her account of the first vision from the Long Text, where she was shown, lying in the palm of her hand, "a little thing, the size of a hazelnut," which was so tiny that she thought that it might "suddenly have fallen into nothing." In this object she perceived three properties:

"the first is that God made it, the second is that God loves it, the third is that God sustains it." From this she understood that God is "the Maker, Keeper and Lover" and that she can have no happiness until there is no created thing between herself and her creator.[42] Here we see a powerful sense of God's loving immanence within the world together with a yearning for transcendence. This dialectic is expressed more abstractly in terms of the distinction Julian draws between "substance" (or "nature"), which remains in God, and "sensuality," which is our mode of existence in the world. It is only in the incarnation that this antinomy is finally resolved:

> I saw that in God our nature is complete. There are different expressions of it, of which he is the source, all created to do his will. Their own nature preserves them, while mercy and grace restore and perfect them. None of these shall perish, for the higher part of our nature was united to God at our creation, and God united himself to our nature in its lower part when he became incarnate. In Christ therefore both parts are made one. For Christ means the Holy Trinity in whom our higher part is rooted and grounded; and he, the Second Person thereof, has taken our lower part, which had already been prepared for him.[43]

With a remarkable ingenuity which is typical of the best in medieval women's religious writing, Julian makes use of the motif of divine motherhood in order to give unity to the love of God as it creates us, and redeems us through incarnation and the sacraments:

> A mother's is the most intimate, willing and dependable of all services, because it is the truest of all. None has been able to fulfil it properly but Christ, and he alone can ... We know that our own mother's bearing of us was a bearing to pain and death, but what does Jesus, our true Mother, do? ... He carries us within himself in love and is in labour until the time has fully come for him to suffer the sharpest pangs and most appalling pain possible – and in the end he dies ... The human mother will suckle her child with her own milk, but our beloved Mother, Jesus, feeds us with himself, and, with the most tender courtesy, does it by means of the Blessed Sacrament, the precious food of all true life.[44]

Julian's struggle with the problematics of particular revelation, together with her distinctively female sensibility, richly expressed for instance in the memorable passages on the motherhood of Christ, have endeared Julian – in the English-speaking world at least – to a readership concerned with the place of the body in Christian tradition and the role of the feminine. Also, her conviction that "all shall be well" has seemed to speak to many in today's society, afflicted as we are by anxieties which are as much increased as they are reduced by advances in technology.

All the texts we have surveyed here represent the highest literary quality, but it is notable that the texts by men are in general more tightly bound into the conceptual worlds of the Middle Ages, with their subtle biblical symbolism and passion for extended numerical structures and intricate distinctions.[45] It is perhaps the women, and maverick men such as the Eckhart of the sermons or the author of the *Cloud of Unknowing*, whose medieval characteristics are no less profound but perhaps less evident to the modern eye, who appeal to us most convincingly today.

Notes

1 For the history of the terms "mystic" and "mysticism," see the article on "Mystique" in the *Dictionnaire de Spiritualité*, vol. 10, Paris: Beauchesne, 1980, cols. 1889–1984. Michel de Certeau's study *The Mystic Fable* (trans. Michael B. Smith, Chicago: University of Chicago Press, 1992) remains a seminal examination of the origins of the "mystical" in early seventeenth-century France, as he traces the evolution of mystical discourse from its origins in radical religion to forms of social and cultural marginalization.

2 This is a central theme in Denys Turner, *The Darkness of God*, Cambridge: Cambridge University Press, 1995.

3 In his recent work *Mystical Theology* (Oxford: Blackwell, 1998), Mark McIntosh has appealed for the reintegration of spirituality and theology.

4 For an exhaustive history of this term, see *Dictionnaire de Spiritualité*, vol. 14 (1990), cols. 1142–73.

5 Bernard McGinn develops the typology of "vernacular," "scholastic," and "monastic" mystical theology in his "The Changing Shape of Late Medieval Mysticism," *Church History*, 65 (1996), 197–219.

6 Bernard McGinn, *The Growth of Mysticism, The Presence of God*, vol. II, London: SCM Press, 1994, 405.

7 *Journey of the Mind into God*, Prologue, 2 (ed. and trans. Ewart Cousins, *Bonaventure*, The Classics of Western Spirituality, New York: Paulist Press, 1978, 54).

8 Ibid., I, 6 (Cousins, *Bonaventure*, 62).

9 Ibid., I, 15 (Cousins, 67).

10 Ibid., II, 7.

11 Ibid., III, 1 (Cousins, 79).

12 Ibid., III, 4 (Cousins, 84).

13 Ibid., III, 5 (Cousins, 84).

14 Ibid., IV, 3–5.

15 Ibid., V, 1 (Cousins, 94).

16 Ibid., V, 6 (Cousins, 98).

17 Ibid., VI, 2 (Cousins, 103). For the principle that goodness is self-diffusive, see Pseudo-Dionysius, *On the Celestial Hierarchies*, IV, 1.

18 Ibid., VI, 5 (Cousins, 107).

19 Ibid., VI, 4.

20 Ibid., VII, 4 (Cousins, 113).

21 Ibid., VII, 1.

22 Ibid., VII, 2 (Cousins, 112).

23 Ibid., VII, 6 (Cousins, 115).

24 For an overview of Eckhart's life, see Oliver Davies, *Meister Eckhart: Mystical Theologian*, London: SPCK, 1991, 22–50.

25 Alain de Libera, *Introduction à la Mystique Rhénane*, Paris: OEIL, 1984, 25–72. Other figures in this school included Dietrich von Freiberg, Ulrich von Strasburg, and Bertold von Moosberg.

26 LW III, 4–5 (J. Quint et al., *Meister Eckhart. Die deutschen (=DW) und lateinischen (=LW) Werke. Hrg. im Auftrag der deutschen Forschungsgemeinschaft*, Stuttgart, 1936–).

27 For a discussion of the theme of the "image" in Eckhart, see Loris Sturlese, "Mystik und Philosophie in der Bildlehre Meister Eckhart," in *Festschrift für Walter Haug und Burghart Wachinger*, Tübingen: Max Niemeyer Verlag, 1992, 349–61.

28 German Sermon 28 (English trans., O. Davies, *The Rhineland Mystics: An Anthology*, London: SPCK, 1989, 31).

29 J. Quint, ed., *Meister Eckhart: Deutsche Predigten und Trakate*, Munich: Carl Hanser Verlag, 1936, 425–6 (in ibid., 36).

30 I have sought to outline Eckhart's indebtedness to and critique of female piety in my *Meister Eckhart: Mystical Theologian*, London: SPCK, 1991, 51–84.

31 Mechthild's text has a complex history of transmission in both Latin and Alemannic translation. Its history can be found in Hans Neumann, "Beiträge zur Textgeschichte des 'Fliessenden Lichts der Gottheit' und zur Lebensgeschichte Mechthilds von Magdeburg," *Nachrichten der Akademie der Wissenschaften in Göttingen*, Göttingen, 1954, 27–80.

32 Caroline Walker Bynum discusses Mechthild's troubles against the background of the Helfta writers as a whole in her *Jesus as Mother*, California: University of California Press, 1982, 237–42.

33 Book V, ch. 28.

34 Book VII, ch. 55.

35 Book V, ch. 11; Book VI, ch. 13; Book V, ch. 22.

36 Book V, ch. 26.

37 Book I, ch. 23.

38 Book I, ch. 44.

39 Book VI, ch. 31.

40 *Revelations of Divine Love*, ch. 2.

41 Ch. 3.

42 Ch. 5 (English trans., Clifton Wolters, *Julian of Norwich: Revelations of Divine Love*, Harmondsworth: Penguin Books, 1966, 68; slightly emended).

43 Ch. 57 (Wolters, 163).

44 Ch. 60 (Wolters, 169–70, slightly emended).

45 Steven T. Katz's thesis of the interpenetration of language and experience in mystical discourse remains an important contribution to the "textuality" of mysticism ("Mystical Speech and Mystical Meaning," in Steven T. Katz, ed., *Mysticism and Language*, Oxford and New York: Oxford University Press, 1992, 3–41). Michael A. Sells draws out the particular parameters of mystical language in his *Mystical Languages of Unsaying*, Chicago: University of Chicago Press, 1994.

Academic Controversies

Takashi Shogimen

The condemnation of March 7, 1277 has been much studied in modern historical scholarship on medieval universities and medieval philosophy and theology. Bishop Stephen Tempier's condemnation of 219 philosophical and theological propositions has been described as a "watershed" in medieval intellectual history. The consensus among scholars is that the condemnation was essentially a reaction to the surging Aristotelian movement in the Faculty of Arts, and possibly also in the Faculty of Theology, which its opponents claimed was in conflict with the Christian faith. The doctrinal significance of the condemnation, however, remains a contested issue. Pierre Duhem, for example, viewed Tempier's action as severing Christian theology from Aristotelian natural philosophy; he assessed the condemnation as a momentous event in the birth of modern science.[1] Pierre Mandonnet and Etienne Gilson, on the other hand, interpreted Tempier's condemnation in the context of the emerging rationalism in the University of Paris. The condemnation was a reaction against the assumption that the truth not filtered through the Christian orthodoxy could be discovered by means of philosophical enquiry.[2] *What* doctrines were condemned is highly debatable; however, *whose* teachings were condemned is also unclear. The condemnation resulted in a sharp nadir in the fortunes of the disciples of Aristotle and Averroes, such as Siger of Brabant and Boethius of Dacia, and the corresponding ascendancy of the theologians of the Augustinian tradition, such as John Duns Scotus and Henry of Ghent. Yet the condemnation did not identify specific scholars.[3]

What made the 1277 condemnation the epoch-making event for the intellectual world in the late thirteenth century, however, was the fact that it was a bishop who took the initiative in the condemnation. The Bishop of Paris, who had jurisdiction over the University of Paris, conducted a doctrinal enquiry into its theologians. Doctrinal censures took place typically in the university context: the chancellor or the regent masters of theology were in charge of censures as a disciplinary measure. But, in the condemnation of 1277, Tempier was involved and led the procedure from the beginning.[4] The condemnation of 1277 therefore concerned the parameters of ecclesiastical authority, rather than disciplinary action. Its historical significance lies in the fact that it was uniquely a serious blow to academic freedom, which arguably drew the curtain on the "Enlightenment" era in the history of medieval theology.[5]

Yet, this is perhaps only one side of the story. Despite the condemnation, or perhaps because of it, theologians recognized the pressing need for enquiring into the question of academic freedom in the Church. The condemnation provoked Godfrey of Fontaines to become a militant defender of the freedom of theological investigation. Godfrey considered that the condemnation became a serious impediment to the academic advances of students. Many of the propositions condemned by Tempier concerned issues that were not necessarily settled; therefore, the condemnation deprived students of the chance to study them. Worse still, the condemnation put some of the doctrines of Thomas Aquinas "out of bounds" for the students of theology.[6] Godfrey maintained that erroneous condemnations must be opposed by doctors and revoked by prelates because they impeded students in their search for knowledge and because they gave rise to scandal.[7]

Godfrey assigned experts in theology with considerable powers to correct ecclesiastical decisions because he thought that theologians were fully entitled to discuss everything pertaining to the divine and natural laws. There was virtually no intellectual boundary that theologians could not transgress. Hence, the ecclesiastical laws and government, for example, should not be left in the hands of canonists; theologians should have the final word on them.[8] To be sure, Godfrey was certainly not the first theologian to claim the superiority of theologians over canonists in the ecclesiastical hierarchy. Thomas Aquinas, Bonaventure, and Roger Bacon all expressed displeasure over the intervention of canonists in doctrinal and ecclesiological matters.[9] Godfrey, however, was unique in that he stressed the magisterial authority of theologians in doctrinal and ecclesiastical questions. He rejected the right of the prelates to define heresy, and called for action against the errors contained in the condemnation of 1277. Godfrey insisted that it was not merely a right, but a duty, of theologians to protest against ecclesiastical errors and to defend the truth. To remain silent when doctrinal matters are at stake were to risk the charge of sycophancy.[10]

Godfrey's elevation of the authority of theologians above that of ecclesiastics was rooted in his rationalism: it was the function of reason to enquire into doubtful matters, and after enquiry, to make judgments and determinations. Hence, when papal decisions appeared to be erroneous, the wise, represented typically by theologians, could not only discuss the decisions but also reach conclusions about them.[11] Godfrey's notion of the authority of theologians was cognitive, not institutional. He was not arguing for the transfer of magisterial authority from ecclesiastics to theologians. Rather, he indicated that theologians, who were professionally trained experts on the Christian faith, should dedicate themselves actively to the assertion of truths as well as rejection of errors.[12] Godfrey's view was not unique but was shared by such theologians as Henry of Ghent and John of Paris. John of Paris wrote that, if the pope acted contrary to the divine law, the "men of learning" ought to inform the Christian community concerning the error, in order that the pope might be brought before its tribunal.[13]

Godfrey's protest against the condemnation of 1277 anticipated the fundamental themes of academic controversies in the later Middle Ages. The defense of academic freedom in opposition to ecclesiastical oppression and the assertion of the doctrinal authority of theologians were to become the undercurrent in the various theological disputes in the post-1277 era. From the late thirteenth century onwards, theologians strengthened their influence on doctrinal and ecclesiastical issues, which inevitably generated clashes between ecclesiastics and doctors. Cardinal Benedict Gaetani, the future Pope Boniface VIII, was disturbed at the rapid ascendance of doctors of the universities. He stated to Parisian theologians in 1290: "you sit in your chairs and think that Christ is ruled by your reasonings . . . They [the theologians] have filled the whole world with their pestiferous teachings."[14] Of course, the distinction between ecclesiastics and doctors was not always well defined: there were overlaps between the two, as some theologians were appointed to higher ecclesiastical offices. Nonetheless, from the times of Godfrey's protest onwards, there was a clear tendency for theologians increasingly to emphasize their own doctrinal authority.

The expanding "magisterial" authority of theologians not only clashed with ecclesiastical authority, but it also became the sword of Damocles for theologians themselves. Theologians came under the threat of doctrinal censure by other theologians. Peter John Olivi, a leader of the Spirituals in the Franciscan Order, was one such theologian who was subjected to doctrinal censure by Parisian theologians. Olivi's early career was distinguished: Pope Nicholas III consulted him in the preparation of his decree *Exiit qui seminat*, which officially regulated the Franciscan way of life. Olivi's *Questions on Evangelical Perfection*, however, threw him into a very stormy controversy over mendicant poverty. At the heart of dispute was Olivi's idea of *usus pauper*: rigorous practice of poverty by restricting use of goods. Olivi maintained that the poverty envisaged by the Franciscan vow involved not merely lack of the ownership of property but also *usus pauper*.[15] This claim was not unprecedented: Hugh of Digne, Bonaventure, and Nicholas III maintained this. Olivi was, however, original in that he rehabilitated this aspect of the Franciscan doctrine of poverty that has long been overlooked.[16] The question of whether *usus pauper* was a part of the vow of the Franciscan way of life invited controversy among Olivi's followers and his adversaries, which resulted in the censure of Olivi's views conducted by the forum of Bonagratia of San Giovanni, the Minister General of the Friars Minor, and his advisers. In 1283, Bonagratia of San Giovanni commissioned four masters and three bachelors of theology at the University of Paris to examine Olivi's works, chiefly his lectures as a bachelor of theology.

As an academic controversy developed to doctrinal censure, the problem of academic freedom from authoritative oppression emerged. The committee produced a list of censured statements and a list of 22 assertions that Olivi was ordered to subscribe as orthodox. To the latter document, known as the *Letter of the Seven Seals*, Olivi assented with reservation. He maintained that the committee's excerpts of his writings were misleading; however, the central issue for him was whether the committee had the right to do what it did.[17] Olivi questioned whether the committee possessed such doctrinal authority as it claimed by censuring his theological writings. His position was clear: he approved in a traditional manner the authorities of the saints, masters, and the pope, whilst he explicitly rejected the committee's right to impose obedience on himself unless it demonstrated to him clearly that its opinion "is that of the Catholic faith and Holy Scripture." He reduced ecclesiastical obedience to a matter of conscience.[18] He squarely refused to obey anyone against orthodox faith, and in matters that do not concern the catholic faith, he was prepared to obey, provided that "purity of conscience" was preserved.[19] Olivi envisaged a situation in which he was unable to obey both catholic truth and ecclesiastical authority, and opted for the former.

The consequence of Olivi's idea of dissent was far-reaching. While he emphasized the supreme authority of the Roman Church, he was preoccupied with the idea that individual popes might attempt to lead the church away from the catholic faith. Above all, he feared that the papal decrees that approved the orthodoxy of the Franciscan way of life would be revoked. Olivi's celebrated doctrine of papal infallibility was built upon this fear. It was essential for him that the decrees of true, orthodox popes, that is those who had authorized the Franciscan doctrine of poverty, should be "not only authoritative for the present, but immutable, irreformable for all time to come."[20] Consequently, Olivi's teaching of papal infallibility was double-edged: it showed that the generally accepted doctrine of indefectibility of the church implied the existence of an infallible pope, whilst it also implied that any pope who departed from the doctrinal decisions of a predecessor would automatically fall into heresy, and *ipso facto* cease to be pope.[21]

Another noteworthy censure is the case of John of Pouilli. John of Pouilli, a student of Godfrey of Fontaines at Paris, was a regent master in theology from 1307 onwards. He was involved in polemics through the dispute over the mendicant privileges between mendicants and secular masters, and defended the latter's case. The background of this antimendicant campaign was the mendicants' attempt to overturn Boniface VIII's decree *Super cathedram* on the occasion of his death. *Super cathedram* required parishioners who had confessed to friars to repeat their confessions to their parish priests. Boniface's Dominican successor, Benedict XI, promulgated *Inter cunctas*, in which he restored the mendicants' privileges, and this, once again, provoked such seculars' attacks on mendicants as John of Pouilli's. In his quodlibetal disputations in 1312 and 1314, John was particularly forceful in questioning the validity of the license to hear confessions granted by the pope. Assuming that Benedict XI's *Inter cunctas* was void, John argued that *Super cathedram*'s stipulations were once again valid; therefore, those who confessed to friars must repeat their confessions to a parish priest.[22]

Not surprisingly, John's antimendicant campaign was met with an immediate counterattack by mendicants. In his quodlibetal questions in Advent, 1314, the Dominican Pierre de la Palud offered an extensive response to the question of whether a bishop can grant permission to hear confessions to someone who has not been licensed by a parish priest. Seculars argued typically that the apostles and disciples in the early church were succeeded by the bishops and parish priests, and thereby did not allow mendicants to occupy any place in the ecclesiastical system stemming from the original church.[23] Pierre, in response, took a far more conciliatory view of the ecclesiastical order, stating that deacons, secular canons, monks, hermits, university doctors had an essential role in the church. He in turn questioned the competence of parish priests in performing sacraments for the salvation of those who confess.[24] Indeed, parish priests were often ignorant of theology, and in some cases their literacy was doubtful. Pierre asserted the cognitive authority of theologically trained friars in achieving sacramental efficacy, thereby aligning himself with other contemporary theologians who viewed themselves as the ultimate doctrinal authority.

Like Olivi's case, the controversy over John's antimendicant campaign resulted in censure against him. Pierre de la Palud was one of those who took the initiative in investigating his views: he produced a theological denunciation of John's 13 articles for Pope John XXII. Likewise, unidentified Franciscans and perhaps a few Dominicans drew up a charge against John, containing a list of his 13 articles, and this document formed the basis for his citation in 1318. In 1321, the three theses made by John of Pouilli in reply to his charges were condemned. His fate was not so propitious as Olivi's: John surrendered and recanted the errors publicly.

The turn of the thirteenth and fourteenth centuries witnessed a new development in the Poverty Controversy (indeed, the controversies triggered by the theological views of Olivi and John de Pouilli constituted important parts of the story). The poverty dispute was no longer a debate over the interpretation of evangelical poverty. It was increasingly focused on the privileges of mendicants and seculars and, concomitant with this, a new literary genre – the treatise on ecclesiastical power – emerged. A massive number of treatises on ecclesiastical – above all papal – power were written at the turn of the thirteenth and fourteenth centuries (for instance, Giles of Rome's *De ecclesiastica potestate*, John of Paris's *De regia potestate et papali*, and Augustinus Triumphus's *Summa de ecclesiastica potestate*, to name a few), and this was not coincidental. The problem of mendicant privileges was ultimately boiled down to the question of papal authority. When John of Pouilli argued that *Inter cunctas* was void, for example, he assumed that the decision by the Council of Vienne entailed greater authority than that of the pope. Pierre de la Palud, by contrast, maintained that the conciliar decrees could only take effect by papal authorization: the pope might or might not endorse conciliar decisions.[25] The central issue here was the locus of papal authority in the church, and this led theologians into an exegetical debate on the nature of the Petrine Commission: whether Christ had given jurisdictional power to the pope alone or to all other priests as well. If the pope is *primus inter pares*, that is, the pope and the other bishops are equal in that they both receive power directly from God, then the pope's primacy remains on the level of practice. The pope enjoys no more than the constitutional status of the elected monarch within the church. Indeed, secular masters such as Godfrey of Fontaines and John of Pouilli upheld this position. To do so, they relied on the authority of St. Jerome; according to his exegetical view, the 12 apostles and 72 disciples were represented by bishops and parish priests. Christ conferred sacerdotal powers to all of them directly. The key biblical text for this position were Matthew 18:18 and John 20:21–3, where Christ's conferment of powers was arguably addressed to several individuals.[26] Mendicant theologians, however, maintained a contrasting view: the pope received all the power directly from God, from whom the bishops derived their authority. The implication of this is that papal authority is the sole, God-given power in the Church, and the pope is an absolute monarch. The key biblical texts for this were Matthew 16:18–19, Luke 22:32, and John 21:17, where Christ's commission of powers was seemingly addressed to Peter alone. This view originated in the papal, not theological, exegetical tradition, readily traceable to Popes Damasus and Leo I.[27] It was, however, not until the turn of the thirteenth and fourteenth centuries that this papal exegesis was adopted by theologians. The mid-thirteenth-century giants in scholastic theology such as Thomas Aquinas and Bonaventure offered no primatial reading in their biblical commentaries, while, a generation later, a number of leading theologians such as Giles of Rome, Augustinus Triumphus, Hervaeus Natalis, Pierre de la Palud, and Guido Terreni introduced papal readings into their interpretation of these key verses. Ironically, the exegetical foundations of papal absolutism were laid by theologians, when papal authority showed signs of decline as symbolized by the ignominious arrest and death of Boniface VIII.

The pontificate of John XXII continued to witness a fierce controversy over the Franciscan doctrine of poverty, which formed the context against which theologians of differing political leanings claimed their influence on ecclesiastical matters. The year 1316 was marked by the ascension of Jacques Duèse to the Papal See as John XXII, as well as the appointment of Michael of Cesena as the Minister General of the Franciscan Order. Michael was confronted by the daunting task of resolving the longstanding conflict between the Conventuals and Spirituals within his Order. The central issue was the idea of *usus pauper*. The Conventuals maintained that the essence of evangelical poverty was the renunciation of all positive rights to any property whatsoever not only individually but also communally. The Spirituals, inspired by Peter Olivi, argued that not only the abandonment of rights but also the practice of restricted use were indispensable to evangelical poverty. Pope John XXII was openly hostile to the Spirituals: the pope attacked them in the bull *Quorundam exigit* (Oct. 1317), followed by the bull *Sancta Romana* (Dec. 1317). The Spirituals fell into disarray, and Michael of Cesena called for obedience to the pope, managing to settle the disorder at the general chapter at Marseille in 1319.[28] As Malcolm Lambert noted, *Quorundam exigit* was purely administrative, aimed at condemning the Spirituals' disobedience, whilst *Sancta Romana* entailed doctrinal implications.[29] The pope was aware of the Spirituals' criticism that the Roman Church was the *ecclesia carnalis* whereas they represented the *ecclesia spiritualis*. Hence he shifted his attention from mere administrative issues to the doctrine of the Spirituals, above all their source of inspiration: Peter Olivi.

An investigation into intricate theological discourses required John XXII, a lawyer by training, to consult specialists. Marsilius of Padua complained that the

Pope regarded theologians as "useless" and favored "shyster lawyers."[30] Contrary to Marsilius' allegation, however, the Pope showed favor to some theologians, whom he commissioned to act as theological consultants. John XXII frequently called on Jacques Fournier (the future Pope Benedict XII), Pierre Roger (the future Clement VI), the Dominican Pierre de la Palud, and Durand de St. Pourçain.[31] Moreover, Guido Terreni, the General of the Carmelite Order, participated in the examination of Olivi's commentary on the Apocalypse and, along with Pierre de la Palud, served the Pope by producing a report on the writings of an anonymous Catalan Beguin.[32]

The renewed investigation into the doctrine of Olivi and his followers by those "curial" theologians resulted in the Pope's doctrinal definition that it was heretical to assert that Christ and the apostles did not own anything individually or communally. In his bull *Quia nonnunquam* (March 1321), John XXII rejected and revoked Pope Nicholas III's *Exiit qui seminat*, which officially endorsed the orthodoxy of the Franciscan doctrine of poverty. At the general chapter of Perugia in 1322, the Franciscans reaffirmed the orthodoxy of their doctrine of poverty in two encyclicals. In them, the leading Franciscan theologians asserted the timeless immutability and irreformability of the official decision of the Roman Church, and therefore, they maintained that *Exiit qui seminat* stood irrevocably.[33]

Michael of Cesena was determined to combat the heretical pope and sought the protection of Ludwig of Bavaria. In 1328, Michael escaped from Avignon, along with other Franciscan colleagues, including the canonist Bonagratia of Bergamo and the Oxford philosopher and theologian William of Ockham. Ockham had already been in Avignon since 1324, and was commissioned by Michael of Cesena to examine the papal bulls that rejected the orthodoxy of Franciscan poverty. Michael's appeals against John XXII were largely anchored in the idea of the irreformability of the decrees enacted by Nicholas III.[34] Since the issue of the two Perugia encyclicals, the Franciscan objections to *Quia nonnunquam* centered upon its legal validity. Michael's legalistic arguments, which are similar to that of his fellow canonist Bonagratia of Bergamo, reflected the new situation. The opponent who confronted Michael was no longer the secular masters as in the previous century but the pope. Hence, Michael's strategy was to defend the legal standing of the Franciscan doctrine by appealing to another authority: Pope Nicholas III. Olivi's nightmare was Michael's reality.

Among the Franciscan pamphleteers in Munich, William of Ockham's response to the Poverty Controversy was novel. He endeavored to restore the theological link between poverty and Christian perfection, which was first formulated by Bonaventure. Bonaventure maintained that Christ's poverty was grounded in charity, the essential virtue of Christian perfection.[35] John XXII's attack on Franciscan poverty was directed towards this Bonaventuran link between poverty and Christian perfection: he severed the link by declaring that charity alone, not poverty, represented perfection.[36] Ockham's Franciscan colleagues in Munich never attempted to restore the Bonaventuran nexus of poverty and perfection. By contrast, Ockham demonstrated in the light of numerous biblical verses that Christ was perfectly poor both in his intentions and in practice. By showing that Christ's poverty was perfect in a sense other than his charity was, Ockham restored the theological link between poverty and perfection.[37]

Ockham's concern with the theological foundation, rather than the legal standing, of Franciscan poverty was grounded in his perception that the Pope was ignorant of theological issues. He discerned the Pope's theological ignorance in his handling of one of the hotly debated issues: whether it was possible for use of a consumable to be separated from ownership. Pope John XXII argued that it was impossible because it was repugnant to law and contrary to reason to assert that use by right or use in fact could be separated from ownership of things consumed by use. To this claim Ockham replied that the pope was ignorant of the theological usage of the term and confused it with its legal usage.[38] Obviously, he considered that the debate over Franciscan poverty should take place on a theological rather than a legal plane. Involvement in the Poverty Controversy seems to have convinced Ockham that contemporary canonists – including Pope John XXII – had intervened unjustifiably in doctrinal matters. Indeed, Ockham deplored the fact that since Innocent III most of the popes had been lawyers rather than theologians and, like Godfrey of Fontaines, criticized canon law studies at several occasions. Ockham, therefore, began his gigantic Part I of the *Dialogus* by declaring the superiority of theology over canon law, prior to an extensive theological discourse on the ideas of heresy and heretics.[39]

In the Poverty Controversy, Ockham found himself in a situation where he was unable to submit himself to orthodox faith and the pope simultaneously; he opted for the former. Godfrey's opponent was a bishop; Olivi's was the Minister General of his own Order and his advisers; Ockham's opponent was the occupier of the Apostolic See. Ockham not only examined what institution in the Church was infallible, as Olivi did, but also enquired into the criterion which enabled a Christian to discern what assertions ought to be believed. His originality, however, is most evident in his elaboration of the possible ways for a Christian to censure a heretical pope. Ockham appealed to the traditional scholastic argument that the higher the office an individual occupied in the ecclesiastical order the more knowledge of orthodox faith he is expected to have, thereby criticizing the pope's erroneous doctrinal definitions due to his ignorance or temerity.[40] Also he reworked the ecclesiological implications of the theological notion of fraternal correction, seeking a justification for an inferior's correction of papal errors.[41] On a practical level, he preferred doctrinal disputes to be settled by means of the free discussion of masters rather than a papal authoritative decision. By "masters" and "experts," however, he did not refer to any corporate body but simply to any informed, individual Christian. This "cognitive" (as opposed to "institutional") notion of "experts"[42] epitomizes his radical rejection of any institutional warrant of the Christian faith; in his later polemical works, he clearly denied doctrinal infallibility to any ecclesiastical institution. Yet he believed that the universal church was infallible; he insisted that the true faith had remained, and would remain, in the Church at all times, at least in one individual, a woman, or even an infant.

Ockham's "cognitive" notion of "experts" might be idiosyncratic, and it was certainly not widely accepted. Rather, the Faculty of Theology in the University of Paris, for instance, was increasingly recognized as a corporate body of experts that should have the final word on doctrinal matters. When Meister Eckhart was investigated by Henry of Virneburg, the Archbishop of Cologne, from 1326 onwards, he pointed out the flaws in the method of extracting his views,[43] insisted on his orthodoxy, and appealed to the judgment of the pope or the University of Paris.[44] This illustrates the fact that, among some theologians, the magisterial power of the University of Paris was considered almost on a par with that of the pope. This is also precisely the point that Pierre d'Ailly made clear in his dispute with John of Monzón, OP, in the last quarter of the fourteenth century. In 1387, John of Monzón was accused by the Faculty of Theology in the University of Paris of having taught a false doctrine regarding the Immaculate Conception. He refused to withdraw the error, and appealed to the papal court. Pierre d'Ailly represented the University at the papal court. Monzón argued that the Faculty of Theology and the Bishop of Paris did not have the authority to censure doctrinal errors. D'Ailly, in reply, distinguished judicial authority from doctrinal authority: the former belonged to the pope and, by delegation, to the bishops, whereas the latter pertained to the theologians. However, d'Ailly went further by declaring that the Faculty of Theology also possessed judicial authority to condemn erroneous doctrines. The Faculty of Theology not only had authority to condemn errors *doctrinally* but was also able to condemn *judicially* erroneous views of its members. The Faculty possessed such coercive power over masters and bachelors because of the papal privileges which the university and each of its faculties had been granted as a corporation.[45] The university or the faculty, as a corporation, could demand sworn obedience from its members to the statutes, and compel them to correct their errors.

The acceptance of the superiority of theologians, however, was not simply the doing of theologians themselves. The popes recognized the authority of theological experts, as Pope John XXII frequently consulted select theologians. Ironically, however, the Pope who promoted consultations with theological experts became himself a victim of their doctrinal deliberation. John XXII's notorious sermons on the Beatific Vision and the subsequent controversy that surrounded them provided an opportunity for Parisian theologians to act as supreme judges on doctrinal matters. In 1331, the pope preached that the souls of the righteous did not enjoy the contemplation of the divine essence before the resurrection of the body and the Last Judgment. In later sermons, he went further in stating that before the resurrection of the body, souls enjoyed neither eternal life nor beatitude, and that demons and the souls of the damned were not in hell until the Last Judgment. These opinions were explicitly condemned by the Faculty of Theology in the University of Paris between 1241 and 1244. Many theologians were clearly opposed to the doctrine expounded in the pope's sermons; nonetheless, they did not instigate any serious attempt to correct the pope, until Thomas Waleys, an English Dominican theologian, preached in Avignon that the pope's sermons were manifestly erroneous. Waleys attacked the papal errors as scandalizing the Church, and labeled theologians who favored the papal view as "flatterers." Waleys was soon summoned, examined, and imprisoned.[46] The persecution of Waleys, however, led to another doctrinal censure. Pope John XXII commissioned Durand de St. Pourçain, one of his favored theologians, to examine Waleys' views. Contrary, no doubt, to what the pope might have expected, Durand concluded that it was the pope's view that should be rejected. From 1331 to 1334, the controversy over the Beatific Vision and the investigation into the views of Thomas Waleys and Durand de St. Pourçain continued. The team of theologians commissioned to examine them failed to reach any conclusive decision. From late 1333 onwards, theologians from the University of Paris took up the investigation in earnest. In an assembly of French prelates and theologians, convoked by the king of France, 29 Parisian theologians judged against the pope. The king wrote to the pope: "our doctors know what ought to be believed in matters of faith better than the jurists and other clerks who inhabit your court and who know little or nothing of theology."[47] Thus the doctrinal authority of theologians was recognized as superior to that of canonists by the secular ruler. John XXII excused himself by maintaining that he did not make any doctrinal assertions to laymen but simply stated his own opinions to prelates and theologians. It was universally acknowledged among theologians and churchmen that as far as Christian doctrine was concerned, any erroneous assertion was subject to coercive censure, whereas merely stating an opinion was subject to correction. However, the pope's apologetic statement demonstrated that he recognized the doctrinal authority of theologians over doctrinal issues. Confronted by the decisions of the theologians the pope not only accepted a humiliating defeat in the controversy, but also indirectly allowed theologians to condemn the doctrinal views of the occupant of the Apostolic See.[48]

As papal authority waned, contemporary critics of the papacy began to undermine the theological foundations of papal primacy. Marsilius of Padua's view was perhaps the most radical: he explicitly rejected papal primacy. His argument rested ultimately on the authority of St. Jerome. Marsilius argued that in the early church, the presbyters – elder persons – elected their supervisors who adopted the title of bishop (*episcopus*). Such human election, however, did not confer any sacerdotal power on the elected but what he called "household power" to control other ecclesiastics without coercive power. Every priest received the same authority directly from Christ, and so priests and bishops were equal in terms of sacramental and penitential power.[49] Marsilius appealed to St. Jerome in stating that the 12 apostles and 72 disciples were represented by bishops and parish priests respectively: an argument the secular masters had favored in the previous century. However, Marsilius' use of St. Jerome was perhaps more radical than the secular masters in that the latter acknowledged the priests' and bishops' receipt of jurisdictional power from Christ, while the former rejected any coercive element in ecclesiastical authority. The Marsilian view was condemned by John XXII as heretical.

Ockham's discourse on papal primacy is more nuanced. He did not discuss papal primacy as such, but narrowed the problem down to a specifically historical question of whether Christ actually commissioned Peter with special power. Ockham's argument, aimed at undermining the position of Marsilius, was essentially a logical exegesis of primatial texts such as Matthew 16:19 and John 21:17, to demonstrate the historical fact of the Petrine commission.[50] However, for Ockham, the historical necessity of the *Petrine* commission did not necessarily suggest the necessity of *papal* primacy. Ostensibly Ockham defended papal primacy, maintaining that it resulted from the historical succession by election; his use of the Aristotelian discourse was intended to demonstrate of the expediency of papal monarchy.[51] However, he never attempted to show the necessity of papal primacy or monarchy. He envisaged a situation where there would be two or more popes when necessary, and this was not simply a hypothetical possibility for him, but a realistic course of action whenever it was expedient.[52] In essence, this amounts to a radical criticism of the "papalist" discourse on papal primacy.

The undermining of the papal monarchy, however, did not remain merely on a theoretical level. In April 1378, Bartholomew Prignano was elected pope and adopted the name Urban VI. The election of Prignano was the outcome of compromise; the conclave finally opted for a candidate who was not a cardinal and belonged to no curial factions. The compromise candidate soon turned out to be the most undesirable one. Urban VI was a man of theory rather than practice: his belief in papal absolutism would not allow cardinals to take part in papal government, and therefore the relationship between the pope and cardinals deteriorated rapidly. In September 1378, a group of mainly French cardinals, under the protection of the Count of Fundi, challenged the election of Urban VI by electing one of themselves, Cardinal Robert of Geneva, to be the new pope, Clement VII. They justified their action by maintaining that the April election had taken place under the duress of invasion of the conclave by mobs. Urban VI insisted on remaining pope in Rome, while Clement VII established his own papacy in Avignon. Thus the Great Schism had begun.

It may appear inappropriate to discuss the Great Schism in the chapter on "academic" controversies; it was of course not an academic controversy in the strict sense of the term, but rather a constitutional crisis in the Church. At the heart of the problem was the legal validity of the action of the renegade cardinals: they maintained that their earlier election of Urban VI had been illegal, implying that the Apostolic See was in fact vacant, and therefore Clement VII was the true pope. Clearly the problem was primarily one of law, and indeed a number of canonists such as Baldus de Ubaldis and Franciscus Zabarella contributed actively to resolve this constitutional crisis.[53] Nonetheless, theologians too were deeply involved in their corporate bodies; by 1383, all the universities in Europe had expressed an allegiance to one or other of the popes. In 1379 the University of Paris declared its support for Clement VII, whereas the University of Toulouse became a bastion for the supporters of the Roman pope.[54]

The principal reason why the Great Schism requires our attention, however, is that the claim for the doctrinal authority of theologians reached its culmination during the crisis. At this time, university academics, above all theologians, claimed and exercised power in Church politics; arguably, the magisterial authority of theologians and their freedom of discussion from ecclesiastical control had never been so emphasized. The debates over ecclesiastical government were no longer the monopoly of ecclesiastics, but were subjected to the influence of academic theologians.

From the early 1380s onwards the University of Paris expressed interest in exploring possible solutions to the grievous division in the Church. Leading theologians such as Conrad of Gelnhausen, Henry of Langenstein, and Pierre d'Ailly produced pamphlets to this end. Among these theologians, Jean Gerson was emphatic in declaring the leading role of the University of Paris in this crisis; he glorified his university, and above all its Theology Faculty. Gerson served the University of Paris as Chancellor from 1395 to his death in 1429. He regarded the University as the source of all knowledge and the intellectual capital of the world. He questioned the theological capacity of the curial theologians due to their partiality to the pope they adhered to, and demanded intellectual excellence and moral quality in theologians in his university.[55] In Gerson's mind, the University of Paris was the guardian of the Christian faith.[56] Hence, he assigned to the Faculty of Theology in Paris the role in determining ecclesiastical government. He considered that the pope and theologians were the successors of Peter and Paul respectively; just as Paul rebuked Peter at Antioch in Galatians 2:11–14, so theologians possessed the right and duty to correct the pope, when necessary, concerning doctrinal matters.[57]

Similarly, Gerson's elevation of the role of theologians determined his view on the relationship between theologians and bishops. Gerson never dismissed the significance of the ecclesiastical order, and noted that the role of bishops and theologians was complementary, not mutually exclusive. Like Pierre d'Ailly, he drew on the distinction between judicial and doctrinal decisions. The bishop gives authoritative enforcement to teachings expounded by theologians. The converse is that the bishop cannot make any doctrinal decisions without consulting theologians.[58]

Gerson acknowledged that the University of Paris consisted not only of theologians but also of lawyers and arts masters. Their functions differed according to the law they studied; the Faculties of Arts and Law in Paris studied natural and positive laws respectively, while the Faculty of Theology enquired into divine law, the highest of all the laws. Gerson attributed to the theology faculty the task of clarifying and defining divine law, thereby differentiating it from positive ecclesiastical law.[59] The background of this was the increasing confusion between divine, canon, and civil laws. Ever since the beginning of the fourteenth century, there was a trend towards the fusion of theology and canon law. Pierre de la Palud's legalistic commentary on Peter Lombard's *Sentences* and the English Carmelite John Baconthorpe's "canon-law-type" exegesis of Scripture represent such a phenomenon.[60] Contemporary dissenters such as Dante, Marsilius, and Ockham were critical of this trend, and their view was shared by Gerson; he maintained that canon law studies should be subordinate to theology. The schism, for Gerson, was a consequence of the stagnated interpretation of ecclesiastical laws, and its resolution required recourse to divine law. Therefore, Gerson argued that canon law as well as divine law fell within the remit of the theologians. Having said this, Gerson did not support the limitless intervention of theologians into canon law studies. He considered that canonists were intellectually ill equipped to master theology, whereas theologians should be sufficiently trained to grasp canon law; therefore, for Gerson, a theologian should also be a canon lawyer (the reverse is also desirable but not plausible).[61]

Gerson's claim, however, was not consistent with the reality of Paris as the intellectual center in Europe. The University of Paris was largely in opposition to Pope Benedict XIII, and he attempted to form his influence there. Gerson's appointment to the post of chancellor thus resulted from the promotion of Pierre d'Ailly, who was chancellor of the University of Paris, to the bishopric of Le Puy in 1395. D'Ailly and Gerson were both supporters of the Avignonese pope; Gerson endeavored to persuade the University to follow the decision of the theology faculty and to support Benedict XIII.[62] It is paradoxical that Gerson's glorification of the University of Paris was concomitant with the undermining of its superior status in Europe. The Schism brought about the exportation of leading Parisian theologians who embraced different political leanings to that of the university. Henry of Langenstein, for example, moved to the University of Vienna, and Marsilius of Inghen to Heidelberg. Benedict XIII also conspired to undermine the status of the University of Paris by creating a new theology faculty in Salamanca. The concentration of authority in the University of Paris gradually diminished, and the universities in Europe were increasingly politicized and fragmented.[63]

Theologians' simultaneous pursuit of intellectual freedom and doctrinal authority in the church was the equivalent of steering a course between Scylla and Charybdis. The theologians who fought for academic freedom and the "cognitive" authority of doctors, such as Godfrey of Fontaines, Peter Olivi, and William of Ockham, were all dissenters from ecclesiastical authority. It is ironic that, once the theologians institutionalized their own role within the church from the late fourteenth century onwards, they emerged, instead of popes and bishops, as an oppressive force on new dissenters among their fellow theologians. One such case is the censure against John Hus.

Before he was tried in Constance, Hus, rector of the University of Prague, was in dispute with Zbynek, Archbishop of Prague. He was then a renowned leader of the reform party inspired by John Wyclif's theological teachings. Hus's election into the rectorship of the University of Prague created a tension between the Czech and German masters, the latter being predominant. The focal point of the dispute was the question of papal obedience. The University's decision to support the 13 Cardinals in abandoning both Gregory XII and Benedict XIII could not win the support of the Germans, who remained loyal to Gregory, resulting in the departure of the Germans to form the University of Leipzig. The Council of Pisa failed to depose the two popes and succeeded only in adding the third pope, Alexander V. The University of Prague expressed its support for the new pope, while Archbishop Zbynek and his entourage remained faithful to Gregory. Zbynek charged Hus with Wyclifite heresies and excommunicated him.[64]

Zbynek's death terminated the dispute; however, Pope John XXIII's call for a crusade against King Ladislas of Naples fueled another controversy in the

University of Prague. The theologian Stephen Palec, along with the Faculty of Theology, defended the papal right of issuing the Bull against the king, whereas Hus rejected that the popes had the "right" to wage war. The new dispute, which triggered public protest in support of Hus, led King Wenceslas to suppress Hus and his followers. Although Hus was manifestly influenced by Wyclif, he was not merely the latter's mouthpiece. Among Wyclif's disputed 45 articles, Hus rendered his support, with reservation, to no more than five articles. Nonetheless, the reason that Hus was charged with heresy and eventually burned to death was precisely because of his alleged subscription to Wyclif's theological doctrines.[65]

One of the tasks of the Council of Constance (1414–18) was the extermination of heresy, and moral reform within and throughout the church. John Wyclif was officially condemned and his remains were exhumed and burned. Hus was, along with his comrade Jerome of Prague, tried and condemned. The Council commissioned Pierre d'Ailly, Jean Gerson, and Franciscus Zabarella to investigate. What was at issue was ecclesiological. Hus believed that the true Church consisted of the predestinate alone, implying that ecclesiastics not among the predestinate do not constitute the true church. Consequently, he could not subscribe to either papalism or conciliarism. Hus was in dispute with such papalist theologians in Prague as Stephen Palec and Stanislav of Znojmo over the question of whether the pope was the head of the Roman Church as the mystical and ecclesiastical *compositum*. He rejected his opponents' view by asserting that Christ was the sole head. Similarly, Hus could not endorse the idea that the councils consisted of the predestinate. By arguing so, he did not dismiss the judicial authority of the ecclesiastical offices; however, he explicitly rejected blind obedience to them, scrutinizing the circumstances under which Christians ought to withdraw ecclesiastical obedience.[66] Hus's concept of the church was precisely the idea that the committee led by d'Ailly, Gerson, and Zabarella regarded as heretical. His testimony that he was prepared to recant his errors if his errors were manifestly demonstrated did not save him from official condemnation.[67]

The theologians' ever-expanding doctrinal authority, which culminated in the Great Schism, did not mute their search for intellectual freedom, which indeed persisted beyond the Council of Constance. Juan de Segovia was probably not a successful statesman like Gerson but, instead, nurtured "Basle conciliarism" by promoting open discussion within the church. This professor of theology at the University of Salamanca contributed to the Council as the sole representative of the university. Segovia believed that "there must be freedom of speech within the council . . . so that everyone may state his opinion."[68] He approved of the fact that the Council of Basle gave even Hussites freedom of speech.[69] His emphasis on open discussion stemmed from the conviction that discussion resulted in better decision. This idea echoes the Ciceronian, and arguably Marsilian, belief in the associative power of humans through such means of linguistic communication as oration and discussion.[70] Marsilius of Padua, for example, maintained that open debates in the councils will eventually arrive at the discovery of the truth: "by each one listening to the others, their minds are reciprocally stimulated to the consideration of the truth at which none of them would arrive if he existed apart or separately from the others."[71]

Segovia was once described as "Ockham redivivus," and this is not absurd.[72] In his conflict with heretical popes, Ockham elaborated 20 modes of heretical pertinacity. He defined pertinacity as a believer's failure to assent to catholic truth, implying that pertinacity was not necessarily the disobedience of a believer to the doctrinal decisions made by the ecclesiastical authority. Ockham's discourse on pertinacity was reproduced by Segovia in his account of heresy.[73] Ockham's idea of heresy provided a firm theological ground for Segovia's defense of freedom of speech in general councils. The Council of Basle, as an ecclesiastical event, ended in a disastrous failure of conciliarism and a revival of papalism. Nonetheless, the voices of the early fourteenth-century academic dissenters found a loyal heir in Juan de Segovia.

Notes

1   Pierre Duhem, *Medieval Cosmology*, trans. Roger Ariew (Chicago, 1985), xxii–xxiii.

2   Pierre Mandonnet, *Siger de Brabant et l'averroisme latin au XIIIe siècle*, 2 vols. (Louvain, 1908–11), vol. 1, pp. 191–5; Etienne Gilson, *La philosophie au moyen âge* (Paris, 1947), p. 559.

3   J. M. M. H. Thijssen, *Censure and Heresy at the University of Paris, 1200–1400* (Philadelphia, 1998), pp. 50–2.

4   Ibid., pp. 48–50.

5   K. Flasch, *Aufklärung im Mittelalter? Die Verurteilung von 1277. Das Dokument von Bischofs von Paris übersetzt und erklärt* (Mainz, 1989).

6   Godfrey of Fontaines, *Quodlibet*, XII, q. 5, in *Les Philosophes Belges*, V (Louvain, 1932), pp. 100–5. Cf. Thijssen, *Censure and Heresy*, pp. 99–100.

7   Thijssen, *Censure and Heresy*, p. 103.

8   Godfrey of Fontaines, *Quodlibet*, XI, q. 11, in *Les Philosophes Belges*, V (Louvain, 1932), p. 55. See Mary Martin McLaughlin, *Intellectual Freedom and its Limitations in the University of Paris in the Thirteenth and Fourteenth Centuries* (New York, 1977), pp. 238–9.

9   G. H. M. Posthumus Meyjes, "Exponents of Sovereignty: Canonists as Seen by Theologians in the Late Middle Ages," in *The Church and Sovereignty, c. 590–1918: Essays in Honour of Michael Wilks* (Studies in Church History: Subsidia, 9), ed. Diana Wood (Oxford, 1991), pp. 291–312.

10 Godfrey of Fontaines, *Quodlibet*, IV, q. 13, in *Les Philosophes Belges*, II (Louvain, 1904), pp. 274–7.

11 Godfrey of Fontaines, *Quodlibet*, III, q. 10, in *Les Philosophes Belges*, II (Louvain, 1904), p. 218.

12 McLaughlin, *Intellectual Freedom*, pp. 245ff.

13 John of Paris, *De regia potestate et papali*, ed. Fritz Bleienstein (Stuttgart, 1969), ch. 22.

14 T. S. R. Boase, *Boniface VIII* (London, 1933), p. 22; Guy Fitch Lytle, "Universities as Religious Authorities in the Later Middle Ages and Reformation," in *Reform and Authority in the Medieval and Reformation Church*, ed. Guy Fitch Lytle (Washington, DC, 1981), p. 74.

15 David Burr, *Olivi and Franciscan Poverty: The Origins of the Usus Pauper Controversy* (Philadelphia, 1989), chs. 2 and 3.

16 Ibid., pp. 45–6.

17 Ibid., p. 189.

18 David Burr, "Olivi and the Limits of Intellectual Freedom," in *Contemporary Reflections on the Medieval Christian Tradition*, ed. G. H. Shriver (Durham, NC, 1979), pp. 185–99.

19 As cited in Burr, "Olivi and the Limits of Intellectual Freedom," p. 194.

20 Brian Tierney, *Origins of Papal Infallibility, 1150–1350: A Study on the Concepts of Infallibility, Sovereignty, and Tradition in the Middle Ages* (Leiden, 1988), p. 125.

21 Ibid.

22 Jean Dunbabin, *A Hound of God: Pierre de la Palud and the Fourteenth-Century Church* (Oxford, 1991), pp. 57–8.

23 Y. M.-J. Congar, "Aspects ecclésiologiques de la querelle entre mendiants et séculiers dans la seconde moitié du xiiie siècle et le début du xive," *Archives d'histoire doctrinale et littéraire du moyen âge*, 28 (1962), pp. 35–151.

24 Dunbabin, *A Hand of God*, p. 60.

25 Ibid., pp. 58–9.

26 Karlfried Froehlich, "Saint Peter, Papal Primacy, and the Exegetical Tradition, 1150–1350," in *The Religious Role of the Papacy: Ideals and Realities, 1150–1350*, ed. Christopher Ryan (Toronto, 1989), pp. 3–44.

27 Ibid. See also Walter Ullmann, "Leo I and the Theme of Papal Primacy," *Journal of Theological Studies*, 11 (1960), pp. 25–51, and Henry Chadwick, *The Early Church* (London, 1993), pp. 239–40.

28 For Franciscan history, see, for instance, J. R. H. Moorman, *The History of the Franciscan Order* (Oxford, 1968) and H. Holzapfel, *The History of the Franciscan Order*, trans. A. Tibesar and G. Brinkmann (Teutopolis, Ill., 1948).

29 M. D. Lambert, *Franciscan Poverty: The Doctrine of the Absolute Poverty of Christ and the Apostles in the Franciscan Order* (London, 1961), pp. 216–17.

30 Marsilius of Padua, *Defensor pacis*, ed. C. W. Previté-Orton (Cambridge, 1928), II, xxiv, 7, p. 371.

31 Thijssen, *Censure and Heresy*, pp. 24–5.

32 Thomas Turley, "Infallibilists in the Curia of Pope John XXII," *Journal of Medieval History*, 1 (1975), pp. 71–101.

33 The shorter encyclical is to be found in *Bullarium Franciscanum*, 5, ed. C. Eubel (Quaracchi, 1891), p. 233 n. 5, and the longer one in Luca Wadding, *Annales Minorum*, ad ann. 1332, no. 55, VI (Rome, 1733), pp. 397–401, and E. Baluze, *Miscellanea*, ed. J. D. Mansi (Lucca, 1914–27), vol. 3, pp. 208–11.

34 Baluze, *Miscellanea*, p. 209.

35 Bonaventure, *Apologia pauperum*, in *Opera omnia*, 10 vols. (Quaracchi, 1882–1902), vol. 8, pp. 235–9.

36 Extravag., Iohann, XXII, 14.3 (De verborum significatione), cols. 1225–9.

37 William of Ockham, *Opus nonaginta dierum*, in *Opera politica*, ed. H. S. Offler et al., 4 vols. (Manchester, 1940–63; Oxford, 1997), vol. 2, pp. 467, 469, 477, 636–7.

38 Ibid., pp. 509–53.

39 T. Shogimen, "The Relationship between Theology and Canon Law: Another Context of Political Thought in the Early Fourteenth Century," *Journal of the History of Ideas*, 60 (1999), pp. 417–31.

40 T. Shogimen, "William of Ockham and Guido Terreni," *History of Political Thought*, 19 (1998), pp. 517–30.

41 William of Ockham, I *Dialogus*, iv, cc. 13–21, in *Monarchia Sancti Romani Imperii*, ed. Melchior Goldast (Frankfurt, 1614), vol. 2, pp. 454–60.

42 Arthur Stephen McGrade, *The Political Thought of William of Ockham: Personal and Institutional Principles* (Cambridge, 1974).

43 Thijssen, *Censure and Heresy*, p. 30.

44 McLaughlin, *Intellectual Freedom*, p. 282.

45 Thijssen, *Censure and Heresy*, p. 109.

46 See Thomas Käppeli, *Le procès contre Thomas Waleys, O.P.* (Rome, 1936).

47 Lytle, "Universities," p. 76.

48 McLaughlin, *Intellectual Freedom*, pp. 282–8.

49 Marsilius of Padua, *Defensor pacis*, II, xv, 5–8, pp. 267–70.

50 William of Ockham, III *Dialogus* I, iv, 13–16, pp. 859–61. See T. Shogimen, "Ockham's Vision of the Primitive Church," in *The Church Retrospective* (*Studies in Church History*, vol. 33), ed. R. N. Swanson (Woodbridge, 1997), pp. 163–75.

51 William of Ockham, III *Dialogus* I, ii.

52 William of Ockham, III *Dialogus* I, ii, 28, pp. 816–17.

53 R. N. Swanson, *Universities, Academics and the Great Schism* (Cambridge, 1979), ch. 2.

54 Ibid., p. 45.

55 Jean Gerson, *De examinatione doctrinam*, in *Opera omnia*, ed. L. Ellies du Pin, 5 vols. (Antwerp, 1706), vol. 1, col. 18 C-D. See also Louis B. Pascoe, *Jean Gerson: Principles of Church Reform* (Leiden, 1973), pp. 86–7.

56 Pascoe, *Jean Gerson*, p. 87.

57 Jean Gerson, *An liceat in causis fidei a papa appellare*, in *Oeuvres complète*, ed. Palémon Glorieux, 7 vols. (Paris, 1960–8), vol. 6, p. 284. See also Pascoe, *Jean Gerson*, pp. 90–1.

58 Ibid., p. 96.

59 Ibid., p. 89.

60 Shogimen, "The Relationship between Theology and Canon Law," pp. 418–20.

61 John B. Morrall, *Gerson and the Great Schism* (Manchester, 1960), pp. 83–4, 120; Pascoe, *Jean Gerson*, pp. 91–3.

62 Swanson, *Universities*, ch. 5.

63 Ibid., p. 206.

64 Matthew Spinka, *John Hus: Biography* (Princeton, 1968), chs. 2 and 3.

65 Ibid., chs. 8 and 9.

66 John Hus, *Tractatus de ecclesia*, ed. S. Harrison Thomson (Cambridge, 1961), chs. 19–21.

67 Matthew Spinka, *John Hus at the Council of Constance* (New York and London, 1965), pp. 46–79. For Hus's idea of the church, see also Spinka, *John Hus: The Concept of the Church* (Princeton, 1966); Paul de Vooght, *L'hérésie de Jean Hus* (Louvain, 1960), and de Vooght, *Hussiana* (Louvain, 1960).

68 As cited in Antony Black, *Council and Commune: The Conciliar Movement and the Council of Basle* (London, 1979), p. 155.

69 Ibid.

70 On the Ciceronian tradition in medieval political thought, see especially Cary J. Nederman, "Nature, Sin and the Origins of Society: The Ciceronian Tradition in Medieval Political Thought," *Journal of the History of Ideas*, 49 (1992), pp. 3–26, reproduced in Nederman, *Medieval Aristotelianism and its Limits: Classical Traditions in Moral and Political Philosophy, 12th–15th Centuries* (Aldershot, 1997).

71 Marsilius of Padua, *Defensor minor*, in Marsiglio of Padua, *Writings on the Empire: Defensor minor and De translatione imperii*, trans. Cary J. Nederman (Cambridge, 1993), p. 42.

72 Georges de Lagarde, *La naissance de l'esprit laïque au déclin du moyen âge*, 5 vols. (Paris, 1956–70), vol. 5, p. 312ff. Cf. Black, *Council and Commune*, p. 135.

73 J. D. Mann, "William of Ockham, Juan de Segovia and Heretical Pertinacity," *Mediaeval Studies*, 56 (1994), pp. 67–88.

Duns Scotus and William Ockham

Alexander Broadie

The project of natural theology is based on the idea that we can learn about God, about his existence and his attributes, by a consideration of the natural world as a whole and of individual things in it. Thus for example there are causes of movement in the world, and theologians have argued from the existence of those causes to the existence of an unmoved first mover, a cause of all movement in the world, a cause who is understood to be God. Likewise there are things in the world that have contingent existence, contingent in the sense that though existing they have also the possibility of ceasing to exist, and theologians have argued from the existence of contingent beings to the existence of a being with necessary existence, who is called God. Likewise we find some things to be better than others, and theologians argue from the existence of these relatively good things to a being who is good in the highest possible degree, good without qualification, who is called God.[1] Likewise consideration of human artifacts can tell us something, perhaps a good deal, about the people who made them, about for example their intelligence, aesthetic sensibility, manipulative skill, and self-discipline. And theologians, carrying forward a doctrine familiar at least since the time of Plato,[2] have held that the natural world as a whole and individual things within it, such as human beings, likewise bear signs of artifice, and that, much as we draw conclusions about the existence and attributes of the human artificer by a careful reading of the artifact, so also we can draw conclusions about the existence and attributes of a divine artificer by a careful reading of the natural world.[3] In particular it is commonly concluded from a reading of nature that the divine artificer has certain intellectual and moral perfections.

These arguments of the theologians, though formidable, are also deeply problematic. Our concept of wisdom is formed by us creatures looking out upon the created order, and observing and reflecting upon the behavior, linguistic and otherwise, of creatures, particularly of course the behavior of human creatures. In that case our concept of wisdom is evidently creaturely through and through, in which case to bring God under our concept of wisdom is to bring him under the concept of something creaturely. Which is to imply that God is a creature. But to deny that God can in truth be brought under our concept of wisdom is surely to imply that he is not wise. If we say that he has wisdom but it is wholly unlike the wisdom with which we are familiar from our observation of human beings, an observation that is the basis of the formation of our concept of wisdom, then a question arises as to why we are justified in using the term "wise" of God. The same points might be made of other intellectual and moral perfections attributed to God, such as knowledge, justice, and mercy. They can be made also of the concept of a cause. Is it not a concept formed in light of our experience of the created order, and how then can it be applicable to God? And in respect of the theologian's move from contingent to necessary existence, these worrying points can be made, above all, as regards the concept of existence. In using even the term "existence" of God are we not seeking to bring him under a concept which is creaturely through and through and is therefore not truly applicable to God?

Famously Aquinas argued that terms signifying moral and intellectual perfections are predicated analogically of God.[4] This doctrine is conceived as a virtuous intermediate position between two errors, on the one hand the doctrine of the univocity of terms according to which terms signifying intellectual and moral perfections have the same sense when predicated of creatures and of God, and on the other hand the doctrine of the equivocity of terms according to which the terms have a totally different sense when predicated of God. The latter supposed error, which is especially associated with Moses Maimonides (1135–1204), was thought to lead to the doctrine of agnosticism if not atheism,[5] whereas the former doctrine was thought to lead to anthropomorphism, if indeed it is not a formulation of it.

Aquinas applies the doctrine of analogy not only to the terms signifying attributes of God, but also to the term "exists" in the proposition "God exists." The very being or existence of God, therefore, is to be understood analogically. Whatever we mean by "God exists," the term does not, and for Aquinas cannot, have the same sense that it has in "A human being exists,"[6] though its sense is not totally different in the two cases. It does not have the same sense, for human existence is only an imperfect representation of divine existence; and on the other hand the sense is not totally different in the two cases, for though human existence represents divine existence imperfectly, it does at least represent it no matter how imperfectly it may do so.[7] This in brief is Aquinas's doctrine of the "analogy of being," and the doctrine, by the greatest Dominican thinker, was a major target of John Duns Scotus[8] and William Ockham,[9] the two greatest Franciscan thinkers, both of whom argued on the contrary for the "univocity of being," that is, for the doctrine that it is possible to isolate a sense of "exists" such that in that one and the same sense of the term it can truly be said that God exists and Socrates exists. Likewise Scotus and Ockham both held, as against Aquinas, that terms for the intellectual and moral perfections can be predicated univocally of God and creatures. That is, it is possible to isolate a sense of "wise," and so on, such that in one and the same sense of the term it can truly be said that God is wise and a creature is wise, and similarly with "just" and other terms signifying such perfections.

Although the doctrines of univocity, analogy, and equivocity are commonly expressed as doctrines about the sense of terms, those doctrines rest upon, and derive such credibility as they have from, doctrines concerning what, if anything, we can know about God. In particular the doctrine of equivocity is the central plank in negative theology. It holds that we can know of God only what he is not, not what he is, and that therefore when we predicate terms affirmatively of God those terms have to be understood negatively. Even "exists" is to be understood negatively, for the only concept of existence that we creatures have is a concept of creaturely existence, and "existence" or "being" as so understood cannot truly be applied to God.

Scotus discusses these matters in the course of answering the question: "Can God be known by natural means by a human being in this life?"[10] As an opening move he argues that it is impossible that all terms truly and affirmatively predicated of God should be understood negatively, for if we deny some predicate X of him this is because we wish to affirm something Y of him and the affirmation that he is X is incompatible with the affirmation that he is Y. In short, we never negate as a first move, only as a move subsequent to an affirmation. It can only be in the light of something that we know God to be that we consider ourselves in a position to deny anything of him.[11] To take Scotus's example, how do we know that God is not a stone unless we know something about God that is incompatible with the affirmation that he is a stone? Perhaps we believe (as no doubt we should) that God is a pure spirit. We therefore infer that he is incorporeal, and since stones are corporeal we infer that he is not a stone. The negative proposition that he is not as tone is deduced from the affirmative proposition that he is a pure spirit.

To take the argument a stage further, though there are many things we can and should deny of God, we cannot *only* deny things of him. For if we say that God is not X and is not Y and is not Z and so on for all affirmative predicates, then the implication is that there is nothing that God is. But there is no difference between saying that there is nothing that God is and saying that he is nothing. But to be nothing is not to exist. A systematic application of the negative way appears therefore to lead to a denial of God's existence and therefore to atheism. Scotus's position seems however to be tougher than this. He affirms: "I never know, as regards something, whether it exists, unless I have some concept of that thing whose existence I know."[12] The real problem with the systematic application of the negative way is that the way ends with the denial of the existence of a God of whom we have no concept. But if we have no concept of God then the proposition that God does not exist, or that there is no God, does not even make sense to us. This is not atheism, for at least the atheist has a concept of God; what he says is that nothing falls under the concept. The negative way on the contrary leaves us without even a concept of God. For Scotus therefore the doctrine of equivocity reduces to incoherence.

Scotus is less unkindly disposed to the doctrine of analogy. At least he accepts some Thomistic doctrines regarding analogy. Aquinas held that terms for intellectual and moral perfections are predicated primarily of God and secondarily and derivatively of creatures, and that accordingly God, insofar as he is primarily wise, just, and so on, is the measure by which we should measure us creatures in respect of our wisdom, justice, and our other mental and spiritual attributes. Indeed the being of God is the measure or standard by which we measure the being of creatures, and as our being falls short of his and therefore imperfectly represents the divine being, so also our wisdom and justice fall short of his and imperfectly represent the divine wisdom and justice. Hence although God has being, wisdom, and justice in an analogical sense of the terms, the terms are more properly predicated of God than of us. For it is creatures that imperfectly represent the Creator, not the converse.

Scotus fully accepts that one reason why terms such as "wise" and "just" do not have precisely the same sense when predicated of God and human beings is that creatures are only imperfect representations of the divine. Nevertheless, as he insists, it does not follow from the terms not having the same sense that there is nothing common to the two senses, no univocal element in them. One metaphor commonly deployed in this context is, as just noted, that of the relation between measure and the thing measured. Another is that of the relation of excedent (that which exceeds) to excess (that which is exceeded). Scotus takes up these metaphors in his discussion of the relation between God's attributes and ours. He does not deny the propriety of saying that insofar as God's wisdom is the measure of ours, or that God's wisdom exceeds ours by a certain proportion, God has wisdom in an analogical sense. But Scotus makes what he evidently takes to be a logical point, namely that analogy presupposes univocity. If of two things one is the measure of the other, then they must have something in common that permits the first to be the measure of the second, and the second to be measured by the first. If of two things one exceeds the other by some quantity or degree, however great, then they must have something in common in respect of which the first exceeds the second.

Scotus writes: "Things are never related as the measured to the measure, or as the excess to the excedent unless they have something in common . . . When it is said: 'This is more perfect than that,' then if it be asked 'A more perfect what?,' it is necessary to ascribe something common to both, so that in every comparison something determinable is common to each of the things compared. For if a human being is more perfect than a donkey, he is not more perfect *qua* human than a donkey is; he is more perfect *qua* animal."[13] In the phrase "human animal," "animal" is the determinable and "human" the determinant which qualifies "animal." Likewise in "asinine animal" (referring to a donkey), "animal" is the determinable and "asinine" the determinant. The idea behind this medieval terminology is evidently that the term "animal" signifies any and every animal whereas "human animal" signifies more determinately, since the phrase signifies only those animals that are human. Thus Scotus is saying that the determinable term "animal" must signify equally humans and donkeys if a human is to be more perfect than a donkey, for it is not *qua* human that the human is more perfect, nor is it *qua* donkey that the donkey is less perfect. It is *qua* animal that the human is more perfect than the donkey *qua* animal. Let us then say that God is more perfect, even infinitely more perfect than human beings are. We are then asked "A more perfect what?" or "More perfect *qua* what?" and reply "*Qua* wise being." And just as in the preceding case "animal" must be predicated, with the same sense, of humans and donkeys if the comparison between humans and donkeys is not to be incoherent, so in this case also "wise" must be predicated, with the same sense, of God and humans if the comparison between God and humans in respect of wisdom is to be coherent. In short, comparison implies univocity.

This is not of course to say that God and humans are wise in exactly the same way, or even in much the same way. It is to say instead that if we cannot form a univocal concept of wisdom under which we can bring both God and humans, then we are wholly unable to compare humans with God in respect of wisdom and conclude that God's wisdom is greater, even infinitely greater, than ours. I assume that we can make the comparison in question. In that case we can form a concept of something, wisdom, which we can predicate of God and humans. We can also make these predications more determinate by saying that God has wisdom to an infinite degree and we have it to a finite degree only. But that God's is infinite and ours is finite does not prevent it being the same thing which is infinite in the one case and finite in the other.

What has just been said about wisdom can be said also in respect of the other intellectual perfections that are traditionally attributed to God. In each case univocity is assumed if we make a comparison between God and us and say that God is infinitely more just or more merciful than we are, and so on for the other perfections. We can form a concept of wisdom, not of finite wisdom or infinite wisdom. We can form a concept of wisdom which is antecedent to these determinants or qualifiers, and can then think of wisdom as qualified in the one way or the other. This is roughly how Aquinas proceeds. But this procedure implies that there is after all an affirmative or positive content to the concept predicated of God, namely the concept of wisdom which is antecedent to the employment of the determinant "infinite." We are therefore drawn again to the conclusion that, as Scotus holds, analogy implies univocity.

This is true no less of being than of intellectual and moral attributes. As against the doctrine of the analogy of being, which is perhaps the central doctrine in Aquinas's religious philosophy, Scotus holds that it is possible to form a concept of being which is neutral as between the being of God and the being of creatures, and is contained in both. He writes: "The intellect of a person in this life can be certain that God is a being though doubtful as to whether he is a finite or an infinite being, a created or an uncreated being. Hence as regards God the concept of being is other than this concept [i.e. of infinite or uncreated being] and that concept [i.e. of finite or created being]. And thus in itself the concept is neither of these and is included in each. Hence it is a univocal concept [of being]."[14] We can form a concept of finite being and one of infinite being. We can also form a concept of being while thinking of being neither as finite nor infinite, but instead as being *simpliciter*. Having this latter concept we can then construct a more determinate concept by adding the determinant "finite" or "infinite" to it. But the two concepts, of finite being and infinite being, are both formed by adding a determinant to one and the same concept, that of being *simpliciter*, a concept which is logically antecedent to the more determinate concepts. The main point here is that removal of the determinant "finite" from the concept "finite being" does not leave a concept of being which, not being finite, is therefore infinite. It leaves, on the contrary, a concept of being which is neutral as between finite being and infinite and is therefore equally predicable of both a finite being and an infinite one.[15] This neutral concept is therefore, as Scotus holds, a univocal concept of being contained as an element in each of the two more determinate concepts just discussed.

There is no suggestion, in this doctrine of univocity of being, that there is, or can be, in the world, something that has being but does not have determinate being; whatever has being has finite being or infinite, has created being or uncreated. For being *simpliciter* is known, not directly or by an intuition, but only by an intellectual act of abstraction, by which, starting from the concept of determinate being, we form a concept of what remains if we think away the determinant, that which determines the being. This is not to say that being *simpliciter* does not exist; it can be said to exist so long as nothing more is meant by this than that (i) we can form a concept of the being or existence of things that have determinate being, and (ii) by a process of abstraction from that concept we can reach the concept of being *simpliciter*. Determinate being is divisible into infinite being and finite, and into uncreated being and created. No doubt we have to say that God, as having infinite and uncreated being has an utterly different mode of being from that enjoyed by creatures, but it is of being, univocally understood, that God has one mode and creatures have another. That is the doctrine of the univocity of being, within the theological context provided by Scotus. He is very clear on this matter: "Take, for example, the formal notion of 'wisdom' or 'intellect' or 'will.' Such a notion is considered first of all simply in itself and absolutely. Because this notion includes formally no imperfection nor limitation, the imperfections associated with it in creatures are removed . . . Retaining this same notion of 'wisdom' and 'will,' we attribute these to God – but in a most perfect degree. Consequently, every inquiry regarding God is based upon the supposition that the intellect has the same univocal concept which it obtained from creatures."[16]

If we deny this kernel of univocity to our concepts of being and of the perfections, what follows? For Scotus two closely related consequences flow from such a denial. First, he thinks that a doctrine of analogy that does not presuppose univocity is in fact a doctrine of pure equivocity. That is, the terms "being," "wise," and so on have a totally different sense when applied to God and to creatures and we are unable to give a more than merely negative characterization of the concepts of being, wisdom, and so on, as those terms are applied to God. This position, as already noted, is unacceptable to Scotus because he holds that it can only be in the light of something affirmative we conceive God to be that we are in a position to deny anything of him. A doctrine that declares our concept of God to be negative through and through is therefore incoherent.

Secondly, and here I give a richer context to a point made at the start, the denial of the doctrine of univocity strikes at the medieval project of natural theology by which conclusions were to be drawn about God's being and his attributes on the basis of a suitably slanted investigation of the created order. Thus, to return to the argument sketched at the start: that there are causes of movement in the world and that therefore there is an unmoved first mover, a cause of all movement in the world, a cause who is understood to be God. This argument, or rather the full-scale version of it, works (if at all) only if the term "cause" has the same sense when applied to God and to creatures. Likewise as regards the argument that moves from signs of intelligence which bespeak an intelligent creature to signs of intelligence in the world as a whole which therefore bespeak the existence of an intelligent artificer who created the world, this move has plausibility only if it is assumed that the term "intelligent" has the same sense when applied to God and to creatures.

Scotus is explicit. From rejection of the doctrine of univocity an absurd consequence follows, namely: "that from the proper notion of anything found in creatures nothing at all can be inferred about God, for the notion of what is in each is wholly different. We would have no more reason to conclude that God is formally wise from the notion of wisdom derived from creatures than we would have reason to conclude that God is formally a stone."[17] It is plain therefore that a good deal depends on the doctrine of univocity.

William Ockham did not accept in every detail all of Scotus's arguments for univocity. Far from it. But his endorsement and defense of the doctrine are no less strong than are those by Scotus himself. For example, Ockham considers the outcome of an act of abstraction by which we think away the imperfection of creaturely wisdom:

> This is nothing other than to abstract from created wisdom a concept of wisdom which points neither to a created thing nor to something uncreated. For every created thing implies imperfection; and hence to abstract imperfection from the wisdom of a creature is nothing other than to abstract a concept of wisdom from an imperfect creature, and the resulting concept does not refer more to a creature than to a non-creature, and hence what results is attributable to God by means of predication . . . For unless such a concept could be abstracted from a creature we could no more reach knowledge of divine wisdom (for example, the knowledge that God is wisdom) *via* the wisdom of a creature, than we could reach *via* the cognition of a stone the cognition that God is a stone.[18]

Here Ockham envisages a process by which, starting from a concept applicable to creatures (and where else can we start?), we reach a concept under which God can be brought. The concept we reach however is one which is not the less applicable to creatures. It is a concept of creaturely wisdom *minus* those elements and features of it that signify imperfection. Elements or features expressly signifying divine perfections are not added, but concepts implying creaturely imperfections are no longer present. As Ockham states: "The concept does not more refer to a creature than to a non-creature," for it refers equally to both. This is precisely the route by which Scotus too reached the concept of terms univocally predicable of God and creatures.

Likewise with the concept of being, which Ockham believes can be reached by abstracting all determinants from our concept of determinate being. The process of abstraction does not result in a concept of being which is applicable to God and not to creatures; it is univocally applicable to both God and creatures. And, as with Scotus, for Ockham also there cannot be, in the world (or out of it), a being which is a pure indeterminate being, a being which *is* without being something, and which is therefore nothing, and which therefore does not exist. That is, though we have a *concept* of wholly indeterminate being, there is no thing "out there" which is a wholly indeterminate being. In *that* sense being *simpliciter* does not exist. Ockham is explicit: "Being [that is, the term 'being'] stands only for a concept in the mind, not for a substance nor an accident."[19]

At first blush this is hard doctrine. In particular, it seems to imply that univocal being exists only in the mind and not at all or in any way in God or in creatures. But if it does exist only in the mind then there seems no sense in which it is true of God or of creatures. The obvious thing to say is that unless God and creatures have univocal being in themselves and independently of whether we predicate it of them, then they simply do not have being in the univocal sense. Nor therefore is being, in the univocal sense, truly predicable of God and creatures. Yet Ockham, like Scotus before him, sought, and believed he had found, a concept of being which is univocal in that it is neutral as between created being and uncreated, and between finite being and infinite, and therefore equally predicable of both. The difficulty of this doctrine is greatly lessened if it is seen within its wider context. The context is Ockham's nominalism or, to use a more helpful term, his "conceptualism," which arose in response to other doctrines, most importantly, Scotus's doctrine of the formal distinction. I shall now return to Scotus, to his formal distinction, as a pushing-off point for more detailed consideration of Ockham's account of the significance of terms used of God and especially the term "being."

God is one not only in the sense that there is only one God but also in the sense that he is simple, that is, is not composite. His simplicity was seen as a problem by many theologians for whom the fact of divine simplicity had to be reconciled with the fact that God is powerful, good, wise, just, merciful, and so on. If internally he has no multiplicity, how is it possible, logically possible, that he should also have these many perfections? One strength, perhaps the chief strength, of the negative way, lies in the fact that it can deal easily with this problem. If all affirmative predicates are to be understood negatively then the ascription of the perfections to God does not imply that he has many attributes. To say that God is wise and just is to say that he is neither foolish nor unjust. But to deny that he is foolish or unjust is not to ascribe an attribute to him, and many such negations do not therefore imply a multiplicity of attributes in God. Simplicity appears therefore not to be a problem for negative theology. On the other hand negative theology has, as we saw, other and very serious problems. Let us enquire next therefore how the doctrine of analogy fares in relation to the concept of simplicity. But the way of analogy, on the Scotistic analysis, implies the doctrine of univocity, and therefore from a Scotistic perspective a question arises, for both the analogical and the univocal ways, as to whether they can be demonstrated to be compatible with the doctrine of divine simplicity. More briefly, is the doctrine of divine simplicity a problem for the way of univocity, granted that God has many attributes?

The doctrine that he has many attributes is warranted by numerous biblical proof texts. The doctrine of divine simplicity was believed to have the support of strong theological arguments. To sketch one of them lightly: in a composite thing the parts are in a sense antecedent to the whole, for it is the parts out of which the whole is composed. They have to be in order for the whole to be, and not vice versa. But there can be nothing, nor even any part of him, antecedent to God. Hence he cannot have parts, and hence is simple. All stages of this argument need to be watched. I present it solely to indicate that the doctrine of simplicity, as supported by rational considerations, could not lightly be jettisoned. The question therefore was how the doctrine of divine attributes was to to be interpreted, if the doctrine of divine simplicity was not to be jettisoned. Scotus had an answer, one almost totally rejected by Ockham, to whom I shall come shortly. First Scotus.

If there are many divine attributes then they must in some sense be distinct from each other. But if they are distinct then what sort of distinction is at issue? Two sorts, the real distinction and the distinction of reason, were common currency in the Middle Ages. At the end of the thirteenth century Scotus added a third.[20] A is really distinct from B if it is separable from B. That is, even if A and B form some sort of unity, it is possible for B to be annihilated while A remains in existence. A pencil is a unity, but the wood and the lead of which it is composed are really distinct from each other, for either can be destroyed while the other remains. The unity of a pencil is however not a possible model for the oneness of God, since no attribute of God can be annihilated, and hence it cannot be true that one attribute of God is annihilated while another remains in existence. It might be added that in any case the wood and the lead are antecedent to the whole of which they are the two parts, and, as noted, nothing is antecedent to God.

As contrasted with a real distinction between two things, a distinction which gets along even if there is no mind making it, a distinction of reason is one produced and maintained solely by a mental act. That is to say, the distinction exists because, and for as long as, a mind *makes* the distinction, or is distinguishing. The distinction is therefore a mental act. Thus the distinction between a definiens and a definiendum, the two parts of a definition, is a distinction of reason. Granted Aristotle's definition of a human being, then outside the mind there is no distinction between a human being and a rational animal. All and only human beings are rational animals, for by definition that is what a human being is. The distinction is entirely in the mind, and has the metaphysical status of an act of mind. But should we say that the distinction between the attributes of God, between for example his wisdom and his justice, is nothing more than a distinction of reason? If we do not *make* the distinction does it therefore not exist? Scotus replies that it *does* exist, but that it is not a *real* distinction. On the contrary, the distinction between the divine attributes is less than real but more than a distinction of reason. It is a formal distinction. The divine attributes are distinct "formalities" in God. I shall expound this claim by reference to creaturely and therefore more familiar territory. My approach therefore is the relational approach of natural theology. *Qua* natural theologians our knowledge of God derives from our knowledge of the things he has made: "By his works shall ye know him."

To take a clear example of a formal distinction: Scotus holds that the distinction between the mental faculties of intellect and will is not a mere distinction of reason, for it is not by our making the distinction between those two faculties that the distinction exists. It is a distinction, as he puts it, "on the side of the object," and is certainly more than the distinction between a definiens and a definiendum, for the concept of a will neither contains nor is contained by the concept of an intellect. But the distinction is not real, for the intellect and the will are absolutely inseparable. On the one hand will cannot perform an act of will unless intellect presents it with a concept of an act that is to be willed, and on the other hand once the intellect has a concept then whether it retains it, or destroys it (by, say, diverting attention from it), or develops it, depends on an act of will.[21] In short, intellect needs will if intellect is to do anything, and will likewise needs intellect, and hence there cannot be an intellect in a mind that does not have a will, nor a will in a mind that does not have an intellect. For Scotus the mind is not the less a unity for having these two faculties. When willing, the mind takes on the form or formality of a willer; when thinking, it takes on the form or formality of an intellect. It is one and the same active principle, mind, that engages in these two sorts of act, and in virtue of being able to engage in the one it is a will and in virtue of being able to engage in the other it is an intellect. And the unity of mind, *qua* will and intellect, is irrefragable. The two faculties are therefore really identical with each other and with mind, while at the same time being formally distinct. Scotus holds that the attributes of God are likewise really identical with each other and with God, while at the same time being formally distinct. We can form a concept of one attribute without forming a concept of another, and hence one of those concepts can exist in our mind when another of them is absent; but unless there is in God something corresponding to all the concepts we form of his attributes, we falsely ascribe these attributes to him.

I should like to offer one further example of Scotus's formal distinction here, and then use the example to lead us back to Ockham. Members of a natural species have something in common, a nature in virtue of which they are members of the species; and yet they also differ for the members are many, not one. According to Scotus, each natural individual has both a nature, which is to be thought of as a systematically related collection of formalities, and also a thisness which is unique to it.[22] If its thisness is unique to it, the same surely cannot be said of its common nature, for that nature is, after all, common. Yet, as Scotus saw, there is a problem with the concept of a common nature, say human nature, the common nature of humanity, for from a given perspective it is not common at all. The humanity of Plato is unique to Plato; he and he alone has *his* human-ity. It is different from the humanity of Aristotle. Plato's humanity is Plato's and no one else's, and Aristotle's is Aristotle's alone. They are plainly different. Each nature is one, and is a different one from the other. In what sense then is human nature, or any common nature, common, and therefore universal among mem-bers of the species?

For Scotus an individual's thisness and the individual's nature are really ident-ical – not even God can annihilate an individual's nature and maintain in existence the *this* which has that nature. As regards any *this*, there must therefore be an affirmative answer to the question: "This *what?*" But the common nature and the thisness are formally distinct, for the nature considered in itself does not constrain the nature to be the nature of *this* rather than of some other unique individual. For if it did then the common nature would be a determinate common nature, the common-nature-of-*this*, in which case the common nature, as individuated by the *this*, would not be truly universal. The common nature as *universal* can exist only in the mind. It does so as a concept of the nature in question. We can conceive of the nature separately from any thisness, for the nature is formally distinct from every thisness and can therefore be conceived as distinct from any thisness, and therefore can be conceived as unindividuated and therefore as uni-versal. Thus when we say that human nature is a universal, then primarily it is of human nature considered as a concept in the mind that the term "universal" is predicated. Nevertheless if a given individual has a human nature then that indi-vidual can be brought under the universal concept of human nature, and that human nature which is "contracted" to that individual can also be described as universal in virtue of the relation the individual has to the universal concept in the mind. Thus Scotus.

William Ockham on the other hand rejects this account of common natures, and in particular rejects the formal distinction that Scotus brings to bear in the course of developing his account. It is crucial to Scotus's account that (i) the thisness proper to a given individual and (ii) the nature of that individual, a nature common to the many members of the species, are really the same and only formally distinct. But for Ockham there is a contradiction lurking in this account. He writes: "The same thing is not both common and proper. But according to them [Scotus and those who agree with him] the individual difference [the thisness] is proper, but the universal is common. Therefore no universal is the same thing as an individual difference."[23] The point seems clear. If, as Scotus affirms, the thisness of an individual and the common nature in the individual are the same thing, then this one and the same thing is both universal (since it is common to many individuals), and also proper (since it is unique to this indi-vidual). But nothing can be both common to many things and proper to one. Scotus's account of the relation between an individual and its common nature is therefore false.

The solution, in Ockham's view, is to jettison the formal distinction, and to allow instead that there are just real distinctions and distinctions of reason.[24] Since the nature of an individual is not really distinct from the individual which has that nature, there is really just the one thing there, the individual, with a nature proper to that individual. For Ockham whatever exists is singular, and natures are as singular as anything else, for there are not degrees of singularity. As said earlier, Plato's human nature is as individual as Plato is and it is proper to Plato. Aristotle does not have Plato's human nature; he has his own. Whatever the mode of existence of those universals I have been calling *common* natures, therefore, they cannot exist in the extramental world, in individuals whether as part of them or separate from them. What then is their mode of existence?

Let us distinguish between two types of cognition.[25] I open my eyes and see my room. The visual experience is of such a nature that I immediately and confidently assent to the proposition that the room exists. It is literally *evident* that it does, for I am looking at it. With my eyes open and while looking at the room I cannot will to believe in its existence, or in its non-existence. My assent to the proposition is by natural causation and is irresistible. This cognition is termed "intuitive cognition" or "intuition." Scotus put this concept of "intuition" firmly on the philosophical map and Ockham developed the concept further. The central feature of intuitive cognition is that it gives rise immediately and irresistibly to a judgment concerning the existence of what is cognized.[26]

At a later time I shut my eyes and think about the room of which I had previously had an intuitive cognition. I again have a cognition of the room, but one of a quite different nature, for this time it does not give rise irresistibly to assent to the proposition that the room exists. While I am not in sensory contact with the room, but am instead merely thinking about it, it could be destroyed by natural means or God could annihilate it. So I have a cognition of the room but one which, so to say, abstracts from existence. Because a cognition such as this one abstracts from existence it is termed "abstractive cognition" or "abstraction." Since intuition implies existence and abstraction abstracts from it, Ockham holds that we are dealing here with two different kinds or species of cognition.

An abstraction of this sort is not necessarily universal. My abstractive cognition of my room is, though abstractive, not a universal concept since it is predicable of my room and not of any other. It is therefore a singular concept. Ockham emphasizes that an intuitive cognition and an abstractive one can have the same object.[27] That is, it may be the same thing that is cognized. What makes the difference is the *way* the object is cognized, and in particular whether it is cognized in such a way as to give rise to an evident judgment concerning the existence of the object.

I can have intuitive cognitions of many rooms and, each time, form a singular abstractive cognition of the room. But a further act of abstraction can be performed. For I can abstract from those singulars the elements in respect of which they do not resemble each other. The product of such an abstraction is a concept which is universal in the sense that it is equally predicable of many things. And for Ockham this is the only mode of existence that a universal can have; a universal is a mental act of conceiving that in respect of which many things resemble each other. It is therefore a sign of many things. I have a concept of a room, not of this room nor of that one, but simply of a room which is indeterminate, in the sense that the room I conceive does not have a determinant, such as "big," "small," "bright," "dingy," "Plato's," "Aristotle's," and so on. It is the concept of a room *simpliciter*, indeterminate but determinable. Because of its indeterminateness it signifies anything you can indicate while saying truly: "That is a room." Any room indicated is of course singular and therefore determinate down to the last detail. But the concept under which each and every room is brought is universal. We can therefore think of a universal as a kind of higher-order abstraction, a concept which, *qua* concept, exists only in the mind.

With Ockham's account of universality to the fore, I shall return now to our problem about the concept of being *simpliciter*, which Ockham, like Scotus, believed to be univocally true of God and creatures. I quoted him as affirming, "Being [that is, the term 'being'] stands only for a concept in the mind, not for a substance nor an accident," and wondered how the concept of being *simpliciter* can be true of beings in the world if being *simpliciter* is to be found nowhere in the world but only as a concept in the mind. It should now be clear that, from Ockham's perspective, being *simpliciter* is much like universals, and indeed is a universal. I have an intuitive cognition of many beings, and the product of an abstractive process starting from those intuitions is a concept which is universal in the sense that it is equally predicable of every being. As completely indeterminate being it is predicable of everything whatever that exists. This is not to imply that each being, that is, everything that exists, somehow contains indeterminate being. It is to say no more than that all beings resemble each other precisely as *being*, and that we can form a concept of that in respect of which they all resemble each other. It is only as a concept in the mind that being *simpliciter* exists, but that fact about it in no way precludes its predicability of all beings. Since, as argued earlier, it is possible to form a concept of being which is neutral as between infinite being and finite, uncreated being and created, this concept is predicable univocally of God and creatures. Likewise, as already argued, we can form a concept of wisdom *simpliciter*, a wisdom which prescinds from infinitude and finitude, from uncreatedness and createdness. And the fact that this is predicable univocally of God and creatures does not imply that there is indeterminate being and indeterminate wisdom in God and creatures. It implies only that the concepts of being and wisdom are truly predicable of God and creatures, where these concepts are not qualified by the determinants "infinite" or "finite," and so on.

It may be thought that the univocal concepts of being, wisdom, justice, concepts drained of the specifically creaturely and the specifically divine, are very thin, almost diaphanous as compared with such concepts as creaturely being and creaturely wisdom. But all the same they do have some affirmative content, and in the view of Scotus and Ockham that is sufficient for natural theology. Reject that affirmative content, and we must reject also the argument from, for example, the existence of creaturely causes to the existence of God as cause of everything, or from the existence of contingent being to the existence of a necessary being. If the senses of the term "cause" in premiss and conclusion of the first argument have nothing in common then the argument fails, as does the second argument if the senses of "being" in premiss and conclusion have nothing in common. From this perspective the doctrine of univocity promoted by Scotus and Ockham is central to the whole project of natural theology. A point touched on earlier should however be stressed here, that the doctrine of analogy is not necessarily in conflict with that grand project of natural theology. Insofar as analogy presupposes univocity, analogy is not inimical to the project but can on the contrary be used as a starting-point for it.

Notes

1 These are three of Aquinas's "Five Ways." See *Summa Theologiae*, pt. 1, q. 2, art. 3c.

2 Plato, *Laws* X, 886a; cf. XII, 966e. For Plato "the earth and the sun and the stars and the universe and the fair order of the seasons and the division of them into years and months, is the most harmonious and beautiful artifact, and consequently must have the finest cause."

3 Cf. Aquinas, *ST.* 1, 14, 8c: "For God's knowledge is related to all created things as an artificer's knowledge is related to his artifacts."

4 For illuminating recent discussion on Aquinas's doctrine of analogy see William Alston, "Aquinas on Theological Predication: A Look Backward and a Look Forward," in Eleonore Stump (ed.), *Reasoned Faith*, Ithaca and London, 1993, pp. 145–78; also Norman Kretzmann, *The Metaphysics of Theism*, Oxford, 1997, pp. 142–57.

5 For discussion of some of the issues see A. Broadie, "Maimonides and Aquinas on the names of God," *Rel. Studies*, 26, 1986, pp. 157–70.

6 It should be noted that for Aquinas "God" is not a proper name; it is the name of a nature, as is "human being" (*Summa Theologiae* pt. 1, q. 13, art. 8). That is, "God exists" and "A human being exists" each affirm that there exists a being of a given nature. Aquinas proves first that there is a God, and then that there cannot be more than one such being.

7 There are several layers of reasons why the representation must be imperfect, but fundamental to them is the doctrine that God's existence is identical with his essence, and there cannot be a created thing whose existence is identical with its essence.

8 The Blessed John Duns Scotus was born ca. 1266 in Duns in south-east Scotland, and studied and taught at Oxford and Cambridge, before going to Paris where he incepted as Master of Theology. He commented on Peter Lombard's *Sentences* at all three universities. He died in Cologne in 1308, and is buried there in the Minoriten Kirche.

9 William Ockham was born in Ockham in Surrey, England (ca. 1285), and studied at Oxford, where he commented on the *Sentences* of Peter Lombard from ca. 1317. He went to London ca. 1320 and there taught logic and physics, worked on his commentary on the *Sentences*, and wrote his *Summa Logicae*, one of the great logic works of the Middle Ages. Thereafter he went to Avignon to defend himself against a charge of heresy, a charge of which eventually he was in effect acquitted. Meantime he had become involved in a dispute regarding the limits of papal power, in consequence of which he fled from Avignon in 1328, first to Pisa and then to Munich. Thereafter, till his death in 1349, he spent most of his time writing about the politics of the papacy. On his flight from Avignon he was excommunicated. It is not known whether there was a formal reconciliation.

10 See *Opus Oxoniense*, Bk. 1, dist. 3, pars 1, q. 1, in *Ioannis Duns Scoti Opera Omnia*, Vatican (1950–), vol. 3, pp. 1–48. The question is printed with *en face* translation in Allan Wolter, OFM, *Duns Scotus: Philosophical Writings*, Indianapolis, 1993, pp. 14–33.

11 . . . negatio non cognoscitur nisi per affirmationem . . . Patet etiam quod nullas negationes cognoscimus de Deo nisi per affirmationes, per quas removemus alia incompossibilia ab illis affirmationibus. ("A negation is not known except via an affirmation . . . It is also obvious that we

know no negations about God except by means of affirmations. It is on the basis of those affirmations that we deny other things that are incompatible with them.") Ord. 1, dist. 3, par. 1, q. 1–2; Vatican edn. vol. 3, p. 4. Also in Wolter, ibid., p. 15.

12 Numquam enim cognosco de aliquo si est, nisi habeam aliquem conceptum illius extremi de quo cognosco esse. Vatican edn. vol. 3, p. 6; Wolter, ibid., p. 16.

13 . . . quia numquam aliqua comparantur ut mensurata ad mensuram, vel excessa ad excedens, nisi in aliquo uno conveniant . . . Quando enim dicitur "hoc est perfectius illo," si quaeratur "quid perfectius?", ibi oportet assignare aliquid commune utrique, ita quod omnis comparativi determinabile est commune utrique extremo compartionis; non enim homo est perfectior homo quam asinus, sed perfectius animal. *Opus Oxoniense*, Bk. 1, dist. 8, par. 1, q. 3, Vatican edn., vol. 4, p. 191.

14 Sed intellectus viatoris potest esse certus de Deo quod sit ens dubitando de ente finito vel infinito, creato vel increato; ergo conceptus entis de Deo est alius a conceptu isto et illo, et ita neuter ex se, et in utroque illorum includitur; igitur univocus. Vatican edn. vol. 3, p. 18; Wolter, ibid., p. 20.

15 In the compound phrases "finite being" and "infinite being" the determinants "finite" and "infinite" do not, for Scotus, signify properties of being. He is explicit on this matter as regards "infinite being" but the same sort of point can be made about finite being also. Infinity, he tells us, is not a property or an attribute of infinite being. "Infinite" in "infinite being" signifies instead what he terms an "intrinsic mode of that being." Infinity is not something that the being has, but is the *way* it is, *how* it exists. Scotus compares "infinite being" to "intense whiteness." The intensity is an intrinsic grade of the whiteness, not an accident extrinsic to it. See Ord. 1, d. 3, pt. 1, qq. 1–2; Vatican edn. vol. 3, p. 44. Wolter, ibid., p. 27.

16 Exemplum de formali ratione sapientiae vel (intellectus) vel voluntatis. Consideratur enim in se et secundum se, et ex hoc quod ista ratio non concludit formaliter imperfectionem aliquam nec limitationem, removentur ab ipsa imperfectiones quae concomitantur eam in creaturis et reservata eadem ratione

sapientiae et voluntatis attribuuntur ista Deo perfectissime. Ergo omnis inquisitio de Deo supponit intellectum habere conceptum eundem univocum quem accepit ex creaturis. Vatican edn. vol. 3, pp. 26–7; Wolter, ibid., p. 25. (One witness has *includit* in place of *concludit*.)

17 . . . quod ex nulla ratione propria eorum prout sunt in creaturis, possunt concludi de Deo, quia omnino alia et alia ratio illorum est et istorum; immo non magis concludetur quod Deus est sapiens formaliter, ex ratione sapientiae quam apprehendimus ex creaturis, quam quod Deus est formaliter lapis. Vatican edn. vol. 3, p. 27; Wolter, ibid., p. 25.

18 Hoc non est nisi abstrahere a sapientia creata conceptum sapientiae, quae nullam rem creatam vel increatam dicit, quia quaelibet res creata dicit imperfectionem. Et ideo abstrahere imperfectionem a sapientia creaturae non est nisi abstrahere conceptum sapientiae a creatura imperfecta, qui non plus respicit creaturam quam non creaturam, et tunc illud quod resultat attribuendum est Deo per praedicationem . . . Nisi enim posset talis abstrahi a creatura, modo non plus per sapientiam creaturae deveniretur in cognitionem sapientiae divinae, puta quod Deus sit sapientia, quam per cognitionem lapidis devenitur ad cognitionem quod Deus sit lapis . . . Ockham, *Reportatio* 3, q. 8, in P. Boehner, OFM, *Ockham: Philosophical Writings*, Edinburgh, 1962, p. 112.

19 . . . ens supponit tantum pro conceptu in mente, non pro substantia nec accidente. *Reportatio* 3, q. 8. *Opera Theologica*, vol. 6, eds. F. E. Kelly and G. I. Etzkorn, St. Bonaventure, NY, 1982, p. 345; see also P. Boehner, OFM, p. 113.

20 The distinction was not invented by Scotus but it was he who brought it to center stage.

21 For a detailed discussion of these points see A. Broadie, *The Shadow of Scotus*, Edinburgh, 1995, chs. 2, 3; also A. Broadie, "Duns Scotus on Sinful Thought," *Scottish J. Theol.*, 49, 1996, pp. 291–310. For detailed discussion of the formal distinction in Scotus see Allan B. Wolter, OFM, "The Formal Distinction," in John K. Ryan and B. Bonansea (eds.), *John Duns Scotus, 1265–1308*, Washington, DC, 1965, pp. 45–60, and Allan B. Wolter, OFM, "The Realism of Scotus," in

J. Phil., 59, 1962, pp. 725–36. The latter two articles are reprinted in Allan B. Wolter, OFM, *The Philosophical Theology of John Duns Scotus*, ed. M. M. Adams, Ithaca, 1990, chs. 1, 2.

22 The thisness is not something that we can know directly, at least in this life. It can instead be known only *via* the various qualities of the individual, including of course the qualities that go to form the individual's nature. Nevertheless, though not directly aware of the thisness we can know it must be there for we intuit, that is, have immediate experience of, individuals, and there can be no individual that is not a *this*.

23 Item, eadem res non est communis et propria; sed secundum eos differentia individualis est propria, universale autem est commune; igitur nullum universale et differentia individualis sunt eadem res. *Summa Logicae*, pars I, cap. 16; see *Opera Philosophica* vol. 1, eds. P. Boehner, OFM, G. Gál, OFM, S. Brown, St. Bonaventure, NY, 1974, pp. 54–5.

24 Ockham's rejection is not total. He deploys the distinction in just one case, that of the Trinity, where he is concerned with the question of how God who is one is also three. Evidently therefore he did not think the concept of the formal distinction incoherent. (He did however think it as mysterious as the doctrine of the Trinity itself.)

25 For detailed discussion see Marilyn McCord Adams, *William Ockham*, Notre Dame, Ind., 1987, ch. 13, esp. pp. 501–9.

26 In the natural order the judgment is to the effect that what is cognized exists, though Ockham argues famously that it is possible, by God's help, to have an intuitive cognition of a non-existent object. In the latter case the judgment to which the cognition gives rise is to the effect that the object does not exist. However, here I shall be attending to what happens according to nature.

27 *Ordinatio*, Prologue q. 1, art. 1. See *Opera Theologica*, vol. 1, eds. G. Gál and S. F. Brown, St. Bonaventure, NY, 1967, pp. 36–70.

Dissent

17 The Waldenses
Euan Cameron

18 Dualism
Gerhard Rottenwöhrer

19 Ecclesiology and Politics
Matthew S. Kempshall

20 Wyclif and Lollardy
Stephen Lahey

The Waldenses

Euan Cameron

Introduction

An anonymous but well-informed churchman, writing in the 1260s, claimed that the Waldenses were the most dangerous of all the heretics then faced by the Church. They were the most long-lived of all; they were the most widespread; and finally, while other heretics taught repellent errors of faith, the Waldenses lived piously, believed everything in the Christian creeds, and differed from the rest only in the "blasphemies" with which they attacked the Roman Church, its clergy, and its rituals.[1] Heretics called "Waldenses" or "Poor of Lyons" were being described, discussed, criticized, and persecuted from their first formal condemnation at the Council of Verona in 1184 right up to the Reformation era.[2] Even beyond that religious watershed, a branch of the reformed Protestant communion in the former Waldensian heartlands of Piedmont retained its identity as a "Waldensian" church. The truism that heresy is defined by reference to the orthodoxy which it rejects, is particularly evident in the case of the Waldenses. As the medieval Church evolved and developed, so the character of Waldensian dissent could change and develop in response to it. The reverse is also true. When the Waldenses opposed the claims to sacral power and exclusive authority made by the Western Catholic Church, their attacks often forced preachers and theologians to sharpen their definitions and defenses of the faith.

Before Heresy: Valdesius and the Poor of Lyons

Valdesius, after whom the Waldenses were named, did not set out to found a movement of religious protest or opposition to orthodoxy. Even with hindsight, the chroniclers who described the origin of his "heresy" acknowledged that its roots lay in entirely traditional Christian instincts: to renounce the riches of the world, to read and study the Scriptures, and to preach the Gospel to the people. The Chronicle of the Anonymous of Laon[3] reports how one Sunday in early 1173

Valdesius heard from a *jongleur* the story of St. Alexis, a fifth-century Roman patrician who had left a wealthy bride for a life of mendicancy and almsgiving in Syria.[4] The following day Valdesius asked the local theologians the most "certain and perfect" way to reach God. He was duly told of Jesus' advice to the rich young man, "if you wish to be perfect, go and sell everything that you possess . . ."[5] Valdesius took the text literally. With part of his property he endowed his wife with an income. The remainder was spent in making restoration to those from whom he had profited through "usury," and in settling his daughters in a house of the Order of Fontevrault. During a famine he gave prodigal handouts of food to the poor, and was reduced to begging for alms himself. His wife persuaded Archbishop Guichard de Pontigny of Lyons to direct him to take alms only from her.

According to Richard of Poitiers, Valdesius (whom he calls *Valdensis*) at once sought to have "some passages of the Bible and the Fathers" translated for him (a collection rather than a complete translation).[6] The translator Stephanus de Ansa and the scribe Bernardus Ydros were entirely orthodox, and clearly saw nothing untoward in preparing translations of religious works for a pious, literate layman who could read the vernacular but not Latin.[7] Valdesius soon began to preach his mission of apostolic poverty in public, and to attract a band of followers, men and women alike. In 1177, according to the Laon Anonymous, "those who followed his example, giving everything to the poor, became exponents of voluntary poverty."[8] Gradually, the chronicle adds, they began to criticize their own and others' sins both privately and in public. Étienne de Bourbon described Valdesius's preaching as spouting publicly what he had learned by heart from his Bible translations.[9]

It is impossible to ascertain just how much of the traditional story of Valdesius represents embroidering by chroniclers from a stock of images or *topoi*. However, it is very significant that some of the details closely resemble those found in the lives of saints. The sudden conversion under the influence of a saint's life told by a minstrel, recurs in the life of St. Aybertus, for example.[10] Valdesius's ambition to turn from a married, lay existence to one of voluntary asceticism and public preaching, though unusual, was not self-evidently wrong or threatening to the Church.[11] However, this eccentric individual, like many other religious individualists, raised an issue of control and authority. While there is some disagreement between the sources, it seems likely that as late as 1179/80 Valdesius was still under a form of probation: his voluntary poverty was encouraged, but he was permitted to preach only with approval from the local priesthood.[12] This "probationary" state was embodied above all in the so-called "Profession of Faith" subscribed by Valdesius at a council held at Lyons under Archbishop Guichard and the prominent Cistercian Henri de Marcy, newly appointed cardinal-legate, in 1180 or 1181.[13] The document consisted, first, of an affirmation of theological orthodoxy, probably drafted by Henri de Marcy and clearly based on earlier documents. Secondly, it contained a "proposal of a way of life." Valdesius and his "brethren" affirmed that they had "renounced the world" and resolved to give their goods to the poor and become poor themselves. They would keep no money for their own use, and would accept nothing but their immediate supplies of food and clothing from others. They would keep the "evangelical counsels" as rules: that is, follow all the advice found in the Gospels about the apostolic way of life literally. Preaching was neither included nor forbidden in the document; it would have been naive of the presiding clerics to expect Valdesius to abandon it.[14]

In practice, relations between Valdesius and his followers broke down almost at once, soon after the death of Archbishop Guichard (1181 or 1182). The new archbishop of Lyons, John of Canterbury (also called Jean Bellesmains, 1122–1204?) is recorded as having expelled them from Lyons, some time around 1182–3.[15] There is an enticing suggestion that local conditions at Lyons, and differing attitudes on the part of successive archbishops towards pressure for reform, contributed to the breakdown.[16] On November 4, 1184 Pope Lucius III promulgated the decree *Ad Abolendam* at the Council of Verona, which for the first time anathematized "those who falsely call themselves *Humiliati* or *Poor of Lyons*." It condemned all those who claimed authority to preach, or who presumed to preach publicly or privately against the orders or without the permission of pope or bishop. A married ex-layman had laid claim to a religious vocation and a self-authenticating mission which clashed, predictably, with the desire of the local clergy to keep control.

Responding to the Cathar Challenge

One primary aim of Valdesius and his followers was to resist the Cathar heresy in the Languedoc by force of argument and example. Several clauses in the "Profession of faith" subscribed by Valdesius in 1180/1 seem designed specifically to exclude Cathar beliefs. He accepted that John the Baptist was divinely inspired, that Christ had a true human nature, that eating meat was not blameworthy, and that those who were to be resurrected would rise in their own flesh and no other.[17] Catholic theological treatises dating from the early years of the movement prove that the Waldenses were distinguished from the Cathars even by hostile witnesses.[18] In his *Liber Antiheresis*, the exceptionally erudite Waldensian theologian Durand of Osca[19] described how God had chosen "Lord Valdesius" to fulfill the apostolic task of preaching against error, when Christ saw that the prelates "were dedicated to greed, simony, pride, avarice, feasting, . . . lechery, and other disgraceful acts." Durand's primary task was to refute the "heretics", i.e. the Cathars, and his secondary one to resist "others who spoke ill of them," that is, hostile Catholic critics.[20]

Most of the first recension of Durand's work, and nearly all of the later chapters, could have been written by a contemporary Catholic. The Trinity, the divine calling of John the Baptist, the full humanity and full divinity of Christ, were all buttressed by Scriptural references and arguments.[21] Durand upheld the unity of the one Church and the seven traditional sacraments. Rain and storms came from God, not the Devil. There were many ways to holiness, not the one way of the Cathar *perfecti*. Meat-eating was licit, while usury, condoned by the Cathars, was not. The Last Judgment would weigh the merits of each individual soul:

transmigration of dead souls into other bodies was rejected.[22] Durand traced the Cathars' errors to Gnostics, Manicheans, other early heretics and even the ancient Pythagoreans.[23] In the second part he attacked Catharism even more exclusively. There was one God, not two, who created everything, not just the spiritual world. The angels who fell from heaven were irredeemably damned. The Mosaic Law was holy and good, not a creation of the devils. At the general resurrection all would rise in their own flesh.[24]

Durand's logical dexterity and use of Scriptural, patristic, and canonical authorities should have made him a formidable opponent. However, the very sophistication of his work may have limited its impact. Durandus wrote in a complex, *recherché* Latin, its word-order gratuitously tortuous and obscure, its vocabulary bristling with words adapted from the Greek.[25] Durand reconverted to Catholicism following the disputation at Pamiers in autumn 1207, and led a fair proportion of the first Waldensian brethren across with him.[26] As the "Poor Catholics," Durand and his companions devoted themselves, under the indulgent if cautious patronage of Innocent III, to reading, exhorting, teaching, and holding disputations against the heretics for some 40 years after.[27] Durand and his companion Ermengaud of Béziers wrote further anti-Cathar works during this period.[28] Meanwhile, the remaining Waldensian brethren continued to argue against the Cathars in the towns and villages of Languedoc, while their appearance and lifestyle grew closer and closer to that of the Cathar *perfecti*. Several testimonies recorded by the inquisitor Pierre Seila in the Quercy in 1241–2 refer to the Waldenses holding public disputations with the "heretics," as the Cathars were always described.[29] One B. Remon described listening to the Waldenses and Cathars in turn, to choose which were the better.[30] Typical Waldensian teaching, like most of the *Liber Antiheresis*, would have defended beliefs shared by Catholics and Waldenses alike.

Contradicting the Sacral Church

The first Waldenses set themselves to tasks which they felt the official Church neither could nor would perform. They argued that the Catholic Church lacked the authority to forbid them to preach, contrary to their consciences and mission. Systematic disobedience to ecclesiastical authority, a refusal to cease preaching when told to do so, was initially the only "heresy" of the Waldenses. The *Book against the Sect of the Waldenses* by Bernard, the Premonstratensian abbot of Fontcaude, written ca. 1184–91, criticized the Waldenses for disobedience and lack of respect for the hierarchy. It did *not* accuse the Waldenses of disobeying the prelates on the grounds that those prelates had forfeited their office through sin.[31] Durand of Osca, when discussing ordination in the *Liber Antiheresis*, upheld the orders of bishop, priest, deacon, and so forth, though he and his like did not receive them themselves. Prelates were true bishops, insofar as they upheld the faith and the sacraments, and not otherwise. If they commanded anything contrary to the word of God, the Waldenses must disobey. When they commanded things pleasing to God and according to Scripture, however, the Waldenses would obey them, *even though they were bad people.*[32] Despite the hypothetical arguments addressed by Alain of Lille,[33] the Waldenses of the Languedoc were not, in their early decades, "Donatist" heretics. They did not allege that the clergy's sins deprived them of ecclesiastical authority or spiritual power. As late as ca. 1320 the Waldensian Raymond de Sainte-Foy, from La Côte-St.-André in the Isère, refused to admit to "Donatist" heresies. He insisted that the priesthood of the Roman Church, and his own order's ministry, were branches of the same thing, and that each was valid in its own sphere. He avoided anticlerical attacks on the Church, let alone rejection of its sacraments. Twice he insisted that the value of a sacrament did not depend on the moral status of the priest. Though pressed hard by Jacques Fournier, he would only say that the Catholic Church was in error ("but not seriously") over oath-taking and purgatory; it was still the Church.[34]

On the other hand, "Donatist" rejection of the sacral Church surfaced early on in Italy, and became a major point of contention between the Italian Waldenses[35] and the "ultramontanes," those living in present-day France. Differences between the two groups came to a head at a conference held in Bergamo in May 1218. While submitting to the Lombards' positions on many issues, the "ultramontanes" insisted that in the consecration of the Eucharist "the substances are changed by virtue of the words of God alone" and "the prayer of an adulterer or malicious man may ... be heard and received by the Lord." The Lombards replied that "evil ministers will not have their prayers heard by God," and with this issue unresolved the letter reporting the conference ended.[36] Bernardus Primus, a Poor Lombard who reconciled himself to Rome around June 1210, had been accused of teaching "that of men only righteous ones should be obeyed" and that "a bad priest is of no value and his prayers and masses are worthless."[37] Peter of Verona explained the schism between the two groups of Waldenses in that the ultramontanes accepted that there were many good men in the Roman Church and that an evil priest or prelate fulfilled his office, which the Lombards denied.[38] Cathars and Poor Lombards alike, said Moneta of Cremona, taught that bad prelates' prelacy was worthless, and their sacraments void. In contrast, the ultramontanes believed that the Roman Church held the priesthood, and they sought its sacraments.[39]

The Lombards' radical opposition to the spiritual claims of the Church cast the longest shadow across the "Waldensian" movements in the later Middle Ages. Its effects were felt most in Germany.[40] By the mid-thirteenth century, Waldenses had grown to intimidating strength in the Danube valley in the south-eastern corner of the Holy Roman Empire. By ca. 1300 they had spread northwards among the Germanic townspeople in Bohemia and Moravia, and up to the Baltic coast. Already by the 1230s, they were vehemently opposed to the spiritual claims and ministrations of the clergy. Some rejected the real presence in the Eucharist, or denied that evil priests could consecrate it. Others entertained doubts about other sacraments, or offerings for the dead.[41] One report claimed that the heretics in Germany "sent an annual tax to Milan, where the leadership of various heresies and errors was run."[42] The earliest of several surviving lists of their heresies, written in the 1260s by an anonymous churchman in Passau diocese, begins by attributing to the Waldenses a complete rejection of the Roman Church.[43] Though long and multifarious, these lists resolve themselves into a few major themes. First, the Waldenses refused to hold the sacred institutions of the Church, its priesthood, its cults and its holy objects in the required degree of respect, instead denouncing them as worthless.[44] Their quasi-"Donatist" denial of spiritual power to the priesthood flowed from this source (though they show little sign of having actually distinguished between "bad" and "good" priests). So did their rejection of purgatory, as the place where the souls of the departed supposedly required the services of the priesthood. This antisacerdotal sentiment led to virulent and occasionally violent anticlericalism. In Kematen in the Traunkreis, the local heretics killed their parish priest some time before ca. 1266, and his murderers went unpunished.[45] The Passauer Anonymous candidly explained the augmented anticlericalism of the Waldenses as a predictable consequence of the poor pastoral standards of the clergy. Church laws were too numerous, and the clergy were too slapdash in their administration of the sacraments, handling supposedly holy things clumsily and carelessly.[46]

However, even at the height of their influence and numbers, Waldensian heretics did not constitute a comprehensive alternative Church, as the Cathars did in the Languedoc and parts of Italy.[47] They continued to attend church, make offerings, confess their sins to priests, take communion, and hear sermons. They also observed the fasts and feasts of the Church calendar.[48] The "brethren," the celibate, traveling pastors of the movement, did not baptize children, consecrate the Eucharist, or perform any other "priestly" functions. All they did was to preach, lead their followers in prayer, hear confessions, and administer penances. When some important and well-educated German "brethren" defected from the movement to the Catholic Church ca. 1368, their letters to the remaining Waldensian leaders focused sharply on the resulting inconsistencies. If they were the true Church, why did they not administer the sacraments? The Waldenses offered only half a sacrament, their inadequate form of confession; for the rest they sent people to the papal Church, which offered all seven sacraments and much more.[49] Would Christ, who loved the Church, have denied to his faithful people the administration of the sacraments, and entrusted it to strangers and infidels?[50] As late as 1530 Georges Morel, the learned pastor of those Alpine Waldenses who settled in Provence, wrote with unconscious paradox that the sacraments were given to the people "not by ourselves, but by the limbs of Antichrist."[51] While at various times some Waldenses toyed with the idea of consecrating Eucharists, it seems always to have been controversial and divisive among the "brethren" to try to do so.[52] "Donatism" was a recipe for theoretical and practical muddle among all the Waldenses in later medieval Europe. The Waldenses never offered a comprehensive sacramental provision. Neither was it practical to trace back the "rightness" of the ordinations of a given group of priests to see whether they had, in fact, been duly ordained by a righteous bishop. "Donatist" Lombards and their heirs, in Germany and the south-western Alps alike, found their practice and their beliefs at odds.

The Traditions of a "Minority Church"

Were the "Waldenses" one tradition or several? Several striking similarities in their way of life, their teachings, and their religious customs over time and space have suggested that they represent a continuous, interconnected filament of dissent spanning much of Europe through the later middle ages.[53] However, there are discontinuities as well as continuities, and dissimilarities as well as resemblances. One modern Italian scholar, viewing the diverse heresies in fourteenth-century Piedmont, writes of "Waldensianisms" in the plural.[54] Some resemblances can be explained by the clumsiness of inquisitorial writers, who wrote up accounts of Waldenses in one place with literary evidence from another area and epoch.[55] Ecclesiastics generally assumed that heretics called "Waldenses" were *doctrinally* homogeneous; they did not assume that they formed a uniform, interconnected movement. On the contrary, a fourteenth-century German ecclesiastic argued that they could not be the true Church, because "some of their heresiarchs are called Romans, others Piedmontese, others Germans, nor does any of these receive authority or jurisdiction from any other, nor confess himself subject to any other."[56]

The Waldenses themselves were very vague about their origins and interconnections. In 1335 Peroneta, sister of Michael Plancha, related a version of the source of Waldensianism which she had heard from her pastors in the Giaveno district of Piedmont:

> When Christ ascended to heaven he left twelve apostles in the world to preach his faith. Four of these kept his books; but the other eight went to make gardens and chanted from other books, not understanding them. However, the other four chanted from Christ's books and understood them all. Hearing this, the eight were stronger, and drove the four out of the Church. When the four had gone out into the square and chanted there, the eight were stronger and drove them out of the square. Then the four began to go about secretly and by night. The Waldenses added "we keep to the way of the four to whom the books of Christ remained; the priests and clergy follow the way of the other eight who wished to keep to a life of indulgence."[57]

In 1368, during a controversy between German heretic leaders who had defected to the Catholic Church, and others who remained Waldensian, some Italian brethren wrote to the German defectors enclosing the "Book of the Elect," a Latin summary of around 1,000 words which described the supposed origin and history of the Waldensian movement.[58] The "Book of the Elect" manipulated the familiar medieval legend of Constantine and Sylvester. Constantine, suffering from leprosy, called on Pope Sylvester to baptize him, and was cured of his leprosy. As a reward, Constantine gave Sylvester power and authority over the (western) Empire. While Sylvester accepted the proffered wealth (here the Waldensian account differed from the traditional story), a companion or companions[59] of his broke away from the wealthy and decadent Church, and remained in their former state of poverty. Eight hundred years later "Petrus Waldis,"[60] a good rich man, heard the Gospel precepts on poverty, sold his goods and gave to the poor, gathered disciples, and confronted the "heresiarch" (the Pope) at Rome. He was eventually expelled and excommunicated. He traveled throughout Italy and he and his successors gathered many supporters. For 200 years they were able to preach in public. Thereafter persecutions arose which had continued to the present time.[61]

The "Book of the Elect" was full of implausibilities, which the convert German masters pointed out mercilessly in their letters.[62] However, both this and Peroneta's simple legend from Piedmont explained Waldensian heresy as a protest by a minority of the Church's priesthood against the wealth and power acquired by the majority. They harked back (like so many late medieval ecclesiastics) to an apostolic age of simple poverty; unlike reforming churchmen, they believed that they somehow represented the minority survival of that apostolic tradition. The Italians of the 1368 correspondence believed that they had an alternative apostolic succession of priesthood (they thought Valdesius had been a priest) despite not fulfilling priestly ministries.[63] The defended their lack of a clear succession by saying that in persecutions their entire literature had been destroyed; barely the Bible had survived.[64]

The Waldensian pastorates comprised, at various times, highly literate and barely or semiliterate people side by side. Face-to-face teaching and a large amount of rote learning filled the gap created by a lack of books. Catholic critics like Stephan Bodecker (Bishop of Brandenburg 1421–59) claimed that most heretics were illiterate and relied on knowing their Scriptural texts by heart.[65] Another critic pointed out that as they had few or no books of their own to show, they disparaged those written by the Fathers of the Church out of envy.[66] In late fourteenth-century Germany, a young, chaste man whom the seniors thought fit to become a master was sent to accompany one of them on his travels for a year or two. The initiate was presented to the "council" and asked if he wished to become one of their number. He made confession of his sins and avowed a simple creed in seven articles. He was then bound to perpetual chastity, to live only from alms, not to swear falsely if captured, and to go wherever he was sent. He was then "ordained" by the laying-on of hands, though he was only allowed to hear confessions later.[67] In 1530s Provence, prospective *barbes* were taken from herding or husbandry at around the age of 25 or 30 on the encouragement of a sponsor among the pastorate. If approved by an assembly of the *barbes*, they were taught over three to four winters and their moral conduct was scrutinized. They learned to read and write, but also learned large portions of the New Testament by rote: Matthew and John's Gospels, the so-called "canonical epistles," and parts of the Pauline corpus. At the end of the process the *barbes* laid hands on the trainee, admitted him to their ministry, and sent him out to preach and teach with a senior companion, to whom the junior would always defer.[68] Both these accounts explained that the "tours" of the pastors were changed every two or three years to escape detection.

The worship of the Waldensian pastorate consisted, from a relatively early date, of repeated regular daily prayer, largely consisting of the Lord's Prayer in Latin.

The "Burgundian" Waldenses, who settled in the Languedoc ca. 1280–90, knelt down after meals, leaning on a bench, and prayed for long periods, while their hosts did the same. While praying in this posture they said the *Pater Noster* from 10 times up to as many as 80 to 100 times over.[69] The same appears to have been true of the leaders in fourteenth-century Germany and sixteenth-century Provence.[70] At different times various little rituals arose, like the "blessed bread and fish," which the Waldenses in mid-thirteenth-century France consumed ritually on Maundy Thursday. Semi-public in the 1240s, this had become a secret rite for brethren only by the 1300s.[71] By far the most important activity of the Waldensian leaders, from quite early on, was preaching to their lay followers and hearing their confessions. The practice of hearing confessions is attested as early as the 1240s in the Languedoc, and became a characteristic activity of all subsequent Waldensian pastors.[72] In preaching and penance pastors met their followers: collectively in the preaching gathering, in the house or cellar of the lay believer;[73] one-to-one in confession, after appropriate and often cautious introductions.[74] This occasional confession supplemented rather than replaced the annual Lenten confession to a priest. Five lay people from the Uckermark, in Brandenburg, claimed that someone who confessed to one of the heretic masters could not be damned if they should happen to die within that year.[75]

The Waldensian Laity and Popular Catholicism

Cathar preachers, by their peculiar dietary and other abstinences, needed a class of "believers" not yet fully "perfect," from whom they received lodgings, food, and support. Cathar society was intrinsically a two-tier affair.[76] There was no such intrinsic need in the Waldensian movement, except that preachers need someone to preach to. Nevertheless, records of the early inquisitions often carry over the term "perfect one" (*perfectus*), which properly describes a "hereticated" Cathar, to denote a Waldensian traveling preacher, and use the term "believer" (*credens*) to describe their sedentary lay hearer or "friend."[77] Inquisitors attributed this same structure to the Waldenses; their activities ensured that this structure was the only means for the movement to sustain itself. Preachers and confessors were celibate itinerants; "believers" or "friends" were sedentary married lay people, who lived amongst Catholics and within the structures of the official Church, but who received the confessors in their homes, listened to their teachings, and escorted them from place to place.[78]

The believers' behavior combined aspects of clandestinity with aspects of self-conscious and even public distinctiveness. As time went by and inquisitors became bolder, the aggressive behavior found in mid-thirteenth-century Germany was replaced by extreme caution, as one Bohemian heretic reported to Gallus of Neuhaus in the mid-1340s:

> Now I tell you: it is not the way it was before, because now they arrive most
> secretly and leave secretly, such that one person, no matter how close a friend he

is, does not allow another to know about the arrival of the said confessors; hence, when they enter or leave a house, they leave and enter secretly and hidden, allowing no-one to know where they are going or where they come from. Thus I know nothing about their arrival and departure.[79]

The believers met in cellars and secret rooms, often at night, which contributed, quite independently, to both the German and Piedmontese Waldenses acquiring a reputation for practicing secret sexual vices, or indeed of worshiping the Devil, at their assemblies.[80] On the other hand, at Buffa, in Piedmont, in the 1330s, meetings were held at night in the home of Marguerita of Pragelato; the neighbors when they saw them going said, "they are only going to hear *Valdesia.*"[81]

While it might be uncertain just *what* the Waldenses did at their meetings, few of their neighbors can have been in doubt as to who they were. From early on Waldensian followers were conspicuous by their speech and manners. In thirteenth-century Austria, they used private words to describe the Church and the clergy.[82] They would ask each other if any "bent wood" (nonheretics) were present.[83] Peter "Smelczo," consul of Budweis, told Gallus of Neuhaus in 1338 that Heynczlin the hatter, Pezold the painter, and Johlin the tailor had "a peculiar way of living and a special *conversacio* amongst themselves."[84] The most conspicuous oddity about Waldensian speech was its cleanliness. Early Waldenses, under the influence of biblical literalism, rejected the swearing of all oaths whatever.[85] Yet ordinary lay people could barely subsist in society without swearing civil oaths, and did so. The last Waldenses of the south-western Alps took formal oaths freely, not only before inquisitors when under trial, but in ordinary legal contexts and sometimes even between each other.[86] However, Waldenses of every century still made themselves conspicuous by avoiding blasphemies and profanity: they would not utter a casual oath even to emphasize a statement. Strict German-speaking Waldenses would refuse even to say "truly," "indeed" (*treuen, warlich*) to confirm the truth of anything.[87] In the 1430s Johannes Nider claimed that so notorious was this Waldensian avoidance of profanity, that Catholics went to the opposite extreme to compensate: "so that no-one might be marked out as a Waldensian, . . . it came about that blasphemies in words, by the limbs of Christ true or imagined, honourable or dishonourable, are far too commonly found on the lips of many people."[88] In the south-western Alps, heretics, and their literature, habitually quoted the texts, "Do not accustom your mouth to oaths" and "One who swears many oaths is full of iniquity."[89] Some Waldensian followers became, literally, a people apart. The communities of migrants from the south-western Alps which established themselves in vacant lands in Provence, Apulia, and Calabria remained ethnically, linguistically, and socially distinct from the indigenous Catholic population.[90] They sought partners in marriage from within their own community: this endogamy was sufficiently pronounced both to show up in the demographic records and to figure in the reports made to the ecclesiastical authorities by Catholic neighbors. They were regarded, in the Alps at least, as a self-consciously superior set of people who looked down on those around them.[91]

Despite this distinctiveness, the followers of the Waldenses had to find a means of accommodation with the majority religious culture. At all periods in their history they attended church services.[92] An early fourteenth-century Austrian text claimed that when the Waldenses entered church, they said to themselves quietly that all that was sung, said, and done was a lie. The heretics of Budweis, when the host was elevated during Mass, refused to look at the body of Christ but instead stared around the Church.[93] However, mere attendance at the weekly mass did not make one a "good Christian."[94] Lay people were expected to participate in the voluntary as well as the obligatory aspects of the official cult, including the cult of saints and the offerings made for the souls of the dead presumed to be in purgatory. In both Germany and the south-western Alps the *theory* of Waldensian dissent rejected those practices. Nevertheless, in both these regions the pull of the saint-cults and the service of the dead was too strong. In Brandenburg numerous confessed heretics actually prayed to saints, whether from habit or to appear more Catholic.[95] Some half-dozen claimed that they believed in the power of the Virgin Mary to intercede, and prayed to her, but not to the other saints.[96] In the Dauphiné, no less than 13 suspects from Freissinières and L'Argentière prayed to both God *and the Virgin Mary*. In at least a dozen cases *barbes* were reported to have enjoined saying the *Ave Maria* as part of a heretic's penance.[97] Although Jakob Welsaw, of Prenzlau in the Uckermark, said graphically in 1392 that praying for the dead was like putting food in front of a dead horse, several of his Waldensian neighbors admitted to praying for the dead or even buying masses for them.[98]

Towards the Reformation

The history of Waldensianism at the very end of the middle ages is one of successive overlapping influences, which tended to absorb or reshape the movement in the manner of other, later dissenting trends. Austrian and German Waldensianism, which had migrated into the German-speaking communities of Bohemia, was overlaid and more or less obliterated by the Hussite movement from the 1420s onwards. There is no agreement as to what extent, if any, Germanic Waldenses influenced Czech followers of the Taborites or the later Unity of Brethren. That debate is made more confusing by the adoption of the term "Waldensian brethren" to describe the Unity by at least the early sixteenth century.[99] Only the Waldenses of the south-western Alps had really survived this sort of supercession by ca. 1480.

Even among the Alpine Waldenses there appear in the early sixteenth century signs of influence from other heresies. Around a dozen surviving manuscripts, none earlier than the 1520s, contain miscellaneous digests of pastoral, pietistic, and catechetical treatises translated into a form of Franco-Provençal, which probably originated with the Waldensian brotherhoods of the Alps and Provence.[100] These treatises draw extensively on the Catholic tradition, including a version of the *Somme le Roi* composed by Laurent de Bois, or Laurent d'Orléans ca. 1279.[101] Even among the authentically Waldensian poems there are borrowings: The "Ship" (Barca) includes a mordant and depressing lament on the miseries of the human condition, based closely on Innocent III's *On the Miseries of the Human Condition*.[102] Interspersed within these are some selected, mostly short treatises originating from the Hussites, the Taborites, and the Czech Unity of Brethren, which in turn often encapsulated ideas derived from John Wyclif.[103] On the whole, ethical, moralizing advice predominated over everything else in the Waldensian literature. Even Christ himself was depicted as the source of a new, stricter code of laws: Jesus made the law of Moses more demanding and more complete, forbidding adulterous thoughts and looks, forbidding divorce, encouraging virginity, forbidding all swearing and all vengeance, and commanding forgiveness to evil-doers.[104] The extracts from Catholic literature tended to omit references to the consoling and cleansing power of the sacraments and other rituals; the Taborite treatises in some ways reinforced traditional Waldensian skepticism about the power of priestly ritual to wash away sin.[105]

Some of the original Czech treatises were only written in the 1520s, so there can have been little time for this Anglo-Bohemian leaven to penetrate the Waldensian religious temperament before the Reformation supervened. No evidence of its effects can be deduced from the surviving trial register evidence. By the late 1520s some of the Alpine *barbes* were already showing an interest in the nascent reforming ideas. Georges Morel made a tour of reformed centers in Switzerland in the autumn of 1530, which led to the compilation of a long digest in dialect of the reactions of Johannes Oecolampadius and Martin Bucer to Waldensian teachings and customs.[106] From the period 1531–2 there survive somewhat confusing reports of preaching visits by Guillaume Farel and Antoine Saunier, reformers of the French-speaking Pays de Vaud, which challenged the *barbes* over their ritualistic conservatism and adherence to their traditions.[107] The anonymous Propositions of Angrogna of September 1532 contain a programatic attack on traditional Waldensian "good works."[108] The early reformers seem to have envisaged the Waldensian *barbes* somehow converting themselves into a model Protestant Church.[109] In practice, there was neither the time, resources, nor the inclination to make such a change before the next phase of the Franco-Habsburg Italian wars supervened in 1536. In 1545 the Waldensian communities of the Luberon in Provence were savaged by François I of France.[110] Between 1555 and 1560 the Alpine communities were drawn into the orbit of Genevan Protestantism: they were given an entirely new cadre of ministers, the vast majority of whom were imported from outside, and the formal structure of "settled churches." Those which were returned to the rule of Emanuele Filberto of Piedmont-Savoy in 1559 soon had to fight for their survival, while those which remained under the French Dauphin were subsumed in the Huguenot church-in-arms of the Wars of Religion.[111] In Piedmont, the Waldensian name and identity, and many of the actual family surnames of its supporters, would survive; yet nothing else remained of its medieval heritage as a dissenting strain within the Catholic establishment.

Conclusion

Waldensian protest was, initially, a disciplinary rather than a doctrinal matter. Valdesius and his followers could not accept the hierarchy's claim to control preaching of the Gospel. The first Languedocien "Waldenses" did not doubt the status and worth of the Church, or claim like "Donatists" that its sins deprived it of authority. However, the heretical atmosphere in Lombardy soon grafted on to the Waldensian stock and name a vehemently antisacerdotal strain of dissent. This antisacerdotalism managed to subsist, as it were parasitically, on Latin Catholicism: its followers used the Church's services while doubting its grander spiritual claims. Despite its internal contradictions, it remained extraordinarily tenacious throughout the Middle Ages in a range of territories in Germany, Italy, and south-eastern France. It would be rash to infer that Waldensianism was part of a wider nemesis against the spiritual claims of the late medieval Church, or that sacral priesthood must necessarily generate such a reaction against itself. It is striking, though, how successfully a skillfull preacher against heresy could deploy arguments in favor of the "sacral Church." Peter Zwicker, an inquisitor who sought and won converts rather than martyrs, was provoked by Waldensian doubts to formulate some extraordinarily homely defenses of the *opus operatum*, the idea that sacraments purified one irrespective the merits of the priest who administered them. "A rose glows just as much in the hands of an emperor as of a polluted woman." "A pearl is as beautiful in the hands of a king or a peasant." "My servant cleans the stable just as well with a rusty iron fork as with one made of gold and studded with precious stones."[112] Against such sacramentalism, and the allure of the cultic popular religion of the later Middle Ages, most Waldensian protest ultimately foundered.

Notes

1   The so-called "Anonymous of Passau," in A. Patschovsky and K.-V. Selge, eds., *Quellen zur Geschichte der Waldenser*, Texte zur Kirchen- und Theologiegeschichte, 18 (Gütersloh, 1973), p. 73; also in J. Gretser, *Lucae Tudensis Episcopi Scriptores aliquot succedanei contra Sectam Waldensium*, in M. de la Bigne, ed., *Magna Bibliotheca Veterum Patrum* (15 vols., Cologne, 1618–22), xiii, p. 299.

2   For the Council of Verona see A. L. Richter and E. A. Friedberg, eds., *Corpus Juris Canonici* (repr. Graz, 1955), ii, cols. 780–2; G. Gonnet, ed., *Enchiridion fontium valdensium (Recueil critique des sources concernant les Vaudois au moyen âge) du IIIe Concile de Latran au Synode de Chanforan (1179–1532)*, (Torre Pellice, 1958), i, pp. 50–3.

3   *Chronicon universale anonymi Laudunensis*, in *Monumenta Germaniae Historica, Scriptores (MGH SS)*, vol. 26, pp. 447–9; trans. in R. I. Moore, ed., *The Birth of Popular Heresy*, Documents of Medieval History, 1 (London, 1975), pp. 111–13, and W. L. Wakefield and A. P. Evans, eds., *Heresies of the High Middle Ages: Selected Sources Translated and Annotated* (New York and London, 1969), pp. 200–3.

4   See Wakefield and Evans, *Heresies*, p. 707 and refs.

5   Matthew 19:21.

6   For Richard of Poitiers' *Vita Alexandri Papae III* see Gonnet, *Enchiridion*, i,

pp. 164–6; for Étienne de Bourbon, A. Lecoy de la Marche, ed., *Anecdotes historiques, légendes et apologues tirés du recueil inédit d'Étienne de Bourbon dominicain du XIIIe siecle* (Société de l'histoire de France, vol. 185, Paris, 1877), pp. 290–2, and Patschovsky and Selge, *Quellen*, pp. 15–16. The recent discovery of the testament of Stephanus de Ansa has corroborated this account: see A. Patschovsky, "The Literacy of Waldensianism from Valdes to c. 1400," in Peter Biller and Anne Hudson, eds., *Heresy and Literacy, 1000–1530* (Cambridge, 1994), p. 115.

7   Patschovsky, "Literacy of Waldensianism," in Biller and Hudson, *Heresy and Literacy*, pp. 113–17.

8   *MGH SS*, 449; Moore, *Birth of Popular Heresy*, p. 112.

9   K.-V. Selge argued, in "Caractéristiques du premier mouvement vaudois et crises au cours de son expansion," in *Cahiers de Fanjeaux*, 2, "Vaudois languedociens et pauvres catholiques" (1967), pp. 114–20, that preaching, not apostolic poverty, was always the core activity for Valdesius.

10 K.-V. Selge, *Die ersten Waldenser mit Edition des Liber antiheresis des Durandus von Osca*, 2 vols. (De Gruyter, Berlin, 1967), i, pp. 232ff. and ref.; Selge, "Caractéristiques," pp. 118–19.

11 But see Moore, *Birth of Popular Heresy*, p. 111.

12 The Laon Anonymous (above, n. 3) implies that in 1179/80 Valdesius was still within the fold of the Church; Étienne de Bourbon, as e.g. in Patschovsky and Selge, *Quellen*, p. 17, claimed that he and his group were judged schismatics at the Third Lateran Council, though they are not named in its records.

13 For the council see Geoffroy of Auxerre in Gonnet, *Enchiridion*, i, pp. 45–9; for the Profession of faith see A. Dondaine, "Aux origines du valdéisme: Une profession de foi de Valdès," in *Archivum Fratrum Praedicatorum*, 16 (1946), pp. 191–235; C. Thouzellier, *Catharisme et valdéisme en Languedoc* (Paris, 1966), pp. 27–34; also in Gonnet, *Enchiridion*, i, pp. 32–6; for doubts concerning the date of council see Wakefield and Evans, *Heresies*, pp. 204, 709.

14 Selge, *Die ersten Waldenser*, ii, p. 5n.

15 The expulsion from Lyons is inferred from the chronicles listed above, nn. 3 and 6; neither is precise as to date.

16 See M. Rubellin, "Au temps où Valdès n'était pas hérétique: hypothèses sur le rôle de Valdès à Lyon (1170–1183)," in M. Zerner, ed., *Inventer l'hérésie? Discours polémiques et pouvoirs avant l'inquisition* (Collection du Centre d'Études médiévales de Nice, vol. 2, Nice, 1998), pp. 193–217.

17 For the Profession see n. 13 above.

18 For instance, Alain of Lille's *De fide catholica* of ca. 1190–1202 includes separate books on Cathars and Waldenses: J.-P. Migne, *Patrologiae Cursus Completus*, Series Latina, vol. 210, cols. 305ff.; bk. iii on the Waldenses occupies cols. 377–400.

19 The standard edition is that in Selge, *Die ersten Waldenser*, ii, *passim*. The usual rendering of "Osca" as "Huesca" is not certain, therefore the original Latin form has been preserved here.

20 Selge, *Die ersten Waldenser*, ii, pp. 6–9.

21 Ibid., ii, pp. 12–39.

22 Ibid., ii, pp. 39–77.

23 Ibid., ii, pp. 93–9.

24 Ibid., ii, pp. 110–99, 202–47.

25 As remarked by Patschovsky, "Literacy of Waldensianism," in Biller and Hudson, *Heresy and Literacy*, pp. 119 and n. 22.

26 Sources are in Gonnet, *Enchiridion*, i, pp. 126–8, 131–2 and refs.

27 Migne, *Patrologia Latina*, vol. 215, cols. 1510–14, further correspondence concerning the "Poor Catholics" is found ibid., vol. 216, cols. 29–30, 73–7, 256, 274–5, 601–2, 607–9.

28 Wakefield and Evans, *Heresies*, pp. 634–5 and refs.; Migne, *Patrologia Latina*, vol. 204, cols. 1235–72; vol. 178, cols. 1823–46.

29 H. C. Lea, *History of the Inquisition of the Middle Ages*, 3 vols. (London, 1888), ii, pp. 582f.

30 Lea, *Inquisition*, ii, p. 583.

31 Bernard's work is found in Migne, *Patrologia Latina*, vol. 204, cols. 793–840.

32 Selge, *Die ersten Waldenser*, ii, pp. 59–62, esp. 61: quote; cf. ibid., ii, pp. 93–9, esp. 95–6.

33 Alain of Lille, in *De fide catholica* (as above, n. 18) says in bk. ii, sec. 5, that "Perhaps certain heretics might say, that one should

obey good prelates, . . . but not those who do not live the life of the apostles or retain their office." He casts this argument as a possibility, and does not explicitly attribute it to the Waldenses.

34 J. Duvernoy, ed., *Le Registre d'inquisition de Jacques Fournier, évêque de Pamiers (1318–1325)*, 3 vols. (Toulouse, 1965), i, pp. 62f., 68f., 80–5.

35 For origins of the Italians see texts in J. J. Ignaz von Döllinger, ed., *Beiträge zur Sektengeschichte des Mittelaters*, 2 vols. (Munich, 1890), ii (*Dokumente vornehmlich zur Geschichte der Valdesier und Katharer*), pp. 64, 74; Wakefield and Evans, *Heresies*, pp. 269–78 and refs.

36 Patschovsky and Selge, *Quellen*, pp. 20–43, with fullest apparatus; also Gonnet, *Enchiridion*, i, pp. 169–83; Wakefield and Evans, *Heresies*, pp. 278–89.

37 Migne, *Patrologia Latina*, vol. 216, col. 292.

38 Wakefield and Evans, *Heresies*, pp. 274–8.

39 Moneta of Cremona, *Adversus Catharos et Valdenses libri v*, ed. T. A. Ricchinius (Rome, 1743), pp. 433–4; cf. 406.

40 The (obscure) origins of German Waldensianism are related by short entries in chronicles and letters, e.g. Gregory IX's *Vox in Rama* of june 13, 1233, in *MGH Epistolae Saeculi XIII Selectae*, i (Berlin, 1883), no. 537, pp. 432–5; *Chronica Albrici Monachi Trium Fontium*, ed. P. Scheffer-Boichorst, in *MGH Scriptores*, 23 (1874), pp. 931–2.

41 *Gesta Treverorum Continuatio IV*, ed. G. Waitz, in *MGH Scriptores*, 24 (1879), pp. 400–2.

42 *Annales Marbacenses*, ed. R. Wilmans, in *MGH Scriptores*, 17 (1861), 176; later references to links with Lombardy occur in e.g. M. Nickson, "The 'Pseudo-Reinerius' Treatise, the Final Stage of a Thirteenth-Century Work on Heresy from the Diocese of Passau," in *Archives d'Histoire Doctrinale et Litteraire du Moyen-Age*, 34 (1967), pp. 282, 302, and in Gretser, *Lucae Tudensis . . .*, in La Bigne, *Magna Bibliotheca*, vol. xiii, 308.

43 Patschovsky and Selge, *Quellen*, pp. 77–103.

44 Compare Nickson, "'Pseudo-Reinerius' Treatise," 296–303; E. Martene and U. Durand, eds., *Thesaurus Novus Anecdotorum*, V (Paris, 1717), pp. 1777ff.; W. Preger, *Der Tractat des David von Augsburg über die Waldesier* (Munich, Abhandlungen der königlichen bayerischen Akademie der Wissenschaften, historische Klasse, vol. 14, pt. 2, 1879), pp. 206–9; cf. Nickson, "'Pseudo-Reinerius' Treatise," 304ff., 311ff.

45 Ibid., pp. 294, etc.

46 Patschovsky and Selge, *Quellen*, pp. 78–9, 81, 83–4, 86–7; W. Preger, *Beiträge zur Geschichte der Waldesier in Mittelalter* (Munich, 1875), pp. 242–5.

47 See e.g. P. Biller, "The Cathars of Languedoc and Written Materials," in Biller and Hudson, *Heresy and Literacy*, p. 62.

48 Gretser, *Lucae Tudensis . . .*, in La Bigne, *Magna Bibliotheca*, vol. xiii, p. 307.

49 Peter Biller, "Aspects of the Waldenses in the Fourteenth Century Including an Edition of their Correspondence" (Oxford University D.Phil. thesis, 1977), p. 327; cf. p. 305.

50 Biller, "Aspects," pp. 338–9.

51 V. Vinay, *Le Confessioni di fede dei Valdesi riformati, con i documenti del dialogo fra la "prima" e la "seconda" riforma* (Collana della Facoltà valdese di teologia, 12, Turin, 1975), pp. 42–3; Trinity College, Dublin, MS 259, pp. 48–50.

52 Wakefield and Evans, *Heresies*, p. 277; Migne, *Patrologia Latina*, vol. 216, col. 291; see also Martene and Durand, *Thesaurus*, v, cols. 1754–5, for a description of an irregular Eucharist; the "Index errorum" as ed. in Gretser, *Lucae Tudensis . . .*, in La Bigne, *Magna Bibliotheca*, vol. xiii, p. 340, and in Döllinger, *Beiträge*, ii, p. 339; the "Cum dormirent" treatise as ed. in Gretser, *Lucae Tudensis . . .*, in La Bigne, *Magna Bibliotheca*, vol. xiii, p. 313.

53 This is the assumption inherent, for example, in J. Gonnet and A. Molnar, *Les Vaudois au moyen âge* (Turin, 1974).

54 G. G. Merlo, *Valdesi e valdismi medievali: itinerari e proposte di ricerca* (Turin, 1984); G. G. Merlo, *Valdesi e valdismi medievali II: Identità valdesi nella storia e nella storiografia: studi e discussioni* (Turin, 1991).

55 For example, The Toulouse inquisitor Bernard Gui, describing the "Burgundians" of Languedoc, incorporated into his *Pratica*

Inquisitionis Heretice Pravitatis literary evidence relating to the more radical Italian and German Waldenses: see Bernard Gui, *Manuel de l'inquisiteur*, ed. and trans. G. Mollat and G. Drioux (2 vols., Paris, 1964), i, pp. 39–53, 62–75 and nn.

56 Döllinger, *Beiträge*, ii, pp. 304, 344–5.

57 G. G. Merlo, *Eretici e inquisitori nella società piemontese del trecento, [con l'edizione dei processi tenuti a Giaveno dall' inquisitore Alberto de Castellario (1335) e nelle valli di Lanzo dall'inquisitore Tommasso di Casasco (1373)]* (Turin, 1977), pp. 219–20.

58 For a modern edition of the "Book of the Elect" see Biller, "Aspects," pp. 264–70; cf. Döllinger, *Beiträge*, ii, 352–5 (with errors); Cambridge University Library MS. Dd.xv.29 fos. 230ʳ ff. contains a paraphrase in dialect of the "Book of the Elect," illustrated in A. Brenon, "The Waldensian Books," in Biller and Hudson, *Heresy and Literacy*, p. 143.

59 There is a discrepancy here between the "Book of the Elect" and the "Letter of the Italian brethren" which accompanied it: see Biller, "Aspects," pp. 283–5 and compare with pp. 264–5.

60 This was the first occasion that the name "Peter" was attributed to Valdesius.

61 Biller, "Aspects," pp. 264–7.

62 See e.g. Biller, "Aspects," pp. 316–18, 346–51.

63 Ibid., p. 290; cf. ibid., pp. 326, 351.

64 Ibid., p. 289.

65 D. Kurze, ed., *Quellen zur Ketzergeschichte Brandenburgs und Pommerns* (Veröffentlichungen der historischen Kommission zu Berlin, Bd. 45, Quellenwerke Bd. 6, Berlin, 1975), p. 280.

66 Döllinger, *Beiträge*, ii, pp. 304, 345.

67 Kurze, *Quellen*, p. 281, and cf. Döllinger, *Beiträge*, ii, pp. 367–9.

68 Vinay, *Confessioni*, 36–9; Trinity College, Dublin, MS 259, pp. 7–8; cf. G. Audisio, *Le Barbe et l'inquisiteur: Procès du barbe vaudois Pierre Griot par l'inquisiteur Jean de Roma (Apt, 1532)* (Aix-en-Provence, 1979), pp. 105–7, 125–7.

69 This is drawn from the Book of Sentences of the inquisitors of Toulouse, as printed in Philippus van Limborch, *Historia Inquisitionis. Cui Subjungitur Liber sententiarum inquisitionis Tholosanae ab anno Christi MCCCVII ad annum MCCCXXIII*

(Amsterdam, 1692) [in a separately paginated appendix], pp. 353–4, 356–8, 367–9, 375–6, 378.

70 See the "Index errorum" as ed. in Gretser, *Lucae Tudensis . . .*, in La Bigne, *Magna Bibliotheca*, vol. xiii, p. 340, and in Döllinger, *Beiträge*, ii, p. 339; also ibid., ii, p. 307; Audisio, *Barbe*, p. 109; Vinay, *Confessioni*, pp. 38–9.

71 Patschovsky and Selge, *Quellen*, pp. 52, 68–9; Lea, *Inquisition*, ii, pp. 581–2, 584; Thouzellier, *Catharisme et valdéisme*, p. 295 n. 105; Duvernoy, *Registre d'inquisition*, i, pp. 67–8.

72 Patschovsky and Selge, *Quellen*, p. 51; Lea, *Inquisition*, ii, p. 582; Gonnet, *Enchiridion*, i, pp. 155–7.

73 For special places being built to accommodate gatherings in Bohemia, see Alexander Patschovsky, ed., *Quellen zur böhmischen Inquisition im 14. Jahrhundert*, MGH Quellen zur Geistesgeschichte des Mittelalters, vol. ii (Weimar, 1979), pp. 182–3, 197, 232, 234, 238.

74 For a Catholic description of how followers were introduced to confession, see Gretser, *Lucae Tudensis . . .*, in La Bigne, *Magna Bibliotheca*, vol. xiii, pp. 314–15.

75 Kurze, *Quellen*, pp. 200, 237–8, 247–8.

76 See e.g. M. Lambert, *The Cathars* (Oxford, 1998), pp. 141–58.

77 E.g. Martene and Durand, *Thesaurus*, v, col. 1781; Preger, *Tractat des David von Augsburg*, pp. 209–10.

78 For early evidence see Patschovsky and Selge, *Quellen*, pp. 51–3, 56, 59–61, 63–4, 68–9; Lea, *Inquisition*, ii, pp. 579–84.

79 Patschovsky, *Quellen zur böhmischen Inquisition*, p. 211.

80 On German "Luciferans," see Nickson, "'Pseudo-Reinerius' Treatise," 304–5, also Kurze, *Quellen*, pp. 61, 88, 91, 96, 132; D. Kurze, "Zur Ketzergeschichte der mark Brandenburg und Pommerns vornehmlich im 14. Jahrhundert, Luziferaner, Putzkeller und Waldenser," in *Jahrbuch für die Geschichte Mittel- und Ostdeutschlands*, 16/17 (1968), pp. 50–94; on sexual allegations from Piedmont, see G. Amati, "Processus Contra Valdenses in Lombardia Superiori, Anno 1387," in *Archivio Storico Italiano*, series 3 (1865), I, pt. 2, pp. 17–18; and II, pt. 1, pp. 7–14; E. Cameron, *The Reformation of the Heretics: The Waldenses of the*

Alps, 1480–1580 (Oxford, 1984), pp. 108–9, nn. 36–8, 110 n. 42; ibid. 109 n. 40, 110 n. 46.

81 Merlo, *Eretici e inquisitori*, p. 172.

82 Nickson, "'Pseudo-Reinerius' Treatise," pp. 293.

83 Ibid., pp. 293, 307.

84 Patschovsky, *Quellen zur böhmischen Inquisition*, pp. 177–8.

85 See e.g. Martene and Durand, *Thesaurus*, v, cols. 1779, 1784.

86 The reality of oath-taking among the Waldenses of Dauphiné and Provence is demonstrated in both Cameron, *Reformation of the Heretics*, pp. 114–16 and nn. 73–84, and also Audisio, *Luberon*, pp. 206–8.

87 Patschovsky and Selge, *Quellen*, p. 74; Patschovsky, *Quellen zur böhmischen Inquisition*, pp. 216–17, 230; "Modus Examinandi Haereticos," in Gretser, *Lucae Tudensis . . .*, in La Bigne, *Magna Bibliotheca*, vol. xiii, 342; Kurze, *Quellen*, pp. 117, 131, 148, 190, 198.

88 Johannes Nider, *Formicarius* (published as *De Visionibus ac revelationibus . . .*) (Helmstedt, 1692), p. 425 (here the quotation has been somewhat compressed).

89 Ecclesiasticus 23:9, 23:11; Merlo, *Eretici e inquisitori*, pp. 219–20; Cambridge University Library MS. Dd.xv.30, fo. 24^r; Cambridge University Library, MS. Dd.xv.32, fos. 58^v–59^r; Trinity College, Dubin, MS. 260, fo. 206^v.

90 Audisio, *Luberon*, pp. 57–70, 99–147.

91 Ibid., pp. 110–14; for comments see sources cited in Cameron, *Reformation of the Heretics*, pp. 105 nn. 10–11, 124 n. 30, 105 nn. 13–14.

92 Patschovsky and Selge, *Quellen*, p. 74.

93 Krems notes, p. 6; Patschovsky, *Quellen zur böhmischen Inquisition*, pp. 175–6, 181.

94 For the criteria of a "good Christian" at this epoch, see e.g. E. Cameron, *The European Reformation* (Oxford, 1991), p. 12.

95 Kurze, *Quellen*, pp. 82, 85, 169, 173, 177, 195, 199–200.

96 Ibid., pp. 123, 145, 159, 178, 226–7.

97 Sources are cited in Cameron, *Reformation of the Heretics*, p. 72 n. 39; pp. 90–1 nn. 41–4.

98 Kurze, *Quellen*, p. 96, and cf. ibid., pp. 128, 139, 148, 155, 237. The reasons given for such prayers or offerings varied from ambivalence to an attempt at concealment.

99 For instances of this phenomenon see e.g. M. Flacius Illyricus, ed., *Confessio Waldensium* (Basel, 1568); B. Lydius, *Waldensia*, 2 vols. (Rotterdam and Dordrecht, 1616–17): see E. Cameron, "Medieval Heretics as Protestant Martyrs," in D. Wood, ed., *Martyrs and Martyrologies: Papers Read at the 1992 Summer Meeting and the 1993 Winter Meeting of the Ecclesiastical History Society*, Studies in Church History, 30 (Blackwell, Oxford, 1993), pp. 198–200.

100 Cambridge University Library, MS. Dd.xv.29–32, Trinity College, Dublin, MSS. 260/1/2/3/7, Geneva, Bibliothèque Publique et Universitaire, MSS. 206–9a, Dijon, Bibliothèque Publique, MS. 234; bibliographical details of these, and the related manuscript translations of the Bible, are supplied in A. Brenon, "The Waldensian Books," in Biller and Hudson, *Heresy and Literacy*, pp. 137–59. My own researches suggest that Cambridge UL MS. Dd.xv.33 probably has no connection with the rest of the corpus.

101 Cambridge University Library, MS. Dd.xv.30, fos. 125^r–237^v.

102 Cambridge University Library, MS. Dd.xv.30, fos. 111^r–118^v; the adaptation is noted in Gonnet and Molnar, *Vaudois au moyen âge*, p. 331 n. 76.

103 Texts of Hussite origin are found in Cambridge University Library, MSS. Dd.xv.29, 32, Dijon, Bibliothèque Publique, MS. 234, Trinity College, Dublin, MSS. 267, 260, 262, 263, Geneva, Bibliothèque Publique et Universitaire, MS. 208.

104 Cambridge University Library, MS. Dd.xv.30, fos. 101^r–102^v [*Noble Lesson*]; Trinity College, Dublin, MS. 260, fo. 287^r [*Enterrogacions Menors*].

105 Cf. Trinity College, Dublin, MS. 260, fos. 288^r ff. [*Enterrogacions Menors*].

106 Trinity College, Dublin, MS. 259, pp. 1–117.

107 The sources are listed in Cameron, *Reformation of the Heretics*, pp. 140–3 and nn. 52–66.

108 The Propositions of Angrogna are found in Trinity College, Dublin, MS. 259, pp. 118–25, and edited in Vinay, *Confessioni*, pp. 139–43.

109 Cameron, *Reformation of the Heretics*, p. 206.

110 Audisio, *Luberon*, pp. 347–407.

111 Cameron, *Reformation of the Heretics*,
pp. 155–66; Audisio, *Luberon*, pp. 409–
39, concurs in dating the effective incorporation of the Waldenses into the reformed
churches to ca. 1560.

112 Taken from the "Cum dormirent" treatise
as ed. in Gretser, *Lucae Tudensis* . . . , in
La Bigne, *Magna Bibliotheca*, vol. xiii,
p. 316.

Dualism

Gerhard Rottenwöhrer

chapter 18

There are several medieval versions of the "dualism" of ancient Gnosticism. They mostly have in common the belief that there are two powers in the universe, a power of good and a power of evil, eternally at war. Christian orthodoxy takes God to be good and also omnipotent. So although he has the Devil as his enemy, there is no doubt who will win in the end. The war between good and evil is finite. The problem with this hypothesis, and the main reason why the dualist solution repeatedly surfaced, was the fact that it left the problem of evil unexplained. For how can an omnipotent and wholly good God permit evil?

Dualist sects were attracted by a series of associated notions. They took matter to be evil and spirit good. That led them into condemnation of the created world and the human body. They argued, for instance, that the war in the universe was carried on in microcosm inside each human being, where a portion of the spiritual universe was trapped in a portion of the material universe.

This was linked with a common practice of identifying an elect of *perfecti*, special human beings, who had powers to transmute matter into spirit. In many dualist sects there was such a division between ordinary followers and these elect, with the followers serving the elect as their contribution to the winning of the war.

There was also tendency for dualist sects to accrue a mythology of demigods. That made the battles more graphic and exciting, but it greatly cluttered the clean lines of such theology as there was.

The first and most notable of our authors to touch on dualism was Augustine. His "Manichee" period is described in chapter 1. When he became a Christian he had to find another solution to the problem of evil. He took the only logical route, which was to see evil as an absence of good, in essence a "nothing." Thus he was able to "save" both the omnipotence and the goodness of the one God.

The Paulicians

Study of the sources, the historical facts and doctrine, shows that there were two forms of Paulicians: one Armenian and one Byzantine.[1] This heterodoxy, which is strongly Pauline in tendency, emerged around the middle of the seventh century. Its existence can be reliably traced up to the tenth century. It seems to have focused on the warfare between an earthly and a heavenly kingdom, governed by the evil and the good God.

The Armenian sources provide only a single mention of the dualism of the Paulicians in the letter written around 1050 by Grigor Pahlavuni, Magistros to the Katholikos (Patriarch) of the Syrians:

> They say: "We love Paul and will curse Peter; and Moses saw not God but Satan." For they consider Satan the creator of heaven and earth, and also of the entire human race and all creature; . . .[2]

Greek sources see the Paulicians as advocates of a doctrine of dual principles, but it is difficult to be quite sure about the nature and distribution of this dualism.

The only undoubted Paulician sources are extracts from eight letters by one Sergios/Tychikos.[3] He was a *didaskalos* or religious teacher from about 800/1 to 834/5, and in addition a tireless and successful wandering preacher until about 820. Passages from his letters read:

> I went from east to west, from north to south, preaching the Gospel of Christ, and that on my knees.

> Let no one lead you astray in any manner. Since we have received these promises made by God, be of good cheer! We have confidence in your hearts, and we write to you: I am the doorkeeper and the good shepherd and the leader of the body of Christ and the candlestick in the house of God. I am with you always until the end of the world. Even if I am absent in the body, yet I am still close to you in the spirit. For the rest, be joyful, become perfect, and the God of peace will be with you.

> The first sin of the flesh that we had of Adam is a benefit, but the second is more weighty. It is said of that sin: "He that committeth fornication sinneth against his own body' [I Cor. 6:18]. . . . We are the body of Christ. If a man deviates from the traditions of the body of Christ – that is to say, from mine – he sins, for he is hastening towards those who teach other doctrines, and is removing himself from the words that are right.

As P. Lemerle correctly comments, these few extracts do not allow us to draw any conclusions about the entire body of the author's writings. They merely illustrate his main concern for the unity of the congregation of the faithful under him, the true *didaskalos*. Nor is there any account of the typical doctrines themselves.[4]

The Bogomils

According to the sources, the Bogomils too were of two kinds, one Greek and one Slav.[5] Pop Bogomil, possibly their founder but in any case their outstanding leader, is named in one Greek and two Slav sources, but remains a faceless figure. This heterodoxy emerged at the beginning of the tenth century and can be traced, at least in Byzantium, until the fourteenth century.

The Bogomils recognized only *one* God, creator and ruler of the kingdom of heaven, but able to influence the earthly sphere as well. The sources do not allow us to say whether his sons – Satan and Christ – were regarded as divine or created beings. Satan rebelled against his Father, fell, and became creator and "God" of the kingdom of this world. The dualism of the Bogomils, then, was a "moderate" dualism, or rather one based on the idea that salvation is to be seen as central to history.

Euthymios Zigabenos, in his *Panoplia dogmatica* of around 1100, cites statements made in a Bogomil commentary on the Gospel of St. Matthew.[6] It is the only text of this group to have been preserved, if more or less indirectly. I cite here some of the important passages:

> [On Matt. 5:25] They call the Devil the adversary of man, and say in their derangement that one must be well-disposed to him and honour him in prayer . . . so that he will not turn against the disobedient, cast them down and deliver them to God as their judge. On the day of judgement they will be brought to answer for their trickery.[7]

> [on Matt. 7:22ff.] Interpreting these words of the Gospel, they say: these are our holy hierarchs and fathers in God, who were dignified with the gift of prophecy and drove out demons and did many other miracles. For the demons that possessed them did all these miraculous things to confound the ignorant.[8]

> [on Matt. 5:1–16] They claim that Christ intends all bliss for their faithful alone, that is, the Bogomils. They are "the poor in spirit," "they that mourn," "they which do hunger and thirst after righteousness," and so forth. They would be called "the salt of the earth" and "the light of the world," and in addition claim what Christ said of the apostles [as being true of them].[9]

These statements make it difficult to determine exactly what the Bogomils thought of the power of Satan and of demons, of themselves and of the orthodox Church.

The Cathars

Other heterodox believers – individually and as groups – are often said to have been dualists. This tendency is most evident when they are taken to be the same as Cathars.[10] The lion's share of this chapter, for many reasons, will be devoted to the Cathars.[11] They represent what was not only the most important dualistic heterodoxy of the Middle Ages, but also the most widely distributed and complex. Moreover, more of their original writings are extant than in the case of any other heterodoxy. Acknowledging no founder, Catharism seems to have arisen in the eastern Balkans and western Anatolia in the second half of the eleventh century. These eastern Cathars probably split off from the Bogomils and organized their community more strictly on New Testament principles and Church practice, as is suggested not only by statements made in various sources but by comparison with Bogomil doctrines,[12] and the theory is confirmed by the position of the Eastern local churches as mother churches to those in the West. Around 1100, participants in the First Crusade met the group in Constantinople, joined it, and founded a local Latin church side by side with the Greek one. Several of them later returned to northern France, where they also founded a church, sent missionaries to the Rhineland – where the first mentions of them are found around 1145 – and won adherents in southern France and Italy. Between 1130 and 1180 Catharism arose and developed in the West.[13] It can still be traced in the second half of the fourteenth century in northern Italy and Bosnia.[14]

The Cathars were theologically fragmented, a feature evident first in their having two fundamental schools, one accepting the existence of two principles, the other accepting only one. To the first group Satan was an independent God, to the second a fallen angel. This difference may have developed around 1150/60 in the East, to be subsequently introduced into the West and become established there. These are the only two movements found in France. Elsewhere, they appear in the form of three confessions: in the East as the Dragovitsan, Bulgarian, and Slavonic confessions, and in Italy as the Albigensian, Concorezzensian, and Bagnolensian confessions. There is evidence of their presence there around 1180. Besides these fundamental distinctions, there were "Reformations" among the Concorezzensians and Albigensians, as well as many groups or individuals who diverged from the general doctrines of their respective communities.

The *Interrogatio Iohannis*

These "Questions of the Apostle and Evangelist John"[15] to Christ seem to be the only extant text we have from the Eastern Catharist or more accurately Bulgarian church, a fact that emerges from comparison of its statements with those made by the Bogomils, and from the fact that they were current among the Concorezzensians,[16] whose mother church was the Bulgarian confession.

Examination of the theology of this document shows that it is unmistakably based on the doctrine of redemption. It dwells, with differing degrees of detail, on the history of salvation, from its initial position to its nadir and thus to the final outcome. God is always in charge; even Satan, for all the divinity ascribed to him and its influence, cannot change that. He is able to disrupt relations between God and the angels severely, but in the face of God's will to salvation he will fail. God liberates fallen souls from their illusions in order to follow the true God,

Christ, whose teachings, together with baptism, enable mankind to see through the deceptions of Satan and thus escape his clutches. While the rigors of life "lived like the angels" are rewarded by return to the heavenly home, those who cannot be taught or converted, with their master Satan and his angels, must perish miserably in the burning ruins of the kingdom of this world, his creation.

To give an idea of the style and approach of the unknown author from a concrete example, I quote the following mythological narrative of Satan's activities:

And it was in his mind to set his throne above the clouds and be like the Most High [see Isaiah 14:13–14]. When he had ascended into the air, he came to the angel that was above the air and said to him: "Open unto me the gate of the air!" And the angel opened it. Descending, he found the angel that held the waters and said to him, "Open unto me the gate of the waters!" And the angel opened it. Descending lower, he found the whole earth covered with water. As he went around on the earth below, he found two fishes. They lay upon the waters, as it were bound together. The whole earth was thus at the command of the invisible Father. Descending still lower, he found great clouds. They held the waters of the sea. Descending lower yet he found his underworld, hell with its fires. But then he could go no lower, because of the burning fiery flames. So Satan then turned back. He filled himself with evil, and rose up to the angel that was above the air, and the angel that was above the waters, and said to them: "All this is mine. If you will heed me, I will set my throne above the clouds and be like the Most High. I will raise the waters above the firmament and gather the rest of the waters into seas, and then there will be no water above the whole of the earth. And I will reign with you for ever and ever." So spoke he to the angels, and he ascended up to the third heaven. As he went, he led the angels of the invisible Father astray, saying to one: "How much do you owe your lord?" The first angel replied: "A hundred measures of oil." And he said to him: "Take your bill, and sit down quickly, and write fifty!" And to another he said, "And how much do you owe your lord?" And he said: "A hundred measures of wheat." And he said to him: "Take your bill and sit down quickly, and write fourscore!" [Luke 16:5–7] Then he rose up to the other heavens until he reached the fifth, and spoke likewise, tempting the angels of the invisible Father. Then a voice came out of the throne of the Father [Rev. 19:5] saying: "What are you about, wicked one, tempting the angels of the Father? O sinner, do quickly what you have in mind!" Then the Father ordered his angels: "Take away the robes and thrones and crowns from all the angels that pay heed to him." And the angels took away the robes and thrones and crowns from all the angels that paid heed to him.

And I, John, asked the Lord again: "When did Satan fall? Where did he dwell?" In answer he said to me: "My Father commanded, and he was transformed because of his pride. He took the light of his glory from him. His countenance became like red-hot iron. The whole appearance of his face became that of a man. He had seven tails, and these tails drew down one-third of God's angels. He was cast down from the throne of God and those that ruled in heaven. Satan came down from heaven to the firmament, but he and those who were with him could find no rest there. He prayed to the Father and said: "I have sinned. Have patience with me, and I will pay you all" [Matt. 18:26]. Then the Father took pity on him, and gave him peace until the seventh day, that he might do his will.[17]

Here, and in other passages, it is clear that the skeleton of the text consists of biblical quotations or echoes. They are explained and complemented by other ideas, making them sound both traditional and genuine. Their readers were presumably impressed by the idea that profound mysteries were being imparted to them.

The Albigensians

Iohannes of Lugio

Iohannes, from northern Italy, was not only the "Reformer" of the Albigensians, but Elder Son of his bishop, Belesmanza, between about 1230 and 1250, and was designated and ordained the bishop's successor. It is not known whether he ever actually held the office of bishop himself. His doctrines created a split among the Albigensians. The younger members of the sect and a few of the older members followed him, while the reverse was the case with his bishop's more traditional teachings. Of his life, work, and theology we know only what the Dominican monk Raynerius Sacconius, a former Cathar, tells us in his *Summa de catharis et Leonistis seu pauperibus de Lugduno*.[18] He writes:

> and he made a large volume in 10 parts out of them [the errors of the sect]. I have a copy, and have read it, and I extracted from it the errors cited above. One must take great care that the said Iohannes and his colleagues do not venture to communicate their errors to their believers, to prevent those believers from leaving them on account of these new errors, and on account of the schism prevailing among the Albigensian Cathars because of them.[19]

Iohannes undertook to construct a system of Albigensian doctrine and exegesis in his own unique and characteristic manner. He tried, for instance, to reconcile the basic attitudes of the confession with the statements of the Bible as a whole, although always avoiding presenting his ideas as a mirror image. His most striking theological characteristics are as follows: he recognizes the validity of all the books of the Old Testament. Biblical events – including the more unedifying of them – take place only on God's earth, which is populated by real people. He presumably does not recognize the existence of angels. Finally, he probably regards Christ as the true Redeemer. It seems that in spite of his large number of adherents his doctrines as a whole did not succeed in carrying the day. However, they did not vanish without trace, as the next work shows.

The Liber de duobus principiis

This work[20] is the only extant original document of Albigensian theology, and the most extensive Catharist text that we have. Its author is anonymous, but he wrote it at some time between 1230 and 1250 in Lombardy. It is clear that he belonged to the Albigensians from the content, from his opposition to the Concorezzensians, and from the following remark: "as is said by all opponents of those true Christians who are rightly called Albigensians."[21] He is more concerned with Catholic doctrine even than with that of the "enemy brothers." The work is a collection of seven separate pieces, not arranged in any particular order. The author states his intentions in his first words:

> Since many are prevented from recognizing the truth aright, I have called upon the power of the Father, Son and Holy Ghost, and have undertaken to set out our true faith through the witness of Holy Scripture and the most genuine of proofs. It is to be an inspiration to those who admonish understanding persons, and to please my own mind.[22]

He does indeed cite many biblical passages. In the process he employs philosophical principles of cause and effect, possibility and reality, and his view of what is irreconcilable and cannot coexist in either God or man. A good illustration of his approach is the following passage from the first section:

> If anyone were to study closely the reasons adduced above, he would see that the idea of free will – that is to say, the free power, or the ability that, according to their [his opponents'] claim, is given to them [the angels] by God, to do good or evil at their pleasure – does not affect me. For it seems to the wise impossible that anyone should simultaneously, at one and the same time, have two opposites at his disposal. That is to say: that anyone should have power to do good at any time and to do evil at any time. This is yet more true of God. He knows all that is to come, and everything necessarily happens according to his wisdom, for all eternity. Above all, one must wonder how the good angels could hate that which was good and was like them from all eternity, being the cause of their goodness, and turn to the love of evil, which is very much opposed to goodness, and do so for no cause, if – as the ignorant say – there was no cause of evil. This is even more true in that we read, in the book of Jesus the son of Sirach [Ecclesiasticus]: "Every beast loveth his like, and every man loveth his neighbour. All flesh consorteth according to kind, and a man will cleave to his like" [13:15ff.].[23]

In the second section, "The Creation," the author writes:

> I understand "create" or "make" in the Bible in three ways. For I say "create" or "make" when something was added by the true God to the nature of those that were very good, enabling them to be appointed to assist those who are to be saved. Thus the Lord Jesus Christ was ordained bishop by the true God and anointed with the Holy Ghost and with strength, that he might free all oppressed by the devil. Thus the angels and servants of God the Father were created to help those who were to inherit salvation. And sometimes I say "create" or "make" when something is added by that same God to the nature of those who had been evil, to fit them for good works. I also say "create" or "make" when God allows something even to one who is basically evil, or to his servant who could not fulfil his wish if the good Lord did not patiently remove his wickedness for a while, for his own instruction and to the confusion of that worst enemy of his.[24]

This is an illustration of an important principle of dualism, which is the separation of the spiritual and material worlds, with the concomitant anxiety to remove the good God from any contact with matter. The following passage is concerned with general terms:

> Thus one must know that the general terms above – though they are called "general" by grammarians – yet simply cannot by any means be thus understood by theologians, since a general term entirely embraces all essences and activities, and all accidental properties too. It is clear, therefore, that they are called "general" by the wise in so far as they denote the intentions of speakers, and not because all good and evil can be simply and directly subsumed under any kind of general term, more particularly because good and evil can have no part of each other, nor be entirely of each other, for they destroy and resist one another with great and constant opposition.[25]

The last section, on "Persecutions," conveys an impression of the way in which the author sees his task in view of his community's persecution by the mainstream Catholic church:

> When, as I very often do, I read the witness of the Bible, it seems to me that it very frequently confirms the evil once suffered by the prophets, by Christ and by his apostles, who did good works for the salvation of souls and gave forgiveness, and also confirms the way in which followers of Christ have recently been obliged to suffer much harassment, oppression, persecution, suffering, pain and even death through the agency of false Christs and prophets, wicked men and tempters, and shows how they must forgive and pray for those who persecute and slander them by doing them good and not defending themselves. So do true Christians now seem to act; so do they fulfil the Holy Scriptures, for their own good and to their honour. And so do the godless and sinners now seem to act to their own detriment, by always committing sins as their fathers did before them.[26]

On the one hand, the writer imparts the main doctrines of his confession. Again, he is thinking in terms of the centrality to history of salvation. But a distinction must be drawn when we compare him with Iohannes. At first he seems to have much in common both with him and with generally accepted orthodox doctrine, but then, again with Iohannes, he contradicts that doctrine. Finally, he contradicts Iohannes himself on some important points: God and Satan are creators in the real sense, not just causes, and Satan is distinguished from the principle of evil – this is a unique distinction in Catharist doctrine; there are angels, just as there is only an *earthly* kingdom of this world. He therefore relates theologically to Iohannes in one way, but in another stands alone. This can mean only that his work was written under the influence of Iohannes and his followers, but that he was not slavishly dependent on them. Besides his view of the centrality to history of salvation, certain other ideas consistently run through the work: the relationship of cause and effect; his total dismissal of the idea of free will; his view that God is always in charge of events in the shape of the destiny of his angels.

The Latin Ritual

This work on divine service[27] – it describes the delivery of the Lord's Prayer and the rite of *consolamentum*, that is to say the reception of a candidate as a full Cathar – is an interpolation into the last section of the manuscript of the *Liber*. It may have been written in the thirteenth century. The unknown author proves himself a very independent-minded theologian, as the following statements, among others, show:

> It is believed that St. Peter spoke of this Noah in his second epistle: "And [he] spared not the old world, but saved Noah the eighth person, a preacher of righteousness, bringing in the flood upon the world of the ungodly" [2:5]. It is said: from time immemorial the Father gave his people the law and the covenant. All were saved who entered that ark, that is to say, who observed his covenant. And so will all be saved who enter the ark of the New Testament and remain within it.[28]

> "And lead us not into temptation," that is to say, do not allow us to be led into temptation any further. But there is one temptation of the flesh and another of the devil. The temptation of the devil is that which proceeds from the heart at the devil's prompting, as error, wicked thoughts, hatred and so forth. The temptation of the flesh comes because of the nature of humanity, as hunger, thirst, cold, and so forth, and this we cannot avoid. Therefore the apostle writes, in his first Epistle to the Corinthians: "There hath no temptation taken you but such as is common to man: but God is faithful, who will not suffer you to be tempted above that ye are able, but will with the temptation also make a way to escape, that ye may be able to bear it" [10:13].[29]

As a whole, the work displays certain striking characteristics by comparison with orthodox doctrine. The writer seems to have seen God's people not as angels but as earthly human beings, made up of an earthly body and a human soul. God redeemed his people even in Old Testament times through the law and observance of the law. The *consolamentum* is added in the New Testament, when the soul first rises to the kingdom of heaven after the death of the body.

Other theologians

The *Liber* contains the teachings of one Magister Guillelmus, and its writer says he heard them with his own ears, which would mean that Guillelmus must have lived in the first half of the thirteenth century. He holds that God can create nothing equal to or resembling himself, and consequently the angels were not created as perfect beings. They can thus desire the beauty and grandeur of God himself, as the example of Lucifer shows.[30]

Another Albigensian teacher, Lanfrancinus of Vaure/Naure, thought that not all the fallen angels were incarnated; some were cleansed in the dark air, without earthly bodies, and suffered greater pain, but were redeemed more swiftly.[31]

A certain Tetricus, who must have lived in the first half of the thirteenth century, wrote a book divided into several parts and chapters. Characteristic of his views is his belief that God created his people in former days, in the other world and in heavenly glory. God's people are as old as God himself, have existed from eternity, and are of heaven. They are reborn in the kingdom of this world, and Christ comes to redeem them. The fundamental idea of this teacher is of the eternal existence of God's people, and here he is close to the theological "school" of Iohannes of Lugio, but remote from other Albigensians.[32]

Desiderius

This Concorezzensian "Reformer"[33] was the Elder Son and theological opponent of his bishop, Nazarius. He thus caused a schism between his coreligionists, probably around 1190–1200, at the beginning of his activities. He wrote a book in which he studied the views of the mainstream Church, dealing with such subjects as Christology, the Resurrection, and poverty. The book and his teachings are known to us only at second hand.

Desiderius regarded Christ and the Holy Spirit as *divine* beings, while Christ incarnate and the Virgin Mary are truly "human" beings with human souls. They and St. John the Evangelist live in an earthly paradise until the Last Judgment. In some respects these ideas resemble those of Iohannes, both in his book and in his attitude to mainstream theology. Desiderius was not very successful in gaining acceptance for his opinions. Even his own adherents modified at least his views on Christ.

The Cathars of Southern France

The Catharist Tractate

The former Waldensian, Durandus Oscensis, quotes in his *Liber contra manichaeos* 19 fragments of a work usually known as the *Catharist Tractate*.[34] It consisted of two books, and was written in Latin by an anonymous author immediately after 1220. The writer aims to present and explain the true nature of Cathar views and the doctrine of the dualist principle, as opposed to the views of those who disputed them, no doubt the theologians of the mainstream Church. It is also a polemical work. The treatise concerns itself in particular with the activities of God, as creator, and in salvation-based history. The extant fragments consist largely of biblical quotations, and many passages show that these quotations were accompanied by an evaluation and/or presentation of the statements in them. The writer therefore supports his views chiefly by biblical quotation, thus meeting his opponents on common ground.

Some quotations may help to illustrate his approach. The following was probably the beginning of the *Tractate*:

Since some make bitter accusations against us, with reference to God's divine works or creations, we now confess with both word and heart what we think of these matters, so that those who oppose us out of ignorance may see the truth of the matter more clearly.[35]

The fourth passage runs:

If the world is bent on evil, and what it contains is not to be loved, then one must not believe it is of the substance of Christ because it is not of the Father. For if it is not of the Father, then it is not of Christ. For he says: "And all mine are thine, and thine are mine; and I am glorified in them" [John 17:10]. Further: if the kingdom of Christ is not of this world, and Christ does not plead for it, and those of his that are of his substance are not of the world, but the world hates them and they are oppressed in the world, which persecutes and overcomes both them and Christ, then one must not believe that it is his, for it neither recognizes nor knows him.[36]

The eighth section is concerned with the parable of the tares and the wheat (Matt. 13:24–30, 36–43). The writer says, of the Pharisees:

But we believe that one and the same person made them within and without. Some ignorant people loudly claim, however, that this is said of both the flesh and the spirit. They claim the spirit is within but the flesh without. So they say, the Lord has said: he who made the flesh also made the spirit. But one need not concede that Christ spoke of the spirit to the Pharisees, who cleansed neither the spirit within nor the flesh without.[37]

In the thirteenth section, on the concept of "nothing," the writer says:

If all evil spirits and evil men, and all that is visible in this world, are nothing because they are without love, then they were made without God. God therefore did not make them, because "without him was not anything made" [John 1:3]. So also says the apostle: "[if] I have not charity, I am nothing" [1 Cor. 13:2].[38]

In spite of their fragmentary nature, and the possibly arbitrary way in which Durandus made his selection, the extant passages provide a reasonably good impression of the writer's theology. He is in agreement with general Catharist views, particularly with respect to the doctrine of dual principles, and in his statements on God, Satan, Christ, New Testament figures, mankind, creation, heaven/the kingdom of God, the kingdom of Satan, and in part in his ideas of the terms "all" and "nothing."

The Interpretation of the Lord's Prayer

With the *Ecclesiological Tractate* and a fragment, the *Interpretation of the Lord's Prayer* has been preserved in one of the so-called Waldensian manuscripts.[39] The

Interpretation was probably written in Old Provençal by an anonymous author in the thirteenth century, and has not been preserved complete. It is a Catharist work, but its nature cannot be more precisely determined. The text consists largely of biblical quotations with either introductions or evaluations arising sometimes from expressions or phrases derived from the quotations themselves, sometimes from theological ideas that are supposed to substantiate them. Another feature of the text is that quantities are given various names and considered from different points of view. Apart from Satan and certain figures of the Old and New Testaments, this approach is taken first to heaven, then to essences, to figures in the history of salvation, and to quantities mentioned in the Lord's Prayer.

In interpreting the opening of the prayer, the author speaks of Christ and God:

> This is why the Redeemer was first sent: to bring penance, for they were afflicted, and to bring the same spirit that is described by that same Lord, in order to observe the commandments of the Gospel, and to say this prayer. And further we must know that the Lord who is the Father of light and of mercy, of love and affliction and of spirits, is also the Father of all other essences, that is to say of lives and souls and hearts and bodies; . . .[40]

On the third request expressed in the prayer, he writes:

> The earth upon which God's will is to be done is the earth of life, which is set beneath the sky, that is the spirit. Therefore these people, that is to say the assembly of spirits, pray that the merciful Lord will have mercy on their lives too and bless them, so that as the Lord works in the spirit, so he may work in their lives.[41]

As in the *Latin Ritual*, the sixth request in the prayer leads to the subject of temptation:

> And one must know that the two-fold temptation to which God's people are exposed, that is to say the temptation of God and the temptation of the devil, comes of two causes: the temptation of God to life and the temptation of the devil to death.[42]

The work does not simply interpret the prayer but uses it as a literary, conceptual, and theological framework to describe the fate of God's people, and the various levels of language and subject matter on which the writer moves are set in this framework. The division of the kingdom of God into seven heavens may echo the seven requests made in the Lord's Prayer, and the same can inevitably be said of the essences. The names on the second plane of consideration come from the Bible. On another plane the author does not cloak his meaning under covering names, and the figures in the history of salvation appear as such. On the last plane, finally, the writer uses terms from the Lord's Prayer such as Name, Kingdom, Bread, Power, Glory, Ever and Ever, Amen. This method is responsible for the confusing initial impression made by his statements.

The Ecclesiological Tractate

The *Tractate*[43] – written in Old Provençal by an anonymous author – is probably also from the thirteenth century. It consists of eleven sections and quotes a variety of more or less extensive biblical passages. It is concerned mainly with the church of God, its nature, its authority to forgive sins and give baptism in the spirit, its moral rules which forbid murder, unchastity, theft, lying, taking false oath, blasphemy and swearing, and adjure it to keep all God's commandments, and finally the work is concerned with the church's persecution by the Catholic church. Again, we may at least assume that the author was a Cathar. The activities of the mainstream Church are described in the tenth section:

> Mark how all these words of Christ are contrary to the wicked Roman Church. For that Church is not persecuted for the sake of the good or for any justice it has in itself. On the contrary: it persecutes and kills all who will not agree to its sinful deeds. It does not flee from city to city; instead, it rules cities, villages and provinces, and reigns in the grandeur and glory of this world. It is feared by kings, emperors and other folk. Nor is it like a lamb among the wolves, but like a wolf among the lambs and the goats. For it strives to rule heathens, Jews and nations. Above all, it persecutes and kills the holy Church of Christ. That Church endures all patiently, like the sheep that does not defend itself against the wolf.[44]

The Provençal Ritual

The manuscript consists, beside the *Ritual*,[45] mainly of an Old Provençal New Testament, and like that work is probably of the thirteenth century. It offers extensive doctrinal statements. These statements are largely to be found in the confession provided for the performance of the ritual of *apparellamentum* – a rite of penitence – and in the remarks of the officiating priest delivering the Our Father and administering the *consolamentum*. Again, as in the Latin *Ritual* that is the counterpart to this work, the statements are closely linked to biblical passages, which serve to substantiate these acts of worship and to describe them in spiritual terms.

The following passage is from the model address given in connection with the delivery of the Lord's Prayer:

> For the people of God separated itself of old from its Lord. It separated itself from both the counsel and the will of its holy Father, because of deception and subjugation by evil spirits. For these and many other reasons it is made known that the holy Father will have mercy on his people, and will receive it into his peace and harmony through the advent of his son Jesus Christ.[46]

The next is from the passage on the *consolamentum*:

> This holy baptism, through which the Holy Spirit is given, has been preserved in God's Church from the time of the apostles until today. It came from the Good Men to the Good Men until the present time, and so it will do to the end of the world. For you must understand that power was given to the church of God to bind and to release, to forgive sin and to reserve forgiveness of sin.[47]

The statements on doctrine deal with fewer subjects and are briefer than those in the *Latin Ritual*, and do not have a theological character of their own.

Other Writings

Various sources show that Catharist literature was even more extensive. Saluus Burtius, in his *Liber supra Stella*, mentions one such work, entitled *Stella*,[48] and Lucas of Tuy mentions a *Perpendiculum scientiarum* in *De altera uita aduersus albigensim errores*. This work is said to have been dressed up with philosophy and interspersed with biblical passages,[49] and in this respect must have been rather like the *Liber de duobus principiis*. The maxims of Petrus Seilanus, OP, mention "two volumes of Catharist errors."[50] The *Liber sententiarum inquisitionis Tolosanae* speaks of a book "which contained certain errors of the heretics, particularly . . . that the baptism given by the Roman church is worthless."[51] The *Register of Jacques Fournier* makes one mention of a book "in which the sect of the Manichaeans and their doctrine is contained."[52] Another passage runs:

> a book on paper in the vernacular, bound in old parchment . . . in which he said he had found and read arguments and counter-arguments, in the vernacular, on the deeds, words and opinions of the Manichaean heretics and of Catholics. In the said books the deeds, words and views of the Catholics are despised, but approval is given to the deeds, words and views of the Manicheans, although sometimes the opposite is the case.[53]

Study of the three "dualist" heterodoxies of the Middle Ages shows that although they had many points in common, there was great variation in both the dualist model and its literary products, and in the weight given to thinking in terms of salvation-based history. The heterodox did not merely see themselves within the jurisdiction of powers opposing God, but experienced the hold on them exerted by those powers in the form of the mainstream church, political power, and society, both in their communities and as individuals. This lends an existential tone to their thinking and writing and their theology alike. In all, the forms taken by medieval "dualism" show it as a serious attempt to live life on earth appropriately, through an understanding of past events in the history of salvation and of its significance for the present, and in hopes of an ultimate future founded on both.

Notes

1 See N. G. Garsoïan, *The Paulician Heresy: A Study of the Origin and Development of Paulicianism in Armenia and the Eastern Provinces of the Byzantine Empire*, The Hague and Paris: Mouton, 1967; P. Lemerle, "L'histoire des Pauliciens d'Asie Mineure d'après les sources grecques," *Travaux et Mémoires*, vol. V, Paris: de Boccard, 1973, pp. 1–144; G. Rottenwöhrer, *Unde malum?: Herkunft und Gestalt des Bösen nach heterodoxer Lehre von Markion bis zu den Katharern*, (Bad Honnef): Bock & Herchen, 1986 [also Munich, theological dissertation, 1986], pp. 289–303.

2 Tr. K. Ter Mkrttschian, *Die Paulikianer im byzantinischen Kaiserreiche und verwandte ketzerische Erscheinungen in Armenien*, Leipzig: Hinrichs, 1893, p. 148.

3 Quoted by Petros of Sicily, *Historia utilis et refutatio atque euersio inanis et uanae haereseos Manichaeorum qui et Pauliciani dicuntur Bulgariae archiepiscopo nuncupata*, 153, 157, 158, 160, 161, 163, 166, 167, ed. and tr. P. Lemerle et al., "Les sources grecques pour l'histore des Pauliciens d'Asie Mineure: Texte critique et traduction," *Travaux et Mémoires*, vol. IV, Paris: de Boccard, 1970, pp. 57, 59, 59f., 61, 63; Photios, *Narratio de Manichaeis recenter repullulantibus*, 115, 118, 119, 121, 123, ed. and trans. ibid., pp. 161, 163.

4 "Histoire," p. 122; see 116–22.

5 See D. Angelov, *Le Bogomilisme en Bulgarie* [*Bogomilstvo v Bulgarija*, Fr.], tr. L. Pétrova-Boinay, intro. J. Duvernoy, Toulouse, private publication, 1972; D. Obolensky, *The Bogomils: A Study in Balkan Neo-Manichaeism*, Cambridge: University Press, 1948 [repr. Twickenham: Hall, 1972; New York: AMS, 1978]; H.-C. Puech, "Cosmas le Prêtre et le Bogomilisme," ibid. and A. Vaillant, *Le traité contre les Bogomiles de Cosmas le Prêtre, Traduction et étude*, Travaux publiés par l'Institut d'Etudes slaves, vol. XXI, Paris: Imprimerie Nationale, 1945, pp. 129–43; G. Rottenwöhrer, op. cit., pp. 305–54.

6 27.27–52/PG, vol. CXXX, cols. 1321–32, and G. Ficker, *Die Phundagiagiten: Ein Beitrag zur Ketzergeschichte des byzantinischen*

Mittelalters, Leipzig: Barth, 1908, pp. 102–11 (from another manuscript and with different numbering).

7 Op. cit. 27.38/Ed. 1325 = ed. G. Ficker 27.51/106.

8 Op. cit. 27.46/Ed. 1329 = ed. G. Ficker 27.59/108.

9 Op. cit. 27.35/Ed. 1325 = ed. G. Ficker 27.48/105.

10 G. Rottenwöhrer, *Der Katharismus*, vol. III (Bad Honnef): Bock & Herchen, 1990, pp. 131–441.

11 See A. Borst, *Die Katharer*, vol. XII, Stuttgart: Hiersemann, 1953 [repr. New York, 1963; also Göttingen, phil. diss., 1951]; J. Duvernoy, *Le catharisme: Le religion des cathares*, 3rd edn., Toulouse: private publication, 1989 [1st edn. ibid., 1976]; ibid., *Le catharisme: L'histoire des cathares*, 2nd ed., ibid., 1989 [1st edn. ibid., 1979]; M. D. Lambert, *The Cathars*, Malden, Mass.: Blackwell, (1998); G. Rottenwöhrer, *Der Katharismus*, 4 vols. in 8, op cit., 1982–93 [vol. I also Munich, theol. diss., 1982].

12 See G. Rottenwöhrer, op. cit., vol. III, pp. 74–114.

13 See op. cit., pp. 453–581.

14 See op. cit., vol. IV/3, 1993, pp. 63–95.

15 Ed. and trans. E. Bozóky, *Le livre secret des Cathares: Interrogatio Iohannis, Apocryphe d'origine bogomile*, Textes, dossiers, documents, vol. II, Paris: Beauchesne, 1980, pp. 42–87.

16 See G. Rottenwöhrer, op. cit., vol. III, pp. 17–64; vol. IV/1, pp. 313–27.

17 Ibid., 44/46/48/50/52/54 (ed. W).

18 Ed. F. Sanjek, "Raynerius Sacconi OP Summa de Catharis", *Archivum Fratrum Praedicatorum*, 44 (1964), pp. 52–7.

19 Ibid., 57. On Iohannes and his teaching see G. Rottenwöhrer, op. cit., vol. IV/1, pp. 165–210.

20 Ed. and trans. C. Thouzellier, SC, vol. CXCVIII, Paris: Cerf, 1973, pp. 160–455. See G. Rottenwöhrer, op. cit., pp. 211–79.

21 Ibid., 318, 362.

22 Ibid., 160.

23 Ibid., 204/6.

24 Ibid., 240/2.

25 Ibid., 272/4.

26 Ibid., 408/10.

27 Ed. and trans. C. Thouzellier, SC, vol. CCXXXVI, Paris: Cerf, 1977, pp. 194–261. See G. Rottenwöhrer, op. cit., pp, 35–67.

28 Ibid., 242.

29 Ibid., 214.

30 See G. Rottenwöhrer, op. cit., pp. 280–4.

31 See ibid., p. 284.

32 See ibid., pp. 290–4.

33 See ibid., pp. 411–22.

34 Ed. C. Thouzellier, *Une somme anti-cathare, le Liber contra Manicheos de Durand de Huesca, Text inédit publié et annoté, Spicilegium Sacrum Lovaniense*, vol. XXXII, Louvain: Publications universitaires, 1964, p. 87f., 98f., 116f., 147f., 160, 166f., 175, 181f., 197, 208f., 216f., 227, 244f., 255f., 272–4, 287, 298; ibid., *Un traité cathare inédit du début du XIIIe siècle d'après le Liber contra manicheos de Durand de Huesda, Bibliothèque de la Revue d'histoire ecclésiastique*, vol. XXXVII, ibid., 1961, pp. 85–113. See G. Rottenwöhrer, op. cit., vol. IV/2, pp. 17–66.

35 Ibid., 87f.

36 Ibid., 116f.

37 Ibid., 166.

38 Ibid., 217.

39 Ed., T. Venckeleer, "Un recueil cathare: Le manuscrit A. 6. 10. De la 'Collection Vaudoise' de Dublin," *Revue belge de philologie et d'histoire*, 39 (1961), pp. 762–85. See G. Rottenwöhrer, op. cit., vol. IV/3, pp. 105–38.

40 Ibid., 763.

41 Ibid., 772f.

42 Ibid., 779f.

43 Ed. T. Venckeleer, op. cit., 38 (1960), pp. 820–31. See G. Rottenwöhrer, op. cit., pp. 139–51.

44 Ibid., 828.

45 Ed. and trans. L. Clédat, *Le Nouveau Testament traduit au XIIIe siècle en langue provençale suivi d'un rituel cathare, Reproduction photolithographique du manuscrit de Lyon publiée avec une nouvelle édition du rituel*, Bibliothèque de la Faculté des Lettres de Lyon, vol. IV, Paris: Leroux, 1887 [repr. Geneva: Slatkine, 1968], IX–XXVI. See G. Rottenwöhrer, op. cit., pp. 156–66.

46 Ibid., XIV.

47 Ibid., XVII.

48 Ed. Ilarino da Milano, "Il 'Liber Supra Stella' del piacentino Salvo Burci contro i Catari e altre correnti ereticali," *Aevum*, 19 (1945), p. 308.

49 *Maxima bibliotheca veterum patrum*, vol. XXV, Lyon, 1677, col. 241A.

50 Doat, vol. XXI, fol. 229^r.

51 Ed. P. von Limborch, *Historia Inquisitionis, cui subjungitur Liber Sententiarum Inquisitionis tholosanae ab anno Christi MCCCVII ad annum MCCCXXIII*, Amsterdam: Wersteen, 1692, p. 152.

52 Ed. J. Duvernoy, *Le Registre d'Inquisition de Jacques Fournier, évèque de Pamiers (1318–1325), Bibliothèque Méridionale*, 2. R., vol. XLI/2, Toulouse: private publication, 1965, p. 204; see pp. 207, 484, 504; vol. XLI/3, op. cit., p. 370.

53 Op. cit., vol. XLI/2, p. 196f.

Ecclesiology and Politics

Matthew S. Kempshall

The period 1250–1350 is sometimes treated as a watershed in the history of political thought, the moment at which a hierocratic conception of human society began to dissolve under the influence of an incipient process of laicization or even secularization. The catalyst for this transformation, it is argued, was the rediscovery of Aristotle's *Ethics* and *Politics*, texts which effectively undermined the hitherto secure foundations of medieval political theology, namely a neoplatonic or pseudo-Dionysian model of the hierarchy of human society and an Augustinian justification of the origins of political authority as a providential remedy for sin. Once Aristotle could be used to legitimize political society through its origins in nature rather than within a framework of salvation, the die was cast. Aristotle's observation that "humankind is by nature a political animal" (*Politics* I.2: 3) thereby liberated the individual from a repressive medieval theocracy, transforming the subject into the citizen and ushering in a so-called "secular" theory of the state.

Interpreting scholastic political ideas as a mighty clash of systems, neoplatonism versus Aristotelianism, Aristotelianism versus Augustinianism, has all the advantages of providing a solution which is neat and simple and wrong. Aristotle's *Politics*, pseudo-Dionysius's *De Caelestis Hierarchia*, and Augustine's *City of God* were sources shared by, authorities common to, all scholastic theologians. While interpretations and emphases could certainly differ from one theologian to another, and differ significantly, this is not the same as having an exclusively Aristotelian political philosophy pitted against an exclusively Augustinian political theology as if these were separate systems to which individual theologians subscribed as a complete package. Likewise, just because one theologian may have favored a broadly "Augustinian" or "Aristotelian" school of thinking in his metaphysics or epistemology does not necessarily mean that the same alignment also governed his political ideas. One reason for this was the way in which aspects of Aristotle's moral and political philosophy could, in fact, be readily harmonized with Augustine. There are thus several occasions on which terms drawn from Aristotle simply served to formalize concepts which already existed, sometimes with a change in vocabulary, sometimes not. For Aristotle to emphasize the centrality of friendship to the human community in Book VIII of the *Ethics*, for example, or to analyze the critical differences between selfish love and self-love in Book IX, or even to beg the question of the relative superiority of a life of contemplation and a life of action in Book X, all had clear resonances with Augustine's account of the operation of Christian *caritas* in Book XIX of the *City of God*.

This is not to deny either the reality or the significance of the questions which originally suggested a schematized view of medieval hierocracy. Given that humans live in society, in what ways should life in the political community relate to their ultimate goal of eternal beatitude? Does it lead them to this end directly or does it merely assist? Is the political community the means by which individuals are brought to their higher goal of eternal beatitude, a community in which law, for example, makes people morally and spiritually good? Or is the political community merely a barrier to the worst consequences of sinful human conduct, of the effects of unrestrained self-interest and self-love, a society in which law simply prevents people from tearing each other's throats out? These are questions to which one reading of a neoplatonic or pseudo-Dionysian hierarchy appears to give a ready answer. It does so on the basis of two fundamental principles – first, the emanation of multiplicity from unity and the reversion of the resulting multitude back towards the One (*omnis multitudo ab uno derivatur et ad unum reducitur*); second, the ascent of individual elements within this multitude back towards union with the One by virtue of being ranked or ordered such that those individuals which occupy a superior grade direct or mediate those immediately below them towards their ultimate end (*infima per media reducuntur*). In theory, the consequences for human society are straightforward. The universe is to be understood as a single, articulated hierarchy of goodness in which superior ranks act on inferior ranks in order to bring them to their ultimate goal such that, without this subjection to, and participation in, a superior community, an individual part of creation will never attain its completeness or perfection. Society must therefore also be understood as hierarchy in which the spiritual power of the Church is superior to the temporal power of kings in such a way that it discharges its responsibility for directing humans towards their ultimate goal of eternal beatitude with whatever means will secure their salvation.

One difficulty with this interpretation of a pseudo-Dionysian hierarchy is its assumption that a metaphysical principle of order in the universe will neatly translate into a political principle of government in human society. Such a transfer *could* happen, but the equation was far from being automatic. Indeed, the potential *disj*unction between metaphysics and politics could mean that the mediation of stratified orders within a terrestrial hierarchy was not so strict as to preclude the possibility either that an intermediate rank could be bypassed (*praetermissio ordinis*) or that an inferior rank could influence and act upon its superior (Luscombe 1988). Likewise, the introduction into a hierarchical economy of salvation of an opposition between an analysis of society which locates its origins in sin and one which traces them to nature is not as stark as it might appear. For Augustine, political authority was providentially instituted by God in order to counteract the worst effects of the Fall. It acted, in other words, as a remedy for sin (*remedium* *peccati*). The function of the temporal power could therefore be understood to be to secure a degree of peace and concord, to serve the spiritual power by imposing a bridle on humanity so that individuals might be rendered more manageable by the Church in its provision of the means of salvation. Augustine, however, still thought humankind sociable and gregarious by nature. Inequality may have originated with the Fall, and political authority may then have been instituted to provide a remedy for the worst effects of this sin, but these Christian concepts were not necessarily incommensurable with Aristotle's understanding of aristocracy as government of the whole community by the virtuous few and of law as rule by reason unaffected by passion.

Understanding the operation of hierarchy in human society and understanding the connection between human nature and political organization within that society are clearly central to an analysis of how scholastic theologians approached the role of the spiritual authority of the Church in this world and its relation to the authority exercised by temporal rulers. Viewed from this perspective, however, the key questions arose, not over the consequences of Aristotle's argument that political society originates in nature, but over the implications of his argument that the purpose of life in the political community is not just to live but to live well, not just to attain material self-sufficiency and physical security but also to attain perfection in the activity of virtue. For scholastic theologians to accept such a principle demanded a discussion of how Aristotle's happiness, the life of moral and intellectual virtue, should be connected to Christian happiness, the life of faith, hope, and charity. For the scholastic theologian, in other words, the issue was not so much the legitimacy of political society in nature as the relationship between moral virtue and theological virtue, between temporal happiness and eternal happiness. The different ways in which individual theologians approached *this* question and, above all, the reasons *why* they took the approaches they did, might therefore give a better insight into the impact of Aristotle's *Ethics* and *Politics* than looking for "schools" of thought or "traditions" of thinking which assume that Aristotelian and Augustinian were necessarily mutually exclusive terms.

Understanding the political thought of scholastic theologians can start with a deceptively simple question. What was it? Would scholastic theologians themselves have recognized such a theoretical categorization for what they were doing when discussing particular moral and institutional questions in a manner which might now be classified as ecclesiology or political philosophy but which at the time was some way from sharing modern assumptions of such systematic rigor? The fact that the political thought of even so systematic a thinker as Thomas Aquinas cannot be found within a single text but has to be fashioned into a corpus of "Thomist" doctrine from a wide range of disparate and variegated sources provides one indicator that, in general, scholastic political *theory* may be more a matter of scholastic political *ideas* which were in turn dependent upon specific historical and intellectual contexts for their formulation and significance. Politics and ecclesiology were not thrashed out by scholastic theologians in a vacuum of theoretical or textual abstraction. Appreciating the particular contexts within which their political ideas were formed, the specific purposes for which they were forged, the individual events to which they provided both a response and a commentary, may provide a more helpful starting-point than assuming that these political ideas were the necessary concomitants of a systematic body of doctrine.

This is not to say that scholastic theologians were themselves either unaware of or uninterested in classifying this particular area of their knowledge. In the twelfth century, Hugh of St. Victor had divided "practical philosophy" into three kinds – the individual, the family, and the public or civil (*Didascalion* III.1: 83). Dominic Gundissalvus, meanwhile, had drawn on the Arab philosopher Alfarabi in order to identify the substance of this "civil science" as the regulation of relations between rulers and their subjects. Thus, by the early thirteenth century, the schools of Paris were teaching this tripartite division of moral science by means of three key texts. Individual *mores* were approached via Aristotle's *Nicomachean Ethics,* household *mores* through Cicero's *De Officiis,* while political *mores* were analyzed through "decrees and laws," that is, through the canon law contained in Gratian's *Decretum* and the Roman law contained in Justinian's *Digest.* The predominantly legal basis which this classification gave to discussion of specifically public matters (*res publicae*) accordingly gave a significantly legal characteristic to scholastic political thinking. Familiarity with canon and Roman law provided a vital underpinning, for example, to Aquinas's theoretical synthesis of the relationship between eternal, divine, natural, and positive law (*Summa Theologiae* IaIIae 90–5) but also to his more practical defense of the position of his own Dominican Order within the Church as a whole. Such legal knowledge continued to be exhibited by subsequent generations of theologians, by secular masters such as Henry of Ghent and Godfrey of Fontaines, by Augustinians such as Giles of Rome and James of Viterbo, and by Dominicans such as John of Paris.

By the second half of the thirteenth century, however, scholastic theologians were beginning to move beyond the confines of basing their ecclesiological and political arguments merely on decrees and laws. They took their cue from Albertus Magnus, who, in the late 1260s, was swift to voice his dissatisfaction with the intellectual limitations of exclusively juristic study. For Albertus, the empirical citation of individual laws would not, and could not, be raised to the status of a science without a rigorous examination of the abstract principles on which these laws rested. Without an understanding of the goal of life in the political community, or of the different types of constitution by which that community could be governed, knowledge of political science was impossible. In order to do that, however, a theologian would require, not Gratian and Justinian, but Aristotle (Kempshall 1999: 135). Indeed, it was Aristotle who suggested to Albertus that the unscientific citation of law was no better than sophistry (*Ethics* X.9: 274–5). It was this recognition which effectively opened up the study of ecclesiology and politics as an extension of moral theology and philosophy.

The translation of Aristotle's *Politics* provided scholastic theologians with a concrete demonstration of how such questions as the goal of life in the human community, the distribution of authority within it, and the role of law could all be made subjects of scientific inquiry (Dunbabin 1965, 1982). In one sense, therefore, it was when the *Politics* was added to the canon of Aristotle's natural philosophy in the early 1260s that scholastic theologians were able to give real analytical substance to *civilis scientia*. By the same token, however, ever since the complete translation of the *Ethics* in 1246–7, scholastic theologians already had a theoretical definition of the intellectual and moral value of engaging in such an undertaking. According to Book I of the *Ethics*, moral conduct, the subject-matter of politics, qualifies as a branch of knowledge but does not possess the determinacy of, say, geometry or mathematics because it is not the subject of a science which demonstrates necessary and universally applicable truths from first principles. Instead, it comprises what is true in most cases and for the most part. As a moral science, moreover, politics, like ethics, has the goal not just of teaching people knowledge of what is good but also of ensuring that people actually put this knowledge into practice by leading virtuous lives and performing virtuous actions (*Ethics* I.3: 2–3). By raising, first, the issue of the determinate nature of ethics and politics and, second, the issue of willing rather than just knowing moral goodness, Aristotle presented scholastic theologians with both a theoretical and a practical agenda. What was the nature of the truth which they were investigating and how could it be put into practice? The significance of the connection between the two halves of this question was driven home in ca. 1269 by the revised translation of a third Aristotelian text, the *Rhetoric*.

Often treated as if it were a sleeping partner in the reception and interpretation of Aristotle's ethical and political thinking, the *Rhetoric* is a work whose impact should not be underestimated. In part, this is because of the digest which it provided of material duplicated from the *Ethics* and the *Politics*, often in a more accessible form. Still more important, however, was the significance of the contention with which Aristotle had opened the work, namely that rhetoric is a counterpart of dialectic, an offshoot of logic, ethics, and politics (*Rhetoric* I.1.1: 28–9, I.2.7: 39). By subordinating rhetoric to dialectic and then connecting it to ethics and to politics, Aristotle invited an examination of the precise relationship which should exist within the study of moral and political matters between the scientific nature of such inquiry and the way in which its results should be communicated. Dialectic was defined as the use of logic to demonstrate the truth of a proposition by appealing to human reason, to the deliberative faculty of human beings. Rhetoric, on the other hand, was defined as the use of linguistic techniques to make human beings act by persuading their emotions and thereby moving their wills. This naturally raised the question of just how these very different disciplines should be combined in the study of ethics and politics. Scholastic theologians were swift to respond. Giles of Rome, for example, thought the issue sufficiently important to devote considerable time and space to it in the early 1270s in the opening section of his commentary on the *Rhetoric* (Robert 1957). He thus took care to provide a detailed refutation of the suggestion that Cicero might be a better guide than Aristotle in this respect in that Cicero had preferred to classify politics with rhetoric rather than with dialectic (Bruni 1932). For Giles, as for Aristotle, rhetoric was certainly an instrument to be used in politics, but it should always be directed by the rigors of logic. With this qualification, however, Giles was content to accept that rhetoric provided the means by which the broad truths of ethics and politics could be put into practice. Dialectic would discover general political truths and rhetoric would make them persuasive.

The combination of dialectic with rhetoric raises significant methodological questions for the interpretation of scholastic political ideas. First, there is the pre-supposition that ethics and politics do not have the determinacy or universality of a science such as geometry. Having accepted that ethics and politics dealt with what was true only "for the most part," scholastic theologians were accordingly careful to deploy in their discussion of political issues one of the most versatile of their conceptual distinctions – a conclusion may be true in an absolute or un-qualified sense (*per se, simpliciter*), but the opposite may be the case in certain circumstances or within certain terms of reference (*per accidens, secundum quid*). Thus, Giles of Rome, for example, was prepared to use Book III of the *Politics* to argue that, in an absolute sense, it is better to be ruled by good laws than by a good man while at the same time insisting that, in certain circumstances, it is better to be ruled by a good man. Likewise, James of Viterbo and Peter of Auvergne used the same book to argue that election may provide a better means of securing a virtuous ruler than hereditary succession in an absolute sense, but that, within certain terms of reference and in certain circumstances, the reverse could be true (McGrade et al. 2000).

A recognition of the potential contingency of political truths, moreover, an acceptance that different principles might be applicable at different times and in different places, was accompanied by an awareness of the different rhetorical forms through which these truths could be conveyed and put into practice. This presupposed an understanding of the different demands which were appropriate to different genres of writing. In an academic commentary upon an Aristotelian text, for example, Giles of Rome was insistent that his primary goal was to elucidate the words and intention of Aristotle himself and not to put forward his own opinion on the subject. A public treatise of exhortation or polemic was altogether different. For Giles, as for Aristotle, it was essential not just to know political and ethical truths but to put them into practice and, in order to be put into practice, they had not only to convince the intellect but be made persuasive to the will. Using rhetoric in the service of moral and political action, however, was not the same as using dialectic to demonstrate the principles of political theory. It could call for a much greater degree of flexibility as the theologian tailored particular arguments to suit his audience. A striking feature of the Capetian royal court at Paris under Louis IX, for example, had been the contribution of members of the mendicant orders to a revival of interest in the "mirror for princes" genre of advice literature. It should come as no surprise, therefore, to find that during (or immediately after) the completion of his academic commen-tary on Aristotle's *Rhetoric*, Giles wrote a treatise of his own on the government of rulers, *De Regimine Principum*, addressed to the king of France. Nor is it necessarily surprising that, some twenty years later, Giles saw fit to compose another public treatise, *De Ecclesiastica Potestate*, this time addressed to the pope and defending papal authority from the challenge of exactly the same king of France for whom Giles had earlier written *De Regimine Principum*. The juxtaposition could not be more striking. However, there is no necessary inconsistency in the political principles which underpin the two works. The differences in their form and content stem from the fact that they were written for different purposes and for different audiences.

Aristotle's *Ethics*, *Politics*, and *Rhetoric* enabled scholastic theologians to transcend the limitations of basing political ideas on canon and Roman law in two fundamental ways. Studying each of these three texts demonstrated that relations between human beings within society could be made the subject of scientific inquiry. Studying the connection *between* these three texts, however, also demonstrated that this process should produce practical and not just intellectual results. The combination of dialectic and rhetoric with which scholastic theologians thereby became familiar strongly suggests that the assumptions of abstraction and systematization which often accompany the phrase "scholastic political thought" need to be qualified by a recognition that it could also serve more specific, even pragmatic, concerns. What is critical to the development of scholastic political ideas, in other words, is not just the discovery of, and commentary upon, these works of Aristotle but the practical historical contexts by which this theoretical analysis was conditioned and to which it was composed as a response. Rather than look at scholastic political ideas simply as the result of the discovery of texts, it is thus more helpful to trace why they read these texts in the way in which they did, that is, how they applied the ideas contained in these texts in the light of contemporary historical events.

An interest in the practical purpose which should accompany ethical and political inquiry did not, of course, originate only with the rediscovery of Aristotle's *Ethics*, *Politics*, and *Rhetoric*. These texts may have provided an intellectual rationale for such an intention but, as with the continued use of canon and Roman law, scholastic political thinking was thereby reinforcing an existing link with the moral and pastoral theology of the late twelfth- and early thirteenth-century schools. Associated in particular with Peter the Chanter, this movement had provided the intellectual motor behind the Fourth Lateran Council of 1215 and had inspired its attempts to create a literate and learned clergy as the instruments of an efficacious system of pastoral care. Preaching and confession were the touchstones of this reform and their subsequent impact on thirteenth–century moral theology was marked, not least by contributing to Robert Grosseteste's motivation for having the complete text of Aristotle's *Ethics* translated in 1246–7. Continuity with the same pastoral concern can subsequently be traced, for example, in Thomas Aquinas. Not only did he seek to provide a broad treatment of moral and political issues in a teaching manual such as the *Summa Theologiae*, but he also responded to needs well beyond the university in such texts as his letter to the Duchess of Brabant (*On the Government of the Jews*). These applied societal concerns are evident, above all, in the form of academic disputation which soon came to flourish in the faculty of theology, namely the quodlibet.

Delivered during Lent and Advent, the *quaestio quodlibetalis* constituted a regent master's discussion of a question asked about any subject whatsover (*de quolibet*). As such, the subject chosen for debate was often a difficult and contentious issue of pressing contemporary concern. This was accordingly the format in which academic controversies over more speculative issues in theology were conducted, such as whether the intellect was superior to the will in cognition, or whether there was a unicity of substantial form in creatures. However, quodlibets also provide an index of those issues of more practical and political import about which theologians were sufficiently concerned to want an answer. Indeed, the wider pastoral matters which these quodlibetic questions reveal serve to reinforce the view that scholastic political ideas developed as a result of, a reaction to, and a commentary upon, specific political and ecclesiastical events on which individual theologians were called upon to give their considered opinion.

The first important issue which elicited sustained reflection in this manner was firmly ecclesiological and centered on the conflict between secular and mendicant masters within the university of Paris. Originally a controversy over academic opportunity and preferment, this rapidly turned into a much broader debate over the position of religious orders within the Church as a whole. The dispute flared up in the 1250s, and again in the early 1270s, but it was given its sharpest political edge in 1281 when Pope Martin IV issued *Ad fructus uberes*. By removing an individual's obligation to reiterate confession to a parish priest which had already been made to a mendicant friar, this bull seemed to grant a dispensation from *Omnis utriusque sexus*, that is, from the terms of canon XXI of the Fourth Lateran Council (*Decrees* I: 245). In thereby raising the issue of the relative authority of a papal bull and a conciliar decree, *Ad fructus uberes* succeeded in precipitating an extended debate over the theory and practice of dispensation or equity. If dispensation could be made from a law only on grounds of necessity or of some benefit to the whole Christian community, who was to judge when such preconditions had been met? Was it the pope or was it the Church as a whole? If it was evident that these stipulations had not been fulfilled but a pope neverthe-less went ahead with his decree, did this provide sufficient justification for bishops and clergy to disobey such a statute on the grounds that the pope's command would thereby constitute an act, not of dispensation, but of dissipation?

A second issue which came to bear increasingly heavily on the secular clergy was the burden of taxation to which the Church was being exposed as successive popes made grants of ecclesiastical tenths to temporal rulers to prosecute cam-paigns of purported utility to the Church. This action raised the same fundamen-tal considerations of exactly who should judge the presence, or absence, of necessity and benefit to the Christian community. It also hinged upon a similar assessment of the relative weight which should be given to obeying a pope and obeying a conciliar decree. According to canon XLVI of the Fourth Lateran Council, eccle-siastical property could be given voluntarily to temporal rulers as an act of love, as a "caritative subsidy," only on grounds of necessity or evident benefit to the community (*Decrees* I: 255). It had not specified, however, what the nature of this necessity should be, nor whose consent was required before such benefit could be judged self-evident. Was it the consent of the temporal ruler, of the pope, or of the Church as a whole?

Taken together, opposition to *Ad fructus uberes* and hostility to both the burden and the misappropriation of clerical tenths formed a potent stimulus to ecclesiological debate in the 1280s and 1290s as each issue had its own sources in particular texts of canon and Roman law. However, at a time of increasingly thorough familiarity with the *Ethics* and the *Politics*, the underlying principles provided fertile ground for political and not just ecclesiological speculation. It was axiomatic to Aristotle, for example, that good forms of government could be distinguished from perverse forms by assessing whether they secured the common good of the whole community rather than the private good of those in authority. The quodlibets of leading secular masters such as Henry of Ghent and Godfrey of Fontaines reveal just how far this argument could be developed. As a litmus test for the legitimacy of all government, temporal as well as ecclesiastical, the common good became the measure by which the exercise of authority should be judged. For a ruler to secure his private interest rather than the common good identified that ruler as a tyrant. Failure to secure the common good was therefore to be corrected, ideally by counsel but, if necessary, by disobedience, resistance, and ultimately deposition (McGrade et al. 2000). This applied to both pope and king.

If the secular–mendicant controversy and the burden of papal tenths invited an examination of the general principles which underpinned the exercise of both spiritual and temporal power, then they also prompted an analysis of the particular issue of property. In the case of the former, this took the form of examining the mendicant vow of poverty and how it could be reconciled with a teaching role within the university. In the case of the latter, it resulted in an assessment of whether the power of the pope over the goods of the clergy was more or less extensive than the power of a temporal ruler over those of his subjects. Was the pope a lord (*dominus*), or was he a steward (*procurator*), that is, an official charged with administering goods which belonged to the whole church and for the benefit of the entire Christian community? In both cases, the ensuing debate on the nature of rights over property drew on a conceptual terminology which had been developing within the Franciscan Order itself in the course of the thirteenth century.

Definitions of property had become the cause of increasingly bitter divisions amongst Franciscans from the moment Francis of Assisi's original commitment to absolute poverty had begun to be modified by his (largely clerical) successors. As a result, Franciscan theologians in Paris, most notably Bonaventure, had developed a series of increasingly sophisticated conceptual distinctions whereby the use (*usus*) of material goods could be separated from their ownership (*proprietas*). With the consequent establishment of principles of legal right (*ius*), Franciscan theologians developed a language which could be applied to the exercise of temporal as well as ecclesiastical authority and thereby came to have a much broader impact on the history of political thought (Tierney 1997). By the second half of the thirteenth century, moreover, internecine strife over the poverty of

Christ had become enmeshed, for some radical Franciscans, in much broader apocalyptic expectations of a new age of the Holy Spirit in which the entire ecclesiastical order would be superceded. For these radical or "spiritual" Franciscans, the resulting combination of poverty and apocalypticism created an ecclesiological agenda even more potent than opposition to papal dispensation and taxation. As the vehicle for a critique of a Roman Church wedded to property, legalism, and territorial aggrandizement, the championing of the *vita apostolica* became a vigorous call for the reform of an institutional Church immired in material and temporal concerns. As successive popes began to clamp down on this movement, these spiritual Franciscans were drawn, once again, into a debate over where the ultimate source of authority within the Church should be located and under what circumstances it would be legitimate to disobey an erring, or even heretical, pope.

The historical events which required practical pastoral attention in the late thirteenth century and which therefore elicited extensive theoretical analysis by scholastic theologians were clearly interconnected. Controversy between secular and mendicant masters, opposition to clerical taxation, and Franciscan disputes over the nature of poverty, all raised fundamental issues of lordship and authority within the Christian community. In each case, ecclesiological arguments were given explicit parallels in the political sphere and vice versa. With the issue of clerical taxation, however, it was not just a question of ecclesiological and political arguments proceeding in parallel. Once lordship in the sense of ownership of property was connected to lordship in the sense of legal right (*ius*), discussion of the respective claims of spiritual and temporal authorities to the goods of the Church rapidly turned into a debate over their respective claims to jurisdiction (*iurisdictio*) and thereafter into an analysis of the relationship between the temporal and the spiritual powers themselves. This was the connection which crystallized in the two disputes between Philip IV and Boniface VIII between 1296 and 1303 which brought forth three of the most significant political treatises written by medieval scholastic theologians.

Conflict initially broke out between Boniface VIII and Philip IV in 1296–7 over the king's right to tax the Church at a time of such pressing necessity and self-evident benefit to the community that it precluded the prior consent of the pope. However, it was the king's arrest of Bernard Saisset, Bishop of Pamiers, in 1301 which raised these stakes still higher, escalating a debate about the king's *dominium* over property into a wide-ranging disagreement over his *dominium* over individuals. In *Ausculta fili* (1301), Boniface VIII accordingly summoned masters of theology, alongside archbishops, bishops, and abbots, to a council to be held at Rome the following year in order to dicusss Philip IV's maladministration of his kingdom (Tierney 1964: 185–6). Philip IV responded by claiming that this was an unprecedented exercise of temporal lordship by the pope and promptly summoned his own assemblies to Paris in order to provide consent and legitimacy for an appeal to a council of the Church to take action against the pope. In 1301–2, Giles of Rome (Archbishop of Bourges since 1295) threw his full weight behind Boniface VIII and composed *De Ecclesiastica Potestate*, a treatise which is often regarded now as the swansong of hierocratic papalism. In 1302, James of

Viterbo (Giles's succccessor as the Augustinian master in theology who had then also left Paris, in his case to head the Augustinian school at Naples) followed suit with *De Regimine Christiano*, a treatise which has been called the first systematic treatise on the Church in the history of theology. John of Paris, meanwhile, their erstwhile Dominican colleague at Paris, and a witness to the Louvre assembly which ratified the king's action against the pope in 1303, composed *De Potestate Regia et Papali*, a treatise which provided "the most complete formulation of conciliar doctrine before the Great Schism" (Tierney 1955: 157–78).

Central to the disputes between Philip IV and Boniface VIII was the claim that the exercise of papal authority in spiritual matters could, and should, extend to those cases which required direct intervention in temporal jurisdiction. This doctrine of "plenitude of power" (*plenitudo potestatis*) had been articulated nearly a century earlier by pope Innocent III. The intervention of the spiritual power in temporal jurisdiction was primarily justified by a straightforward appeal to the principle "wherever sin is involved" (*ratione peccati*). In bulls such as *Novit* and *Per venerabilem* (Tierney 1964: 134–8), however, Innocent III had provided the basis for successive generations of canon lawyers to set about amassing long lists of specific cases in which such intervention could be legally justified – temporal gifts to the Church, oath-breaking, usury, heresy, dowries, inheritances, and, more generally still, whenever justice was found wanting (*defectus iustitiae*), whenever there was difficulty or ambiguity, and whenever there was benefit to the Church and to the public good. In protesting that the summoning of a council to discuss the maladministration of the French kingdom was no more than the assertion of a traditional legal right, Boniface VIII may therefore have been canonically correct. However, he could not, and seemingly did not want to, conceal just how wide a scope for intervention this principle would comprise. It was the implication of such a carte-blanche which was latched upon by Philip IV's own jurists as they argued that the pope was claiming nothing less than supreme temporal lordship over both the goods and the people of Philip IV's kingdom. The battle-lines of the debate into which scholastic theologians were then drawn were therefore quite clear. For Giles of Rome and James of Viterbo to defend Boniface VIII, they would have to provide a theoretical justification for the exercise of papal *plenitudo potestatis*; for John of Paris to moderate the apparent consequences of such hierocratic papalism, he would have to show both its theoretical and practical limitations.

At the heart of *De Ecclesiastica Potestate* are two sentences taken from Augustine's *City of God*: "there is no true justice except in the *res publica* whose founder and ruler is Christ" (II.21: 75) and "when this true justice is absent, kingdoms are nothing but large bands of robbers" (IV.4: 139). Giles's deduction was simple. Justice is defined as giving to each person their due; any political community which does not give God His due (that is, any community which is non-Christian or which does not accept the authority of Christ's vicar on earth) is, for that reason, lacking in justice; such an unjust community accordingly has no right to either the jurisdiction or the temporal goods to which it lays claim. Giles's conclusion was unequivocal. There can be no true lordship, no true *dominium*, either over material goods or over individuals, unless there is a correct relationship towards God and, by extension, towards the pope as God's representative on earth. Giles draws the same conclusion from the premise that the spiritual power can be compared to the soul and the temporal power to the body. Just as the soul is superior to the body, he argues, so the spiritual power is superior to the temporal, and just as the soul directs and commands the body, so the spiritual power directs and commands the temporal. Giles supports this analogy by appealing to a pseudo-Dionysian hierarchy of ends. Just as the goal of the soul (namely eternal happiness in heaven) is superior to the goal of the body (namely material well-being on this earth), so the goal of the body must be directed towards the attainment of the goal of the soul. Since material well-being on this earth must be ordered towards the attainment of eternal happiness in heaven, the power which is responsible for the soul, namely the spiritual power, must supervise and direct the power which is responsible for the body, namely the temporal power.

It is on this theoretical basis that Giles is then able to run through all the standard canon law texts justifying the pope's capacity to intervene in the exercise of temporal jurisdiction and, in particular, the allegorical exegesis of the two swords in Luke 22:38 ("The disciples said, 'See, Lord, here are two swords.' 'That is enough,' he replied."). Taking their cue from Christ's words to Peter at Gethsemane, canonists had argued that the Church must be understood to possess ultimate authority over the exercise of both spiritual and temporal power, both the spiritual and the temporal "swords," but that it had conceded to political authorities the use of the temporal sword on condition that its use should be subject to the Church's approval and ratification (Watt 1988). Giles of Rome accordingly never argues that papal intervention in temporal jurisdiction should be a regular occurrence. Indeed, he is careful to point out the dangers of propounding such an extreme position. The Church may have *dominium* over everything temporal but the exercise of such "superior and primary" jurisdiction is not always "immediate and executive." Instead, it should be "incidental" or "casual," leaving the normal and regular exercise of temporal jurisdiction as the responsibility of the temporal power. Giles thus accepts that the Church should not show too much concern for temporalities lest it be distracted from its true spiritual function. He also insists that any resulting action should be appropriate to the nature of the Church (a qualification which thereby manages to accommodate the canonical bar on the shedding of blood). With these practical reservations, however, Giles leaves the theoretical scope for papal intervention undiminished.

De Ecclesiastica Potestate was an influential text. In the short term, it provided the theoretical basis for many of the arguments which were issued by Boniface VIII immediately after his 1302 council in the bull *Unam sanctam*: the analogy of the soul's rule over the body, the direction of inferior entities by superior entities within a hierarchy of ends, and the subjection of each human being to the spiritual power in everything which concerns the well-being of their souls (Tierney 1964: 188–9). Giles of Rome's theoretical defense of papal plenitude of power was rooted firmly in arguments drawn from Augustine and pseudo-Dionysius. As such, it bears close comparison with *De Regimine Christiano*, a justification of *plenitudo potestatis* in which James of Viterbo puts forward arguments from canon law not dissimilar to those in *De Ecclesiastica Potestate*. Thus, *De Regimine Christiano*, like *De Ecclesiastica Potestate*, demonstrates that the spiritual power has superior and prior possession of all temporal jurisdiction, and proceeds to outline its casual exercise of this jurisdiction in the particular instances laid down by canon law. It is therefore, in many respects, a round-up of the usual texts, not least Jeremiah 1:10 ("See, today I appoint you over nations and kingdoms to uproot and tear down, to destroy and overthrow, to build and to plant"), a favorite citation of both Innocent III and Boniface VIII and a text which was carefully expounded to the French king's ambassadors in June 1302. According to James of Viterbo, the spiritual power is entitled to judge, correct, direct, and command the temporal power, to punish it with temporal as well as spiritual penalties, and, if the crime was a sin of sufficient severity, to secure its overthrow. All these hierocratic conclusions, however, cannot disguise the fact that, in comparison to Giles of Rome, James of Viterbo proceeds along a rather different route from his Augustinian confrère.

What is so striking about *De Regimine Christiano* in contrast to *De Ecclesiastica Potestate* is the way in which James deploys the central tenets of Aristotle's *Ethics* and *Politics*. As an ecclesiological treatise, this results in a demonstration that the Church is, in fact, Aristotle's perfect political community, a "kingdom" in which bishops have the function, if not the name, of kings. As a polemical political treatise devoted to establishing the correct relationship between the spiritual and the temporal power, this results in a demonstration of how Augustine and Aristotle support the same hierocratic papalism. According to Giles of Rome, the function of political authority is to secure peace and is therefore limited to the provision of material and corporeal goods. James of Viterbo argues quite differently. Not only does James insist on Aristotle's first premise that humankind is by nature a political animal but he also cites the second, and far more significant, tenet that the function of life in political society is not just to live but to live well, not just to achieve material self-sufficiency, peace, and security, but also to lead a life of moral virtue. James succeeds in incorporating both Aristotelian principles into a thoroughly hierocratic argument by appealing to Thomas Aquinas and to the axiom which has often served as a shorthand for the Thomist synthesis of Christian theology with Aristotelian philosophy – "grace does not abolish nature but perfects it" (*Summa Theologiae* Ia 8.2: *gratia non tollit sed perficit naturam*). It is on this basis, therefore, that James argues that, although political authority may originate in nature, in order to be complete, to be "perfect," it still needs to be guided by grace, by the action of the spiritual power. Temporal power which does not possess such grace is comparable to moral virtue which has not been informed by theological virtue – it is not illegitimate, as Giles of Rome had argued, but it is still unformed, "imperfect," until such time as it receives the ratification of the spiritual power. This is why, in contrast to Giles, James is content to argue that political authority is not limited to the provision of material and corporeal goods but can be credited with the moral purpose of ensuring that individuals lead virtuous lives. By doing so, in fact, he makes an even stronger case for the subordination of political authority to the spiritual power. The syllogism is simple. According to Aristotle, virtue is a good of the soul; the good of the soul is, by definition, the responsibility of the spiritual power; a political community whose goal is the life of virtue must therefore be subject to the jurisdiction of the Church. With this argument, James's appropriation of Aristotle for the cause of hierocratic papalism was complete. Political authority which was legitimated by its origins in nature still needed to be perfected by being ratified by the spiritual power, just as moral virtue which was legitimated by its origins in natural reason still needed to be perfected by grace. A definition of political authority which had virtue at its heart *necessarily* implied subordination to the Church.

In composing *De Potestate Regia et Papali* in Paris at the height of the second dispute between the French king and the pope, John of Paris declares a (no doubt highly prudent) intention to chart a *via media*, a middle way between two extreme positions. Initially, at least, this claim appears to be borne out, as John sets up a series of elaborate parallels between the authority which is exercised by the spiritual power and the authority which is exercised by the temporal power. For example, rather than follow Giles of Rome and conflate the ideas of *dominium* as lordship over material property and *dominium* as jurisdiction over individuals, John carefully establishes that ownership of property belongs, strictly speaking, neither to the king nor to the pope. Strictly speaking, temporal goods in the kingdom belong to the individuals who possess them; the king merely serves as an arbiter when disputes over ownership arise. Temporal goods in the Church, meanwhile, belong to ecclesiastical communities and to the Church as a whole; the pope merely serves as their steward and administrator for the benefit of the whole. The consequences of both types of relation are the same, in theory at least, for both king and pope. Each ruler can appeal to evident utility, necessity, and the common good as justifications for overriding the rights of individual property holders, or for dispensing the goods of the Church, but each of them is accountable for such an action should it fail to prove justified. This much was already familiar territory from Henry of Ghent and Godfrey of Fontaines. The king is accountable (although John spends noticeably little time discussing this) to the barons and peers of the kingdom. The pope, meanwhile, can be deposed by a council of the Church, not just for the legal crimes of heresy, fornication, drunkenness, and conferring prebends for his own private advantage, but also for maladministration.

Such apparent even-handedness is repeated when John comes to discuss papal plenitude of power. At no point does John deny the capacity of the spiritual power to exercise a "casual" or "incidental" power of jurisdiction in the temporal sphere. Thus, if the king becomes a heretic, or if he transgresses a broad category of ecclesiastical crime, then the pope can indeed excommunicate him, absolve his subjects from their oaths of obedience, and thereby (indirectly) secure his overthrow. Once again, however, these are consequences which John spends little time elaborating. He is far more concerned to demonstrate that the temporal power has a reciprocal right of casual and incidental intervention in the spiritual sphere. John does not go as far as calling it a temporal plenitude of power, but the terms in which it is described are too similar to have been unintended. The temporal power can therefore intervene in the affairs of the Church if it is a case of "urgent necessity" and "evident benefit"; if, that is, such action will secure the common good of the whole community. In the first instance, this means that Philip IV should indeed be able to demand exactions of temporal goods from the Church in order to secure the defense of his kingdom. In the second instance, it means that Philip IV was justified in supporting any attempts which a council of the Church might make to remove an heretical, corrupt, or incompetent occupant of the papal see.

John of Paris bears eloquent testimony to the very real dilemma which was facing scholastic theologians, and indeed all bishops and clergy, within the kingdom of France. His solution was to accept a theoretical definition of papal plenitude of power but make the pope accountable for its abuse in practice, to accept the right of the spiritual power to intervene in the jurisdiction of the temporal power but insist that this power is reciprocal. In conceding reciprocal rights of intervention in each other's affairs, John of Paris is clearly a long way from arguing for the autonomy or independence of the temporal power. Viewed in these terms, he is largely justified in claiming to be charting a *via media*. In the context of the papal council of 1302 and the royal assemblies of 1303, however, this parallelism was a delicate line to tread, less of a *via media*, perhaps, and rather more of a political tightrope. Indeed, when John discusses the relationship between the spiritual and the temporal power in terms of the operation of a hierarchy of ends and the life of virtue, the radicalism of his treatise begins to emerge.

One of the most decisive arguments used by Giles of Rome in *De Ecclesiastica Potestate* was his appeal to a particular conception of hierarchy. Eternal beatitude is superior to temporal happiness in the same way that the soul is superior to the body; as a result, just as the body must be ruled by the soul, so temporal happiness must be directed towards eternal happiness. Applied to the spiritual and the temporal powers, this model produced a relationship of simple subordination. The spiritual power is superior to the temporal power in such a way that the exercise of authority by the temporal power must be controlled by the spiritual power, because the power which is concerned with attaining a superior goal must be able to command those powers which are only concerned with secondary goals. This is the strict mediation of ends which John of Paris sets out to dismantle, not by abandonning the notion of hierarchy as such, but by putting forward a different interpretation of how its operation needs to be understood. John accordingly establishes a clear distinction between two types of hierarchy, between a hierarchy of intrinsic worth or dignity and a hierarchy of causality. Being superior in intrinsic worth or dignity, John maintains, does not necessarily mean being absolutely superior in command or authority since, when an inferior discipline is subject to a superior in one respect, it does not follow that the same subjection applies in all respects. John draws an analogy with the relationship between a doctor and an apothecary. Both the doctor and the apothecary receive their power directly from the king or lord of the community; while the doctor may instruct or guide the apothecary, and even judge the correctness of his medicine, he does not institute him in his post or remove him from it; only the king or lord can do that. Likewise, both the pope and the king receive their power directly from God and, while the pope may indeed be superior in dignity to the king, this does not translate into a capacity to exercise authority over him (*De Potestate Regia et Papali* XVII: 185). John delivers a similar riposte to the way in which James of Viterbo had sought to apply to a hierarchy of ends the moral teleology of Aristotle's *Ethics* and *Politics*. John agrees with James that the function of authority in the political community is to secure the life of virtue, to make individuals lead virtuous lives. However, he also insists that a life of virtue is a good in its own right and not only when it is directed towards the further goal of eternal beatitude. Unlike James, therefore, John maintains that it *is* possible to exercise perfect moral virtue without the additional presence of grace (*De Potestate Regia et Papali* XVIII: 191). The inference is unmistakable. It is possible to credit the temporal power with a moral purpose, with an authority which extends to more than just the provision of material goods, without making it necessarily subordinate to the supervision of the Church.

The ecclesiological treatises which were precipitated by the disputes between Philip IV and Boniface VIII demonstrate three key features of scholastic political thinking. In the first instance, these works were written as academic analyses of, but also contributions to, public political events. Giles and James wrote their treatises explicitly for the pope in the period immediately preceding the Rome council of November 1302. Given James's rapid promotion to the archbishopric of Naples, and given the similarities between Giles's ideas and the formulations which were soon issued in *Unam sanctam* (Luscombe 1976), this conjunction would seem to be more than just coincidence. In the second instance, these treatises reveal how theologians took as a starting-point for their abstract theorizing the more empirical basis of the dispute in a series of canon law texts on the nature of *plenitudo postestatis* and the justification for intervention *ratione peccati*. In the third instance, these treatises reveal how misleading it is to envisage any "secular" theory of politics being precipitated by the reintroduction of Aristotle's *Ethics* and *Politics*. Rather than treat such scholastic political thought as the effect of a conflict polarized between "conservative Augustinianism" and "radical Aristotelianism," it is much more helpful to think in terms of different combinations of, and citations from, *both* Augustine *and* Aristotle by the same authors. The results may be less schematic, and certainly less straightforward, but they are more reflective of the complexity of the respective texts. Giles of Rome, James of Viterbo, and John of Paris read Augustine and Aristotle in different ways to produce different conclusions. James of Viterbo, in fact, shows how Aristotle's life of virtue could be used to construct a particularly powerful justification of the subordination of the temporal power to the Church.

De Ecclesiastica Potestate, *De Regimine Christiano*, and *De Potestate Regia et Papali* exemplify how scholastic political thinking depended on a combination of the theoretical with the practical, the academic with the public, dialectic with rhetoric, moral theology with canon and Roman law. If these respective fusions of Aristotle with Augustine reveal that the *Ethics* and the *Politics* were far from being intrinsically "secularizing" texts, they nonetheless indicate that the reintroduction of Aristotle did condition the *way* in which scholastic theologians could tackle moral and pastoral issues of pressing political concern and therefore the *form* which their political treatises would take. The impact of such an approach was not limited to the confines of the university of Paris. Textually, this can be traced via the dissemination of manuscripts of the *Ethics*, the *Politics*, and the *Rhetoric* themselves but also, and perhaps more significantly, via the distribution of distillations of their ideas in the form of *florilegia*, their incorporation into such vernacular encyclopedias as Brunetto Latini's *Livre dou Tresor*, and their dispersal through vernacular translations of Giles of Rome's *De Regimine Principum*, copies of which were rapidly made into French, German, and English. Likewise, the intellectual fall-out from the disputes between Philip IV and Boniface VIII left a much longer-term textual legacy as the ecclesiological treatises of Giles of Rome, James of Viterbo, and John of Paris all continued to be copied, and to influence debates over the nature of authority in the Church, throughout the fourteenth and fifteenth centuries. Just as important as such textual transmission, however, was the experience of those individuals who listened to quodlibets and disputed questions being discussed at the university of Paris but who then went back to their churches and mendicant houses in order to incorporate this new learning into their own sermons and homilies. A prime example of the potential significance of this more personal transmission of scholastic political ideas is the Dominican Remigio dei Girolami.

Remigio dei Girolami attended the university of Paris in the 1260s, and again the late 1290s, but his career was otherwise devoted to teaching at the Dominican *studium* at Florence until his death in 1319. In preparing a cross-referenced edition of his own sermons and treatises for the community at Santa Maria Novella, Remigio provides a direct link between the theology of the Paris schools and a generation of northern Italian Dominicans. More specifically, by composing two explicitly political treatises, *On the Common Good* (1302–3) and *On the Good of Peace* (1304), as well as giving a detailed summary of the arguments to be used in resolving the relationship between the spiritual and the temporal powers in *Contra Falsos Ecclesiae Professores* (before 1314), Remigio provides a detailed commentary both on the factionalism which was endemic to late thirteenth- and early fourteenth-century Florence and on the series of specific events which this factionalism precipitated, most notably Boniface VIII's invitation in 1301 to Philip IV's brother, Charles of Valois, to restore Tuscany to "peace and good order".

Remigio dei Girolami's significance, however, rests on more than just his transmission of Aristotelian political ideas beyond the university of Paris and their application to the city-states of northern Italy. Once again, it lies in what his writing reveals about the way in which Aristotle was being read and, in particular, how a hierarchy of ends and the life of virtue had become central to the debate over the relationship between the spiritual and the temporal power. In the case of hierarchy, for example, Remigio is clearly prepared to follow John of Paris in modifying the operation of a strict mediation of ends. According to Remigio, a final cause, an end which is, in an absolute sense, superior in intrinsic worth or dignity to those things which are ordered towards it, can nevertheless, in certain circumstances, be ordered towards something which is of less intrinsic worth or dignity. This accordingly provides Remigio with his solution to how ecclesiastical goods can be directed towards a temporal goal without thereby subordinating the Church to temporal authority. Still more striking is Remigio's approach to Aristotle's life of virtue. Despite his willingness to cite so much else from the *Ethics* and the *Politics*, including the observation that humankind is by nature a political animal, Remigio is careful not to make the life of virtue the goal of the political community and therefore the defining characteristic of the exercise of political authority. Instead, Remigio consistently maintains that the goal of the temporal ruler is to provide peace and harmony, a position which he supports with extensive citation from Augustine. For a scholastic theologian who is often cited as a political theorist who used Aristotle's account of the perfect human association to propound a "dangerous idealization" of the commune (Davis 1960), this restraint is worth noting. Given the circumstances of early fourteenth-century Florence, this may, of course, be simply the reflection of a pragmatic realization that a degree of material security is the most which could be expected from sinful humankind. On the other hand, viewed in the light of James of Viterbo's *De Regimine Christiano*, Remigio's reluctance to cite the life of virtue may reflect his recognition of the carte-blanche which such a moral goal would offer to the intervention of the Church in temporal jurisdiction. Like John of Paris, Remigio had already criticized the Donation of Constantine on the grounds that the direct assumption of such temporal power had ended up distracting the Church from its true spiritual function. If Remigio's refusal to cite Aristotle's life of virtue stems from a similar awareness of the dangers such scope could pose for the Church's own well-being, then this may help resolve some of the tensions apparent in his thinking. At one and the same time, Remigio was arguing for the theoretical supremacy of the spiritual power while attempting to restrict the practical exercise of that power over matters of temporal jurisdiction.

The impact of Remigio's ideas on his fellow Florentines is hard to gauge but, to judge from the sermons which he preached before the Priors (the ruling oligarchic elite to which he had himself close familial ties), his audience would have comprised influential laymen as well as clergy. Indeed, what makes Remigio's political and ecclesiological ideas so intriguing is the fact that he is a prime candidate for providing the "disputazioni de li filosofanti" at the "scuole de li religiosi" which were attended by Dante Alighieri. Dante, himself condemned to a lifelong exile following the expulsion of the "White" Guelfs in 1301, developed his own political ideas in the decade which followed, producing first the philosophical and Aristotelian idealism of the *Convivio* (1304–8) but then the more somber and polemical realism of the *Commedia*, the first two sections of which, *Inferno* and *Purgatorio*, were composed during these years. It was the expedition to Rome of Henry VII of Luxembourg (1310–12), however, and in particular the papal volte-face which accompanied its failure and the emperor's death, which prompted Dante to compose his major political treatise, *Monarchia* (1310–14). Dante was not, of course, a theologian but, as *Paradiso* was to demonstrate, his knowledge of scholastic theology was considerable. His political ideas are thus an intriguing mixture of familiarity with scholastic commentary on Aristotle's *Ethics* and a keen interest in classical Roman history. This is a combination which appears, too, in the work of Remigio dei Girolami although, in Dante's case, it was a classicism which prompted an extensive defense of the providential role of the Roman Empire against no less an attack than the critique put forward in Augustine's *City of God*.

Judged in the context of scholastic political ideas, the interest of Dante's *Monarchia* lies in its invocation of two ends or goals for humankind, an earthly and a heavenly beatitude, as the respective responsibilities of the temporal and the spiritual power. The separation which such an argument seems to envisage has led some historians to refer to an "uncompromising dualism," even "secularism," in Dante's political thinking. There are, however, strong grounds for contesting such claims. In writing a treatise which set out to combat the excesses of papal intervention in temporal affairs, the effects of which he had personally experienced in Florence, Dante faced exactly the same dilemma presented in John of Paris's *De Potestate Regia et Papali*. How can the spiritual power be separated from the temporal power without making that separation absolute? Having established his "twofold goal" (*duplex finis*), therefore, Dante concedes in the closing paragraph of his treatise that there is still a certain sense (*quodammodo*) in which the temporal power remains subordinate to the spiritual power, namely in the manner that a son receives a blessing of grace from his father (*Monarchia* III.16: 149). This is a passage which, not unnaturally, has caused some consternation for the more secularist of Dante's interpreters. These parting words may represent a grudging concession, it is argued, but it is a concession which effectively undermines everything which Dante has hitherto tried to construct, qualifying the autonomy of the temporal power and exposing it to precisely the sort of supervision and ratification by papal *plenitudo potestatis* which the remainder of the treatise had been attempting to avoid (Reeves 1965).

If internal consistency is to be salvaged for *Monarchia*, then its closing paragraph clearly has to be made integral to Dante's political thinking. One way of doing so is to treat it as a carefully worded allusion to the Thomist model of nature and grace which had been so central to the argument of James of Viterbo – grace does not abolish nature but perfects it (Gilson 1963). For James, the relationship between the temporal power and the spiritual power should be understood as a relationship between nature and grace, between moral virtue and theological virtue, in which the former may be legitimate in its own terms but, in order to be perfect, must be completed by the latter. For Dante, therefore, a closing appeal to the blessing of grace marks his recognition that the relationship between moral virtue and theological virtue, which so interested (and troubled) him in *Paradiso*, had a directly political import. Dante explains a little more when he attacks the analogy drawn from Genesis 1:16 which had been favored by many papal polemicists – just as the moon is inferior to the sun and receives its light from it, so the temporal ruler is inferior to the spiritual and receives his power from the Church. The sun and the moon, Dante retorts, both receive their existence directly from God and the moon is therefore not dependent upon the sun for either its existence or its power (*Monarchia* III.4: 107, 111–13). However, Dante again inserts a significant concession, in this case that the moon's relation to the sun still gives it light "in abundance" (*habundanter*) and enables it to function "better and more virtuously" (*melius et virtuosius*). By adding these final qualifications, Dante reinforces the formula attached to the end of his treatise. The spiritual power and the temporal power are separate, they are both directly dependent upon God, but this does not mean that a relationship to the spiritual power is without benefit to the temporal power. Whether such a relationship is necessary, as James of Viterbo had argued, or whether it is accidental, as John of Paris had argued, Dante does not reveal. Just as in his discussion of the morally virtuous pagan in *Paradiso* XIX, it is a question which he chooses to leave open.

Dante's understanding of the political implications of the relationship between moral and theological virtue provided him with one possible model for separating the temporal from the spiritual power without making that separation absolute. On the one hand, the temporal power possessed an intrinsic legitimacy from nature; on the other hand, this nature could be perfected by grace. By failing to specify whether this nature *should* be perfected by grace, or whether it was, in fact, possible to have perfect moral virtue without the supervenience of grace, Dante effectively ducks the issue which had proved such a crucial point of disagreement between James of Viterbo and John of Paris. However, this was not his final word on the matter. In disagreeing over whether the perfection of moral virtue by theological virtue was necessary or accidental, James of Viterbo and John of Paris had both kept firmly to the Aristotelian principle that the function of life in the political community is not just to live but to live well, and that the goal of those in political authority is therefore to make their subjects virtuous. Indeed, it was precisely because Aristotle's life of virtue lay at the center of both their definitions of temporal authority that the relationship between moral virtue and theological virtue carried such a significant political corollary in *De Regimine Christiano* and *De Potestate Regia et Papali*. It is on this point that Dante's *Monarchia* marks a revealing departure.

For Dante, the earthly goal of humankind is the "actualization of the potentiality" (that is, the perfection) of the human intellect. The goal of temporal authority, meanwhile, is to ensure the peace between humans which will make the attainment of this moral and intellectual perfection possible. The means by which the earthly goal of humankind is facilitated is thus the establishment of a single world monarch whose rule (*imperium*) will provide both justice and freedom (*libertas*). It is the implications of this final term which are significant. By making law the guarantor of freedom rather than the instrument of virtue, by pointedly avoiding the moral perfectionism of an Aristotelian or Thomist account of political authority, Dante ends up with a much looser conception of what the temporal ruler will actually do in practice. The world monarch will simply provide a framework of peace and material security within which individuals will be free to actualize the potentiality of their intellect. What Dante has done, in other words, is to separate virtue from peace, the earthly goal of humankind from the means by which that end is made possible. There are several possible explanations of why Dante should have sought to limit the role of temporal authority in this way. As with Remigio, it may be the result of a bitter political realism which had taught Dante that a degree of peace and security was the most he could ever hope for in northern Italy. It may also be the result of an Augustinian acceptance that peace is the most anyone could expect anywhere in a sinful world. Or it may be the result of an attempt to combine the authority of a single world monarch with a federation of subordinate but "free" city-states. Alternatively, Dante's concern with peace rather than with virtue may stem from a realization that the best means of keeping the spiritual power separate from the temporal power was to remove the life of virtue from his definition of the scope of political authority and with it the main justification for ecclesiastical intervention. In itself, this idea was certainly not new. Giles of Rome, after all, had used Augustine to limit the exercise of political authority to material and corporeal concerns in *De Ecclesiastica Potestate*. For Giles, however, this was a means of expanding the corresponding scope of spiritual authority to comprise the exercise of all virtue, moral as well as theological. What makes Dante's argument so different, therefore, and what makes him take it one step further than Remigio, is that when he comes to discuss the corresponding exercise of authority by the Church, he limits that too, in this case to preaching, teaching, and administering the sacraments. Dante does so by appealing to a Franciscan ideal of the *vita apostolica* and to the model of the early Church recorded in the book of Acts.

In 1245, the Emperor Frederick II had already exploited the polemical possibilities of holding up the New Testament against papal claims to temporal jurisdiction by championing the paradigm of a Church devoted to poverty and to preaching (Tierney 1964: 145–6). For all his advocacy of a single world empire, however, Dante's familiarity with the ideals of the spiritual Franciscans, primarily through Ubertino da Casale (but maybe also through having heard Pierre Jean Olivi preach at Santa Croce), makes such an overtly political expropriation of the *vita apostolica* unlikely. Indeed, read alongside the *Commedia*, and in particular the vivid apocalyptic imagery of the pageant (*Purgatorio* XXIX–XXXIII) and the bitter denunciations of the Donation of Constantine (*Inferno* XIX, *Paradiso* XX), Dante's advocacy of the *vita apostolica* reads as a committed, even prophetic, call for reform of the Church from within. Read in this context, indeed, Dante's closing paragraph to *Monarchia* is far from a grudging concession. The paternal blessing of grace *should* be bestowed by the spiritual power upon the temporal power but this is a spiritual power whose authority is measured according to the New Testament rather than papal decretals. A spiritual Franciscan conception of a reformed Church, when coupled with a material conception of a temporal power which is limited to the provision of peace and material security, has left Dante with a clear and consistent conclusion. He has achieved a *de facto* separation of the temporal from the spiritual power while continuing to allow a theoretical relationship of subordination. Removing the life of virtue, the contested ground between the two powers, was the key. It provided the means by which the Church would be made to concentrate on its true spiritual functions of poverty and preaching, the temporal power would be left to secure peace and material security, while individual human beings would be freed to perfect their moral and intellectual potential. Taken together, Dante's *Monarchia* and *Commedia* present a coherent account of the way in which the apostolic ideal of poverty and preaching could be deployed as a powerful critique of how "the sword is joined to the crook" (*Purgatorio* XVI) to the detriment of both the spiritual life of the Church and the temporal peace of northern Italy. Dante's imperialism may have been his political solution to this crisis, but this conception of temporal authority was the direct result of his ecclesiology, not the other way around.

Ten years after Dante had completed *Monarchia*, another northern Italian, Marsilius of Padua, tackled the same fundamental issues of spiritual and temporal authority in his *Defender of the Peace* (1324). Once again, this was not the work of a theologian as such (although as a member of the faculty of Arts in Paris, Marsilius's familiarity with Aristotle left his work much closer to the rigor of scholastic commentary) and once again it was precipitated by external events, in this case the conflict between the Emperor Ludwig IV of Bavaria and Pope John XXII. The *Defensor Pacis* is a prime example of the difference which is made by approaching a scholastic text as a work not just of dialectic but of rhetoric, in this case by treating it as polemic and not as systematic political philosophy drawn from abstract first principles. What otherwise come across as so striking to a modern reader of Marsilius are the apparently familiar echoes of positivism and voluntarism. Thus, whereas Aquinas had defined law as "an ordinance of reason directed towards the common good and promulgated by the authority who is charged with care of the political community" (*Summa Theologiae* IaIIae 90.4), Marsilius defined law as whatever was determined by the legislative authority of the community and was therefore capable of being enforced (*Defensor Pacis* I.10.4: 36). Likewise, whereas Aquinas had followed Aristotle in distinguishing good forms of government from perverse forms according to whether they secured the common good of the whole community, Marsilius used the *Politics* to argue that political legitimacy derived from the consent or will (*voluntas*) of that community rather than the correspondence of this will to an absolute standard of the common good. Marsilius thereby picks up the one passage in the *Politics* which conceded that, taken together, there might be greater wisdom in the whole community than there is in the virtuous few who are ruling that community, even though, taken separately, individuals within that community may not be as wise as those virtuous few in authority (*Politics* III.15: 76). The whole community is thus *almost always* a better judge of what is in its own interest. Even if the community consents to something which is not so much to its advantage, in other words, which does not secure the *communis utilitas*, then it is still legitimate as law in virtue of the fact that it has been willed by the whole community (*Defensor Pacis* I.12.6: 47).

The first question to ask, clearly, is why should Marsilius seem so modern, why does he emphasize consent and coercive command (*praeceptum coercivum*) as the twin foundations of legal and political legitimacy, stripping down the rule of law to its bare essentials without reference, apparently, to the need (as opposed to desirability) for its correlation with the traditional higher norms of reason and the common good? The answer lies in the singular cause of strife which Marsilius himself identifies as the primary target of his treatise. In order to understand what Marsilius is arguing *for*, it is essential to understand what he is arguing *against*, and what Marsilius is setting out to dismantle is the theoretical basis of papal *plenitudo potestatis*. Marsilius approaches this task from two directions. On the one hand, he emphasizes that the goal of political authority is the life of material self-sufficiency rather than an Aristotelian life of virtue. Like Dante, Marsilius thereby limits the scope of temporal power to the provision of peace and security rather than the promotion of activity in accordance with perfect virtue. On the other hand, Marsilius emphasizes the spiritual nature of the Church, appealing, again like Dante, to the *vita apostolica* of poverty and preaching as the true scriptural paradigm for the Church. In both instances, Marsilius reinforces his argument by appealing to his own particular definition of law as a command which is capable of being enforced. His aim throughout is to provide a definition of human law which will place it entirely within the competence of the temporal sphere. Since divine law is subject to coercive punishment only in the next life, strictly speaking it cannot be regarded as "law" within the confines of this life but only as counsel, as the subject of teaching rather than command, the sphere of interior ("immanent") rather than exterior ("transient") action. Moreover, by avoiding natural law in the traditional sense of a higher norm to which human law must correspond in order to be legitimate, by defining human law instead in the more neutral sense of something which secures peace, order, stability, and common benefit, and which only needs to be willed and enforceable in order to be legitimate, Marsilius removes the theoretical basis for the clergy's intervention in the government of the political community. When Marsilius then takes up the Franciscan paradigm of poverty and humility, making the distinction between ownership and use so universal that the Church should be disendowed of all temporal goods not needed for worship, maintenance, and acts of charity, his reform program is complete. Having restricted the sanctions of divine "law" to the next life and having removed the grounds on which the Church can intervene in temporal jurisdiction, Marsilius has succeeded in freeing the Church not just from lordship in the sense of ownership of property but also from lordship in the sense of jurisdiction. Any papal claim to exercise its plenitude of power in temporal matters wherever sin is present, wherever a spiritual good is involved, or wherever the common good is threatened, would, on this basis, carry no legitimacy at all.

The second question to ask is *why* Marsilius should be so concerned, on the one hand, to limit the function of political authority to the preservation of peace and, on the other, to remove the Church from the temporal sphere. Much the same possibilities apply as to Dante. Is this the result of a political realism born of bitter personal experience at Padua (Rubinstein 1965)? Is it an Augustinian recognition that political authority will only ever serve as a barrier to worse evils rather than as the means to a higher end because, compared to humankind, nothing is more sociable by nature but more quarrelsome by corruption (*Defensor Pacis* I.4.4: 13; *City of God* XII.28: 508)? Or is Marsilius's advocacy of the *vita apostolica* motivated by purely secular political goals, that is, by his imperialism, in which case the New Testament is, as it was for Frederick II, simply a convenient stick with which to beat the papacy? Again, however, one final possibility remains, namely that Marsilius was motivated by the profoundly religious concerns revealed by the closing lines of the entire treatise. In this case, the *Defensor Pacis* should be read as a genuine call to reform made by a committed radical who saw the disendowment of the Church to be for its own good. Unlike Dante, for whom the eliptical closing paragraph of *Monarchia* can be juxtaposed with the prophetic fervor of *Purgatorio*, Marsilius has unfortunately left little supporting material beyond what the internal evidence of *Defensor Pacis* can supply. What there is, therefore, turns on the practical implications of Marsilius's discussion of consent.

The apparently modern resonances of Marsilius's attachment to coercion and consent should not be allowed to conceal the more conventional foundations of his thinking. This is particularly true of his belief that any elaborately constructed dualism of jurisdiction between the spiritual and the temporal power would still always lead to conflict and that the only means of securing peace was therefore to advocate a single source of *dominium*. This was, of course, an assumption shared by his papalist opponents. For Marsilius, the crucial difference was to make this single source of jurisdiction the temporal, not the spiritual, power. It was thus a principle common to both Marsilius and papal theorists alike that peace requires a unity of jurisdiction. What Marsilius did, quite simply, was to turn this argument on its head. Rather than establish any dualist principle of coordinate spiritual and temporal powers, he resorted to political monism, arguing that the temporal power must possess jurisdiction over all bishops, priests, and clergy in order to avoid the destruction of society by a multiplicity of governments. Marsilius is only able to do this, however, because of his particular understanding of the nature of the human legislator. For Marsilius, again as for his papalist opponents, society was the Church and the Church was society. It is on the implication of this numerical identification that a "religious" interpretation of Marsilius's text rests.

The *Defensor Pacis* has often been seen as running into difficulties when it connects the political community with the Christian faith. Political life, for Marsilius, should be concerned with exterior, not interior, actions. The interior spiritual life of each Christian should therefore be a matter not for precept but for counsel, not for the legislator but for the individual's own conscience. Nevertheless, Marsilius does accept that exterior action can include the temporal consequences of spiritual acts and that, as such, there are some spiritual acts which may fall within the purview of the legislator. It is on this basis that Marsilius argues that excommunication and heresy – always the acid tests for a "secular" political theory – can, in fact, be the subject of temporal legislation. This concession has always proved a stumbling block to the more secularist interpretations of his treatise (Gewirth 1951: 155–66). Although the determination of articles of faith is necessary to preserve the unity of the faith, Marsilius certainly does not condone their enforce-ment outright. What he does say is that the authority to coerce on such matters belongs to the human legislator "if it is permissible for this to happen" (*Defensor Pacis* II.5.7: 136). This phrase, *si liceat hoc fieri*, can be read in two ways. Either it means that divine law can be made the subject of human law if it has external repercussions, if, that is, it affects the peace and security of the community. Or it means that divine law can be made the subject of human law if it has been willed by the whole community, if, that is, it has been consented to by a legislator who also happens to be Christian.

In the first part of the treatise, Marsilius outlines a theoretical model of a legitimate political community, arguing that it can be justified on entirely rational and philosophical grounds. As such, the one reference to religion treats it quite dispassionately as something which can be useful to the political community – the fear of eternal punishment helps citizens to observe those measures which are necessary for peace and security. In the second part of the treatise, however, Marsilius moves on to the reality of northern Italian city-states and a community of citizens which also happens to be a community of Christians. In this instance, the lawful sovereign, the body of citizens (*universitas civium*), will happen to be the same group of people as the body of the faithful (*universitas fidelium*). It is this accidental, numerical identity which makes the lawful sovereign in the Chris-tian political community also the sole authority in the government of the Chris-tian Church. The connection between them may be accidental rather than necessary, but the consequences for the laws of that community are considerable. This is because of Marsilius's insistence on the centrality of consent, since the *Defensor Pacis* remains open to the interpretation that a Christian community which listens to the teaching and counsel of its clergy will give its consent to correspondingly Christian legislation. While it is possible, therefore, to read Marsilius's treatise as a "secular" theory, the numerical identity of citizens and Christians within the same community will, in practice, prevent the separation of human and divine from being absolute.

William of Ockham presents the difficulties posed by the relation of metaphys-ical principle to political ideas in their most acute form. On the one hand, there is a distinct lack of political comment in his speculative works and, on the other, there is a paucity of philosophical passages in his political works. Modern scholars have accordingly examined the relations between his theology, philosophy, and politics only to conclude that Ockham worked at two different levels, of abstrac-tion and of polemic. It is thus, in every sense of the word, unrealistic to look for a precise correlation between an inductive empiricism in epistemology and a refusal to treat the community in terms other than those of aggregate composi-tion (McGrade 1974). Ockham is also a prime example of the difficulties which can arise as a result of differences in the genre of political writing, in his case by distinguishing the personal views put forward in a treatise such as the *Breviloquium* from the more impersonal collection of arguments in the *Dialogus*, a work which invites its readers to establish the truth for themselves. Given this dichotomy, therefore, and given the fragmented nature of his political writings, it is perhaps not surprising that Ockham's work appears to yield little in the way of a "theory" of the political community. His political ideas are developed instead as polemical responses to specific political events. Ockham's investigation of the consequences of papal heresy, for example, is a point by point refutation of John XXII's bulls attacking the separation of ownership from use and declaring that it was heretical to hold to the doctrine of the absolute poverty of Christ (*Ad conditorem* 1322; *Cum inter nonnullos* 1323; *Quia quorumdam* 1324). Likewise, Ockham's denial that the pope can do anything not forbidden by divine or natural law is a demonstration of the illegitimate and tyrannical nature of the pope's actions against Ludwig of Bavaria. Ockham's approach throughout is characteristically Franciscan. The result is political thought based first and foremost on scriptural and patristic sources rather than on philosophy. Thus, his attempt to establish the independence of the Empire, and of temporal power in general, draws primarily, not on any Aristotelian account of the needs and fulfillment of human nature, nor on any detailed theory of popular sovereignty, but on biblical and patristic texts which recognize the legitimacy of dominion and jurisdiction amongst non-believers.

Perhaps the most important feature to emerge from Ockham's political writings when they are compared with those of earlier scholastic theologians is the pragmatic separation of the spiritual from the temporal power. Ockham's primary concern is to widen the distance between the temporal and the spiritual power by limiting the practical scope of their respective jurisdictions. Like Dante and Marsilius, therefore, Ockham achieves this separatism by, on the one hand, re-moving the moral end of the political community and, on the other, replacing the legalistic emphasis of papal government with the apostolic ideal of a pastoral ministry. Like Dante and Marsilius, then, Ockham's political theory depends ultimately on a particular reading of the New Testament. For the spiritual power this means accepting a much more restricted definition of its legitimate exercise of coercive command. As a pastoral ministry, the Church will exercise its power only when it is vitally necessary for the good of the Church or the salvation of its members. In *theory*, this was a traditional reading of canon law – papal plenitude of power must be exercised to give clear benefit to the common good up to, and including, casual intervention in temporal affairs. Ockham's aim, therefore, is to limit the application of this principle in *practice*. Papal plenitude of power is never denied by Ockham, nor is Petrine primacy and authority over the Church. Ockham therefore does not preclude the casual exercise of *plenitudo potestatis* when it is warranted by occasions of evident necessity and utility. What he *is* intent on doing, however, is establishing limits to its *regular* exercise. It is here that the absence of a moral end to politics is of central importance. Where the function of the temporal power is discussed by Ockham, it is expressed as the same Augustin-ian minimalism which characterized Remigio, Dante, and Marsilius. Temporal power is instrumental, it is a means to social existence, a way of preventing or punishing injustice. It is not an embodiment of higher values. The common good is not the life of perfect moral virtue but the social necessity of peace and security. By treating the promotion of virtue as a non-essential function of temporal government, Ockham aimed to keep the material goal of temporal rulers separate from the spiritual goal of the Christian Church. Like John of Paris, Remigio, and Dante, therefore, and unlike Marsilius, Ockham accepts the need for two powers, each with their respective functions, and like Remigio and Dante, Ockham is careful to restrict these functions to carefully defined spheres of activity. The role of the Church, therefore, is driven by a Franciscan critique of property and temporal jurisdiction. Its paradigm is the apostolic life of poverty, preaching, administering the sacraments, and exercising charity towards the poor. Like John of Paris, Dante, and Remigio, Ockham accordingly denounced the Donation of Constantine as a grant which had distracted the Church from its true spiritual function. The role of the temporal power, meanwhile, is limited to punishment of the wicked and to the preservation of peace, concord, and tranquillity; it is not an instrument of virtue and happiness but a guarantor of material security, an authority which ensures a political framework within which individuals will be free to exercise their rights and liberties. The result is a *de facto* separation of the spiritual from the temporal power which does not deny the presence of a theoretical connection between the two, or even a right of reciprocal intervention in each other's jurisdictions, but which carefully circumscribes the functions of each in such a way as to limit the implementation of this theory in practice.

Ockham's belief in limited jurisdictions for both the spiritual and the temporal power had its origins in a particular conception of individual liberty based, characteristically enough, on the New Testament and James 1:25: "the perfect law that gives freedom" (*lex evangelica lex libertatis*). This concept of freedom, however, is primarily negative in its formulation in that it is used by Ockham to demonstrate that the subjects of both spiritual and temporal rulers must not be reduced to the status of slaves. Within the Church and the empire, Ockham argues, there are some liberties and rights which have been legitimized by consent, by just war, or by falling outside an explicitly scriptural remit, and which therefore cannot be overridden without a ruler becoming a tyrant and reducing his subjects to slaves (Kilcullen 1999). The individual is thus subordinated only to those external obligations which are imposed by spiritual and temporal authority to enable humans to live together in peace and tranquillity. Such freedom, however, is also circumscribed by these requirements. The legitimate rights of individuals should therefore always give way to considerations of necessity and the common good.

Such pragmatism is as central a feature of Ockham's political thinking as his emphasis on evangelical poverty. Precisely because there was so little scriptural prescription of the institutional organization of both the spiritual and the temporal powers, Ockham is always careful to hedge his political arguments with practical qualifications. Monarchical government, for example, is preferable, in an absolute sense, for both the temporal and the ecclesiastical powers but, in both cases, Ockham insists that allowance has to be made for those changes which can be brought about by circumstance, namely when rulers become corrupt, tyrannical, or heretical. On these occasions, the advice of "the wise" (*periti*) must be sought, either informally or as a council, in order to restore the common good of a society which has become endangered by its ruler's sins. Such contingent measures may prove a short-term or a long-term expedient depending on the exact historical circumstances. Insofar as this is given a theoretical basis, it rests on Ockham's understanding of equity, that is, the capacity to dispense from a general law or principle so that the demands of a particular case can be met while maintaining the original purpose of that law or principle, namely the preservation of the common good. Ockham therefore remains critical of Marsilius's absolute prescription of conciliarism. At no point does he wish to deny the scriptural basis of the Petrine commission nor of the desirability of a monarchical form of government. However, Ockham does accept that circumstances – most notably papal error and heresy – can be such that, at particular historical moments, conciliar procedures will have to be implemented.

The rediscovery of Aristotle's *Ethics, Politics,* and *Rhetoric* in the late thirteenth century showed scholastic theologians how the conduct and organization of human beings in political communities could be examined more analytically than merely by laws and decrees. However, these texts also indicated that the resulting truths were general rather than universal and that the purpose of such an investigation was to will the good rather than just to know the truth. Viewed in this light, the subsequent Renaissance caricature of scholastic political thought as too abstract, speculative, or even abstruse, to be of any practical importance or value clearly requires substantial modification. More significantly, Giles of Rome, James of Viterbo, John of Paris, Dante, Marsilius of Padua, and William of Ockham reveal the intimacy of the resulting connection within scholastic political thinking between ecclesiology and politics. This amounts to more than just saying that scholastic political writing concerned itself with the relationship between the spiritual and the temporal powers. This subject was certainly central to the form which it took in the late thirteenth and early fourteenth centuries, as a succession of highly public disputes, between Boniface VIII and Philip the Fair, Clement V and Henry of Luxembourg, John XXII and Ludwig of Bavaria, called forth a succession of scholastic treatises on this subject. However, in devoting their attention, accordingly, to the conception of papal plenitude of power which was so central to these disputes, scholastic writers applied principles of government which operated in one sphere to principles which operated in the other.

This can be seen in the late thirteenth century when the controversies over *Ad fructus uberes* and over clerical taxation caused scholastic theologians to examine the exact location of authority within *both* temporal *and* ecclesiastical communities. Godfrey of Fontaines, for example, established the common good as the measure of political and legal legitimacy when he discussed the justification of opposition to royal taxation but then applied the same concept to the justification of opposition to papal grants of dispensation from conciliar decrees. It was this transfer which then became so central to John of Paris's argument that a pope could be made accountable to the common good of the Church and should therefore be removed, not just for heresy and other manifest crimes, but also for mismanagement of his stewardship of the goods of the Church. John of Paris thereby made a powerful connection between Aristotle, Roman law, and canon law, locating authority within the whole Church rather than just in the pope. Marsilius of Padua drew a similar, if more extreme, conclusion from Aristotle's *Politics*. In establishing his principle of collective wisdom, Marsilius is careful to point out that the human legislator can be "the whole body of the citizens or its weightier part" (*valentior pars*). This final phrase is, again, originally Aristotle's (*Politics* IV.12: 99) and its immediate importance is to give Marsilius a sufficiently flexible political principle to cover city-states, kingdoms, and the Empire. However, it also applies to the community of the Church, where Marsilius can now maintain that it is the whole body of the faithful or a general council which can determine matters of faith and doctrine. William of Ockham, finally, made the common good the basis of a theory of Church government which could justify a general council as a contingent response to a specific set of historical circumstances. Taken together, the critique of *plenitudo potestatis* which was established by Henry of Ghent and Godfrey of Fontaines and then expanded upon (in their different ways) by John of Paris, Marsilius of Padua, and William of Ockham, came to exercise a profound influence on conciliar ecclesiology in the fourteenth and early fifteenth centuries.

It is, perhaps, too often taken for granted that late medieval political theory witnessed the origins of the idea of a "secular state" as the product of man's political nature, a process of secularization caused directly by the rediscovery of Aristotle's *Ethics* and *Politics*. If the reception of Aristotle reveals anything, it is instead the flexibility with which the twin principles of the natural origin of the political community and the common good of the life of virtue could be applied. The question which proved such a bone of contention between Giles of Rome, James of Viterbo, and John of Paris was not so much the natural origin of society as the relation of moral virtue to theological virtue, the life of virtue to eternal beatitude. It is clear from Dante, Marsilius, and Ockham, however, that any "secularizing" tendencies which appear in subsequent scholastic writings were not provided by championing the moral autonomy of Aristotle's political community. Precisely the opposite. It was the absence of this life of virtue, the dropping of this moral requirement from their definition of the political community, which formed the distinctive feature of this political thinking. This was achieved by appealing, not to Aristotle, but to Augustine. By removing moral virtue from their theoretical definition of the goal of the political community, by insisting instead on material peace and security, all three writers were intending to remove a central support for the justification of papal intervention in temporal jurisdiction. They did so, moreover, from a profound commitment to a New Testament ideal of the *vita apostolica* of poverty and preaching (Leff 1967). Removing the Church from the temporal sphere was intended to correct the baleful effects of papal plenitude of power. Such a separation was for the benefit of the Church and was not designed to be absolute. John of Paris's conception of accidental perfection, Dante's paternal blessing of grace, Marsilius's numerical identity of *universitas civium* and *universitas fidelium*, and Ockham's emphasis on pragmatism and contingency, were all designed to acknowlege a continuing connection between the temporal and the spiritual power. Viewed in this light, the advocacy by Dante, Marsilius, and Ockham of distinctively Franciscan ideals becomes all the more important. If the "birth of the lay spirit" is to be located in the early fourteenth century, then it originated, not in a positive alternative of "secular" power, but in criticism and reform of the Church from within. From this perspective, the truly radical texts in scholastic political thought were provided, not by Aristotle, but by Augustine and the Bible.

References

Aristotle, *Nicomachean Ethics*, trans. D. Ross, rev. J. L. Ackrill and J. O. Urmson, Oxford, 1980.

Aristotle, *Politics*, trans. S. Everson, Cambridge, 1988.

Aristotle, *On Rhetoric*, trans. G. A. Kennedy, Oxford, 1991.

Augustine, *City of God*, trans. H. Bettenson, Harmondsworth, 1972.

Bruni, G., "The *De Differentia Rhetoricae, Ethicae et Politicae* of Aegidius Romanus," *The New Scholasticism*, 6 (1932), pp. 1–18.

Burns, J. H., ed., *The Cambridge History of Medieval Political Thought c.350–c.1450*, Cambridge, 1988.

Coleman, J., "Medieval Discussions of Property – *ratio* and *dominium* According to John of Paris and Marsilius of Padua," *History of Political Thought*, 4 (1983), pp. 209–28.

Coleman, J., "Property and Poverty," *Cambridge History of Medieval Political Thought*, ed. J. Burns, Cambridge, 1988, pp. 607–48.

Dante, *Monarchia*, trans. P. Shaw, Cambridge, 1995.

Dante, *The Divine Comedy*, trans. C. S. Singleton, Princeton, 1970.

Davis, C. T., "An Early Florentine Political Theorist – Fra Remigio de' Girolami," *Proceedings of the American Philosophical Society*, 104 (1960), pp. 662–76.

Decrees of the Ecumenical Councils, ed. and trans. N. Tanner, 2 vols., London, 1990.

pseudo-Dionysius, *The Celestial Hierarchy*, trans. C. Luibheid, in *Pseudo-Dionysius, The Complete Works*, New York, 1987.

Dunbabin, J. H., "Aristotle in the Schools," in B. Smalley, ed., *Trends in Medieval Political Thought*, Oxford, 1965, pp. 65–85.

Dunbabin, J. H., "The Reception and Interpretation of Aristotle's *Politics*," in N. Kretzmann, A. Kenny, and J. Pinborg, eds., *The Cambridge History of Later Medieval Philosophy – From the Rediscovery of Aristotle to the Disintegration of Scholasticism 1100–1600*, Cambridge, 1982, pp. 723–37.

Gewirth, A., *Marsilius of Padua and Medieval Political Philosophy*, in *Marsilius of Padua – The Defender of the Peace*, 2 vols., New York, 1951, vol. I.

Giles of Rome, *On Ecclesiastical Power*, trans. R. W. Dyson, Woodbridge, 1986.

Gilson, E., *Dante and Philosophy*, trans. D. Moore, New York, 1963.

Hugh of St. Victor, *Didascalion*, trans. J. Taylor, New York, 1961.

James of Viterbo, *On Christian Government*, trans. R. W. Dyson, Woodbridge, 1995.

John of Paris, *On Royal and Papal Power*, trans. J. Watt, Toronto, 1971.

Kempshall, M. S., *The Common Good in Late Medieval Political Thought*, Oxford, 1999.

Kilcullen, J., "The Political Writings," in P. V. Spade, ed., *The Cambridge Companion to Ockham*, Cambridge, 1999, pp. 302–25.

Leff, G., "The Apostolic Ideal in Later Medieval Ecclesiology," *Journal of Theological Studies*, 18 (1967), pp. 58–82.

Luscombe, D. E., "The *Lex Divinitatis* in the Bull *Unam Sanctam* of Pope Boniface VIII," in C. N. L. Brooke, D. E. Luscombe, G. H. Martin, and D. Owen, eds., *Church and Government in the Middle Ages*, Cambridge, 1976.

Luscombe, D. E., "Thomas Aquinas and Conceptions of Hierarchy in the Thirteenth Century," *Miscellanea Mediaevalia*, 19 (1988), pp. 261–77.

Marsilius of Padua, *The Defender of the Peace*, trans. A. Gewirth, New York, 1951.

McCready, W. D., "Papal *plenitudo potestatis* and the Source of Temporal Authority in Late Medieval Hierocratic Theory," *Speculum*, 48 (1973), pp. 654–74.

McGrade, A. S., *The Political Thought of William of Ockham – Personal and Institutional Principles*, Cambridge, 1974.

McGrade, A. S., Kempshall, M. S., and Kilcullen, J., *Translations of Medieval Philosophical Texts – Ethics and Political Philosophy*, Cambridge, 2000.

Minio-Paluello, L., "Remigio Girolami's *De bono communi* – Florence at the Time of Dante's Banishment and the Philosopher's Answer to the Crisis," *Italian Studies*, 11 (1956), pp. 56–71.

Reeves, M., "Marsiglio of Padua and Dante Alighieri," in B. Smalley, ed., *Trends in Medieval Politcal Thought*, Oxford, 1965, pp. 86–104.

Robert, S., "Rhetoric and Dialectic according to the First Latin Commentary on the Rhetoric of Aristotle," *The New Scholasticism*, 31 (1957), pp. 484–98.

Rubinstein, N., "Marsilius of Padua and Italian Political Thought of his Time," in J. R. Hale, J. R. L. Highfield, and B. Smalley, eds., *Europe in the Later Middle Ages*, London, 1965.

Thomas Aquinas, *Selected Political Writings*, ed. A. P. d'Entreves, trans. J. G. Dawson, Oxford, 1959.

Tierney, B., *Foundations of the Conciliar Theory – The Contribution of the Medieval Canonists from Gratian to the Great Schism*, Cambridge, 1955.

Tierney, B., *The Crisis of Church and State 1050–1300*, Englewood Cliffs, NJ, 1964.

Tierney, B., *The Idea of Natural Rights – Studies on Natural Rights, Natural Law and Church Law 1150–1625*, Atlanta, 1997.

Watt, J. A., "Spiritual and Temporal Powers," in J. Burns, ed., *Cambridge History of Medieval Political Thought*, Cambridge, 1988, pp. 367–423.

William of Ockham, *A Short Discourse on Tyrannical Government*, ed. A. S. McGrade, trans. J. Kilcullen, Cambridge, 1992.

Wyclif and Lollardy

Stephen Lahey

John Wyclif's place in the history of Christian ideas varies according to the historian's interest. As scholastic theology, Wyclif's thought appears an heretical epilogue to the glories of the systematic innovations of the thirteenth century. Historians of the Protestantism, on the other hand, characterize him as a pioneer, the "Morning Star of the Reformation," acknowledging his theology and the Lollard and Hussite movements associated with it as forerunners of sixteenth-century change. It has been difficult to understand Wyclif as a man of his age because the late fourteenth century itself is easily viewed as a period of transition from "Late Medieval" to "Early Modern." Recent scholarship has helped to change this by showing how the decline of systematic Thomism and Scotism, the developing Ockhamist *Moderni* movement, and a vibrant Augustinianism contributed to form an atmosphere in which Wyclif's theological innovations were a recognizable, albeit unorthodox, expression of the period. The beginning of the fourteenth century saw a shift in the practice of theology, from the magisterial *Summa* to an interest in terminist analysis of specific theological problems. Theology had become "mathematized," reduced to a set of problems soluble through examination of the concepts involved.[1] Ockham's *Moderni* movement is most associated with this methodological shift, and most theologians of the period, whether philosophical Ockhamists or not, embraced it. Robert Holcot and Adam Wodeham are among the best-known analysts of terms, concepts, and propositions associated with understanding the divine nature and attributes, and the psychological elements of human willing, loving, and enjoyment relevant to merit and grace, among other problems.

Ockham's approach to the thorny problem of divine foreknowledge and future contingents is particularly significant for understanding later fourteenth-century theological controversy. Ockham believed his account of divinely known future contingent truths preserved the contingency of the future action without detracting from God's perfect knowledge; further, he argued that the human will was capable of actively eliciting its enjoyment of God above all things. If our will achieves this through its own agency, independently of God's foregoing causal knowledge, critics responded, the Pelagian heresy in which one can merit grace through one's works is resurrected.[2] The most notable of these critics was the Mertonian Thomas Bradwardine, whose *De Causa Dei* argues that God predestines all created action, including all human willing; no one can will without God having eternally willed that they will as they do.[3]

Bradwardine's determinist position is important not only because of its effect on academic treatments of merit, grace, and the future contingents problem into the sixteenth century; it also highlighted a revival of Augustinianism at Oxford that achieved its fullest expression in Wyclif's thought. The Paris condemnations of 1277 had set the stage for an increase of interest in orthodox Augustinian theology, and theologians of the following years like Gregory of Rimini emphasized the need for faithfulness to Augustine's writings over *Moderni* innovation. In Oxford, Uthred of Bolton had formulated a position redolent of the controversial Pelagianism, and Rimini's disciple John Klenkok imported the new Augustinianism into England to combat Uthred. The influence of the Augustinian, or "Austin," friars in Oxford was instrumental in helping to transport Augustinianism across the channel, particularly in the form of arguments specifying the need for grace for any just exercise of authority.[4] Giles of Rome's papalist *De Ecclesiastica Potestate* was the first to formulate this thesis, and effectively defined the new Augustinianism. Giles's arguments were particularly appealing to the Irish scholar Richard Fitzralph, whose *De Pauperie Salvatoris* responded to Franciscan Minorites using Giles's contention that grace alone justifies authority, in this case, over temporal goods. Fitzralph's innovation was to introduce the term *dominium* to the discussion, making grace-founded *dominium* an important concept in mid-fourteenth-century Oxford.[5] By mid-century, despite the depradations of Black Death, theological discourse at Oxford was lively, enriched by Bradwardine's determinism and Fitzralph's Augustinianism; scholars like Richard Brinkley, Thomas Buckingham, and Peter of Candia enjoyed an atmosphere in which philosophically innovative Augustinian theology could flourish.

Wyclif arrived at Oxford from Yorkshire in the 1350s, and following an education in the systematic theology of Thomism, Scotism, and the new learning of the *Moderni*, he rose to become Master of Balliol College and his generation's foremost logician and realist metaphysician.[6] He began theological studies in 1363, and was ordained six years later. As was then common for ordained scholars, he held benefices in Lincolnshire, Buckinghamshire, and Gloucestershire while at Oxford, until 1381, when he retired to Ludgershall, Leicestershire, where he died in 1384. While these facts suggest a placid life as scholar and rector, events in Wyclif's life and his own inability to accept compromise on the priest's ecclesiastical responsibilities led to a tumultuous career. He entered the service of John of Gaunt, Duke of Lancaster, in 1372, representing the Crown at negotiations with papal nuncios in Bruges in 1374, and supported Gaunt in parliamentary disputes in 1376 and in the Hauley-Shakyll incident in 1378. Shortly after he began his royal service, Wyclif decided that he was obliged to turn from metaphysics to more practical matters. "It is time for me to give the rest of my life to matters as much speculative as practical, according to the capacity that God has given."[7] So his writings shifted from the academic pursuits of pure logic and metaphysics to the need for ecclesiastical reform, the right relation of secular to sacred authority, to issues of fraternal and papal responsibilities, Scriptural interpretation, and the Eucharist.[8]

Wyclif's earlier writings on the need for royal divestment and control of the English Church earned him lasting ecclesiastical antipathy. In 1377 Bishop William Courtenay attempted formally to confront Wyclif but was foiled by popular unrest. Shortly thereafter Gregory XI demanded Wyclif's arrest and examination, and Courtenay attempted again in 1382 to force Wyclif into submission at Blackfriars, where 24 propositions characterizing Wyclif's ecclesiology were condemned as heresy. In each instance, the Duke of Lancaster's protection ensured Wyclif safety in what would otherwise have been life-threatening confrontations.[9] The Council of Constance declared Wyclif an heresiarch in 1415, unjustly condemned and burned the Bohemian Jan Hus for having espoused Wyclifism, and ordered Wyclif's remains to be exhumed, burned, and thrown into the river Swift. Connections between Wyclif's realist metaphysics and his ecclesiological ideas were sufficiently evident to scholars in Prague to prompt them to embrace his ecclesiology after having accepted his ontology, which played an important role in the tumultuous Hussite rebellion of the fifteenth century. Following Constance and the defeat of the Hussites, there were no significant instances of this realism again in the scholastic tradition.

Most twentieth-century scholarship of Wyclif's theology has been predicated on the influence of his earlier philosophical writings on his later, more practical theology.[10] Indeed, throughout his logical and metaphysical treatises one occasionally catches glimpses of Wyclif's mounting frustration with the state of the Church, while his formal philosophy undergirds many of the arguments of the later treatises, occasionally resurfacing in his arguments for the need of logical training in interpreting Scripture and understanding the Eucharist. While Wyclif did not disagree with Ockhamism on many points, including sensitivity to the relation of language to thought and to extralinguistic reality, he adamantly rejected Ockham's denial of the existence of universals outside the mind. In fact, he felt that advocacy of such a spare ontology contributed to society's downfall. "Thus, beyond doubt, intellectual and emotional error about universals is the cause of all the sin that reigns in the world."[11] Wyclif contended that God knows creation primarily through universals and only secondarily as individual creatures. This need not entail the existence of some realm of universals apart from divine and created being; universals exist primarily in God as second intentional concepts and secondarily in created essences as first intentional concepts.[12]

While Wyclif accepted the reality of traditional universals like genus and species and so on that had been introduced to scholasticism by Boethius and disputed in the schools for centuries beforehand, he departed from contemporary realists like Walter Burley and Gregory of Rimini by arguing that universals are the foundation for relations as well. Thus, any relation holding between creatures has a reality beyond the creatures themselves; its being is founded in God's conception of the paradigm of that relation.[13] Hence, Adam's paternity relation to the rest of humanity is real through God's conception of paternity as such and its connection to Adam's being as the first instantiation of the species Man. In this sense, Wyclif explains, all mankind existed potentially in Adam by virtue of his causal priority as the first father. This is a radical departure from the Aristotelian understanding of relations, and was to have important consequences for Wyclif's conception of the Church and of human dominion in creation. Certainly the most obvious consequence has to do with salvation; if some will be saved and others damned at judgment, some will have a relation of "justification through grace" to their Creator that others will lack. And while the "justification" relation is a consequence of how the saved act, it has reality by virtue of God's understanding of justification and who will enjoy it. "The entire species of man is complete through God's mediation, and . . . the multitude of the predestined are one genus, whose principle is the celestial Adam [Christ], while all the damned are a lesser generation, whose father and prince is the devil."[14] As a result, Wyclif's relational realism involves a deterministic theology evocative of and reliant upon Bradwardine's anti-Pelagianism.

Bradwardine held that God's perfect foreknowledge and omnipotence meant that every created action is directly caused by God's participation in the activity. Indeed, Bradwardine held that this coeffiency of activity extends to cases of human sin; here, God's moving causal primacy is as much a cause of the mechanics of the physical act of the sin as is the sinning agent. Only the sinner's will acts alone, although in any case in which the created agent wills the good, God's causal power moves along with the agent's willing, and is the reason why it is good.[15] Wyclif felt that Bradwardine's position could too easily be taken to eliminate the possibility of merit and demerit in human activity, suggesting that clarity about the necessity with which God foreknows future events dispels theological error.[16] The means by which Wyclif addresses this determinism is distinguishing between the kind of necessity by which God knows who will be saved and the kind of necessity of truths not dependent upon created action, like mathematical or definitional truth. That God necessarily knows who will be among the saved is undeniable, but a consequence of the activity of created wills.

This could suggest that God's knowledge is caused by created events, compromising the divine essence's perfection. Wyclif hastens to distinguish between the way in which our knowledge is causally reliant upon and temporally consequent to created action, and the way in which divine knowledge is eternal, and so neither temporally consequent to, nor causally reliant upon, temporal events. *That* we will freely, God eternally wills with absolute necessity, but *how* we will is only hypothetically necessary. Although God eternally knows, and wills, that I will X at a given time, I might have willed otherwise then, in which case it would have been absolutely necessary that God know and will that I will otherwise. Our action only has causal power over eternal knowledge after the fact; there is no reduction in God's power, because as eternal knower God is prior ontologically to creation. So while there is a sense in which our action "causes" divine knowledge, that sense does not entail contingency in the divine nature.[17]

Wyclif's metaphysical realism about relations is important not only because it illustrates how Wyclif's thought diverges from Bradwardine's, but also because it provides the theoretical framework on which his ecclesiology rests. Two conclusions follow from it. First, God knows who are the Elect, predestined for salvation, and so the real members of Christ's earthly body. This means that the true Church is the congregation of the Elect, free of sin and favored by grace through Christ's redemption to live the ideal life. Anyone tainted by sin claiming membership in the church must be an imposter, and anyone so stained claiming ecclesiastical authority must forcibly be stopped. Second, every just action for which we are responsible is an instantiation of God's justice, and every law-grounded relation we enjoy is only a real relation through divine law. These two concepts lead directly to Wyclif's indictment of the existing Church's hunger for secular authority, to his insistence on the need for clerical reform and for royal divestment of Church property, and to his contention that Scripture must be available in the vernacular for the proper instruction of the Elect on earth.

Wyclif's conception of the Church's identity is the foundation of his ecclesiological program. "The holy doctors are in agreement stating that all the elect are, from the beginning of the world to the day of judgement, one person which is the mother Church."[18] This definition of the true Church as the congregation of the Elect causes some problems, notably in determining exactly who are saved, and who are damned. That it is impossible to know who is predestined, Wyclif explains, should help us recognize that Church membership is no basis for claims of earthly authority. "Without a special revelation, no one should assert that he is predestined, and similarly, he should not assert that he is a member of the Church, or for that matter, its head."[19]

It follows that, if the Church is the congregation of the elect, whose identity remains unknown in this life, the need for clerical authority is likely to be decreased, if not eliminated altogether. It is tempting to interpret Wyclif as having endorsed the abolition of the priesthood altogether, given his claim that "all the predestined are at once kings and priests."[20] While this could follow from his definition of the Church, Wyclif explains that the Church has need of a class of "evangelical lords" who instruct Christians by teaching and exemplifying *lex Christi*. There is need for a clerical hierarchy of authority, however; bishops are useful primarily to prevent clerical abuse of authority, while the pope can serve as spiritual exemplar for the entire Church. The existing papal machinery of ecclesiastical control is an abomination, existing to attain and maintain the mundane power inimical to the priestly office. The arguments papalists present to justify this authority are without Scriptural foundation. Where in the Petrine commission is anything said of special powers of the absolution of sin or excommunication granted to some of Christ's servants but not to others? "How dare anyone say that he alone has the singular power of absolving any sinner from punishment and blame?"[21] Surely such authority is God's alone to assign to as many as He will, without restriction. Nor is excommunication a tool for anyone to trifle with for their own ends, "for it is certain that anyone sinning mortally excommunicates himself, that is, places himself outside the community of the faithful, and accordingly a minister of the church publishes that fact by denouncing the excommunicant and forbidding him from any communication with others in God's name . . . [T]he Church today is without any foundation in pretending to excommunicate to obtain temporal goods; neither the apostles nor any of Christ's disciples knew that sort of power; rather than scandalize the church by demanding even the necessities of life, . . . they would endure hunger, thirst, and scant clothing, and would set themselvs to manual labor."[22] Throughout Wyclif's works, he stresses that excommunication is a matter between God and sinner, without need for clerical interference, that anyone claiming the authority to excommunicate pretends to divine authority, thereby indicating his or her own sinful state.[23]

Priestly authority may be necessary for guidance, but when priests assume that the office allows its holders secular power, they confuse two kinds of law. The Church is defined by Christ's law, which is exemplified by Christ's life and illustrated by the purity of the early Church. Secular power is different from spiritual authority, and the law that serves as its foundation is grounded not in Christ's life, but in original sin and the institution of private ownership, from which Christ's law liberates us. Those who accept the responsibility of instructing others in Christ's law are bound, Wyclif holds, to obey it scrupulously, to turn away from the world's temptations not only to strengthen their own spiritual resolution but also to embody the Christian life. Of primary interest for Wyclif is the clergy's tendency to use their authority to wield secular power, from papal claims of superiority over emperors and kings down to the lowliest priest's claiming ownership of property. While anyone can rationalize a hunger for temporal goods by pretending to be concerned for the Church, they should not fool themselves. "Because they have cold intentions towards temporal goods for which they strive, they are hypocrites, as abominable to God as the tepid water which causes vomiting."[24]

Property ownership is part of a concept that lies at the heart of Wyclif's theology, *dominium*, which also includes jurisdiction and enforcing what is right. *Dominium* is the chief relation holding between Creator and creation, consequent upon God's creative act, entailing His governance and sustenance of all things as well as His ultimate authority in any action associated with ownership of creation, including giving, receiving, and lending any created thing. In fact, God's *dominium* lies at the foundation of anything in creation having the capacity to exercise any kind of power whatever. Recall that Wyclif held that all relations in creation are prefigured and ontologically reliant upon God's being; the justice of any created being's exercise of power is grounded in divine justice, and the actual exercise of that power is causally reliant on God's willing that action. Hence, a creature's having any capacity to give, receive, or lend, and to exercise jurisdiction or authority, is causally reliant upon, and prefigured by, God's own *dominium*. In Aristotelian terms, any creature's having, which Wyclif explains is the tenth category in Aristotle's list of predicables, is reliant upon God's antecedent having: "And the dominion of God . . . his lordship over every creature, is the principle of the final category."[25] So God's *dominium* serves as a universal relation in which all created instances of *dominium* participate.

Wyclif describes God's *dominium* in *De Dominio Divino*, the first major treatise he produced after having decided to turn his attentions to "more practical" matters. Here he explains that God's *dominium* is the "standard and presupposition" for all relations involving jurisdiction or ownership in creation, including the natural lordship mankind enjoyed before the Fall, the evangelical lordship exercised by priests, and the coercive, civil lordship that characterizes secular power. "The lordship of God is the measure, as prior and presuppositum, of every other [lordship] assigned; if one creature has lordship over another, God has prior lordship over it, so any created lordship follows upon God's lordship, and not otherwise."[26] In keeping with his realist metaphysics, Wyclif explains that God's *dominium* over creation is secondary to His *dominium* over the universals that provide its order and structure. This means that God knows and has authority over humanity as such before having it over individual people. And since God's *dominium* is the paradigm for all created instances of lordship, it follows that *dominium* as such is ideally over whole classes of things, rather than over individual objects.[27]

That the concept has come to mean the exercise of authority and ownership over particular things in the world illustrates how man's understanding has been weakened by sin. As created, Wyclif explains, man enjoyed true *dominium* over creation, and the lordship Adam exercised was a true instantiation of, and participation in, God's *dominium*. Characterizing this natural *dominium* was the absence of distinction between lord and subject as we have come to understand it; natural lords were as much servants as lords, because "all men have a dual nature, both elements of which, namely body and soul, serve the other in serving themselves, and they serve the just if the man is in a state of grace. Accordingly any man is corporally subservient to his spirit, and spiritually subservient to that of his brother, so he is at once lord and servant."[28] Any human being was a lord as much as subject in prelapsarian natural *dominium*, because nobody had a will bent on serving itself to the exclusion of God; thus, distinctions of "mine" and "thine" were foreign before the Fall. "Natural *dominium* extends across the entire world: heaven, earth, and the universe in which the heavens are contained . . . [it] requires no solicitude or looking after by any secular lord, janitor, or lesser minister, . . . [it] is not eradicable from human nature, despite the obstacles of sin."[29] The stamp of natural lordship remains with us even if the innocence in which we exercise it is lost, by virtue of the ideal exemplar humanity by which we have our being and are known primarily by God.

Sin destroyed man's capacity for natural *dominium* by introducing the illusion of exclusive ownership, in which one selfishly assumes exclusive control of property. Since creation alone is the foundation for such exclusive ownership, and only God creates, this supposition is grounded in illusion. To claim unrestricted authority over what someone else has brought into being is to suppose that the other agent is capable of giving over absolute control of the object. But, Wyclif explains, it is impossible to abdicate *dominium* in this sense; bringing something into being entails remaining responsible for it throughout its being. The requirement of creation as necessary condition for ownership is based securely in Wyclif's philosophical theology, in which "God produces all works most principally, most immediately, and most exclusively . . . creatures do nothing unless previously motivated through and helped by God's movement."[30] When God gives to us, He never loses control over the gift; God keeps all of creation in being, so what God gives remains to a real extent God's. "Because God is omnipotent and His multiple creation is required by any creature, it follows that He cannot alienate through giving any of His gifts because of the plenitude of His dominion."[31]

Private property ownership is a fiction founded on the belief that God can abdicate His *dominium* over the owned sufficiently to allow the owner real control over it. Wyclif was certainly not the first to have suggested this; his theory of ownership is heavily reliant on the literature of the Franciscan Poverty Controversy, and distinctions between ownership, possession, and various kinds of use were fully developed in William Ockham's *Opus Nonaginta Dierum* and in Richard Fitzralph's *De Pauperie Salvatoris*. Wyclif's understanding of the ultimate impossibility of exclusive property ownership among men and of the consequential artificiality of postlapsarian civil *dominium* is reliant on Fitzralph's treatise, in places so much so that critics have accused him of having cribbed from Fitzralph. While there is no question that Wyclif made use of Fitzralph, the results of his incorporation of Fitzralph's conception of *dominium* into his own philosophical theology are sufficiently original to rule out this accusation.

Until Christ's coming, the specter of property ownership eliminated any possibility of man's serving God as a natural lord. God would never deprive the just of any gift without recompense, and Wyclif argues that those made righteous through Christ's redemption and His institution of *lex Christi* regain the lost natural *dominium* by living in the apostolic purity of evangelical *dominium*. "Man in a state of innocence had lordship over every part of the sensible world, and the virtue of the passion of Christ is [the basis] for righteous remission of all sins and for restitution of lordship, so the temporal recipients of grace have justly complete universal lordship."[32] Christ lived a communal life with the apostles, sharing everything in the *caritas* of His sinless nature, and those who follow His example, realizing through grace the restored *caritas* of apostolic purity, regain the natural lordship now called evangelical *dominium*. "For all men coexisting in *caritas* on this side of Christ communicate in the things over which they exercise lordship . . . since all members of the church hold unmediatedly their lordship from Christ their chief lord, which I call natural, evangelical, original, or grace-endowed lordship . . . restored by the gospel, beyond which any superadded lordship would be superfluous."[33]

It is difficult at this point to see why Wyclif would later attack the friars so vehemently, given the obvious similarities uniting his ideal of evangelical surrender of civil lordship and the mendicant ideal defended by Michael of Cesena, Ockham, and others. The theoretical seeds for his later indictment of the friars lie in Wyclif's distinction between St. Francis's ideal and Christ's: followers of Francis are called Franciscans, while followers of Jesus Christ are not "Jesuans," reliant upon the rule of a man, but Christians. In an order instituted by man, obedience of the rule may or may not be a necessary condition for grace, while a life faithful in Christ, a divinely-instituted ideal, is needed to receive grace. Franciscans follow a rule constructed by a man, while Christians live by Christ's divinely appointed law.[34] So long as the friars argue that Christians ought to surrender civil ownership to enjoy apostolic purity, they are correct, but when they suppose that their Order is the foundation for the righteousness of this purity, they err greivously. Wyclif's later writings became increasingly directed against the Friars, whom he nicknamed "Caim," an acronym referring to Carmelites, Augustinians, Dominicans (Jacobites), and Franciscans (Minorites). In the *Trialogus* Wyclif outlines the six chief evils perpetrated by the mendicant orders. They oppress Christians with the burden of their physical needs and the greedy prices they charge for their services as confessors, they avoid labor, they sully Christ's law with impertinent additions that benefit themselves, they ignore the rebukes of non-friars, they hunger for wealth and worldly honor, and "what is worst of all, they seduce to their ruin in spiritual things those of the people who rashly put their faith in them."[35] Many of the shorter Latin pieces of Wyclif's later life are directed against the friars, as are a considerable number of the vernacular tracts attributed to him.[36]

We must not suppose that lacking private ownership is all that is needed to regain our lost birthright. There have always been poor people, but their suffering does not mean they live in the righteous state of prelapsarian man. The poverty characterizing evangelical *dominium* is a state of one's spirit, and not only a matter of having or not having things. "Evangelical poverty has nothing to do with the possession of temporal goods, but [is a] mode of caring having, which augments wealth neither by increasing nor by taking away from it, just as on the other hand it neither augments nor decreases a privation of goods."[37] Evangelical *dominium* is so different from the civil *dominium* resulting from sin that defining it must not take civil elements into consideration.

The doctrine of natural *dominium* restored through Christ's redemption of original sin provides the basis for Wyclif's demand that all priests live in apostolic poverty and humility, removed from the taint of private property and secular authority, and for his contention that the king ought to bring this about through divestment of ecclesiastical authority and property. It would appear that the justification for royal control of the Church is precluded by Wyclif's rejection of the justice of civil *dominium*; how can someone be sufficiently righteous to cleanse the Church when he embodies the institution caused by original sin? Had Wyclif desired, he might have argued as Marsilius had, for a complete separation of the two realms of Church and State, with secular authority having total control over all temporal goods. This was certainly how Gregory XI interpreted Wyclif, for the bulls condemning *De Civili Dominio* accuse it of Marsilianism.

Wyclif differs importantly from Marsilius, though, because his political theory is nested in his theology. The justice of civil rule is only real through participation in divine justice; *De Civili Dominio* begins with the motto "Divine justice is presupposed by civil justice; Natural lordship is presupposed by civil lordship."[38] Wyclif's idea is that a just civil lord is just through grace, since, as he had argued in his philosophical theology, God's will is the primary cause of a given individual's acting justly. Thus it is possible for someone to exercise proprietative and jurisdictive authority with God's justice, but only if he is eternally foreknown to be among the Elect favored by grace. A just king, then, is first and foremost a member of the Church, but one who is not free to abandon the cares of civil ownership. His place is to serve as God's minister in the postlapsarian world, a steward of temporal goods acting as a human lord on behalf of the interests of the divine lord.

> Since the king is the minister of God, according to the correspondent eminence of virtue, it is clear that he should rule following the divine law by which the people are ordered. Since it is the part of justice to decline from evil and to do good, the king should coerce rebels against divine law and other authorities, and advance the factors of justice according to the laws of *caritas*. The king should have the power of ministratively ruling his subjects from God, and not by human law lacking divine sanction.[39]

Wyclif's just king is the central aspect of a political theory that emerges from his ecclesiology, and is better understood as a follower of *lex Christi* shouldering the responsibilities of postlapsarian life on behalf of the other evangelical lords than as a secular officeholder.[40] That priests have come to embrace the secular encumbrances from which Christ freed His flock is the greatest threat now facing the Church, and should be the king's chief concern. This is because the king is as much Christ's vicar as any bishop is, realizing Christ's divinity to exercise *dominium* over physical goods just as prelates realize Christ's humanity to exercise a different kind of *dominium* over spiritual affairs.

> It is right for God to have two vicars in His church; namely a king in temporal affairs, and a priest in spiritual. The king should strongly check rebellion as did God in the Old Testament. Priests ought minister the precepts mildly, in a humble manner, just as Christ did, Who was at once priest and king.[41]

The cancer of private property ownership and its attendant hunger for secular authority was introduced into the Church by the Donation of Constantine, Wyclif explains, and can be purged only by a grace-endowed civil lord using his office as God intends to protect the Church from its own sin. Ideally, the Church would be nothing more than an apostolic community enjoying the purity of evangelical poverty, but circumstances require the intercession of secular authority. "It would be best for the Church to be ruled wholly by non-avaricious successors of the apostles following the rule of Christ; less good would be a regime mixed through with co-active secular civil powers and lords, but worst of all is when prelates rule who are immersed in the worries and cares of civil lords."[42]

The place of the evangelical lord is to serve as God's steward in spiritual concerns, just as the civil lord serves God in temporal matters. Evangelical *dominium* is the fullest realization of the natural *dominium* mankind lost with the Fall, and the evangelical lord is entrusted with the care for that which is most valuable in creation, the spiritual reality that undergirds earthly life. The Church as Christ's living presence in the world is the vehicle by which this responsibility is carried out, and those entrusted with it must focus their whole lives upon it. Priests are most precisely the stewards of Christ's body, and "must give themselves in their service by promulgating, working, and manifesting such that they glorify God through their continued actions, taking this service upon themselves in humility."[43] These spiritual shepherds must lead their flock by embodying the *caritas* made possible by an apostolic life devoted to Christ's law. "The pastor must instruct his charges through virtuous works so that they might live their faith as he does."[44] Accordingly, an evangelical lord living a vicious life fails to instruct his charges, ignoring his duties as God's spiritual steward. And because of the exalted nature of spiritual authority, this kind of failure is far more onerous than secular tyranny or some more mundane transgression; the dignity of the office, and of the giver of the office, is defiled by an evangelical lord's turning from his spiritual responsibilities, warranting redress far more than does material iniquity.

The history of the Church embodies this failure. Initially the Church lived the ideal life of apostolic purity and poverty that had been revealed through Christ's teachings and exemplary life, but the Donation of Constantine destroyed any possibility that this would continue on an institutional level. The Church had become yet another secular organ, "perverted by temporal affairs from the honor of *caritas*, as prodigal in rich ornament as civil and secular lordship, prone to more richness in food, families, and clothing . . . than the secular laity."[45] This wealth of material possessions makes evangelical lords incapable of the spiritual purity required by their office. "As one overburdened with a multiplicity of clothing is thereby oftentimes rendered unfit for travel, so the man who is burdened with things temporal is often made less capable of serving the Church."[46] Wyclif frequently refers to material possessions as the vilest elements in the church, "the dung of the mystical body of Christ," contending that nullification of the Donation and the divestment of ecclesiastical office of all material authority are the only means by which evangelical lords will be cleansed of this filth.[47] If the well-being of the Church requires using material things, he suggests, then let it be sustained by alms provided by the grace-favored civil lords. The ecclesiastical industry presently thriving on this dungheap, the selling of benefices and indulgences, and the proliferation of canon law, a perverse monster created by grafting secular juridical practices onto the living body of *lex Christi*, all must be obliterated for the Church to realize its true identity. Then, Wyclif contends, the church will be able to instruct mankind through its exemplary *caritas*, and the war and confusion that now troubles the world will die away.

> If, according to the Old Testament, it is licit and obligatory to remove a yoke that weights down a neighbor's mule, much more so in the New Law should a brother's soul not be burdened by the weight of so-called alms by which Christ's religion is lost and dragged to the lower depths by the devil's snare; and in these matters, we ought not to trust the appetites of sick men who have embraced in their need dungheaps in the Pauline sense. If, therefore, temporal possessions are necessary for us, let them be given to us according to the manner and measure the Gospel has determined; for then temporal possessions will be dispersed in the world as fruitfully as the rains, and dissensions and wars and sects and other fruits

of the flesh that the Apostle mentions will be laid to rest, and the word of God will enter . . .[48]

Our source for understanding Christ's law is Holy Scripture, which is the source not only of all order in the Church, but the special link between the eternal logic of the Ideas understood by God and any understanding possible in the human mind. If Wyclif's name is remembered at all in common parlance, it is as the first to have translated the Bible into the English language; however, contemporary scholars suggest that the Wyclif Bibles that have survived are likely not to have been the products of Wyclif's own translating efforts, but the work of his disciples. This does not diminish Wyclif's importance in the history of the place of Scripture in Christian theology, though; his theory of Scriptural interpretation was one of the key elements of the Lollard and Hussite movements, and remains a landmark of late medieval philosophical theology.

Augustine had long ago urged the primacy of Scriptural authority above all other sources of knowledge, and had argued that cases in which Scripture appeared to fly in the face of reason demanded greater perspicacity in Scriptural interpretation. What had changed by the late fourteenth century was the depth of logical analysis to which Scripture might be subjected; throughout Wyclif's works on understanding the Bible, he rails against those who would use new-fangled logical tools to demonstrate the incompatibility of cold, clear Aristotelian reason with revealed truth. Every truth, however it might appear to conflict with Scripture, must be, if it is indeed true, found primarily in Holy Scripture. This, Wyclif contended, is because Scripture is the embodiment of the eternal logic of divine understanding, the source of all truth. Since God's knowing a thing to be true is that by which the thing is true, and since Scripture is the primary source of every truth in creation, "all law, all philosophy, all logic and all ethics is in Holy Scripture"; if our reason judges something to be so, the foundation for that judgment must rest in Scripture primarily, and only secondarily in the operation of created reason.[49]

Wyclif had early on argued that Augustine's call for a careful interpretation of Scripture required a sensitivity to the fundamental truths of logic, suggesting that too many logicians had confused means with ends, making logic appear incommensurate with studying Scripture.[50] A careful student of the relation of terms to objects will recognize the primacy of the ontological nature of the object to the truth of the term, and correspondingly, the primacy of the universal to the particular nature. The Ockhamist logicians erred in supposing that universals play no part in the signification of terms, which led to a misunderstanding of the nature of truth. Following Grosseteste, Wyclif argues that a term or word's signifying force is dependent upon its conformity to that which it signifies, and since the first and most primary universal signification is the Word's embodiment of the eternal ideas known by God through which creation occurs. Thus, the duty of the student of Scripture is to begin with a recognition that the Word of God is the perfect expression of, and universal in which, all created truths have their being.[51]

In fact, the nature of Holy Scripture realizes a universal–particular relation. Scripture has five levels of being, of which four have an ideal, universal status instantiated in the physical book.

> It has been my custom to list five degrees of sacred Scripture. The first is the Book of Life mentioned in Apocalypse 20 and 21. The second is the truths written in the Book of Life in their ideal being . . . In the third sense Scripture means the truths which are to be believed in general, which, in their existence or effect, are written in the Book of Life. In the fourth sense Scripture means a truth to be believed as it is written in the natural book which is a man's soul . . . In the fifth sense, Scripture means the books or sounds or other artificial signs of truth.[52]

The physical book is not the end of the relation; the active participation of the individual, believing reader engaging with the text is the final instantiation of the chain that begins with the ideal truths understood by God. What I truly understand when I read Scripture is my mind's realization of an instantiation of the eternal Truth that makes use of the written medium of the Bible as a means. In fact, Wyclif holds that, as the source of all truth in creation, Scripture serves as the paradigm for any linguistic expression of the truth, and is the means by which God teaches man how to express all truth. "Scripture should be the exemplar of all types of human speaking, [since] it includes in itself every type of possible speech."[53] As with any other true relation, God's willing the reality of the relation is necessary for the understanding that blossoms in my mind instantiating the universal eternal Word, which means that grace is necessary for successful Scriptural understanding.[54] Thus Wyclif identifies two elements necessary for understanding the truth of Scripture: the most basic element, the movement of the Holy Ghost in the reader's mind illuminating the eternal truth that Scripture embodies, and secondly, schooling in logic and grammar sufficient to aid the reader in understanding how the words in the Bible refer to eternal truths. With these two elements, a Christian reading Scripture has no need of "authoritative" intermediaries explaining how to understand the truth it contains. "The whole of Holy Scripture . . . is an infinitely greater authority than any other writings regarding its authenticating the propriety of human authors . . ."[55]

Since Scripture is the first and final authority, it must be available to all seekers of truth. Certainly without ready access to Scripture justice will be impossible in society, as is salvation for anyone deprived of the living Word of God.

> It has been said that there should be a mirror of secular lords in the vulgar tongue by which they can rule in total conformity with the law of Christ . . . for Holy Scripture is the faith of the church and as much as it is plainly understood in the orthodox sense, so much for the better . . . Similarly because the truths of the faith are clearer and plainer in Scripture than the priests know how to express, since many priests . . . are ignorant of it while others conceal the points of Scripture which speak of humility and clerical poverty, it seems useful for the church that the faithful reveal this true sense . . . In each language by which the Holy Ghost gives knowledge is the faith in Christ disclosed for the people.[56]

Wyclif's belief that Scripture ought to be available in the vernacular, and the movement to translate it that followed, are not all for which Wyclif is commonly remembered. While it is easy to report Wyclif's denial of transubstantiation occurring during celebration of the Eucharist, it is not so easy to understand the complexity underlying his motivation for doing so. From one standpoint, Wyclif's eventual rejection of transubstantiation, an explanation of Christ's real presence at the Sacrament approved by Innocent III in 1215, can be explained as a rejection of the scholastic Aristotelian accounts propounded by Aquinas and Scotus based on his philosophical rejection of their synthetic Aristotelianism.[57] In this account, Wyclif the philosopher denies the possibility that the substance of the elements are annihilated at consecration because it demands that one act entail two simultaneous yet independent movements: the bread ceases to be at the same instant and place that Christ's body begins to be. Yet the schoolmen insist on calling this an act of conversion, which requires a subject in which the conversion occurs. What, Wyclif asks, is converted, if the bread's substance is annihilated when Christ's body begins? If one responds that the accidents remain constant while the underlying substance shifts, then it appears that our sense perception, the foundation of our understanding of the material world, might never perceive things as they are. The certainty of natural knowledge would vanish; how would we know that the perceived object X is not some other object Y with the perceptible accidents of an X?[58] If the answer is that some accident-like quantity causes the other accidents to remain constant in the absence of underlying substance, the problem still exists: in what do these accidents inhere? If something, it must be substantial according to Aristotelian ontology, but if not, then nothing is the subject of conversion. The explanation that Wyclif's rejection of transubstantiation grows out of his metaphysics has been widely accepted, but frequently followed by a dissatisfaction with the apparent vagueness of Wyclif's alternative account of Christ's real presence in the elements.[59]

A different view is possible if one concentrates on Wyclif's interest in redefining Christian authority through a reassessment of Scriptural hermeneutics. Throughout *De Eucharistia* Wyclif blasts "modern doctors" for having run roughshod over the distinction between the literal and figurative interpretations of Christ's words. In too many cases theologians have twisted the ideas of the Evangelists and the Church Fathers to benefit themselves, thereby creating a tendency amongst prelates to value the words, the signifiers, rather than the truths signified. Did not Paul, Augustine, Rhabanus, and John the Damascene indicate that the sacrament remained bread and wine while signifying Christ's body and blood? This fixation with appearances rather than true underlying meanings is symptomatic of a priestly disease that manifests itself in other forms, including a hunger for material goods, for political power, and an aversion to spiritual discipline. What is sorely needed, Wyclif believes, is an approach to Scripture guided not by earthly concerns but by a prayerful seeking of eternal truths. Attention to the fundaments of proper logical analysis of Scripture is fundamental here; its absence leads to undue emphasis placed on pilgrimage, the cult of relics, and transubstantiation, all merely signs of eternal truth, not true in themselves. Here Wyclif the Scriptural commentator and ecclesiastical reformer proves the abuse of clerical authority through examination of the biblical foundation for transubstantiation, making his redefinition of the Eucharist a vehicle through which his vision of a Church reborn can be realized.

While this interpretation improves on the view that Wyclif's eucharistic doctrine is primarily philosophically motivated, by incorporating other elements of his theological vision, it requires a fuller understanding of his logic and philosophy of language than one might suppose. Underlying his arguments for correct interpretation of Scriptural language and of the relation of sign to signifier is an assumption that his audience is familiar with formal scholastic linguistic analysis, including supposition theory, the nature of denomination, and similar concerns of the late fourteenth-century Oxford schoolman. Nor is Wyclif's logic the only concern. Recently Heather Phillips has argued convincingly that Wyclif's "remanence" theory, in which Christ's being has spiritual reality in the physical essence of the host, is best understood through an awareness of his interest in optics. Phillips explains that Wyclif's alternative to transubstantiation incorporates the imagery of light and its refraction pioneered by Alhazen, Witelo, and Roger Bacon to explain how Christ's being is wholly and really present in the host, just as an image is present in a mirror. While the object reflected is not itself substantially "in" the mirror, the mirror certainly undergoes a change such that the reflected object is really present in the mirror in a way that it is not when no reflection occurs. So it is with the Eucharist; while Christ is not substantially "in" the elements, they serve as mirror by which Christ's being is really present in them when consecrated.[60]

Wyclif's thought serves as the foundation for many Lollard doctrines, although attempts to trace secure ties from surviving Lollard writings to particular elements of Wyclif's thought are bound to be affected by the movement's shift from formal academic circles to popular vernacular preaching and debate. Nevertheless, in each of the three general areas of Lollard ideology – theology, ecclesiology, and politics – Wyclif's theological influence is unmistakable. Lollardy, the popular English movement rooted in Wyclif's theology, is divisible into three distinct periods. In the first, the "Oxford period," from 1378 to 1413, the fates of Wyclif, his writings, and the careers of important figures in Lollardy are closely associated. The movement was recognized as sufficiently threatening to warrant parliamentary authorization of the death penalty for its members in 1401, with the enactment of *De Heretico Comburendo*. In 1409, Archbishop Thomas Arundel issued the *Constitutions*, which in its attempt to stamp out Wyclifism restricted all public preaching to licensed representatives of the episopal authority. In 1413, Sir John Oldcastle and other rebellious knights, all of whom identified themselves with general tenets of Lollardy, rose unsuccessfully against Henry V. 1415 proved a significant year for Lollardy, for Wyclif's writings were formally condemned as heresy at the Council of Constance just as the doomed Oldcastle revolt marked Wyclif's disciples as guilty of treason. From 1415 into the 1560s, Lollardy was an underground movement associated with a host of anticlerical reformative preachers, firebrands, and common citizens situated largely in England's northern counties. Thus, Lollardy was three things: at its inception, it was a movement among scholars and students at Oxford, at which point it was heretical; it became a cause used by anti-Lancastrian knights, making it treasonous as well as heretical; finally, it waned but remained as glowing embers among the people in the north country, at which point it was mainly heretical again.[61]

Theologically, Lollardy embodies a reaction against much of the practice of late fourteenth-century Christianity. The cult of saints, the proliferation of clerical profit from administration of the sacraments, and a fondness for pilgrimage and image-worship, drew the ire of preachers and believers inspired by the spirit of Wyclif's reforming zeal. Underlying all Lollard theology was the conviction that Scripture alone provides the basis for legitimate Christian practice. "It is said often that we desire not that men believe us, unless we base ourselves in the faith or in the reason of God's law. And then men believe us not because we say a thing, but because God says it – and woe to him who then believes not!"[62] One of later Lollardy's greatest foes, Bishop Reginald Pecock, described the movement's theology as poisoned by three connected misconceptions.

> No ordinance is to bind Christian men to the service of God save that it is grounded in the Holy Scripture of the New Testament . . . That whatever Christian man or woman humble in spirit desiring true understanding of Holy Scripture shall without fail find [it] . . . wherever he or she shall read or study . . . and the more meek he or she shall be, the sooner he or she shall come into the true understanding of it . . . Whenever a person has found the understanding of Holy Scripture . . . he or she ought turn away their hearing, reading, and understanding from all reasoning and arguing or proof which any cleric might make by any kind of evidence of reason or Scripture, and especially of reason, to the contrary.[63]

Bound up in the *sola scriptura* theological orientation are virtually all of the elements of Lollard theology.[64] While most Lollards did not deny the need for sacraments to attain salvation, their extant writings describe a vehement reaction against ecclesiastical sacramental practices. Most easily recognizably Wyclifite among these is the Lollard denial of transubstantiation. Just as a man seeing a statue does not think first about its being of some kind of wood but thinks what the statue is meant to represent, suggests an early vernacular sermon, so someone considering the Eucharist should think of Christ, and not bread or wine, nor any metaphysical subtleties. Many Lollard texts rely heavily on the substance of *De Eucharistia*: "The bread of the sacred host is true bread in its nature, and is eaten physically, but it is God's body figuratively . . . This host is eaten physically and spiritually by some men, but Christ's body in His nature is not physically eaten."[65] Some later Lollards even rejected the real presence of Christ, holding that the Eucharist was but a memorial of Christ's passion, while other, more extreme individuals actively denigrated the sacrament; one Lollard knight is said to have taken the host from his mouth and consumed it later with a dish of oysters.

The other sacraments came under similar scrutiny, although the basis for criticism tended more towards Scriptural interpretation than metaphysical arguments. Various texts discuss the need for infant baptism, the possibility of marriage for clergy, and the legitimacy of laymen hearing confession and absolving sins, in each case starting with the possibility that Scripture allows for more freedom than contemporary Church practice admits. Typifying Lollard rejection of clerical profit from sacramental authority, many texts decry the contemporary traffic in indulgences with arguments that would prefigure Luther's: how can the pope be truly charitable if he does not relieve all suffering souls from the torments of purgatory? How can the pope justly release from purgation living supplicants who might well be eternally damned? To clerical arguments that money is asked to cover the physical costs incurred by the Church, "certainly a little lead costs many thousand pounds each year to our poor land . . . truly they deceive people and mock them, for they sell a fat goose for little or nought, but the garlic costs many shillings!"[66]

Much that embodies late medieval Christian practice drew Wyclifite fire. Wyclif had rejected prayers to individual saints as based in the confused belief that the saints have powers based in their own sanctity, apart somehow from divine giving.[67] Enthusiastic followers pursued this line of reasoning, resulting in iconoclastic occurrences like using the image of St. Katherine as fuel to cook supper and similar destruction of pictures, statues, and relics. Prayer as a whole underwent a serious revision: Latin prayers spoken by non-Latin-speaking people were worthless, and the activity of a faithful life serves as a more effective prayer than any mere collection of words. Likewise, the practice of pilgrimage was criticized as but an opportunity for revelry and entertainment. True pilgrimage, these preachers suggested, involves giving alms to the poor and serving God faithfully in daily life; few Lollards would countenance the hijinks of Chaucer's merry band.

Lollard ecclesiology is recognizably a vernacular adumbration of Wyclif's *dominium* writings, based on the premise that the true Church is the congregation of the Elect. While Wyclif was clear that its true members were unknowable save by God, his Lollard disciples tended towards a variety of interpretations of this idea. Some followed Wyclif, holding the Church's membership to be unknowable. The author of the *Lanterne of Liȝt*, a well-known early Lollard text, expands on Wyclif's definition, saying "The Church is not in men by power or spiritual or temporal dignity, for many princes and high bishops and others of lower degree . . . are found to be apostate . . . The Church stands in those persons in whom is acknowledgement and true confession of faith and truth."[68] Others interpreted the membership to be the "holy saints of God," "the congregation of just men for whom Jesus Christ shed his blood," or "true Christian men and women."[69] The obvious conclusion to be drawn from these later definitions – that "true Christians" are recognizable as just, godly men and women – is contrary to Wyclif's idea, but dovetails neatly with the issue of whether priests who sin can minister to their flock. Here, Wyclif's belief that clerics pursuing worldly goods or acting sinfully are not fit to serve as spiritual lords provided sufficient foundation for his followers to embrace a Donatism that he had struggled to avoid. Earlier Lollards followed Wyclif's approach, arguing that "Antichrist's sophisters should know well that a cursed man fully doth the sacraments, though it be to his damnation, for they are not the authors of these sacraments, but God keepeth that dignity to Himself."[70] Nevertheless, Donatism loomed over the development of Lollard conceptions of the priesthood, so that the Carmelite Thomas Netter was to identify Wyclifism with the heresy in his later *Doctrinale Fidei Catholicae*.[71]

Wyclif's sentiments towards the Church and its present state are echoed throughout Lollard writings. Regarding the physical being of the Church, Wyclif's opinions suggest later, Tudor innovations; in *De Officio Regis* he advises the king to dismantle the churches in times of national emergency and use the stones to build fortresses.[72] Similar attitudes surface in Lollard texts; one suggests that worship is "commonly better done in the air under heaven, but often in rainy weather, churches are good."[73] His antipathy towards papal striving for political power surfaces repeatedly in Lollard indictments of the ecclesiastical hierarchy. If there is any need for a chief spiritual lord, should he not embody Christ's law in his person and actions? "God gave power to Peter being a good and holy man to bind and to loose, and to his successors who are as good as he was – and otherwise not."[74] Likewise, the Church's crying need for reform must be addressed by the just civil lord as his chief duty, although some later Lollards surpassed their teacher in their zeal for reform by arguing that if the king be incapable of divesting the church of its wealth, then the duty falls to the common people.[75]

While the impact Wyclif's thought had on the theological landscape of the fifteenth century was significant, it is difficult to describe direct influence it might have had on the Lutheran movement of the early sixteenth century. Elements of Wyclif's reformative vision certainly suggest Luther's, notably the appeal for a "top-down" reform model in which the aristocracy takes responsibility for the Church's reform, as well as the deterministic theology, the emphasis on the place of Scripture in the Christian's daily life, the savage attacks on clerical abuse of power, and the rejection of transubstantiation. Yet Luther was in many senses a product of his schooling, and the Council's condemnation of Wyclif in 1415 discouraged further formal academic pursuit of the philosophical theology that had germinated into Wyclifism.[76]

Bohemia proved a more fertile ground for Wyclifism. Jan Hus, a professor and preacher at the university of Prague, began a theological movement based in Wyclif's thought that would grow into a nationalist crusade that would influence eastern Europe's Christianity into the seventeenth century. In the early fifteenth century, Prague intellectuals discovered Wyclif's realism, which flew in the face of the nominalist thought universally accepted by German academics, and Czech intellectuals eagerly embraced it as definitive of their Bohemian identity. While Hus was by no means foremost among Prague's Wycliffites, he became familiar with Wyclif's reformative ecclesiology and theology in pursuing his doctorate, and incorporated some of the English reformer's revolutionary sentiment into his sermons.[77] Hus's *De Ecclesia* incorporates none of Wyclif's *dominium*-centered philosophy and little of his antiproprietary theology into its argument, retaining primarily the argument that the Christian church is nothing more than the universal body of the predestinate. While many of Hus's arguments for clerical reform find their origin in Wyclif's *De Ecclesia* and *De Potestate Pape*, the philosophical complexity that characterizes Wyclif's theology is absent. Arguments that Hus embodied a Bohemian incarnation of Wyclifism are overstated; at best, Hus used Wyclif's thought as an inspiration.[78] Hus supported Utraquism, the belief that the communicant must take both bread and wine, but did not deny transubstantiation, as did Wyclif, and later reformers. While Luther's exclamation on reading Hus's *De Ecclesia*, "We are all Hussites without knowing it," is celebrated as evidence of Hus's proto-reformation status, it is more accurate to view the treatise as the chief document of the Hussite revolution in fifteenth-century Bohemia.

Notes

1 See Courtenay, 1987, pp. 171–306.
2 Normore, 1982, pp. 358–82.
3 Oberman, 1957; Leff, 1957; De La Torre, 1987.
4 Gwynn, 1940; Trapp, 1956, pp. 146–274.
5 Walsh, 1981; Dawson, 1983.
6 Workman, 1926; Robson, 1966; Kenny, 1985; Catto, 1992, pp. 175–261.
7 *De Dominio Divino*, I.1, p. 1.6.
8 For a bibliographical and chronological account of Wyclif's writings, see Thomson, 1983.
9 Dahmus, 1952; McFarlane, 1952.
10 Thomson, 1931.
11 *De Universalibus*, ch. 3, 161–4.
12 See Kenny, 1986, pp. 17–30. Also, *De Universalibus*, ch. 2.
13 *De Universalibus*, ch. 7.
14 *De Dominio Divino*, I.10, pp. 68.29–69.2.
15 *De Causa Dei contra Pelagium*, I.9, p. 190D.
16 *De Universalibus*, ch. 14.
17 *De Dominio Divino* I.14–18.
18 *De Ecclesia*, ch. 1, pp. 20.32–4.
19 Ibid., pp. 5.24–8.
20 *De Officio Regis*, ch. 6, p. 133.20.
21 *De Potestate Pape*, ch. 2, p. 31.20.
22 *De Civili Dominio* I, ch. 38, pp. 276.16–277.19.
23 See also *De Ecclesia*, ch. 7, pp. 153–6; *De Potestate Pape*, ch. 7, p. 141; *De Officio Regis*, ch. 7, pp. 226–38; *Trialogus Supplementum*, ch. 4.
24 *De Ecclesia*, ch. 3, pp. 61.21–7.
25 *De Universalibus*, ch. 10, 1.680.
26 *De Dominio Divino* I, ch. 3, pp. 16.17–22.
27 Ibid., ch. 8.
28 *De Civili Dominio*. I, ch. 11, pp. 77.32–78.6.
29 Ibid., III, ch. 13, pp. 228.8–229.4.
30 *De Dominio Divino* I, ch. 10, p. 75.
31 Ibid., III, ch. 1, pp. 200.27–31.
32 *De Civili Dominio* I, ch. 9, p. 62.9–13.
33 Ibid. III, ch. 13, pp. 230.5–15.
34 Ibid. III, ch. 2, pp. 15.5–23.
35 *Trialogus* IV, ch. 35, pp. 204–7.
36 For Wyclif's antifraternal Latin works, see Thomson, 1983; also Szittya, 1985, pp. 152–83; for vernacular tracts attributed to Wyclif see Matthew edition of *The English Works*, 1902; see also Aston, 1987, pp. 281–330; Gradon and Hudson, 1996, pp. 121–45.
37 *De Civili Dominio*, III, ch. 8, pp. 119.34–120.2.
38 Ibid. I, ch. 1, pp. 1.1–2.
39 Ibid. I, ch. 26, pp. 188.14–24.
40 For Wyclif's political thought, see Daly, 1962; Lahey, "Wyclif and Rights," 1997; McGrade, 1991; Wilks, 1965.
41 *De Officio Regis*, ch. 1, pp. 13.2–8.
42 *De Civili Dominio* I, ch. 28, pp. 195.24–30.
43 *De Potestate Pape*, ch. 2, pp. 30.16–19.
44 *De Ecclesia*, ch. 2, p. 43.24.
45 *De Civili Dominio* III, ch. 13, pp. 217.26–9.
46 *Trialogus*, IV, ch. 17, p. 305.
47 *De Civili Dominio* III, ch. 22, p. 158.4.
48 *De Simonia*, ch. 3, pp. 38.15–25, trans. Terrence McVeigh, *On Simony*, Fordham, 1992, p. 75.
49 *De Veritate Sacrae Scripturae*, ch. 2, p. 22, quoting Augustine, *Ep. ad Volusianum*, III.
50 *De Logica, proemium*, p. 1.
51 Levy, 1998.
52 *De VSS*, ch. 6, pp. 108.2–109.2, trans. Anthony Kenny, as quoted in Kenny, 1985, p. 60.
53 Ibid., ch. 10, pp. 205.4–6.
54 Ibid. ch. 9, p. 201.
55 Ibid. ch. 15, p. 394.4.

56 *Speculum Secularium Dominorum*, ch. 1, *Opera Minora*, pp. 74.9–75.24.
57 As late as 1375, Wyclif had espoused transubstantiation; see *De Civili Dominio*, I.36, p. 260.7.
58 *De Eucharistia* 3, pp. 78.9–83.9.
59 Workman, II, p. 30; Leff, 1957, II, p. 550; Keen, 1986.
60 Phillips, 1987.
61 The chief scholarly authority for this period is Hudson, 1988; see also Hudson, 1978; Hudson, 1985; Aston, 1984; McFarlane, 1972; Dickens, 1959.
62 Quoted in Hudson, 1988, p. 280.
63 Reginald Pecock, *Repressor of Overmuch Blaming of the Clergy*, I, ch. 1, pp. 5–7. See Brockwell, 1985.
64 For a thorough analysis of Lollard theology with reference to extant MSS, see Gradon and Hudson, 1996.
65 Quoted in Hudson, 1988, p. 283.
66 Ibid. p. 300.
67 *De Ecclesia*, ch. 2, pp. 44–6.
68 *The Lanterne of Liyt*, London, 1917, 2/20.
69 Gradon and Hudson, 1996, pp. 89–92; Hudson, 1988, pp. 320–1.
70 Quoted in Hudson, 1988, p. 316.

71 Netter's *Doctrinale* is a collection of six books compiled before 1430 meant to address the substance of the Wyclifite movement from an orthodox standpoint. The *Fasciculi Zizianorum* is another Carmelite collection of documents describing the church's attempts to combat the spread of Wyclifism. See Hudson, 1985; "Wyclifism in Oxford 1381–1411" and "Wyclif and the English Language," in Kenny, 1986, pp. 67–105, in addition to Hudson, 1988.
72 *De Officio Regis*, ch. 7, p. 185.
73 Gradon, *English Wyclifite Sermons*, II, 73/23; see also Hudson and Gradon, p. 92.
74 Hudson, 1988, p. 329.
75 Gradon, *English Wyclifite Sermons*, II, 64, pp. 48–53.
76 For Wyclif's Reformation reputation, see Lytle, 1987; Aston, 1984. For Luther's background, see Oberman, *The Harvest of Medieval Theology*, Harvard, 1963.
77 See Kaminsky, *A History of the Hussite Revolution*, Berkeley, 1967.
78 Spinka, *John Hus' Concept of the Church*, Princeton, 1966; see also Jan Hus, *De Ecclesia*, ed. S. Harrison Thomson, Colorado, 1956.

References

Margaret Aston, "Wyclif and the Vernacular," in Hudson and Wilks, 1987, pp. 281–330.

Margaret Aston, "John Wyclif's Reformation Reputation," in her *Lollards and Reformers*, London, 1984, pp. 219–72.

Margaret Aston, *Lollards and Reformers*, London, 1984.

C. W. Brockwell, *Reginald Pecock and the Lancastrian Church*, Lewiston, 1985.

Jeremy Catto, "Wyclif and Wyclifism at Oxford 1356–1430," in J. Catto and G. R. Evans, *History of the University of Oxford*, vol. 2, Oxford, 1992, pp. 175–261.

William Courtenay, *Schools and Scholars in Fourteenth Century England*, Princeton, 1987.

Joseph Dahmus, *The Prosecution of John Wyclyf*, Yale, 1952.

L. Daly, *The Political Theory of John Wyclyf*, Chicago, 1962.

James Doyne Dawson, "Richard Fitzralph and the Fourteenth Century Poverty Controversies," *The Journal of Ecclesiastical History*, 34, 1983.

Bartholomew De La Torre, *Thomas Buckingham and the Contingency of Futures*, Notre Dame, 1987.

A. G. Dickens, *Lollards and Protestants in the Diocese of York*, Oxford, 1959.

Pamela Gradon and Anne Hudson, *English Wyclifite Sermons*, vol. 4, Oxford, 1996.

Aubrey Gwynn, *The English Austin Friars in the Time of Wyclif*, Oxford, 1940.

Anne Hudson, *The Premature Reformation*, Oxford, 1988.

Anne Hudson, *Lollards and Their Books*, London, 1985.

Anne Hudson, *Selections from English Wyclifite Writings*, Cambridge, 1978.

Anne Hudson and Michael Wilks, eds., *From Ockham to Wyclif*, Studies in Church History Subsidia 5, London, 1987.

Jan Hus, *De Ecclesia*, ed. S. Harrison Thomson, Colorado, 1956.

Maurice Keen, "Wyclif, the Bible, and Transubstantiation," Kenny, 1986, pp. 1–16.

Anthony Kenny, *Wyclif*, Oxford, 1985.

Anthony Kenny, "The Realism of the De Universalibus," in *Wyclif in His Times*, ed. Anthony Kenny, Oxford, 1986, pp. 17–30.

Norman Kretzman, Anthony Kenny, and Jan Pinborg, eds., *The Cambridge History of Later Medieval Philosophy*, Cambridge, 1982.

S. Lahey, "Wyclif and Rights," *Journal of the History of Ideas*, 58, 1997, pp. 1–20.

Gordon Leff, *Bradwardine and the Pelagians*, Cambridge, 1957.

Ian Levy, "John Wyclif and Augustinian Realism," *Augustiniana*, 48, 1998, pp. 87–106.

Guy Fitch Lytle, "John Wyclif, Martin Luther, and Edward Powell: Heresy and the Oxford Theology Faculty at the Beginning of the Reformation," in Hudson and Wilks, eds., 1987, pp. 465–81.

K. B. McFarlane, *Lancastrian Kings and Lollard Knights*, Oxford, 1972.

K. B. McFarlane, *John Wyclif and the Beginnings of English Nonconformity*, London, 1952.

A. S. McGrade, "Somersaulting Sovereignty: A Note on Reciprocal Lordship and Servitude in Wyclif," Hudson and Wilks, 1991, pp. 261–8.

Calvin Normore, "Future Contingents," in Kretzman, Kenny, and Pinborg, eds., 1982, pp. 358–82.

Heiko Oberman, *Archbishop Thomas Bradwardine: A Fourteenth Century Augustinian*, Utrecht, 1957.

Heiko Oberman, *The Harvest of Medieval Theology*, Harvard, 1963.

Heather Phillips, "John Wyclif and the Optics of the Eucharist," in Hudson and Wilks, eds., 1987, pp. 245–58.

J. A. Robson, *Wyclif and the Oxford Schools*, Cambridge, 1966.

Matthew Spinka, *John Hus' Concept of the Church*, Princeton, 1966.

Penn R. Szittya, *The Antifraternal Tradition in Medieval Literature*, Princeton, 1985.

S. H. Thomson, "The Philosophical Basis of Wyclif's Theology," *Journal of Religion*, 11, 1931, pp. 86–116.

Williel R. Thomson, *The Latin Writings of John Wyclyf*, Toronto, 1983.

Damasus Trapp, "Augustinian Theology in the Fourteenth Century," *Augustiniana*, 1956, pp. 146–274.

Katharine Walsh, *A Fourteenth Century Scholar and Primate: Richard Fitzralph in Oxford, Avignon, and Armagh*, Oxford, 1981.

Michael Wilks, "Predestination, Property, and Power: Wyclif's Theory of Dominion and Grace," *Studies in Church History*, II, London, 1965, pp. 220–36.

H. B. Workman, *John Wyclif*, Oxford, 1926.

John Wyclif, *Tractatus de Universalibus*, ed. Ivan Boh, Oxford, 1985.

John Wyclif, *The English Works of Wyclif*, ed. F. D. Matthew, Early English Text Society, 74, 1902.

John Wyclif, *Trialogus*, trans. Robert Vaughn, *Tracts and Treatises of John De Wyclif, D.D.*, London, 1845.

Conclusion

21 Robert Kilwardby, Gabriel Biel,
       and Luther's Saving Faith
              G. R. Evans

22 Augustine, the Medieval Theologians,
              and the Reformation
              Paul Rorem

Robert Kilwardby, Gabriel Biel, and Luther's Saving Faith

G. R. Evans

This short chapter is included here not because Kilwardby is an author of sufficient individual importance to merit a chapter to himself but because it is instructive to take stock through comparison with his workmanlike thinking, of the manner in which fashions of emphasis changed in the later Middle Ages, in ways which eventually opened the gates to Reformation. Luther asked what it takes to be saved, with the intention of substituting for all the complex requirements he thought he saw around him, the simple essential of a "saving faith." The idea that faith saves, even that faith alone saves, was not in itself new, although Luther gave it a fresh focus. It was an important strand, and from an early stage, in discussion of Peter Lombard's comments in the *Sentences* on faith, hope, and charity. What Robert Kilwardy made of it, and, briefly, Gabriel Biel, helps us to see how current controversial heat posed or failed to pose at one time, questions which later became crucial, even Church-dividing.

Robert Kilwardby, born in England in about 1215, first taught as a master of arts at Paris. Then he became a Dominican and, in 1261, Prior Provincial of the English Dominicans. He moved to the archbishopric of Canterbury in 1272. He did not lose his interest in academic affairs. In March 1277 he sought to interfere in the curriculum at Oxford by listing 30 propositions which were not to be taught.

In Robert Kilwardby's *Quaestiones in Librum Tertium Sententiarum*, Question 6 of the set on "faith" asks what is the written text which contains everything which must be believed in order to obtain salvation: *quae est illa Scriptura quae continet omnia ad salutem credenda?*[1] The suggested answer is that it is the creed. That means that the focus is being taken to be the subject-matter of the faith, *what* is believed, not the *mode* of believing (its fiduciary or trusting or committed character), or the personal *object* of faith (Christ). Kilwardby partly covers this point in Question 1, with references to Book II, distinction 27 of the *Sentences*. There he had taken Augustine's definition that "believing" is "thinking with assent": *credere est cum assensione cogitare.*[2]

Kilwardby recognizes that faith – like other terms such as *opinio* and *scientia* – is equivocal, and can stand for natural powers, *habitus*, the *use* of such powers or the expression of such *habitus*, or for their objects. If faith is to be understood as *habitus*, he says, it may depend upon a rational cause, as in the Ciceronian notion that *argumentum est ratio rei dubiae faciens fidem.*[3] Having such a cause, that is, having a reason for it, lodges faith between opinion and knowledge.[4] Alternatively, it can be taken to be something caused by affection and love, and in that case it does not have a place on a continuum from uncertainty, but on a line running from a small degree of confidence to full adherence.[5] This is manifestly a relatively undeveloped treatment of the aspects of faith which have to do with the mode of its being held, and with its personal object, Christ.

The concepts of *habitus* and *virtus* are closely linked. Kilwardby recognizes the distinction, however, between political virtues, which are not "informed" by grace and love (*non informentur a gratia vel caritate*), and the theological virtues, which are.[6] This "informing" makes faith *multo fortius*, and that strength consists in the sublimity of its acts and the nobility of its objects: *sublimior est actus fide et nobilius obiectum eius quam politicarum.*[7] But again the sharp focus on Christ as object of faith is missing.

"The creed" does not prove to be a satisfactory answer to Question 6. Kilwardby distinguishes in Christian learning between those things which precede faith, those which follow from it, and its principal objects: *fidei antecedentia, consequentia,* and *principalia obiecta.* The antecedents of faith are those things which are knowable by natural reason and do not require revelation; the *consequentia* are derived from the main points of faith. It is these *principalia* which Kilwardby thinks have to be believed for salvation (*ad salutem credenda*), not the antecedent or consequent points. Those *principalia* he would deem to be in the creed.[8]

But being "in" the creed is not itself a concept without complications. There are many ways in which something may be "contained" in something. In particular, Kilwardby has in mind the fact that something may be explicitly stated in the creed or it may be merely understood. *Contineri aliqua in aliquo multipliciter est, scilicet vel explicite vel implicite.* The creed contains on the face of it only the articles which may be read there. But *implicite* it contains the whole of Holy Scripture. So it has to be asked whether believing all the articles, or believing them all equally in their fullness of implication, is necessary for salvation.

Here Kilwardby turns to a familiar difficulty of medieval discussion. Those who were born before Christ could not have knowledge of the full span of points of faith in the creed. Was it enough for them to believe those points which relate to the Godhead, which it was agreed could be arrived at by the light of reason, as, in large measure, ancient philosophy had done? Kilwardby argued that it was not.[9] But if it is to be held that all the *antiqui* were bound to adhere to the faith in full, it must be asked how they could do so.[10]

Kilwardby argues in terms of a requirement to "trust" in something which was "to come."[11] Believers could have had a faith that redemption was to come in the way that it was to come, coupled with a longing for it: *credendo et desiderando cognoscentibus et credentibus adhaeserunt.*[12] This introduces an element of "trust" into the notion of "holding" an appropriate set of ideas to be true, and that was to prove crucial to the later debate.

A "trusting" faith in the inexplicit is all that those who lived before Christ can have had. But those who came after Christ do not have the excuse that they could not believe what had not yet been revealed to them. Does it follow that they must believe explicitly? That is Kilwardby's next question. Here he makes three distinctions. It could not be enough (*diminutum ad salutem*) to believe everything merely implicitly. No one is so ignorant that he has not heard that God is three in one and was incarnate, and things of that sort.[13] He thinks that it is enough for salvation to believe some things implictly and some explicitly (depending on one's degree of knowledge; for in that way the simple and uneducated are not denied salvation). But the best thing (*fidei provectae*) is to believe everything explicity and point by point: *explicite et distincte*.

Kilwardby moves on naturally, from faith, to hope and charity. But taking things in this sequence is in itself partly determinative of the questions which present themselves. It becomes pertinent to ask whether hope and charity are virtues and thus whether they are *habitus*. That takes us into the realm of the *mode* of believing that which it is necessary to salvation to believe, and thus to the question whether it is also necessary to salvation to believe in a particular way.

Caritas is of special interest in connection with the sixteenth-century debate, because, in order to give faith sole prominence, it became important to deny that love was effective for salvation. Kilwardby argues on the basis of their difference of object that the three virtues involve different *habitus*. He speaks in terms not only on the mode of adherence involved, but of the personal character of the object of faith, hope, and love. These refer to God, not to the "facts about God" contained, explicitly or implicitly, in the creed. Faith is concerned with the truth about God; love with his supreme goodness; hope with God's satisfaction of human desires. So, since their objects differ, so do their *habitus*. (*Fides est summi boni ut veri tantummodo, caritas est eiusdem ut summi boni, spes eiusdem est ut boni perfectivi et sufficentis humanis desideriis, ergo cum objecta differant, et habitus.*)[14]

But love has a claim to be a general and embracing thing, the *ars recte vivendi continens omnes virtutes*. In that sense, Kilwardby thinks, it may be the same thing as righteousness.[15] The sixteenth-century debate takes it in that sense, too, and that is where the difficulty arises, for that may mean that a person could be worthy of salvation on the basis of righteousness if he or she "loves" enough in the sense of "living rightly." Kilwardby certainly interprets this broad "charity" in terms of obedience to prescribed rules: *ars communis recte vivendi incommutabilis continet leges vel regulas partiales sufficienter dirigentes hominem in omnibus actionibus et passionibus*. To live like this has, he argues, the effect of conforming the soul to God and making him capable of loving God above all things and for his own sake.[16] This all has to do with actually "being that which God can approve" so that salvation is "deserved." And that of course was what Luther later saw as standing in irreconcilable opposition to a salvation which depended solely on faith and not at all on love (or the conduct of life). For Kilwardby the opposition is not so clear. Faith itself is associated with actions.

Kilwardby begins his *Quaestiones de fide* by contending that it is not the *habitus* but actual actions which are meritorious: *habitibus non meremur proprie sed actibus*. Faith intends acts which express the *habitus* and in that way it is fulfilled and completed. But that is not the end of the matter. Merit wins reward. So if it is true that the acts of faith are meritorious, then it is reasonable to hold that they may earn reward. *In quo est actio meritoria, in eodem subseque debeat praemium illius meriti.*

Kilwardby has no difficulty in identifying that reward. Faith is by definition in things not seen. So its reward must be sight, the sight of God being – in Augustine's view – itself eternal bliss. The sight is not all, for joy goes with it. *Praemiatur etiam affectus in eodem ut gaudeat de visione aspectus, quia ipse bene usus est aspectu ipsum dirigens et convertens as consensum non visi.*[17]

Kilwardby includes in Question 18 a discussion of the *comparative* importance of faith, hope, and charity, which obliquely addresses this question whether faith (or love) can stand alone. He defines them all as *qualitates animae ipsam gratificantes*, qualities of the soul through which it has grace.[18] On that definition it looks as though love comes first, for it brings grace *per se* and the others do so only through *caritas*.[19] But in temporal terms faith and hope precede love. He does not, however, ask whether one of the virtues is alone sufficient for salvation.

The *Collectorium circa quattuor libros Sententiarum* of Gabriel Biel (1415–95), Rector of the university of Tübingen from 1485–9, is a natural *point de départ* from which to address these questions in the fifteenth century, and begin to see whether there has been a sea-change in the contemporary anxieties they reflect. Biel is known to have influenced Luther. He was himself conspicuously indebted to Ockham. So one strand of continuous reflection at least is plain in his work.

Biel is brief on the subject of Peter Lombard's Prologue. He has three questions, he says. The first is what theology is (*de theologia in se*). This is considered in relation to its nature, its internal coherence, and its object. In connection with the first, Biel says that the Lombard asks what kind of knowledge is theological knowledge (*qualis notitia sit theologia*); and whether theology is a science or not. And since the unity of theology depends upon the unity of the subject-matter with which it is concerned, we have to ask what that is.[20] The term *theologia* now uncontroversially covers the whole subject-span as it did not in the twelfth century.

If we turn for comparison to Gabriel Biel's salvation theory in the fifteenth century, we see that the theologian is a *viator*. Therefore he is not at the end of his journey, but still upon it. That is important because it immediately places us in the context of the coming debate about salvation. "For there are two ends of a rational creature, that is final blessedness and final misery."[21] A pilgrim's destination, suggests Biel, is not yet clear: *Viator ergo est quisquis, qui neque beatus est neque finaliter damnatus.*[22]

For Biel it appears to be still knowledge (not faith) which leads to blessedness: *notitia intuitiva Dei beatificat.* If the direct knowledge of God is blessedness it is also salvation. There is some discussion of the case of St. Paul, when he was caught up *in raptu* (2 Cor. 12:2ff.), and the point is made that there is a difference between a temporary and a permanent experience of that communication.[23]

Veritas theologia est veritas necessaria viatori ad aeternam salutem habendam. Here we come much closer to the idea that knowledge of God is salvific because it is in fact faith. *Veritas theologica est veritas necessaria viatori ad aeternam salutem habendam.* This *veritas theologica* is then further defined. *Veritas theologica est veritas, cuius notitia adhaesiva necessaria est ad salutem explicite vel implicite habenti usum rationis ad eam apprehendenti.*[24]

It is striking that the emphasis of the debate on *notitia* in Biel is still on faith as "knowledge," rather than on faith as "trust." The security of adherence to what is believed thus depends on having sufficient grounds for rational conviction. And that immediately takes a medieval thinker, especially of the later medieval centuries, into the realm of the debate on necessity and probability in proving.

Biel asks whether a knowledge (*notitia*) of this kind of theological truth (that is, of matters of faith) is strictly speaking knowledge (*scientia*). *Utrum notitia evidens huiusmodi veritatum theologicarum sit scientia proprie dicta.* First we must ask what a "knowable proposition" (*propositio scibilis*) is. Then we must look at what is a *scientia proprie dicta.* Then at last we can try to answer the question.[25] Biel approaches this task in Ockhamist terms by looking at the mode of the knowledge. He cites Ockham's view: *quod propositio scibilis scientia proprie dicta est propositio necessaria, dubitabilis, nata fieri evidens per propositiones necessarias evidenter per discursum syllogisticum ad eam applicatas.*[26]

A knowable proposition thus has to have three properties (the first is to be "necessary," the second to be capable of being doubted (*dubitabilis*), the third to be demonstrable (*demonstrabilis*)).[27] Biel argues that *propositiones demonstrabiles* are of two sorts. The first are resolvable into *principia per se nota* and the second into *principia nota per experientiam.* This is important because, as Biel points out, *per se nota* are not the same thing as *indemonstrabilia* or *immediata.* Some *indemonstrabilia* are known *per experientiam.*[28] If that is the case, certain propositions are excluded, argues Biel. A *propositio scibilis* cannot be contingent, *contingens*, or self-evident, *per se nota*, or known by experience *notum per experientiam.*[29] We do not need to pursue this further to see that far greater refinements of distinction are in play than Kilwardby was juggling with, and that they are concentrating attention on the epistemological issues about the nature of faith as knowledge and thus, by implication, directing it away from concepts of faith as trust and faith as commitment to the person of Christ.

If we move to Biel's discussion of Peter Lombard in connection with what is necessary to salvation, we find a similar concern, with a greater technical refinement than is detectable in Kilwardby. On the one hand, that seems to take us away from what were later to be Luther's concerns. On the other, it affords tantalizing glimpses of preoccupations which are germane to the early Reformation debates. Distinction XVII, Question 1, of Book I of the *Sentences* deals with the theme of justification. The notion being explored is pneumatological not Christological – that the Spirit is the love (*caritas et amor*) by which we love God.

Biel suggests that if that is held *formaliter*, it is not tenable. But if we understand it in terms of its effect (*effective*), it is true. He argues that the Spirit pours upon us the "habit" of love (*quia ipse infundit habitum caritatis*), and that is the love by which we love God.[30]

This pouring out is seen as salvific: *ad salutem et ad diligendum Deum*.[31] It has that effect because it pleases God, and thus the link is made between salvation and acceptability in the sight of God. But it is asked whether there has to be something actually "in" the created soul to make it "dear and acceptable to God," or whether the Spirit's outpouring is the necessary condition: *Utrum praeter Spiritum sanctum necesse sit ponere caritatem absolutam creatam animam formaliter informantem ad hoc quod sit cara Deo et accepta*.[32]

On this question Ockham disagrees with Peter Aureoli, as Biel observes. Peter Aureoli holds three things:

i.   That there is a created form, which in the nature of things is pleasing to God (*que ex natura rei de necessitate cadit sub complacentia Dei*), and through which the soul is made full of grace in his eyes (*gratificatur*).

ii. That such a form is antecedent to that acceptance, not consequent upon it. That is obvious, it is argued, from the fact that the soul is not *accepta* except through that form, and that form presupposes his acceptance: *quod talis forma non profluit ex divina acceptatione in animam. . . . per illam formam et ita illa forma presupponitur acceptationi eius.*

iii. This form is a *habitualis dilectio* which does not come from nature alone but has to be infused by God.[33]

Biel sets out Ockham's objections to this.[34] Biel takes it with Ockham that it is the same thing to be "pleasing to," *grata*, "dear to," *cara*, or "accepted by," *accepta*, by God (*quod pro eodem habetur*). He understands this to mean being in such a *status* that God wishes to give the person in question eternal life. (A baptized infant is in that condition, until it sins.)

But the *complacentia* of God with respect to the creature is twofold. The first is general, and that consists in the divine will that whatever can be good shall be good. In this sense *complacentia Dei* simply means *voluntas Dei*. But there is particular or *specialis complacentia*, and that has three kinds. God wants all things for the best, but he also wants some things to be better than others (*velle aliquid esse perfectius alio*). Thus substance is better than accident and reason than unreason. Thirdly, he wants some individuals to have the best, that is blessedness or eternal life.[35]

He can be "dear to" God, who is in the condition in which God can give him eternal life, provided that he does not prevent that by his own fault: *Ille potest esse carus Deo, qui est in statu, in quo Deus (si non impedit culpabiliter) potest sibi dare vitam aeternam.* God can bestow that blessedness on anyone if he wills, even in a natural state where the individual does not possess that form. *Sed Deus posset, si vellet, alicui in puris naturalibus (id est non habenti illam formam) dare beatitudinem.*[36] God could make anyone blessed even without this "form," *et sic esset carus Deo.*[37] It is acknowledged that this theory of a *qualitas infusa* cannot be proved by reason, only by authority,[38] and it is held not to be necessary to salvation to have it. But there is a set of concerns here both encouraging a type of analysis which Luther wants to sweep aside, *and* presenting him with a matrix of key points to address. These are:

i.   whether it is faith or love that matters to God;
ii. whether it is the state or the actions which count;
iii. whether the crux of the matter is now recognized to be not what you believe but how you adhere to God, the relationship which exists, whether of love or faith.

The Christology of the discussion of what is necessary to salvation therefore remains on the periphery for Biel as much as for Kilwardby, two centuries earlier. Kilwardby approached Christology with questions in his mind still largely formed by the debates of the twelfth century. He asks *cur deus homo*, and why only the Son was Incarnate, and he addresses the traditional problems about the relationship of body and soul in Christ. It is, for example, asked whether Christ could have assumed a human person while his own personality remained: *quaeritur an posset assumpsisse personam humanam, dico mantentem in sua personalitate.*[39] Linked with these are questions about the nature of Christ's suffering in the Passion. Was it in his body or in his mind, *secundum potentiam sensitivam* or *secundum potentiam rationalem?* Did it involve infinite bitterness? If no penitent ought to suffer eternal punishment how could that suffering of Christ be infinite? Did Christ have to suffer?[40]

It is clear how intricate, how nuanced these debates are, how the tides of preoccupation and debate shift about. The question this volume must leave hanging for the next, is how and why these issues reshaped and represented themselves in the sixteenth century in a way which divided the Church.

Notes

1 Robert Kilwardby, *Quaestiones in Librum Tertium Sententiarum*, ed. Gerhard Leibold, Bayerische Akademie der Wissenschaften, 12 (München, 1985), p. 22.

2 *De praedestinatione sanctorum*, II.v, PL44.963.

3 Kilwardby cites this tag from Boethius *In Topica Ciceronis*, 1, PL64.1048; ed. Orelii-Baiter, V.277.

4 Kilwardby, *Quaestiones in Librum Tertium Sententiarum*, Question 1, p. 8.

5 "Pro habito causato ab affectu et amore, et sic essentialiter habitus fidei non est (medius) illarum duarum, sed sic est fides media illorum habituum solum secundum effectum et secundum certitudinem. Secundum effectum, quia efficit in aspectu consensum credulitats qui est medius inter opinari et sciere. Secundum certitudinem, quia certior est fides opinione et minus certa quam scientia, sicut ibidem dicit Hugo." Hugh of St. Victor, *De Sacramentis*, I.10.2, PL176.330 and 331.

6 Kilwardby, *Quaestiones in Librum Tertium Sententiarum*, Question 2, p. 11.

7 Ibid.

8 Ibid., p. 23.

9 Ibid., Question 7, p. 32.

10 Ibid., Question 8, p. 34.
11 Ibid.
12 Ibid., p. 35.
13 Ibid., Question 9, p. 36.
14 Ibid., Question 16, p. 50.
15 Ibid., p. 51.
16 Ibid.
17 Ibid., Question 1, p. 8.
18 Ibid., p. 59.
19 Ibid.
20 Gabriel Biel, *Collectorium circa quattuor libros Sententiarum*, Prologue, eds. W. Werbeck and U. Hofmann (Tübingen, 1973), 4 vols., I, p. 8.
21 Ibid., p. 9.
22 Ibid.
23 Ibid.
24 Ibid., p. 12.
25 Ibid., p. 32.
26 Ockham, Prologue, q.2 B (O.76.13–6).
27 Ockham gives three senses for *demonstratio*. It has a broad general sense (*largissime*) in which it refers to any syllogism *ex necessariis*. It has a less broad sense: *pro syllogismo ex necessariis prioribus conclusione, non curando an propositio sit per se nota an dubitabilis.*

On these two definitions a proposition *per se nota* is *demonstrabilis*. Strictly, "demonstrative" ought to be used of a syllogism whose premisses are necessary, *natae causare notitiam adhaesivam conclusionis.* Biel, Prologue q.2.a 1.A, p. 33; Ockham, Prologue D (I.81).

28 Ibid. Cf. Augustine, *Retractationes*, 1.8.n.2.
29 Gabriel Biel, *Collectorium*, I, p. 33.
30 Gabriel Biel, *Quaestiones de justificatione*, ed. C. Feckes (Aschendorff, 1929), p. 7.
31 Ibid.
32 *Sentences*, Dist. XVII.q.1.
33 Ockham, I *Sent.*, d.17, q.1, and Petrus Aureoli, *Sent*, d.17.a.2, props. 1–3.
34 Biel, *Quaestiones de justificatione*, p. 8.
35 Ibid., p. 9.
36 Ibid., p. 10.
37 Ibid.
38 Ibid.
39 Kilwardby, *Quaestiones in Librum Tertium Sententiarum*, Question 9, p. 43.
40 Ibid., Questions 46, 47, 48, 49, 50.

Bibliography

Gabriel Biel, *Quaestiones de justificatione*, ed. C. Feckes (Aschendorff, 1929).

Gabriel Biel, *Collectorium circa quattuor libros Sententiarum*, Prologue q.2.al. B, eds. W. Werbeck and U. Hofmann (Tübingen, 1973), 4 vols.

Robert Kilwardby, *De ortu scientiarum*, ed. A. G. Judy, Auctories britannici Medii Aevi (London, 1976).

Robert Kilwardby, *Quaestiones in Librum Tertium Sententiarum*, ed. Elisabeth Gössman, Bayerische Akademie der Wissenschaften, 10 (München, 1982).

Augustine, the Medieval Theologians, and the Reformation

Paul Rorem

At the end of the Middle Ages, the momentous transition into the sixteenth-century controversies suggests looking back over all these medieval theologians according to the useful yet limited categories of the well-known epitaph by Benjamin B. Warfield (1851–1921). "The Reformation, inwardly considered, was just the ultimate triumph of Augustine's doctrine of grace over Augustine's doctrine of the church." For our retrospective purposes, this quotation conveniently points to four aspects of medieval theology.

First, we must respect the long and broad legacy of the Bishop of Hippo throughout this entire millennium of theology, not only on the two major themes named but on several other theological topics as well. An overview can indicate this legacy's breadth, namely, the sheer frequency of references to Augustine by so many medieval theologians of such diverse orientations, but it must defer to more specialized studies for any demonstration of its depth. (Since not everything about medieval theology can be subsumed under Augustinian influence, a prominent exception will also be noted.)

Second, the medieval doctrine of the Church was developed within Augustinian parameters, broadly speaking, including aspects of ministry, sacramental theology, authority, and the relationship of the church to the civil government.

Third, Augustine's doctrine of grace (in Pauline terms, encompassing sin, free will, grace, justification, election, predestination, in short, salvation) was obviously central to our theologians, already being a "famous question" in Anselm's day.

Fourth, how do these two enormous fields of doctrine (Church and grace) relate to each other? Augustinians could and did differ on how to correlate salvation and ecclesiology, how to relate election and the sacraments. On this last point especially, Warfield's own perspective needs to be reassessed or even reversed regarding the Reformation as an Augustinian debate, not to mention his Protestant leap over all of the medieval theologians in appealing directly to St. Augustine.

Augustinian Legacies

As John Rist said in the opening sentence of this volume's opening chapter, Augustine's writings "set the Western theological tone for more than a thousand years." Even before engaging the enormous issues of church and grace, we should note how important these works were for other theological topics, such as the nature of God and the doctrine of the Trinity, creation and evil, biblical interpretation, spiritual contemplation and the ascent toward God, and finally eschatology. These and other issues received their Augustinian imprint in the Middle Ages not only because our authors read the Bishop of Hippo directly but also because so many other transitional figures mediating the legacy of antiquity to the early medieval world were themselves so steeped in the same corpus: Boethius, Cassiodorus, Gregory the Great, Isidore of Seville, the Venerable Bede, and many of the Carolingians.

Anselm's contributions to the medieval doctrine of God began from his own reading of Augustine's *On the Trinity*. His fundamentally interior perspective on God and the soul made in the image of the triune God is thoroughly Augustinian, as presented in Evans' chapter. Even Anselm's ontological argument has a precursor in Augustine, as Rist noted above. Augustine was also immensely influential on the entire Western development of the doctrine of the Trinity, although here the question is more complex than it might seem. Ecumenical dialogues and histories of doctrine often portray the dispute between Western Latin Church and the Eastern Orthodox Churches over the procession of the Holy Spirit as a simple case of Augustinian insistence that the Spirit proceeds from the Father and the Son (the *filioque* addition to the Nicene Creed) because God's unity logically precedes the Trinity, whereas the Greeks taught that the Holy Spirit proceeds from the Father (indeed, since the ninth-century involvement of Patriarch Photius, from the Father alone), because they on the other hand started with the three persons and then affirmed the divine unity. This is partially true, but misleading in two ways. First, the logical priority of "unity" to "Trinity" is not so "Augustinian" as claimed, whether in the Bishop of Hippo himself or in an Augustinian doctrine of the Trinity like Peter Lombard's. This form of Aristotelian logic, developed in the late neoplatonism of Proclus, was applied to the doctrine of the Trinity by Boethius, but in a suggestive and preliminary way; it fully entered the Western theological tradition only with Thomas Aquinas. Second, Augustine's own doctrine of the Trinity was not so exclusively identified with the Western position on the *filioque* as to be completely alien to the Easterners after all. Gregory Palamas read and appreciated a Greek translation of *On the Trinity* in the fourteenth century and in fact found in Augustine some support for the Orthodox arguments against the *filioque*, as Andrew Louth notes in his chapter.

Thus, the Augustinian influence on later views of the Trinity is not as monolithic as often portrayed. It shared the stage with other factors in the West and was not so completely absent in the East.

The complex history of medieval dualists like the Cathars or Albigensians includes the persistent belief, then and now, that these were "medieval Manichees" and therefore could be opposed with Augustine's own anti-Manichean arguments about creation and the source of evil: the material world comes from God and is therefore good, although a lesser good; evil stems not from some cosmic source of its own but from our own mistaken entanglements with this lower realm. Ironically, Augustine's anti-Manichean works may have not only provided good arguments against such dualists but also supplied some of the Manichean details for the Albigensians to adapt and appropriate for their own use.

Although Augustine did not establish the fourfold system of exegesis, Scripture was understood in the Middle Ages along the lines of Augustine's own exegesis and principles of interpretation, especially in his widely circulated *On Christian Doctrine*. His basic teaching about language, about signs, about multiple meanings to a biblical text, were all foundational for medieval hermeneutics from the Carolingians to the Humanists. His own specific interpretations also lived on in many forms, not least the *Glossa ordinaria*. The conviction that biblical contemplation led to spiritual ascent toward God is another common medieval theme with Augustinian lineage. Bernard of Clairvaux and Bonaventure were openly indebted to Augustine on these things, as in the former's teaching on love and the will, or the latter's *Itinerarium* or journey from the exterior things perceived by the senses to the interior realm of the soul (made in God's triune image) upwards to that superior realm of God who is one and three. The chapters on these authors and the chapter on the later medieval mystics all testify to the enduring legacy of Augustinian spirituality on this front. Finally, Augustinian eschatology also prevailed over much of Western medieval theology, in that his teachings on the "end," especially in the overall theology of history in *The City of God*, effectively replaced several versions of the millennial expectation that identified the kingdom of God with some earthly reality and anticipated a period of radical improvement in human history. Augustine's sober view of human institutions, especially after the fall of Rome in 410, discouraged millennial hopes for any earthly version of paradise, at least until the challenge, only partially successful, of Joachim of Fiore in the twelfth century.

The chapters in this volume have also traced a different type of influence, since not everything about medieval theology should be attributed to Augustine. From Dionysius the Areopagite, a programmatic use of negations (apophatic theology) entered into Western intellectual history with John the Scot Eriugena, and continued on through Hugh of St. Victor (within his largely Augustinian framework) to Albert the Great, Thomas Aquinas, and their various heirs. That human language fails before the transcendence of the divine was common theological property, including Augustine himself, who had a healthy respect for the inexpressible majesty of the eternal God. Although the Bishop of Hippo could therefore resort often enough to negations about God, he was not systematic about it and certainly did not see it as the best way to approach God. For such a programmatic and central place for the apophatic, our medieval theologians could and did cite the Dionysian corpus, considered apostolic throughout this period. The methodological principle that negations about God are preferable in theological discourse because they are plainly true, whereas affirmations about God always need qualifications befitting the transcendent subject-matter, had its own vigorous life among our medieval theologians, and they owed little of it to the Bishop of Hippo. There were, after all, other Fathers. Yet even the occasional dash of Dionysius seems in long retrospect like an exotic oriental spice lightly seasoning the standard Augustinian loaf. It was well-known but not to everyone's taste and not essential to the basic medieval diet.

The Church, Ministry, and Sacraments

When Warfield spoke of Augustine's doctrine of the Church, he narrowly meant what he considered Cyprian's equation of "Church" with the empirical (and episcopal) institution. When ecclesiology is defined more broadly to include the Church, ministry, sacramental theology, questions of authority and polity, as well as issues of church and state, the question of Augustinian influence becomes broad indeed. Augustine's numerous writings and varying emphases allowed later disputants to invoke him on both sides of an argument, sometimes with limited understanding of what had actually been his own position.

A prominent example stems from the Donatist controversy. The church's ministry and especially the efficacy of the sacraments do not depend upon the history and the subjective integrity of the ministers themselves, argued Augustine, but upon the objective promise of Christ himself as worked out in the performance of the sacrament itself. This principle of "objectivity" informed the entire development of medieval sacramental theology, as well as understandings of ministerial office. When Carolingians disputed over the eucharistic presence of the body and blood of Christ in the Mass, for example, the arguments for an objective or "real" presence by Paschasius Radbertus could cite this side of Augustine's thought. On the other hand, there was also a subjective side to Augustine's sacramental theology, wherein the efficacy of the Eucharist *was* related to human participation, not to the (Donatist) integrity of the officiant but to the Christian faith of the recipient. Here Augustine's interest in signs and symbols, especially regarding the Bible, was applied to the sacraments. If the bread and wine were signs, there was necessarily some distinction between them and that which they signified, namely, the body and blood of Christ, which were objects of faith. At this point, the other side of the Carolingian controversy, in the person of Ratramnus of Corbie, could and did claim the Augustinian legacy as well. Using terminology taken directly from Augustine's sign theory, especially in biblical exegesis, Ratramnus argued that the bread and wine are *figures* of the body and the blood, and point the believer to them. Both sides not only believed in the presence of Christ, they also invoked the same Bishop of Hippo, but on different aspects of the question and from different emphases within the Augustinian corpus.

When Berengar and Lanfranc argued through their eleventh-century version of this question, the landscape was equally Augustinian regarding a sacrament as a "sacred sign," but new ways of formulating the particulars were developing. The Aristotelian language of substance and accidents gradually helped the scholastic theologians go beyond Augustine in specifying just how the bread was outwardly bread and yet substantively Christ's body. Yet in this early development of scholastic sacramental theology, we also see the long reach of Augustinian categories. The Victorines were thoroughly Augustinian regarding signs and signification, and this heritage was applied by Peter Lombard to a full-scale theology of the sacraments. Lombard's pivotal *Sentences*, as discussed in this volume by Marcia Colish, emphasized and expanded Augustine's fundamental concepts of signs and things, to be used and to be enjoyed. The concept of transubstantiation held together the objective and the subjective dimensions of the question, but when Wycliffe and then the Protestant Reformers started arguing about the presence of Christ in the sacrament (the Protestants, among themselves), we can see these two dimensions of sacramental theology, equally Augustinian, pitted against each other. Except for some Waldensians, with their "quasi-Donatist" denial of priestly efficacy as discussed above, medieval theologians and their Reformation heirs were generally Augustinian and thus anti-Donatist in their sacramental theology and views on ministry. (Even if John Eck accused the Protestants of being new Donatists, just as the Protestants accused the Anabaptists of the same anti-Augustinian error!) Yet Augustinian theologians could still differ on whether to emphasize the objective or the subjective side of his legacy in sacramental theology.

When it came to the doctrine of the Church itself, including ecclesiastical authority and the relationship of church and state, there are several starting-points in Augustine's works, but also considerable medieval development far beyond the Bishop of Hippo's own thoughts. The development of the Roman papacy, for example, owes little to the North African, but cited him (and Cyprian and others) regarding episcopal authority generally. The concept and vocabulary of "hierarchy," for one thing, entered the Latin scene later, courtesy of the Pseudo-Dionysian corpus. Similarly, Augustine's views of the Roman government were justifiably famous through his magisterial work *The City of God*, with influences upon a host of people, including Charlemagne, and upon diverse topics, including the complex question of a "just war." But the medieval efforts, especially by some popes, to subordinate the temporal governments of kings and emperors to the ecclesiastical power went beyond Augustine's own views. Yet they cited him so often that this ecclesial takeover of the state is known today as "political Augustinianism." Insofar as the starting-points are some rhetorical comments by Augustine about secular government, often taken out of context, perhaps this too is an example of his long influence; but insofar as this view of ecclesiastical and secular government was actually developed by Gregory the Great, Isidore of Seville, and various medieval popes, "political Augustinianism" cannot claim Augustine himself among its adherents.

Grace and Predestination

The difficulty in assessing Augustine's legacy regarding the doctrine of grace lies not so much in its breadth, but rather its depth, the sheer complexity of the issue. Here especially, and perhaps more than any other Father, Augustine "set the Western theological tone" for this whole millennium through his particular exegesis of the Pauline presentation of sin, grace, free will, election, justification, and predestination.

The "Semi-Pelagian" controversy which took place in Augustine's own lifetime was replayed a century later, yielding a statement by the Second Council of Orange (529). Sometimes considered "Semi-Augustinian," this text combined Augustine's divine election to salvation with human free will and responsibility, especially for the unbelief which leads to damnation. Yet this synthesis settled nothing for most of the later disputes; it was unknown to the Carolingians and their successors until Thomas Aquinas. What further bedeviled the later debates over grace and election was the misattribution of key sources. Pelagian materials survived under the names of Jerome and Cassiodorus, and even under Augustine's own name.

When Gottschalk and Hincmar squared up to one another in the Carolingian dispute over election, part of the problem was whether the foreknowledge solution was genuinely Augustinian. Gottschalk and his supporters cited Augustine's later treatises against the Semi-Pelagians, and an interpretive tradition headed by Isidore of Seville which summarized this strong view of divine election as "double predestination," that is, both to salvation and to damnation. To Hincmar's eye, Gottschalk had neglected free will and missed Augustine's own understanding of foreknowledge and predestination, wherein God foreknows human choices and *thereby* predestines people to their chosen fates. That this generous place for an independent human will came from a Pseudo-Augustinian "Memorandum" of Semi-Pelagian stock escaped Hincmar and most contemporaries, but not Gottschalk's ally, Florus of Lyons.

By Anselm's day, this debate was already a "famous question," but it had several more stages of development yet to come, too many to rehearse here. Thomas Aquinas started out with an inherited synthesis of free will and grace, but in his rediscovery of Augustine's later treatises and the Semi-Pelagian controversies he then (in the *Summa Theologiae*) carefully emphasized the divine initiative for every part of what had become the process of justification, from humanity's initial desire to its subsequent perseverance. Even this strong Augustinian position did not settle the debate for the later Middle Ages, not to mention the Reformation. Thomas's great centuries of influence, after all, were not his own or any of those immediately subsequent, but rather the sixteenth to the twentieth centuries. Late medieval controversies over grace and election continued to proliferate, with Kilwardby, Wyclif, Gregory of Rimini, Bradwardine, and Gabriel Biel among the Augustinian disputants, as indicated in earlier chapters. The problem was in identifying what "Augustinian" meant, and even more pointedly, what it meant to charge an opponent with "Pelagianism." The labels seemed to shift with the theological climate.

The late medieval Augustinian revivals went separate ways on this front, as seen in Luther himself over against the head of his erstwhile order, Jerome Seripando (1493–1563). Luther, like Calvin after him, claimed that Augustine was entirely on his side; Seripando, Prior General of the Order and delegate at the Council of Trent, was equally adamant about faithfully representing Augustine's doctrine of healing or transforming grace. Even if Protestants and such Tridentine theologians might (sometimes) agree on justification by grace alone, there was still the question of grace's effects on and in the Christian. From the human side, was the result of such grace a (forensic) justification by faith alone, as taught by Luther and condemned at Trent, or was it a (transforming) justification by faith formed in love, which a Seripando (or a Kilwardby before him) could claim as the authentically Augustinian position? Despite Warfield's implication, Augustine's doctrine of grace was not so easily identified and was certainly not so captive to a Protestant monopoly. In Jaroslav Pelikan's variation on Whitehead, if Western philosophy is a series of footnotes to Plato, the Western theological doctrine of grace and predestination is a series of footnotes on Augustine, and we have not even come yet to John Calvin and Cornelius Jansen.

Church and Grace, in Conclusion

If issues of Augustinian ecclesiology are broader than Warfield knew, and issues of grace deeper and more complex, no wonder that his linking of the two sounds so unsatisfactory today, namely, that the Reformation was the "ultimate triumph" of the latter over the former. Before revisiting Warfield's basic understandings of these two doctrinal topics, we should inquire into their linkage, starting with the medievals themselves. Gottschalk and Hincmar nicely illustrate the problem with pitting grace against the Church. The former was committed to Augustine's understanding of God's eternal decrees of election as the final goal or end. As an independent thinker, not to mention a maverick opponent of churchly authorities, Gottschalk gave little importance to the intermediate ends of the Church and the sacraments as God's ecclesial *means* of grace. But to a Hincmar, God's eternal decrees would remain abstract and distant without the intermediate realm of the church, its ministry of mediation, and especially the sacraments. Hincmar was an archbishop, after all, and not about to let Gottschalk's emphases render his churchly enterprise irrelevant. Hincmar thus stressed Augustine's anti-Donatist doctrine of the Church, the earthly means of grace (including the human response), and various forms of mediation. Along with the related intercession of Mary and the saints, this emphasis on ecclesial mediation grew throughout the Middle Ages. On one level, the Protestant agenda was to reemphasize the sole mediatorship of Christ, even if Luther and Zwingli, for example, could not agree on the Christological relationship of the divine and the human natures, and therefore on the presence of the body of Christ in the Lord's Supper. Surely Warfield the

Calvinist would have taken Gottschalk's rigorous theological side over against Archbishop Hincmar's interest in ecclesial mediation. But Augustine himself was both a rigorous theologian and a bishop, and his legacy cannot be so simply bifurcated.

In fact, perhaps Warfield's dictum could be reversed. Instead of setting Augustine's (Protestant) doctrine of grace over against his (institutional) doctrine of the church, perhaps Trent had its own valid claim on an Augustinian doctrine of justification by grace through faith formed in love, and perhaps Augustine's doctrine of the church, as seen in some newly rediscovered sermons, was not so institutionally "Cyprianic" after all, but a "low" ecclesiology of the "communion of saints" gathered for worship. In such a reversal of affiliations, the Reformation could then be called not a triumph but a failure, the failure to keep a Protestant or low-Augustinian doctrine of the church together with the Tridentine-Augustinian doctrine of a healing or transforming grace. Of course, this forced reversal is just as flawed and oversimplifying as Warfield's original, but the very possibility of reformulating the material illustrates the rich complexity of Augustine's legacy. As John Rist said above, in many controversies both sides could claim Augustinian parentage. In both oversimplified caricatures, however, the linkage of grace and the means of grace, of election and the sacraments, is lost. For the Bishop of Hippo, God gives the means as well as the ends. Otherwise, the Augustinian tradition comes apart, as indeed it did in the sixteenth century.

Bibliographical Note

B. B. Warfield's comment, reprinted in *Calvin and Augustine* (Philadelphia: Westminster, 1956), p. 322, is used by J. Pelikan, *The Christian Tradition*, vol. 4, *Reformation of Church and Dogma (1300–1700)* (Chicago: University of Chicago Press, 1984), p. 9 and elsewhere, and is discussed in Pelikan's "An Augustinian Dilemma: Augustine's Doctrine of Grace versus Augustine's Doctrine of the Church?," *Augustinian Studies*, 18 (1987): 1–29. See also Pelikan's volume 3, *The Growth of Medieval Theology (600–1300)* (Chicago: University of Chicago Press, 1978); Karlfried Froehlich, "Justification Language and Grace: The Charge of Pelagianism in the Middle Ages," in *Probing the Reformed Tradition: Historical Studies in Honor of Edward A. Dowey, Jr.*, eds. Elsie Anne McKee and Brian G. Armstrong (Louisville: Westminster/John Knox Press, 1989), pp. 21–47; and *Augustine Through the Ages, an Encyclopedia*, ed. Allan D. Fitzgerald, OSA (Grand Rapids, Mich.: William B. Eerdmans Publishing Company, 1999).

Index

abstraction 261
academic freedom 234
academic theology x, 89
accidents 118, 120, 179, 219, 262
Achard of St. Victor 144
Adalman of Liège 86, 87
Adam 9, 16, 29, 72, 175, 188, 191, 192, 334, 340
Adam Parvipontanus 102
Adelmann 88
adoption 9
adoptionism 65–9, 69, 71, 81
Aelred of Rivaulx 139
aestimatio 132
Agapetus I Pope 31
Aidan 61
Alain of Lille 273
Alberic of Reims 165
Albert the Great 202, 204, 208, 217, 367
Albertus Magnus 306
Albigensians xiv, 89, 290
Alcuin 30, 65–9, 71, 81, 161
Alexander of Hales 187, 189, 190, 217, 223
Alfarabi 306
altar 194
Ambrose of Milan xii, 25, 31, 57, 75, 140, 189
analogy 214, 251, 252, 257, 263
Anastasius of Antioch 32
Andrew of Crete 47
Andrew of St. Victor 143

angels 13, 41, 99, 174, 181, 192, 204, 215, 226, 272, 291, 292, 294
Anglia 31
animal, political 303, 315
animals 209
Anonymous of Laon 269
Anselm of Besate 90
Anselm of Canterbury xii, 12, 80, 85, 90, 91, 94–101, 129, 131, 137, 142, 146, 189, 191, 192
Anselm of Laon 104, 114, 116, 131, 161, 164, 165
anthropology 219
anthropomorphism 132
Antichrist 169
antisacerdotalism 281
Antoine Saunier 280
apocalypse 46, 181
apocalyptic 311
apologetic x
apophatic fideism 213; mysticism 139; theology 41
Apostolic See 243
apostolic poverty 347; purity 346
Aquinas, Thomas 96, 201, 206, 209, 221, 234, 238, 251, 252, 254, 234, 306, 316, 320, 371
Arabic 182, 196, 202
Arabs 45, 204, 306
Arians xiii, 25, 33
Aristotle xii, 11, 26, 43, 88, 94, 130, 143, 171, 172, 174, 179, 187, 195,

Aristotle (*cont.*)
  196, 197, 202, 203, 205, 207, 208,
  209, 225, 233, 233, 258, 261, 303,
  305, 306, 309, 311, 315–36, 344, 352,
  371
Ark 223
Ark of the Covenant 145
Armenians 38
Arnald of Bonneval 129
artificer 250, 255
ascension 218
ascent 223
asceticism 31
assent 177
assumed person 67
astrology 17
astronomy 25
Athanasius 15, 38, 44
atheism 12
Athos 50
atonement 14
Augustine ix, xii, xiii, 3–23, 27, 29, 51,
  57, 60, 61, 67, 75, 78, 79, 87, 95, 96,
  97, 108, 113, 137, 140, 142, 169, 189,
  191, 202, 207, 221, 224, 226, 287,
  303, 313, 314, 318, 319, 320, 369–76
Augustine of Canterbury 33
Augustinian hermits 207
Augustinus Triumphus 237, 238
autobiography 103
avarice 271
Averroes 195, 206, 233
Avicenna 204, 225
Avignon 241, 243
axioms 118

Baldus de Ubaldis 243
Baptism 15, 41, 274, 178, 179, 218, 219
  and *passim*
Bari, Council of 100
Barlaam 50, 51
Bartholomew Prignano 243
Basil of Ancyra 73
Basil the Great 39, 44, 60, 189
Basle 246, 247
beatific vision 241
beatitude 218, 304
Beatus of Liebana 67
Bede xi, xii, 57–64

Beguines 228
Benedict Biscop xi
Benedict of Aniane xi
Benedictines 33, 34
Berengar 365
Berengar of Tours xiii, xiv, 85, 86, 87,
  88, 161, 166
Bernard of Clairvaux xii, xiv, 102, 105,
  114, 115, 129–55, 168, 189, 192, 222,
  229, 361
Bernard of Fontcaude 272
Bernardus Primus 273
betrothal 180
Bible xii, 30, 31, 72, 96, 129, 156–67,
  230 and *passim*; *see also* Scripture
bishops x, 15, 129, 242 and *passim*
blasphemy 278, 299
blessed 174
body 136
Boethius x, xi, xv, 24, 25–7, 28, 30, 94,
  112, 116, 117, 118, 145, 204, 341,
  371
Bogomils 289
Bonagratia of San Giovannis 235
Bonaventure 187–200, 217, 224, 225,
  225, 226, 234, 239, 311
Bride of Christ 134
Bruno of Chartreux 161
Bulgarian Church 290
Byzantium 37–54, 29, 81

Calvin 367
canon law 162, 221, 240, 245, 309, 314,
  318
canonical authorities 272
canonists 180, 234
Cappadocians 44
cardinals 208, 243
caritas 16, 304, 343 *and see* love
Carolingians 65–82, 159, 160
Carthusians 140, 222
Cassian 60
Cassiodorus xi, 24, 28–30, 60
catechetics x
catena aurea 205
Cathars 271, 272, 272, 289–300
cause 255
cause, first 171
celibacy 277

celibacy, clerical xiv, 85
Chad 61, 62
Chalcedon, Council of (451) 29, 37, 38, 45
character 219
charism xiv
charismatics 216
charity 77, 135, 178 *and see* love
Charlemagne xi, 68, 71, 94
Chrism 41
Christ 10, 39, 40, 43, 60, 65–9, 69, 100, 112, 134, 209, 212, 215, 218, 225, 229, 238, 242, 246, 274, 297 and *passim*; divinity of 271; humanity of 271
Christendom 132
Christology 27, 38, 44, 65, 66, 72, 73, 81, 132, 145, 168, 218, 367
Chrysostom 60
Church 14, 85, 89, 129, 176, 179, 304, 321, 322, 323, and *passim*; teaching office x; universal 73
Cicero xi, 20, 21, 22, 94, 95, 246, 307
circumcision 219
Cistercians 146, 129
Claudianus Mamertus 29
Claudius of Turin 161
Cloud of Unknowing 231
cognition 261
collegial xiv
commentary 157
communis utilitas 326
Concordat of Worms 1122 xiv
Concorezzensians 293–6
concupiscentia 16
confession 180
confessors 44, 228, 277
confirmation 178, 218, 219
congregation of the faithful 288
Conrad of Gelnhausen 244
conscience 175, 236
consent 180
consolamentum 299
Constance, council of 246
Constantine, Donation of 275, 320, 349
Constantine, Emperor 275
Constantine of Cyprus 73
contemplation 50, 135, 145, 202, 223, 225

contrition 180
convenientia 99
Copts 38
Corpus Christi, Feast of 205
Cosmas of Maiouma 47
cosmos 41, 44
Council of Constance 341
Council of Lyons (1274) 187, 206
Council of Nicaea (787) 70
Council of Vienne 237
Councils, ecumenical, *see* Councils, General
Councils, General 189
counsel 324
courtly love 229
creation 45, 136, 146, 190, 228, 250, 291, 293; creatures 119, 121
Creator 135, 193
creatures 119, 193, 215, 253, 262
Creed 69
Creed, Nicene ix, 25, 372
creeds 203
Cross 9, 10, 45, 192, 225
Crusade 131, 290
cults 181, 274
cupidity 196
Cur deus homo 367
curia 70, 115
curiositas 17
Cuthbert 14, 60, 63
Cyprian 365
Cyril of Alexandria 37, 38, 44
Czech Unity of Brethren 280

Damascene, John 42
Damasus, Pope 238
damnation 79
damned 174, 272
Dante Alighieri 131, 244, 321–37
Deborah 228
decentia 99
demons 289
demonstrative method 27
Desiderius 296
determinism 335
Deus-homo 191, 192
Devil 96, 191, 192, 271, 278, 289 *and see* Satan
devotional writing 100, 192

Diadochos of Photike 44
dialectic 91, 107, 130 *and see* logic
Didymos the Blind 39–40
Dionysius the Ps.-Areopagite 40, 41, 42,
    44, 142, 144, 189, 203, 204, 205, 207,
    223, 303, 304, 376
discipline 281
dispensation 311
disputatio 130
disputations 272
dissent 236, 245, 269–86
divine being 106
divine law 196
divine power 90
divine sovereignty 90
divine substance, nature, essence 108, 109
divorce 28
Dominicans 202, 205, 207, 208, 236,
    306, 357
dominium 311, 314–31, 342, 343, 345–8
Donatists xiii, 14, 20, 33, 273, 274
dowries 312
Drogo of Tours 161, 166
dualism 287–300, 326
Duns Scotus 251
Durand de St. Pourçain 240
Durand of Osca 271, 272, 297

earthly kingdom 294
ecclesiastical authorities 273
ecclesiology x, xiv, 73, 76, 81, 89, 134,
    168, 246, 305, 310–37
Eckhart, Meister 225, 226, 231, 241
ecumenical councils 37, 45
elect 78, 343
election 242
Elipandus Migetius 67, 68
emanation 170
encyclopedia 157
end of the world 31
energies 41
enthememe 79
Ephesus, Council of 69
Epiphanios 46
epistemology 138, 330
equivocation 214
equivocity 252
Eriugena, John Scotus 38, 78, 79, 80, 81,
    87, 161, 371

Ermengaud of Béziers 272
eros 10
eroticism 229
error 181, 195
essence 212
essence, divine 337
eternity 26, 90
eternity of the word 195
ethics 176, 177, 205, 280, 209, 305ff.
Étienne Tempier 195
Eucharist xiv, 41, 66, 73, 74, 86, 87, 88,
    134, 140, 172, 178, 179, 192, 193,
    219, 273, 274, 341, 352–6
Eudes Rigaud 187
Eugenius III, Pope 115, 134
Eusebius 60
Euthymios Zigabenos 289
Eutyches 27
Evagrios 39–40, 42, 44
evangelical counsels 271
Eve 175, 188, 191, 192
evil 174, 287
ex nihilo 13, 173
excommunication 338
exegesis 46, 49, 57, 59–60, 340
existence 261
exitus 212
excommunication 179
experience 138, 139, 222
extramental world 261

faith alone 359–63
faith and works 87
faith ix, x, 61, 94, 117, 123, 130, 135,
    138, 244 and *passim*
Fall 13, 72, 99, 175, 176, 190, 192, 340
Father, the 27, 100, 106, 107–10, 112,
    113, 120, 172, 177, 224
Fathers ix, xii, 37, 43, 46, 58, 69, 70, 72,
    75, 80, 106, 189, 270, 272, 352
fear 18
Felix III Pope 31
feudalism 99
figurative speech 108, 119
filioque 40
first mover 250
florilegia 37, 38, 46, 115, 319
Florus of Lyons 78, 370
foreknowledge 22, 172, 173

Fortune 26
Fourth Lateran Council 193, 194, 309, 310
Francis of Assisi 133, 190, 187, 192, 208, 236, 238, 311
Franciscans 311, 328–36
Franciscans, conventual 238
Franciscans, spiritual 238, 311, 323
Franciscus Zabarella 243, 246
free choice 137
free will 13, 22, 76–80, 100, 174, 177, 135, 137, 215
freedom of speech 246
friars 195, 203, 206, 347
Fulbert of Chartres 161
funeral 41

Gabriel Biel 357–63, 371
Gelasius I 72
Geoffrey of Auxerre 139
geometry 306, 307, 307
George of Cyprus 47
Georges Morel 274
Georgians 38
Gérard d'Abbeville 194
Gerard de Borgo San Domingo 203
Gerson, Jean 26, 246
Gertrude of Hackeborn 228
Gilbert Crispin 98
Gilbert of Poitiers 102–28, 162
Gilbert the Universal 164, 165
Giles of Rome 207, 237, 238, 306, 307, 313–37
Glossa ordinaria 97, 156–67
Gnosticism 287
Gnostics 272
God, existence of 251, 252; nature of 85
Godfrey of Fontaines 197, 234–5, 237, 240, 245, 336
good 10, 26, 97, 106, 119, 174, 204, 213, 224, 257, 287
good works 16
goodness 304
Gospel precepts 276
Goths 25, 28
Gottschalk of Orbais 77, 78, 79, 80, 374
governance xiv
governance, divine 172

grace 76–80, 77, 81, 88, 123, 130, 145, 172, 174, 175, 175, 178, 181, 190, 195, 204, 214, 215, 228, 314–35, 348, 369–76 and *passim*
grammar 85, 94, 122, 124
Gratian 306
Great Schism 243, 245, 246, 313
Greek 100, 156, 182, 196, 202, 205, 207, 272, 289
Gregory Nazianzen 43, 49, 60, 189
Gregory of Nyssa 44, 133, 189
Gregory of Rimini 340, 341, 374
Gregory Palamas 51
Gregory the Great ix, xii, 24, 30–6, 57, 60, 71, 140, 146, 189, 192, 202, 207
Gregory the Theologian 44
Guido Terreni 238
Guigo I 222
Guillaume Farel 280
Gundissalvus, Dominic 306

habitus 357–63
Haimo of Auxerre 161
happiness, pursuit of 26
healing 194
heaven 88, 174
heavenly kingdom 288
Heinrich of Halle 228
Heiric of Auxerres
hell 174
Henry of Ghent 233, 234, 336
Henry of Langenstein 244
heresiarchs 276
heresy x, 42, 43, 45, 46, 86, 98, 105, 240, 324, 326
heretics 31, 88, 132, 179, 269–86
Herluin 94
hermeneutics 106, 221
Hervaeus Natalis 238
hesychasm 50, 51
hexaemeron 174
hierarchy 41, 44, 171, 178, 303, 304, 317
hierocracy 304
Hilary of Poitiers 60, 189
Hilda 61
Hincmar of Reims 29, 76, 77, 78, 81, 372
history 10, 19

holy orders 178, 179
Holy Roman Empire 273
Holy Spirit xiv, 27, 91, 100, 105, 106,
    107–10, 112, 113, 141, 142, 172, 180,
    215, 216, 312 and *passim*
homo assumptus 67
honor 191
hope 177
Hugh of Digne 235
Hugh of Langres 86, 88
Hugh of St. Victor xii, xv, 129, 131, 134,
    142, 168, 178, 189, 222, 223, 306,
    371
human nature 130, 175
humanism 130
humanity 136, 181, 305
Humbert, Cardinal 49
Hus, Hussites 246, 279, 280, 334–54
hylomorphism 209
hypostasis 39, 43
hypostatic union 176, 209, 217

iconoclasm 42, 45, 47, 48, 70–3
icons 45, 71
idolatry 45, 46
illumination 41, 42
image 73, 140, 145, 224, 227
image, divine 218
image of God 96
images 70
images (literary) 119
imago dei 81, 141
imitation of Christ 180
immaculate conception 132, 218
immanence 213, 230
immortality 137
immutability 213
imperialism 19, 321
Incarnation x, xv, 12, 27, 40, 69, 72, 85,
    100, 133, 175, 190, 191, 197, 212,
    216, 218
infideles 134, 274
infinity 213
Innocent II, Pope 105
Innocent III, Pope 272, 280
Inquisition 275, 277, 278, 281
intellect 117, 255
intention 177, 227
intuition 261

Investiture 85
Investiture Contest xiv
inwardness 227
Iohannes of Lugio 292
Irenaeus 15, 38
Isaac of Stella 139
Isidore of Seville 60, 163, 166
Islam 45
itinerants 277
iurisdictio 311
Ivo of Chartres 92

Jacques Fournier 239, 300
James of Viterbo 306, 313–37
Jean de la Rochelle 187, 190, 195
Jean Gerson 244, 245
Jerome xii, 14, 38, 57, 58, 143, 189,
    237, 242
Jerome of Prague 246
Jerusalem 47
Jesus 1
Jews 33, 46, 89, 91, 99, 106, 204, 205,
    219
Johannes Oecolampadius 280
Johin of Ravenna 32
John Baconthorpe 244
John Chrysostom 189
John Damascene 46–7, 48, 57, 169, 213,
    352
John Donne 167
John Duns Scotus 197, 233, 253, 255,
    257, 258, 259, 260–3
John Eck 373
John Italos 50
John Klentok 340
John of Caesarea 39
John of Damascus 189, 216
John of Fécamp 130
John of Paris 234, 306, 316, 317–36
John of Parma 223
John of Pouilli 236, 237
John of Salisbury 102, 131
John of Vercelli 208
John Pecham 197
John the Scot, *see* Eriugena
John XXII, Pope 238
John Wyclif 245, 246, 280
Joseph the Hymnographer 47
Juan de Segovia 246, 247

Julian of Eclanum 38
Julian of Norwich 221; Norwich 229, 230
jurisdiction 180, 242, 316, 323
justice 13, 97, 191, 251, 253, 257, 348
justification 204
Justin, Emperor 25, 39
Justinian 306

Kilwardby 370, 371
koinonia 62

laity 58, 134, 327
Lambert of Utrecht 162
Lanfranc 85, 86, 87, 91, 94, 95, 96, 98, 130, 161, 166, 373
Langenstein, Henry of xii, xvi
language 97, 114, 118; philosophy of 88
Last Judgement 190, 241, 270
last things 218
law 308
law, divine 234, 244, 324
law, human 324
law, Mosaic 272
law, natural 234
law, Roman 162, 306, 309, 318
Leander of Seville 32
lectio 130
lectio divina 132
Lent 277
Leo I, Pope 37, 238
Leontios of Jerusalem 39
lex evangelica 329
liberum arbitrium 137 *and see* free will
Libri Carolini 70
light 120
likeness 140, 145
literalism 278
liturgy 44, 47–8, 60, 88, 139, 201, 207
Livy 29
logic 12, 46, 85, 94, 97, 102, 106, 118, 122, 123, 124, 132, 350 *and see* dialectic
Lollards xiv, 334–54
Lombards 33
Lord's Prayer 276, 277, 298, 299
love 18, 224
Luther, Martin 132, 362–8, 375
Lyons, Council of 270

Macrobius 108
magic 17
malice 196
Manegold of Lautenbach 158, 161
Manichees xiii, xiv, 11, 45, 86, 207, 272, 287
Manuel Paloudis 51
marriage 20, 21, 136, 178, 181, 218, 278; clandestine 180
Marsilius of Padua 238, 239, 242, 244, 246, 324–37
Martin Bucer 280
Mary, Virgin 90, 132, 218, 228, 279
Mary Magdalene 133
Mass 279
Masses for the dead 279
Master, regent 236
masters 130
mathematics 25
matter 287, 294
Matthew of Aquasparta 197
Maundy Thursday 277
Maximos the Confessor 39, 40, 42, 44, 45–6
Mechthild of Magdeburg 228, 229
medicine 194
meditation 95
memory 96, 224
mendicant masters 310
mendicants 194, 237, 238
Mercurius Trismegistus 113
mercy 13, 97, 251, 257
merit 135, 177, 181, 340
metaphysics 172, 304
Michael Keroularios 49
Michael of Cesena 238, 239
Michael Plancha 275
Michael Psellos 44, 49–50
Michael the Synkellos 47
mind 224
ministry 372–6
miracles 90
mission 272
missionaries 205, 290
moderni 334, 340
monenergism 42, 43
Monophysites xiii, 41
Monothelites xiii, 42, 43
Monte Cassino xi, 201

moors 67
moral science 307
morals 18, 211
Moses 280
Moses Maimonides 251
motivation 9
Muslims 205
mystery 88
mysticism 71, 134, 139, 216, 221–32, 371

names 119
natural reason 172
natural theology 212, 250, 259, 262, 263
nature 27, 124, 212; divine 118, 216
natures 9, 10
necessary being 262
necessary for salvation 211
necessity 90
negative theology 252, 257
neoplatonism x, 9–12, 16, 41, 100, 225
Nestorianism 67
Nestorius xiii, 27
Noah's Ark 143
nominalism 257
notitia 138, 360–1

Ockham, William of 242–51, 257, 258, 259, 260–3, 327–37, 366
Odo Rigaud 217
omnipotence xiii, 13, 287
omniscience 119, 172
ontological argument 97
ontology 41, 118, 120, 172
optics xii
opus conditionis 143
opus restaurationis 143
order xiv
Orderic Vitalis 95
Ordination 41, 180
Origen 32, 38, 39–40, 60, 140
original sin 175, 215
orthodoxy 270
orthography 30
Oswald 61
Otto of Freising 102, 114
ownership 311, 346

pagan 89, 177
Pahlavuni 288

papal absolutism 238, 243
papal primacy 243
parousia 81
participation 172
Paschasius Radbertus 73–6, 80, 87, 161
Passion 193, 212, 229
pastoral care 33
pastoral ministry 328
patriarchs 100
patristics 201, 207, 213
Paul 347
Paul, St. ix, 15, 206, 207
Paul of Burgos 156
Paul the Deacon 61
Pelagians 9, 15, 340, 376
Pelagius xiii, 29
Pelagius II, Pope 31, 32
penance 106, 178, 179, 180, 194, 218, 279, 298, 299
perfecti 277, 287
perfection 213
person 39, 91, 106–12, 114, 120, 121, 171, 225
Peter, St. 15
Peter Abelard xiv, 102–28, 129
Peter Comestor 166
Peter Damian 89, 90, 91, 130
Peter Lombard 97, 115, 116, 131, 162, 165, 166, 168–83, 203, 205, 244, 361, 371, 376
Peter of Candia 335
Peter of Celle 129
Peter of Ireland 202
Peter of Spain 207
Peter the Chanter 164, 309
Peter the Venerable 105, 129
Petrus Manducator 167
Petrus Olivi 235, 236, 237, 240, 245
Petrus Seilanus 300
Philo of Alexandria 32
philosophers 106, 112
philosophy xv, 204
Photios 48, 44, 47
physis 43
Pierre d'Ailly 241, 244, 245, 246
Pierre de la Palud 236, 237, 238, 239, 244
Pierre Roger 239
pilgrimage 350

plants 209
Plato 12, 19, 20, 26, 97, 108, 110, 113, 173, 250, 261
platonism 141
plenitude of power, papal 313, 316, 326, 328
Plotinus 9, 10, 12, 22
plurality 100
polemic 43
political institutions 18
politics 303–37
poor, relief of 33, 34
Poor of Lyons 269–86
Pope, *passim*
Porphyry 12
poverty 194, 236, 238, 240, 276, 311, 312, 334–7; apostolic 270; voluntary 270
poverty controversy 237
power 90, 106, 112, 119, 172
prayer 41, 350
preaching x, 202, 271, 272, 277, 355
precept 324
predestination 22, 76–80, 172, 341; double 77, 78
prelates 272
Premonstratensians 273
presbyters 242
prescience 79, 172
pride 271
priesthood 273
priestly functions 274
priests 242, 323, 347 and *passim*
procession 100, 113
Proclus 26, 41
property 311, 337, 344
prophecy 86, 123, 180, 204, 216
protestants 379
providence 26, 41, 45, 172
Prudentius of Troyes 60, 78
Psalms 29–30
purification 41, 42, 223
Pythagoreans 100, 272

quadrivium 27
quodlibets 310

Rabanus Maurus 30, 159, 161, 166
Radbertus 81

Ralph of Laon 162, 165
rational animal 258
Ratramnus of Corbie 73–6, 78, 80, 81
Raymond de Sainte-Foy 273
Raynerius Sacconius 292
real presence 135
realism 341, 355
reason and authority xv
rectitudo 99
rectus ordo 98, 99
redemption 90, 136, 176, 192
Reformation ix, 269, 339–58
regio dissimilitudinis 177, 178, 181
relation 121
relics 71, 347
Remigio dei Girolami 319–37
Remigius of Auxerre 161, 163
renaissance 130, 309; Carolingian 78
reprobate 78
res publica 312
res sacramenti 178
resurrection 12, 212, 218
revelation 188, 211
Rhabanus 347
rhetoric 91, 94, 95, 308
Richard Brinkley 335
Richard of Middleton 197
Richard of Poitiers 270
Richard of St. Victor 129, 144–6, 189, 222, 223
rightness 98
rites 178, 219
rituals 277
Robert Grosseteste xii, xvi, 190
Robert Holcot 329
Robert Kilwardby 208, 361–7
Robert of Bridlington 165
Robert of Melun 115, 167
Robert of Poule 131
Roger Bacon 234, 344
Roger Marston 197
romanitas 28
Romanos the Methodist 40
Roscelin of Compiègne xiii, 91–2, 98, 104
Rufinus 38, 60
Rupert of Deutz 129, 140

Sabellianism 114, 116
sacerdotal powers 238

sacra doctrina 210
sacramentology 89
sacraments 15, 74, 75 81, 85, 87, 176, 178, 180, 190, 218, 219, 273, 372–6
sacred doctrine 211
saints 71, 236
Sallust 19
Saluus Burtius 300
salvation 14, 43, 77, 81, 123, 172, 178, 214, 300, 303, 342, 354, 364; history 298
Satan 15, 289, 290–1, 297, 298 *and see* Devil
satisfaction 180, 191
schism 100, 115, 117, 188
schismatics 179
science 118, 227, 233, 307
Scotism 257, 335
Scripture 72, 88, 97, 190, 213, 224, 350 and *passim and see* Bible
Scythopolis, John 41
secular city 20
secular power 344
secular state 337
Sedulius 60
self 222
self-knowledge 135
semantics 122
Sens, Council of 132
sensuality 230
Sentences 168–83
Seripando 375
sermons 274, 318
sex 16, 17, 136, 181, 278
Siger of Brabant 206, 233
signs 87, 218, 219
simony xiv, 85, 89, 271
Simplicianus 9, 10
simplicity 120
sin 15, 26, 69, 106, 137, 176, 181, 194, 299, 317 and *passim*
Skeptics 8–12
slaves 16, 19, 20
Slavs 289, 290
Soisson, Council of 92, 106
Son 27, 106, 107–10, 112, 113, 120, 172
soteriology 90, 134

soul 26, 28, 29, 136, 141, 175, 176, 209, 211, 224, 290, 314; origin of 100; transmigration of 26
souls of the dead 279
sovereign 324
speech 110
spiritual classics 221
spiritual power 274, 303–37
spirituality 89, 222, 226
staff, episcopal 85, 86
Stanislav of Znojmo 246
state xiv, 85, 180
Stephan Bodecker 276
Stephen Harding 131
Stephen Langton 167, 207, 233
Stephen Palec 246
Stoicism 9, 12, 18, 26
substance 118, 171, 179, 262
Suger of St. Denis 115
supreme being 171, 178
swearing 280, 299
swords 313
Sylvester I, Pope 275
Symeon the New Theologian 48, 49, 50
Symmachus 25
synesthesia 138
Syriacs 38

taxation 311
teaching 219, 272
temporal authority 303–37
temporalities 313
temptation 218
tenses 173
Terence 21
Theobald of Etampes 92
Theodore 47, 48
Theodoric 25, 28
Theoduin of Liège 69, 70–3, 86
theological language 69
theology xv and *passim*
Theophanes 47
Theophylact 49
Thierry of Chartres 114
thisness 260
Thomas Arundel 348
Thomas Bradwardine 340, 342, 343
Thomas Buckingham 335
Thomas Waleys 241